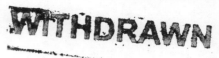
THE EMERGENCE OF RUS
750–1200

LONGMAN HISTORY OF RUSSIA
General Editor: Harold Shukman

The Emergence of Rus 750–1200
Simon Franklin and Jonathan Shepard

*The Crisis of Medieval Russia 1200–1304
John Fennell

*The Formation of Muscovy 1304–1613
Robert O. Crummey

*The Making of Russian Absolutism 1613–1801
(Second Edition)
Paul Dukes

*Russia in the Age of Reaction and Reform 1801–1881
David Saunders

*Russia in the Age of Modernisation and Revolution 1881–1917
Hans Rogger

The Russian Revolution 1917
Steve Smith

*The Soviet Union 1917–1991
(Second Edition)
Martin McCauley

*already published

LONGMAN HISTORY OF RUSSIA

The Emergence of Rus
750–1200

SIMON FRANKLIN
AND
JONATHAN SHEPARD

LONGMAN
London and New York

Longman Group Limited
Longman House, Burnt Mill,
Harlow, Essex CM20 2JE, England
and Associated Companies throughout the world.

*Published in the United States of America
by Longman Publishing, New York*

First published 1996

ISBN 0 582 490901 CSD
ISBN 0 582 49091X PPR

British Library Cataloguing-in-Publication Data

A catalogue record for this book is
available from the British Library

Library of Congress Cataloging-in-Publication Data

Franklin, Simon.
  The emergence of Rus : 750–1200 / Simon Franklin and Jonathan
Shepard. — 1st ed.
    p.   cm. — (Longman history of Russia)
  Includes bibliographical references and index.
  ISBN 0–582–49090–1 (csd). — ISBN 0–582–49091–X (ppr)
  1. Kievan Rus—History—To 862.   2. Kievan Rus–
–History—862–1237.   I. Shepard, Jonathan.   II. Title.
III. Series.
DK73.F73   1996
947'.02—dc20   95–49326
                                                                         CIP

Set by 5 in 11/12pt Garamond
Produced by Longman Singapore Publishers (Pte) Ltd.
Printed in Singapore

Contents

List of Maps

INSET MAPS

GENERAL MAPS

REGIONAL MAPS

List of Genealogies

Acknowledgements

Our prime debt – immense but unquantifiable – is to Dimitri Obolensky, who provided both the inspiration and the excuse for the writing of this book. The first volume in the Longman series was originally to have been produced by him. We took over the project at his suggestion and with his encouragement.

Others have helped along the way. Francis Thomson, Constantine Zuckerman, Alexander Kazhdan and Andrzej Poppe kindly allowed us to see proofs or typescripts of forthcoming articles. Christopher Ward and Lesley Abrams read and commented on draft chapters. Anna Richardson offered valuable last-minute assistance with some tricky points in Arabic sources, Metin Kunt advised on a Turkic term and Rosamond McKitterick loaned a book at a critical moment. The Law of the Dog and the Forest is cited with the permission of Ihor Ševčenko.

Special thanks are due to our publisher, Longman, who consistently contrived to give a plausible impression of optimism in the face of delay. Last and least one should mention the Higher Education Funding Council for England (HEFCE), without whose multiple initiatives the book would undoubtedly have been finished sooner.

A Note on Spellings, Dates and References

i. SPELLINGS

In controlled tests, the inconsistent transliteration of foreign names and terms might emerge as one of the main causes of high blood-pressure in the academic community. Transliteration is like gambling: however subtle the system, the odds will always defeat one in the end. Our own guidelines are as follows.

For Slavonic words we use the modified Library of Congress system, without diacritics: hence Andrei, rather than Andrey, Andrej or Andrew; Iurii, rather than Yury, Yuriy, Jurij or George. In certain place-names, however, we retain 'ë', pronounced 'yo', as in yacht. Medieval word-forms are transliterated according to modern spelling conventions, i.e. rendered without nasal or reduced vowels. In the modernized forms the 'soft sign' ('), showing that a consonant is palatalized, is included in bibliographical references and in italicized terminology, but omitted when the word appears as an ordinary part of the text: hence Suzdal rather than Suzdal', Rus rather than Rus', but *volost'* rather than *volost*. In rendering Turkic or Arabic or Scandinavian words we follow the equivalent convention.

In general we prefer to reflect linguistic diversity rather than to impose familiarity. The practice of monolingual standardization seems needlessly condescending, as if readers are incapable of spotting equivalent forms. The names of Greek-speakers are therefore Greek rather than Latin: hence Nikephoros rather than Nicephorus; unless they are culturally active among the Rus, in which case they are Slavonized: hence Metropolitan Nikifor. This is illogical, except that it helps to circumvent the problem of having to make a choice of spellings when ethnic origins are unknown. Very famous people must, however, remain English: hence St Andrew, or Constantine the Great.

That is the simple part. Consider the name of the prince of Kiev at the turn of the eleventh century. The modern Russian equivalent is Vladimir, the modern Ukrainian equivalent is Volodymyr. Either choice could be seen as tendentious. So we turn to the sources. In the chronicles the prince tends to be *Volodimerŭ*, with local East Slav vocalization, closer to the Ukrainian. But on the coins which he himself issued, he is *Vladimirŭ*, with Church Slavonic vocalization, closer to the Russian. There is no right or wrong. We plump for Vladimir. Other names, too, appear in variant forms, forcing an arbitrary solution. A similar problem can arise with respect to some place-names in modern Ukraine and Belarus: Russian Belgorod or Ukrainian Bilhorod, Russian Galich or Ukrainian Halych? In cases of doubt, our map is medieval: hence Belgorod and Galich; and hence also, incidentally, a small and not very significant place called Moskva, which would sound too grand for its context if it were to be called Moscow.

So much for rules and systems. Within these broad limits we have tried to be consistent, except where we judge it appropriate to be inconsistent. We hope that the results are less confusing than their prefatory explanation.

ii. DATES

Some readers may wish to follow up the references and look at the 'authentic' versions of the tales of the Rus. They will notice frequent discrepancies between the dates in the sources and the dates in our own narrative. Our dates are not – we hope – misprints, nor are we particularly maverick in our chronological hypotheses. It may be helpful to provide in advance a general indication of why such discrepancies occur so often.

The chronicles of the Rus date events from the Creation, not from the Incarnation. As is well known (at least to medieval eastern Christian chronologists), Christ was born around the middle of the sixth cosmic 'day'; that is, around the middle of the sixth millennium; that is, around the year 5500 after the Creation. But the precise sums could be added in a variety of ways, producing different 'eras'. The Rus adopted the 'Constantinopolitan' era. In order to convert an AM (*anno mundi*) date from this era into an AD date, one has to subtract 5508, not 5500.

That, at any rate, is the basic rule. The complication here is that the Constantinopolitan year began in September, whereas the standard year in the Rus chronicles begins in March: usually in the March *following* the start of the equivalent Constantinopolitan year (this is called a 'March year'), but sometimes in the March *preceding* it (an 'ultra-March year'). Thus, for example, the date 6658 would cover the period from September 1149 to August 1150 according to the Constantinopolitan year, or from March 1150 to February 1151 if the chronicler is using a 'March year', or from March 1149 to February 1150 if the chronicler is using an 'ultra-March year'. Just for good measure, some native Rus sources also use the Constantinopolitan year, starting in September. No author ever explains his own usage. Some compilers unwittingly mix all three. One should also bear in mind that the annalistic framework for the first couple of centuries of dated local narrative was constructed by chroniclers writing long after the events. In short, dating is a problem even when the sources make it appear straightforward.

iii. REFERENCES TO SOURCES

Where there is a choice of editions, we tend to cite from that which is likely to be most convenient, unless a particular variant reading is important in context. Most of the translations are our own, although we also provide references to published translations where they are likely to be useful, which is not always the case.

List of Abbreviations

Abramovich/Müller, *Erzählungen*	L. Müller (introd.), *Die altrussischen hagiographischen Erzählungen und liturgischen Dichtungen über die heiligen Boris und Gleb*
Abramovich/Tschiźewskij, *Paterikon*	D. Tschiźewskij (introd.), *Das Paterikon des Kiever Höhlenklosters*
AEMA	*Archivum Eurasiae Medii Aevi*
ASSSR SAI	*Arkheologiia SSSR. Svod arkheologicheskikh istochnikov*
Berezhkov, *Khronologiia*	N. G. Berezhkov, *Khronologiia russkogo letopisaniia*
BNJ	*Byzantinisch-neugriechischen Jahrbücher*
CFHB	*Corpus Fontium Historiae Byzantinae*
DAI	Constantine VII Porphyrogenitus, *De administrando imperio*
DC	Constantine VII Porphyrogenitus, *De cerimoniis aulae byzantinae*
DGTSSSR	*Drevneishie gosudarstva na territorii SSSR*
DGVEMI	*Drevneishie gosudarstva Vostochnoi Evropy. Materialy i issledovaniia* (continuation of *DGTSSSR*)
DOP	*Dumbarton Oaks Papers*
EP	*Russkaia Pravda*, 'Expanded' redaction
Franklin, *Sermons and Rhetoric*	S. Franklin, *Sermons and Rhetoric of Kievan Rus'*
GVNP	S. N. Valk, ed., *Gramoty Velikogo Novgoroda i Pskova*
Heimskringla, tr. Hollander	Snorri Sturluson, *Heimskringla*, tr. L. M. Hollander
Heppell, *Paterik*	M. Heppell, *The 'Paterik' of the Kievan Caves Monastery*
HLEUL	*The Harvard Library of Early Ukrainian Literature, English Translations*

Hollingsworth, *Hagiography*	P. Hollingsworth, *The Hagiography of Kievan Rus'*
Holtzmann, *Die Chronik*	R. Holtzmann (ed.), *Die Chronik des Bischofs Thietmar von Merseburg und ihre korveier Überarbeitung*
HUS	*Harvard Ukrainian Studies*
Ianin, *Aktovye pechati*	V. Ianin, *Aktovye pechati Drevnei Rusi X–XV vv.*
JGO	*Jahrbücher für Geschichte Osteuropas*
JÖB	*Jahrbuch der österreichischen Byzantinistik*
Kaiser, *The Laws*	D. Kaiser (tr.), *The Laws of Rus' – Tenth to Fifteenth Centuries*
KSIA	*Kratkie soobshcheniia Instituta Arkheologii*
Leo Deac.	Leo the Deacon, *Historia*
MGH	*Monumenta Germaniae Historica*
MIA	*Materialy i issledovaniia po arkheologii SSSR*
Moldovan, *Slovo*	A. M. Moldovan, ed., *'Slovo o zakone i blagodati' Ilariona*
NGB	*Novgorodskie gramoty na bereste*, ed. Artsikhovskii et al.
NPL	A. N. Nasonov, ed., *Novgorodskaia pervaia letopis' starshego i mladshego izvodov*
Ob upravl. imp.	Constantine VII, *Ob upravlenii imperiei*
ORIAS	*Otdelenie Russkogo Iazyka i Slovesnosti*
OWS	*Oldenburg–Wolin–Staraja Ladoga–Novgorod–Kiev. Handel und Handelsverbindungen im südlichen und östlichen Ostseeraum während des frühen Mittelalters. Internationale Fachkonferenz der Deutschen Forschungsgemeinschaft vom 5.–9. Oktober 1987 in Kiel.*
PG	J.-P. Migne, *Patrologia graeca*
PLDR	*Pamiatniki literatury Drevnei Rusi*
PSRL	*Polnoe sobranie russkikh letopisei*
PVL	D. S. Likhachev and V. P. Adrianova – Peretts, eds, *Povest' vremennykh let*
RA	*Rossiiskaia arkheologiia* (= continuation of *SA*)
RIB	*Russkaia istoricheskaia biblioteka*
RES	*Revue des études slaves*
RM	*Russia Mediaevalis*

Rozanov/Tschiževskij, *Avraamij*	D. Tschiževskij (introd.), *Die altrussischen hagiographischen Erzählungen und liturgischen Dichtungen über den Heiligen Avraamij von Smolensk*
SA	*Sovetskaia arkheologiia*
SEEJ	*The Slavic and East European Journal*
SEER	*The Slavonic and East European Review*
Skyl.	John Skylitzes, *Synopsis Historiarum*
Sotnikova and Spasski, *Russian Coins*	M P. Sotnikova and I. G. Spasski, *Russian Coins of the X–XI Centuries A.D.*
SP	*Russkaia Pravda*, 'Short' redaction
Sreznevskii, *Materialy*	I. Sreznevskii, *Materialy dlia slovaria drevnerussko ioazyka*
TM	*Travaux et Mémoires*
TODRL	*Trudy otdela drevnerusskoi literatury*
UHV	*Untersuchungen zu Handel und Verkehr der vor- und frühgeschichtlichen Zeit in Mittel- und Nordeuropa*, IV, *Der Handel der Karolinger- und Wikingerzeit*, eds, K. Düwel, H. Jankuhn, H. Siems and D. Timpe.
Uspenskii sbornik	O. I. Kniazevskaia et al., eds, *Uspenskii sbornik XII-XIII vv.*
ZDR	V. L. Ianin, ed., *Zakonodatel'stvo Drevnei Rusi*

For Dimitri Obolensky:
teacher and friend

Introduction

This book is and is not an account of the emergence of a thing called Russia. The further we pursue the thing into the past, the more misleading our modern vocabulary becomes. Only in nationalist fantasy can the word 'Russia' stand for a kind of Platonic form, immanent even when invisible, constant in essence though variable in its historical embodiments. If we picture Russia as a state with its focus of power in Moscow or St Petersburg, or as an area inhabited mainly by people who think of themselves as Russians – if, that is, our notion of Russia is coloured by current political or ethno-cultural geography – then most of this book is not about Russia at all, or at least not about Russia alone. Instead it is about *russia* in the original Latin sense: about a land ruled by people known as the Rus (pronounced *rooss*). The story of the land of the Rus could continue in one direction towards modern Russia, or in other directions towards, eventually, Ukraine or Belarus. The land of the Rus is none of these, or else it is a shared predecessor of all three. Modern state boundaries are irrelevant here, as are the distinctions between modern national identities. So as not to confuse the main plot with its divergent sequels, the subject is labelled 'Russia' neither in the title nor in the text.

Who were the Rus and what was their land? Visitors at different times would have produced dramatically different answers. Around the turn of the ninth century the Rus were barely visible: small bands of traders trekking along the rivers through the dense and sparsely populated northern forests between the Baltic and the Middle Volga, lured towards the silver of the east; faint specks on a vast landscape; transient Scandinavians among Finno-Ugrian tribes. Returning after a couple of centuries the visitor would have found the Rus firmly established in thriving fortified cities, fattened with trade and tribute; but based in a new place, hundreds of miles to the south, on the Middle Dnieper, near the frontiers of the steppes; speaking a new language, since significant numbers of the Scandinavian Rus had become assimilated to the Slavs among whom they had settled; and promoting a new culture, for their rulers had accepted Christianity, the faith of the 'Greeks' (i.e. of the Byzantines). Two centuries more, and the lands of the Rus stretched from the Carpathians almost to within sight of the Urals: centres of wealth and power had proliferated across a network of territories in many respects diverse, but lent coherence (if not always cohesion) through sharing a single dominant dynasty, a single dominant language and a single dominant faith.

These are large changes. The Rus and their lands are, so to speak, moving targets. The first task is to track the changes in sequence, to construct a framework of political or geopolitical narrative. The second and concurrent task, more interesting and important, is to explore the texture of change, the interlinked transformations in economic, social and cultural life which give substance and sense to the plain political chronology. The Rus therefore provide a convenient peg, but the theme of this book is not so much the people as the processes in which they participated.

To drape a history of the period around a history of the Rus is an old device. It was used by the Kievan compiler of the earliest surviving large-scale native narrative, the *Povest' vremennykh let*, literally the 'Tale of the Years of Time', better known as the *Primary Chronicle*, which seeks to relate 'whence the land of the Rus came into being' and 'who first began to be prince in it'.[1] The *Primary Chronicle* is an immensely rich and colourful source, lively and varied, ambitious and informative. Nobody now would accept it as precise or adequate 'fact': the extant manuscripts date from much later than the work itself, the compiler was far removed from all but the most recent of the events described, his own sources of information were patchy and tendentious, and the whole was shaped to fit the political morality of a section of the Kievan elite in the early twelfth century. Yet despite the continual emergence of new material, and of new kinds of historical inquiry, the chronicle has in many ways proved remarkably resilient. Its uses are adapted rather than diminished, and the old device – to explore the age through an account of 'whence the land of the Rus came into being' – can still be effective in serving new purposes.

Over the past few decades specialized auxiliary studies have moved far ahead of general syntheses. There have been regional histories, economic histories, urban histories, church histories, social analyses, legal and diplomatic histories, textual reconstructions and deconstructions, theoretical ruminations, cultural interpretations and evaluations, plus enormously productive archaeological excavations. Yet there have been few attempts to draw the themes together, to reconsider the entire period, to re-integrate the particulars into a thorough reassessment of the whole: no extensive monograph in English for 50 years, and surprisingly little of the requisite scope even in Russian or Ukrainian. The gap that this book aims to fill is therefore not entirely parochial. While our main brief is to introduce the period to those who know little about it, the fresh synthesis may also be of some use to those who already know quite a lot.

---

1 Note the variant 'in Kiev': *PSRL*, I, cols 1–2; *PSRL*, II, col. 2.

'The period' is a chronological abstraction, to which historians try to give shape. Shape is inevitably a product of hindsight: one picks the beginning which fits the end. The Rus of the early ninth century would be a very minor footnote were it not for the Rus of the eleventh and twelfth centuries. Nevertheless, to focus on a particular people (the Rus) as narrative device remains justifiable, so long as one remembers that the end is not necessarily implicit in the beginning. But the *Primary Chronicle* employs another shaping device which has proved equally durable, although in more recent retrospect it ought to be more questionable. This is its focus on a particular place: on the city of Kiev. Political assessments of 'the period' take as almost axiomatic the view that the Kiev-based polity of the eleventh century – preferably ruled by a monarch – was and is the proper yardstick by which success and failure, or virtue and skulduggery, are to be measured; that it was the necessary culmination of all that went before and the proper aspiration for all that followed afterwards. Hence the catch-all label 'Kievan Rus' (or 'Kievan Russia') – not, as it happens, a medieval term – frequently applied to the entire span of some 400 years from the legendary origins of the ruling dynasty to the Mongol conquests of 1237–41. Hence also, from a 'Great Russian' perspective, the common division of Russian history into three parts, as a tale of three cities: Kiev, Moscow, St Petersburg.

The city of Kiev was enormously important to the economic, political and cultural life of the Rus, and must figure prominently in any narrative or analysis. The problem with using Kiev as an emblem for the period is that the story of the land(s) of the Rus and the story of the Kievan Rus are different: though they overlap significantly in the middle, they do not coincide either at the beginning or at the end. An acceptance of normative, kievocentric values has led historians from the twelfth century to the twentieth to shape the politics of the period in terms of rise and fall, triumph and decline: first the prehistory of Kievan dominance, then the Golden Age, then political decay and the erosion of Kievan authority. But this leads to a paradox: the time of Kiev's political 'decline' was also a time of economic and cultural expansion for the Rus as a whole. If one abandons the Kiev-based, centralist schema, then there was no rise and fall, but rather a rise and rise, a continual growth and expansion. The paradox disappears: the lands of the Rus flourished economically and culturally not *in spite of* political decay but in part *because of* political flexibility.

The adaptability of the Rus is a *leitmotif* throughout the present book. We do not see the Rus at any stage as implementing a single grand plan or as operating according to a fixed system. They explored and exploited opportunities, improvised, probed for alternatives. They adapted and modified their own conventions, both in order to initiate change and, increasingly, in order to cope with its effects: in order to stay abreast of the social and political consequences of their own economic and territorial success. It was a kind of success that implied continual 'failures': false starts, paths tried and abandoned. Such 'failures' are as necessary to an explanation of the 'rise' as they are deceptive as an indication of a 'decline'. The dynamic adaptability of the Rus should be obvious even from the brief summary of their transmutations. But in the writing of their history it has tended to be overshadowed by schematic structures, whether of medieval providentialism, or of Soviet determinism, or of nostalgic nationalism.

To stress that the Rus were flexible is not, of course, to argue that change was random or amorphous. Rather the opposite: it is simply to emphasize that patterns of political behaviour among the Rus were closely tied to shifting patterns of circumstance and development around them. This raises a question of form. One could choose to separate the various strands and devote a different sub-section to each: a chapter on the physical setting, a chapter on political chronology, a chapter on modes of production, a chapter on social structures, a chapter on culture, a chapter on dealings with neighbours. The result might be a very convenient work of reference, mirroring the division of the subject into distinct sub-disciplines, but with little sense of process and interrelationship. We prefer to integrate the narrative rather than to segregate the themes. By and large, therefore, we stick to a linear sequence, while accumulating sub-themes as appropriate along the way. Thus, for example, the reader will find the main discussion of military recruitment in Chapter Five; of the economy of steppe peoples in Chapter Two; of the status of women in Chapter Eight; of ecclesiastical organization and finances in Chapter Six; of architecture in Chapter Nine and so on. The thematic digressions look forwards and backwards in time, but they are anchored in their narrative context and do not pretend to be comprehensive. The inconvenience is mitigated to some extent by the use of copious cross-references.

Further sins of omission ought also to be confessed in advance. Readers can be spared a certain amount of frustration if they are warned of what *not* to expect.

We have concentrated more on the variables than on the constants, more on processes than on events, more on the dynamics of change than on the description of routine. The result is elitist, in that we devote relatively little space to what most of the people through most of the lands were doing most of the time. Worse still, we virtually ignore the huge quantities of scholarly debate as to the precise status of various groups among the rural population, or on the precise meanings of social terminology relating to dependent or semi-dependent or semi-free categories of people: when or where or whether one might or might not detect what features of what stage of feudalism, or of the predominance of slave-ownership, or of democracy. Indeed, most of our remarks on social structures are deliberately approximate. For this we are only slightly apologetic, since the majority of the debates lie on the wrong side of the line between hypothesis and guesswork. Systematic reconstructions, so high on the agenda for Soviet historians, tend to push the available evidence a long way beyond what it can persuasively be made to show; which is why different historians have been able to produce radically different versions of the most basic sets of social relationships.

Other conventionally major questions likewise loom small. In setting priorities we have been acutely aware of Ševčenko's Law of the Dog and the Forest. A dog approaches a virgin forest, goes up to a tree, and does what dogs do against trees. The tree is chosen at random. It is neither more nor less significant than any other tree. Yet one may reasonably predict that future dogs approaching the same forest will focus their own attentions on that particular tree. Such is often the case in scholarship: the scent of an argument on one issue draws scholars into more arguments on the same issue. We have not felt obliged to linger at all the traditional landmarks.

Not that we imagine our own agenda to be in every respect beyond question. In a field where evidence is notoriously sparse even by normal medieval standards, the very simplest facts are often extremely fragile. The modern criterion of forensic proof – beyond reasonable doubt – can rarely be applied. There are only grades of hypothesis, from the almost certain to the probable to the plausible to the just conceivable. For purists, all statements should be recast as investigations, and narrative should dissolve into source-annotation. As far as possible we attempt to convey the flavour of the evidence, but in a single volume it is not practicable to remain constantly in the investigative mode or to spend much time discussing the received opinions. Where there is a legacy of major dispute, notes can guide readers towards it. However, we cannot requisition extra space so as to justify or qualify in detail every judgement which may happen *not* to coincide with received opinion. To do so would be to distort the balance of narrative by making a fetish of innovation; and to repeat the word 'perhaps' every other sentence would be tedious. However responsible one may try to be, no account of the Rus is definitive.

Finally, a word about dual authorship. Historians tend to be nitpickers by professional habit and often by temperament. The eye is trained to scan quickly across areas of consensus before focusing sharply on points of disagreement. When we started on this project we were by no means certain that we would be able to reverse the procedure so as to arrive at a common perspective. In practice it was easier than we had feared and more productive than we had suspected. Our individual interests and preoccupations turned out to be complementary rather than contradictory. Each of us took on a separate set of chapters for first drafting, and these preliminary versions were then revised after long sessions of what the diplomats would call 'frank and open' discussion. The final product is not quite seamless. Intonation and emphasis vary to some extent, but it would have been absurd to try to standardize all aspects of style, and a mildly stereophonic effect might be no disadvantage. For those who may be curious, Part I was initially drafted by Jonathan Shepard, Part II and most of Part III by Simon Franklin. Work on the first sub-section of Chapter Nine was shared in ways too complicated to be worth explaining. We are jointly to blame for the results.

PART I:

Roots and Routes

The Silver-Seekers from the North (c. 750–c. 900)

1. BEGINNINGS

When the compilers of the *Primary Chronicle* tried to explain where in the world their land lay, they conceived of it largely in terms of rivers and riverways. Tribes and peoples are named in connection with them, and great thoroughfares are described, together with journeys of famous men. Surprisingly, perhaps, for a work which sets out to record the deeds of a series of princes and of their subjects, the chronicle's opening pages treat the land as essentially one of transit, somewhere between other, more famous, places. There is a clear bias in the direction of the river Dnieper, and in favour of those living around one section of it. We are told that St Andrew, wanting to travel from a town on the Crimea to Rome, travelled up the Dnieper until he halted one night on the bank below some hills. Getting up next morning, he exclaimed to his disciples, 'Do you see those hills, how God's Grace shines forth upon them? God will cause a great town to stand there, and many churches to be built'.[1] Andrew blessed the hills and planted a cross on what was to become the site of the town of Kiev. He made his way further up the Dnieper and came eventually to the land of the Slovenes and the site of the future town of Novgorod. He observed their daily practice of beating themselves with young branches within an inch of their lives after baths of scalding hot water; having finished their self-flagellation, they plunged into cold water. Andrew continued on his journey and arrived in Rome. He recounted all that he had learnt and seen, and that the Slovenes 'do this as their way of bathing, not battering'. Andrew's listeners are said to have 'marvelled'.

The anonymous contributor of this tale to the chronicle was fostering the sense that the northerners were different, and comically inferior; it was Kiev, and not the wooden bath-houses of Novgorod, that evoked the saint's prayers and prophecy. This bias reflects the outlook of Kiev-based authors of the later eleventh and early twelfth centuries, wishing to demonstrate that churches and refinement were preordained for the banks of the Middle Dnieper. They had only hazy notions about

1 *PVL*, I, p. 12.

events of more than three or four generations before their own, and their picture of Rus' extent and place in the world was not clear-cut. Yet in their attention to rivers as markers of settlements and as the means of travelling huge distances the contributors to the chronicle were not simply reading back the conditions of their own time into a distant past. As we shall see, rivers were used by a variety of people and peoples, sometimes to traverse the land mass, but far more often for the purpose of short trips, or simply as a source of food and water. Other animals besides man came to the river bank, and could be hunted or trapped, and finds of fish-hooks and weights for nets are common in settlements throughout the 'prehistoric' and 'medieval' periods. River-basins were channels for gradual, piecemeal migrations of groups of people living from hand to mouth in the seventh and eight centuries as in previous periods. Such movements were still under way at the time of the compilation of the chronicle, when several groupings bore the names of 'tribes' (see below, p. 77, 336). The chronicle's editors assumed that most of the ancient inhabitants of their land were Slavs. But in fact the Slavs were relatively recent arrivals to most regions north-east and north of the Dnieper, and even c. 1100 they probably constituted only a minority of the population in the north-east (see below, p. 131, 332).

The chronicle's assumption is that the Dnieper is the pivot of its story, and some of the most dramatic events which it relates are set there, for example the mass-baptism of the inhabitants of Kiev c. 988 (see below, p. 163). In its awareness that rivers are more important than frontiers, it is responding to, and highlighting, one of the distinctive features of the history of Rus, in contrast to that of many other peoples or political structures. Frontiers were developed in Rus, and became defined by fortifications, from the end of the tenth century onwards (see below, pp. 170–3). But they were seldom clear-cut, and they could not usually be marked by natural barriers. There were dense forests, and marshes which were impenetrable in spring and summer. These stretched for thousands of kilometres across the plain in no particular pattern, save that in a wavering line running mostly to the south of the 57th parallel the pine forests gave way to those mixing conifers with deciduous trees such as chestnut and oak; further south still, the forests thinned out and eventually gave way to what Rus chroniclers called 'the open field'. There was no obvious focal point in this wilderness, nor were there the roads or ruins of more ancient cultures – nothing man-made to facilitate travel or direct attention towards some central place or half-forgotten authority. Rome was little more than a name even to the bookmen contributing to the chronicle and, as we shall see, awareness of the achievements and the ideology of the Roman empire was very slight (see below, p. 240). The best legitimizing myth that the editors of the chronicle could come up with was the tale of St Andrew planting his cross in the hills above Kiev. St Andrew is not said to have preached there, or anywhere else in the eastern lands. He was merely a traveller, passing through.

The tale of St Andrew's journey is probably a fairly late contribution to the chronicle. It seems to have been inserted in a geographical description of the land of Rus, and it is in this description that we find a more coherent attempt to give the land a shape, in terms of routes. The chronicle comes close to providing it with a kind of centre – but a forest, not a city or a trading post. We are told that one could travel along the Dnieper to the Greeks or from the Dnieper, by way of other rivers, to 'the Varangian sea' (the Baltic), and on from there to Rome and thence to Tsargrad (Constantinople) and ultimately back to the Dnieper's mouth: 'the Dnieper flows from the Okovskii forest and flows to the south, but the Dvina flows from the same forest and goes to the north, and enters into the Varangian sea. Now from this same forest the Volga flows to the east'.[2] Thus in so far as there is any basic starting-point inside the Rus lands, it is the forest of Okovskii, which stretched from Lake Seliger to the upper reaches of the Western Dvina and south-westwards as far as the river Kasplia. Even though it straddled the head-waters of great rivers which offered geographical bearings of a sort to the inhabitants of Rus, it was densely packed with trees and undergrowth, and parts of it were still virtually impenetrable in the later middle ages. Thus even where nature provided fairly convenient means of communications and some sort of focal point, it threw up massive barriers, hindering the concentration of populations in any one area.

Not that travel by means of the great rivers was easy for those covering long distances. Rafts, canoes of stretched hides and dugout canoes enabled the native inhabitants to get about for the purposes of fishing or pursuit of the deer, beaver, wild fowl and other game which tended to congregate near the banks. But they were less suitable for long distances, especially if laden with passengers or bulky cargo. Besides, there were many natural hazards facing anyone sailing far from his home waters. This was the case even along the Volga, which is, rightly, seen as one of the great waterways of the later medieval and modern periods. There were numerous sandbanks, shoals and stretches of white water to be negotiated, and towards the end of summer the water-level could fall so low as to make navigation in all but the smallest and lightest craft awkward and slow. For example, there were more than eight sandbanks along the Volga in the region of modern Iaroslavl, where some important trading settlements would arise in the ninth century. These navigation hazards literally vanished each spring, when the snows melted into the tributaries feeding the river and burst its banks. During the weeks of the thaw, a boat could be

2 Ibid., p. 12.

swept quite rapidly downstream towards the point where, according to the *Primary Chronicle*, the river flowed into the Caspian Sea through 'seventy mouths'.[3] The speed and turbulence of the flood waters posed new dangers, especially for small, light, craft, while the breadth of the expanses of water and the lack of landmarks posed navigational problems for boatmen unfamiliar with local conditions. Moreover, a return journey after the force of the current slackened involved coping with the sandbanks and other hazards which now re-emerged from the waters.

The Volga was the longest river in the eastern land and its floods were among the most spectacular of all. But there is no reason to suppose that navigation was significantly easier or safer elsewhere. So while the major rivers offered a means of piercing the forested land mass, they did not present a particularly soft option for those planning a round trip across great distances. By the time the final version of the *Primary Chronicle* was being compiled, there were settlements of boatmen, pilots and hauliers at the more difficult stretches of water, and the growing number of villages strung along the river banks could provide food or overnight shelter to the crews of oarsmen. Long-distance commercial travel with a cargo of goods depended on these services, especially if the cargo was a human one of slaves, in need of food. These back-up facilities for regular travellers were not available 400 or so years earlier, at the beginning of our story, and it is likely that the riverways were then most in use for short journeys by boat, or were followed in winter by those able to travel by ski or sledge.

In these circumstances, the case for staying at home might seem to have been overwhelming, and for the vast majority of persons in the eighth and ninth centuries, it was. But 'home' was itself a movable and uncertain affair for the inhabitants of the river valleys and the depths of the forests alike – part hunter-gatherers, part fishermen and part agriculturalists. They had few ties other than, in some areas, burial-grounds and ancestor worship to bind them to a particular spot, and dearth and hunger offered periodic stimuli to move on, while the increase in mouths which prolonged freedom from dearth could engender would ultimately have the same effect. Therefore the population of major river valleys was never wholly immobile and the small but fairly numerous promontory settlements in the region of the Upper Volga seem to have been meeting-points and places of co-residence of diverse ethnic groups over a protracted period. These settlements came into being there between the fifth and the end of the seventh or the earlier eighth centuries. The majority of their inhabitants belonged to one variant or another of the Finno-Ugrians, an

3 Ibid., p. 12.

ethnic group characterized by a basically common language of which modern Finnish is one descendant, Hungarian another. Members of this group inhabited the expanses from northern Scandinavia to the Urals, and their ability to talk with one another perhaps went some way towards offsetting all the obstacles to travel. Finds of metal ornaments and decorative bonework at one of the earliest of the promontory settlements, Berezniaki, on the banks of the Volga, suggest the gradual infiltration there of Finno-Ugrians from as far east as the basin of the river Kama. But a community of language cannot be the sole, or even the main, reason for these movements of small groupings of people. Finds of pottery and ornaments at some of the settlements point to the presence in them of Balts, members of a quite different ethnic group, whose language belongs to the Indo-European stock of languages. They must have made their way from the west to the Volga through forests such as the Okovskii. The pace, scale and dating of the Balts' seemingly piecemeal migration across the land mass is still very unclear, but that they were on the move is not in doubt.

There were also, in the sixth and seventh centuries, some long-distance exchanges which can reasonably be classified as 'trade' and which involved deliberate journeying. The evidence for them is very sparse, but it is important as an indication that long before the appearance of towns or the rudiments of politico-military organizations, the land mass could be traversed in its entirety, seemingly fairly regularly. The historian of the Goths, Jordanes, wrote in the sixth century of the 'Swedes', 'a people famed for the dark beauty of their furs', who 'send by way of trade through innumerable other peoples the sapphire-coloured skins for Roman use'.[4] Jordanes does not state that the 'Swedes' themselves made the long journey down to trade with the 'Romans' (i.e. Byzantines). But he leaves no room for doubt that commercial ties existed, and the Swedes had gained their reputation for sables by visits to the regions where high-quality furs were to be had, such as Lake Ladoga and the lands to its north and north-east. There is also archaeological evidence of exchanges much further east. The sixth- and earlier seventh-century Persian and Byzantine silverware and Byzantine coins found in the basins of the rivers Kama and Viatka reached the far north by means of trade rather than some non-commercial method such as gifts, plunder or tribute. The Byzantine silver coins and the cups and bowls, many of them bearing the stamps of the Constantinopolitan authorities or Persia's ruling dynasty, the Sasanians, had most probably been exchanged for furs. They had, presumably, been brought north to the Kama by Persian or other oriental traders. The vessels were highly valued by the Kama region's inhabitants. Some were used for

---

4 Jordanes, *Romana et Getica*, III.21, *MGH Auctores Antiquissimi*, V, p. 59; tr. C. C. Mierow, *Gothic History* (repr. Cambridge, 1966), p. 56.

ritual purposes, but they were also kept as treasures, and occasionally drawings were scratched on their sides. Others were melted down and turned into ornaments responding to the Finno-Ugrians' tastes.[5] These two commercial nexuses linking the Byzantine and the Persian civilizations with the extreme north were, however, fragile. They slackened drastically in the course of the seventh century, although it is not certain that contact between the Middle East and the Middle Volga region was, or could be, totally severed. The change had less to do with the arrival of new groups of nomads in the Black Sea and Kazakh steppes – zones which had not been notably tranquil during the sixth century – than with the collapse of the market for sables and similarly high-priced furs in Byzantium and Persia. The Sasanian dynasty was overthrown by Emperor Heraclius and soon afterwards, in the 630s, the Arabs overran Persia and the ruling elite suffered impoverishment. The manufacture of elaborately ornamented silver vessels appears to have ceased. For more than a century the Arabs were at odds not only with the Byzantines but also with the people which had installed itself in the northern Caucasus and along the north-west shores of the Caspian, the Khazars. This people will be discussed later (see below, pp. 82, 95), and here we will note simply their prolonged confrontation with the Arabs. This reached a climax in 737, when an Arab army surged north of the Caucasus and advanced upstream along the Volga. The Khazars' ruler was obliged to submit and even agreed to accept Islam, albeit not for long. During this period of hostilities the risks for those contemplating a journey to the far north, never negligible, became formidable and elaborate series of short-distance exchanges between the Middle East and the far north could scarcely have avoided dislocation.

Even so, there were in place several of the links in a possible chain of long-range contacts and exchange. Excavations have uncovered small Scandinavian settlements at various points along the eastern coast of the Baltic. There had been exchanges of goods and some circulation of persons between Central Sweden and Estonia and Finland since the early Iron Age. Such contacts are not very surprising, seeing that Sweden lies little more than 150 kilometres from the Finnish mainland and the Åland Islands and the archipelago of islets off the south-west coast of Finland offer many landfalls. There is archaeological evidence suggesting periodic voyages of Swedish kin-groups as far as Lake Ladoga already in the sixth century. Their objective, at a time when the area lacked any permanently settled inhabitants, is very likely

5 V. P. Darkevich, *Khudozhestvennyi metall Vostoka VIII–XIIIvv.: proizvedeniia vostochnykh torevtik na territorii evropeiskoi chasti SSSR i Zaural'ia* (Moscow, 1976), p. 188; T. S. Noonan, 'Khwarazmian coins of the eighth century from Eastern Europe: the post-Sasanian interlude in the relations between Central Asia and European Russia', *AEMA* 6 (1986) [1988], 253–4 and n. 36, 256.

to have been fur-clad animals. Later, in the course of the seventh century, a substantial Scandinavian settlement was established on the main island of Åland and pottery was regularly imported there from Finland and perhaps also from Estonia. Finds in Finland of bronze, and of glass beads most probably of West European manufacture, point to commerce as being one of the activities in which the Åland islanders engaged. By the eighth century, some seem to have been taking Finns from the mainland as wives.[6]

The handful of Scandinavian settlements known on the eastern side of the Baltic took diverse forms. A unique complex of settlements arose at Grobin, a few kilometres inland from the coast of Kurland. The numbers of the settlers and the extent of the territory which they occupied seem to have been sufficient for them to keep their identity distinct from the local Balts for over 200 years, until the mid-eighth century. This was the case even though the settlers traded with the inhabitants of the hinterland. Grobin was, in that sense, a 'colony'. Recent excavations have disclosed a commemorative stone depicting what appears to be a sea-going vessel of the sort which would have kept the settlers in touch with their homeland. Other Scandinavian settlements lay south of Grobin – on a navigable river in the case of Apuola, some 40 kilometres south-east of Grobin; and in an inlet in the Bay of Gdansk in the case of the settlement at Elbing. That some Scandinavians were interested in the forests' produce, or simply in seizing their human contents, is suggested by sagas which relate the expeditions of Scandinavian heroes to raid the eastern lands and also the imposition of tribute on the inhabitants by Swedish kings. These tales are largely fictitious and gained their present form in the twelfth and thirteenth centuries, or later still. However, they probably relay an echo of a Scandinavian interest in the eastern Baltic coastal regions of low intensity, but long standing.

These various forms of contact between Scandinavians and the Balt peoples were not of momentous significance in themselves. The forementioned settlements are few in number and scattered along a lengthy coastline. Yet their presence along the fringes of the Eurasian landmass helps account for the speed with which long-distance commercial ties appear to have knitted together, once a commodity generally deemed even more valuable than furs was to be had from the east. Such a commodity became available quite suddenly, in the middle of the eighth century. It is something still of value today, silver.

There is controversy concerning many aspects of the process whereby the forested landmass became a meeting-point for members of various

---

6 J. Callmer, 'Verbindungen zwischen Ostskandinavien, Finnland und dem Baltikum vor der Wikingerzeit und das Rus'–Problem', *JGO* 34 (1986), 358–60; idem, 'The clay paw burial rite of the Åland islands and Central Russia: a symbol in action', *Current Swedish Archaeology* 2 (1994), 28–30.

different peoples, united by the one common aim of material gain. The part played in this, and in the eventual formation of some form of political structure, by the Scandinavians is still more hotly contested. Much will always be unclear, and one reason for this is that the number of persons directly involved in the exchanges was exiguous, a minute proportion of the total number of inhabitants of the interior – itself in all probability a modest enough figure. But there are three developments which can be traced through the murk.

Firstly, major changes in the Middle East followed the Abbasids' seizure of power from the Ommayad dynasty in 749. No further attempt was made to advance beyond the northern Caucasus and overrun the steppes. Instead, the Abbasids in 762 moved their capital from Damascus to Baghdad. This city was their own foundation and they instituted markets, seeking to attract traders with privileges and the protection of their caravans. From that time onwards their mint in Baghdad began to strike silver dirhams in quantities markedly greater than those of any other mint. The total annual output of Abbasid mints seems to have been substantial for the rest of the century, while much effort went into maintaining a high silver content. Many courtiers and officials populated the caliph's huge palace complex. Thus a ruling elite with a strong purchasing power and a penchant for luxury goods re-emerged in the neighbourhood of the Sasanians' old centre of power. And they disposed of a metal much prized by the inhabitants of the frozen north. In c. 759 Yazid, the emir of the Abbasid province of Arminiya (Armenia), married the daughter of the Khazar khagan, upon the instructions of the caliph. Peace was instituted between the two powers and even when armed clashes resumed at the end of the eighth century, they were now local affairs between the Khazars and the petty emirs and factions of Moslems of the border districts of Darband and Sharvan. Thus some of the man-made deterrents to journeys northwards along the Volga or across the adjacent steppe were lessened.

Already in the 730s Khazar merchants were frequenting the port of Darband, on the north-west Caspian coast, while Darband's merchants could, upon payment of a tenth of their goods to the authorities, travel north from there 'to the countries of the Khazars'.[7] During the second half of the eighth century the town expanded and became the most important channel of trade between the Khazars and the Moslem world. Silver dirhams and such manufactures as glazed pottery, metal ornaments, glassware and beads were offered to the Khazars. The Khazars were living an essentially nomadic way of life in the steppes north of Darband and the Lower Volga and they do not seem to have

7 *Derbend-Nameh*, cited in T. S. Noonan, 'Why dirhams first reached Russia: the role of Arab-Khazar relations in the development of the earliest Islamic trade with Eastern Europe', *AEMA* 4 (1984), 265.

grown or manufactured things which were of commercial interest to the Moslems. Such, at least, was the view of the mid-tenth-century Persian geographer, al-Istakhri. So they needed to procure goods from elsewhere to exchange with the Moslems and to a large extent that meant furs. The identity of those who ventured northwards in quest of them is obscure. It probably included Moslems as well as Khazars and members of the Burtas, a people living up-river from the Khazars on the Volga. This was, after all, an era when Arabic literature celebrated the daring and resourcefulness of merchants, and Sinbad the Sailor plied the seas as far as China.

A second development of this period was that silver dirhams (then averaging around 2.8–2.9g in weight, but subsequently subject to much fluctuation) began to be transported to the north-western extremity of the forested land mass, and on to central Sweden or the island of Gotland. Dirhams are found individually or in 'hoards', which can vary in size from a handful to several hundreds or even thousands. No comprehensive catalogue of dirham hoards found on the territory of the former USSR has been published to date, and this leaves much obscure. Serious problems anyway attend the use of the dirhams – like all early medieval coin finds – as evidence for fluctuations in trading patterns or even as evidence of trade at all. Stray finds of one or two coins made outside an archaeological context need have nothing to do with the date when they were (according to their inscriptions) struck. They may have reached the area in which they were discovered long afterwards, entering the earth later still. Hoards, defined as finds of not less than 20 coins,[8] are a less random form of evidence in that their constituent parts can tell us something about the date when they were deposited. Unfortunately, many of the hoards known for Russia were reported in the nineteenth or early twentieth centuries, and were not systematically described before being dispersed. Only fractions of several once-large hoards have been published, and the 'youngest' coin in these remnants of hoards may not have been the youngest in the original hoard. So it cannot be taken for a reliable guide as to the date when that hoard was deposited, a function which many archaeologists are willing to give to the youngest coin in reasonably large and accurately described hoards. Moreover, a hoard deposited for long-term safe keeping or as a religious offering might contain coins of a particular sort, perhaps long treasured as an heirloom or favoured on aesthetic grounds. So the inferences made from even a fully studied hoard about the date of its deposit contain an element of hypothesis.

---

8 T. S. Noonan, 'Ninth-century dirham hoards from European Russia: a preliminary analysis', in M. A. S. Blackburn and D. M. Metcalf, eds, *Viking-Age Coinage in the Northern Lands. The Sixth Oxford Symposium on Coinage and Monetary History* (British Archaeological Reports International Series 122; Oxford, 1981), p. 59.

Nonetheless, patterns do emerge from bits of evidence strung across vast tracts of territory. In north-west Russia there have been found several hoards of dirhams whose youngest pieces date from the late eighth or the first quarter of the ninth centuries. In one of them, the youngest coin dates from as early as 786–7. If one makes the common, if contentious, assumption that only ten to fifteen years elapsed between the date of issue of the youngest coin and its deposit, one may conclude that dirhams were trickling into the north-west by c. 800. Hoards possessing youngest coins of about the same date have been found in Central Sweden and on the south side of the Baltic. That there really is some correlation between these hoards' youngest coins and their date of deposit is suggested most spectacularly by a gold coin of King Offa of Mercia, England. Its Kufic inscriptions are said to be skilful, if uncomprehending, copies of an Abbasid gold dinar struck in 773–4, and they may be the work of an English moneyer. Since Offa died in 796, a specimen of Caliph al-Mansur's dinar was available to his moneyer in or before that year. The dinar may well have made its fairly rapid way from the Middle East to the west via East European riverways and trails. The same goes for another gold coin, struck for Offa or his next successor but one, Coenwulf. It was copied from an Abbasid dinar of 789–90 or 792–3.[9]

A third new feature was the appearance in the mid-eighth century of a settlement at Staraia Ladoga. This was situated beside the inflow of a settlement at Staraia Ladoga. (See Map A). This was situated beside the inflow of the little river Ladozhka into the river Volkhov, 13 kilometres up the Volkhov from Lake Ladoga. At Staraia Ladoga in the late twentieth century only the area nearest the town is cultivated. The surrounding countryside consists of forests and enormous stretches of bog, no less impenetrable in the early middle ages. A surface area of 2,500 metres has been excavated systematically. The bottom-most substratum of the lowest stratum, 'Horizon E_3', has been dated precisely with the help of dendrochronology, the technique which seeks to establish an absolute chronology from the sequences of tree rings discernible in the wood used for structures, paving and so forth. Dendrochronology's methods of dating are more or less free of controversy and the dating of the settlement's earliest 'micro-horizon' to the 750s has met with general acceptance.[10] Almost as certain has

9 I. Stewart, 'Anglo-Saxon gold coins', in R. A. G. Carson and C. M. Kraay, eds, *Scripta nummaria romana: essays presented to Humphrey Sutherland* (London, 1978), pp. 155, 165.

10 E. A. Riabinin and N. B. Chernykh, 'Stratigrafiia, zastroika i khronologiia nizhnego sloia staroladozhskogo Zemlianogo gorodishcha v svete novykh issledovanii', *SA* 1988, no. 1, 77, 80, 98 and chronological chart of datable timbers on 99; E. Mühle, *Die städtischen Handelszentren der nordwestlichen Rus'. Anfänge und frühe Entwicklung attrussischer Städte (bis gegen Ende des 12. Jahrhunderts)* (Quellen und Studien zur Geschichte des östlichen Europa 32; Stuttgart, 1991), pp. 20–1.

been the attribution to a Scandinavian craftsman of a set of smith's tools, found in a 'production complex' for working in wood and metal in this same substratum. The 26 pincers, hammers, tongs and so forth found in the 'complex' have precise analogies in kits found in Scandinavia proper. In other words, persons from afar were working at Staraia Ladoga from the first.

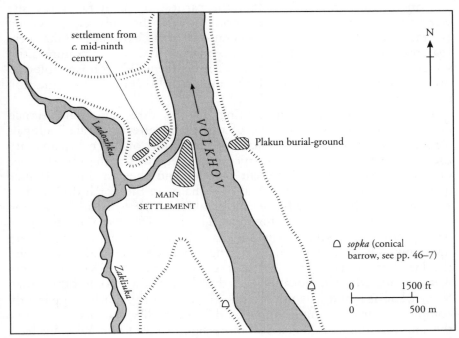

Map A.   Staraia Ladoga

In construction technique and lay-out the large wooden houses with heating apparatus in their centres are not dissimilar to those of indisputably Finno-Ugrian settlements, but they could as well be Scandinavian workmanship, and the virtual absence from the stratum of the eighth and earlier ninth centuries of finds of ornaments or tools classifiable as Finnic is striking. The indigenous population of the surrounding countryside was Finno-Ugrian, but it was very sparse indeed. Thus outsiders, and probably only outsiders, were the founders. This is shown most clearly by the finds of leather shoes, combs and other personal belongings characteristic of Scandinavians. The combs are found from the lowest substratum onwards. They are believed to have been made by itinerant craftsmen (see below, p. 16).

The earliest types of combs are likely to have been brought to Ladoga by their owners, or were worked up on the spot: they were not objects of barter or gift exchange. For most Scandinavian adults of either sex possessed a comb, and made frequent use of it on their hair. Combs were valued, and had some decorative features, but they were not *de luxe*. Clay pitchers of the type known as 'Tatinger ware', made somewhere in Francia, have also been found at Staraia Ladoga – as well as at other trading settlements in the Baltic region. Scandinavian-style tools and everyday articles have, then, been found at Staraia Ladoga, and an obvious inference is that the earliest frequenters of the site were Scandinavians. They were not, though, the only ethnic group at Staraia Ladoga in the first generations of its existence: Balts were also present.[11] There must have been some activity or commodities which attracted a medley of persons to this seemingly inhospitable and previously uninhabited spot in the mid-eighth century. The question is: what?

The answer comes from joining up the three above-mentioned developments in a straight line of cause and effect. Staraia Ladoga's formation may be seen as a function of the influx of silver dirhams into the north-west, while this in turn could be regarded as the consequence of the Abbasids' less belligerent policies and their striking of huge quantities of dirhams. The arrival of dirhams in the north does in fact seem most likely to have been a by-product of the Abbasids' accession and active promotion of commerce. The hoard whose youngest coin dates from 786–7 is the earliest to have been discovered in the north up to now. This suggests that exchanges between the Middle East and the far north-west started or resumed soon after the Khazaro–Arab warfare abated. The location of this hoard was none other than Staraia Ladoga, and it is not a freak phenomenon. Another apparently complete hoard, having a youngest dirham of 808, has been found to the south of Staraia Ladoga. Still more significantly, oriental coins have been excavated on the site of two successive wooden buildings at the bottom of the settlement's 'Horizon E_3'. Thus silver coins from the Middle East were to be had at Staraia Ladoga in the very earliest buildings and in effect they constituted its basic *raison d'être*. This would mean that news of the Abbasids' output of silver coins reached the shores of the Baltic within a few years. But we cannot be sure that trade between the Middle East and the fur-yielding regions to the north of the Kama ever stopped entirely. And the Swedes probably continued to go on hunting or bartering expeditions to Lake Ladoga after the sixth century, while their settlements on the Åland islands continued. They may also have been intermediaries in the long-distance connections between the Arctic north and Anglo-Saxon England: by

11 O. I. Davidan, 'Etnokul'turnye kontakty Staroi Ladogi VIII–IX vekov', *Arkheologicheskii sbornik* (Gosudarstvennyi Ordena Lenina Ermitazh) 27 (1986), 101–3.

the late eighth century walrus ivory was being used in Anglo-Saxon carvings. If movement of populations along the great river valleys of the northern forest zone was more or less incessant, news of traders bearing silver from the Moslem south could have travelled quite rapidly. And that silver could move fast between the Middle East and the north-west is shown by the sequence of coins in structures at Staraia Ladoga. A silver piece struck in Tabaristan in 783 has been found in a structure built over one containing an earlier Tabaristan coin, issued in 768.[12] Silver is not the only commodity of external origin to be found in the earliest substrata of Staraia Ladoga. Amber from, most probably, the coasts of the southern and south-eastern Baltic occurs in the form of small ornaments and also as unworked raw material. The lumps of amber were carved and drilled (without any heating process) into beads and pendants in workshops such as the 'complex' where the 26 smith's implements were found. Amber was highly valued and it was frequently reworked. Finds of amber are fairly plentiful at Staraia Ladoga, in stark contrast to anywhere else in the north-west. Glass beads have been found in very great profusion at Staraia Ladoga. In the lowest two substrata of 'Horizon E_3', the variety of shapes and colours is particularly wide, and these layers contain some of the most inherently valuable types, silvered beads and silver beads covered with light-brown glass to give the effect of gold. A workshop for glass-making has recently come to light at Staraia Ladoga and it appears to have started functioning at the beginning of the ninth century. But it probably depended on imported scrap for its raw material, and it cannot have produced every type of bead found at Ladoga. Many, probably most, of the beads represent imports. Furthermore, the beads found are too numerous to have been intended only for use by the earliest *habitués* of Ladoga. They were continuously being brought or manufactured so as to be exchanged for other commodities, and while at first many of them were made of silver or were of intricate construction, these types gave way during the ninth century to simpler, though still brightly coloured ones. Presumably the latter were less valuable, and reflected growth in the volume of commercial activity.

This archaeological evidence points unmistakably to the original function of Staraia Ladoga. It was a trading post, and diverse crafts to service the trade were practised there. In fact, there is evidence that amber beads were being fashioned on the spot even before the first wooden structures were built at Staraia Ladoga. There may have been a brief period when workshops with drainage channels were in seasonal operation but no actual settlement had been established. Craftsmen were making things from the 750s in the forementioned

12 E. A. Riabinin, 'Novye otkrytiia v Staroi Ladoge (itogi raskopok na Zemlianom gorodishche 1973–1975 gg.)', in V. V. Sedov, ed., *Srednevekovaia Ladoga* (Leningrad, 1985), pp. 51, 73.

'production complex', whose forge had walls of light wickerwork and lacked any solid roofing. Clearly, business developed rapidly. The decision of the 'founding fathers' then to take up permanent occupation and build a number of wooden residences and workshops would have been quixotic, had they not felt reasonably confident of at least an intermittent supply of goods to buy and to sell (see below, p. 35). The site of Staraia Ladoga was probably chosen on account of its water-communications. Downstream lay Lake Ladoga, which seems to have debouched directly into the sea in the earlier middle ages, while a few kilometres upstream lay a series of treacherous rapids. Staraia Ladoga's relative isolation, set back from Lake Ladoga itself and in a kind of no-man's-land, recommended it to outsiders seeking to enrich themselves without risk of disturbance from local inhabitants. It was bleak, yet accessible by water.

Staraia Ladoga's contacts also reached far to the west, judging by the finds of Scandinavian-style combs and Tatinger-type pitchers. These are among the more humdrum of the objects which form a kind of trail, spidery but persistent, eastwards from Hedeby across the Baltic via Central Sweden or along the southern Baltic coast. The earliest firmly datable hoards of dirhams in the Baltic region, of c. 800, form a similar distribution pattern and amber, albeit a natural product on the south shore of the Baltic, is found in only a very few other sites, notably Birka and Staraia Ladoga. Beads belonging to several of the types known in Ladoga have been found in ample quantities at Birka. Their place of manufacture is uncertain, but at least some types were probably made in the Rhineland or elsewhere in Francia or the Mediterranean basin. These scattered bits of evidence imply a nexus of long-distance exchanges and ventures which were essentially for the purpose of gain. They were not primarily objects of gift-exchange between members of ruling or noble elites. The combs made of bone or deer antlers are particularly suggestive in this respect, for they belong to types which have been found as far west as Dorestad in Frisia, York and Dublin. They were everyday objects, of less value than ornaments of precious metal, and so less likely to be kept in use, or on display, indefinitely. They were therefore sensitive to changing fashions in design and decoration and, one might suppose, responsive to the peculiarities of local tastes. Yet combs of the same date show a striking uniformity of size, proportions and ornament. It seems that they were made by itinerant craftsmen who shuttled constantly from trading post to trading post in the Scandinavian world. Using materials which they obtained on the spot, they worked up these combs for local customers.[13]

13 K. Ambrosiani, *Viking Age Combs, Comb Making and Comb Makers in the Light of Finds from Birka and Ribe* (Acta Universitatis Stockholmiensis. Stockholm Studies in Archaeology 2; Stockholm, 1981), pp. 53–6, 157–8; maps: fig. 11, p. 35; fig. 13, p. 39; fig. 19, p. 48.

The settlements and market-grounds of Birka and Hedeby seem to have come into existence at about the same time as the trading post on the Volkhov. Hedeby is thought to have been occupied as early as the mid-eighth century. The traditional date for the foundation of Birka, c. 800, is now open to revision, partly because some of the combs found there are identical to examples found in the earliest substratum in Staraia Ladoga. It appears possible that Birka may have been functioning as a settlement as early as the mid-eighth century.[14] It is not certain that these two settlements were from the first involved in long-distance trade, but the connections of Birka, in particular, with Staraia Ladoga are obvious and it is probable that demand for silver stimulated other significant commercial activities such as the manufacture of beads and dealing in amber. A furnace for melting glass to make beads, together with numerous moulds and other materials from metal workshops, have been found in the early, central, part of the settlement at Hedeby. It is possible that some of these products were destined for sale in markets such as Staraia Ladoga. Hedeby probably owed its commercial significance to its position on a convenient route for the transport of goods by river and, for a short distance, overland across the neck of the Jutland peninsula. Finds of Arab silver coins in Hedeby or points further west are rare, but we have already noted Offa's 'dinar' and, from 789, Charlemagne's edicts pay considerable attention to the imposition of new standards of weights and measures; around the same time a new, heavier, silver denier was introduced into the Frankish lands.[15] Access to a new supply of silver from the east would be one explanation of why fuller recourse to this metal now seemed feasible.

The overall weight and the quantity of the goods in play was not, however, very great, judging by the totals of finds of 'imported wares' and tools found in strata of the eighth and ninth centuries at Staraia Ladoga. The number of persons directly involved in handling them was correspondingly small. This was the case in the earlier stages of settlement at Birka and Hedeby, too. The round-the-year residents at Birka probably amounted to no more than 700–1,000 men, women and children – and perhaps considerably fewer. Numbers were swollen by visitors to the markets, and there were most probably winter fairs at Birka to which full- and part-time traders and itinerant craftsmen could bring their wares. Likewise, Staraia Ladoga's settled area does not appear to have been extensive, even after expansion during the ninth century (see below, pp. 58–9). But the limited scale of these exchanges raised the kudos attached to, and the price placed upon, luxury goods, above all, silver: scarcity generated value. The physical constraints on

---

14 H. Clarke and B. Ambrosiani, *Towns in the Viking Age* (Leicester, 1991), pp. 63, 75.
15 R. Hodges and D. Whitehouse, *Mohammed, Charlemagne and the Origins of Europe* (London, 1989), pp. 109–10.

trading were immense: the carrying capacity of the boats was modest and it was only worthwhile for Frisians or Scandinavians regularly to brave the seas if there was a robust enough demand for high-priced goods obtainable from the east. Clearly, such a purchasing power did exist in Charlemagne's Francia. But there were few royal courts besides Charlemagne's with the patronage and revenues capable of sustaining a steady demand for luxury goods. And there were few other population or patronage centres with strong purchasing power. The scarcity of luxuries could trigger off enterprises of a different sort, piratical raids, either to relieve traders of their goods or to acquire commodities which could then be exchanged for exotic luxuries. The handful of emporia which dealt in them regularly thus stood out from their immediate surroundings. Almost from the first, the nexus to which they belonged involved elements of violence as well as exchanges by consent.

It may seem rash to connect events in the North Sea with those occurring in the Gulf of Finland, but the vitality of the link provided by Birka is demonstrated by the *Vita* of Ansgar. This German missionary visited Birka in 830-31 and again in 852. The boatload of merchants with whom Ansgar set off from Francia on his first visit to Sweden was attacked by pirates; they lost their boats and nearly all their goods. Subsequently, Birka was the target of an exiled Swedish king, named Anund. He mustered a fleet of Danish adventurers with promises 'that there were many wealthy traders there and an abundance of every good thing and loads of money [*pecunia thesaurorum multa*]'.[16] When Anund was mollified by the 100 pounds of silver promptly offered by the merchants in Birka, his followers objected that 'any one of the merchants there possessed more than they had been offered, and that they could in no way bear such calumny'. The *Vita* depicts a get-rich-quick society of long-distance entrepreneurs, in which trading intermingled with raiding. Slaves were an important source of Birka's prosperity and they had been seized from distant places, in Western Europe: Ansgar encountered 'many . . . Christian captives' there. They had presumably been imported as commodities, to be exchanged for eastern silver. Wine was to be had in the town, and a pious woman named Frideburg bought some for use as a viaticum, in the belief that she was dying and for want of a priest. When eventually the rich old woman lay on her death-bed and thought of deserving candidates for her charity, the place which sprang to mind was Dorestad in Frisia, rather than Birka, where there were few poor persons; at Dorestad, in contrast, 'there are very many churches, priests and

---

16 Rimbert, *Vita Anskarii* 19, in W. Trillmich and R. Buchner, eds, *Quellen des 9. und 11. Jahrhunderts zur Geschichte der Hamburgischen Kirche und des Reiches* (Ausgewählte Quellen zur Deutschen Geschichte des Mittelalters 11; Darmstadt, 1978), pp. 58-61.

clergymen . . . [and] a crowd of the needy'.[17] Her daughter's journey to Dorestad in fulfilment of her wishes is treated as praiseworthy, but not extraordinary. Through their tenuous but resilient network of contacts with points such as Dorestad to the west and Staraia Ladoga to the east, Birka's inhabitants grew rich.

Staraia Ladoga was most probably the principal source of the pounds of silver which attracted to Birka merchants as well as pirates. But it is questionable whether things were as insecure at Staraia Ladoga as they appeared to be to Ansgar's party at Birka. Staraia Ladoga is not even mentioned in any western source other than the Norse sagas, which are much later in date. The impression that Staraia Ladoga lay beyond most people's horizons in the ninth century emerges from the *Vita* of Ansgar. Journeys across the Baltic are made, but they are southwards, where King Anund and his fleet sack a town 'in the confines of the Slavs', or south-eastwards to Kurland, where first the Danes and then the reigning king of the Swedes attacked the inhabitants of, seemingly, Grobin and Apuola (see above, p. 9). The Swedes are said to have reimposed tribute which had long since lapsed. But no journey north-eastwards features in the *Vita*'s anecdotes and Ansgar himself apparently interpreted his mission to Birka as being in fulfilment of Isaiah's prophecy of salvation brought 'unto the end of the earth', as if nothing lay beyond it.[18] The archaeological evidence from Staraia Ladoga is incomplete, but it, too, suggests that the settlement was set apart from goings-on in the rest of the Baltic region. For Staraia Ladoga seems to have been unfortified during the first 150 or so years of its existence, and finds of weapons in the settlement and the burial-ground are not particularly abundant. There are few signs of a warrior elite capable of intervening in defence of the inhabitants, as was sometimes the case at Birka. Yet Staraia Ladoga does not seem to have paid a price for this. The conflagration which it suffered during the later ninth century may well have resulted from a raid, but it seems to have been the first major upheaval (see below, pp. 56–7).

If this impression of relative tranquillity at Staraia Ladoga is valid, a question arises as to the reason for its neglect by predators. Sheer remoteness and the lack of alternative ports of call in the vicinity put a dampener on piratical ventures. There was no major trading

---

17 Rimbert, *Vita Anskarii* 20, in Trillmich and Buchner, eds, *Quellen*, pp. 64–7. The story of Frideburg illustrates the vitality of Birka's ties with Dorestad, whether or not she was herself of Frisian stock: see S. Lebecq, *Marchands et navigateurs frisons du haut moyen âge*, I (Lille, 1983), pp. 31–2, 61–2, 81–4, fig. 46 on pp. 198, 202. Seals-cum-amulets of Frisian merchants have been found in tenth-century sites in the eastern lands: V. P. Darkevich, 'Mezhdunarodnye sviazi', in B. A. Kolchin, ed., *Drevniaia Rus'. Gorod, zamok, selo* (Moscow, 1985), p. 395.

18 Rimbert, *Vita Anskarii* 25, in Trillmich and Buchner, eds, *Quellen*, pp. 84–7; Isaiah 49:6.

settlement, monastery or treasury between Birka and Ladoga, either to yield plunder or to act as a market for the proceeds of a successful strike on Staraia Ladoga. Moreover, the general thinness of the native population in the region had deprived raiders of easy opportunities for acquiring slaves. Nonetheless, Staraia Ladoga's stocks of silver might have been expected to attract some predators or self-styled 'protectors'. Perhaps Staraia Ladoga was shielded by its function as a kind of 'flow-valve' of eastern silver, too intricate for any one group of outsiders to master, a kind of silver goose which must not fall victim to casual destruction. This is to impute enlightened self-interest to the leaders of war-bands. But any who got as far as contemplating a raid on Staraia Ladoga probably concluded that they could easily obtain all the silver their boats could carry by other means: delivery of a consignment of slaves or furs gathered through some kind of bartering, raiding, 'tribute' or extortion in the coastal regions of the Baltic or further west. Moreover, little fame was to be had from sacking so remote an outpost. In contrast, expeditions in quest of slaves from relatively well-populated countries in Western Europe provided the slave-traders with the means to obtain silver at markets in the Baltic, and relieved them of the need to travel all the way to Staraia Ladoga itself. The number of persons who made that journey each year during the second half of the eighth century was probably tiny, perhaps less than a hundred. And knowledge about the spot where they acquired most, if not all, of their silver was correspondingly restricted.

Staraia Ladoga's locale and the pattern of archaeological finds there suggest that it became the node of exchanges of considerable complexity. Produce and products converged from many directions and it was essentially as a meeting-point that Staraia Ladoga's unique economic role developed. One of the functions of its workshops, from the mid-eighth century onwards, was to produce rivets and planks for boats. From the Baltic region and beyond came slaves who could be exchanged directly for eastern dirhams. The North Sea and Mediterranean regions were probably the source of most types of beads and also provided the glass scrap for the manufacture of those made at Staraia Ladoga. Fur-bearing animals roamed the forests throughout the northern regions, but those with coats of finest quality in terms of colour, texture or thickness mostly lived in the furthest north, towards the Arctic Circle. Lake Ladoga was well connected with the far north by riverways, being linked by the Svir to Lake Onega, whence one could travel by lake and river due northwards to the Northern Dvina, itself rich in furs. The forms of barter which had probably long been in play between Swedish fur-traders and the Finno-Ugrians living near Lake Ladoga and further north could now be invigorated by the beads and inexpensive bronze ornaments stored in the new trading post. It is probable that these suppliers of furs were the main customers for the beads, although Scandinavian women, too, wore them in abundance. The use of force, or threat of force, was not of decisive advantage as a means of regularly extracting furs from the more northerly peoples. They tended to be scattered across a huge area, thus denying Scandinavians opportunities for sudden, devastating, assault. And, no less importantly, aboriginal peoples living to a large extent as hunter-gatherers were not rooted to any one spot and could permanently withdraw from areas easily reached via waterways. This is what they seem to have done, even in the relatively circumscribed vicinity of Staraia Ladoga itself. The fur-traders' task was to lure them to a meeting-point and motivate them to seek out the finest pelts. Staraia Ladoga played an essential role in this – partly as a manufacturing centre, but above all as a kind of giant warehouse, where the beads and other goods could be brought by water during the summer, stored and then, in late winter or spring, exchanged for the winter's harvest of furs. For a long time, Staraia Ladoga's role seems to have been more or less unique, a reflection upon the small scale of the trading operations.

These considerations prompt two basic questions: why did the Scandinavians trouble to probe far beyond Staraia Ladoga into the interior? And what routes were used to convey the silver to the north? The original *raison d'être* of Staraia Ladoga was as an aid to bartering and, unlike most of the Scandinavian settlements on the Baltic coast, it was very well placed for journeys into the interior: cargoes could be unloaded onto river vessels capable of negotiating the formidable Volkhov rapids, or ships could put in at Staraia Ladoga before sailing up another river from the south-eastern shore of Lake Ladoga. It is most probable that the silver was extremely highly valued in the period when it first began to arrive, in very limited quantities. The fact that some of the earliest types of bead contained silver suggests that the Finno-Ugrians needed substantial inducements to part with their furs (see above, p. 15). There was accordingly every reason for entrepreneurs to hasten into the interior, vying with one another for more abundant supplies of both furs and silver. This, in turn, would lead one to expect that a variety of trails was followed. Secrecy may well have been of the essence. There is no reason to suppose that these journeys were made exclusively by water, or that Scandinavians were the sole travellers. In fact, the speed with which dirhams reached Staraia Ladoga in the mid-eighth century indicates conveyance by persons well acquainted with part, or all, of the way from Tabaristan. They are unlikely to have been newcomers from the Baltic region.

This raises the questions of who were the bearers of the dirhams, and whether the coins were transported in one long-haul journey, or in several stages by different traders. To this, as to so many questions about happenings in the eastern lands, the answer is that the scanty evidence does not permit a decisive answer. But a few clusters and trails of archaeological finds offer pointers to strong tendencies in what was, most probably, a far-flung and volatile series of contacts and *ad hoc* arrangements. Thus it is clear that some Finno-Ugrian settlements near the Upper Volga were involved in the movement of silver within about a generation of the foundation of Staraia Ladoga, and probably earlier still. One of the most significant clusters was in the vicinity of Lake Nero, approximately 50 kilometres south from the Volga. Lake Nero's district became the centre of a Finno-Ugrian grouping known to the *Primary Chronicle* as the Mer. Near the lake has been excavated a settlement on a promontory overlooking the valley of the river Sara. Four earthen ramparts blocked off the neck of the promontory and they give the settlement the status of a 'fort'. Precise dating is not possible, for the stratigraphy of the settlement was not recorded by its excavators in the 1920s, but it seems clear that while the site was occupied by Finno-Ugrians from the sixth or the beginning of the seventh centuries, significant enrichment in their material culture, together with expansion of the settlement, occurred some time later. In, apparently, the eighth century the inhabitants of the 'Sarskii fort', as it is known to Russian archaeologists, began to make extensive use of iron tools and spearheads and arrowheads appear. This was also the time when metal ornaments in the form of wire triangles with jingling pendants made their first appearance among the Mer of the Sarskii fort and elsewhere. This development is probably connected with the fact that three dirham hoards, deposited in, apparently, the early ninth century have been found at the Sarskii fort or nearby. They are among the earliest hoards to be uncovered outside the district of Staraia Ladoga. In the settlement on this promontory fort have been found Scandinavian ornaments and tools or weapons, two of them datable to the beginning of the ninth century, or earlier still. The only other place where both early hoards of oriental silver and Scandinavian objects of c. 800 or earlier have been found is Staraia Ladoga. They probably attest a Scandinavian presence at the Sarskii fort rather than simply the import of objects of exchange. These are not, however, sure signs of permanent settlement.[19]

The elasticity of archaeological periodization precludes a decisive answer to the questions: did the coming of the Scandinavians trigger off the other developments, or were Scandinavians drawn to the area by the presence of silver there already? But the materials for an answer may come from the fact that the Sarskii fort is *not* situated on a major river. The region of Lake Nero was fertile and the fish in the

---

19 On the beginnings of the Finno-Ugrian settlement at the Sarskii fort, and the Scandinavian objects (and also dirhams) found in and near it: E. I. Goriunova, *Etnicheskaia istoriia volgo-okskogo mezhdurech'ia* (*MIA* 94; Moscow, Leningrad, 1961), pp. 95–109; A. E. Leont'ev, 'Skandinavskie veshchi v kollekstii sarskogo gorodishcha', *Skandinavskii sbornik* 26 (1981), 144–8; idem, 'Volzhsko-Baltiiskii torgovyi put' v IX v.', *KSIA* 193 (1986), 4–5; I. V. Dubov, *Novye istochniki po istorii drevnei Rusi* (Leningrad, 1990), pp. 86–7.

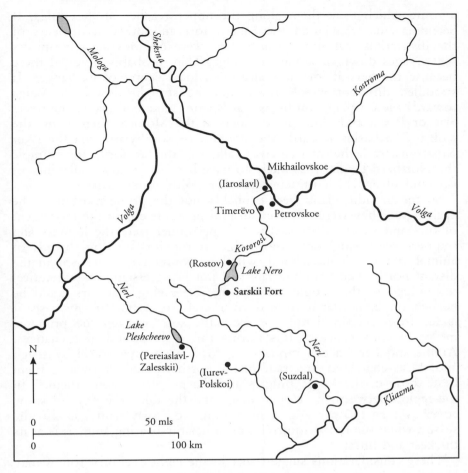

Map B.   Sarskii fort

lake supplemented the inhabitants' diet of milk and meat from their domestic animals and the hunters' kills. It was, most probably, for reasons such as this that a number of settlements arose there, as they also did in the vicinity of Lake Pleshcheevo, about 40 kilometres to the south-west. But the very fact that these districts were, so to speak, oases of human habitation amidst largely unpopulated forests made them convenient points of exchange. And for those local inhabitants familiar with the rivers, lakes and crossing-points, there was fairly easy access to the Volga and, in the south, to the Kliazma, which flowed into the Oka. On the other hand, the region could have had no inherent attraction for persons travelling from Staraia Ladoga on a route which took them along the upper reaches of the Volga. If Scandinavians frequented the Sarskii fort and other settlements of the district, it was not because they were obvious stopping-places for voyages down or along the Volga. They probably diverted there because the Sarskii fort was already a local centre of exchanges. It straddled different routes from the one straight down the Volga towards the Caspian: south-eastwards from Lake Ladoga up the rivers Sias or Pasha and along rivers such as the Mologa, then *across* the Volga–Oka basins towards the steppes; or southwards via the river Kostroma from the fur-rich river valleys of the far north, for example the Northern Dvina. It is likely to have been the ready availability of furs and silver which attracted travellers to the Sarskii fort.

So the Scandinavians were probably not the prime movers of the exchanges. They were not even an indispensable cog in the movement of furs and silver dirhams. The key personnel were the hunters and trappers possessing local knowledge of the fur-runs and breeds of animal in the neighbourhood, whether around Lake Nero or in the distant north. The Scandinavians did not bring essential new nautical technology to the peoples of the interior, seeing that furs could be heaped on light, flat-bottomed river craft, or rafts. In any case, it is far from certain that boats were the sole or even the principal means of conveyance of furs during this early period of exchanges. Arabic and Persian geographers regarded fast winter travel by sleigh and ski as characterizing trade in the northern lands known to them best, those of the Volga Bulgars and the peoples beyond them.[20] In the region between the Upper Volga and the Oka, the days of snow cover average 140 per year. Late autumn and early winter is also the season when the fur of squirrels and other fur-bearing animals is at its thickest and finest.

These considerations suggest that in the eighth century routes may have run from the far north and the north-west to the region between the Volga and the Kliazma, perhaps revitalizing a more ancient one. But their direction south of the Kliazma has not been determined and anyway there were probably various alternative trails towards the dirhams' sources. There is most probably commercial significance in the numerous hoards of dirhams found near the Middle and the Upper Oka, a notable concentration being around the settlement which grew, during the eleventh century, into the town of Riazan. The hoards nearly all occur on the right, southern bank of the Oka, or on its southern tributaries. They form an elaborate curve around the head-waters of the Don, where it spearheads a broad salient of

---

20 On the Volga Bulgars' use of sleighs and skis to cover great distances and to transport goods to the far north, see J. Martin, *Treasure of the Land of Darkness. The Fur Trade and its Significance for Medieval Russia* (Cambridge, 1986), pp. 20–1, 28; below, p. 63.

wooded steppe reaching northwards towards the Oka. This could have served as a convenient meeting-ground between forest-dwellers and inhabitants of the steppe.

Such suppositions would remain just that, were it not for the evidence of several dirham hoards along the Don and the Severskii Donets, and further south. Their location is suggestive in itself, but the dates ascribed to the earliest hoards and their composition are even more striking. The three earliest hoards from the Don and the Kuban steppes date from c. 800, while dirham hoards first appear in the southern Caucasus region around the same time. Since the late eighth and early ninth century is also the date of the earliest hoards in or near Staraia Ladoga, and the Sarskii fort hoards are datable to the early ninth century, the obvious inference is that the distribution pattern of these roughly contemporaneous hoards registers the principal route by which the Staraia Ladoga dirhams reached the north. Such an inference gains support from a study of the date and composition of these early hoards. They indicate that the principal area where the dirhams left Moslem territory was Caucasia. Taking into consideration the other indicators, one may conclude that their route further northwards ran along the rivers Don or Donets, passing the white stone 'fortresses' of the semi-nomadic peoples living in the Khazar ambit.[21]

This conclusion gains support from finds of a variety of rock-crystal and cornelian beads of similar, and sometimes identical, types at Birka, Staraia Ladoga and burial-grounds in Dagestan. The cornelian beads are found in 'Horizon E_3' at Staraia Ladoga, and they occur in sites in Dagestan – the northern Caucasus, encompassing the port of Darband – from the sixth or seventh century onwards. Over 10,000 examples have been found in the burial-ground of Agach-Kala and they have long been known to archaeologists. Finds of small cornelian pendants carved in the form of a 'dung-beetle' have also been made in roughly contemporaneous sites in Birka, Staraia Ladoga and Dagestan. The examples from Sweden and Dagestan are very similar in design. Such pendants are extremely rare in sites of the ninth to eleventh centuries, and this alone would suggest a special relationship between the places where they are found. The question of where exactly the cornelian was worked up into ornaments – Dagestan, Iran or India – remains unanswered. But the probability that their route northwards, together with that of the beads and dirhams, ran along the Don and the Donets valleys seems overwhelming. Some of the objects

---

21 In five of the six fairly fully published Russian hoards of the late eighth or early ninth centuries, southern Caucasian dirhams are among the youngest coins in the hoard. It is most likely that these dirhams were added to the other pieces as the latter were being conveyed across the Caucasian lands: Noonan, 'Why dirhams first reached Russia', 155, 159, table II on 161, 163, 165. On the white stone 'fortresses' and the Khazars, see below, pp. 79–84.

were probably manufactured or worked up in the Khazar sphere of influence. Crescent-shaped ornaments of dark-blue glass are found at Verkhnee Saltovo, in the central section of the foothills of the northern Caucasus and in Dagestan. Their only other find-location appears to be in various substrata of 'Horizon E' at Staraia Ladoga, datable to between the late eighth and the late ninth centuries. Small lumps of amber are a very common find in the burial-ground at Dmitrievskoe, a fortress on a northern tributary of the Donets. These lumps, used as amulets, may well have originated in the Baltic region.[22] There is, then, evidence pointing clearly to the existence of a trade-route from the Moslem lands of the Caucasus towards the steppes north of the Sea of Azov. And there seems to have been a strong tendency for traders to follow – though not necessarily to navigate – the course of the Don northwards to the Middle Oka and the forest zone.

However, this was not the sole route taken by the bearers of silver. The Severskii Donets could as well lead to the Vorskla and other tributaries of the Middle Dnieper as towards the Upper Oka. Groups of dirham hoards found between the Western Dvina and the Upper Dnieper suggest that some silver was carried this way up to Staraia Ladoga, or directly down the Dvina to the Baltic, at least by around the mid-ninth century.[23] Evidence of trade up the Volga from its mouth is much scantier. Earlier ninth-century hoards have been found on or near the rivers Kama and Viatka, which linked the Middle Volga with the far north, and a hoard whose youngest coin dates to AD 821 has been found near the Volga itself. Silver vessels of oriental origin have also been found in the regions of the Kama and the Viatka. There is no reason to deny the possibility of travel further upstream from the Middle Volga, but the lack of hoards or other silver objects reported along the 700–kilometre stretch of the Volga above the junction with the Kama contrasts sharply with the configuration of evidence on

22 For find-locations of the cornelian beads and pendants, and of the crescent-shaped, dark-blue glass ornaments, see M. V. Fekhner, 'K voprosu ob ekonomicheskikh sviaziakh drevnerusskoi derevni', *Ocherki po istorii russkoi derevni, Trudy Gosudarstvennogo Istoricheskogo Muzeia* 33 (1959), 152–4; O. I. Davidan, 'Stratigrafiia nizhnego sloia staroladozhskogo gorodishcha i voprosy datirovki', *Arkheologicheskii sbornik* (Gosudarstvennyi Ermitazh) 17 (1976), 115; Davidan, 'Etnokul'turnye kontakty Staroi Ladogi', 101; O. I. Davidan, 'Skarabei iz Staroi Ladogi', *Arkheologicheskii sbornik* (Gosudarstvennyi Ermitazh) 29 (1988), 112–14; E. A. Riabinin, 'Busy Staroi Ladogi (po materialam raskopok 1973–1975gg.)', in A. D. Stoliar, ed., *Severnaia Rus' i ee sosedi v epokhu rannego srednevekov'ia* (Leningrad, 1982), p. 171; I. Jansson, 'Wikingerzeitlicher orientalischer Import in Skandinavien', *OWS, Bericht der Römisch-Germanischen Kommission* 69 (1988), 586–8. For the amber, see S. A. Pletneva, *Ot kochevii k gorodam. Saltovo-Maiatskaia kul'tura* (*MIA* 142; Moscow, 1967), pp. 140, 176 and illustration 49: 18, p. 177.

23 L. V. Alekseev, *Smolenskaia zemlia v IX–XIII vv.* (Moscow, 1980), pp. 75, 78; Leont'ev, 'Volzhsko-Baltiiskii torgovyi put'', fig. 1, p. 4 (map). See also below, p. 101.

the Oka and around Lake Nero. Arguments from silence cannot be conclusive when no dirham hoards have been found on or near the *Lower* Volga, even though some dirhams presumably passed that way *en route* to the Kama. But it could well be that there were at least two different major routes to the north, one along the Lower Volga valley and then northwards from the Middle Volga to the best fur-yielding regions; and the other from the Caucasus north-westwards across the steppes up the valleys of the Don, the Donets and other rivers towards the Middle Dnieper or centres such as the Sarskii fort beyond the Oka. Most importantly of all, however, a plurality of routes, and frequent fluctuation in the degree of usage of them, may well have been the norm.[24]

The one constant in this kaleidoscope, and the one common interest which bound together individuals and small groups from a variety of different peoples, was a quest for self-enrichment through exchanges of luxury goods. Only a minority of the anyway exiguous population of the forest zone was directly engaged in this activity at any one time. This was not the first nexus to have been spun between the inhabitants of the far north or the Baltic region and the trading zones of the southern civilizations. There was no development in the eighth century to suggest that the revived arrangements would be more durable or larger-scale than their predecessors.

2. FIRST REPORTS ON THE RUS

The lack of clear evidence of a single dominant route across the Eurasian land mass in the ninth century fits in with a pattern of exchanges being conducted by a variety of peoples: Scandinavians, often in competition with one another in their undertakings to Lake Nero, as far as the Oka or beyond; the Mer of the region of Lake Nero, some of them making journeys to their Finno-Ugrian cousins in the far north; the semi-nomadic inhabitants of the settlements along the Don, the Severskii Donets and their tributaries, acting sometimes as agents of the Khazars and sometimes on their own account; and Khazar and Arab merchants making the journey to the edge of the steppes or still further northwards.

There was little need for complex social structures to carry out these exchanges in the forests north of the steppes. So long as the

---

24 Contacts between the silver-endowed regions of the Middle East and Central Asia and the far north may not have lapsed altogether, even during the second half of the seventh and first half of the eighth centuries. Nonetheless, the establishment of the Abbasids in Baghdad and emergence there of a moneyed elite vastly strengthened demand for furs; much of the trafficking may have been along a third major route, through Central Asia. See Darkevich, *Khudozhestvennyi metall Vostoka VIII–XIII vv.*, pp. 147, 179; Noonan, 'Khwarazmian coins of the eighth century from Eastern Europe', 253–8.

entrepreneurs operated in small numbers and kept to the north, they did not catch the attention of observers or writers in the Moslem or Christian worlds. But the silence of these sources is broken towards the middle of the ninth century, by references to a grouping or 'people' previously unheard of. The name varies slightly, from *Rūs* in Arabic to *Rhōs* in the Greek, and the earliest Latin-language mentions of it. But their various references are undoubtedly to the same grouping and it is equally clear that the name *Rus'* which later Slavic sources employ is a version of the same term. The bearers of the name had their haunts far to the north, and they came to the notice of Moslems and Christians by virtue of their journeys down to their respective regions. The sheer length of the journeys is commented upon by several writers, and so is the extraordinary ferocity of the northerners when they appeared as raiders. The Rhos attack on Constantinople in 860 was compared to a 'thunderbolt from heaven' by Patriarch Photios in a sermon delivered at the time.[25] But these occasions were few in comparison with the journeys made for the purposes of trading or gift-exchanges.

But who were the *Rūs/Rhōs*, and where exactly did they come from? Controversy over the answer has raged for over 200 years. They are at the heart of what is known as 'the Normanist controversy' over the role of the Northmen or Scandinavians in the formation of what became the Rus 'state'.[26] From what has been said in Section I, the front-runners for the label are already clear. The Finno-Ugrians or a particular grouping of them such as the Mer are eligible, seeing that they engaged in trade and their haunts were within fairly easy reach of the Moslem world. But the trading post at Staraia Ladoga would in itself deserve very serious attention, while the finds of Scandinavian-type personal ornaments at the Sarskii fort suggest that Scandinavian traders travelled far into the forested interior (see above, pp. 14–15, 22). It is also a fact that the name for Swedes in Western Finnic languages is *Ruotsi* and the Estonian for Swede is *Root'si*. Conversely, there is no unequivocal evidence of any Finno-Ugrian people carrying out raids of the sort which stunned Patriarch Photios in 860. In contrast, the Scandinavians' potential for devastatingly successful raids is notorious (see above, pp. 18–19; below, pp. 55–6).

---

25 Photios, *Homiliai*, ed. B. Laourdas (Thessaloniki, 1959), p. 40; tr. C. Mango, *Homilies* (Washington, D.C., 1958), p. 96. See also below, pp. 50–1.

26 There are useful summaries of issues and bibliographies in R. J. H. Jenkins, ed., *De administrando imperio: II Commentary* (London, 1962), pp. 20–3, 40–2 (Obolensky); several contributions in K. Hannestad et al., eds, *Varangian Problems* (Copenhagen, Munksgaard, 1970), especially by Schmidt, Shaskol'skii and Obolensky; *Ob upravl. imp.*, pp. 293–307 (Mel'nikova and Petrukhin). See also G. Schramm, 'Die Herkunft des Namens Rus': Kritik des Forschungsstandes', *Forschungen zur osteuropäischen Geschichte* 30 (1982), 7–49; E. A. Mel'nikova and V. J. Petrukhin, 'The origin and evolution of the name *Rus*", *Tor* 23 (Uppsala, 1990–91), 203–34; *Encyclopaedia of Islam*, VIII, pp. 618–20 (Golden).

Taken together, this evidence suggests that *Rūs/Rhōs* was used by southern writers to denote a grouping of predominantly Scandinavian characteristics. The term need not have been used wholly consistently or accurately. The label may well have been slapped onto virtually any new arrival from the far north by confused and sometimes apprehensive Byzantines and Arabs. Recent research has emphasized the ambiguousness with which terms such as 'Burgundian' could be used in the early medieval west, and warns against taking them at face value. They apparently had at least as much to do with social roles as with ethnic origins.[27] However, an entry in a set of Frankish annals records that in the 830s persons calling themselves *Rhōs* appeared to belong to 'the people of the Swedes' to investigators who specifically enquired into their origins.

The *Annals of St Bertin*, which were written up at the time, recount that a Byzantine embassy arrived at the court of Emperor Louis the Pious in Ingelheim in 839. Travelling with the party were some men whom the Byzantines presented to Louis. A letter from the Byzantine emperor requested Louis to give them every assistance in returning home: their outward journey to Constantinople had, according to the letter, been 'among barbarous and most savage peoples of exceeding ferocity'. These strangers had told Emperor Theophilos that they belonged to a people named 'Rhos', but when Louis made his own enquiries as to the reason for their arrival, he 'discovered that they were of the people of Swedes' (*comperit eos gentis esse Sueonum*). Louis is said to have suspected that they had come as 'spies of that realm [i.e. Byzantium] and of ours rather than as seekers after friendship'. He accordingly detained them for further interrogation.[28] Louis' ability to recognize a 'Swede' when he saw one – or several – has not been seriously contested by modern scholars. Louis and his counsellors were reasonably well qualified to judge. Some years earlier he had sponsored the mission of Ansgar to the Swedes and, as we have seen, Ansgar travelled to Birka (see above, p. 18). This does not in itself mean that the Rhos viewed by Louis originated from Central Sweden, but it suggests a more than passing resemblance between them and other Swedes in Louis' experience. Moreover, there is evidence that the Central Swedish coastal region facing the Åland islands and Finland was, in the thirteenth century, called 'the country of Rodhen'

---

27 For a review of recent scholarship on 'ethnicity', the rhetorical and political uses to which it could be put, and the fluidity of terms denoting groupings, see P. Amory, 'The meaning and purpose of ethnic terminology in the Burgundian laws', *Early Medieval Europe* 2 (1993), 1–5, 8–10, 24–8. On the problems of applying the ideas of R. Wenskus and subsequent scholars to the source-poor East Slavs and early Rus, see C. Goehrke, *Frühzeit des Ostslaventums* (Erträge der Forschung 277; Darmstadt, 1992), pp. 150–4.

28 *Annales Bertiniani* s.a. 839, ed. F. Grat, J. Vieilliard and S. Clémencet (Paris, 1964), pp. 30–1; tr. J. L. Nelson, *The Annals of St-Bertin* (Manchester, 1991), p. 44.

or 'Rodhs'. The precise way in which a term such as *Ruotsi/Rōtsi* might have been transmuted into *Rus'* remains unclear, but that there is a connection between them seems very likely.[29] Distinctive features of ritual objects and ornaments also point to a particular link between a number of settlers in the eastern lands and the inhabitants of the Åland islands and, probably, of Central Sweden itself (see below, pp. 66–7). The looseness and fluidity of 'ethnic' designations in the early middle ages should never be underestimated, especially when used by one people of very distant ones who were known chiefly through intermediaries. But Louis the Pious and his counsellors were dealing with the Rhos at first hand. That there were persons who regarded themselves as belonging to a 'people' of 'Rhos' or 'Rus' in the ninth century and that their original homeland had been the Central Swedish coast and the Åland islands seems a fair conclusion.

A few other scraps of evidence besides the *Annals of St Bertin*'s entry suggest that individual Scandinavians (a term henceforth used interchangeably with *Rhōs* and *Rūs*) began to impinge on southern civilizations during the first half of the ninth century. The name 'Ingeros' was borne by two Byzantine notables of the earlier ninth century, and if the name is derived from the Scandinavian 'Inger' it probably suggests a Nordic origin for them.[30] One further hint that the Scandinavians could have encountered Greek-speakers not long after beginning their long-range eastern ventures comes from a name, 'Zacharias', scratched in Greek letters on a dirham. The dirham formed part of a hoard found on the southern shore of the Gulf of Finland, not far from modern St Petersburg. The hoard's youngest coin dates from 804–5 and on several of the dirhams are scratched Scandinavian runes. This is obviously no proof that the runes were carved far to the south of their find-spot; but the inscription naming Zacharias suggests that the dirham passed through that part of Khazaria which abutted on Greek-speaking communities in settlements on the Crimea and the shores of the Sea of Azov. The majority of the earliest Scandinavian dealers in furs were probably content to exchange their goods for silver somewhere north of the steppes, but the piecemeal and competitive nature of their trade may well have led some to probe down the Don or Donets valleys in quest of the sources of silver.

29 A. V. Soloviev, 'L'organisation de l'État russe au X siècle', in A. Gieysztor and T. Mannteuffel, eds, *L'Europe aux IX–XI siècles. Aux origines des États nationaux* (Warsaw, 1968), p. 264 and n. 87, repr. in Soloviev's *Byzance et la formation de l'État russe* (London, 1979), no. 1. See also S. Ekbo, 'The etymology of Finnish *Ruotsi* "Sweden"', in R. Zeitler, ed., *Les pays du nord et Byzance (Scandinavie et Byzance). Actes du colloque nordique et international de byzantinologie tenu à Upsal 20–22 avril 1979* (Acta Universitatis Upsaliensis. Figura, nova series 19; Uppsala, 1981), pp. 143–5; Schramm, 'Herkunft des Namens Rus''', 13–16; *Ob upravl. imp.*, pp. 297–8.

30 C. Mango, 'Eudocia Ingerina, the Normans and the Macedonian dynasty', *Zbornik Radova Vizantoloshkog Instituta* 14–15 (1973), 17–18, 20, 27, repr. in Mango's *Byzantium and Its Image* (London, 1984), no. 15.

There are indications that in the south, as in the Baltic, the search for self-enrichment could lead to a pooling of resources and the formation of war-bands. Some time in the ninth century a party of Rus raided the town of Amastris on the north coast of Asia Minor. They took prisoners and tried to dig up and loot the tomb of a local saint, who bore the name of George. Some scholars maintain that the miracle story recounting the paralysis which struck these sacrilegious looters was written before 842, and that therefore the attack which it embroiders occurred before that time.[31] No mention of any such raid is made in the Byzantine chronicles for the first half of the ninth century, but their silence is less than damning, given the thinness of their coverage of events in the provinces. It is not impossible that the Rhos embassy which arrived in Byzantium in 838 'for the sake of friendship' was dispatched in the aftermath of the raid on Amastris. However, there is no necessary connection, and much could be done by one group of Rus without the knowledge, let alone the prompting, of another.

What is certain is that by c. 838 some sort of political structure had been formed among the Rus. It was headed, according to Emperor Louis' guests, by the *chaganus* (i.e. khagan, ruler) who had sent them to Constantinople and this title was considered well known by the Byzantine government a generation later (see below, p. 38). A capacity to send out long-range embassies does not necessarily denote effective power, but the very existence of a polity of sorts in the eastern lands is a striking advance on what the bits and pieces excavated at the trading post of Staraia Ladoga might lead one to expect.

This leads to a fundamental question which the debate over the ethnic identity of the Rhos has overshadowed: where was the envoys' *chaganus* based? Four areas present themselves as candidates: Central Sweden; Staraia Ladoga; Riurikovo Gorodishche, near the point where the Volkhov flows out of Lake Ilmen; and the region of the Upper Volga. Neither Kiev nor the Middle Dnieper region deserve serious attention, for reasons which will be discussed below (see pp. 94–103). It may seem bizarre to regard the kings of Central Sweden as any worthier of attention. But the route of the returning Rhos envoys would have been fairly well chosen, if Sweden were their objective. Moreover, there is evidence, in the form of a lead seal, that Byzantine officials were seeking contact with persons in the Baltic region, perhaps at this very time. The seal, excavated at Hedeby, belonged to a certain Theodosios. The seal's publisher proposed to date it between 820 and

---

31 See I. Ševčenko, 'Hagiography of the Iconoclast period', in A. Bryer and J. Herrin, eds, *Iconoclasm* (Birmingham, 1977), p. 122 and n. 67, pp. 123–4. A contrary view was taken by A. Markopoulos, 'La vie de Saint Georges d'Amastris et Photius', *JÖB* 28 (1979), 78–82.

860, and to identify Theodosios with the Byzantine emissary of that name sent to Venice and the court of Lothar I between 840 and 842.[32] The identification is highly probable and in any case the seal indicates diplomatic contacts, actual or attempted, between Byzantium and the Scandinavian world. This could have been a follow-up to the more celebrated embassy of the Rhos of 838–9.

The title of 'khagan' (chaganus) was borne by the rulers of Khazaria in the eighth and ninth centuries. It could easily have been well enough known for a Swedish konungr to think it worth appropriating for himself. Silver dirhams were reaching Birka and its hinterland, and so were small ornaments such as cornelian and rock-crystal beads and, occasionally, elaborate oriental belts. Some of the dirhams were put to decorative use on, for example, necklaces, and they clearly had a fashionable cachet. The purchasers, wearers and hoarders of these goods were probably aware of Khazaria, the land through which most of these products had passed, and might have been impressed by a local king's adoption of the Khazar khagan's title. The term would not appear to have been known to Emperor Louis II, if one takes literally his profession of unfamiliarity with the term chaganus ... Northmannorum in a letter addressed to Basil I in 871. Louis denied that the titles 'chaganus of the Northmen' or even 'khagan of the Khazars' were known, in answer to a letter of Basil which had cited them.[33] But Louis' letter was a polemical riposte and his protestation of ignorance is not conclusive evidence as to whether or not a chaganus of the Swedish Northmen was known to the Franks.

Staraia Ladoga might also have some claim to be the principal residence of the chaganus who sent the envoys to Byzantium. Excavations have not disclosed traces of fortifications before the late ninth or early tenth centuries. The earliest inhabitants raised structures on the low bank of the river Ladozhka, for ease of access to the river rather than from any strategic considerations. Staraia Ladoga was a very loosely knit settlement, open to all who ventured there, and to that extent it stands in contrast with Birka, where the settlement was surrounded by a rampart to the north-east and overlooked by a hill-fort to the south. Birka is described as having a rex by the Vita of Ansgar, but he was not strikingly effective in defending the town during Ansgar's visit and the fort itself is described as being 'not very strong'.[34] One cannot absolutely rule out the possibility that this

---

32 V. Laurent, 'Ein byzantinisches Bleisiegel aus Haithabu', Bericht über die Ausgrabungen in Haithabu 12 (1978), 36–7; J. Shepard, 'The Rhos guests of Louis the Pious: whence and wherefore?', Early Medieval Europe 4 (1995), 55–8.

33 Ludovici II. Epistola ad Basilium I., MGH Epp. Karolini aevi, V, p. 388.

34 Rimbert, Vita Anskarii 19, in Trillmich and Buchner, eds, Quellen, pp. 60–1.

Swedish *rex* had a counterpart in or near Staraia Ladoga. Extensive areas of the settlement remain unexcavated, while it is conceivable that an overlord might have resided somewhere as yet unidentified, out of town. Such a location for the '*chaganus* of the Northmen' would the better explain, and vindicate, Louis II's profession of ignorance as to the existence of such a title, while a return journey via the Rhineland from Byzantium would have been circuitous, but not extraordinarily so.

Similar geographical considerations could be adduced in support of the third candidate for the khagan's seat, Gorodishche. This settlement, sometimes known as 'Riurikovo Gorodishche' (i.e. 'Riurik's fortress') in modern works was built on what was in medieval times raised ground entirely surrounded by rivers, the Volkhov, the Volkhovets and the Zhilotug. The most important of these three was the Volkhov, which flows out of Lake Ilmen just above this point. Its island-like character would have been particularly striking after the spring thaw, when floods lingered for weeks, if not months, in the Volkhov flood plain. Excavations of Gorodishche had uncovered little more than 1,500 square metres by the early 1990s, but the size of the site's total area – well over 10 hectares – and the nature of the finds point to a basically Scandinavian trading emporium of first-class importance. The finds of 'equal-armed' brooches and a tortoiseshell brooch suggest that Scandinavian women settled here, as they did at Staraia Ladoga.[35] But the position seems to have been chosen for its strategic significance. The settlement was fortified from the outset, the highest part of the elevation being separated from the much lower ground by a narrow hollow which was most probably filled with water, and by a ditch which joined up with the hollow. The outhouses were put up in the lower-lying, oft-flooded, part of the island site.

Gorodishche's site was the least assailable of several plots of raised ground just over a kilometre from the outflow of the Volkhov from Lake Ilmen. As the first such rising downstream from the lake, it was a prime site. The axis of a series of unfortified settlements near the lakeside and along the Volkhov seems to have had Gorodishche at its pivot. There is evidence that by the early ninth century some of them were already in existence and that they had some sort of commercial contact with the steppe regions and the Moslem world. In the initially unfortified settlement of Georgii, excavations have revealed glass beads, a few oriental coins deposited 'no later than the ninth century',[36] and a bronze finger-ring of 'Saltovo-type' – belonging to

---

35 T. A. Pushkina, 'Skandinavskie nakhodki iz Gorodishcha pod Novgorodom', *Skandinavskii sbornik* 31 (1988), 100–3; E. N. Nosov, 'Ryurik Gorodishche and the settlements to the north of Lake Ilmen', in M. Brisbane, ed., *The Archaeology of Novgorod, Russia* (Lincoln, 1992), p. 35.
36 Nosov, 'Ryurik Gorodishche', p. 18.

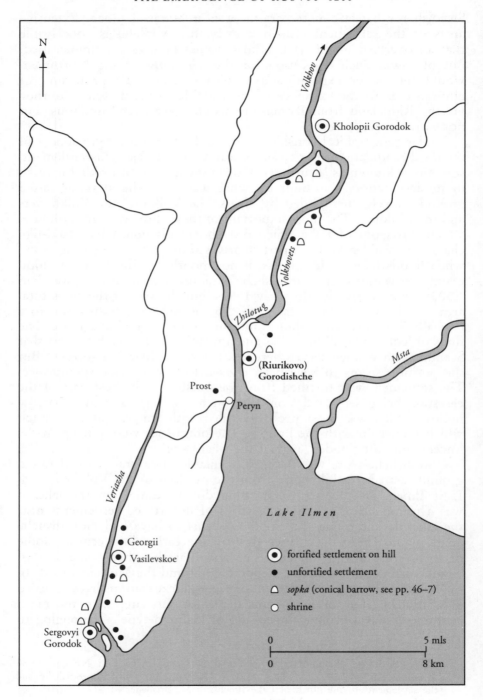

Map C. Gorodishche

a type manufactured somewhere in the lands of the Saltovo-Maiatskii 'culture' between the end of the eighth and the mid-ninth century. A bronze finger-ring of the same type has been found in Gorodishche.[37] A hoard of oriental silver coins apparently datable to the beginning of the ninth century has been excavated at another settlement, Kholopii Gorodok. This naturally-fortified site was on a rise near the point where a branch of the Volkhov, the Volkhovets ('Little Volkhov'), rejoined the main stream. It thus stood at the opposite end from Gorodishche of the 12-kilometre-long island site which the Volkhovets formed together with the Volkhov. It is therefore noteworthy that the (exclusively) hand-modelled pottery, glass and cornelian beads and other ornaments found there are mostly datable to the eighth or ninth centuries; the beads and ornaments have close analogies with finds in Staraia Ladoga, Birka and other trading centres in the Scandinavian world. A hoard of tools, agricultural implements and bridle-bits is especially suggestive. The iron plough-blades were of the sort most appropriate for working areas of ground newly cleared from the forest and their closest analogies occur in strata of the mid-eighth to mid-ninth centuries at Staraia Ladoga.[38] These finds suggest that the early inhabitants of Kholopii Gorodok and Staraia Ladoga to a considerable extent grew their own foodstuffs. Presumably the volume and value of exchanges was not yet large enough to permit total reliance on manufacturing and trade for one's livelihood. The similarity between the pattern of finds in the two settlements also suggests that their early inhabitants were preponderantly Scandinavians. In the light of these indications of the existence in the early ninth century at the opposite end of the Volkhov from Staraia Ladoga of such settlements as Georgii and Kholopii Gorodok, it would be strange if the best-appointed island site of all had been left vacant for long.

The lack of positive evidence of occupation at Gorodishche itself before the mid-ninth century does not, therefore, debar identification of it with the seat of the Rhos *chaganus* of 838–9. He need not, after all, have been established there for very long. The despatch of an embassy to the famed *basileus* of the Greeks might have been a means of announcing the formation of a new power structure. The embassy of 838–9 could well have been the first, or one of the first, to have been sent by the Rhos *chaganus* to Byzantium. The *Annals of St Bertin* give the impression that a Rhos embassy was unusual for the Byzantines as well as the Franks, and that Theophilos was looking for a safe return route for them. A further inducement to identifying Gorodishche as the *chaganus*' seat might be the find in the infill of one

---

37 E. N. Nosov, *Novgorodskoe (Riurikovo) Gorodishche* (Leningrad, 1990), p. 175. For the Saltovo-Maiatskii 'culture', see below, pp. 79–82.
38 Nosov, *Novgorodskoe (Riurikovo) Gorodishche*, p. 181.

of the structures of a copper *follis* of Theophilos. The coin was, most probably, deposited there before the beginning of the tenth century. In other words, it could have been brought to the citadel by the same party – or embassy – that brought coins of the same emperor to Hedeby and Birka. Ninth-century hoards containing Byzantine copper coins, or individual finds of such coins in ninth-century archaeological contexts, are extremely rare in Russian or Scandinavian sites.[39]

The fourth candidate as the starting-point of the 838–9 embassy is the Upper Volga region. The Sarskii fort is the only site beside Staraia Ladoga where *both* Scandinavian objects of c. 800 or earlier *and* hoards of around the same date have been found (see above, p. 22). Craftsmen worked there and it possessed long-distance trading connections through the ninth and tenth centuries. Much of this activity seems to have been in the hands of the Finno-Ugrians, but the ninth century saw the emergence of at least three other complexes, albeit of a somewhat different type, approximately 70 kilometres away, in the neighbourhood of modern Iaroslavl. The largest site is that at Bolshoe Timerëvo, standing beside a small stream near the stream's confluence with the river Kotorosl; this river rises near Lake Nero and flows into the Volga not far from Timerëvo. The site had the advantage of awesome natural defences, overlooking river valleys on two sides and reportedly being, in its first phase, screened off from the remainder of the hillside by a palisade. It was quite close to the Volga, but hard of access. Excavations have only uncovered a fraction of the surface area (approximately 6,000 metres^2), but they show that the settlement was involved in long-range commerce from the outset. Two hoards of Arab dirhams have been unearthed. One of them is thought to have been deposited at the end of the ninth century. The other, supposedly deposited before 870, contained at least 2,751 coins, a figure which each successive investigation of the find-site raises. The date of the settlement's first phase is uncertain, and the location of the earliest buildings of all may have escaped detection so far. In the burial-ground adjoining the settlement one barrow, containing the cremated remains of a woman and child, has been assigned to the first half of the ninth century. Most of the others, however, have been dated to the very end of the ninth or to the tenth centuries.[40] At some time in the late ninth century a settlement complex arose on the opposite, northern, side of the Volga, at Mikhailovskoe, and in the burial-ground there have been found graves with more or less firm ethnic indicators. Foremost among these are pairs of tortoiseshell-shaped brooches (worn at the shoulders to fasten the straps of a Scandinavian woman's outer garment

39 Ibid., pp. 101, 148–9; Shepard, 'Rhos guests', 51–3.
40 I. V. Dubov, 'Novye raskopki timerevskogo mogil'nika', *KSIA* 146 (1976), 82–6; N. G. Nedoshivina and M. V. Fekhner, 'Pogrebal'nyi obriad timerevskogo mogil'nika', *SA* 1985, no. 2, 114.

to her shift or chemise), and sizable iron rings on which miniature 'hammerlets of Thor' were strung.[41] Another settlement arose in the late ninth century at Petrovskoe. The sites seem to have been chosen for their strategic significance. Mikhailovskoe, set back 4 kilometres from the actual banks of the Volga, was a potential watch-post to regulate traffic coming down the Volga towards the point where the Kotorosl flowed into it. Timerëvo, set back 12 kilometres from the Volga, dominated traffic passing along the Kotorosl valley to Lake Nero, the Sarskii fort and the various routes leading southwards from there.

Of these four serious candidates as the Rus *chaganus*' seat, none is utterly implausible. Staraia Ladoga does not, however, have any really compelling claim, while a *chaganus* based in Birka might be expected to have been called by this title in, for example, the *Vita* of Ansgar. Moreover, if he and his people regularly called themselves Rhos or Rus, the name should have been more familiar to Louis the Pious. The archaeological evidence of some sort of politico-military organization in the interior makes Gorodishche or the Iaroslavl settlements the stronger candidates. The fewest anomalies are created by the supposition that the Rhos envoys set out from the citadel of Gorodishche. Admittedly, this is to give it the benefit of the doubts which the limited excavations and lack of unequivocally early ninth-century finds inevitably raise. But other considerations tell in its favour. Gorodishche's position seems to have been chosen for the purpose of dominance as well as defence: all boats sailing up the Volkhov to Lake Ilmen and further into the forested interior passed beneath its slopes. In contrast, Timerëvo, Mikhailovskoe and Petrovskoe lack the evidence of extensive building-work of the middle to later ninth century which Gorodishche offers. Moreover, there is a question of geography, or at least, of a sense of direction. One might expect an embassy from the Upper Volga to have had a fairly straightforward passage along a valley such as the Don's to the Sea of Azov. The Khazar fortress of 'S-m-k-r-ts' watched over the straits between this sea and the Black Sea and the journey from Khazaria to Constantinople by sea reportedly took only nine days in the tenth century.[42] So the emperor's professions of concern about the 'most savage peoples' menacing the Rhos on their return journey would have

41 On the oval brooches and rings, see I. Jansson, 'Communications between Scandinavia and Eastern Europe in the Viking Age. The Archaeological Evidence', *UHV*, *Abhandlungen der Akademie der Wissenschaften in Göttingen*, philol.-hist. Klasse, Folge, no. 156 *Dritte*, pp. 776–7, 781–2. A tenth-century dating for the rings in the burial-grounds at Timerëvo and Mikhailovskoe is favoured by G. L. Novikova, 'Iron neck-rings with Thor's hammers found in Eastern Europe', *Fornvännen* 87 (1992), 86. See also fig. 1, 76 (map of finds).

42 N. Golb and O. Pritsak, *Khazarian Hebrew Documents of the Tenth Century* (Ithaca, London, 1982), pp. 119–21. On S-m-k-r-ts, see below, pp. 107–8.

been rather exaggerated. In contrast, Gorodishche's location would fit well enough with the account of the Rhos envoys' apprehensions as to the 'most savage peoples' interposed between their base and Byzantium, and also with the return route which the Byzantines proposed for them. The existence and the title of a '*chaganus* of the Northmen' based on Lake Ilmen might be presumed (albeit falsely) to be known to Frankish emperors (see above, p. 32). Moreover, Lake Ilmen was linked by its outflow and tributaries to a network of riverways leading southwards or, from the nearby Lake Seliger and the head-waters of the Volga, to the east. It was a natural communications centre.

Three further items of evidence weigh in favour of Gorodishche. It is, firstly, worth noting that the district of Gorodishche is recorded as the residence of a prince as soon as relatively detailed and reliable literary evidence about the Rus becomes available. Gorodishche may well be identifiable with the 'Nemogardas' where, according to Constantine VII, Sviatoslav, the son of Prince Igor, was installed while merely a child. The symbolic presence of a child-prince suggests the high standing of the place in princely calculations.[43] This accords with the *Primary Chronicle*'s indication that by the later tenth century it was well established as a political centre, accustomed to being the seat of princes. The citizens of the town which the chronicle calls 'Novgorod' were threatening c. 970 that if Sviatoslav did not come to rule over them in person, they would call in a prince for themselves.[44] The inhabitants of the district may first have come to expect a resident potentate at a much earlier date.

Further evidence seemingly suggestive of the peculiar significance of the area of Lake Ilmen comes from the *Primary Chronicle*. This connects it with a story purporting to recount the formation of the earliest political structure in the eastern lands. The diverse native peoples are said to have sent a message 'to the Varangians [i.e. Scandinavians], to the Rus . . . . The Chud, the Slovenes, the Krivichi and the Ves said "Our land is vast and abundant, but there is no order in it. Come and reign as princes and have authority over us!" ' Three brothers came with 'their kin' and 'all the Rus' in response to this invitation. The eldest brother, Riurik, made what the chronicle calls 'Novgorod' his seat and upon the deaths of his brothers a couple of years later, he took over their possessions, too. The chronicle states that Riurik assigned his men to various 'towns' which already had their own 'aboriginal inhabitants' (*per'vii nasel'nitsi*) – 'in Novgorod, the Slovenes; in Polotsk, the Krivichi; in Rostov, the Mer; in Beloozero, the Ves; in Murom, the Muromians. And Riurik ruled over them all.'[45]

43 'Nemogardas' is the manuscript reading in Constantine's *DAI*, ch. 9.4, pp. 56–7. See below, p. 130, n. 36.
44 *PVL*, I, pp. 49–50.
45 Ibid., p. 18.

This story, with its casting of Riurik and his brothers as state-builders by invitation, has an obvious bearing on the 'Normanist question' and it remains highly controversial.[46] The motif of brothers acting in partnership occurs in the mythology of various European peoples concerning the origins of their ruling dynasty, and this should serve as a warning against assuming the literal truth of even the outline of the tale, let alone details such as the names of men and places. Moreover, the compilers of the *Primary Chronicle* in its final form seem themselves to have been unsure how to reconcile the traditions and stories which were to hand. Hence their paradoxical statement that 'the people of Novgorod are of Varangian stock, for formerly they were Slovenes'.[47] Nonetheless, in representing 'Novgorod' as the pivot, they were not simply relaying the *esprit de corps* and territorial claims of their own day. For the distant town of Murom on the Lower Oka was of no particular concern to the Novgorodians around the beginning of the twelfth century, and it was then a princely residence of barely even secondary status. But the district of Murom had been closely involved with the trade in silver, judging by the large quantity of early dirham hoards found there, and so it was likely to have attracted 'Varangian' traders. Excavations at Murom and in its hinterland have been too small-scale to clarify the northerners' role in the formation of the settlement. It most probably arose independently as a local population centre, although Frankish swords, a sword chape and a tortoiseshell brooch attest a Scandinavian presence in the tenth century, if not before. At any rate, the *Primary Chronicle*'s depiction of some sort of political structure, based in the region of Lake Ilmen and stretching as far as the Upper Volga and Murom on the Lower Oka, does not clash with the impression given by the archaeological evidence. The chronicle may well be offering a caricature, and a gross over-simplification, but a picture of Scandinavians gravitating towards 'towns' (when they did not found them outright) emerges from archaeological findings as well as from the chronicle's pages. The weaponry, fortifications and strategic location of Gorodishche and the Iaroslavl settlements point to the presence in them of some sort of armed elite consisting mainly, if not exclusively, of Scandinavians, and the pattern of the above-mentioned settlements (see p. 33) in

---

46 On the ways in which the tale of the summoning could have arisen, see D. S. Likhachev, 'The legend of the calling-in of the Varangians, and political purposes in Russian chronicle-writing from the second half of the XIth to the beginning of the XIIth century', in K. Hannestad et al., eds, *Varangian Problems* (Copenhagen, Munksgaard, 1970), pp. 178–85. The possibility that the story contains (distorted) echoes of actual events is advocated by, e.g., I. I. Froianov, 'Istoricheskie realii v letopisnom skazanii o prizvanii variagov', *Voprosy Istorii*, 1991, no. 6, 10–13; cf. E. A. Mel'nikova and V. I. Petrukhin, '"Riad" legendy o prizvanii variagov v kontekste rannesrednevekovoi diplomatii', *DGTSSSR* 1990 (1991), pp. 219–29.

47 *PVL*, I, p. 18.

the vicinity of the Volkhov's outflow from Lake Ilmen clearly points to the central role of Gorodishche.

A third item of evidence points in the same direction. Our earliest fairly full account in Arabic of the habitat of the *Rūs* is provided by the geographer, ibn Rusta. He is believed to have compiled his encyclopedic work between AD 903 and 913, but for his information about the Rus he may partly have been drawing on one or more somewhat earlier sources. According to ibn Rusta, the Rus resided on an 'island' (*jazira*), surrounded by 'lakes'. This 'island', three days' journey in extent, consists of 'forests and bogs overgrown with vegetation. It is unhealthy and the ground is so sodden that it moves under one's feet'.[48] The 'king' (*malik*) is said to bear the title of '*khāqān* of the *Rūs*' and a farrago of further information is provided: the Rus are said to possess 'many towns' and to have no property, villages or agricultural land; they make their living from 'razzias against the Slavs', trading in furs and in the Slavs whom they take captive. ibn Rusta offers a number of vignettes to illustrate the courage, religious rites, modes of settling disputes and treachery of the Rus. Allegedly, mistrust was so prevalent that a man could not even go to relieve himself without three companions to stand guard over him, 'holding their swords'. Such details have something of the flavour of travellers' tales or imaginary exotica and one hesitates to attach significance to particular points in ibn Rusta's description. It is nonetheless interesting that he conceives of the Rus as living on a large 'island' set among lakes and consisting in large part of marshes. *Jazira* is a rather imprecise term, which can mean 'enclave' or 'peninsula' as well as 'island', and one might argue that it could denote any one of the four candidates, in that Birka stood, like Gorodishche, on an island, Staraia Ladoga was on a wedge of land formed by the junction of two rivers, and the settlements near Iaroslavl might loosely be conceived as forming part of some sort of 'enclave' between the Volga and the Kliazma. Even so, the peculiarly insular character of Gorodishche among the settlements in the eastern lands was expressed, apparently from the outset, in its name, if one accepts that Scandinavian sources denote it by 'Holmgarthr' (literally, 'island compound'); and that this name was only later transferred to the emerging town of Novgorod nearby.[49] In that case, ibn Rusta, possessing an explanation of the

---

48 ibn Rusta, *Kitab al-A'lak al-nafisa* [*Book of Precious Jewels*], ed. T. Lewicki, *Źródła arabskie do dziejów słowiańszczyzny*, II.2 (Wroclaw, Warsaw, Cracow, Gdansk, 1977), pp. 38–9, 40–1; tr. G. Wiet, *Les atours précieux* (Cairo, 1955), p. 163.
49 Mühle, *Städtischen Handelszentren*, pp. 77–8, 86; idem, 'Von Holmgardr zu Novgorod. Zur Genesis des slavischen Ortsnamens der Ilmensee-Metropole im 11. Jahrhundert', in *Ex oriente lux. Mélanges offerts en hommage au professeur Jean Blankoff, à l'occasion de ses soixante ans*, I (Brussels, 1991), pp. 251–2.

name, but without means of gaining further elucidation, could well have mistaken the part for the whole and supposed that the entire region occupied by the Rus was in fact an 'island', rather than just their focal point. He might have added the detail of the 'three days' journey' in an attempt to explain an island-expanse which, on his information, contained 'many towns'. This confusion of ibn Rusta – or his source – could account for his slightly anomalous portrayal of an 'island' or 'enclave' which is surrounded by lakes yet which itself consists to a large extent of 'bogs'. And it may be no accident that ibn Rusta's description of a sodden island site is directly followed by mention of the ruler and his title: his source may have stated that 'Holmgarthr' was the residence of the '*khāqān* of the *Rūs*'.

The balance of probability among these items of evidence and more general considerations weigh heavily in favour of Gorodishche-Holmgarthr as the starting-point, and ultimate destination, of the Rhos envoys of 838–9. However, there is no reason to assume that the situation was static or that change, when it came, was invariably gradual. Nor should one suppose that the Rus *chaganus* had tight control over all the Scandinavians settled in, or roaming, the forest zone. In fact the nature and extent of his powers are uncertain and, whether or not Gorodishche was his base throughout the ninth century, he may have regulated and profited from the commerce only to a limited extent. He need not have functioned as its 'hands-on' protector. This would reflect less on the norms and assumptions about kingship then prevailing in the Swedish homeland than it would on the extraordinary and often protean nature of the Scandinavians' activities in the eastern lands. For although we have sketched some of the most commonly visited emporia, it must be emphasized that no one place enjoyed a monopoly: no single route could have been imposed to the exclusion of all others, even from the vantage-point of Gorodishche. In fact, although finds of boat rivets together with tools for making them and for repairing boats are common at Staraia Ladoga and Gorodishche, transport by water was not the invariable means of conveying goods and slaves. Winter seems to have been a convenient time for fur-traders to travel to the far north, while hoards strung along the southern banks of the Oka suggest an exchange-zone between traders from the north-west and the south-east (see above, pp. 24–5). So while boats and rafts were probably the most convenient form of transport for Rus goods in spring, there were alternatives. And bone skis, sledges and steppe ponies had, together with dugout canoes, already been in use in the east before the Scandinavians probed beyond Staraia Ladoga. Land-routes were therefore a feasible option, and an Arabic account of the journeys of Jewish merchants – the Radhanites – indicates that, by the mid-ninth century and quite possibly earlier, they were travelling eastwards from Christian Europe overland to the

Khazars' principal town.[50] Seeing that greed, or material want, led the Scandinavians to the eastern lands, they might be expected to have competed fiercely for supplies of the finest primary produce and for dealers who could offer them the highest prices. They had a strong incentive constantly to be investigating new routes, on the look-out for lucrative markets. Given the diversity of river valleys criss-crossing the forest zone and providing routes along iceways by winter as well as downstream in summer, there was not very much that a *chaganus* could do to govern their movements. A base at Gorodishche could not guarantee commanding oversight of traffic between the Western Dvina and the Upper Volga, or over movements south-eastwards from Lake Ladoga.

Some notion of the plurality of the trading ventures of the Rus is offered by Arabic geographers and travellers. Our earliest extant mention of them comes in the *Book of Ways and Realms* of ibn Khurradadhbih, the writer who also supplies the description of the Radhanites. He inserts into his account of the Radhanites the itineraries of the Rus, whom he regards as just another group of 'merchants', dealing in beaver, black fox skins and swords. ibn Khurradadhbih cites various routes which they took. The Rus can go down to 'the sea of the Rum (Byzantines)', i.e. the Black Sea, where the Byzantine emperor levies a 10 per cent tax on their goods. Boats are not mentioned for this journey, nor is the name of any river which the Rus might have plied to reach the sea.[51] The likeliest spot for the exaction of a tithe by the Byzantine authorities is Cherson, on the Crimea, and the seals of *kommerkiarioi* of Cherson – officials whose duties included collection of customs dues – are known from the first half of the ninth century. Cherson could be reached from a ford across the Dnieper by a land-route which a tenth-century Byzantine work mentions (see below, p. 93). Thus we have no hard and fast evidence that the earliest Rus traders came to the Black Sea by boat. ibn Khurradadhbih proceeds to list other routes used by the Rus. He mentions two terms, one of which has been variously reconstructed as 'Tanais' or 'Tin' (i.e. the Don), while the other unquestionably means 'the river of the Slavs'.

---

50 ibn Khurradadhbih, *Kitab al-Masalik wa'l Mamalik* [*Book of Ways and Realms*], ed. T. Lewicki, *Źródła arabskie do dziejów słowiańszczyzny*, I (Wrocław, Cracow, 1956), pp. 76–7; tr. M. Hadj-Sadok, *ibn Khurradadhbih, ibn al-Faqih al-Hamadhani et ibn Rustih: Description du Maghreb et de l'Europe au III=IX siècle* (Algiers, 1949), pp. 24–5; M. Gil, 'The Radhanite merchants and the land of Radhan', *Journal of the Economic and Social History of the Orient* 17 (1974), 299–328; *Encyclopaedia of Islam*, VIII, pp. 363–7 (Pellat).

51 ibn Khurradadhbih, ed. Lewicki, pp. 76–7; tr. Hadj-Sadok, pp. 22–3; tr. of 'reconstructed' text by O. Pritsak, 'An Arabic text on the trade route of the corporation of Ar-Rūs in the second half of the ninth century', *Folia Orientalia* 12 (1970), 256. See also T. S. Noonan, 'When did Rūs/Rus' merchants first visit Khazaria and Baghdad?', *AEMA* 7 (1987–91), 213–19; *Encyclopaedia of Islam*, VIII, pp. 620–1 (Golden).

Whichever, or however many, rivers ibn Khurradadhbih had in mind – and his own conceptions need not have been crystal-clear – the Volga is plainly one of the rivers in play. For the Rus are depicted as journeying past the Khazars' principal town, which lay near the mouth of that river. It is quite possible that ibn Khurradadhbih is, deliberately or not, referring to alternative routes. In any case, the Rus pay a tithe to the Khazars and evidently do business with them. But they also sail across the Caspian 'and disembark on whichever shores they please . . . Sometimes they carry their goods on camels from Gurgan [a region on the south-east shore of the Caspian] to Baghdad where Slav eunuchs serve as their interpreters'. ibn Khurradadhbih states that they claimed to be Christians, in order to pay only the poll-tax. This remark may well be trustworthy, since ibn Khurradadhbih himself resided in Baghdad, as Director of Posts and Intelligence. It is of great significance, as a sign not merely of Rus guile but also of their efforts to minimize costs incurred during their long journeys: profit was the driving force, and this is in keeping with the picture of competition, experiment with alternative routes and searching for favourable markets which is beginning to emerge. The Rus were presumably travelling in groups, but they do not seem to have been trading continuously under the aegis of, or on behalf of, a ruler. Those getting as far as Baghdad had their own devices for minimizing outlay on taxes, while others are said to put in 'on whichever shores they please', in the Caspian.[52] (See Map 3).

A similar air of somewhat spasmodic trading is provided by an eye-witness of the Rus engaging in business, ibn Fadlan. Trading patterns had altered greatly during the 40 or more years separating ibn Khurradadhbih's final version of the *Book of Ways and Realms* from ibn Fadlan's visit to the Middle Volga in 922: many Rus now did their business there, rather than heading further south (see below, pp. 65–6). Those whom ibn Fadlan observed came in a group, by boat, and they built on the river bank a number of large wooden cabins, each sleeping between ten and twenty men. They are not depicted as carrying out their trading as a corporation, or in a closely regulated manner. If, says ibn Fadlan, a trader enters a cabin 'to buy from one of them a young slave, and finds him in the midst of copulating with her, [the slave-owner] does not detach himself from her before he has satisfied his needs'.[53] The Rus seem to have done much of their business at

---

52 ibn Khurradadhbih, ed. Lewicki, pp. 76–7; tr. Hadj-Sadok, pp. 22–3; tr. Pritsak, 257. On Arabic writers' terms for the Caspian, Volga and Don, see M. Espéronnier, 'Le cadre géographique des pays slaves d'après les sources arabes médiévales', *Welt der Slaven* 31 (1986), 5–19.

53 ibn Fadlan, *Risala*, ed. T. Lewicki, A. Kmietowicz and F. Kmietowicz, *Zródła arabskie do dziejów słowiańszczyzny*, III (Wroclaw, Warsaw, Cracow, Gdansk, Lodz, 1985), p. 68; tr. M. Canard, *Voyage chez les Bulgares de la Volga* (Paris, 1988), p. 74. See also below, pp. 65, 68.

markets held 'at brief intervals'. A sanctuary consisting of wooden idols and seemingly peculiar to the Rus stood there: upon arrival, each of them would make an offering of bread, meat and onions before the principal idol around which the smaller ones were grouped. He would, according to ibn Fadlan, say ' "O my Lord, I have come from a distant land and have brought with me so many young girl-slaves, so many marten-skins" and so forth, until he has listed everything which he has brought in the way of merchandise'.[54] He prays for a merchant possessing many dinars and dirhams, ' "who buys from me all that I could wish him to, and who does not enter into dispute with me". If he has difficulties in selling, and his visit is prolonged, he returns with another gift' and makes repeated offerings to the idols. From this, it would appear that each Rus was trading on his own account, and would leave town once a satisfactory deal had been struck. No doubt ibn Fadlan simplifies matters, and his reportage aims to show up the idolatry of pagans. But the Rus do seem to have been able to come and go quite freely. They may well have tended to belong to kin-groups, like the sixth-century visitors to Lake Ladoga (see above, p. 8). ibn Fadlan takes it for granted that various kinsmen took charge of the funeral arrangements for a wealthy Rus. It was 'the man most closely related to the deceased' who – 'completely naked' – lit the pyre, thus giving ibn Fadlan the opportunity to observe a boat-burning.[55] 'An old woman whom they call "the Angel of Death" ', together with her two daughters, officiated at the funeral. These rites, like the negotiations with the idols, bespeak fairly loose-knit groups of traders and piecemeal transactions. The traders do not appear to have been in need of special protection, although we are told that each man 'has with him an axe, a sword and a knife, and never parts with any of them'.[56]

Trading conditions and patterns were very different in 922 from those of the mid-ninth century. Most importantly, the number of Rus active in the eastern lands had greatly increased since the earlier period (see pp. 66–7; below, pp. 125–7). Yet ibn Fadlan's well-observed portrayal of the Rus in business and in death is unique, and many traits were probably common to both periods. Loose-knit bands of traders and their kin were travelling huge distances for a season at a time, intent on profit. Their activities did not require long-term settlement and so did not, for the most part, leave remains of

54 ibn Fadlan, ed. Lewicki, p. 69; tr. Canard, pp. 74–5.
55 Ibid., ed. Lewicki, p. 74; tr. Canard, p. 82. The main features of the funeral which he describes are consistent with those discernible in boat-burnings at Birka and other sites in the Scandinavian world: A.-S. Gräslund, *The Burial Customs, Birka* IV (Uppsala, 1980), pp. 55–8; E. Roesdahl, *The Vikings*, tr. S. M. Margeson and K. Williams (London, 1991), pp. 156–7. See below, p. 127.
56 ibn Fadlan, ed. Lewicki, pp. 73, 67; tr. Canard, pp. 78, 72.

the sort associated with strongholds or burial-grounds. Those Rus who perished during an enterprise were buried or burned individually, and even the most elaborate barrows, such as the one ibn Fadlan watched being raised, have left no trace. Many, perhaps most, of the Rus traversing the eastern lands did not intend to leave their bones there: they were birds of passage, acquiring silver and homing back to the Baltic area, especially Central Sweden (see below, pp. 20–1, 22, 27–8). This has a bearing on the polity over which a *chaganus* was presiding by the 830s. It emerges as a loose association of ruthless entrepreneurs. ibn Rusta's Rus distrust one another intensely, and every man must look after himself (see above, p. 40). Greed seems to be rampant: 'even the man who has only modest wealth is still envied by his brother, who would not hesitate to do away with him in order to steal it'.[57] ibn Rusta states that every dispute is submitted to the ruler for arbitration and this presupposes some degree of customary procedure. But he also states that if a disagreement persists, it is decided by single combat. ibn Rusta maintains that this is done upon the ruler's command, but since he also states that the 'kin-groups' of the two parties fight it out with one another, he seems to be describing a society in which vendettas were commonplace. Judging by ibn Rusta's own account, great respect was accorded to 'shamans', who have authority over the ruler 'as if they themselves were masters', and can summarily order the sacrifice of man or beast.[58] That the ruler was essentially a figurehead is suggested by ibn Fadlan. He maintains that he resides on an immense and richly ornamented throne, shared with 'forty slave girls destined for his bed. And it happens that he lies with one of them in the presence of his fellows, without descending from his throne'. He does not leave the throne even to relieve himself, and if he wishes to ride somewhere, he mounts a horse directly from his throne, subsequently dismounting straight back onto it. The ruler's 'bravest companions' and kinsmen are said to number 400, and they live with him in his 'palace'. These 'are men who die with him, and kill themselves for him'.[59] The ruler has a lieutenant, who commands troops and fights battles on his behalf. There may well be fantasy in ibn Fadlan's account and the differentiation between the figurehead and the effective ruler recurs, together with other aspects of court life, in his account of Khazaria.[60] But his description of the Khazar ruler's court is by no means identical

---

57 ibn Rusta, ed. Lewicki, pp. 42–3; tr. Wiet, p. 165.
58 Ibid., ed. Lewicki, pp. 40–3; tr. Wiet, p. 164.
59 ibn Fadlan, ed. Lewicki, p. 75; tr. Canard, pp. 83–4.
60 Ibid., ed. Lewicki, p. 76; tr. Canard, pp. 84–6 (using the fuller text preserved in Yaqut's entry on the Khazars in his *Geographical Dictionary*: see M. Canard, 'La relation du voyage d'Ibn Fadlan chez les Bulgares de la Volga', *Annales de l'institut d'études orientales* 16 (Algiers, 1958), 41, n. 2; 135, n. 362); D. M. Dunlop, *The History of the Jewish Khazars* (Princeton, 1954), pp. 109–13.

to that of the Rus ruler's; there would be nothing extraordinary in the lifestyle of the Rus *chaganus* aping that of the ruler from whom his title was borrowed. So ibn Fadlan's account of the Rus ruler's court cannot be dismissed out of hand.[61] His picture of the Rus court was based, presumably, on what he heard in 922. The ruler's standing was sufficient for his name to be carved, together with that of the deceased, on a post set up on the barrow covering the boat-burning site. But ibn Fadlan's portrayal of wealth-seekers owing nominal allegiance to a splendiferous ruler is comparable to the essentially individualistic, atomized society outlined by ibn Rusta a generation or so earlier.

The overriding impression, then, is one of diversity and flux. Things may well have appeared ambivalent and even inconsistent to contemporaries in the ninth and earlier tenth centuries, as they do today. If the Rus formed only a tiny – maybe transient – minority of the population at Murom or the Sarskii fort, they seem at first to have made up the bulk of the population at Timerëvo and the other settlements near Iaroslavl. They clearly were the predominant grouping of the forest zone in the eyes of the two Arabic writers. To ibn Rusta the Rus were a people based in numerous 'towns', who made their living from trading in furs and slaves. For the men, this meant living by the sword: allegedly, the father of a new-born boy would place a sword before him and announce that this would be his sole inheritance: the rest must come by the sword.[62] Finds of toy wooden swords at centres such as Staraia Ladoga and Gorodishche partially bear out ibn Rusta's account, but the archaeological evidence also shows him to have over-simplified matters. This is the case with his picture of the Rus as having a wholly predatory relationship with the other inhabitants, who are falsely termed 'Slavs' (*Ṣaqāliba*). Here, ibn Rusta betrays his ignorance, for the native peoples whom the Rus first encountered in the regions of Lake Ladoga and the Upper Volga were for the most part not Slavs at all, but Finno-Ugrians. Slightly further south, at places such as Izborsk and the neighbourhood of Lake Ilmen, there were Slav immigrants and some groups of them arrived from the south in the eighth century. But there are no compelling reasons for ascribing exclusively to Slavs the groups of large conical barrows, each ringed by stones and containing several cremations, which are concentrated in the basin of Lake Ilmen and which also occur along the Volkhov (especially near Staraia Ladoga). It is more likely that these barrows, known today as *sopki*, are mainly the work of Balts, who had a penchant for stone constructions which provided facings or internal cores for their burial-mounds. Groupings

---

61 See Canard, *Voyage*, nn. 337, 340 on p. 126. Only a generation after ibn Fadlan's journey, the collaboration of prince and commander (*voevoda*) is attested in the *Primary Chronicle*: see below, p. 117.

62 ibn Rusta, ed. Lewicki, pp. 40–1; tr. Wiet, p. 163.

of Balts were probably drawn northwards from Lake Ilmen by the prospect of enrichment once business got under way in Staraia Ladoga: they could work as boatmen, provisioners or repairers at points where boats halted for the night, or at the two sets of formidable rapids along the Volkhov. Some may have engaged in commerce for themselves. The elements of funerary ritual and pottery characteristic of the Slavs found in a number of *sopki* in the region of Lake Ilmen can be taken as evidence of a Slav migration there. It is unclear whether they formed separate communities: the evidence of the *sopki* suggests that they soon intermingled with their fellow-immigrants. What is undeniable is that the relations of the Rus with the raisers of the *sopki* and other ethnic groups were more variegated and multi-storied than ibn Rusta supposed.

It is likely that diverse methods were used by Rus and others in the common pursuit of furs, slaves and silver. A comparison could be drawn with the North American wilderness in the seventeenth and eighteenth centuries. There, too, over a still lengthier period, trappers, traders, *voyageurs* and, eventually, settlers put in an appearance. Their relations with one another were often ambivalent, sometimes downright hostile; conversely they often allied, traded, hunted and slept with native Americans. But there are significant differences between conditions in the two wildernesses. Rus numbers were, in most places, too limited to enable the Rus to engage in labour-intensive activities. They enjoyed technical advantages – in weaponry above all; in metal-working tools; riding-gear and, most probably, agricultural implements. But these differences were not as clear-cut or comprehensive as those between redskin and paleface in North America. At the same time, the inhabitants of the forest zone were thinly scattered, and few of them belonged to political formations which rooted them firmly to one spot. This inevitably affected, and on the whole tempered, the behaviour of the Rus towards them. Similar expediency led the Rus to dress their slaves with care and to treat them humanely, 'for to them they are articles of commerce'.[63]

This does not mean that the Rus invariably established themselves in existing centres of population. The environs of Staraia Ladoga and Gorodishche were thinly populated at the time when the Rus began to reside there. Conversely, Izborsk did not develop into a settlement of primarily Scandinavian character, although there is archaeological evidence suggesting the presence, and perhaps residence, of Scandinavians there in the ninth century. Izborsk had already emerged as a settlement in the eighth century, with a population consisting of Finno-Ugrians and, to some extent, Slavs: finds of two hoards of dirhams and of the weights from scales suggest that Izborsk

---

63 Ibid., ed. Lewicki, pp. 40–1; n. 261, p. 138; tr. Wiet, p. 164.

was involved in long-distance trade, and a Scandinavian presence from the ninth century onwards is suggested by finds of ornaments and weapons such as spear- and arrowheads. The early importance of Izborsk, together with Beloozero, is suggested by the role which the *Primary Chronicle*'s tale of the summoning of the Rus assigns to them, as the respective residences of Riurik's two younger brothers, Sineus and Truvor (see above, p. 38). Yet Izborsk did not develop into a major Scandinavian politico-military centre. Neither, it seems, did Beloozero, although Scandinavian ornaments, including combs, have been excavated there and its location on a route from Lake Ladoga towards the Volga made it a frequent port of call; moreover, Scandinavians occupied 'village'-type settlements to the south-west of Lake Beloozero, judging by finds of such essentially ritual objects as Thor's hammerlets. Another settlement which existed well before the coming of the Rus was the Sarskii fort. It is the next earliest site to show signs of the presence of Scandinavians after Staraia Ladoga, and these signs become more marked for the late ninth and above all the tenth centuries, judging by the finds of ornaments and weapons. Among the latter is a sword of ninth-century Frankish type, on whose blade can be read a Latin inscription: 'Lun fecit' – 'Lun made'.[64] Swords are among the items mentioned by ibn Khurradadhbih as being brought by the Rus to the Black Sea, and later Arabic writers mention 'Frankish swords' as forming one of the Rus exports to the Moslem world. Yet if Scandinavians played a part in commerce at the Sarskii fort, they made up only a small proportion of the predominantly Finno-Ugrian population. Further to the south-east, Murom continued predominantly to be occupied by Finno-Ugrians, although, if we believe the chronicle, it came under Rus overlordship in the ninth century. It is to the north, at Timerëvo and Mikhailovskoe, that we find the clearest evidence of predominantly Scandinavian settlements arising on what seem to have been 'green field sites' (see above, pp. 36–7).

The variegated and apparently random pattern of Rus activity is not surprising in view of the vast distance between Lake Ladoga and Murom, the proliferation of routes and trails and the ability of traders to pick and choose between them, or to prospect for new ones. If the Rus were the prime movers in the region of Staraia Ladoga, hundreds of kilometres to the south-east they seem to have

---

64 I. V. Dubov, *Velikii volzhskii put'* (Leningrad, 1989), p. 129. The sword corresponds to Petersen's E-type. On the approximately 115 sword-blades inscribed with the name 'Ulfberht' found in Western Europe, Scandinavia and the eastern lands and probably mostly manufactured in the Rhineland, see A. N. Kirpichnikov, 'Connections between Russia and Scandinavia in the 9th and 10th centuries, as illustrated by weapons finds', in K. Hannestad et al., eds, *Varangian Problems* (Copenhagen, Munksgaard, 1970), pp. 57–61; A. Stalsberg, 'O proizvodstve mechei epokhi vikingov', *Vestnik Moskovskogo Universiteta, seriia 8, Istoriia* 1991, no. 2, 75.

latched onto a pre-existing nexus of exchanges which hinged on the district of Lake Nero. Different arrangements were appropriate in areas with different 'mixes' of inhabitants, and while the Rus at Staraia Ladoga and even around Gorodishche may initially have aspired to self-sufficiency and engaged in agriculture (see above, p. 35), this was unnecessary where population centres already existed, together with markets where foodstuffs could be acquired. Moreover, the aims of a given person or group of persons may well have altered over time. As we have already seen, the first Scandinavian visitors to Staraia Ladoga appear quite rapidly to have decided to set up permanent installations and some, at least, to stay. Similar decisions were probably taken a generation or two later, in the vicinity of Gorodishche. But such decisions need not have been taken exclusively from considerations of profit. After several years of hard travel, a man might simply opt for a more sedentary way of life and decide to invest his wealth in the eastern lands rather than bringing it back to Sweden, as the earliest traders may have done. There is, after all, no evidence besides the tale of the summoning of the Rus of a planned Scandinavian immigration or settlement. It was presumably open to persons from anywhere in the Baltic world, West Slavs as well as Scandinavians, to seek their fortune in the east. Some persons of Scandinavian stock settled along the eastern and south-eastern feeder-rivers of Lake Ladoga, and they engaged in agriculture as well, most probably, as the fur trade which had drawn Scandinavians to the area in the first place. Their numbers became substantial, judging by the quantities of finds of rings with hammerlets of Thor and tortoiseshell brooches in the graves. In fact, the Scandinavians' presence to the south-east of the lake was sizable enough for such brooches to be used by Finno-Ugrian women of the region. Subsequently, in the eleventh century, they started to wear imitations of these brooches, as did women in Finland and those east Baltic coastal regions which had most dealings with the Scandinavians. There is no evidence that the settlers to the east or south-east of Lake Ladoga were concentrated into anything that could be described as a 'town'. Here, the Rus were scattered in numerous small settlements, in breach of ibn Rusta's generalization about them (see above, p. 40). One of the rare other instances of the Rus presence in small, 'rural' settlements is provided by those on the south-west side of another lake, Beloozero.

ibn Rusta can, then, be shown to have simplified matters, particularly in respect of the regions most remote from the Moslem world, such as Lake Ladoga. But the variegated and widely scattered nature of the archaeological evidence is compatible with the free-wheeling society which he depicts. The Rus had a *chaganus* who maintained an elaborate household at a fixed point, most probably Gorodishche, and according to ibn Fadlan he disposed of a standing force of 400 fighting men. But he seems to have been an essentially ceremonial figure and while he may have been capable of launching embassies and even occasional expeditions, he relied heavily on the collaboration of his 'companions', and not even 400 of them could suffice to regulate closely or police the far-flung archipelago of settlements which was beginning to emerge in the mid-ninth century. The Rus do, in certain areas such as Gorodishche, seem to have formed a kind of elite, but ibn Rusta's portrayal of the mobility, self-reliance and appetite for self-enrichment of individual Rus rings true. This wide-meshed political order rested on some form of consensus among the newcomers from the Baltic region, a tacit assumption that silver was the common pursuit. It relied no less on the assent and active cooperation of the existing inhabitants of the eastern lands, the majority of whom were only in the loosest sense the subjects of the Rus in general or the *chaganus* in particular. The essential fact that such a consensus underlay the Rus operations in the east is captured, albeit schematically and mythically, in the *Primary Chronicle*'s tale of the summoning of the Rus.

3. RAIDS AND NEIGHBOURS (c. 860–c. 900)

By the mid-ninth century, some sort of socio-political order had formed under the aegis of a Rus *chaganus*. Neither the origins of this order nor the territorial range of the *chaganus'* sway is certain. One must not assume that matters were necessarily cut and dried at the time. Even when literary evidence about the Rus begins to appear, it tends to raise as many questions as it answers. Set-piece descriptions and the partial excavations of archaeological sites can hardly begin to do justice to what was, most probably, a volatile and fluctuating situation; no-one at the time could have had an overview of all the local scenarios. There were many links in the chain of exchanges between the Middle East and the ultimate markets for some of the silver, in the Baltic region and still further west. A decline in purchasing power on the part of later ninth-century Carolingian rulers or members of the Abbasid elite could have had marked repercussions on the level of demand for luxury goods, and one axis of exchanges may have grown more active as another one waned. Further analysis of the chronology and contents of ninth-century Moslem coin hoards should show how far patterns are common to widely separated areas. What is certain is that from the second half of the ninth century the Rus began to have a discernible impact on other peoples, an indication, very probably, of the increasing numbers of Scandinavians who were now living in, or at least sounding out, 'the East Way', to use the name applied by later sagas to the regions east of the Baltic, and frequently to those under the rule of Rus princes.

The most celebrated of the Rus bouts of activity took the form of a raid on Constantinople. It is repeatedly likened to a 'thunderbolt' by

Patriarch Photios in the sermons which he delivered at the time.[65] A large fleet, said to have numbered 200 ships, arrived in the Bosporos without warning. The raiders pillaged along its shores and devastated the countryside and settlements outside Constantinople. They made a point of trying to terrify the capital's citizens; at one point they sailed past the walls and raised their swords, 'as if threatening the city with death by the sword'.[66] They ravaged the Princes' Islands off Constantinople and may have penetrated further into the Sea of Marmara. They are described as slaughtering anything that moved, women, infants, even oxen and poultry and, according to Photios, the citizens supposed 'the barbarian tribe' to be 'irresistible'. Presumably, the Rus had hoped to take the Byzantines by surprise, and in fact they encountered no resistance outside the city's massive walls. They are said to have amassed 'immense wealth' from their pillaging and this may well have been their prime objective, as it was of many of the Viking assaults on Western Europe. Their sojourn around Constantinople was brief, perhaps only a week or two, and they withdrew as abruptly as they had come. It seems that they were overwhelmed by a storm very soon afterwards, allowing imperial propaganda to impress upon foreigners that the Rus departure had been due to divine intervention. The Byzantine chronicle which makes out that the Rus had been 'utterly defeated' is our sole source for the precise date of their arrival at Constantinople – 18 June 860. The chronicle, compiled in its present form at a considerably later date, perhaps in the eleventh century, cannot be regarded as an unimpeachable source.[67] But no compelling evidence that the attack must have occurred significantly later than 860 has been published, and the traditional dating can be retained.

Photios' sermons form the earliest extensive Byzantine account of the Rus, and scholars have combed them for clues as to their abode. Photios harps upon a few specific details. The Rus are 'a savage tribe' who appeared suddenly 'out of the farthest north', following an 'unbelievable course'. Photios emphasizes the lowly status of the attackers, 'obscure, insignificant and not even known' hitherto, and he laments that now their assault has brought them fame. They are 'an uncaptained army, equipped in servile fashion', 'nomadic' and 'leaderless'. Such remarks cannot be accepted to the letter: the Rus were not wholly 'unknown' to a state which had received an embassy of Rhos twenty years earlier, assimilated individual Nordic immigrants and perhaps already undergone at least one raid (see above, p. 31). Photios was not, after all, trying to give his listeners a detailed briefing

---

65 Photios, ed. Laourdas, pp. 29, 40; tr. Mango, pp. 82, 96; see also above, p. 28.
66 Ibid., ed. Laourdas, p. 44; tr. Mango, p. 101.
67 *Anecdota Bruxellensia*, I, ed. F. Cumont (Ghent, 1894), p. 33 and n. 2; A. Külzer, 'Studien zum Chronicon Bruxellense', *Byzantion* 61 (1991), 413, 425, 446–7.

on the background to the current raid or to propose a particular course of terrestrial action. He was citing the disaster as a sign of God's wrath with the Byzantines for their sins, and he was calling for penitence, prayer and higher moral standards. Constantinople had been all the more humiliated because the blow had been struck by a rabble drawn from a totally obscure people. Photios' derogatory references to the 'uncaptained army equipped in servile fashion' could be rhetorical touches intended to demonstrate how wretched a foe had reduced 'the queen of cities' to trepidation. Likewise with his rather bizarre claim that the Rus had been 'destitute' before their recent bout of plundering.[68]

But if Photios highlighted certain traits of the attackers, he was not inventing them outright. That the Rus behaved savagely in 860 is attested by other, independent sources, while their parties of looters and chicken-slayers may well have looked ill-disciplined to Byzantine eyes. So his stress upon the extraordinary journey of the Rus – 'out of the furthest north' – may not simply be a function of their alleged obscurity. Photios' statement that they had journeyed via 'numberless rivers and harbourless seas' suggests a point of departure far to the north of the Black Sea, and likewise with his assertion that the enemy had been 'sundered off from us by so many lands and kingdoms'.[69] The emphasis on 'the distance', while consistent with the statement that 'nations have been stirred up from the end of the earth', is no warranty in itself. But the possibility that it rested on specific information about the habitat of the Rus, gained before the attack, should be considered. Photios had, after all, some experience of Byzantine diplomacy, having participated in an embassy to Baghdad. Moreover, his stress on the quantity of 'lands and kingdoms' separating the attackers' abode from Byzantium recalls Emperor Theophilos' underscoring of the 'barbarous and most savage peoples' interposed between Byzantium and the land of origin of the Rhos envoys of 838–9 (see above, p. 29).

The analogy is only a loose one, and does not prove that the raiders of 860 set off from Gorodishche as, most probably, the envoys had. But a number of other considerations bring this politico-military centre into play. Above all, one should note the substantial size of the raiding force. The figure of 200 vessels given by the foresaid chronicle tallies with Photios' description of 'the massed aspect' of the Rus, and Photios indicates that they were numerous enough to fan out across the countryside. If there is any substance in the figure of 40 men per boat which the *Primary Chronicle* gives for a later expedition (supposedly launched against Byzantium in 907: see below, p. 106), a force of approximately 8,000 struck terror into the Byzantines in 860. While Photios indicates that the boats benefited from a tranquil

68 Photios, ed. Laourdas, p. 42; tr. Mango, p. 98.
69 Ibid., ed. Laourdas, p. 34; tr. Mango, p. 88.

sea, he does not deride their size or seaworthiness, as he might have done in order to highlight the humiliation of the Byzantines at the hands of unworthy foes. On the contrary, the boat crews threatened the city 'with swords raised'.[70] While neither Photios' description nor the probable allusions to the Rus attack in the hymns of Joseph the Hymnographer enable us to specify the type or types of vessel used,[71] they do not appear to have been dismissable as mere dugout canoes or hollowed-out tree-trunks. Photios' assertion that the Rus had gained 'immense wealth' suggests that their boats could carry a substantial amount. A saint's *Life* tells of their appetite for booty and that one of the boats was solid enough for 22 captives to be dismembered with axes on part of its stern.[72]

If this was the case, considerable resources and organization were needed, both to build or muster the fleet and to prepare means of manhandling fairly weighty vessels down to the Black Sea. A considerable amount of portaging would have been inevitable, which-ever river was to be navigated, the Don, Volga or Dnieper (on which, see below, pp. 91–3). While it is quite possible that a large number of Scandinavia-based Vikings joined forces and clubbed together to mount an attack on Byzantium, it is hard to believe that they could have sailed southwards without cooperation and, indeed, guidance from persons more familiar with the rivers. In other words, it is probable that the politico-military structure centred on Lake Ilmen was connected with the expedition, but the *chaganus* may not have initiated it. This is not, of course, to imply that there was any permanent Rus establishment further south at that time (see below, p. 71). The assumption of the *Primary Chronicle* that the attack of 860 was launched from Kiev is most probably an anachronism, for the contributors to the chronicle relied almost wholly on a Byzantine chronicle of the tenth century for their information about the raid. That chronicle, the *Continuation* of the *Chronicle* of George the Monk, makes no mention of the raiders' point of departure. There is no firm archaeological evidence to demonstrate a significant Rus presence on the Middle Dnieper as early as the mid-ninth century, and the evidence of ibn Khurradadhbih does not expressly state that the Rus travelled to the Black Sea by boat (see above, p. 42). In fact the sheer astonishment of the Byzantines in 860 recalls the bewilderment of the letter which Alcuin wrote after the Vikings sacked Lindisfarne

70 Ibid., ed. Laourdas, p. 44; tr. Mango, p. 101.
71 *Mariale* of Joseph the Hymnographer, *PG* 105, cols 1005–6, 1009–10, 1011–12, 1015–16, 1023–6; A. Kazhdan, 'Joseph the Hymnographer and the first Russian attack on Constantinople', in R. Thomson and J.-P. Mahé, eds, *From Byzantium to Iran. Armenian Studies in Honour of Nina G. Garsoian* (Atlanta, Georgia, 1996) (forthcoming).
72 *Vita Ignatii, PG* 105, cols 516–17.

in 792. The possibility of a large-scale, direct attack on Constantinople – as against fleeting and minor depredations in the provinces – does not seem to have entered into Byzantine strategic thinking about the Black Sea before 860. Photios' mention of 'the unbelievable course of the barbarians'[73] suggests that the Rus were not then regularly plying riverways to reach the Black Sea. It also tends to suggest that the Middle Dnieper was not yet a Rus base; for had a settlement of any political, military or economic significance been established there, their activities might be expected to have come to the attention of statesmen and strategists, if of nobody else, at Byzantium.

Our considerations so far have led us to suppose that the Rus host of 860 enjoyed at least the cooperation and guidance of the *chaganus* whose residence was, most probably, in Gorodishche. That he was in fact involved is strongly suggested by subsequent events. 'Not long after' the attack, according to Byzantine chronicles, the Rus sent envoys professing a desire to be baptized.[74] The date of their *démarche* is not known, but by 867 Photios was proclaiming that 'the oft-talked-about-by-many' people 'known as Rhos' had accepted Christianity, received a 'bishop and pastor' and were showing great zeal for Christian worship.[75] Photios had his reasons for representing the Rus as reformed characters and obedient associates of the Byzantine empire to the other eastern patriarchs, who were the addressees of his round-robin notice. He was writing at the height of his dispute with the papacy concerning jurisdiction over another newly converted people, the Bulgarians, and he was trying to highlight his patriarchate's missionary feats in a bid for the eastern patriarchs' support. But he is unlikely to have invented outright the mission to the Rus, and his assertion that the Rus had 'subjugated those around them' before presuming to take up arms against the empire is probably not sheer fantasy.[76] This makes it reasonably likely that he was talking about Rus who had established some sort of order, rather than about roving pirates or 'kings' based in Scandinavia proper. If the Rus *chaganus* requested a religious mission soon after an apparently quite unsuccessful expedition, this was presumably because he had played a leading role, whether as initiator or collaborator. Photios in his circular letter clearly identifies the newly baptized Rus with the ex-raiders.

A later Byzantine work also presupposes that the missionaries were sent to a hierarchically structured, albeit barbarous, people. It recounts a mission led by an 'archbishop' (rather than a bishop) which Basil I

---

73 Photios, ed. Laourdas, p. 34; tr. Mango, p. 88.
74 Theophanes Continuatus, *Chronographia*, IV.33, ed. I. Bekker (Bonn, 1838), p. 196; Skyl., p. 107.
75 Photios, *Epistulae et Amphilochia*, ed. B. Laourdas and L. G. Westerink (Leipzig, 1983), I, p. 50.
76 Ibid., I, p. 50.

is credited with having launched. This Byzantine source is dedicated to the praise of Basil and the denigration of his predecessor, Michael III, and it was unquestionably during Michael's reign (not Basil's) that the mission was launched. Nonetheless, Basil, on becoming emperor, may have reinforced the mission. Our source's portrait of Rus society as being headed by a prince (*archōn*) and as being regulated by him in conjunction with 'elders' (*gerontes*) meeting in an assembly could be a back-projection from the writer's own time, the mid-tenth century. And the tale of the archbishop's gospel-book, which was placed in a fiery oven and subsequently extracted from it unscathed, belongs to a genre of miracle-induced conversion stories.[77] But an assembly of the ruler and his elders to deliberate on key issues would not have been out of place in the sort of society pictured by ibn Rusta and suggested by the scattered archaeological evidence (see above, p. 45). One small clue could imply contacts between Basil I and Gorodishche, a silver *miliaresion* of the emperor found in the main, hilltop, part of the settlement. This was the area in which the copper coin of Theophilos was excavated (see above, pp. 35–6). The *miliaresion* was not, unfortunately, found in a closely datable context, being among the objects unearthed in a workshop or store which was in use in the later ninth and tenth centuries.[78] The coin has an eye, enabling it to be used as an ornament, and it is badly worn. It could be a relic of diplomatic or missionary contacts during the reign of Basil, perhaps arriving in the purse of some churchman. At any rate, it may not be accidental that the couple of Byzantine coins found so far at Gorodishche belong to emperors whom reliable literary sources depict as being in contact with the Rus leadership in the ninth century.

The Byzantine chronicles presuppose a political structure within reach of Byzantium, and the one centred on Gorodishche is the obvious candidate. Speculation on what might have induced the Rus *chaganus* to countenance the raid is hazardous, given our ignorance of the extent of his involvement in the expedition. One plausible reconstruction of events might be that he was seeking an outlet for an influx of armed fortune-seekers arriving from the west. There was an upsurge of Viking activity in the Scandinavian world around the time of the Rus attack on Constantinople, and a wealth of far-flung targets came within the raiders' sights. In the later 850s, a series of raids devastated Francia, but once Charles the Bald managed to resolve some of his domestic disputes and repulse or treat with the war-bands menacing the coastline and riverways of Francia, the British Isles began to bear the brunt. Another sizable fleet harried southern and eastern Spain between 858 and 860, and according to Latin and

77 Theophanes Continuatus, *Chronographia*, V. 97, pp. 343–4.
78 Nosov, *Novgorodskoe (Riurikovo) Gorodishche*, p. 94.

Arabic sources, its ships went on to raid Italy. Some Viking pirates are said to have roamed as far as Alexandria and lands of the Byzantine empire. That there should be some connection between outbursts of predatory activity in widely separated areas is not inconceivable. As we have seen, the distribution pattern and uniformity of style of bone- and antler-combs suggest constant perambulation around the Scandinavian world on the part of bands of craftsmen (see above, p. 16). Likewise, the widespread finds of Tatinger-type pitchers and artefacts such as swords of Frankish manufacture point to trading activity between the North Sea and the Baltic regions. It would not be surprising if news of spectacular ventures and spoils moved fast along the seaways and stimulated rival undertakings, which could draw partly on war-bands of already seasoned raiders. In other words, the *chaganus* of the Rus may, in or before 860, have been confronted with one or more bands of fortune-seekers, and have sought a vent for their energies and ambitions in an expedition against Byzantium, encouraging or permitting the arms-bearers of his own realm to join in.

That there was a certain restlessness, or heightening of expectations and recourse to violence, among the Scandinavians in the east around this time is suggested by a Persian historian's mention of a *Rūs* raid on Abaskun, on the south-east coast of the Caspian. The Rus are said to have been defeated and slain by the local Moslem authorities.[79] This occurred some time between c. 864 and 883, and the affair may well have been an offshoot of the same energies that manifested themselves in the attack on Byzantium at almost the same time. These activities were not necessarily wholly to the advantage of the Rus *chaganus'* authority. In fact there is evidence suggestive of turbulence: between c. 863 and c. 871 a massive conflagration destroyed the entire settlement at Staraia Ladoga, judging by those areas which have been excavated. There was also a fire in some of the buildings of the fortified settlement at Gorodishche around this time. In one 'complex' a hoard of dirhams had been deposited and the coins were severely damaged by the heat of the blaze. If, as seems likely, the hoard was deposited shortly before the fire, its owner may well have been acting advisedly. In other words, the fire may have been started deliberately. Taken with the approximately contemporaneous holocaust at the other end of the Volkhov, it suggests some sort of upheaval. For while fires of individual buildings or 'complexes' were not uncommon in towns such as Gorodishche, Staraia Ladoga never underwent at any other time total destruction of the kind that struck between c. 863 and c. 871. Moreover, the town's lay-out was very loose-knit, with the complexes of residences and sheds separated from one another by open ground

---

79 ibn Isfandiyar, *History of Tabaristan*, abridged, tr. E. G. Browne (Leiden, London, 1905), p. 199.

and fences. Even the most vicious wind would have been hard-put so to fan the flames of an accidental blaze as to set every structure alight.

Two further considerations could point to some sort of disruption occurring c. 870: firstly, the silence in Byzantine sources about the fate of the religious mission after Basil I's despatch of the archbishop and his miraculous flame-proof gospel-book; and secondly, the *Primary Chronicle*'s account of the appearance of various Rus potentates and of the strife between them. Neither factor is of much weight in itself: the failure of the mission to take hold, and its seeming evanescence need not have been the result of Viking raids or power struggles; and we have already warned against accepting even in broad outline the chronicle's account of the arrival from Scandinavia of Prince Riurik, his two brothers and their followers (see above, p. 39). This 'event' is one of the first to be assigned a date in the chronicle, 862.[80] The chronicle's heavy reliance on the *Continuation* of George the Monk for its account of the 860 attack on Byzantium does not inspire confidence in such shreds of material as it adds for that event.[81] Nor can its version of subsequent events be taken at face value. Yet there may be glimmerings of truth behind the tales of strife between Rus magnates in the later ninth century, and a glance at them is worthwhile.

The Rus attack on the 'Greeks' is dated by the chronicle, incorrectly, to 866.[82] Kiev is represented – anachronistically – as the starting-point of the expedition; and the leaders of the expedition are depicted as two adventurers, who had taken control of Kiev shortly beforehand. They are named as Askold and Dir, and they are categorically stated to be 'not of his [Riurik's] clan': they were merely 'nobles' (*boiarina*), and not of princely standing.[83] These two men are depicted as continuing to rule Kiev after the unsuccessful raid on Byzantium, while Prince Riurik ruled in 'Novgorod'. Upon the death of Riurik, power was reportedly exercised on behalf of his infant son, Igor, by a certain Oleg, described rather vaguely in the chronicle as being 'of his kin'. Oleg is said to have sailed to Kiev in the guise of a trader bound for the Greeks, and to have lured Askold and Dir down to the river bank. They unsuspectingly came down and his men, who were hidden in his boat, leapt out and killed them. Oleg began to reign in Kiev as prince. The residence of the infant Igor, who had been held up in front of the unprincely Askold and Dir, is left unstated. Riurik's death in 879 is the

---

80 *PVL*, I, s.a. 862 (6370), p. 18.
81 Ibid., s.a. 866 (6374), p. 19; *Continuation* of George the Monk, in Theophanes Continuatus, *Chronographia*, pp. 826–7.
82 *PVL*, I, p. 19. The *Primary Chronicle*'s dates for Byzantine-related events in the ninth and early tenth centuries were computed (accurately or inaccurately) from the *Continuation* of George the Monk or, in two or three instances, from other Byzantine sources: I. Sorlin, 'Les premières années byzantines du *Récit des temps passés*', *RES* 63 (1991), 15–17.
83 *PVL*, I, s.a. 862, p. 18; ibid., p. 20.

sole item of Rus affairs in the chronicle's coverage for the years 866 to 882, the year of the killing of Askold and Dir. These two names may have been borne by historical personages but they did not necessarily live at the time or in the place indicated by the chronicle. Igor was certainly a real person and ruled as a prince of the Rus, but he was active and apparently still in his prime in the mid-tenth century (see below, pp. 115, 117). This raises serious doubts as to whether he can already have been on earth, let alone the political scene, in the later ninth century. The chronicle itself seems aware of the anomaly, and tries to explain it away with the observation that Igor was, at the time of his father's death in 879, 'exceedingly young' (*detesk vel'mi*).[84] It may well be that the *Primary Chronicle* sought to paper over the gaps in its information by stringing together the names from diverse genealogies or stories in a more or less coherent sequence. A not dissimilar attempt to fill in a gap can be observed in the *Anglo-Saxon Chronicle*, where the arrival of the princes Cynric and Cerdic is back-dated to the fifth century.[85] As we shall see (below, pp. 115–16), there is testimony to the existence of a Rus prince named Oleg, or rather, 'H-L-G-W', in the early 940s. In other words, doubts about the chronicle's assigning of these names to the later ninth century need not mean that the names bear no relation to any historical person. The compilers of the chronicle may have believed, from some sort of oral tradition, that there was political turmoil in the decades following the first major assault on Tsargrad. They may have sought to convey these conditions by attaching to their outline knowledge princely names which in fact belonged to later generations of potentates. The chronicle seems to be offering a similar blend of basic fact with fancied incidents in its account of Oleg's take-over of the Middle Dnieper region in the last years of the ninth century (see below, p. 107).

One must not overrate the extent, or the purely destructive aspects, of the turbulence to which the archaeological evidence and the chronicle seem to point. The disruption may in a sense register the growth in Scandinavian interest and activity in the eastern lands. Gorodishche continued to be a political centre. Staraia Ladoga seems before long to have recovered from the conflagration, and eventually came to be built-over more densely. The structures seem to have continued to take the form of large halls surrounded by stores and cattle-sheds, and the general lay-out was still scattered, lacking any kind of planning. However, the tempo of commercial exchanges and economic activity quickened from the late ninth century, judging by the increased quantities of finds of glass beads, their production cast-offs and various

---

84 Ibid., p. 19.
85 *Anglo-Saxon Chronicle*, tr. D. Whitelock (London, 1965), p. 11; B. Yorke, 'The Jutes of Hampshire and Wight and the origins of Wessex', in S. Bassett, ed., *The Origins of Anglo-Saxon Kingdoms* (Leicester, 1989), pp. 85–8, 95–6.

kinds of ornaments. Buildings began to be raised in greater numbers on the left bank of the Ladozhka, the opposite side of the river from the main settlement. It appears that the number of indubitably Scandinavian ornaments found in the substratum above the fire markedly exceeds that in the earlier layers. And Staraia Ladoga became much better-protected than it had been before. A circuit wall of limestone slabs was built on the promontory formed by the confluence of the Ladozhka with the Volkhov. The wall was not especially high – apparently between 2.5 and 2.8 metres – and the slabs were laid directly on the natural soil without any foundations; no mortar was used. But the elongated area which the wall enclosed was clearly intended to act as a citadel, and at least one tower was attached to the inner side of the wall.[86] Nothing comparable is known anywhere else in the eastern lands of the ninth or the first half of the tenth centuries. The stone fortress was built before the 930s or 940s but the precise date of construction remains uncertain. So does the identity and provenance of the builders. But there is no reason why it should not have been built some time in the last quarter of the ninth century, in order to guard the inhabitants of Staraia Ladoga against further marauders from across the Baltic Sea. For if the conflagration of c. 863–c. 871 was started deliberately, Viking raiders or conquerors are the most obvious culprits.

The evidence is too sparse and too ambivalent to allow a fuller or more confident reconstruction of events than this. But there may be a connection between developments at Staraia Ladoga and others which we have already encountered: only from the late ninth century does the datable evidence (in the form of dendrochronologically analysed wood, ornaments or Frankish swords) become relatively full at Gorodishche, Timerëvo and the other Upper Volga sites where some sort of politico-military order seems to have been instituted by the Rus. Thus at Gorodishche the turn of the ninth and tenth centuries saw the construction of bread-ovens on the site of the narrow hollow which had originally divided the hilltop from the settlement's more thinly occupied lower ground.[87] This suggests that the number of immigrants increased around this time, and there were more mouths to be fed.

There is one further phenomenon to which numismatic historians have drawn attention. Relatively few dirhams struck between c. 870 and c. 900 have been found in late ninth-century Russian hoards in comparison with dirhams of earlier date. This is not in itself conclusive evidence, seeing that relatively few hoards deposited in the late ninth century have been reported there, and this will have depressed the number of finds of coins dating to that period. But the dearth of finds of Abbasid dirhams struck in the later ninth century extends

86 A. N. Kirpichnikov, *Kamennye kreposti novgorodskoi zemli* (Leningrad, 1984), pp. 23, 29–32; Mühle, *Städtischen Handelszentren*, pp. 50–3.
87 Nosov, *Novgorodskoe (Riurikovo) Gorodishche*, p. 154.

beyond the Russian lands: a fairly similar pattern is found in Swedish hoards and late ninth-century dirhams are also rare in the few hoards of that period known in Poland or Finland. The historical numismatist, T. S. Noonan, has described the period as that of 'the first major silver crisis in Eastern Europe'.[88] Noonan draws attention to the upheavals in the Abbasid caliphate in the later ninth century, and also to reports of warfare and unrest in the Khazar-dominated southern steppes in the later ninth century. This could have caused dislocation of the routes leading to the northern forests, and thus a reduction in the number of dirhams reaching that area. This interpretation is tenable and can in fact be supplemented by further evidence of disorder in the steppes in this period (see below, pp. 85–6).

One cannot, however, be absolutely sure that there was a marked decline in the number of dirhams *reaching* the north. It is possible that more dirhams were being put to other, non-monetary, uses as raw material for ornaments; or they may have been repeatedly changing hands – circulating – among the Rus in a way which had not happened earlier. This might have left fewer reasons for depositing the dirhams in the ground. And seeing that the majority of Middle Eastern dirhams found in the Baltic region had passed through the lands frequented by the Rus, any marked change in Rus usage or demand for them would have constricted the flow of dirhams further west, inducing a real shortage there. Such a scenario seems as plausible as that of an absolute decline in the number of dirhams being imported to the north in the later ninth century. It is not easy to reconcile the hints of heightened commercial activity at the widely scattered sites of Staraia Ladoga, Gorodishche and the Upper Volga settlements with a silver famine; for although the existing stocks of silver might have sufficed to lubricate exchanges for a while, they are unlikely to have satisfied demand indefinitely. As Noonan himself emphasizes, well-informed Arabic writers such as ibn Rusta and ibn Fadlan indicate that the Rus would only offer up their produce in exchange for the silver dirhams brought from the Islamic world.[89] So the trading nexus relied for its survival on a fairly steady influx of silver, and while the Rus settlements contained ample tools, seeds and skills to sustain their small permanent populations, their *raison d'être* was trade. We cannot, then, be sure that the decline in the number of late ninth-century Abbasid coins found in hoards represents an actual decline in the number of dirhams being brought to the north. It could be that a significant increase in the number of Rus residing and trading in the eastern lands caused the dirhams to be spread more widely and thinly than

---

88 T. S. Noonan, 'Khazaria as an intermediary between Islam and Eastern Europe in the second half of the ninth century: the numismatic perspective', *AEMA* 5 (1985) [1987], 183.

89 Noonan, 'Khazaria as an intermediary', 198.

before, and that more were melted down for ornaments. It seems to be from the later ninth century onwards that finds of rings and other ornaments made wholly or partly of silver become more common.

This second scenario, of burgeoning demand for silver on the part of the Rus, is, in fact, quite compatible with the other, more straightforward, hypothesis – that the inflow of dirhams to the forest zone in the later ninth century was being constrained by turbulence in the steppes. The two phenomena may have come about independently of one another, but have had the overall effect of diminishing the amount of dirhams set aside in hoards. And the decline in the finds of recently minted coins in Russian hoards of the later ninth century anyway suggests some change in the circumstances of the Rus.

There is firm evidence of another change around that time, the formation – or rather, the integration – of a political structure not far to the east, on the Middle Volga. It was a change to which the Rus seem to have been quick to adapt, taking advantage of the loose ascendancy which they already enjoyed in the Upper Volga region to intensify their trading there, and to step up their use of boats. They did not, however, have occasion fully to exercise their military or organizational skills. The distant location of the sources of silver did not encourage such a development. Neither did their formidable eastern neighbours, a non-Slav people known as the Bulgars.

It was to the Bulgars on the Middle Volga that ibn Fadlan was sent on a mission in 922, and while staying in their main town he observed Rus traders going about their business (see above, pp. 43–4). It is easily forgotten that the Bulgar khagan's realm was then of quite recent formation. It seems rapidly to have gained cultural assets which the Rus lacked, and the very fact that already in the early tenth century the Abbasid caliph honoured it with a well-stocked mission suggests a power to be reckoned with. The Volga Bulgars' economic interests converged in important respects with those of the Rus, but they were also rivals and, as we shall see, they remained an indomitable, alien presence on the eastern fringes of the Rus sphere of activity up to the later twelfth century (see below, pp. 156, 333). This robust alternative culture to that of the Rus therefore deserves attention.

The Bulgars were not newcomers to the north. Substantial numbers of them had been living in the Middle Volga region since the eighth century. Judging by their pottery and their burial ritual, they were closely related to those Bulgars who made up one of the principal elements in the Khazar-dominated lands (see below, p. 80). They were formally subject to the Khazar khagan in the first half of the tenth century, and this may reflect a longstanding state of affairs. At any rate, the trade in silver and furs between the inhabitants of the Kama valley and still further north and the traders from southern lands passed along the Middle Volga. This involved continuing exchanges between the Bulgars and their fellows living in the Khazar-dominated steppes. Such contacts were feasible, seeing that the wooded steppe curves north-eastwards to within 100 kilometres of the Middle Volga. The Volga Bulgars' own way of life remained essentially nomadic, and their numbers may well have been reinforced by the periodic arrival of newcomers from the steppes. Conversely, numerous aboriginal inhabitants of the central Urals and Upper Kama regions migrated down the Kama valley in the direction of the Middle Volga in the second half of the ninth and the early tenth centuries. They seem to have made up well over half the population of the area, judging by finds of their pottery and burial ritual there. The Bulgars frequenting the Middle Volga region reportedly kept distinct from the members of another, albeit very similar, material culture, the Karaiakupovskii. The latter were concentrated in the south-eastern Urals and beyond the Urals and, judging by the distribution pattern of their fortresses, they were not on particularly amicable terms with the Bulgars to their west. They have been identified by certain archaeologists with the 'proto-Hungarians'. Sites of the 'Karaiakupovskii culture' become rarer from the ninth century onwards and this would be consistent with the appearance of the Hungarians in force in the Black Sea steppes at that time (see below, p. 84). But it could also reflect migration into the lands of the Bulgars. At any rate, it seems to have been only after the waning of the neighbouring 'Karaiakupovskii culture' that burial-grounds combining substantial proportions of graves of both Bulgars and immigrants from the Urals and Kama regions emerge. This was in the second half of the ninth century, and it marks the beginnings of a more sophisticated politico-military structure.

At the head of this structure stood the Bulgar khagan, supported and perhaps constrained by an arms-bearing elite. Cavalry remained the principal mode of warfare, and although in the tenth century large fortified settlements were built and became home in wintertime, the members of the elite and, apparently, most of the inhabitants of the settlements still dispersed to their iurts – tents of felt – in summer. As in the case of the Khazars, this semi-nomadic way of life was compatible with a sedentary religious culture and intensive trading activity. Already in the ninth century individual Bulgars adopted the Moslem faith, as witness their burial rituals, and some time around the beginning of the tenth century the khagan himself was converted to Islam, together with the rest of the elite. According to ibn Rusta, 'the majority' of the Bulgars were Moslems, 'and in their settlements are mosques and Koranic schools; they have muezzins and imams'.[90] It was in response to a request from the khagan for an instructor in religion and for assistance in building a new mosque that ibn Fadlan was sent to the Middle Volga in 922. At the chief town – located,

90 ibn Rusta, ed. Lewicki, pp. 32–3; tr. Wiet, p. 159.

significantly, by the confluence of the Kama with the Volga – he found a market-ground where markets were held 'at brief intervals', and much costly merchandise was exchanged.[91] The fur trade was the hub of these exchanges and ibn Fadlan states that Bulgar merchants would travel to the land of the '*Wisū*' (i.e. Ves) in quest of marten-skins and black fox. It was they who conducted the 'silent trade' with the inhabitants of the far north, journeying there in sledges drawn by dogs and reportedly carrying out the exchanges without talking to, or even directly meeting, the locals. Weasel skins were used as currency, each being worth two-and-a-half dirhams, according to ibn Rusta, and 'white dirhams . . . from other Moslem countries' were reportedly also in use.[92] This writer, or his source, shows no awareness that the Bulgars issued coins of their own and it may be that none were yet being struck at the beginning of the tenth century. In any case, within a few years dirhams were being struck on the Middle Volga in the name of the Bulgars' ruler, Jafar ibn Abdallah, and coins continued to be struck intermittently for him, his sons and subsequent Bulgar potentates until the late tenth century. The number of these coins has probably been underestimated by modern scholars, because they are liable to be mistaken for dirhams struck in the Middle East or Central Asia. The striking of silver coins is a measure of the khagan's ample resources, and also of the fairly high degree of political organization to be found on the Middle Volga from the beginning of the tenth century onwards. The Bulgars' organization may have owed some stimulus to the Khazars' tribute demands: the khagan paid one marten-skin for each household in his realm. However, when a boat arrived from the land of the Khazars, the contents of the cargo were listed and one-tenth taken as tax. According to ibn Fadlan, the khagan would ride to the riverside, and see to the drawing up of the inventory.

The model which the Volga Bulgars took for their coins is as significant as the fact of their striking them. For the earliest issues were imitations of dirhams of the Samanid rulers of Central Asia. They combine the name of a Samanid emir with the name of the Bulgars' principal town, Bulgar, or with that of Suvar, the other one of their settlements described by a tenth-century Arabic writer as a town. Even after Bulgar dynasts began to issue dirhams in their own name, they continued to strike imitations of dirhams of the Samanids. This is a clear indication that the principal source of their dirhams lay in the Samanid realm beyond the Aral Sea, in Transoxiana. The Samanids began to strike dirhams in massive quantities from the end of the ninth century onwards and they pursued a policy of conspicuously encouraging trade with the northern regions. They drew attention to their new trading links through such gestures as

91 ibn Fadlan, ed. Lewicki, p. 61; tr. Canard, p. 66.
92 ibn Rusta, ed. Lewicki, pp. 32–3; tr. Wiet, p. 159.

the dispatch to the Abbasid caliph in 910 of 'an unusual present of furs, especially sable'.[93] They thereby showed off the new supplies of primary produce at their disposal, even while going through the motions of deference towards Baghdad. The Samanids seem to have regulated trade as a means of gaining dominance over Moslem Central Asia. There is probably a direct connection between their emergence as a *de facto* independent dynasty and the growing importance of the Volga Bulgars as middlemen between traders from the south and the northern providers of the furs.

It was possible, though awkward, for trade to be conducted overland rather than by boat across the Caspian and then through Khazaria up the Lower Volga. There are indications of tension between the Volga Bulgars and their Khazar overlord, who was still capable of exacting tribute in the 920s. In fact, the khagan had asked the Abbasid caliph for assistance in building a fortress as well as a mosque, and the reason he cited was the need for protection against the Khazars, who had imposed a blockade 'and reduced [us] to servitude'.[94] Therefore ibn Fadlan took what seems to have been the most direct land-route avoiding the Khazars – from Bukhara to Khorezm, and on across the Ust-Iurt plateau to the river Ural and, eventually, the Bulgar capital. The route was dangerous and difficult from the moment ibn Fadlan's party, mounted on camels bought *en route*, entered the steppes of the Ust-Iurt plateau. The bands of nomadic Oghuz (known to the *Primary Chronicle* as Torks) were suspicious, if not downright hostile. They anyway had scant respect for their own nominal leaders. When the Moslems protested to an Oghuz that they were friends of the *kūdherkīn* (the Oghuz's deputy-ruler), his response was: 'Who is this *kūdherkīn*? I shit on the *kūdherkīn*'s beard!'[95] ibn Fadlan's route was a direct one from Central Asia to the Bulgars, but it required the crossing of numerous rivers; the travellers negotiated these with the help of camel-skins which were converted into fold-up boats. The journey for caravans laden with dirhams was even more vulnerable to attacks from the nomads, yet it was certainly one of the routes by which silver reached the Volga Bulgars, and most probably the main one. According to Masudi, 'there are caravans continually travelling from their land to Khorezm ... or returning from that realm', and they had to 'place themselves under [the nomads'] protection'.[96] Trade did, however, continue through the land of the Khazars. Masudi mentions ships bringing goods, chiefly furs, down to Khazaria from

93 M. Shaban, *Islamic History: a New Interpretation* (Cambridge, 1976), II, p. 148.
94 ibn Fadlan, ed. Lewicki, p. 50; tr. Canard, p. 56, n. 167 on p. 111.
95 Ibid., ed. Lewicki, p. 40; tr. Canard, p. 43.
96 Masudi, *Muruj al-Dhahab wa Ma'adin al-Jawhar* [*Golden Meadows and Mines of Precious Stones*] 455, ed. C. Pellat (Beirut, 1966), I, p. 216; tr. C. Pellat, *Les prairies d'or* (Paris, 1962), I, p. 164.

the land of the Burtas. Many of the furs probably originated further north. The Bulgars thus had a choice of routes to the Moslem countries and enjoyed access, albeit hazardous, to an abundant new source of dirhams.

This state of affairs presented the Rus with opportunities which they were quick to seize. From the beginning of the tenth century, the composition of hoards found in the Russian lands and the Baltic region alters drastically. Most tenth-century dirhams found in tenth-century Russian hoards are Samanid issues, and their quantity exceeds that of all the dirhams found in earlier hoards. This is unquestionable, even though no comprehensive catalogue of these hoards has yet appeared. It seems that the supply of dirhams was now sufficient to provide raw material for ornaments and other non-monetary uses, while leaving many coins in circulation as a medium of exchange or available for hoarding. In other words, the volume of trade between the Rus and dealers in silver increased markedly around the beginning of the tenth century.

The key importance of the Rus link with the Bulgars is already signalled by ibn Rusta. He twice mentions them as being, like the Khazars, trading partners of the Bulgars, and he states that they bring their goods to the Bulgars.[97] This fits in with the scene painted by ibn Fadlan, wherein Rus boats of some size ply the Volga with their cargoes of slaves (see above, pp. 43–4). It is worth pointing out a couple of facets of the picture which are easily overlooked. Firstly, this situation was of quite recent origin and there is no firm evidence that the Rus were sailing regularly and in substantial numbers down the Volga as far as the Bulgars before the close of the ninth century. If the Rus did not make much use of this waterway earlier, this could reflect not merely the lack of an established market on the Middle Volga, but also the relatively modest amounts of silver involved in trading up to that time. One may suppose that only after the loads of dirhams became really heavy – and the number of slaves and other commodities for sale numerous – did it become profitable for the Rus to maintain vessels for transporting them in bulk. This situation had arisen by the beginning of the tenth century, when ibn Rusta implies that the Rus use boats to bring goods to the Bulgars, 'like all the other people who live on this river's [Volga's] banks'.[98]

A second facet of this picture has not received comment from ibn Fadlan or modern historians. There is probably a connection between the trading which he observed and the development of the Rus settlements on the Upper Volga. For although there were already Rus in the region of Iaroslavl in the second half of the century (see

97 ibn Rusta, ed. Lewicki, pp. 30–1, 40–1; tr. Wiet, pp. 159, 163.
98 Ibid., ed. Lewicki, pp. 30–1, cf. pp. 40–1; tr. Wiet, p. 159, cf. p. 163.

above, p. 36), the use of Timerëvo, Mikhailovskoe and Petrovskoe only intensified around the end of the century. The essential *raison d'être* of these settlements was the trade in furs and silver. One hint of this comes from the small iron weights of scales and miniature bronze bowls for holding them which have been found in the burial-ground at Timerëvo. Weights, the bowls for holding them, or weights together with bowls have been found in 32 graves.[99] This figure is modest, as a fraction of the total of 464 graves excavated, but it is likely that many weights were melted beyond recognition by the heat of funeral pyres. The precise weighing of precious metal – above all, silver – was expected to be a more or less routine activity in the next world as well as this. Weights, bowls and, occasionally, fragments of the miniature portable balances for holding them have been found at Gorodishche and Staraia Ladoga, too, and systematic excavation of a burial-ground there on the scale of the one at Timerëvo would probably reveal many more examples. But it was probably the emergence of a major silver market on the Middle Volga that caused more Rus to take up residence near the junction between the Volga and the river Kotorosl, which led southwards to the Sarskii fort and longer-established trading grounds. A number of Rus went on to settle further afield in the Volga-Kliazma watershed.

The mainly tenth-century burial-ground at Timerëvo is the most scientifically excavated north-eastern site containing substantial quantities of Scandinavian-style ornaments and ritual. The surviving part of the burial-ground has been excavated almost in its entirety. Scandinavian-style women's brooches have been found in 27 graves; rings on which were hammerlets of Thor in four graves; and clay paws in 46 graves. The latter – lightly baked clay figures of what are most probably beavers' paws – are of particular significance, since they occur in so few other areas. Only one example has been preserved from the Scandinavian mainland, and it was found in an early Vendel period context of the seventh century. The numerous examples from the Åland islands date from the Vendel and the (subsequent) Viking periods. In some burial-grounds on west–central Åland, more than one-quarter of the graves contain the paws. The other large concentration of finds is at Timerëvo, Mikhailovskoe and Petrovskoe. Clay paws have also been found in several burial-grounds further south from the Volga, in the region of Lakes Nero and Pleshcheevo, and near Suzdal and Iurev-Polskoi.[100] In the Volga region – though not on the Åland isles – the paws are often accompanied by small rings, likewise of clay. The

---

99 M. V. Fekhner and N. G. Nedoshivina, 'Etnokul'turnaia kharakteristika timerevskogo mogil'nika po materialam pogrebal'nogo inventaria', *SA* 1987, no. 2, 72–4.
100 Map of distribution of clay paws: Jansson, 'Communications', fig. 6, p. 783; cf. M. V. Fekhner, 'Bobrovyi promysel v volgo-okskom mezhdurech'e', *SA* 1989, no. 3, 73, 77; Callmer, 'Clay paw burial rite', 17, 20–3, 32–4.

survival- and detection-rates of these small, unpretentious-looking items of burial ritual are rather chancy, but the distribution-pattern of finds is suggestive. It broadly corresponds with that of the large iron rings on which were hung miniature hammers – hammerlets of Thor – and other pendants. These rings were mainly of ritual significance, as the clay paws certainly were. They are found in large numbers on the island of Åland and in the eastern parts of Uppland and Södermanland. They are found only in a very small number of other Scandinavian sites, but they appear in the Rus lands, at such sites as Gorodishche, Staraia Ladoga and the settlements to the south-east of Lake Ladoga.[101] They constitute another pointer towards some sort of special relationship between Central Sweden and, in particular, the Åland isles on the one hand, and the eastern lands on the other. They suggest that some sort of migration, or wavelets of migration, occurred from the islands and, to a lesser extent, Central Sweden from around the end of the ninth century. There is little evidence (other than the appearance in the east of small clay rings) of 'local variants' or 'hybrid forms' of these two ritual objects, although different patterns of occurrence in male and female graves emerged among the Volga communities as they did on the Åland islands themselves. In other words, there is no indication of a slow Rus migration eastwards, with intensive intermingling with native peoples on the way. As with these objects and with combs (see above, p. 16), so with ornaments in general, and with sword-types: changing designs and techniques are registered in the eastern lands at about the same time as they appear in the Baltic and North Sea regions. This fits in with a picture of close contacts between far-flung areas, and of constant toing and froing on the part of many Rus while in their prime. Timerëvo offers testimony to a kind of migration in the tenth century, as do the burial-grounds near Lakes Nero and Pleshcheevo, Suzdal and Iurev-Polskoi. These burial-grounds underwent highly unscientific excavation in the mid-nineteenth century: they yielded a range of ornaments and weapons comparable to those at the Iaroslavl sites, for example, brooches, rings with coins as pendants, sword-chapes, battle-axes and lancet-shaped arrowheads.[102]

'Migration' may sound too grand a term for what is, admittedly, a fairly puny body of evidence. Even the 46 cremation-graves containing clay paws at Timerëvo constitute only a small proportion of the total, and the overwhelming majority of graves are lacking in goods or other indicators of possible ethnos or 'material culture'. But while they are, strictly speaking, indeterminate, they need not necessarily

---

101 Map of distribution of Thor's hammer-rings: Jansson, 'Communications', fig. 4, pp. 782, 781; Novikova, 'Iron neck-rings with Thor's hammers', fig. 1, p. 76 (distribution map), 77, 84–7.

102 A. Spitsyn, 'Vladimirskie kurgany', *Izvestiia Arkheologicheskoi Kommissii* 15 (1905), 86–9; E. A. Riabinin, 'Vladimirskie kurgany', *SA* 1979, no. 1, 232–4; see also below, p. 132, n. 38.

have belonged to non-Scandinavians. Most graves in Scandinavia itself contain very few goods, or none at all, and tortoiseshell brooches are found in a higher proportion of cremation-graves at Timerëvo than they are even in the cremation-graves of Birka.[103] The Timerëvo burial-ground may therefore contain to a large extent persons of Scandinavian descent, although the evidence of certain graves suggests coupling with Finno-Ugrian women began at an early stage. All this would be compatible with ibn Fadlan's evidence of mobile communities comprising one or more kin-groups (see above, p. 44). These travelling bands could have spent fairly regular periods doing business at places such as Timerëvo. Such a rhythm would account for the discrepancy between the size of Timerëvo's total settlement area – approximately 6 hectares – and the modest scale of its burial-ground: this may have been a kind of giant fair-ground in winter, on the lines of Birka (see above, p. 17). A smallish population of permanent residents would help account for the scantiness of the archaeological traces left by the structures there. As at Staraia Ladoga and Gorodishche, many seem to have been lightweight affairs and were not built to last. New cabins and storehouses could be knocked up within a few days to cater for the changing needs of shifting groups. ibn Fadlan saw the Rus putting up such temporary cabins at Bulgar in 922 (see above, p. 43). In contrast with Staraia Ladoga and Gorodishche, where large numbers of structures were superimposed one on top of another at frequent intervals, new buildings were put up on vacant parts of the slope on which Timerëvo stood. Space was plentiful and security does not seem to have been at a premium, at least by the tenth century.

The better-off inhabitants of Timerëvo, Mikhailovskoe, Petrovskoe and the settlements further 'inland' in the Volga–Kliazma watershed were well-armed, some being equipped in their graves with swords as well as weights for doing business. It is probable that they formed part of a wider political order, under the Rus *chaganus* based at Gorodishche (see above, p. 41). But the *chaganus* and his bed were over 500 kilometres away, and neither ibn Rusta's nor ibn Fadlan's accounts suggest that his political role was a very active or interventionist one. It was neither necessary nor feasible for a systematically exploitative Rus regime to develop in the region. Rus numbers were finite – perhaps 130 persons living at Timerëvo at any one time in the tenth century – and the rest of the population was mostly too diffuse. The weaponry of the Rus might intimidate, but they needed to induce the Finno-Ugrians to come and offer up furs and other marketable commodities rather than slipping away into the forests. They themselves engaged in hunting and trapping, as the prominence of their beaver-paw talismans shows. Thirty of the Iaroslavl burials contain remains of husky-like dogs as well as beaver paws: most probably the dogs were specially trained to prise the beavers

103 Jansson, 'Communications', 786, 789–90.

out of their lairs.[104] The Rus had no need to form themselves into a militarized unit in order to do business with the Bulgars. Judging by ibn Fadlan's account, a fairly high degree of security obtained in the Bulgar markets, and every Rus was preoccupied with the best price which his slaves and furs might fetch, rather than with hostile locals or robbery (see above, p. 44).

Conversely, the Rus did not have the capacity, at least in terms of numbers, to subjugate the Bulgars, even though they could sail directly to them. The Bulgars were well equipped with spears, sabres, bows, arrows and chain-mail and they showed their mettle not long after 912 when they broke up the remnants of a major Rus expedition to the Caspian. The Rus had, on the outward journey, travelled to the Lower Volga where they had made an agreement with the Khazar ruler that half the booty from their rampage round the Caspian should be paid to the Khazars. They proved willing to honour this undertaking upon their return to the Lower Volga, 'sated with plunder and tiring of this way of life'.[105] They were nonetheless attacked by the Moslem subjects of the Khazar khagan, who sought vengeance for their fellow-Moslems whom the Rus had slaughtered or, in the case of women and children, taken captive. The Rus are said to have disembarked from their ships and for three days fought the Moslems and 'some of the Christians' from the Khazar capital, Itil. By the end of it, most of the Rus had been killed or drowned. The survivors, withdrawing on foot, were attacked by the Burtas further up-river, and 'others arrived at the Moslem Bulgars, who massacred them'.[106]

Masudi, our mid-tenth-century source for this episode, puts the total number of Rus slain by the Moslems at one point or another along the Volga at 'about 30,000', and states that there has been no recurrence of such raiding since then. The episode cannot, however, be taken to show an increase in Rus numbers or organization on the Upper Volga, even after leaving aside the unreliability of medieval estimates of armies' sizes. In fact, the raiders on their outward journey had crossed over to the Lower Volga from the Don, presumably after sailing up the latter river from the Black Sea. This is an implicit acknowledgement of the Volga Bulgars' might, in that the Rus had opted for an apparently more circuitous route, rather than sailing down the continuous waterway of the Volga. Thus the episode suggests the futility of any Rus attempt to force the Middle Volga. They may have been weary and encumbered with loot and captives at the time of their defeat near Itil, and of course the Volga Bulgars only had to finish off a fraction of the original force, returning on foot. But, as the Rus themselves seem to have decided after c. 912, the strategic balance of

104 Fekhner, 'Bobrovyi promysel', 76.
105 Masudi, 461, ed. Pellat, I, p. 220; tr. Pellat, I, p. 166.
106 Ibid., 461, ed. Pellat, I, p. 221; tr. Pellat, I, p. 167.

advantage rested overwhelmingly with the two powers established on, respectively, the Middle and the Lower Volga, and the greatest material gains were to be had from trading, not raiding. Moreover, it would seem that the settlements near Iaroslavl were directed against attacks from upstream – from fellow Rus coming eastwards down the Volga – at least as much as against the Volga Bulgars. The Upper Volga region offered ample opportunities for the Rus to enrich themselves and their settlements grew in size and in the volume of their commercial activity during the tenth century. But they relied heavily on the cooperation of the local Finno-Ugrian population, and there was no pressing danger or incentive to forge these local communities into a politico-military formation.

CHAPTER TWO

Turning South

1. SLAVS AND SEMI-NOMADS IN THE NINTH CENTURY

From the end of the ninth century onwards the Rus faced, in the form of the Volga Bulgars, a military power blocking any ambitions they may have entertained of expansion down the Volga. About the same time, they began to instal themselves in the south, in the region of the Middle Dnieper. To state this is at once to stir up controversy. For it has been assumed by the compilers of the *Primary Chronicle* and by modern historians that the Rus attack on Constantinople of 860 was launched from Kiev and that Rus had been living there for at least a few years. However, Photios writes of the attackers as if they were coming from even further north and states that they have already 'subjugated those around them'.[1] This fits better with an attack launched or helped on its way from an established centre, such as Gorodishche (see above, p. 54). As we shall see below (pp. 94–5, 96–102), there is no firm archaeological evidence of Scandinavian settlement, or of any significant political centre at all, on the Middle Dnieper in the mid-ninth century. For want of reliable literary or archaeological evidence of a Dnieper base for the Rus raid of 860, some scholars have supposed an abode for them somewhere on the north coast of the Black Sea, for example, the eastern Crimea.[2] But no convincing archaeological evidence has been produced in support of such theories and the Byzantine sources have nothing to say about any Rus establishment on the Black Sea in the ninth century. Here, their silence is damning (see above, p. 54). That leaves the majority of the Rus sticking to the north through most of the ninth century, with merely a handful of envoys or fortune-seekers venturing as far as Byzantium, or taking goods for sale down to the steppes or a port on the Black Sea (see above, p. 42).

This raises the question why the Rus were so slow to settle on the Dnieper. 'So slow' is a loaded phrase and, before trying to offer some

---

1 Photios, *Epistulae et Amphilochia*, ed. B. Laourdas and L. G. Westerink (Leipzig, 1983), I, p. 50; see also above, p. 51–2.

2 H. Ahrweiler, 'Les relations entre les Byzantins et les Russes au IX siècle', *Bulletin d'Information et de Coordination de l'Association internationale des études byzantines* 5 (1971), 56–7, 65.

answers, we must stop to consider whether the question even makes sense. As has already been seen (pp. 21–2, 36–7), the archaeological evidence of Scandinavian settlement beyond Staraia Ladoga is quite sparse before the late ninth century. Only then do finds of Scandinavian-style artefacts and burials become more common in the Upper Volga region. Even centres such as Gorodishche have so far yielded only limited evidence for settlement before the closing decades of the ninth century. Even if, as is likely, further excavations at Gorodishche point to a substantial Rus population there earlier in the century, the picture of a small-scale and mercurial Rus presence to the south or east of Gorodishche is likely to remain intact. If places of permanent Rus settlement further along 'the East Way' were few and scattered throughout the ninth century, their absence from the Middle Dnieper would not, in itself, be particularly surprising. It was possible for the Rus to pass through a region or to visit its market centres without instituting a permanent trading post or 'colony' there. Bands of Rus were probably traversing the Middle Dnieper region long before they settled there if, as is likely, Rus were involved in the transport of dirhams between the Donets and the Upper Dnieper (see above, p. 26). It is more worthwhile to ask what there was to draw the Rus southwards for good or, alternatively, what might have hindered or deterred them from attempting to do so. This involves a glance at the lie of the land and the peoples who lived off it. The eventual surprise may be that the Rus made the effort at all.

In the far south-west, Slav settlements lined the rivers Dniester, Prut and Siret and the Slavs also formed a fairly dense group of unfortified settlements between the Middle Dniester and the Prut. But this kind of occupation of unfortified sites on the southernmost fringes of the wooded steppe was exceptional and may be explained by their being under the aegis of the Danubian Bulgars. Further eastwards, the Slavs tended to keep to the wooded steppe and the deciduous forest zone, fearing to trespass on lands which offered lush pastures for the nomads' herds of horses, cattle and other livestock. The fertile 'Black Earth' and 'Grey Earth' of, respectively, the wooded steppe and the deciduous forest was quite adequate for the Slavs' agriculture, and the woods offered some protection from casual pillaging by the steppe-dwellers. The Slavs living between the Dniester and the Dnieper were generally reliant on natural defences and some of their settlements are not easily accessible even today, being set among the Pripet marshes or occupying rises in the flood meadows of river valleys. The Slavs' settlements tend to be bunched together in groups of four or five. The inhabitants were bound together by ties of kinship and a common interest in self-defence. But the secluded nature of many settlements, and their diffusion over a vast area, did not make for a tight socio-political structure overall.

The inhabitants of the clusters of settlements probably aimed at self-sufficiency in the essentials of life. Fish from the surrounding streams and rivers, and game and livestock such as cows and pigs, provided protein, as they did to the human population of the more northerly forests, but arable farming was more productive than was the case further north, in the mixed-forest zone. The Slavs grew wheat, barley and rye, including a type of rye sown in the autumn for early harvesting in the following year. The question of whether a metal ploughshare was in use among the Slavs in the eighth and ninth centuries is still controversial. It may be that iron mattocks, a common find in settlements of the wooded steppe and deciduous forest zone, normally served to break the soil for the sowing of corn, as well as for the cultivation of vegetables. What is certain is that only a very narrow range of weapons has been unearthed in the Slavs' settlements. Iron arrow-tips and spearheads are common enough finds, together with axes, adzes, sickles and other implements. They were manufactured on the spot and were probably used for hunting and fending off four-, as well as two-legged, predators. The spears and arrows were not the attributes of a ruling elite, and the general lay-out of the settlements and the uniformity of finds in the graves tells heavily against the existence of any such elite. The dwellings, sunk half into the ground with hearths mostly of stone, are small and could have accommodated only four or five persons. There is no conclusive evidence of groups of larger or more richly furnished buildings, or of a central hall which might have housed a chieftain and his retainers. These intimations of a loose-knit society of agriculturalists lacking in marked variations of wealth tally with many aspects of the way of life of the Slavs living north of the Danube described by the Byzantine emperor Maurice, at the end of the sixth century. Maurice's Slavs are more aggressive, raiding into Byzantine territory, but they, too, prize their freedom, are 'anarchic', and live among forests, bogs and inaccessible lakes where they raise livestock and grow cereal crops.[3] Their lifestyle probably had much in common with that of their descendants, some two centuries later.

But there was movement and, eventually, change. Groups of Slavs moved off in a variety of directions from the relatively densely populated settlement areas between the Western Bug, the river Pripet and the Dnieper. In dribs and drabs they wandered northwards into the less fertile and less easily cultivable mixed-forest zone where conifers grew side by side with chestnuts, oaks and other deciduous trees. One line of migration threaded its way gradually along the Western Bug to the river Neman and the middle reaches of the Western Dvina. Offshoots from this trail of settlements reached the basins of the great lakes Pskov and Ilmen in the eighth century, seemingly anticipating the

---

3 Maurice, *Strategikon*, XI.4, ed. G. T. Dennis, German tr. E. Gammilscheg (*CFHB* 17; Vienna, 1981), pp. 372–5.

first probes of the Rus (see above, p. 21). Another line of movement followed the Dnieper valley upstream, eventually heading further north to the upper reaches of the Western Dvina. Their settlements were few and small. One cluster formed astride the river Svinets' point of inflow into the Dnieper, the site of the future Gnëzdovo (see below, p. 101). But even here, the total number of inhabitants was small before the later ninth century. The Slavs following this northerly line of migration were not moving into a total vacuum. The mixed-forest zone was inhabited by members of various linguistic groups, the most numerous of which were the Balts. They have left their mark on the names of lakes and streams in the Dnieper basin as far south as the Seim and the confluence of the Dnieper with the Pripet, and they also occupied the forest to the north of the Dnieper. Many archaeologists have attributed to them at least some responsibility for the raising of the 'long barrows', which are found between the Upper Dnieper and the southern approaches to Lakes Ilmen and Pskov. The barrows contained rows of cremation-burials. The questions of who raised these barrows, and precisely when, remain controversial, not least because of the diversity of burial rituals found within them. It is probable that the Balts raised the majority but that Finns, Slavs and members of other, nameless groupings also became involved. Soviet archaeologists' preoccupation with these and other burial-grounds was at the expense of close study of the settlements and the most important consideration is in any case a general one. The population density of the mixed-forest zone as a whole was very low, and it was possible for newcomers to move into an area without displacing or necessarily having much to do with existing groups of inhabitants. While groups of diverse origins met and mingled at points along the major waterways (where the 'long barrows' are mostly found), it was often possible for the Balts and other peoples to live out their lives separately from one another, in their respective river valleys and clearings. Their smallish numbers and broadly similar forms of livelihood – through hunting, fishing and subsistence agriculture – made such co-existence feasible and the arrival of Slav immigrants in the eighth and ninth centuries did not at once transform the situation.[4]

Another direction of Slav migration was to the east. The Slavs moved into the handful of pre-existing settlements in the vicinity of the Dnieper, such as Kiev, and founded a few important new ones – for example, Kanev, about 100 kilometres downstream from Kiev at the last important ford before the open steppe. It seems that groups of settlers crossed the Dnieper already in the seventh century,

---

4 C. Goehrke, *Frühzeit des Ostslaventums* (Erträge der Forschung 277; Darmstadt, 1992), p. 35. Goehrke offers a lucid survey of the highly problematic evidence relating to the Slavs' infiltration into the mixed-forest zone and beyond: pp. 27–36.

and moved into the basins of the Lower and Middle Desna and the Lower Seim. But it was apparently the eighth century which saw the main thrust of their settlement eastwards along the Desna and the Seim or south-eastwards to the upper reaches of tributaries of the Dnieper such as the Vorskla, the Sula and the Psël. Its density seems to register a significant continuing migration during the eighth and ninth centuries, rather than just population growth. The Slavs founded many settlements here as far south as the boundary between the wooded and the open steppe, in contrast to their pattern of settlement west of the Dnieper. Others headed north-eastwards, as far as the upper reaches of the river Oka. They settled on the right-hand side of the river, and some settlements formed well away from the Oka, in the valley of a river which rises not far from the head-waters of the Don. Thus their lines of migration veered towards the areas where silver dirhams were to be had, and where the Khazars held sway.

Finds of dirhams individually or in very small quantities are, together with ornaments made of silver, not uncommon in the Slav settlements to the east of the Dnieper. The amounts of silver coins and the size of the occasional hoards are modest, but the numerous silver finger-rings and bracelets found in the settlements or the nearby burial-grounds belonged to persons who were rich in comparison with their fellow-Slavs living west of the Dnieper. There, very few silver coins have been found in settlements and silver or silver alloy ornaments are also very rare. The way of life of the Slavs east of the Dnieper differed in one other important respect. They generally made their homes in or next to strongpoints – on promontories or terraces overlooking river valleys, or among the much earlier earthworks of the Scyths, which they adapted for their own purposes. Ramparts were thrown up and ditches dug across the neck of a promontory, and wooden stockades lined the tops of the ramparts. The promontories did not rise particularly high above the bogs and water meadows, but these natural defences protected the inhabitants from casual molesters. In the winter, when the bogs and streams froze over, nomadic pastoralists tended to take their herds to the southernmost steppes, where the snow cover was likely to be thinnest, and the prospects of finding adequate grazing for the animals were brightest. To the west of the Dnieper, fewer of the Slavs' settlements were equipped with elaborate, man-made, fortifications, save perhaps in the environs of Kiev. Life may have been richer for the Slavs on the fringes of the open steppe country, but it was also riskier. The distinctive material culture of the left-bank settlements of the eighth to the tenth centuries is known as the 'Romny' or 'Romny-Borshevo' culture, after two of the settlements.

Population increase and the fertility of the valleys on the east bank may have provided the main stimuli for the Slavs' migration thither, but the flow of silver dirhams through the region from the later eighth century onwards was most probably an added attraction. One series of silver routes led from the Upper Don northwards across the Oka towards Finno-Ugrian settlements between the Kliazma and the Volga such as the Sarskii fort, or from the Upper Donets across to the Upper Oka. Another skein of routes wound north-westwards from the Donets and its tributaries to the tributaries of the Dnieper and then along the Upper Dnieper valley (see above, pp. 24–7). The role played by the Slavs in the import of the dirhams is unclear and here, too, one must beware of supposing a uniform or constant state of affairs. The number of hoards known from the zone of their settlement to the east of the Dnieper in the ninth century is not great – approximately twenty – and for the most part these are not connected with Slav habitations or burial-grounds. To the north-east, in the basin of the Oka, most of the hoards are on the right bank, exposed to the steppes, and they are commonest along the middle course of the river, whereas the Slav settlements were mostly confined in the ninth century to the upper course. These hoards further downstream may well have been deposited in connection with exchanges between Moslem and Khazar traders or the semi-nomadic inhabitants of the Don steppes, on the one hand, and the Finno-Ugrian inhabitants of the Oka valley and the regions further north on the other. But there was no physical bar to communities of Slavs joining in the enterprises which were essentially a matter of bartering furs for silver. Fur-clad animals such as foxes, marten and beaver lived in the wooded steppes and judging by the fact that only their extremities – skulls, foot-bones and tail-bones – are found in the Slav settlements, they had been caught for their pelts and not for their meat. However, the animals inhabiting this relatively mild clime did not need the thickest or the whitest of furs and their skins were of correspondingly inferior quality, and value. It is quite possible that Slav entrepreneurs tried to supplement what they could earn from locally caught furs by travelling to markets further north. But if they did so, they would still have needed a commodity such as silver to begin bartering for high-quality pelts. One means of acquiring some silver would have lain in providing guides to long-distance traders bearing the silver from the south. If, as is likely, these journeys were made by land, the travellers presumably needed provisions, and the settlements strung along the Desna, the Seim and the upper reaches of the Sula, Psël and Vorskla were well-positioned to supply them at frequent intervals. This may also have been the route taken by Radhanite Jewish merchants (see above, pp. 41–2; below, p. 93).

That some such commercial exchanges went on is indicated by the finds of fragments of amphorae and pitchers of 'Saltovo-Maiatskii' type in the Slav settlements. The amphorae were probably made on the Crimea or elsewhere in the Black Sea's northern zone and they are believed to have arrived in the settlements as containers of oil or wine. These bulky, quite fragile wares could not well have been seized as loot. Their distribution pattern is similar to that of the finds of individual coins and ornaments made of silver or silver alloy. These solitary coins or small handfuls of coins and silver ornaments are found inside the settlements or in graves, in quite sharp contrast to the pattern of the hoards. This points to conditions in which a certain amount of silver and ready-made ornaments, together with the amphorae and pitchers, was reaching the Slavs on the Dnieper's left bank by means of exchange. There has been found in a workshop at a settlement on the Psël a hoard of dirhams and silver ornaments of 'Saltovo-Maiatskii' type. All but one of the ornaments are damaged and they, together with the dirhams, were probably intended to serve as scrap for melting down in the crucibles and matrices also found there. Clearly, dirhams provided the raw material for the many finds of silver rings and bracelets in Slav settlements. Sometimes they were simply pierced and turned into the pendants of necklaces or bracelets.

The Slav settlers to the east of the Dnieper were not, however, free to keep for themselves all the silver which they managed to acquire: nor did they part with all their furs through commercial transactions. The *Primary Chronicle* represents two Slav 'tribes' as paying tribute to the Khazars in the form of a silver coin, the *shchiliag*. This term is the Slavicized form of a word known in Gothic as *skilliggs*, in Old Norse as *skillingr* and in Anglo-Saxon as *scilling*, from which comes the English 'shilling'. The Radimichi, who lived to the east of the Dnieper around the river Sozh, are described as paying tribute this way in 885. The Viatichi are said to have been paying tribute 'by the *shchiliag*' to the Khazars as late as the 960s (see below, p. 144). According to an entry for 859, the Khazars also exacted tribute from the Polianians and the Severians in the form of 'white squirrel' skins 'from each hearth', an indication of some degree of social order among them.[5] The *Primary Chronicle* cannot be trusted as an authority for precise dates for this period and one must query its assumption that the Slav tribes occupying the basins of the Dnieper and the Oka in the tenth and eleventh centuries were fully formed, demarcated and static in earlier centuries. St Andrew's encounter with the Polianians on the hills of the future city of Kiev represents only the wishful thinking of the contributors to the chronicle (see above, p. 3; below, p. 109). Nonetheless, the chronicle is clear, even insistent, that the Slavs living astride, or to the east of, the Dnieper paid tribute to the Khazars on a regular basis. The chronicle is doing this partly for the record but also to demonstrate that the tables are now turned. Thus it relates how the Polianians responded to a Khazar demand for tribute by rendering a two-edged sword from each 'hearth'. The Khazar elders are said to have regarded this kind of payment as ominous. They compared the swords of the Polianians favourably with the weapon which their own people brandished to exact tribute, the sabre, sharp on one side only:

5 *PVL*, I, pp. 18, 20.

'they will have the means to exact tribute from us'.[6] 'And all this came to pass', observes the chronicle, launching into a long and somewhat inept analogy involving the Khazars, the Egyptians and Moses and his people. Just as the Egyptians underwent destruction and, allegedly, subjugation at the hands of their former slaves, so 'the Rus princes rule over the Khazars up to the present day'.[7]

This tale shows how vividly and long the memory of some sort of Khazar dominion over the Dnieper Slavs lingered. Against no other people is such a historicizing thrust directed and this suggests that in so far as the Rus came to regard any other established power as inimical to their autonomy, they thought of the Khazars and not the distant 'Greeks' (see below, p. 240 and n. 94). The story may have a further dimension. As already noted (see p. 42), by the later ninth century Frankish swords were being brought down to the Black Sea by Rus traders. If, as is likely, some passed along the Dnieper valley, it is conceivable that certain Slavs disposed of enough silver to be able to acquire these valuable commodities and that they featured among the items rendered to the Khazars. This surmise is compatible with the chronicle's statement that the Polianians and the Severians paid tribute in the form of white squirrel skins. White squirrel was clearly the chief commodity sought of them, and it was presumably expected to be of the highest quality. This in turn suggests an origin far to the north. It may well be that the Slavs were impelled to seek out furs of quality from the north by the demands of the Khazars. This was not necessarily a matter of blatant coercion. For, as we have seen, the Slavs were migrating into Khazar-dominated lands through the eighth and ninth centuries, settling in considerable density. Their migration would have been more likely to have headed out of the Khazars' range, had their demands seemed exorbitant. And the chronicle offers hints of a *modus vivendi* between them. Oleg, the Rus prince depicted as taking over the Middle Dnieper region in the late ninth century, is said to have imposed only a 'light tribute' on the Severians, telling them, 'I am against them [the Khazars], but not against you in any way'.[8] If there is substance to this report, it implies a situation where the Severians were contented with their Khazar overlords' regimen, and the Rus intruder was trying to gain acceptance by promising terms at least as light, or lighter.

Such a scenario of co-existence, even cooperation, between the Slavs and the Khazars and their confederates gains in credibility from further consideration of their respective patterns of settlements. These straddled the Seim, Upper Sula, Psël and Vorskla, a few sites being stationed on tributaries between the rivers. Another group of

6 Ibid., p. 16.
7 Ibid., p. 17.
8 Ibid., p. 20.

settlements lined stretches of the Upper and Middle Don and its tributary, the Voronezh. The settlements were, for the most part, fortified. It is most improbable that the prime aim of the Slavs' fortifications was to fend off the Khazars. On the contrary, the Slavs' audacity in settling so far south was probably due to the Khazars' strong arm which, at the price of tribute exactions, could ensure a relatively high degree of security from nomadic marauders. A glance at the map suggests a correlation between the areas of intensive Slav settlement and the outer limits of the Saltovo-Maiatskii culture (Map 3). In fact, many Slavs settled within the limits of that culture, to which we must now turn.

The limits of the Saltovo-Maiatskii culture generated by the Khazars' confederates were marked in monumental, even dramatic, fashion by a number of 'fortresses' along the Upper Severskii Donets and in river valleys between the Donets and the Upper Don. Nine of the twelve known 'fortresses' lie beside or near the Donets and while there may be undetected examples elsewhere, this pattern probably does reflect a concentration of fortifications close to the region of dense Slav settlement. The known fortresses are, with one exception, built of blocks of white limestone, laid directly on the earth without any masonry foundations. Situated on promontories or, occasionally, terraces overlooking river valleys, these fortresses enjoyed good natural defences. Only a few show signs of possible occupation all the year round and it has convincingly been suggested that their prime function was as winter compounds for the semi-nomadic elite dominating the region.[9] Their iurts could have been pitched there through the winter months without leaving a deep impression on the soil. Semi-underground dwellings replete with clay or stone hearths and the foundations of stone structures have been found inside the walls of a few fortresses, for example at Maiatskoe on the Don. But these occupied only a fraction of the compounds, which were themselves usually quite small: the winter encampments may have extended beyond the walls. The frequenters of the white stone fortresses, like other members of the Saltovo-Maiatskii culture, used wheel-turned pottery and their craftsmen were capable of producing high-quality metalwork.

The martial character of those who frequented the fortresses is evident from their burial-grounds. The remains of the dead – inhumed or cremated – were laid in underground chambers known to archaeologists as 'catacombs'. Riding gear and weapons such as sabres and axes figure prominently among the grave goods of males and

---

9 S. A. Pletneva, *Na slaviano-khazarskom pogranich'e. Dmitrievskii arkheologicheskii kompleks* (Moscow, 1989), p. 24. The largely peaceable relations of the Slavs in the Don basin with their semi-nomadic overlords are discussed by A. Z. Vinnikov, 'Kontakty donskikh slavian s alano-bolgarskim mirom', *SA* 1990, no. 3, 124–37.

some females. These were the most carefully forged items of iron- and steelwork – and the means by which members of the elite exercised dominance. Horsemanship and an array of weapons provided the means for wide-ranging patrols across the steppes and beyond, while the settlements grouped immediately around the fortresses could provide food, fodder and, if necessary, shelter. They made it easier for the pastoralists to spend the winter quite far north, in an area liable to a thickish blanket of snow cover for several weeks. It was customary for steppe nomads to make for more southerly pastures in winter. Through this logistical arrangement, the mounted elite could be maintained indefinitely on the verges of areas densely settled by the Slavs. In the event of any disturbances or defiance from the Slavs, they could wait until winter froze over the bogs and flood meadows around their habitations, and then pay them a visit. They possessed one further advantage, the functional literacy which is attested by the Turkic rune inscriptions on the stonework of the fortresses, especially at Maiatskoe.

The ethnic identity of this warrior elite on the edge of the Saltovo-Maiatskii culture has been much discussed by archaeologists. It is clear that Alans, speaking an Iranian language, and Turkic-speaking Bulgars were the two most important elements in it. Of the two groups, the Alans were numerically predominant in the zone of the white stone fortresses and individual settlements and burial-grounds belonging to them have been identified at, for example, the fort and settlement at Maiatskoe. The Alans and the Bulgars maintained separate communities, but at fortresses such as Dmitrievskoe there is evidence of some intermingling. The Bulgars apparently adopted from the Alans the practice of burying the dead in catacombs. The inhabitants of the settlements around the fortresses were also of diverse origins. Some were the descendants of much earlier migrants across the steppes, while others were Alans, Bulgars, Slavs and even, exceptionally, Finno-Ugrians. One indication of their heterogeneity is the diversity of types of dwelling and construction techniques in the settlements. The hearths and the post-holes of iurts are intermingled with half-underground dwellings characteristic of the Slavs. There were also many settlements interspersed between the fortresses and a considerable number of these were inhabited mainly by Slavs. For example, there were numerous Slav settlements as far south as the confluence of the river Bishkin with the Donets and there were even a few settlements further south in the open steppes. Individual settlements were dotted along the Middle and Lower Don as far south as its confluence with the Chir. It is quite possible that some of the Slavs were installed in the Donets and Don basins involuntarily and charged with provisioning the *habitués* of the fortresses. But this would hardly explain the appearance of the Slavs in settlements well to the south of the fortresses, and anyway they seem to have moved gradually, only reaching down the Don as far as modern Voronezh and beyond in the ninth century. This suggests a largely voluntary migration, a continuation of the Slavs' movement eastwards from the Dnieper. So, too, does another feature of the pattern of Slavs' settlements. There is a cluster of fortified Slav settlements in the vicinity of Voronezh, just to the north of the stone fortress of Maiatskoe, and a similar cluster lies near a series of stone fortresses on the Donets, in the vicinity of modern Kharkov. A wholly servile population would probably not have been allowed to live behind ramparts, even earthen ones.

There are, then, various clues pointing to a convergence of interests. The warrior elite whose hegemony the forts declared were well equipped to fend off marauders from the southern steppes. It was here that they could provide a worthwhile service to the Slavs, although it is likely that some random pillaging still went on. The lords of the fortresses, semi-autonomous as well as semi-nomadic, were not necessarily tightly disciplined themselves. But their general interest lay in protecting the Slavs from the other nomads of the steppes, conserving them as a source of tribute. Their attentions were keened by the loads of silver being borne along the valleys of the Don and the Donets; some of the tribute which the Slavs paid was in silver, as the *Primary Chronicle* indicates (see above, p. 77). Hoards of dirhams have been found in the vicinity of some of the fortresses on the Donets and also further south-east, on the Lower Don and in the Kuban steppes. We have already noted the configuration of the hoards and inferred that Moslem silver was being borne northwards along the Don and the Donets from the late eighth century onwards (see above, pp. 25–6). The finds of silver ornaments in Slav settlements to the east of the Dnieper support this inference, and so do the silver ornaments from the burial-grounds beside the stone fortresses. Silver was used for making the ear-rings, belt mounts and casings of sheaths of the fortresses' occupants. The quantity of silver used in this way was not great: bronze ornaments are much more common. But conspicuous wealth is occasionally signalled in the burial ritual, as for example in the sets of silver bridle ornaments found in a few catacombs at Dmitrievskoe.[10] The design of these warriors' bridles, with plumes sprouting from silver holders fastened to the horse's head, probably served to overawe the Khazars' tributaries, notably the Slavs. Much the same could be said of the white stone fortresses themselves, with their crenellated battlements. Further south, on the Middle Donets and the Lower Don, fortifications consisted mostly of earthworks, not stone buildings. The fortresses' significance may have been symbolic as much as functionally military, seeing that the dry-stone walls do not seem to have been particularly sturdy.

---

10 Pletneva, *Dmitrievskii arkheologicheskii kompleks*, pp. 79, 81, 84, 88, 91, 113.

The date commonly proposed for the construction of the white stone fortresses is the late eighth or earlier ninth centuries. That they were built at approximately the same time is suggested by the similarities in their construction techniques and ground plans. This dating is, however, not without its critics and the periodization of the Saltovo-Maiatskii culture as a whole has come into question. The consensus among Russian archaeologists is that the culture emerged towards the middle of the eighth century, after the flight of Alans, Bulgars and Khazars away from the north Caucasus region before the advance of the Arabs. They moved into the Don and Volga steppes and, particularly in the Alans' case, northwards into the wooded steppes; this conglomeration of peoples came to be under the dominion of the Khazars.[11] However, it has been pointed out that some of the ornaments found in burial-grounds of the stone fortresses have close analogies with those found in the Crimea or the Caucasus and datable to the first half of the eighth century or earlier still, while in the Dmitrievskoe burial-ground have been found pots characteristic of the 'Penkovka culture'; this primitive culture of the wooded steppe is generally dated no later than the end of the seventh century.[12] Moreover, as we have seen, there are indications that already in the 730s Khazar traders were frequenting the Caspian port of Darband (see above, p. 10). These commercial exchanges were probably of furs and thus involved at least the wooded steppe, if not points further north. They suggest that the Khazars were by that time established and taking a close interest in the northern fringes of the steppes.

These considerations suggest that the Saltovo-Maiatskii culture may have begun to form a generation or more before the mid-eighth century. This does not, however, necessarily mean that the white stone fortresses of the wooded steppe or the major earthworks of the Lower Don were built as soon as the Khazars and associated peoples began to hold sway there. It was only during the eighth century that the Slavs' movement *en masse* eastwards across the Dnieper began. Some settlements on the Donets had been in existence for a considerable time before a fortress was built nearby, and so their burial-grounds might contain ornaments or pottery of correspondingly early date, reflecting the medley of peoples brought under Khazar hegemony. Moreover, there is evidence that the fortress on a promontory overlooking the right bank of the Don at Tsimlianskoe was built some time after Sarkel; that celebrated brick fortress was built on the opposite bank in the 830s. The right-bank fortress was constructed of white blocks in the same dry-stone technique as was used on the other forts. It was most

---

11 E.g. S. A. Pletneva, 'Vostochnye stepi vo vtoroi polovine VIII–Xv.', in S. A. Pletneva, ed., *Stepi Evrazii v epokhu srednevekov'ia* (Moscow, 1981), pp. 64–5.
12 S. Angelova and L. Doncheva-Petkova in *Arkheologiia*, Sofia, 1991, no. 2, 50–3.

probably built in the second half of the ninth century.[13] On balance, then, a dating of these other fortresses to the same century, or perhaps the end of the eighth, can be accepted. By then, but probably not earlier, there were enough Slav agriculturalists living within easy riding distance of the Upper Donets for stations of well-armed horsemen to be sustainable and potentially wealthy, in terms of the tribute that could be extracted from the Slavs. Silver may not have been passing through this area in very large quantities at the time when the first fortresses were built, but the stone structures lining the Donets made for a higher degree of order and thus trading confidence. We have already noted small items besides dirhams which occur in sites along the Don and Donets and in a very few, and far-flung, other places: certain types of bead made of cornelian, and also Cornelian dung-beetles (see above, p. 25). Larger, heavier, objects from afar also reached the wooded steppe. Thus a bronze mirror made in Tang China in the eighth or ninth century has been excavated in a catacomb at Dmitrievskoe. This mirror, together with less costly objects such as amphorae and pitchers from the Black Sea zone, was probably borne there by pack-animal, after changing hands many times. There is evidence that continuous journeys were made to the wooded steppe from the Middle East. The bones of camels have been found at the Slav settlements of Bolshoe Borshevo and Titchikha, while a lifelike camel was carved on a block of the Maiatskoe fortress not far away. The camel is being led on a rein by a man. A similar carving, on bone, has been found at a burial-ground not far from the river Oskol. Here, the driver is wearing a double-breasted kaftan and his upper body is protected by what appears to be chain-mail. Both camels have two humps and long legs, indications that they are of the Bactrian type, native to Central Asia. The bones of camels have also been found lower down the Don, near the stone fortress on the right bank, facing Sarkel.[14] These bones, like the carvings, are testimony to caravans bearing goods such as dirhams from Caucasia, Caspian centres such as Darband, or markets still further east. The finds of the bones in Slav settlements are particularly suggestive: presumably the camels had belonged to Moslem, Caucasian or Khazar traders rather than to the

13 S. A. Pletneva, 'Istoriia odnogo khazarskogo poseleniia', *RA* 1993, no. 2, 63, 65–6. On Sarkel, built by Byzantine craftsmen, see *DAI*, ch. 42.22–55, pp. 182–5; M. I. Artamonov, *Istoriia khazar* (Leningrad, 1962), pp. 298–302; F. E. Wozniak, 'Byzantine policy on the Black Sea or Russian steppe in the late 830s', *Byzantine Studies/Études byzantines* 2 (1975), 56–62; M. McGovern, 'Sarkel – a reflection of Byzantine power or weakness?', *Byzantinoslavica* 50 (1989), 178–80.
14 V. V. Kropotkin, 'O topografii kladov kuficheskikh monet IXv., v vostochnoi Evrope', in *Drevniaia Rus' i Slaviane* (Moscow, 1978), p. 116; S. A. Pletneva, 'Risunki na stenakh maiatskogo gorodishcha', in S. A. Pletneva, ed., *Maiatskoe gorodishche* (Moscow, 1984), pp. 79–80.

nomads, and they imply exchanges directly between the orientals and the Slavs.

The Slav inhabitants of the wooded steppe and the semi-nomadic lords of the stone fortresses seem, then, to have achieved a symbiosis by the ninth century. These were the conditions which Rus traders encountered as they began journeying down to the wooded steppe. There were opportunities for individuals to enrich themselves, but the natural hazards were considerable, while the arrangements between the Slavs and their steppe-based overlords probably restricted the openings and profitable deals available to the Rus. The steppes were inhospitable to outsiders and one may recall the allegation of Theophilos' envoys in 839 that 'barbarous and most savage peoples' lived between their Rhos travelling companions and the Rhos' homeland (see above, p. 29). It is quite possible that the Rhos were telling less than the whole truth in offering this explanation for their avoidance of Khazar-dominated territory. Even so, their claim confirms that the Rus, travelling as individuals or in smallish groups, were vulnerable to interception in the southern lands.

Conditions in the second half of the ninth century became even less promising for individual newcomers from the north. There was upheaval in the steppes on a scale greater than the endemic rounds of pillaging and feuding. The Hungarians made their first, violent, entry upon the European stage in 862, when they ranged as far as the East Frankish lands. According to a Frankish chronicle, these 'enemies called Hungarians' were 'hitherto unknown'.[15] The Hungarians had been at large as a distinct grouping for over a generation before that date, having coalesced out of diverse elements including, possibly, members of the Karaiakupovskii culture in the southern Urals (see above, p. 62). Their language is a branch of the Finno-Ugric family of languages, in itself a clue to origins in the furthest north. The circumstances in which they arrived in the Khazar dominions are unclear. A Byzantine source, the *De administrando imperio* (= *DAI*), contains stories of the early Hungarians' relations with the Khazars which were probably relayed to the Byzantines around the time of the *DAI*'s compilation, the mid-tenth century. While they cannot be believed word for word, they suggest that after a period of close association with the Khazars, the Hungarians moved westwards and were joined by the 'Kabaroi', a group or people which had formerly belonged to the Khazar confederacy.[16]

These goings-on occurred some time before or during the mid-ninth century: from then onwards the Hungarians' raids begin to figure in literary sources. Separate raids on the East Frankish marches by

15 *Annales Bertiniani*, ed. F. Grat, J. Vieilliard and S. Clémencet (Paris, 1964), p. 93; tr. J. L. Nelson, *The Annals of St-Bertin* (Manchester, 1991), p. 102.
16 *DAI*, chs 38, 39, pp. 172–5.

the Hungarians and by the Kabars ('Cowari') are recorded for the year 881.[17] The Hungarians' stamping-ground lay west of the central territories of the Khazars, in a region described by the *DAI* as 'Atelkouzou', a Turkic word meaning 'between the rivers'. The rivers could be the Siret and the Dnieper, or the Dniester and the Dnieper: the name is too general to give clear bearings. What is clear is that the Hungarians had the run of a large part of the steppes north of the Black Sea. They were probably not permanently at odds with the Khazars, and their raids on their western neighbours and in the southern Crimea – where 'Hungarians, howling like wolves', set upon a Byzantine envoy in 860[18] – could be indirect testimony to Khazar power, in that they sought their victims and fortune elsewhere. The Hungarians are, however, prime suspects for the devastation of the settlement which for a short time occupied the promontory at Tsimlianskoe before the forementioned white stone fortress was raised there. The earlier settlement lacked walls, but its natural defences were formidable. The promontory rose 70 metres above the Don's water-meadows, and could be reached only via a narrow isthmus. Some time in the mid-ninth century, the inhabitants of the settlement – apparently identifiable from their skulls' dimensions as Bulgars – were massacred and their iurts set on fire. Some of the women were killed trying to protect the children, but the younger ones seem to have been carried off, perhaps to be sold as slaves.[19] To strike near a carefully guarded control point on the Don was beyond the capacity of ordinary nomads. The Hungarians' relatively sophisticated battle order was one of the reasons why a Byzantine emperor, Leo VI, devoted a longish passage of his *Tactica* to their ways of fighting, at the end of the ninth century.[20]

The Hungarians were not, however, the only movers and shakers in the Khazar domains. During the decade in which Leo VI was writing, the 890s, they gave ground in the Black Sea steppes before a still more ferocious people. The Pechenegs had been living in the steppes east of Khazaria but at some point in the later ninth century they swept or were driven across the central Khazar lands and eventually took over the Hungarians' grazing grounds of 'Atelkouzou'. The Pechenegs' westerly progress could have taken a few years or the best part of a generation. It is equally unclear whether and – if so – how their migration relates to a large-scale anti-Khazar operation which certainly

17 *Annales Iuvavenses antiqui*, MGH SS, XXX.2, p. 742.
18 *Vita of Constantine-Cyril*, 8, ed. B. S. Angelov and K. Kodov, in *Kliment Okhridskii. S'brani s'chineniia* (Sofia, 1973), III, p. 96; tr. M. Kantor and R. S. White, *Vita of Constantine and Vita of Methodius* (Michigan Slavic Materials 13; Ann Arbor, 1976), p. 23.
19 Pletneva, 'Istoriia odnogo khazarskogo poseleniia', 58, 62–5.
20 Leo VI, *Tactica*, PG 107, XVIII.40–76, cols 956–64.

involved them. A coalition of 'all the nations' was marshalled against the Khazar king, Benjamin. The names of these peoples are listed in a report on Khazar history composed by a subject of the Khazaria in the mid-tenth century. The Hebrew text is incomplete at the point where it lists the names, and the form of the names is apparently somewhat corrupt. But the presence of the Pechenegs, Oghuz and 'Macedonians' (i.e. Byzantines) on the enemies-list is clear enough. The text claims that an ally of Benjamin, the ruler of the Alans, 'went against their land and [destroyed it], so that there was no recovery'.[21] The rhetoric is high-flown, but there can be no doubt that major operations took place somewhere north-east of the Black Sea. The Khazar document states that up until the reign of Benjamin (?c. 880–?c. 900) 'the fear of the [officers of Khazaria was over the nations] round about us, and they did not come against the kingdom of Khazaria [for war]'.[22] This portrayal of a contrast may be simplifying a protracted series of developments in the later ninth century, but it fits the picture intimated by other scraps of evidence: of movements of peoples and challenges to Khazar authority on an unprecedented scale.

The Khazars' hegemony over the steppes between the Sea of Azov and the Lower Volga was shaken, but not wholly overturned. They managed at least to hold their own against two successive groupings of nomads, the Hungarians and the Pechenegs. The Hungarians, the weaker of the two, still seemed to a contemporary German chronicler 'most ferocious, and crueller than any beast'.[23] The Khazars proved able to overawe peoples living to the north of the steppes well into the tenth century. The Khazar king repeatedly demanded that the Volga Bulgar ruler should send one of his daughters to be his bride, and had one removed by force; upon her death, he demanded another. It was avowedly in order to resist such pressure that the Bulgar khagan turned to the Abbasid caliph for aid in 921 (see above, p. 64). However, the Khazars' ability to keep order in the Don and Donets steppes was probably impaired and there are signs that the white stone fortresses' defences needed to be reinforced. In the late ninth century an earthen rampart together with a small ditch was constructed to protect the settlement just beyond the stone walls at Dmitrievskoe, and it seems that similar earthworks were raised at other forts on the Don and in the open steppes around that time. The white stone walls of the Maiatskoe fortress were apparently raised about this time. Neither insecurity nor scarcity debarred long-distance trade in luxuries: in fact, rarity value could act as a stimulus to merchant ventures (see above, pp. 17–18).

---

21 N. Golb and O. Pritsak, *Khazarian Hebrew Documents of the Tenth Century* (Ithaca, London, 1982), p. 115.

22 Ibid., p. 113.

23 Regino of Prüm, *Chronicon*, ed. F. Kurze (*MGH* in usum schol.; Hanover, 1890), p. 131.

But there are grounds for supposing that the numbers of Scandinavians frequenting the eastern lands were rising, and silver was still the magnet which drew them on. The coincidence of rising demand for silver on the part of the Rus with an erratic supply probably accounts for the decline in the finds of late ninth-century Abbasid coins in Russian hoards (see above, p. 61). If there was, in some sense, a 'silver crisis', the obvious remedy was to find new routes to the longstanding sources of silver or to seek out new sources of silver or some other highly prized commodity.

Prospecting for silver was not in itself problematic, seeing that there had never been a single, fixed, link between the north and the Moslem world (see above, pp. 26–7). Individual traders and trappers are likely to have been ever on the look-out for fresh openings and better deals, and a variety of peoples was involved in the process of exchanging furs and slaves for silver. The trails along the Don and Donets were simply the most trodden ones. One alternative was offered by the Volga and, as we have seen, the Rus were making use of it to a significant extent by the early tenth century. They sailed to the Bulgars' market on the Middle Volga, where they bartered their goods for silver (see above, p. 44). The importance of this new eastern connection can hardly be over-stressed, in economic terms. It became a principal channel for the influx of silver during the tenth century and while one cannot give figures for the total number of dirhams or weight of silver, they were markedly higher than those for the ninth century. The development of the Rus settlements on the Upper Volga registers the increase in volume of trade. The majority of ornaments found in them date from the tenth century. The opportunities for enriching oneself were good, and ordinary persons seem to have made the journey from Central Sweden and the Åland islands. The numerous poor, inventory-less graves at Timerëvo may well belong to migrants who failed to strike it rich (see above, pp. 67–8).

Yet for all the convenience and economic vitality of this link with a new source of Moslem silver, the Rus were subject to the regulations and taxes imposed by the Volga Bulgars. Clearly these were not such as to render trading unprofitable and the restrictions were not entirely of the Bulgars' making. If there is no firm evidence of Rus boats sailing all the way down the Volga to the Caspian in the tenth century, this may be due to a Khazar ban rather than to any Bulgar embargo on Rus vessels. But in either case, it was somewhat anomalous that the Rus now possessed settlements on the Upper Volga and their own means of transport, yet were apparently unable to take full advantage of the Volga waterway. To force their way through to wealthier lands was not a viable option. We have already noted how a large fleet of Rus went on the rampage round the Caspian not long after 912, but came to grief and eventual elimination at the hands of the Khazars, Burtas and Bulgars (see above, p. 69). The Rus seem to have learnt their lesson in that no further forays into the Caspian are recorded for a generation after this debacle. However, the raid was apparently their third effort within a few years. A small band of sixteen ships had pillaged around the southern Caspian in the autumn of 910. Another, larger, raiding party came to grief a year or so later. Many of the Rus ships were burnt on the shore; others escaped only to be waylaid at sea. These episodes, culminating in the major expedition after 912, amount to rather more than a series of copy-cat raids. The expedition which, according to Masudi, comprised 500 ships, required considerable organization, resources and prior diplomatic negotiations with the Khazars (see above, p. 69). It may be that these attacks represent the reaction of the Rus to a fairly novel situation in which, debarred from approaching the sources of the dirhams as traders, they tried their hands at forcible extraction of the treasure. The way down the Volga, however, was no more open to them as raiders than as traders.

Another outlet for Rus energies and appetite for treasure lay in the opposite direction, Central Europe. A working document detailing customs dues at Raffelstatt provides for visits of Rus and other traders to spots where they may hold temporary markets along a section of the Middle Danube, or in the valley of the river Rodl or the eastern portion of the modern Mühlviertel. Wax is the prime commodity they are expected to bring 'for the purpose of trading', either by the mule-load or carried by men on their backs.[24] Slaves and horses are other commodities which they bring regularly, the slave-girls being valued at around three times the worth of the males.

The charter's text is datable to (most probably) between 903 and 905, but it purports to reaffirm the procedures obtaining in the reigns of Louis the German (840–76) and Carloman (876–80) and their successors. Various other shreds of evidence – including archaeological evidence – suggest that the Rus were frequenting the Middle Danube by then. The place-name 'Ruzaramarcha' appears in a charter of 863 and it has been argued that 'Ruzara-' means Rus.[25] Ruzaramarcha, located somewhere to the south-east of the area covered by the Raffelstatt regulations, on the southern side of the Danube, lay near a trade-route which was undoubtedly used by Rus trading caravans in the twelfth century (see below, p. 328). It could already have acted as a stopping-place in the mid-ninth. The Rus would have reached the Danube and Ruzaramarcha via southern Poland and the river March (Morava) or via the passes across the Carpathians or, in the case of the Raffelstatt regulations, from the north via Prague and the river

---

24 'mercandi causa', *MGH* Leges, II.2, *Capitularia regum Francorum* (Hanover, 1897), p. 251.

25 *MGH* Diplomata, I, *Ludowici Germanici, Karlomanni, Ludowici iunioris Diplomata* (Berlin, 1934), p. 157; A. V. Nazarenko, 'Rus' i Germaniia v IX–Xvv.', *DGVEMI* 1991 (1994), 30–1.

Vltava. The former two routes, which were probably also used by traders such as the Radhanite Jews (see above, pp. 41–2), are likely to have become hazardous from the late ninth century, with the arrival of the Hungarians in Central Europe: the northerly route via the Vltava implied by the Raffelstatt customs tariff probably then became more important. It has been pointed out that 'Dunai', the name for the Danube found in the *Primary Chronicle* and other early Rus writings, is the one used by the Czechs, Poles and other West Slavs living near the Danube above the Iron Gates. A different form was current among the South Slavs living near the Lower Danube.[26] 'Dunai' could be an indication that the Rus first came upon the Danube along its middle course, and this would tally with the hints which are offered by the Raffelstatt regulations and, perhaps, Ruzaramarcha.

What is undeniable is that the Rus did business on the Middle Danube. Individuals or bands of Rus and Slav entrepreneurs were journeying there in the mid-ninth century, if not earlier. The distribution pattern of various types of glass beads suggests a nexus embracing Staraia Ladoga and other far northern markets, the regions abutting on the Middle and Upper Danube, the valleys of the Donets and the Don, Caucasia and Central Asia.[27] Trade was partly in the hands of Bohemians and of Slavs living under Rus hegemony: the Raffelstatt regulations provide for 'the Slavs who come from the Rus [*Rugi*] or the Bohemians',[28] without distinguishing between the kinds of goods these sundry traders brought. The wording of the regulations together with the description of the modes of conveying the goods – by foot, mule pack or on the hoof – indicates that those Rus who made the journey to the Middle Danube travelled in much the same style as the Slav traders. The Rus did not enjoy an overweening advantage, in that they were not travelling by boat. The inhabitants of Bavaria, whether German or Slav, were expressly exempted from paying sales or purchase taxes when they did business in these markets, but there is no such provision for the Rus. So on the Middle Danube as on the Middle Volga the Rus had to trade and pay tolls on terms set by the regional powers. The Rus making for the Middle Danube did not have the use of a continuous waterway, and while the Raffelstatt regulations illustrate

26 G. Schramm, '"Gentem suam Rhos vocari dicebant"', in U. Haustein, G. W. Strobel and G. Wagner, eds, *Ostmitteleuropa. Berichte und Forschungen* (Stuttgart, 1981), pp. 7–8.

27 Z. A. L'vova, 'Stekliannye busy Staroi Ladogi: I, sposoby izgotovlenii, areal i vremia rasprostraneniia', *Arkheologicheskii sbornik* (Gosudarstvennyi Ermitazh) 10 (1968), 92.

28 *MGH* Leges, II.2, p. 251; C. Warnke, 'Der Handel mit Wachs zwischen Ost- und Westeuropa im frühen und hohen Mittelalter. Voraussetzungen und Gewinnmöglichkeiten', in *UHV, Abhandlungen der Akademie der Wissenschaften in Göttingen, philolog.-hist. Klasse*, 3 Folge, no. 156 (Göttingen, 1987), p. 558; Goehrke, *Frühzeit des Ostslaventums*, p. 127 and n. 193.

the Rus' range in seeking out markets, they also indicate the handicaps under which they laboured. Balls of wax, their principal article of trade, were bulky and fairly heavy objects, and the cost of transporting them far overland cannot have been negligible, even if the bearers were slaves. Thus the prospects for making really profitable deals were not bright. Unlike the Rus trader whom ibn Fadlan watched praying for a lucrative transaction in the Bulgar market (see above, p. 44), the trader on the Danube could not expect loads of dirhams or even, necessarily, silver coins at all, in exchange for his goods. And the outlook for a successful raid by the Rus on the Danubian markets was even bleaker than it was on the Volga – although, as we shall see, the Danube continued to exert a certain magnetism on the Rus (below, p. 145).

There was a third outlet for the energies and produce of the Rus, besides the Volga and the Danube – in the south. The Rus were journeying down as far as the Black Sea by the 880s and probably a generation or so earlier in journeys described by ibn Khurradadhbih (see above, p. 42). A stepping-up of their trading ventures in that direction might seem an obvious counterpart to their activities on the Danube and a response to the vagaries of the silver supplies from the Moslem lands. However, there were formidable natural barriers to continuous navigation along the Dnieper (see below, p. 92), and the human obstacles or disincentives were also substantial. There was no outstandingly lucrative market on the Crimea or elsewhere on the north coast of the Black Sea. Cherson, the probable objective of ibn Khurradadhbih's Rus, was an emporium where traders from various lands, including Khazaria and, probably, the Moslem world, converged, but its prosperity could hardly compare with that of towns in the Caspian region. While it began to strike coins in the name of the Byzantine emperor from the mid-ninth century onwards, these were made of copper and there is no evidence that it was particularly rich in silver. Nor did the Byzantine lands as a whole abound in silver in the quantities which oriental merchants seem regularly to have had at their disposal. There was, moreover, a tax of 10 per cent to be paid on their goods (see above, p. 42). If the profits to be had on the Black Sea coast were less than those in the markets of Khazaria or the Moslem world, the routes southwards were risky, and probably growing riskier. The Dnieper basin lay amongst the Hungarians' grazing grounds and was frequented by them during the second half of the ninth century. The Hungarians were then engaged in selling slaves to Byzantine merchants on the Black Sea coast.[29] Individual bands of Rus traders would have presented easy pickings to them. In short, all that we have reviewed in this chapter – the Slavs' lack of ample silver stocks, the *modus*

---

29 ibn Rusta, *Kitab al-A'lak al-nafisa* [*Book of Precious Jewels*], ed. T. Lewicki, *Źródła arabskie do dziejów słowiańszczyzny*, II.2 (Wroclaw, Warsaw, Cracow, Gdansk, 1977), pp. 34–5; tr. G. Wiet, *Les atours précieux* (Cairo, 1955), p. 161.

vivendi of the Khazars and their confederates with the Slavs and the mounting insecurity of the Black Sea steppes in the second half of the ninth century – raises the question of why the Rus should ever have intensified their journeys down to the Black Sea, rather than the question of why they were so slow to do so.

2. THE RUS FOOTHOLD ON THE MIDDLE DNIEPER
(c. 900–30)

From a look at conditions in the steppe and the wooded steppe in the later ninth century, we have been led to alter the question from why the Rus were slow to establish themselves on the Dnieper to what could have induced them to go, let alone stay, there. Clues lie in the indications of disarray in the Khazar-imposed order in the south and in the new openings as well as hazards which this presented to the brave, vigorous and ruthless. That such qualities were attributed to Northmen by diverse contemporaries is virtually a cliché, but that does not mean they should be disregarded. Arabic writers comment on the talent of the Rus for war in descriptions of their trading activities, even though the Rus do not seem to have relied heavily on organized coercion for carrying on these activities. As we have seen, some Rus tried to break through to the Caspian at the beginning of the tenth century and to seize the riches which were seemingly no longer to be had from trading there (see above, p. 88). Rus were already, by the later ninth century, journeying down to the Black Sea and they might be expected to have been on the look-out for lucrative markets or new sources of silver which could be gained by bartering or force, whichever proved the more expedient. Cherson's trading links were wide-ranging, but this was ultimately only a provincial town, defended by massive fortifications. So if the Rus were to look further afield for trading partners or easy pickings, they would need to sail across the Black Sea. And herein lay the fundamental problem. Vessels best-suited for navigating the Dnieper were neither capacious, nor particularly seaworthy.

This was well known to the Byzantine authorities, judging by the *Tactica* compiled by Leo VI in the 890s. The 'northern Scyths' are said to use 'smaller, lighter-weight and faster' craft than the Arabs, 'because, descending upon the Black Sea along rivers, they cannot use larger ships'.[30] This manual focuses on strategic concerns, but what it says of raiding ships would apply to other sorts of vessel, such as those laden with bulky goods. The clear implication is that the Rus boats had to be light enough to cope with shoals and shallows or to be hauled overland. Leo VI is not wholly dismissive of the Rus, but he does not

---

30 Leo VI, *Tactica*, XIX.69, col. 1012 (= *Naumachica*, ed. A. Dain (Paris, 1943), p. 32).

seem to regard them as an overriding threat. This suggests that there had been Rus forays to the Black Sea since the great expedition of 860, but that an expedition on such a scale did not seem likely to be repeated; nor were the forays expected to get out of hand. In other words, the prospects of large amounts of loot accruing from constant piracy were, from the Rus point of view, faint. The Black Sea tends to be even stormier and more given to sudden changes of wind direction than the Caspian. There was, moreover, a massive natural barrier to journeys down the major river flowing into the Black Sea, and this may well have contributed to the slight air of complacency in Leo's manual.

The barrier took the form of a series of granite ridges, nine of them stretching right across the Dnieper and many others projecting part of the way. The river's waters, in full flow, were forced up and over these natural dams. Many sections of the ridges were submerged beneath the flow, but other rocks protruded above the waters, which raced between them. The rapids interrupted a lengthy section – almost 70 kilometres – of the river's course and, in addition to the rapids proper, numerous stray rocks and islets churned up the surface water. The effect was to make navigation at best perilous, at worst, suicidal. And even this held true only while the spring thaw released enough melted snow and ice to raise the water-level above many ridges and outcrops. When the current was weaker, the water-level fell and boatmen had constantly to nose their craft along the bank or haul them overland for kilometres at a time. Such an operation offset most of the normal advantages of water transport, if goods were being carried. It is not surprising that there is little firm evidence for the use of the Dnieper as a waterway during classical antiquity. Fragments of amphorae and Roman and Byzantine coins dating between the first and seventh centuries AD have been found in settlements in the vicinity of the future city of Kiev, but few finds have been made at the Dnieper rapids. The incidence of such finds at the rapids is a kind of register of the use of the Dnieper as a waterway, seeing that this was the place where loss, breakage or theft was likeliest to occur. The fact that the Dnieper long retained separate names for its upper, middle and lower reaches suggests that through-traffic along it was unusual.[31] Mass movements of peoples tended to be latitudinal, whether they were Slavs edging eastwards or Bulgars, Hungarians and Kabars heading westwards (see above, pp. 75, 84). Profitable trading was most obviously to be had from trading the north's furs for luxury goods of the south and yet, as we have seen, the main axis in the eighth and ninth centuries was south-eastwards

31 G. Schramm, 'Fernhandel und frühe Reichsbildungen am Ostrand Europas. Zur historischen Einordnung der Kiever Rus'', in K. Colberg et al., eds, *Mittelalter und Früher Neuzeit. Gedenkschrift für Joachim Leuschner* (Göttingen, 1983), pp. 18, 22, n. 9 on p. 37.

towards the Don and Volga steppes (see above, pp. 25–6). Khazar power and the Middle Eastern sourcing of the silver were the main reasons for this, but they were not the only ones. Light and valuable goods could be borne vast distances across the steppes by pack-animals and camels (see above, p. 83). The Radhanite traders toed and froed incessantly between Western Europe and the Moslem lands during the ninth century. One of their routes ran across 'the land of the Slavs' to the Khazar capital and the Caspian, and then eastwards for China. There may well have been other east–west trading axes which failed to come to a contemporary writer's notice or to seem worth recording. The Hungarians conducted some such trading overland with their kinsmen living far to the east in the tenth century.[32]

For most traders and travellers, then, the Dnieper was an obstacle rather than a thoroughfare and the ford which the Chersonites used to cross the river was also patronized by the steppe nomads. Constantine VII, the source of this information, indicates that the Pechenegs regarded the river as a kind of boundary. Some would cross the Dnieper at the end of spring (after the floods) and passed the summer on the other side.[33] This accords with the picture which the archaeological evidence presents, of a contrast between the Slav settlements on either side of the Dnieper (see above, p. 75). For the Slavs, too, the Dnieper marked some sort of boundary. Moreover, the valley itself does not seem to have held much attraction for them in the eighth and ninth centuries. Migrant Slavs pressed on to the valleys of the Desna and the Seim, or installed themselves well away from the Dnieper, on the upper reaches of its tributaries (see above, p. 76). It is unclear how far this represents a deliberate policy on the part of the Slav settlers or their Khazar overlords. It may well be that the flood meadows of the Dnieper valley were prized as pasture land by the nomads and semi-nomads, rendering a Slav presence unwelcome. There were in any case few promontories overlooking the river to provide sanctuaries for the Slavs.

One of the better-populated areas in the vicinity of the Middle Dnieper was that of Kiev. The ground was fertile and the pine-wooded heights rising 80 to 90 metres above the river made for secure surroundings. Their ravines and streams were natural defences while the conifers offered wind-breaks from the steppe's winter blast and the woods were, according to the chronicle, stocked with game in abundance. There was no such cluster of hills anywhere else along the Middle Dnieper. The heights formed part of a plateau some 15 kilometres long and 3 or 4 kilometres wide. This was a convenient point for crossing the river, and the contributors to the chronicle showed scrupulousness in noting the tradition that Kiev's eponymous

32 *DAI*, ch. 38.63–4, pp. 172–5.
33 Ibid., ch. 8.34–5, pp. 56–7; ch. 9.65–7, pp. 60–1.

founder, Kii, was a ferryman. For the founding father to have been a mere ferryman appeared demeaning, and the editors tried to rebut the slur with a rival tradition: that Kii went to Tsargrad (Constantinople) and paid a visit to 'the *tsar*' and, so it is said, received great honour'; 'if', they argued, 'Kii had been a ferryman, he would not have journeyed to Tsargrad'.[34] The polemic contains a grain of substance in that it highlights the settlement's original significance as a crossing-point. Only later did the route *down* the Dnieper to Byzantium become important, to the point where it outshone but did not wholly eclipse Kii's profession. This detail may well be the remnant of an earlier foundation story.

The questions of what Kii might have founded, and when, do not admit of a firm answer. The heights were occupied in Neolithic times and the forementioned finds of Roman coins and amphorae show that the locale was an emporium or transit point of some vitality during the first centuries AD. But there is no firm evidence that it was of importance as either a tribal or a religious centre. Stray finds of hand-modelled pottery and the excavation of a few semi-sunken dwellings with walls of beaten clay and hearths attest some sort of settlement on the extensive hill which enjoys the best natural defences, the Starokievskaia. This inspired proud citizens of Kiev to celebrate the '1,500th' birthday of their city in 1982, but it is far from clear that the dwellings date from before the seventh century, and they could be datable to the eighth. Only in the latter century did the Slavs – to whom the pottery and the semi-sunken houses probably belonged – migrate eastwards across the Dnieper *en masse*, and from then on crossing-points such as Kiev were probably in frequent use. But the way of life of these early Kievans was probably little different from that of Slavs living on other promontory forts or hill-terraces west of the Dnieper, and it does not seem to have hinged on the arrival of silver dirhams. The Middle Dnieper valley is, in fact, devoid of finds of ninth-century hoards of silver and even individual finds of dirhams of the eighth and ninth centuries are very rare. Such trading bands or caravans as passed this way did not linger.

Excavations on the Starokievskaia hill have uncovered traces of two constructions which are thought to denote the existence of some political or social organization. A defensive ditch (presumably together with a rampart) encircled approximately 2 hectares of the north-west part of the hill; in the middle of the enclosure a small platform of roughly rectangular shape was built out of loosely laid, unworked, stones. This platform has generally been identified as a place of sacrifice and dates as early as the seventh or eighth century have been proposed for ditch and 'pagan sanctuary' alike. But no compelling evidence has been adduced that the population living on or near the hill was large

34 *PVL*, I, p. 13.

enough to warrant an extensive enclosure at that time; there is no reason why the ditch and the platform – which may rather have been the base of a towerlike structure – could not have been constructed in the ninth century, even its second half.[35] It is only from the later eighth century that there is evidence of Slav settlement on at least one other hill, the Zamkovaia. The ditch, if not the platform, would have been within the technical competence of the Slavs, but this earthwork could well have been put up at the behest of the overlord of the inhabitants of the Kievan heights in the ninth century, the Khazar khaganate.

The Khazars' close involvement with Kiev is illustrated by an alternative name for the settlement which seemed to Constantine VII worth citing, 'Sambatas'.[36] This is most probably its Khazar name, being analogous to their names for other fortresses, for example, 'S-m-k-r-ts' (see above, p. 37). A widely accepted derivation of Sambatas is from the Turkic roots *sam* and *–bat*, meaning respectively 'high' or 'top', and 'strong'. At the time when Constantine was writing, the mid-tenth century, there were 'many . . . Khazars' living in Kiev, according to the *Primary Chronicle*.[37] The probable derivation of Sambatas does not in itself prove that Khazars were residing in a fortified enclosure there in the ninth century. But the chronicle, while insisting that the tables are now turned on the Khazars, makes it clear that they once enjoyed ascendancy on the Dnieper (see above, p. 77). The Khazars' links with Kiev have received further attention since publication of a letter in Hebrew among whose eleven signatories there feature non-Semitic, apparently Turkic names. They refer to themselves as the 'community of Kiev'. The existence of the letter in the Cairo Geniza is not particularly surprising, seeing that the ruling elite of the Khazars practised Judaism. They did not attempt to impose it on their subjects, whose heterogeneity and plurality of beliefs was provided for by the spread of judges in the capital, Itil: two apiece for the Jews, Moslems and Christians and one for 'pagans' such as the Rus and the Slavs; there were mosques, minarets and Moslem schools as well as synagogues in the main towns. Various forms of spirit-worship and shamanism prevailed among the Khazars' confederates and agents in the Don steppes. But there is no reason why communities of Judaists should not have existed in the population centres or outposts such as Kiev. The editors of the Hebrew letter

35 J. Callmer, 'The archaeology of Kiev ca A.D. 500–1000. A survey', in R. Zeitler, ed., *Les pays du nord et Byzance (Scandinavie et Byzance), Actes du colloque nordique et international de byzantinologie tenu à Upsal 20–22 avril 1979* (Acta Universitatis Upsaliensis. Figura, nova series 19; Uppsala, 1981), p. 33; E. Mühle, 'Die Anfänge Kievs (bis ca. 980) in archäologischer Sicht. Ein Forschungsbericht', *JGO* 35 (1987), 85–6, 101.

36 *DAI*, ch. 9.8–9, pp. 56–7.

37 *PVL*, I, p. 39.

interpret six characters, apparently contemporaneous with the main text, as Turkic runes meaning 'I have read'; from this they infer that the letter was penned while Khazar officials were still stationed in Kiev, scrutinizing correspondence.[38] They further postulate that the document was drafted 'shortly before the conquest' of Kiev by the Rus, 'that is, it has to be dated c. AD 930'.[39] Their arguments show a welcome scepticism as to the chronology offered by the chronicle, but they do not offer conclusive grounds for dating the letter so late. At any rate, the document is of value in attesting some sort of Jewish Khazar community in Kiev and, assuming that the runes have been read correctly, they offer independent corroboration of the chronicle's allusions to Khazar rule in Kiev. As we shall see, there are further indications that the inhabitants of the Middle Dnieper region were familiar with the symbols of Khazar presence (below, p. 121).

It is, then, possible that the earthwork on the Starokievskaia hill was raised to provide a secure compound for semi-nomadic collectors of tribute on behalf of the Khazars and the storage of their takings. It calls to mind the earthworks of the steppes and it seems to have been designed to be functional, the ditch in places being 4.7 metres deep. One might perhaps connect it with the evidence of supplementary earthworks raised in the late ninth century at sites along the Don and take it as a mark of mounting insecurity (see above, p. 86). The Khazars' interest in gathering tribute could well have intensified in the face of new challenges in the open steppes (see above, p. 63). With the revenues gained from the tribute – whether in the form of silver or marketable furs – they could the better hire warriors or incite groups of the nomads against their enemies. The Middle Dnieper was well situated as a base from which to ensure that the likes of the Radimichi paid up their 'shilling's' worth of tribute (see above, p. 77). It may be that the 'Hungarian hill' on the south side of Kiev did not (as the chronicle maintains) represent the spot where the Hungarians 'camped in their tents' in the course of their migration,[40] but the place where Hungarians in the khagan's employ were encamped for a while. A Hungarian presence in the vicinity of Kiev might explain the 'Hungarian' traits which some archaeologists discern in various types

---

38 Golb and Pritsak, *Khazarian Hebrew Documents*, p. 42. For Arabic accounts of the Khazars, see D. M. Dunlop, *The History of the Jewish Khazars* (Princeton, 1954), pp. 93, 95–6, 98–9, 105, 113–14, 206–7; P. Golden, 'The peoples of the south Russian steppes', in D. Sinor, ed., *The Cambridge History of Early Inner Asia* (Cambridge, 1990), pp. 266–7. Arguments for dating the adoption of Judaism by the Khazar leadership to the early 860s are presented by C. Zuckerman, 'On the date of the Khazars' conversion to Judaism and the chronology of the kings of the Rus Oleg and Igor', *Revue des études byzantines* 53 (1995), 241–50.
39 Golb and Pritsak, *Khazarian Hebrew Documents*, p. 71.
40 *PVL*, I, p. 21.

of bridle ornaments, harness and weapons – not just typical nomads' weapons such as arrows but also the ornamentation of sword-hilts and blades.[41] These objects are found mostly in tenth-century burials and may by then have been in use by non-Hungarians, but their occurrence at Kiev and elsewhere on the Middle Dnieper awaits a conclusive alternative explanation.

The ambivalence of the evidence is partly a function of its scarcity, but it registers a fast-changing state of affairs. Amidst the speculation, three major developments stand out. All three are datable to within two decades of AD 900. They are, firstly, the irruption of the Pechenegs into the steppes north of the Black Sea; secondly, the foundation or marked development of settlements on the Middle and Upper Dnieper; and thirdly, the making of treaties between the Rus and the Byzantine emperor.

The Pechenegs overran the grazing grounds of the Hungarians during the 890s, having been egged on by the ruler of Bulgaria, Symeon (see above, p. 97). The region between the Don and the Donets steppes in the east and the Dniester (and, subsequently, the Danube) in the west lay at their disposal. They were markedly poorer than the Hungarians in terms of material culture – ornaments and riding-gear – but they were, perhaps for that reason, more ferocious. When a Byzantine emissary tried to stir up the Hungarians against the Pechenegs, they protested: 'We cannot fight them, for their country is vast and their people numerous and they are the devil's brats!'[42]

The Pechenegs' ferocity was also daunting for the inhabitants of fortified settlements. One conspicuous feat is their dissolution of the Saltovo-Maiatskii culture. Sarkel, on the left bank of the Don, continued in business as a Khazar fort but the same cannot be said of the stone fortresses along the Upper Don and Donets, or the settlements interspersed between them. The fortresses were for the most part abandoned, rather than taken by storm. Sometimes the decision to flee was taken without much warning, judging by the scene which archaeologists have reconstructed in a dwelling excavated at the main settlement at Dmitrievskoe. Seemingly a pot, newly turned and about to be fired, was left on the wheel, while the clay was left lying uncleared around the potters' wheels in other houses, too.[43] The settlements at Maiatskoe are likewise thought to have been abandoned, albeit rather less hastily. The climate of fear can be traced in many of the settlements of the 'Romny' culture in the wooded steppe. They had the protection of natural defences, with ditches and ramparts on the landward side of promontories, but even large, well-fortified

---

41 C. Bálint, *Die Archäologie der Steppe: Steppenvölker zwischen Volga und Donau vom 6. bis zum 10. Jahrhundert* (Vienna, Cologne, 1989), pp. 114–15.
42 *DAI*, ch. 8.30–2, pp. 56–7.
43 Pletneva, *Dmitrievskii arkheologicheskii kompleks*, pp. 42, 44.

settlements such as that at Novotroitskoe were abandoned around the end of the ninth century. The promontory fort at Donetskoe (near modern Kharkov) suffered a conflagration in the tenth century and many other forts and settlements in the Donets basin were destroyed. These bouts of destruction over a wide area were not inflicted at a stroke, in the manner of the Mongols. The Pechenegs lacked the organization or resources to deliver knock-out blows. But the effect of their incessant raiding was to put an end to the socio-political order which had emerged to the east of the Dnieper. The Khazars' semi-nomadic agents were mostly dispersed, while those Slavs who remained in the wooded steppe settlements east of the Dnieper had a lower standard of living, and risk of death. This is shown by the lack of hoards, or of individual finds of Moslem dirhams, for the period after c. 900, and ornaments made of silver or other valuable metals become markedly rarer in their settlements of the tenth century. So, too, do finds of pitchers and amphorae brought from the central lands of the khaganate or the Crimea. Large settlements with workshops containing forges and matrices for stamping belt mounts ceased to exist, and those Slavs who knew the whereabouts of, or possessed, objects of silver had every reason to leave well alone. Reports of silver caches would have drawn in the Pechenegs. The economic nexus which had arisen under the tutelage and extortion of the Khazars and their confederates disintegrated.

So negative a consequence of the arrival of 'the devil's brats' in the Don and Dnieper steppes is not surprising. Far more remarkable is the second of the major changes which can be dated to within two decades of AD 900. This involves Kiev, a few other sites in the Middle Dnieper area, and, on the Upper Dnieper, Gnëzdovo. The population of the Kiev heights seems to have been small, leaving few signs of activities other than straightforward arable farming, fishing and hunting. The earthwork on the Starokievskaia hill points to the degree of socio-political organization one might expect of a Khazar tribute-collecting outpost, but the ditch could date from as late as the closing years of the ninth century and there is very little sign of a commercially vigorous community enclosed by it. A number of developments transformed the situation around the turn of the ninth and tenth centuries. The most drastic innovation at Kiev was in a district which, unlike the other settlements, occupied low ground near to the Dnieper. From this distinguishing mark it gained its name of Podol, meaning 'in the valley'. Excavations indicate that this land only came into intensive use for commercial or residential purposes around the beginning of the tenth century. The earliest structures were probably few in number, standing in compounds fenced by palisades; there are signs of a street-plan whose main axes linked the Starokievskaia citadel with the water's edge. The structures were of wood and the earliest dates for specimens of timbers are 900 or later, although one example as early as 887 has been reported.[44] These dendrochronological datings have yet to receive the general endorsement which those for Staraia Ladoga enjoy, but they are compatible with such individual coins as have been found in the Podol and also with finds in the burial-ground on the Starokievskaia hill. The earliest coins in the latter are a Samanid dirham of between 892 and 907 and a coin of Leo VI (886–912), and there is nothing among the numerous ornaments and weaponry of the grave goods pointing clearly to a date before c. 900.[45] So the burial-ground probably only came into use early in the tenth century.

Caution is never a vice in dealing with the early history of Rus, but it is possible to take the discussion further in that part of Kiev where change c. 900 is most pronounced, the Podol. This riverside district had long remained unsettled, probably on account of its exposure to floods during the Dnieper's spring thaw, and in the early middle ages, as in the twentieth century, the Podol often underwent prolonged flooding. This was dangerous, rather than merely awkward, and the residences of the tenth century rested on foundations reinforced with cross-beams and earth, while drainage channels and streamlets flowed through and between the compounds. The finds in two successive layers of a tenth-century structure offer clues as to what drew men to the riverside: a Byzantine coin, an amphora, walnut shells and the weights of scales.[46] It was the prospect of trade in valuables – such as silver or silks – that drew people to the water's edge. And the Dnieper's waters offered a means of transporting bulky commodities such as wax and slaves. The Volga was beginning to serve the same purpose as far as Bulgar at about the same time (see above, p. 65).

The structures put up in the Podol in the early tenth century were mostly one-room wooden cabins; some were sheds for livestock and storehouses but the larger buildings – occupying up to 60 m² – were dwellings. They were built of pine logs laid horizontally, one upon another, and interlocking at the corners by a technique called in modern Russian *v oblo*. This technique, like the establishment of a trading quarter so near the river, marks a break with past custom. Earlier buildings on the heights had, so far as is known, been semi-underground. Archaeologists, upon discovering these cabins in the 1970s, commented on the similarity between their construction techniques and those of the structures in Novgorod and Staraia

---

44 M. A. Sahaidak, *Davn'o-kyivs'kyi Podil: problemy topohrafii, stratihrafii, khronolohii* (Kiev, 1991), pp. 82–4, 88.

45 Ibid., pp. 9, 81, 91–2; M. K. Karger, *Drevnii Kiev* (Moscow, Leningrad, 1958), I, pp. 216, 223–6; T. V. Ravdina, *Pogrebeniia X–XIvv. s monetami na territorii drevnei Rusi* (Moscow, 1988), pp. 72–4.

46 Mühle, 'Anfänge Kievs', 95.

Ladoga.[47] The obvious explanation for their appearance at Kiev is that they were brought by migrants from the north. That traffic increased between the northern riverways and the Dnieper is suggested by the development of the settlement at the place now called Gnëzdovo but whose early name was probably Smolensk. It lies a few kilometres west of present-day Smolensk but is identifiable as the *Miliniska* named by Constantine VII as a 'town' of the Rus.[48] The development seems to have occurred in the late ninth and beginning of the tenth centuries.

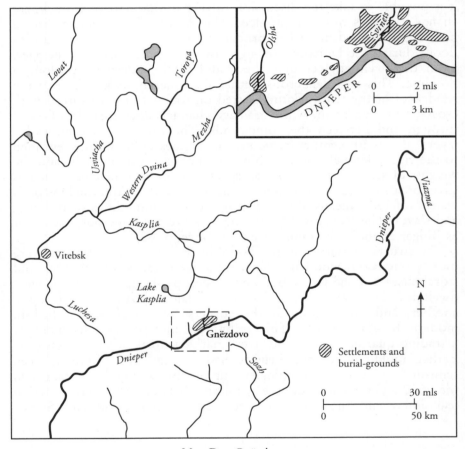

Map D.   Gnëzdovo

47 V. O. Kharlamov, 'Konstruktyvni osoblyvosti derev'ianykh budivel' Podolu X–XIII st.', in P. P. Tolochko, ed., *Arkheolohichni doslidzhennia starodavn'ogo Kyeva* (Kiev, 1976), p. 54.
48 *DAI*, ch. 9.6, pp. 56–7. The shift of the main settlement – and the name – to the present-day site occurred from the late eleventh century onwards: see below p. 335.

Gnëzdovo (i.e. Smolensk) is located not far from the Dnieper's confluence with the Olsha, a small but navigable river from which one could portage boats by various routes to Lake Kasplia and then sail down the Kasplia into the Western Dvina. It was thus a crossing-point from the Dvina to the Dnieper, while the passage from the head-waters of either the Dvina or the Dnieper to the Upper Volga was feasible, although it led through the Okovskii forest (see above, p. 5). The inhabitants of the Upper Dnieper region were mostly Balts, but already by the beginning of the ninth century groups of Slavs had moved up the Dnieper basin, gravitating towards the vicinity of Gnëzdovo. Their numbers were small, and it is only for the second half of the ninth century that there are clear signs of a settlement forming at Gnëzdovo itself. They settled beside the Dnieper, on either side of a tributary, the Svinets.[49] The allure of Gnëzdovo lay in its proximity to several possible routes between the Baltic world and the Khazar-dominated south-east. Near the Upper Dnieper, or between it and the Dvina, have been found a number of hoards datable to the ninth century. At Gnëzdovo individual dirhams and a few ornaments of bronze or silver have been found, for example a silver bow-brooch. These signs of a modest prosperity recall those in the Slav settlements east of the Middle Dnieper (see above p. 73). Significant Scandinavian involvement in the through-trade is suggested both by ibn Khurradadhbih and by archaeology – for example, finds of a ninth-century even-armed brooch on the bank of the Kasplia, and of a half-bracteate characteristic of Hedeby in a hoard also containing Moslem silver at a Balt settlement on a tributary of the Kasplia. Two Frankish swords characteristic of the ninth century have been found, one in a Balt burial-ground near a portage from the Kasplia southwards, the other in a ninth-century barrow at Novoselki, 5 kilometres from Gnëzdovo.[50] A hint that Scandinavians were making the journey to the Western Dvina from northern riverways as well as directly from the Baltic comes from the find of a ninth-century brooch in a woman's grave at a burial-ground near Toropets. Toropets lay on what would develop into a busy network of portages and streams linking the Lovat with the Western Dvina. In the late ninth century the Scandinavians were also beginning to bury their dead, women as well as men, at the burial-ground at Gnëzdovo.

49 E. Mühle, *Die städtischen Handelszentren der nordwestlichen Rus'. Anfänge und frühe Entwicklung altrussischer Städte (bis gegen Ende des 12. Jahrhunderts)* (Quellen und Studien zur Geschichte des östlichen Europa 32; Stuttgart, 1991), pp. 242, 250; see also above, p. 74.

50 The sword in the Balt site (at the modern village of Rokot) belongs to Petersen's E-type: G. S. Lebedev, V. A. Bulkin and V. A. Nazarenko, 'Drevnerusskie pamiatniki basseina r. Kaspli', *Vestnik Leningradskogo Universiteta, ser. Istoriia, Iazyk, Literatura* no. 14, *vyp.* 3 (1975), 168–9.

These finds fit into the picture of a select number of Rus and maybe also Finno-Ugrians journeying from the north with furs and other portable goods and either bartering them with the Balts and Slavs of the settlements between the Dvina and the Dnieper or pressing south-eastwards towards the sources of the silver. Such were the Rus described by ibn Khurradadhbih as carrying furs and swords as far as the Black Sea (see above, p. 43). But there is no sign of the network of settlements and workshops which regular traffic and incessant boat-hauling across the portages required. Such a network – consisting largely of Slav settlements – formed between the Dvina and the Dnieper only during the tenth century. Most of the coins found in the graves at Gnëzdovo date from after 900. Then, and only then, were enough persons passing through to make it worthwhile for others to settle, make a living from trades such as boat repair, and eventually die there (see Map 2). The long-distance travellers went on to build or visit the log cabins which were appearing in the Podol at Kiev from around 900 onwards.

There was also a significant development in and around Chernigov. Numerous Slav settlements lay along the Middle and Lower Desna and especially along its tributary, the Seim. These fertile valleys were more densely populated in the ninth century than the Dnieper valley was. The main thrust of Slav migration followed the valleys and occasional finds of dirham hoards or individual pieces of silver suggest that much silver passed along them or changed hands in their vicinity. But there is little about these promontory forts and neighbouring settlements to indicate significant centres of wealth or power, except for some clustering of sites on the Middle Desna, near Chernigov. Then, from the second half of the ninth century, the settlement at Chernigov began to expand and others sprang up just outside it, for example at the Gulbishche site. The site which has received most exhaustive attention, and which was of outstanding importance, is at Shestovitsy, some 12 kilometres south-west of Chernigov. Ten Byzantine and Moslem coins have been found in the extensive burial-ground, the earliest being a Samanid dirham of 895/96 and two coins of Leo VI. Shestovitsy's pattern of coin finds resembles the Starokievskaia burial-ground's, and the two sites' burial rituals, weapons and other goods have no close parallels elsewhere in the Middle Dnieper region. How far this chronological pattern applies to the other burial-grounds in the vicinity of Chernigov is uncertain. This is partly because of the relative paucity of burial goods, aggravated by the preponderance of cremations and the mass-destruction of barrows in modern times. But of the 60 barrows excavated at Sednev (Snovsk) only six contained a substantial array of weapons, and their inventory is poorer than that of the 30 or so graves of heavily-armed men – 20 per cent of the total – at Shestovitsy. Clearly, the latter constituted an elite. What has come to light suggests the foundation of a settlement at Shestovitsy around the beginning of the tenth century. Its inhabitants were of the same type as those responsible for changes at Kiev at that time, and – starting somewhat earlier – the number of inhabitants of Chernigov and its river valley also increased markedly.

The third of the major developments mentioned above (p. 97) takes the form of the texts of documents issued by the emperors of Byzantium and agreed between them and certain Rus. These treaties (as we shall call them, though the first may well have taken the form of a charter of privileges) feature in entries of the *Primary Chronicle* for 907 and 911; one is in fragmentary form, interwoven with a tale of a Rus attack on Tsargrad, while the other purports to be the full text. There is no serious doubt that they derive from actual charters or treaties, even if the editors of the chronicle omitted or embellished passages. The dates provided for the documents are very plausible. The date of September 6420 (here = 911) is integral to the text of the second treaty, together with the names of the reigning emperors, Leo VI, Alexander and Constantine. Only the first two emperors are represented as responsible for the document which features (fragmentarily) in the chronicle's entry for 907. This corresponds with the constitutional arrangements in Byzantium at that time: the infant Constantine was only crowned as co-emperor in May 908.[51] So a date of 907 for the treaty could well have been in the text from which the chronicle drew extracts. That the treaties were drafted within a few years of one another is clear: the names of all five Rus associated with the first-mentioned document feature among the fourteen listed in the 911 treaty.

The texts are interlinked in another respect: the extracted fragments of the 907 text give the strong impression of being preliminary to the fuller one. Arrangements are laid down for the everyday conditions under which the Rus could trade at Constantinople. They were to 'live at St Mamas', a harbour in the Bosporos north of the city, and the names of them all were to be written out. They were to receive lodging and free provisions for six months, and could enter the city in groups of 50 at a time 'through (only) one gate, in the company of the imperial agent, without their weapons'.[52] Those coming without merchandise would not receive monthly supplies, while the Rus 'prince' must forbid acts of violence 'against the villages of our country'. Judging by these excerpts, the focus was on the practical arrangements for the Rus' stay, rather than on procedures for dispute settlement and other contingencies. The other text addresses these issues and sets

51 J. Shepard, 'Vikings in Byzantium', in T. S. Noonan, ed., *The Vikings in the East* (forthcoming).

52 *PVL*, I, s.a. 907 (6415), p. 25. On some practical aspects of the two texts' provisions, see G. G. Litavrin, 'Usloviia prebyvaniia drevnikh Rusov v Konstantinopole v X v. i ikh iuridicheskii status', *Vizantiiskii Vremennik* 54 (1993), 81–92.

a tariff of compensation for the likeliest forms of injury or offence which the Rus or the 'Christians' might allege against one another. Regulations are laid down for the restitution of the cargo and crew of a wrecked ship; if a wrong-doer seeks sanctuary in Constantinople by prolonging his trading there, 'let the Rus complain to the Christian emperor', and he must be returned.[53] These clauses from the 911 treaty cannot be dismissed as abstract musings of Byzantine clerks. The lengthy provision for shipwrecks applied to the Byzantines' own vessels as well as Rus ones and a later treaty indicates that the Rus did encounter Byzantine-protected vessels in the Dnieper estuary. The provision registers the real dangers of Black Sea navigation, as does a stipulation in the 907 treaty that the Rus are to receive, before their return journey, 'food, anchors, ropes and sails and whatever is needed'.[54]

In effect, the first treaty lays down the house rules for Rus visitors and a few years later a more comprehensive set of procedures, invoking both Rus and Byzantine practices, is issued in the form of a treaty. Taken together, the texts give the strong impression that they are providing for a new situation, rather than codifying a number of existing customs and regulating them more precisely than before. To some extent, the second treaty corroborates this, in stating that there has not previously been a sworn, written, affirmation of the 'love which has existed for many years between the Christians and the Rus'.[55] This implies that the earlier document was not regarded as a wide-ranging, bilateral agreement, ratified by the rulers of two polities or their accredited representatives. The original form of the 907 document may not have been much more elaborate than that of the surviving fragments, a permit to do business in Constantinople, together with particulars concerning accommodation and maintenance grants. Such details were necessary because regular traffic between Constantinople and the Rus riverways was a novelty. The Byzantines' guarantee of whatever supplies and sailing tackle were needed for the return voyage seems to be an acknowledgement of the unusual hazards which the visitors would face. This unprecedented imperial permit was issued at a time when the 'devil's brats' (see above, p. 97) were on the rampage, devastating settlements to the east of the Dnieper, while

---

53 *PVL*, I, p. 28.
54 Ibid., pp. 24, 27, 37 (944 treaty on Chersonite fishermen). On similarities between some of the treaty's stipulations and various twelfth- and thirteenth-century Scandinavian law books, see M. Stein-Wilkeshuis, 'A Viking-age treaty between Constantinople and northern merchants, with its provisions on theft and robbery', *Scando-Slavica* 37 (1991), 39–46. See also J. Malingoudi, *Die russisch-byzantinischen Verträge des 10. Jahrhunderts aus diplomatischer Sicht* (Thessaloniki, 1994).
55 *PVL*, I, p. 26.

craftsmen were driving piles into the Podol's sodden soil and laying the foundations for a new, river-orientated quarter at Kiev.

The negotiating of the treaties occurred, like the Pechenegs' irruption and the building of the first structures in the Podol, within two decades of AD 900, and there is reason to suppose that these developments are interrelated. A trading community arose at Kiev and simultaneously forged links with the markets of Constantinople and with markets which could supply Moslem silver. The fact that dirhams are found on the Middle Dnieper only from c. 900 is an indication of this. That there was a spurt of travelling to Byzantium then is suggested by the type of the earliest Byzantine coins found in the burial-grounds on the Starokievskaia hill and at Shestovitsy. They are copper coins, *folles* of Leo VI, of some curiosity as novelties, but of little inherent value. So they are unlikely to have changed hands many times as objects of barter, and they may represent loose change, carried from Byzantium more or less by accident, and later discarded or kept as a minor ornament. We have noted a string of finds of *folles* of Theophilos which is probably connected with the return to Gorodishche-Holmgarthr of the Rhos emissaries of 838–9 (see above, p. 36). The *folles* on the Starokievskaia hill and at Shestovitsy could be mementoes brought back by some of the pioneers of the sea-link with Byzantium. It may be no accident that a *follis* of Leo VI is one of the earliest Byzantine coins to have been excavated in the burial-grounds at Gnëzdovo, while the first Byzantine copper coin excavated in Sweden after those of Theophilos also belongs to Leo. It was found among 'settlement remains' in the Black Earth at Birka.[56] This would also suggest that persons and goods were journeying all the way from Scandinavia to the Greeks and back. This matches the pattern of finds in the most richly furnished graves in Kiev, Shestovitsy, Gnëzdovo and the settlements at Gorodishche and near Iaroslavl. Ornaments such as belt mounts and weapons such as swords belong to types which were in vogue in the Baltic emporia, too. Bone combs continued to be used in the eastern lands and to keep up with changing fashions in the rest of the Scandinavian world (see above, p. 16). There also appears a type of burial ritual new to the eastern lands but already known at a select number of centres in Scandinavia, chamber-graves (see below, p. 122). This does not mean that all the occupants of the chamber-graves on the Middle Dnieper or on the Upper Dnieper at Gnëzdovo were newcomers from Scandinavia, or necessarily of Scandinavian stock at all. But travel between the Dnieper and the Baltic was frequent, even if the number of those travelling all the way in any one year was small. Many elements of material culture and burial ritual linked the frequenters

---

56 I. Hammarberg, B. Malmer and T. Zachrisson, *Byzantine Coins Found in Sweden* (Commentationes de nummis saeculorum IX–XI in Suecia repertis. Nova series 2; Stockholm, London, 1989), pp. 27, 61.

of Birka, Gorodishche and Gnëzdovo, and they most probably still had a language in common. Even through the filter of Greek and then Slavonic transcriptions the names of the Rus associated with the charter of 907 retain an unmistakably Nordic flavour: Karl, Farlof, Velmud, Rulav and Stemid. So too with most of the additional names in the 911 agreement, for example, Inegeld and Ruald.[57]

The installation of a number of Rus from the north at Kiev, Shestovitsy and a few other settlements around Chernigov around the end of the ninth century is, then, reasonably clear. But once we move beyond coin finds and the treaties, we enter an almost open field of speculation. There is no certainty that the Rus negotiators of these documents were based on the Middle Dnieper. The *Primary Chronicle* would have it so, just as it assumes that the 860 expedition was launched from Kiev or that the deed of 907 was prompted by a Rus attack on Constantinople. The chronicle makes out that a Rus fleet led by Prince Oleg attacked Tsargrad and terrified the Greeks into submitting and offering generous terms. Its tale of the Rus striking terror – sailboats rigged up on wheels bearing down on the city – is redolent of the stratagems related in Old Norse sagas.[58] The absence of any unambiguous reference to the raid in Byzantine sources is in stark contrast to their various mentions of the attacks of 860 and 941. It is most likely that contributors to the chronicle devised a historical background for the 907 document out of the tale of a raid containing the fantastic motif of boats on wheels. That tale may well be an elaboration of the involvement of a certain prince named 'H-L-G-W' in the historical raid of 941 (see below, pp. 115–16). It is true that the name of Oleg is closely associated with the two Rus-Byzantine accords and it features in the text of the 911 agreement. However, this is no guarantee of its presence in the original text. That text may have contained no ruler-name at all, or the name or names of princes which meant nothing to the contributors of the late eleventh or early twelfth centuries.[59] The contributors were prepared to add names by way of explanation, judging by their listing of Pereiaslavl as the 'third' of the towns whose inhabitants were to receive monthly allowances,

---

57 *PVL*, I, pp. 24, 25; V. Thomsen, *The Relations Between Ancient Russia and Scandinavia and the Origin of the Russian State* (Oxford, 1877), pp. 134, 135, 137, 138, 139, 140.
58 *PVL*, I, p. 24.
59 The texts of the Rus-Byzantine accords only became available to the contributors to the *Primary Chronicle* then. The *Novgorod First Chronicle*, which apparently contains an earlier version of the same chronicle, compiled in the 1090s, lacks the accords; nearly all other texts of, or excerpts from, Greek sources are also missing from it. The acquisition by later contributors of the texts of the accords apprised them of contacts between Rus and Greeks at the beginning of the tenth century, a time for which they possessed no narrative sources, whether local oral ones or translations of Byzantine chronicles. The urge to associate the 907 and 911 accords with a known raid on Byzantium involving a prince may well have been irresistible. See *NPL*, p. 108.

after Kiev and Chernigov. This is a glaring interpolation, seeing that
the chronicle itself recounts the foundation of Pereiaslavl in its entry
for 992, and there is no archaeological evidence of a settlement there
before the end of the tenth century.[60] The contributors, faced with a
blank, or with alien names at the head of the texts, may well have
sought to place them in the geographical setting of the recent past,
when Kiev, Chernigov and Pereiaslavl stood in a loose but indubitable
order of seniority (see below, pp. 249, 261). The name of Oleg need
have had no more to do with the original documents than did the name
of Pereiaslavl, and a question-mark hangs over the association of the
other towns' names with those documents. A question-mark also hangs
over the status of Karl and his fellows named in the 907 text. They
could initially have been freelances, without formal affiliations to any
established Rus potentate.

In these conditions of uncertainty, it is futile to attempt a detailed
reconstruction of events. But one can deduce something from the
foresaid changes in the Middle Dnieper and the steppes. The archaeological evidence suggests that by c. 900, but not much earlier, the Rus
were settling at Kiev and Shestovitsy. This is not far off the time when
the *Primary Chronicle* depicts Oleg as seizing power at Kiev from
Askold and Dir, and then imposing tribute on nearby Slav peoples –
the mid-880s.[61] Whether this dating rests on some specific information
available to the chronicle, or is simply a shot at filling the gap between
the first Rus raid on Constantinople and the Russo-Byzantine treaties,
is an open question. While not denying the possibility that Askold,
Dir and Oleg were historical figures, we cannot take at face value the
chronicle's version or dating of their careers (see above, pp. 57–8).
What is clear is that the *raison d'être* of the Rus presence on the Middle
Dnieper was trade, and the chronological margins for their arrival
there overlap with those for mounting disruption to the Khazars'
overlordship of the steppes (see above, p. 86). They also overlap
with the diminution of finds of recently struck Abbasid dirhams in
the hoards of the later ninth century, themselves few in number (see
above, pp. 59–60). As has been seen, the Rus were quick to adapt to
new situations and for some time had been probing alternative sources
of wealth far to the west and to the north-east. So there is nothing
surprising in new *démarches* to the south, especially as Rus traders
had been bearing goods down to the Black Sea for at least a generation.
al-Fakih represents the Rus as paying their tithe to the Byzantine
authorities and then voyaging 'by sea' to 'S-m-kūsh of the Jews', i.e.

60 *PVL*, I, pp. 24–5, 85; J. H. Lind, 'The Russo-Byzantine treaties and the early urban
   structure of Rus', *SEER* 62 (1984), 364–8.
61 *PVL*, I, pp. 20–1.

S-m-k-r-ts, the fortress on the Straits of Kerch.[62] Here al-Fakih adds to the material found in ibn Khurradadhbih or their common source and describes the situation at, or a little before, the time of writing, the beginning of the tenth century. Things seem to have moved on since ibn Khurradadhbih's time. The Rus were now sailing boats to the Black Sea and on to Kerch, perhaps trying to circumvent the turbulence of the Donets and Don steppes. But their goal at the end of the ninth century was still Khazaria and the lands of silver. They did not, at least to al-Fakih's knowledge, sail down to Constantinople (see above, p. 42).

It is possible that those Rus who saw advantages in establishing themselves on the Middle Dnieper were operating on their own account, much like the Rus on the Danube (see above, p. 89). But they could not have operated for long without some politico-military organization. The treaties with Byzantium and the well-equipped warriors in their chamber-graves favour this conclusion (see below, pp. 118, 122-4). The Byzantine government was willing to subsidize the trading activities of the Rus and exempted them from all customs dues, a distinct advantage over the 10 per cent levy which had been, and presumably still was, payable at Cherson. At the same time, the restrictions on the number of Rus let into Constantinople and the requirement that weapons be left outside the walls show wariness. It seems unlikely that such regulations would have been devised just for the members of itinerant, raiding-cum-trading parties, or that detailed procedures for restitution of stolen property and the repatriation of fugitives would have been negotiated for them soon afterwards. It is noteworthy that the 911 treaty's provisions speak of the return of 'wrong-doers' to 'the Rus' as a whole without mentioning a prince or envisaging any role for him in the enforcement of the regulations. But on balance it seems likely that Karl and his fellows, whose numbers rose from five to fourteen in only four years, had or gained affinities, however loose, with an acknowledged potentate or potentates. The 911 treaty's rhetorical reference to the longstanding 'love' between the Byzantines and the Rus would have made some sense if Karl and his colleagues were associated with a northern power which had maintained diplomatic relations with Byzantium for over 70 years, but whose extreme remoteness had rendered a written treaty redundant, or at least not worth saving.

This need not, in itself, verify the *Primary Chronicle*'s portrayal of the Rus as forcibly taking over from the Khazars. One might envisage a situation in which the Khazars, hard-pressed by the Pechenegs,

---

62 al-Fakih, *Kitab al-Buldan* [*Book of the Countries*], ed. T. Lewicki, *Żródła arabskie do dziejów słowiańszczyzny*, II.1 (Wroclaw, Warsaw, Cracow, 1969), pp. 28-9; 82-3 (commentary): tr. H. Massé, *Abrégé du livre des pays* (Damascus, 1973), p. 324; see also above, p. 37.

acquiesced in or even solicited the arrival of a group of Rus on the Middle Dnieper. That they employed Rus mercenaries at their capital, Itil, in the tenth century is attested by Masudi, and a case has been made for regarding the Khazars as still exercising hegemony over Kiev as late as c. 930 (see above, p. 96). This scenario is plausible, provided that it allows for a degree of rivalry between the Khazar authorities and the Dnieper Rus – a rivalry not merely over tribute-collecting rights but also over trade-routes. For many of the Samanid coins found on the Middle Dnieper arrived via Bulgar, being transported along the valleys of the Oka and the Seim. The latter route is identifiable with the route from Bulgar to Kiev served by twenty staging-posts which features in the Persian translation of an Arabic work, made at the end of the tenth century.[63] While the opening-up of this land-route between Central Asia and the Rus may have been primarily in reaction to the dangers of trafficking through the steppes, the effect was to bypass the central regions of the Khazars and further diminish their customs dues. The Khazars' relations with the Volga Bulgars were fraught: the ruler of the Bulgars, nominally under the khagan's overlordship, was by 921 trying to forge ties with the Abbasid caliph against the Khazars (see above, p. 64). This could suggest that the Rus, too, were under Khazar hegemony: they may have paid obeisance to the khagan, playing a role reminiscent of the semi-nomadic peoples occupying the Donets fortresses a generation earlier. That some direct trade continued between Khazaria and Rus on the Middle Dnieper is indicated by the *DAI*.[64] But if the Khazar overlordship persisted into the tenth century, it was probably largely notional.

Kiev had the advantage of good natural defences and the Khazars may have taken advantage of them (see above, pp. 95–6). However, the natural obstacles to utilizing the Dnieper as a continuous waterway were formidable, while the areas besides the environs of Kiev and a few points further south such as Kanev appear to have been very thinly settled. The Polianians, so praised by the locally based – and biased – contributors to the *Primary Chronicle*, cannot have been very numerous, while there is nothing in the archaeological evidence to suggest superior socio-political organization in the Slav settlements along the Dnieper. On the chronicle's avowal, the derivation of Polianians (from *pole*, 'open field', or steppe) is unspecific, lacking firm geographical anchorage. It was the Slavs settled well to the east of the Dnieper who enjoyed a slightly higher level of material culture through the silver exchanges, even if they, like the Slavs west of the river, only began to use the potter's wheel (instead of modelling pottery by hand) from the end of the ninth century. Above all, the Slavs'

---

63 B. A. Rybakov, 'Put' iz Bulgara v Kiev', *Drevnosti Vostochnoi Evropy* (*MIA* 169; Moscow, 1969), p. 189 and map, fig. 1 on p. 191.
64 *DAI*, ch. 42.77, pp. 186–7.

settlements along the Desna and the Seim were plentiful, in comparison with those along the Dnieper.

It is, then, very possible that a firmer socio-political structure lurks behind the chronicle's name for these Slavs, the Severians ('men of the north'), than is the case with the Polianians. This would accord with a detail which it offers concerning the Rus imposition of tribute on them. According to the chronicle, Oleg imposed only a 'light tribute', assuring the Severians that he was opposed to the Khazars, but was not against them.[65] No comparable vignette relates to the Polianians at Kiev. This contrast cannot be pressed hard: the historicity, let alone the chronology, of such episodes is questionable. But if the numbers of the Rus in the south were limited, they had to focus their activities – extorting and exchanging goods – where there were partners or tribute-payers. The regular exaction of tribute seems, from the opening stages of their settlement in the south, to have been of importance to the Rus. It may not simply be the location of the chronicle's composition that led it to give fuller details about tribute-payments to the southern Rus than about tribute paid to those in the north. The Rus heading south needed the cooperation of the better-organized groups of Slavs if they were to utilize such arrangements for tribute-gathering as the Khazars had devised. They could, in return, offer a modicum of protection against the Pechenegs' incursions and it is likely that the population along the Desna and the Seim was swollen by migrants – Slavs and semi-nomads – from the forts and settlements further south-east which had been sacked or abandoned. The settlements in the vicinity of Chernigov housed men whose quite plentiful weaponry and elaborate riding-gear equipped them for coping with nomad raids from a position of relative strength. In contrast, and on the assumption that surrounding sites have not simply vanished, Kiev seems to have lacked counterparts to Shestovitsy, Gulbishche and the other settlements (see above, p. 102). Even Kitaevo, a point of great strategic significance 10 kilometres to the south of Kiev, was apparently fortified and occupied only from the middle of the tenth century onwards.

These bits of evidence point to a fast-developing, heterogeneous society on the Middle Dnieper in the early tenth century. There were probably contrasts in function, as well as population size and composition, between the settlements in and around Kiev and Chernigov. We cannot be sure that Kiev possessed hegemony over Chernigov. There may have been no fixed or formal ranking order. What is certain is that the situation of the Rus on the Middle Dnieper differed from that of their *confrères* journeying to the Danube or the Volga, and even from the settlers upstream at Gnëzdovo. Their numbers were, judging by the paucity of archaeological remains, diminutive at

65 *PVL*, I, p. 20; see also above, p. 78.

the beginning of the tenth century and they faced formidable human threats as well as the barrages hindering navigation down the Dnieper. Their relations with the Khazars were probably uneasy while the Pechenegs needed no prompting to pillage their trading bands or to raid the Middle Dnieper territories. And they were ultimately no less dependent upon the goodwill of established rulers for profitable trading than were the Rus visiting the Volga or the Danube. In fact, as we have seen, the routes which they straddled indebted them to the Volga Bulgars and the Byzantines as well as the Khazars. The Byzantines' privileges gave them the right to stay on at Constantinople in search of a profitable deal, something which they could also do at Bulgar (see above, p. 44). And they were freed from living expenses in Constantinople (see above, p. 103). The concessions, which may well have been made at the request of the Rus, reflect the Byzantines' willingness to make special arrangements for new arrivals within their sphere of interests. But they are also a mark of the dangers of the new-fangled voyage by sea. Without blanket subsidies and exemptions the enterprise would probably not have been worthwhile even for the most intrepid or avaricious Rus. Equally, the apparent generosity of the Byzantine government was probably conditioned by the Rus' paucity of numbers. Neither the monthly provisions nor the exemptions were thought likely to cost much in actual outlay or lost customs dues.

The opening-up of a sea-link between the Middle Dnieper and Constantinople was a remarkable feat requiring a high degree of organization from the Rus who negotiated it – substantially higher than for their trips to the Middle Volga, for example (see above, pp. 43–4). In the face of so many hazards, and having to deal collectively with the Byzantines, the Rus must organize or die. But, in the opening years of the tenth century, a question-mark hung over this southern offshoot from the main zones of commerce: did they have the capacity to adapt?

CHAPTER THREE

The Dnieper Rus (c. 920–60) – Organize or Die: Securing the Way to Byzantium

Our last chapter ended with a question: could the Rus foothold on the Middle Dnieper and the trading ties they forged with Byzantium endure? An answer comes from the much fuller literary and archaeological evidence which emerges fairly abruptly from around the middle of the tenth century. This presents a picture of a resilient political structure. The Rus have a ruling elite which is headed or fronted by a paramount prince, whose authority is hereditable. When Prince Igor is killed by recalcitrant Slavs in the mid-940s, there is no discernible free-for-all among the other princes or senior members of the elite. Instead, the reins of power are taken over by his widow, known to Byzantine writers by her Nordic name of Helga and given the Slavic name, Olga, in the *Primary Chronicle*. She acted as regent on behalf of their small son, Sviatoslav. Most importantly of all, the *locus* of her power lay among the Rus in the south and she possessed two halls at Kiev. One was a stone keep and stood inside the fortified area on Starokievskaia hill, while the other is said to have stood 'outside the town'. Ingenious, but not wholly convincing, attempts have been made to identify the stone hall.[1] They are liable to divert attention from the remarkable fact that such a shift of power southwards occurred within a generation or so of the Rus' installation on the Middle Dnieper. The precise date and the circumstances are unknown, save that by the end of the 930s Prince Igor was ensconced in Kiev. It may be that Igor, or his predecessor, gained authority there essentially in the manner recounted in the chronicle – through the elimination or expulsion of Rus adventurers who had set themselves up in the south. But it is no less possible that the change came about peaceably. Assuming that the *chaganus* at Gorodishche belonged to a hereditary dynasty, he may have considered it expedient to send a relative, perhaps a son, to embody his

---

1 *PVL*, I, p. 40; P. P. Tolochko, ed., *Novoe v arkheologii Kieva* (Kiev, 1981), pp. 180–1; E. Mühle, 'Die Anfänge Kievs (bis ca. 980) in archäologischer Sicht. Ein Forschungsbericht', *JGO* 35 (1987), 89–90.

authority on the Middle Dnieper. There is no archaeological evidence of a conflagration at Kiev, such as a violent take-over in the second quarter of the tenth century might have occasioned.

One of the most vivid witnesses to the emergent power of the Rus is Constantine Porphyrogenitus' *DAI*, compiled c. 950. Chapter 9 is devoted to a description of the Rus' way of life and their yearly trips to Constantinople (see below, pp. 119–20). These journeys were for the purposes of trade, but Constantine's prime concern was to pinpoint, and provide data about, that stretch of the journey where the travellers were at their most vulnerable. At the Dnieper rapids was an important ford (see above, pp. 93–4). There, remarks the emperor, 'the Pechenegs come down and attack the Rus'.[2] The Rus alone are regarded as serious potential aggressors against 'this imperial city of the Romans' and Constantine spells out the policy of containment clearly: the Rus cannot reach the city 'either for war or for trade, unless they are at peace with the Pechenegs, because when the Rus come with their boats to the barrages of the river and cannot pass through unless they lift their ships off from the river and carry them past by portaging them on their shoulders, then the men of this people of the Pechenegs set upon them and, as they cannot do two things at once, they are easily routed and cut to pieces'.[3]

Constantine was pointing out an Achilles heel of the Rus which his own father had mooted more vaguely (see above, pp. 91–2). But whereas Leo wrote generally of the 'rivers' plied by the northerners in order to reach the Black Sea, Constantine writes only of 'the river', without troubling to name it. This shows the extent to which the Dnieper had become the main artery of Rus activity in the south since the end of the ninth century. From its mouth light boats could, with a fair wind, cross the Black Sea to the Anatolian coast in less than 48 hours. Such advantages of surprise were exploited by Cossack raiders in the early seventeenth century, causing panic in Ottoman Istanbul. Similar spectres haunted the citizens of tenth-century Constantinople and the emperor himself. They were concretized by an actual attack in 941. This event probably intensified the efforts to devise safeguards against the Rus enjoined in the *DAI*.

A fairly detailed account of the expedition is provided by the Byzantine chronicles and passing references appear in a saint's *Vita* and an emperor's private letter.[4] There is also a short account by Liudprand of Cremona, whose stepfather visited Constantinople soon afterwards. If we believe Liudprand, the Byzantines were taken by surprise in

---

2 *DAI*, ch. 9.70–1, pp. 60–1.

3 Ibid., ch. 2.16–23, pp. 50–1.

4 Gregory the Monk, *Vita Basilii Iunioris*, ed. A. N. Veselovskii, in *Razyskaniia v oblasti russkogo dukhovnogo stikha, Sbornik ORIAS* 46 (1889), *prilozhenie* 6, pp. 65–8; J. Darrouzès, *Épistoliers byzantins du X siècle* (Archives de l'Orient chrétien 6; Paris, 1960), p. 322.15.

June 941, as they had been in 860, and Emperor Romanos Lekapenos 'spent not a few sleepless nights in reflection' while the Rus devastated areas near the coast.[5] The day was saved by bringing fifteen 'battered old galleys' out of mothballs and rigging up Greek Fire-throwers at the bows, stern and broadside. Liudprand depicts the Byzantines as winning fairly easily, thanks to this non-conventional weaponry. Rus boats swarmed around the galleys, which began to 'project their fire all around; and the Rus, seeing the flames, hurled themselves from their boats, preferring death by water to live incineration. Some sank to the bottom under the weight of their cuirasses and helmets . . .; others caught fire even as they were swimming among the billows; not a man escaped that day save those who made it to the shore'.[6] Liudprand echoes the triumphalist tone which Byzantine chronicles relay. They celebrate at greater length the successive routs and slaughtering which the Byzantine naval and ground forces inflicted on the raiders. These were inconclusive, fairly small-scale engagements, but the Rus never gained the overall initiative. Once the main Byzantine army was withdrawn from the eastern front and began picking off stragglers, the Rus reportedly kept to their boats. From these the Rus had no chance of storming the walls of 'the great city', Micklagarthr, and they are not reported to have captured any walled town or fort. Their depredations struck the countryside and open suburbs, with special attention for priests and churches. The latter were burnt, while nails were hammered into the heads of the former. The role of ordinary prisoners was also unenviable, ranging from targets for archery practice to crucifixion.

These atrocities are in the vein of Viking raids in Western Europe and they call to mind the expedition of 860 (see above, p. 51). Yet there are differences between the two expeditions which register the changing circumstances of the Rus. Firstly, the number of boats was significantly larger in 941. It was probably only a fraction of the 10,000 of the Byzantine chronicles, but even if Liudprand's figure of '1,000 and more' is nearer the mark, this is more than double the number reported for the earlier attack. Secondly, these raiders did not, for all their butchering, fit the description of 'an uncaptained army' given by Photios to the raiders of 860. Liudprand is aware that they had a leader, a 'king named Inger', while the Byzantine chronicles imply a measure of discipline among them. We have already noted the change of tactics, whereby they hove to offshore as a compact unit. They were thus out of range of the land forces but, as Liudprand observed, their lightweight boats could stay in the shallows, where the deep-draft Byzantine galleys could not pursue them. Thirdly, our Byzantine

---

5 Liudprand of Cremona, *Antapodosis*, V, 15, in *Opera*, ed. J. Becker (*MGH* in usum schol.; Hanover, Leipzig, 1915), p. 138; tr. F. A. Wright, *The Works of Liudprand of Cremona* (London, 1930), p. 185.
6 Liudprand, *Antapodosis*, V, 15, ed. Becker, p. 138; tr. Wright, p. 186.

sources, while lamenting the slaughter of victims and torching of buildings, say nothing about the seizing of loot, as against foraging. In 860, in contrast, the Rus reportedly gained 'immense wealth' through their plundering.[7] There may be a connection between this and Liudprand's comment on the Rus vessels' small size. The craft of 941 may have been smaller, less capable of carrying loot, but correspondingly suitable for cruising offshore. This would suggest a rather different objective on the part of 'Inger' (Igor of the *Primary Chronicle*) from that of the Rus in 860: widespread devastation and terror rather than a free-for-all in search of riches. It is even possible that some of the Rus lightweight boats were hauled overland, perhaps on wheels. This would give sense to the sequence of targets implied in the semi-fabulous *Vita of St Basil the Younger*: from Herakleia on the Black Sea to the region of Nikomedeia in the Sea of Marmara.[8] This, too, would suggest careful planning and the Rus tactics of staying offshore imply awareness of the limitations on Greek Fire-power.

Planning and discipline might be expected of an expedition led personally by an established ruler, Igor. But if plunder was not the primary objective, what could it have been? Conquest can scarcely have been on the agenda, and although an attack on Constantinople was characteristically dreaded by the citizens, the Rus stayed well away, ravaging the eastern shore of the Bosporos. A possible explanation for the behaviour of the Rus emerges from the mid-tenth-century Khazar text recounting events of the recent past. It mentions a water-borne Rus expedition against Byzantium lasting four months, in which the Byzantines 'were victorious by virtue of Fire'.[9] The surviving Rus are said to have fled by sea. The details of a naval campaign, four-month stay in Byzantine waters and the successful application of Greek Fire correspond so closely with those of Byzantine chronicles and Liudprand that strong counter-evidence would be needed to refute identification of the campaign with the one discussed above. The one serious embarrassment is that the 'king' of the Rus is named in the Khazar text as H-L-G-W, not Inger/Igor, and his fate – death in the Caspian region – differs from that of Inger/Igor, who was slain by the Derevlians (see below, p. 117 and n. 12). The naming of H-L-G-W is not, however, an insuperable barrier to seeing in

---

7 Photios, *Homiliai*, ed. B. Laourdas (Thessalonica, 1959), p. 42; tr. C. Mango, *Homilies* (Dumbarton Oaks Studies 3; Washington, D.C., 1958), p. 98. See also above, p. 53. The *Primary Chronicle* does claim that 'much property' was taken by the Rus in 941 (*PVL*, I, p. 33), but this probably represents merely a literary embellishment on the Byzantine sources' accounts. See Theophanes Continuatus, *Chronographia*, VI. 39, ed. I. Bekker (Bonn, 1838), pp. 423–6; *Continuation* of George the Monk, in Theophanes Continuatus, *Chronographia*, pp. 914–16.

8 Gregory the Monk, *Vita Basilii Iunioris*, ed. Veselovskii, pp. 65, 67.

9 N. Golb and O. Pritsak, *Khazarian Hebrew Documents of the Tenth Century* (Ithaca, London, 1982), pp. 118–19.

the text a reference to the 941 raid. H-L-G-W could well have answered to the name which features in the *Primary Chronicle* as Oleg and which corresponds more closely to the Nordic form, Helgi (on Oleg's reported exploits, see above, pp. 57, 106). The earliest extant version of the chronicle carries a story about a raid on Byzantium organized *jointly* by Igor and Oleg; it represents Oleg, rather than Igor himself, as leading this attack, which it dates to 922, two years after an expedition of Igor's.[10] Igor and Oleg are, so far as this version is concerned, contemporaries. It is the *Primary Chronicle*'s slightly later compiler, possessing texts of the treaties with Byzantium and able to date Igor's attack correctly to 941 (see above, p. 106, n. 59), who reassigns Oleg to a generation earlier than Igor's and makes him active at the turn of the ninth and tenth centuries. Yet, as we shall see, there is clear evidence in other sources of the existence of other princes and potentates besides the paramount prince (see below, p. 134). Oleg, a.k.a. Helgi or H-L-G-W, could have been a fellow-prince of Igor.

There is, then, reason to suppose that the Khazar text offers an almost contemporary, if one-sided, account of the 941 attack on Byzantium. It holds out an explanation for the conduct of the Dnieper Rus, throwing light on their predicament. Their ruler is a considerable figure, courted by Byzantine diplomacy, possessing military might, but not invincible. H-L-G-W is said to have been incited 'with great presents' by Romanos Lekapenos to seize a city which can be identified as S-m-k-r-ts, a Khazar fortress well known to Rus traders (see above, pp. 107–8). They were dislodged from the fortress by a formidable Khazar commander, who went on to attack and overcome H-L-G-W, apparently on the latter's home ground. The commander is said to have insisted that H-L-G-W should go to war with Romanos. 'Thus against his will did he go and fight against Constantinople.'[11] Again, one may suspect minor distortion or condensation, but nothing more misleading than that. It is questionable whether the Khazars were powerful enough directly to attack the Rus on the Middle Dnieper. But they may have continued to exercise some hegemony there, calling in the services of nomads. This background, of an assault launched for essentially 'political' reasons, is in keeping with the demeanour of the Rus in 941. The Rus would have been able to observe to the letter the terms imposed by the Khazars and to impress their nuisance-value on the Byzantines, lurking offshore for months; but they forebore from large-scale plundering or frontal assault.

This reconstruction of events leading up to the Rus attack on Byzantium is hypothetical, but it offers an explanation why the Rus should have turned on the 'Greeks' after a generation of trading under advantageous terms. The Rus leadership seems to have had

10 *NPL*, pp. 107–8.
11 Golb and Pritsak, *Khazarian Hebrew Documents*, pp. 118–19.

few illusions about their prospects. According to the Khazarian text, H-L-G-W set off reluctantly – 'against his will' – to attack Byzantium, and in the event the Rus vessels came up against Greek Fire. Moreover, there are hints in the sources of the problems which the suspension of trade with Byzantium – or, at least, of trade on privileged terms – posed for the Dnieper Rus. The venture of H-L-G-W to the Caspian after 941 could well represent an attempt by a substantial proportion of the Rus and one of their leaders to enrich themselves, and maybe migrate, at a time when the flow of luxury goods from Byzantium dried up.[12] That treasure was still in short supply in the mid-940s is suggested by a story in the *Primary Chronicle*. Prince Igor's followers or 'retinue' (*druzhina*) are said to have complained that they were 'naked' in comparison with the well-armed and well-clothed followers of a certain Sveneld, whom the chronicle terms the 'commander' (*voevoda*) of Igor.[13] Igor led off his men to raise tribute from a Slav people living to the north-west of Kiev, the Derevlians. These were one of the better-organized Slav groupings but were, judging by the inventories of their graves, strikingly poor even by the modest standards of the East Slavs in general: at most, an iron knife, bronze hoops or a solitary bead.[14] Igor went back with a few retainers to raise a second haul of tribute from them, presumably for want of alternative sources of primary produce. It may have been a mark of his flagging prestige that the Derevlians offered violent resistance. They put Igor and his retainers to death near their principal town, Iskorosten (modern Korosten), some 150 kilometres from Kiev. Then, according to the chronicle, they presumed to propose the marriage of the dead man's widow, Olga, to their own leader, Mal.

By the time of these events, Igor's emissaries had negotiated the renewal of privileged terms of trading with the Greeks. The new treaty was agreed, probably in 944, and its text is incorporated into the chronicle. It contains what look suspiciously like interpolations (in the names of leading towns: see above, p. 107), but it was not radically recast. The contents, while similar to those of the 911 treaty, hint at developments which even the best-inspired reviser

---

12 H-L-G-W's deeds in the Caspian region may well be identifiable with the Rus occupation of Barda'a recounted by Miskawayh, *Tajarib al-umam [The Experiences of the Nations]*, in *The Eclipse of the Abbasid Caliphate*, ed. H. F. Amedroz (Oxford, 1921), II, pp. 62–7; tr. D. S. Margoliouth (Oxford, 1921), V, pp. 67–74; J. Shepard, 'Constantine VII and the "containment" of the Rus', Festschrift for G. G. Litavrin (Moscow, 1996). Such a conclusion, and a broadly similar revision of chronology, has been arrived at independently by C. Zuckerman, 'On the date of the Khazars' conversion to Judaism and the chronology of the kings of the Rus Oleg and Igor', *Revue des études byzantines* 53 (1995), 259–68.

13 *PVL*, I, pp. 34–5.

14 I. P. Rusanova, 'Territoriia drevlian po arkheologicheskim dannym', *SA* 1960, no. 1, 69; C. Goehrke, *Frühzeit des Ostslaventums* (Erträge der Forschung 277; Darmstadt, 1992), pp. 138, 153.

of the early twelfth century could scarcely have divined without documentation. The text focuses on the trading conditions of the Rus at Constantinople, providing in greater detail for problems arising from runaway slaves, or Byzantine-domiciled persons falling into the hands of the Rus as slaves, and also for the theft of goods and the purchase of silks; the Rus were only to buy silks up to the value of 50 gold pieces (*nomismata*) and these were to be stamped by an official. Silks seem to have been of primary interest to the Rus and two silken cloths are now prescribed as the compensation to be paid to the owner whose escaped slave is not returned. The treaty of 944 gives the impression that larger numbers of Rus were now involved in exchanges with Byzantium. Noting that hitherto Rus traders had brought silver seals by way of accreditation, the treaty stipulated that in future they were to be provided by their prince with a 'letter' specifying how many boats had been sent and confirming that they were travelling with peaceful intent. While this is clearly a precaution against another surprise attack, it probably also reflects an increased volume of Rus maritime traffic. By the 940s, the Black Sea was known as 'the Sea of the Rus' to Moslem writers such as Masudi.[15] And the amount of names at the beginning of the new treaty suggests an increase in the number of northerners actively dealing with the Byzantines. Altogether, 76 persons are listed in one capacity or another, whereas the 911 treaty has only fifteen (see above, p. 106).

Still more suggestive of change is the hierarchy evinced by the 944 treaty. The earlier treaty lists Karl and his fellows without any indication of their status, beyond the vague and questionable statement that they had been sent by Oleg and 'all the splendid and great princes and great boiars who are under his hands'. The 944 treaty names the emissaries of 25 persons, starting with Igor and close members of his family: 'Vuefast [the envoy] of Sviatoslav, the son of Igor; Iskusev [the envoy] of Princess Olga; Sludy [the envoy] of Igor, the nephew of Igor', and so on. Several names later comes the emissary of 'Akun, the nephew of Igor'.[16] Presumably the intervening names, including two female ones, belonged to persons of pre-eminent standing but having looser kinship ties with Igor, or none at all. These top people's names are followed by persons categorized as 'merchant' (*kupets*), who only represent themselves. The list was written down by Byzantine clerks, but the pecking order had probably been supplied by the Rus. It denotes a structure revolving round one kin-group, but by no means dominated by it. Igor presides rather than commands, seeing that his

15 Masudi, *Muruj al-Dhahab wa Ma'adin al-Jawhar* [*Golden Meadows and Mines of Precious Stones*], 455, ed. C. Pellat (Beirut, 1966), I, p. 216; tr. C. Pellat, *Les prairies d'or* (Paris, 1962), I, p. 164.
16 *PVL*, I, pp. 34–5; V. Thomsen, *The Relations Between Ancient Russia and Scandinavia and the Origin of the Russian State* (Oxford, 1877), pp. 131–2, 139, 140–1.

nephews, wife and son send their own representatives. Yet a much more prominent role in enforcement is envisaged for the prince than had been the case in 911. While this is partly a matter of military or diplomatic undertakings – protection of Cherson from the Black Bulgars, for example – these are themselves a mark of the armed force presumably at the prince's disposal. The Byzantine government also expected the active cooperation of the prince in more routine matters such as dealing with fugitives who fled to the Rus. Its assumption that the foremost Rus prince was in a position to 'deliver' is likely to have had some foundation.

The apparatus required for drafting letters in the name of the princes to the emperor in Tsargrad need not have been large, any more than was that of earlier steppe confederations. Attila the Hun's correspondence with Byzantine emperors was undertaken by Roman captives or 'gifts' whom he maintained as secretaries. The prince's staff at Kiev was probably minimal – perhaps Greek-speaking clergymen who presumably catered for Christian Rus. Some of the latter swore to honour the treaty by the Christian God in a church of St Elijah. For the treaty to make this provision, a significant number of prominent Rus must have been Christian – some, presumably, sending emissaries to Byzantium. Thus for all the modesty of its scale and the rudimentary nature of its administration, a political structure of some intricacy is apparent. The scene which the treaty seems to presuppose is the more credible because a very similar picture emerges from the *DAI*'s lengthy description of the Rus year. This begins with the spring thaw, when the trunks of trees felled by the Slavs are floated down tributaries of the Dnieper towards Kiev. There, they are sold – not simply handed over gratis – to the Rus, who fit them out as transports and load them with goods. Slaves formed the most conspicuous – and probably the single most valuable – item: such self-propelling commodities were well suited for negotiating the rapids and they are the most frequently mentioned sort of merchandise in both the 911 and the 944 treaties. Judging by the *DAI*, the Rus were operating as a kind of collective. They formed a flotilla which contended with the quadruple hazards of potentially fugitive slaves – kept in chains at the rapid which everyone had to bypass on dry land – as well as the rapids themselves, the Pechenegs and the Black Sea's storms. The travellers were stalked by Pecheneg hopefuls along the coast: 'and every time the sea casts a *monoxylon* to shore, they all put in to land, in order to present a united front against the Pechenegs'.[17] Only when the

---

17 *DAI*, ch. 9.94–6, pp. 62–3. On the simple type of boat – a hollowed tree-trunk built up and widened with ribs and side-planks – denoted by *monoxylon*, see O. Crumlin-Pedersen, Schiffe und Schiffahrtswege im Ostseeraum während des 9.–12. Jahrhunderts', *OWS, Bericht der Römisch-Germanischen Kommission*, 69 (1988), 536–42; P. M. Strässle, 'To monoxylon in Konstantin VII. Porphyrogennetos' Werk *De administrando imperio*', *Études Balkaniques* 1990, no. 2, 99–102, 105–6.

Rus reached one of the mouths of the Danube were they rid of Pecheneg shadows and scavengers. Their journey towards Byzantine territory is described by Emperor Constantine as 'fraught with such travail and terror, such difficulty and danger'. Even in winter-time their way of life is 'hard'.[18] Then, too, they operate as a pack: 'all the Rus' go out with their 'princes' (*archontes*), 'on the "poliudia", which means "rounds" ' to their tributaries; thus, we are told, they are maintained by peoples such as the Krivichi and the Severians through the winter.[19]

Constantine's description is not free from error, but its main lines match the details of the Rus-Byzantine treaties, and also the evidence of archaeology. Political organization and military force featured prominently in the 'hard' way of life of the Rus. The dangers of the long haul made it advisable for them to journey to Byzantium in a group, although the introduction of certificates in the 944 treaty suggests that by then not all the Rus traders belonged to the flotilla described by Constantine. The Rus seem to have been more reliant on tribute-arrangements than were the Rus whom we have observed further north. This may reflect the sedentary and agrarian way of life of the Slavs in comparison with that of the Finno-Ugrians in the Volga basin, and also the fact that the Slavs living to the east of the Dnieper had for some time been paying tribute to the Khazars. As we have seen (see above, p. 81), there appears to have been an understanding that the Khazars and their confederates should provide protection for the Slavs against other, more wantonly predatory, nomads. If the Pechenegs' depredations became more destructive in the early tenth century, the initial installation of the Rus on the Middle Dnieper may have brought some respite and thus have been welcome to the Slavs. This fits in with the *DAI*'s indication that the Rus paid for the tree-trunks which they received from the Slavs each spring. As they had with the Khazars and their allies in previous generations, the Slavs of the wooded steppe became drawn into commercial transactions at the same time as rendering services and delivering goods to their overlords. The symbols of authority – *tamgas* – which the Rus princes came to use are suggestive in this respect. Seals had been in use for some time by the 940s, with the 'envoys' of princes bearing gold seals to Byzantium while merchants presented silver ones.[20] No examples of these early seals are known, but the seals commonly attributed to Sviatoslav Igorevich and the coins indubitably struck by his son, Vladimir, show emblems – variants on the motif of prongs or tridents – which resemble those found on Khazar

18 *DAI*, ch. 9.104, pp. 62–3.
19 Ibid., ch. 9.105–10, pp. 62–3.
20 *PVL*, I, p. 35; see also above, p. 118.

sites associated with the khagan.[21] Such emblems may well already have been adopted by earlier Rus princes. Through using Khazar symbols, the Dnieper Rus could enhance the claim to legitimacy which the title of their paramount prince – *chaganus* or khagan – had long been making. And, as has been noted (see above, p. 112), some time before the late 930s that prince, in the form of Igor or one of his predecessors, took up residence on the Middle Dnieper.

One gains more information about the new politico-military structure by collating the literary evidence with that of archaeology. A considerable number of the graves at Shestovitsy are cenotaphs, devoid of all trace of human remains, and they seem to have been empty from the start, rather than being robbed or dug in acidic soils capable of totally obliterating bodies. Cenotaphs have been found at other Rus sites but the percentage of barrows answering this description at Shestovitsy stands at over 32 per cent, and there seems to be a contrast between north and south. At Timerëvo, for example, the percentage is around 16 per cent, at most. This is the percentage of the total number of graves at the site, the inventoryless graves of the poor or ordinary Rus free man, as well as the graves of those whose relatives or mourners could afford some burial goods or elements of ritual. The publisher of the Shestovitsy burial-ground excavations, D. Blifeld, concluded that the majority of its cenotaphs commemorated men who had perished far from home, on voyages to Byzantium or in combat against the nomads and other predators.[22] There is no reason to doubt their testimony as to the dangers – and brevity – of life on the Middle Dnieper.

The paramount leader of the Rus, Igor, was clearly more than the figurehead described by ibn Fadlan less than a generation earlier. But this is compatible with the impression which the treaties and the *DAI* give of a collective leadership involving a number of 'princes' or chiefs. They head the bands on tribute-collecting rounds in winter, and they are not all based in Kiev. Huge, lavishly furnished barrows such as the mid-tenth-century Chernaia Mogila at Chernigov (replete with figurine of Thor) bespeak wealthy magnates whose status may well have been

21 Whether the signs were intended as symbols of the khagan's authority or had a more banal function remains an open question. The trident is found throughout the Khazar lands and could have been adapted by Rus princes wishing to gain a certain cachet through its associations. Diverse views and useful data in: A. M. Shcherbak, 'Znaki na keramike i kirpichakh iz Sarkela-Beloi Vezhi', *MIA* 75 (Moscow, Leningrad, 1959), pp. 363–5; M. I. Artamonov, *Istoriia khazar* (Leningrad, 1962), p. 430; Ianin, *Aktovye pechati*, I, pp. 40–1 and n. 89; no. 1, pp. 166, 249; V. E. Nakhapetian and A. V. Fomin, 'Graffiti na kuficheskikh monetakh, obrashchavshikhsia v Evrope v IX–Xvv.', *DGVEMI* 1991 (1994), pp. 172–3, 175 and n. 69, fig. 9, p. 174. N. B. Krylasova, 'Podveska so znakom Riurikovichei iz rozhdestvenskogo mogil'nika', *RA*, 1995, no. 2, 193–7.

22 D. I. Blifeld, *Davn'orus'ki pam'iatky Shestovytsi* (Kiev, 1977), p. 35. On Timerëvo: N. G. Nedoshivina and M. V. Fekhner, 'Pogrebal'nyi obriad timerevskogo mogil'nika', *SA* 1985, no. 2, 101–2.

'noble' or 'princely' (although these terms were not technical ones and could have affixed themselves to anyone outstandingly successful in war or tribute exaction). That Chernigov was an important centre, on a par with Kiev, is suggested both by the large number of settlements in its vicinity (see above, p. 110), and by the evidence of an armed elite at Shestovitsy. There, as at the burial-ground on the Starokievskaia hill and other locations in and around Kiev, lie a number of graves which Russian archaeologists have termed 'retainer-graves'. They resemble a type known in western writings as 'chamber-graves', after the chamber-like wooden construction, 1.5 metres or more in width, complete with wooden walls, ceiling and floor, housing the dead and their chattels. Russian archaeologists have been rather freer with the label 'retainer-grave' than western scholars are with 'chamber-grave', applying it to what were essentially heaped-over pyres involving some sort of wooden structure in which the deceased was placed, and which was then set on fire. Earth was heaped over the site of the conflagration, to form a barrow, and barrows also covered the burials underground.[23] In both chamber-graves and heaped-over pyres, the dead man could be accompanied by his horse or horses, his woman, or both. The weaponry, bridle ornaments and saddles together with the silver and gold ornaments of the women attested the male occupants' power and status: basically, the more objects, inanimate or defunct, in the grave, the bigger the barrow, with corresponding claims to social standing.

The chamber-graves in the districts of Chernigov and Kiev signal the bases of the tribute-raising bands described by Constantine Porphyrogenitus. Their male occupants have been described as 'professional warriors' or 'mercenaries' and some probably earned their wealth wholly through the service of lords. However, weights and balances are found in many chamber-graves and constant arms-bearing was quite compatible with frequent engagement in trading. This is shown by the Byzantines' requirement that the Rus entering Constantinople to trade should leave their weapons behind (see above, p. 103). But the equipping of the dead with expensive beasts such as horses and with slave-girls, together with a full set of weapons, represents a development not found in the lands of the Rus before the tenth century. It suggests positive exaltation of the bearing of arms as a mark of status, besides wealth and ostentation. This type of burial ritual is found at very few sites in Scandinavia proper. By far the largest number of chamber-graves in Sweden is at Birka, whose 120 or so chamber-graves form around 10 per cent of the total of graves excavated there. Finds elsewhere in Sweden are very rare and several of them are in Uppland, not far from Birka. In contrast to the chamber-graves on the Middle Dnieper,

---

23 D. I. Blifeld, 'K istoricheskoi otsenke druzhinnykh pogrebenii v srubnykh grobnitsakh srednego Podneprov'ia IX–Xvv.', *SA* 20 (1954), 148–62.

a high proportion – approximately 40 per cent – of the chamber-graves contained women by themselves (rather than as adjuncts to males), and weights have been found in many of them. But at Birka, as in the lands east of the Baltic, the salient characteristic of the men's graves is their formidable array of weaponry, often arranged in order, the sword being at the man's belt, the spear lying beside him and the shield initially resting against the wall of the chamber. Chamber-graves have mostly been found along the East Way leading to Byzantium; relatively few are reported in the north, along the Volga or other routes linking the Baltic lands with Bulgar and the sources of the dirhams. Twelve later tenth-century chamber-graves have been found near the Volga in the burial-ground at Timerëvo, but the site is a lone exception among the several settlements in the north-east where some sort of Rus presence is attested. The majority of the chamber-graves are found along the north–south axis – at Staraia Ladoga, Pskov, Gnëzdovo and, above all, the Middle Dnieper.[24] It is only in the latter area and at Gnëzdovo that they occur in significant numbers. This seems to offer an index of the centres of power-driven wealth among the Rus in the tenth century. The contents of the chamber-graves suggest that in the eastern lands conspicuous wealth was now often associated with the use – or at least the brandishing – of weapons.

While the construction and ritual of the chamber-graves in the Dnieper burial-grounds resemble those of Birka's, the graves mostly lack artefacts of unequivocally Scandinavian type. Furthermore, many of the tools, pieces of pottery or items of riding-gear have no Scandinavian analogies or associations. But it is unsurprising that many everyday items were acquired from the local population, or that some of the Shestovitsy riding-gear and ornaments closely resemble types used by the Hungarians and by Turkic nomads. Constantine VII states that there were dealings between the Rus and the Pechenegs, who sold them sheep, cattle and horses.[25] The archaeological evidence matches Constantine's sketch in two other respects. Firstly, Constantine implies that their military manpower was very limited, since they could not simultaneously go off on an expedition and provide adequate cover for their settlements against the nomads. And in stating that 'all the Rus' go off with their princes or chieftains on the winter round among

24 E. A. Mel'nikova, V. I. Petrukhin and T. A. Pushkina, 'Drevnerusskie vliianiia v kul'ture Skandinavii rannego srednevekov'ia. (K postanovke problemy)', *Istoriia SSSR* 1984, no. 3, 58; Nedoshivina and Fekhner, 'Pogrebal'nyi obriad', 111–12. On Birka's chamber-graves, see A.-S. Gräslund, *The Burial Customs, Birka* IV (Uppsala, 1980), pp. 27–36, 45–6; cf. F. O. Androshchuk and R. M. Osadchii, 'Pro kul'turnyi typ ta konstruktyvno-rytual'ni osoblyvosti kamernykh pokhovan pivdennoi Rusi', *Arkheolohiia* 1994, no. 3, 99–106.

25 Blifeld, *Davn'orus'ki pam'iatky Shestovytsi*, pp. 78, 82–3; *DAI*, ch. 2.6–7, pp. 50–1. The Pechenegs were just 'one day's journey' from the Rus: *DAI*, ch. 37. 47, pp. 168–9. See also T. S. Noonan, 'Rus', Pechenegs and Polovtsy', *Russian History* 19 (1992), 307–9.

the Slavs, Constantine implies a fairly select band of itinerant *rentiers*.[26] Such a picture may, of course, merely reflect imperial ignorance. But in fact the number of chamber-graves or other graves attributable with reasonable certainty to persons of Scandinavian culture in the Middle Dnieper region is not great. Even at Shestovitsy and the Starokievskaia hill in Kiev, no more than 30 chamber-graves apiece have been reported, approximately 20 per cent of the total of graves at each burial-ground. While many may have been destroyed, the total of chamber-graves is unlikely to have exceeded a few hundred, at a generous estimate. The craftsmen and traders from the north who built and settled in the Podol may have been too poor or eclectic in their tastes to be buried in graves with Scandinavian ornaments and in accordance with Scandinavian ritual, while the poorer tribute-gatherers or settlers presumably ended up in graves largely lacking in inventories. Even so, the strong impression given by the Middle Dnieper burial-grounds is of a small minority group, under whose aegis craftsmen and traders from many other areas began to congregate (see below, pp. 141–2, 161, 169). The burial-ground at Shestovitsy probably belonged mainly to persons of Scandinavian culture and language. But most of the graves in the other tenth-century burial-grounds in and around Chernigov should probably be ascribed to Slavs or sedentarized nomads. Some of the men interred in these poorer burial-grounds had borne weapons such as spears and bows and arrows, judging by their grave goods, and they were presumably at the disposal of the Rus leadership for the purposes of defence or the occasional long-range expedition to a lucrative target in the south.

A second way in which Constantine's sketch agrees with the archaeology is in his emphasis on the harshness and perils of the Dnieper Rus lifestyle. The armouries deposited in the chamber-graves suggest a society organized for warfare. There may also be significance in the dearth of graves clearly attributable to Scandinavian women. Very few chamber-graves on the Middle Dnieper housed such women and the total number of finds of tortoiseshell brooches – one of the clearest of ethnic indicators – is small, in comparison with the 34 tortoiseshell brooches excavated in the Timerëvo burial-ground.[27] The paucity of finds of such brooches or other female ornaments of Scandinavian type is probably not an accident, since female ornaments are better-represented than male ones in the north. The pattern of finds suggests that the Rus society on the Middle Dnieper was a 'man's world' to a markedly greater degree than was the case further north. At Gnëzdovo, also on the Dnieper but further from the steppes,

26 *DAI*, ch. 9.105–6, pp. 62–3.
27 M. V. Fekhner and N. G. Nedoshivina, 'Etnokul'turnaia kharakteristika timerevskogo mogil'nika po materialam pogrebal'nogo inventaria', *SA* 1987, no. 2, 77–8.

twelve chamber-graves contain Scandinavian-style ornaments implying occupation by women of substance. These make up almost half the total number of chamber-graves.[28]   This evidence suggests why a politico-military structure with a fairly high degree of self-imposed discipline formed in the south rather than in regions earlier frequented by the Rus. It was a question of organize or die.

This, however, invites a further question. What induced a number of Rus to persevere on the Middle Dnieper, when ample opportunities for settlement or self-enrichment existed elsewhere? For around the middle of the tenth century is the period of fullest evidence of Scandinavian-type objects, and thus of the likely presence of persons of Scandinavian stock, in many of the sites discussed in earlier chapters. And it is to the tenth century that the majority of the known hoards of dirhams belong. Most of the coins were struck in the Samanids' mints in Central Asia. They attest the vitality of the trading links which had been opened up along the Volga and other waterways connecting with the Middle Volga around the turn of the ninth and tenth centuries (see above, p. 65). Even at settlements such as the Sarskii fort, the majority of Scandinavian-type objects date from the tenth century. There are indications of the presence of Scandinavian women in settlements around Lake Pleshcheevo. Tenth-century tortoiseshell brooches have been found in the burial-grounds as well as Samanid coins, weights and balances for scales and clay beavers' paws (see above, pp. 66–7). It is most probable that the dead who were buried with them originated in the Åland islands or Central Sweden, and the beavers' paws and the weights offer clues as to the activity which drew them to the shores of Lakes Pleshcheevo and Nero: the fur trade. It is to the tenth century that most of the Scandinavian artefacts in the Iaroslavl burial-grounds belong – swords, axes, lancet-shaped arrowheads, tortoiseshell and circular brooches, innumerable boat rivets, snow spikes and ritual items such as the paws. Most of the 32 burials containing weights and balances excavated at Timerëvo date from the second half of the tenth or the beginning of the eleventh century.[29] Similar inventories have been reported of the burial-grounds of settlements near Suzdal and Iurev-Polskoi, and here, too, substantial – albeit never massive – immigration from the Scandinavian Baltic may be inferred.

Timerëvo attained its maximum extent – some 6 hectares – around the mid-tenth century. This period also saw a marked expansion in the area of built-up land at Staraia Ladoga. An intensification in development is evident from the 930s, when a new 'Horizon', D, was superimposed on the earlier one. It is characterized by houses which

28 I. E. Zharnov, 'Zhenskie skandinavskie pogrebeniia v Gnëzdove', in D. A. Avdusin, ed., *Smolensk i Gnëzdovo (k istorii drevnerusskogo goroda)* (Moscow, 1991), pp. 207–8.
29 Fekhner and Nedoshivina, 'Etnokul'turnaia kharakteristika', 73–4.

are smaller than the large halls of the earlier stratum, tight-packed and carefully aligned to a street-plan. Judging by the excavations of the main settlement to date, the built-up area greatly expanded from the 930s to the 960s, the lower level of Horizon D. This expansion is connected with the sharp upswing in manufacturing and trading indicated by an increase in the number of finds of amber, cornelian and glass beads – many of the latter locally made. In some of the workshops-cum-dwellings coins have been found, or the weights from scales. Twenty-four weights are known from Horizon D, as against just two from Horizon E.[30]

Development was also under way in the mid-tenth century in settlements by the source of the river Volkhov. At Gorodishche, the low-lying area liable to flooding began to be built over with dwelling-houses (see above, p. 33). Plentiful finds of craftsmen's tools and cast-offs have been made here: as at Staraia Ladoga, the numerous ships' nails and planks attest the importance of ship repairs and shipbuilding in the economic life of the settlements. It is no coincidence that the majority of objects of Scandinavian type or style found at Gorodishche are datable to the tenth century. But the development which would prove most significant of all in the long term was the construction of two groups of buildings a couple of kilometres downstream along the Volkhov. Wooden street paving was laid in them in the 940s or 950s, soon after people began living there, in homesteads aligned neatly to the street-plan. The first inhabitants were well-armed, judging by their axes and lancet-headed arrows, and they, like the inhabitants of Gorodishche, were much involved with shipping: rudders, ships' timbers and rivets abound. There are numerous finds of more or less *de luxe* objects from afar which can only have arrived by means of trade: glass vessels, amphorae, beads of cornelian and rock-crystal, boxwood and dirhams.[31] The settlements' inhabitants did not aim at self-reliance: they counted on being able to meet everyday needs of nourishment and household implements by bartering fragments of dirhams or other more or less *de luxe* objects for them. This was not a development confined to the new town, which is called Novgorod in the *Primary Chronicle* and other sources referring to the period from the eleventh century onwards. It is in the tenth-century sites in general that the greatest number of fragments of dirhams are found: weights

30 E. Mühle, *Die städtischen Handelszentren der nordwestlichen Rus'. Anfänge und frühe Entwicklung altrussischer Städte (bis gegen Ende des 12. Jahrhunderts)* (Quellen und Studien zur Geschichte des östlichen Europa 32; Stuttgart, 1991), p. 25, Diagram 2, p. 27, Table 2, p. 35, pp. 46–7, 59–60. That the development of Rus towns intensified across a wide area from around the mid-tenth century was noted by V. P. Darkevich. 'Proiskhozhdenie i razvitie gorodov drevnei Rusi (X–XIIIvv.)', *Voprosy istorii* 1994, no. 10, 50, 53.
31 Mühle, *Städtischen Handelszentren*, pp. 90–5, 97–8.

and fragments of balances are likewise most common then, especially for the middle and second half of the century.

An expansion of commercial activity and in settlement area can be observed at Gnëzdovo, in whose burial-grounds some 90 weights (from 55 graves) have been found. In the early years of the tenth century the main settlement straddling the river Svinets and lining the Dnieper bank was unfortified and covered at most about 4 hectares. Only in the mid-tenth century was a portion of the settlement fortified with an earthen rampart and ditch; from the 930s the settled area expanded drastically, to cover approximately 15 hectares by the end of the century. That these changes were due to an intensification in trade is suggested by the excavations of the settlements and, above all, the extensive burial-grounds enfolding the main settlement on three sides. Gnëzdovo acted as a repair yard as well as a market. The portaging of boats overland between riverways from the Western Dvina inevitably took its toll on their hulls and fittings, and it is no accident that the smithies of Gnëzdovo were of a technical competence matched only by those of Staraia Ladoga, Gorodishche and Pskov.[32] They manufactured the rivets, brackets and other tackle needed for boats and their high-quality axes and knives could be used for repair work or constructing new vessels. The importance of boats as the means to, and mark of, wealth is demonstrated symbolically by the boat-burials. These were generally accompanied by the richest array of grave goods and the mounds heaped over them were the largest in the burial-grounds. Boat-burials are known from the early days of Scandinavian settlement at Gnëzdovo, around the beginning of the tenth century. The very wealthy were still being treated to cremation in boats towards the end of the century, while such cult objects as Thor's hammerlets and rites such as swords being bent and then driven into the ground occur in graves throughout the century. But just as nearly all the largest barrows date from the middle or second half of the tenth century, so, too, do such firm indicators of a Scandinavian presence as tortoiseshell brooches. Examples have been found in no less than 43 cremations at Gnëzdovo, as well as in several inhumations.[33] The demand for brooches was large and constant enough for craftsmen to manufacture them on the spot, as clay moulds for casting them indicate. The fairly full publication of these ornaments from Gnëzdovo permits a further conclusion to be drawn. The tortoiseshell brooches found there follow the same chronological sequence, and are of the same approximate date, as those excavated in Scandinavia. In other words, the Scandinavian women flashing their jewelry at Gnëzdovo were keeping up with the fashions of Birka. It has been suggested that

32 Ibid., pp. 248–9.
33 Zharnov, 'Zhenskie skandinavskie pogrebeniia', pp. 214, 216.

the two towns, Gnëzdovo and Birka, played similar roles as markets where traders met seasonally and exchanged goods from a wide variety of regions.[34] Both were surrounded by large burial-grounds and their settlements were of comparable size: Birka covered some 12 hectares to Gnëzdovo's 15. The evidence of the tortoiseshells supports the idea of close and frequent contacts between the two markets. It is likely that the expansion of the settlement was due to fresh arrivals from the Baltic region rather than just to demographic increase or internal migration, large as was the influx of Balts and Slavs to Gnëzdovo during the tenth century. Many, perhaps most, of the Scandinavians setting foot there, men and women alike, were birds of passage and had no intention of residing there, let alone of leaving their bones. The same was true of those putting in at Staraia Ladoga and Gorodishche. It may have been the Middle Dnieper area that was regarded as the point of no return: for many, as the cenotaphs imply, it was.

Much of the commerce described above was of the sort which had long been undertaken, directly or indirectly, with the Moslem world. The main differences in the tenth century lay in the increased volume of business and the fact that slaves were now a more important commodity. Slaves acquired in the eastern forest zone rather than from Baltic markets (see above, pp. 18, 20) could prove harder to obtain through barter and they anyway needed guarding. These developments are connected with the greater quantities of weapons found in northern Rus sites in general for the tenth century (albeit less spectacular than the arrays in 'retainer-graves'). Oriental silver was of great importance at Gnëzdovo as well as further north, and analogies to some of the ornaments found at Gnëzdovo have been unearthed in the region of the Volga Bulgars. They are an indication of the route by which much of the silver reached Gnëzdovo.

To a considerable extent these nexuses could function without reference to the Middle Dnieper zone, and those engaged in them were neither involved in nor necessarily amenable to the tighter organization prevailing there. The ultimate destination of much silver was still Central Sweden, Gotland and other Baltic trading centres, as the pattern of the hoards indicates: numerous Swedish hoards of dirhams date from the first half of the tenth century. It is clear that this east–west nexus was interlinked with the Middle Dnieper and beyond. Tablet-woven bands – silk threads on a ground of silver or golden wire – and silks of probable Byzantine origin have been found in tenth-century graves in Birka, while the throne of ibn Fadlan's Volga Bulgar host in 922 was covered in Byzantine

34 Ibid., p. 219; V. A. Bulkin and G. S. Lebedev, 'Gnëzdovo i Birka (k probleme stanovleniia goroda)', in A. N. Kirpichnikov and P. A. Rappoport, eds, *Kul'tura srednevekovoi Rusi* (Leningrad, 1974), pp. 11–17.

brocade. The brocade which the deceased Rus wore may well also have been of Byzantine manufacture (see above, p. 44), and silks of probable Byzantine origin have been found in barrows at Timerëvo and Gnëzdovo.[35] Amphorae fragments found in and around Staraia Ladoga and at Gorodishche and Beloozero and Byzantine coins also register imports from the south in the tenth century. Equally, there was trade between the Middle Dnieper region and the east and south-east. Hoards of Samanid dirhams have been discovered, especially in and around Kiev, where approximately 11,000 coins have been found. As has been noted (see p. 109), a route for transporting dirhams from the Middle Volga to Kiev is mentioned in a tenth-century oriental source. Nonetheless, other, more direct, routes led from the Middle Volga past the Iaroslavl settlements to Gorodishche, Staraia Ladoga or Gnëzdovo and on to the Baltic. And the total number of coins found at Kiev is far inferior to that of finds in the north.

All this sharpens the question raised earlier (see p. 125): what can have induced certain Rus to take up a stand on the Middle Dnieper and to persevere there? Why did they not settle for somewhere like Gnëzdovo – closer to the sources of high-quality furs, accessible to bearers of Arab silver, and still within reach of Byzantium? The answer lies in the conjunction of Rus talents with the circumstances described above. The Rus were impelled by greed and although most of them settled for trading as the most expedient way of obtaining primary produce and eastern silver, unremitting probes and experimentation characterized their way of life. Quietude was the goal of some, such as the agriculturalists working the land to the south-east of Lake Ladoga and beside Lake Beloozero (see above, p. 49), but many were on the look-out for lucrative new marketing arrangements. With self-discipline, ample weaponry and the Khazars' former tribute arrangements, the Rus could take produce and winter keep from the Dnieper Slavs while offering some protection against nomadic marauders. They were thereby freed from having to engage in agriculture for themselves. A further attraction was that they could obtain a considerable amount of produce without needing to offer anything in exchange, transporting it directly to a wealthy market, rather than having to sell to middlemen. Free accommodation and

35 A. Geijer, 'The textile finds from Birka', in N. B. Harte and K. G. Ponting, eds, *Cloth and Clothing in Medieval Europe. Essays in Memory of Professor E. M. Carus-Wilson* (London, 1983), pp. 93–6; I. Hägg, 'Birkas "orientalische Prunkgewänder"', *Fornvännen* 78 (1983), 221; M. V. Fekhner, 'Shelkovye tkani v srednevekovoi vostochnoi Evrope', *SA* 1982, no. 2, 62–3; D. A. Avdusin and T. A. Puškina, 'Three chamber graves at Gniozdovo', *Fornvännen* 83 (1988), 22–3, 26, 28; ibn Fadlan, *Risala*, ed. T. Lewicki, A. Kmietowicz and F. Kmietowicz, *Źródła arabskie do dziejów słowiańszczyzny* (Wroclaw, Warsaw, Cracow, Gdansk, Lodz, 1985), III, p. 58; tr. M. Canard, *Voyage chez les Bulgares de la Volga* (Paris, 1988), p. 63.

other privileges virtually guaranteed them a profit in Constantinople. Moreover the very paucity of numbers of the Dnieper Rus may well have been a positive advantage for those fit enough and willing to brave the risks. They could, if they survived, pile up the treasure from trading without having to share out the proceeds with numerous colleagues. A sizable amount of valuable goods and slaves could be shipped by a fairly small number of Rus, aided by the Slavs who floated tree-trunks down to Kiev every spring (see above, p. 119). Organized arms-bearing, in fact more or less continual soldiering, was thus closely bound up with trading. A few select – and, presumably, to some degree self-selecting – bands of Rus formed an essentially voluntary association in order to take fullest advantage of the opportunities for self-enrichment offered by the new waterway to the Greeks.

This association was, as we have seen, headed by a prince, Igor, and although his roots are placed by the *Primary Chronicle* in the north, he or his predecessors made the Middle Dnieper their base (above, pp. 57, 112). There may be a connection between this fact and the evidence of accelerating development at Gnëzdovo, Gorodishche and Staraia Ladoga from around the 930s onwards (see above, pp. 125–7). Igor still gave high priority to maintaining authority over the north, installing his only son in a town which Constantine VII calls 'Nemogardas', and which is most probably identifiable with Gorodishche, the Holmgarthr of the Norse sagas and the Novgorod of the *Primary Chronicle*'s references to the period before the eleventh century.[36] The infant Sviatoslav's presence there was symbolic – both of the prestige of the paramount family and of the importance which Igor attached to supervising the northern reaches of the waterway. The evidence of overlordship exercised by Igor or other members of the Kievan

36 The 'Nemogardas' of the *De administrando*'s manuscript was emended to 'Nevogardas' by J. B. Bury ('The treatise De administrando imperio', *Byzantinische Zeitschrift* 15 (1906), 543, n. 1). His emendation has been accepted by later scholars, e.g. D. Obolensky in R. J. H. Jenkins, ed., *De administrando imperio: II Commentary* (London, 1962), p. 26; *Ob upravl. imp.*, p. 310 (Mel'nikova and Petrukhin). It is quite possible that the settlement at Gorodishche then bore a name such as Nevogardas, corresponding to the Slavic form 'Novgorod' (literally, 'New Town'). It is no less possible that Gorodishche was known by a number of different names or hybrid forms, reflecting the heterogeneity of its population, and that it was Holmgarthr to newcomers from Scandinavia but Nemogardas in other languages or dialects. Kiev, too, was known by more than one name in the tenth century (see above, p. 95). The Slavic form Novgorod could already have been in currency then, being perhaps an adaptation of Nemogardas, or it could have been a relatively late development, only appearing after the shift of the centre of power and population to the new suburbs north of the old settlement in the eleventh century. See also, for a somewhat different reconstruction, E. Mühle, 'Von Holmgardr zu Novgorod. Zur Genesis des slavischen Ortsnamens der Ilmensee–Metropole im 11. Jahrhundert', in *Ex oriente lux. Mélanges offerts en hommage au professeur Jean Blankoff, à l'occasion de ses soixante ans* (Brussels, 1991), I, pp. 245–52; cf. *Encyclopaedia of Islam*, VIII, p. 622 (Golden).

leadership along the Volga basin is scanty. Admittedly, arguments from the virtually unbroken silence of the literary sources are inconclusive, but the archaeological evidence, too, is mute, save at the Iaroslavl settlements. Only in these are there hints of some sort of politico-military order, and the development of Timerëvo seems to have been much later than that of Staraia Ladoga and on a far smaller scale than there or at Gnëzdovo. A muffled echo of the distinctive nature of Rus activities in the Volga region may be preserved by the Arabic and Persian geographical writings of the tenth century. These speak of three 'kinds' (Arabic, ṣinf) of Rus. Despite or because of the obscurity of the names, much ingenuity has been spent in trying to identify them. Kiev is a convincing candidate for Kūyāba while Ṣalāwiya is presumably a reference to the Slavs living near the regions most accessible to Moslem traders, the Dnieper and the Upper Oka. It would not be surprising if the Rus settled in significant numbers on the Upper Volga were known by a name of their own to Moslem and other oriental travellers, especially since they had been dealing with the Rus and Finno-Ugrians from this quarter for so long. The third term, which is transmitted in many variants – Arsā, Urtāb, Artā, Artāniya – might be such a name.[37] One must beware of pressing the details. These oriental writers had only hazy notions of who the Rus were or where they lived, and their claims that the Arsā Rus 'do not say anything about their affairs' and that they 'kill any traveller who enters their land' do not ring true for the Volga Rus. But they have a certain value, in suggesting some awareness on the part of Moslem observers of divergent customs and trading practices among different groupings of Rus.

It is quite likely that the Iaroslavl settlements were, from their foundation, under the overlordship of a khagan based at Gorodishche, and they presumably remained or became affiliated to the regime which was instituted on the Dnieper. The total of chamber-graves reported at Timerëvo – twelve – is not negligible and if they can be interpreted as symbols of a self-assertive and wealthy elite, they point to links between the Iaroslavl settlements and the regime on the Dnieper. But the three settlements clustered there – Timerëvo, Petrovskoe and Mikhailovskoe – are drops in the ocean of the north-east. They had small permanent populations, whereas settlements such as the Sarskii fort were expanding and new ones forming in the tracts between the Volga and the Kliazma. The majority of their inhabitants were Finno-Ugrians, but groups of Slavs were now arriving in the north-east in substantial numbers, and the burial-grounds near Lakes Nero and

37 al-Istakhri, *Kitab Masalik al-Mamalik* [*Book of Ways of the Kingdoms*], ed. M. J. de Goeje (Leiden, 1870), pp. 225–6; *Hudud al-'Alam* [*The regions of the world*], tr. V. F. Minorsky (Gibb Memorial Series, New Series 11; London, 1970), pp. 434, 436; *Encyclopaedia of Islam*, VIII, p. 622 (Golden).

Pleshcheevo, Suzdal and Iurev-Polskoi also attest significant numbers of Rus men and women in the tenth century. The ornaments found in the barrows include tortoiseshell, circular and equal-armed brooches, ring brooches with long pins (worn only by Scandinavian males) and rings with silver pendants. Sword-chapes, battle-axes, spears, lancet-headed arrows and riding-gear indicate coercive capability, while Samanid dirhams, weights and balances and clay beavers' paws point to the settlers' most lucrative occupation.[38] The unscientific nature of the nineteenth-century excavations of the barrows and lack of investigation of the settlements impede assessment of their size or population composition. There are, as at Timerëvo, elements of Finno-Ugrian ornament and ritual which could denote intermingling between the newcomers and the local Finno-Ugrians. But as at Timerëvo, the absence of goods in a grave or the presence in it of local artefacts need not necessarily mean that a local inhabitant was buried there (see above, pp. 67–8). Whether or not the Rus settlers in the Volga-Kliazma watershed were co-residing with Finno-Ugrians and Slavs in the mid-tenth century, they do not seem to have formed a militarized elite analogous to that on the Dnieper and they were, like the Slavs, incomers from afar. They were rich in silver, numerous – probably exceeding the numbers of the Rus on the Middle Dnieper – and quite widely scattered. Their types of weapons and riding-gear resembled those of the Rus elsewhere, but the numbers of weapons excavated is not strikingly large and few swords have been reported. It seems that the Rus in the north-east did not close ranks to form a tighter organization, either to defend themselves against, or to intensify exploitation of, the Finno-Ugrians. The former course would have been unnecessary, and the latter impracticable. This may help to explain why the *locus* of political authority shifted from the shores of Lake Ilmen southwards to the Middle Dnieper and not to the east, even though it was from the latter quarter that all the silver flowed.

The leaders of the politico-military structure which emerged on the Dnieper had, in every sense, to 'deliver the goods' – produce and slaves – to the markets of Constantinople, and luxury goods and arms to

---

38 A. Spitsyn, 'Vladimirskie kurgany', *Izvestiia Arkheologicheskoi Kommissii* 15 (1905), 96–7 and *figs* 5–89, pp. 129–35; E. I. Goriunova, *Etnicheskaia istoriia volgo-okskogo mezhdurech'ia* (*MIA* 94; Moscow, Leningrad, 1961), pp. 192–4; E. A. Riabinin, 'Vladimirskie kurgany', *SA* 1979, no. 1, 232–41; I. V. Dubov, *Velikii volzhskii put'* (Leningrad, 1989), pp. 131–3; J. Callmer, 'The clay paw burial rite of the Åland islands and Central Russia: a symbol in action', *Current Swedish Archaeology* 2 (1994), fig. 18, p. 33; 36–7, 39. See also above, p. 68. Silver finds in a Merian burial-ground near the Volga are published by A. Belyakov, 'The coins and monetary pendants from the barrows near Pleshkovo village (late Viking age)', in K. Jonsson and B. Malmer, eds, *Sigtuna Papers. Proceedings of the Sigtuna Symposium on Viking-Age Coinage 1–4 June 1989* (Commentationes de nummis saeculorum IX–XI in Suecia repertis. Nova series 6; Stockholm, London, 1990), pp. 35–40.

those who helped them intimidate or police their tributaries. We have seen how pressed Igor was by his retainers in what seems to have been a lean season (see above, p. 117). Maintaining the link with Byzantium was, in effect, the *raison d'être* of the leadership and the choice articles imported from the south were the primary means of marking out the pre-eminent family, or families, and of rewarding associates and retainers. The khagan had, in the north, been essentially a figurehead, albeit supported by 400 warriors (see above, p. 45). So far as one can judge, the leaders of the Dnieper Rus were active warleaders. Their need for a steady inflow of revenue and profits of trade, and thus for amicable relations with the Byzantine emperor, was correspondingly pressing. This consideration may have underlain H-L-G-W's willingness to launch an attack on Khazar-held S-m-k-r-ts at the instigation of Romanos and also his reported reluctance subsequently to attack Constantinople (see above, p. 116). The pattern of needs, constraints and emerging aspirations provides a background to the activities of Olga, Igor's widow, who took over upon the death of Igor at the hands of the Derevlians, c. 945.

Olga's immediate aim after taking over was to put down the Derevlians' uprising, a task which she accomplished firmly and bloodily. Such, at least, is the impression given by the *Primary Chronicle*'s tales of her retribution on her husband's killers. She is said to have mounted an expedition on which her young son, Sviatoslav, served, trying vainly to toss his spear over his horse's head.[39] The Derevlians were defeated (see also below, p. 301), but Olga is said to have had to besiege their main town, Iskorosten, 'for a year' (*leto*), and even then she is depicted as only capturing it by means of a trick. The chronicle records in some detail the arrangements which she made for collecting tribute. She instituted 'camps and hunting grounds', and laid down the rules for payment. She also specified the proportions in which the tribute was to be paid, one-third to Olga's own town of Vyshgorod and two-thirds to Kiev. Olga was trying to introduce some routine into the exaction of tribute, presumably so as to reduce the risk of provoking another uprising. But she was also aiming to increase and regularize the inflow of produce from territories already securely under Kievan rule, along the Desna and the Dnieper itself, where 'netting places' for catching birds were instituted. And she travelled north to the valleys of the Msta and the Luga. The former provides one of the main waterways from Lake Ilmen to the Volga, while the latter rises near Lake Ilmen and debouches into the Gulf of Finland. Olga's itinerary suggests that she was organizing tribute-collection in regions where she disposed of longstanding authority, yet where hitherto tribute had only been collected irregularly, if at all. Pskov had been her home

39 *PVL*, I, p. 42.

town and, according to the chronicle, 'her sledge stands [there] to this day'.[40] Olga was probably not acting solely on her own account. She was rather acting on the part of her kinsmen and colleagues in the Dnieper-based elite to extend their tribute catchment area wherever this looked to be practicable. In further-flung regions, such as the Volga basin, the obstacles to more extensive exploitation were more than a match even for Olga.

The *Primary Chronicle*'s account of Olga's feats gives a clear idea of the sort of produce gathered as tribute – honey, and the furs and feathers of the creatures caught in the hunting-grounds and nets. The immense, thinly populated mixed forests (especially of oak intermingled with pine and spruce) stretching east and west from the Dnieper could yield plenty of high-quality wild bees' wax and honey. The chronicle also gives hints of which market the produce was principally destined for: the Byzantine emperor is depicted as asking Olga for 'slaves, wax and honey'.[41] There were other outlets – in Volga Bulgaria, Birka and the other Baltic markets. But easy access to the Middle Danube was impeded by Hungarian raiding bands, and the development of Gnëzdovo and the Middle Dnieper settlements points to the Byzantine south and specifically Constantinople as the focal point of Olga's exertions. It was to Constantinople, not the Volga or Baltic, that she paid a visit. Just afterwards, Emperor Constantine is depicted as asking her to send produce and also soldiers, maintaining that she had undertaken to do so during her discussions with him.[42] This is a clear sign that matters of trade ranked high on Olga's agenda. Another indication is the sheer quantity of 'traders' who attended the two receptions held in the Great Palace: 43 and 44 respectively, roughly double the number of envoys of the 'princes of Rhosia', and considerably more than the 28 named in the 944 treaty.[43] The involvement of foreign traders was uncommon in ceremonial receptions for embassies and potentates, and its occurrence during

---

40 Ibid., p. 43; Goehrke, *Frühzeit des Ostslaventums*, p. 156 and n. 378. At a site known as Borki III, in the Middle Desna valley, has been excavated a small settlement whose inhabitants specialized in the hunting of fur-clad animals. It probably resembled the sort of 'camps' set up by Olga: E. E. Antipina and S. P. Maslov, 'K voprosu ob organizatsii okhotnich'ego promysla v drevnei Rusi', *Arkheolohiia* 1994, no. 1, 60–4.

41 *PVL*, I, p. 45. On the forests best-suited for high-quality honey, see C. Warnke, 'Der Handel mit Wachs zwischen Ost- und Westeuropa im frühen und hohen Mittelalter. Voraussetzungen und Gewinnmöglichkeiten', *UHV, Abhandlungen der Akademie der Wissenschaften in Göttingen, philolog.-hist. Klasse*, 3. Folge, no. 156 (Göttingen, 1987), pp. 553–5.

42 *PVL*, I, p. 45.

43 *DC*, pp. 597, 598; *PVL*, I, pp. 34–5; A. V. Soloviev, 'L'organisation de l'État russe au X siècle', in A. Gieysztor and T. Manteuffel, eds, *L'Europe aux IX–XI siècles. Aux origines des États nationaux* (Warsaw, 1968), p. 254, repr. in Soloviev's *Byzance et la formation de l'État russe* (London, 1979), no. 1.

Olga's visit highlights the importance of the traders as a group. Traders had also been party to the treaty with Byzantium of 944 (see above, p. 118), and they, together with the representatives of 'the princes of Rhosia', may well have had a say in the negotiations between Olga and the imperial government. An initiative by the Rus leader and other members of the elite to facilitate trade with Byzantium and to amplify it is not especially surprising. They were jointly committed to bringing in the goods, and while the extreme hazardousness of the enterprise gave them the role of organizers and protectors, that role presupposed favourable trading terms and conditions at Constantinople.

Perhaps for this reason, Olga herself seems to have had a rather fuller agenda than trade talks for her stay. She brought two interpreters, a sign that she was expecting to hold substantive discussions. She was baptized and took as her Christian name that of Empress Helena, while Constantine is depicted as becoming her godfather. The *Primary Chronicle* has Constantine develop carnal as well as spiritual interests in Olga, to the point where he proposes marriage. Olga rebuffs him by pointing out that she could not wed a man who had baptized her and called her his daughter. 'Olga', the emperor replies, 'you have outwitted me!'[44] This tit-for-tat may well have its origins in tales told for entertainment in the halls of the princely elite, but there is no reason to dismiss the main points of the story. A Byzantine chronicle and a virtually contemporary German writer who had himself been in Kiev relate that Olga was baptized in Constantinople, while a marriage-tie of sorts could well have been discussed: the Rus are cited as one of the peoples liable to seek them in Constantine's *DAI*.[45] A contemporary Byzantine memorandum mentions a priest, Gregorios, as being a fairly prominent member of Olga's party: he dined and received donations together with the others.[46] While Gregorios' presence is not in itself conclusive, it corroborates the evidence of the other sources that matters of religion were on Olga's agenda.

Olga may have been drawn by personal needs or revelation to contemplate baptism, but her choice of Byzantine Orthodoxy as her creed and her decision – in middle age – to brave the Dnieper Rapids and be baptized in state in Tsargrad accord with the outlines of the political structure traceable in the literary and archaeological evidence reviewed above (see pp. 119–25). Already by 944 enough Rus were Christians for special provision to be made for their swearing to the terms of a treaty in a church. And the memorandum on Olga's receptions in the emperor's Great Palace seems both to register the Rus hierarchy of rank and to show how the ceremonial enhanced her

---

44 *PVL*, I, p. 44.
45 *DAI*, ch. 13.25, 104–10, pp. 66–7, 70–1.
46 *DC*, pp. 597, 598.

status. Olga was accompanied by a number of 'princesses', while male relatives also attended, together with envoys of 'the princes'. But Olga was singled out for special treatment. She stood in front of the empress and 'slightly bowed her head' while the other princesses performed ritual prostration, and she alone took dessert at a golden table together with the emperor and his family.[47] These scenes could only have been orchestrated in advance. Olga's nod of qualified deference or politeness to her hosts showed to her fellow-Rus that she could deal with the Greeks on amicable, if not quite equal, terms; the widow of a financially embarrassed and defunct prince was now accepted as a dining companion by the rulers of the Greeks. At the same time baptism in the Great Palace and adoption of Helena's name forged a personal and lasting bond between her and the royal family, placing her on a pedestal higher than that of the celebrated Kii (see above, p. 94).

However, Olga probably also hoped for more tangible benefits from the ceremonial and discussions which she was carrying out in person. Speculation as to her precise goals is hazardous, but they probably involved lifting restrictions which the 944 treaty had imposed, for example, the ban on the Rus wintering in the Dnieper estuary and the limitation of the amounts of silks purchasable (see above, p. 118). But neither a treaty nor a marriage-tie crowned Olga's stay in Tsargrad, which dragged on until at least late October, when the Black Sea's weather becomes unpropitious for sailing vessels. That the visit did not end on a note of harmony is suggested by the *Primary Chronicle*'s account of Olga's response to the emperor's request for produce and military aid. Olga is depicted as replying, 'If you will stay with me on the Pochaina [in Kiev] as long as I did in the Sound [the Golden Horn], then I will send [these] to you'.[48] This vignette, like the tale of an infatuated emperor's propositioning of Olga, inverts the real balance of play, if the requests were in fact put by her to Constantine.

One further indication that Olga was taking bold initiatives and failed to gain satisfaction at Constantinople comes from the forementioned German chronicler, Adalbert. By autumn 959 Olga was in contact with Otto I, king of the German lands, asking for 'the ordination of a bishop and priests for [. . . her] people'.[49] Adalbert himself was eventually consecrated bishop and sent off. Olga had been trying to dignify and tighten her dealings with the Byzantines, and adoption of

---

47 Ibid., pp. 595, 597.
48 *PVL*, I, p. 45.
49 Adalbert, *Continuatio Reginonis*, ed. A. Bauer and R. Rau, in *Quellen zur Geschichte der Sächsischen Kaiserzeit* (Ausgewählte Quellen zur Deutschen Geschichte des Mittelalters 8; Darmstadt, 1971), pp. 214–15. The validity of Adalbert's indication that Olga was primarily seeking a religious mission is advocated by A. V. Nazarenko, 'Rus' i Germaniia v IX–Xvv.', *DGVEMI* (1994), pp. 65–9.

their form of worship was one means of bringing this about. She was trying to further with the help of a full-blown mission the cult she had taken on, acting as its chief patron and organizer in Kiev. The obvious source of priests and a bishop was Byzantium, with whose ruler and creed Olga was now conspicuously associated: Adalbert, writing in the later 960s, knew her by the baptismal name she had taken from Empress Helena. If Olga turned to Otto of Saxony by 959, it was most probably because she had failed to obtain from Byzantium the sort of mission she wanted. This, too, could account for the rather sour note on which her exchanges with Constantine VII apparently ended.

It is of no very great consequence precisely when Olga visited Tsargrad and received baptism from the emperor. On the whole, the dates of 954–5 or 955–6, indicated by the Kievan sources, or 957, deducible from the Byzantine memorandum on the receptions, are the most plausible.[50] Olga, once baptized, is unlikely to have delayed very long before trying to provide fuller pastoral care for her fellow-Rus. Her *démarche* towards Otto in or before 959 would probably have been in the wake of the Byzantines' rejection. More important is the failure of Adalbert's mission to the Rus. He relates that he returned, since he was labouring in vain and unable to achieve any of 'those things on account of which he had been sent'.[51] On the homewards journey some members of his party were killed and he himself 'barely' escaped. Adalbert claims that Olga's request had been false, but it is questionable whether he or King Otto had ever been fervently interested in evangelizing what was for them a far-away country.

Olga's successive initiatives towards the Byzantines and the Germans are of more general significance. The leaders of the Rus were not very long-established on the Middle Dnieper, and for all the ingenuity of their trading organization and their strenuous efforts to work it, they were far from secure. For that very reason, their paramount princess put out feelers towards established rulers, seeking visible associations and access to the potent cults they patronized. The underlying objective of Olga was to consolidate her leadership of the structure which was emerging on the Dnieper. In a way, this was also a sophisticated variant of the attempts of earlier generations of Rus to seek out new sources

---

50 On the numerous recent attempts to date Olga's visit, see A. Poppe, 'Once again concerning the baptism of Olga, Archontissa of Rus'', in A. Cutler and S. Franklin, eds, *Homo Byzantinus. Papers in Honor of Alexander Kazhdan*, DOP 46 (1992), 271–3; Goehrke, *Frühzeit des Ostslaventums*, pp. 148–9 and n. 333 on p. 252. A dating to 957 is favoured by Nazarenko, 'Rus' i Germaniia', p. 69 and n. 59 on p. 77; Poppe suggests a first trip to Constantinople – and baptism there – in 954 or 955, followed by another visit in autumn 957: 'Baptism of Olga', 273.

51 Adalbert, *Continuatio Reginonis*, ed. Bauer and Rau, pp. 218–19; cf. Poppe, 'Baptism of Olga', 274–5.

of treasure far to the east, south or west. As Olga's commercial and diplomatic initiatives show, Byzantium was the obvious first port of call. But Byzantine cooperation or even goodwill could not be counted upon. In fact, as the *DAI's* opening chapters show, the government of Constantine VII looked on the new power astride the Dnieper with suspicion, and was primarily concerned with methods of containing the Rus to the north of the steppes. The Byzantines' apprehensions were ill-judged, so far as Olga herself was concerned. But their doubts about the future prospects and intentions of the Rus on the Dnieper were not groundless. As events would soon show, the Rus alertness to new opportunities, their quest for more convenient trade-routes and their readiness for experimentation were not yet done.

CHAPTER FOUR

U-Turns and Conversion
(c. 960–1015)

1. THE LAST MIGRATION: SVIATOSLAV ON THE DANUBE

The efforts of Olga to safeguard and further Rus trade with the Byzantines and to propagate her new-found cult have left no direct archaeological trace. Not one Byzantine artefact or church building can be unequivocally attributed to the fifteen years or so Olga spent as a Christian in Kiev, where she was served, presumably, by Eastern Orthodox clergy. In fact the number of solid objects of unquestionably tenth-century Byzantine provenance, whether coins or ornaments, found along the Dnieper Way is small. This, and the apparently inconclusive outcome of Olga's negotiations at Constantinople, tends to blur the implications of other forms of archaeological evidence of the middle and second half of the tenth century.

There are many signs of economic dynamism and population growth in the Rus lands. In the north-east, the Iaroslavl settlements were flourishing as centres of trading, albeit on a more modest scale than Gnëzdovo or Gorodishche, and the Rus settlements in the vicinity of Lake Nero, Lake Pleshcheevo and elsewhere between the Volga and the Kliazma proliferated (see above, pp. 125, 132). A new centre arose near the Sarskii fort, developing into the town known to our sources as Rostov. By the late tenth century a considerable number of Slavs had joined the settlements or formed separate ones of their own. They were probably drawn there by the commercial exchanges involving silver, as well as by the fertility of the tracts of land in river valleys such as the Nerl.

To the north-west, Staraia Ladoga's building development continued, while at the opposite end of the Volkhov the new settlements just outside Gorodishche expanded rapidly. For example, by c. 1000 building development on the site of the later Liudin district stretched far enough north to join up with the group of structures on the site of what would become the Kremlin of Novgorod. New sections of the main streets were being paved with wooden duckboards and by the beginning of the 990s the street which gained the name 'Velikaia' ('Great') was paved along its entire length. A connection between this development and 'the way from the Varangians to the Greeks' is suggested by the growth of settlements along the routes between the Lovat and the Western Dvina from the second half of the tenth century onwards. Mostly these were small communities of boatmen and portagers along rivers such as the Usviacha, but a promontory fort was established at Toropets in the second half of the tenth century and an extensive settlement developed near the fort at Polotsk at about the same time. By the 970s Polotsk was important enough to serve as the base of a Scandinavian magnate (see below, p. 152). Further south, at Gnëzdovo, nearly all the 'big barrows' – those several metres high and 25 or more metres in diameter – date from the middle or second half of the tenth century. Their grave goods are the richest in Gnëzdovo (see above, p. 127).

The foundation and expansion of these settlements cannot be put down wholly to population growth or new arrivals from the Baltic world. There was an influx of Scandinavians to centres such as Gorodishche and Gnëzdovo, but they only made up a small minority of the population at Gnëzdovo. Judging by the burial-ground, a far larger proportion of the thousand or so round-the-year residents were Slavic, and semi-underground dwellings characteristic of the Slavs have been excavated. In and around the huts, dirhams and pendants of silver have been unearthed, offering clues as to what drew the Slavs there from the south and the west.[1] They gravitated towards Gnëzdovo or the settlements at portages and other points along such rivers as the Kasplia, which linked the Upper Dnieper with the Dvina. They did not branch away from the transit routes into the areas where the population – scattered across vast tracts of forest – consisted mainly of Balts. For their part, a number of Balts moved into Gnëzdovo, including the newly emergent settlement on the Olsha (see above, pp. 101, 127). There is no evidence that the settlements at Gnëzdovo or elsewhere between the Dnieper and the Lovat were partitioned between the different ethnic groups. Judging by the combinations of goods and burial rituals in the graveyards, there was intermingling and, most probably, intermarriage between the three main groups at Gnëzdovo in the later tenth century.[2]

The Scandinavians, Slavs and Balts at Gnëzdovo shared an interest in being able to deal easily with one another for the purposes of exchange. It is very probable that they did so in Slavonic. By the mid-tenth century, at latest, the Scandinavians on the Middle Dnieper

1 D. A. Avdusin et al., 'Raskopki v Gnëzdove', *Arkheologicheskie Otkrytiia za 1979 god* (Moscow, 1980), 43–4; T. A. Pushkina, 'Raboty gnezdovskogo otriada', *Arkheologicheskie Otkrytiia za 1981 god* (Moscow, 1983), 82–3.
2 E. Mühle, *Die städtischen Handelszentren der nordwestlichen Rus'. Anfänge und frühe Entwicklung altrussischer Städte (bis gegen Ende des 12. Jahrhunderts)* (Quellen und Studien zur Geschichte des östlichen Europa 32; Stuttgart, 1991), pp. 250–1.

were using Slavic terms and members of the leading princely family were known by Slavic names (see above, p. 118). But the inhabitants of Gnëzdovo and other trading posts further north could well have had reason to speak at least a smattering of Balt or Finno-Ugric. For there is evidence of trade, in the form of small-scale finds of ornaments such as women's rings manufactured in Gnëzdovo but unearthed in native settlements set well back from the north–south riverways.[3] Another, smaller, centre of production of pottery and ornaments as well as boat repairs has been found on the bank of the Upper Lovat, near modern Velikie Luki. The inhabitants of the expanding conglomerates do not seem to have gone in for agriculture. They counted on being able to satisfy their daily wants with produce obtained from growers in the surrounding countryside (see above, p. 126). At the same time, weapons such as bows and arrows, swords and battle-axes are a fairly prominent find in Gnëzdovo, Gorodishche and even Staraia Ladoga for the mid- and second half of the tenth century. Part of the produce was being extracted by means of coercion or the threat of coercion, and wherever the catchment areas for the slave-trade may have lain, weapons were needed to guard the captives, not least from other slave-handlers. A mixture of trade with tribute is what the *Primary Chronicle* gives reason to expect, in relating Olga's measures to institute 'camps and hunting grounds' among the Derevlians and along major rivers in the vicinity of Gorodishche and her native Pskov.[4] The surpluses accumulated through tribute provided an incentive for others to gather goods and exchange them for a few of the luxury goods which the primary produce earned abroad.

Much of this produce, waxen, animal or human, was bound for the south and, ultimately, Byzantium. Dirhams seem to have ceased arriving in the Middle Dnieper region around the middle of the tenth century. Presumably, Kiev's traders and rulers came to rely chiefly on Cherson and Constantinople as outlets, although ever alert for openings elsewhere. There is no sign of Kiev's prosperity faltering during the later tenth century: on the contrary, business and the number of persons engaged in it was expanding, in so far as the finds in the Starokievskaia burial-ground and the Podol can be dated.[5] The stray finds in the graves of silver Byzantine coins probably bear inadequate witness to a trade link whose most valuable imported item was silk and other forms of precious cloth. Fragments of Byzantine

---

3 Ibid., p. 249 and n. 64.
4 *PVL*, I, p. 43; see also above, p. 133.
5 M. K. Karger, *Drevnii Kiev* (Moscow, Leningrad, 1958), I, pp. 226–7; M. A. Sahaidak, *Davn'o-kyivs'kyi Podil: problemy topohrafii, stratihrafii, khronolohii* (Kiev, 1991), pp. 91–2, 94, 126. Survey of urban development elsewhere in V. P. Darkevich, 'Proiskhozhdenie i razvitie gorodov drevnei Rusi (X–XIIIvv.)', *Voprosy Istorii* 1994, no. 10, 53–5.

silks have been found in the burial-grounds of Kiev, Shestovitsy, Gnëzdovo and Birka, and the quite numerous fragments of silks excavated in tenth-century strata at York and Lincoln very probably arrived from Byzantine or Middle Eastern workshops along the East Way.[6] The prominence given to silks in the 944 Rus-Byzantine treaty points clearly to the luxury product which made the hazards of the sea voyage to Constantinople worthwhile for the Rus (see above, p. 118).

However, the voyage was not made easier by the increasing use of the Dnieper route which this commercial activity engendered. In fact, the more traffic plied the river, the more tempting a target it presented to predatory nomads. As we shall see, the Pechenegs could still bar the Rapids (see below, p. 150). Thus the Rus were locked into a kind of 'prosperity trap' which no amount of organization of convoys and collective security could spring. The desire for active Byzantine cooperation in trying to police the route and hold the nomads at bay may well have been one of Olga's objectives in visiting the emperor. The arms and tightening organization of the Rus enabled them to amass ever larger amounts of marketable produce, but they remained vulnerable and so were 'much concerned to keep the peace with the Pechenegs', in the words of the nomads' ultimate paymaster.[7] Judging by the archaeological evidence, the Pechenegs gravitated towards the basins of major rivers, including the Ros south of Kiev. They were thus well placed to exercise a virtual stranglehold over those Rus who ventured southwards.

It is against this background that the deeds of Sviatoslav Igorevich and his son and eventual heir, Vladimir, should be viewed. The volume of trading with the south increased, for all the hazards of the journey. And the princely elite on the Dnieper were expected to try to foster it, as well as engaging directly in the trade. Olga's mission to Tsargrad marks one conspicuous attempt to carry out this role (see above, p. 134). Sviatoslav's campaigns are at first sight wholly at odds with his mother's policies, but there is a fundamental continuity of purpose – to lessen the handicaps under which the Rus operated, if necessary by moving operations to a more convenient vantage-point.

The *Primary Chronicle*, it is true, highlights a contrast between mother and son. Olga is portrayed as trying to persuade Sviatoslav to adopt Christianity. He refuses, pleading, 'My retainers will laugh at this'.[8] And if Olga sat at the dining table reserved for ladies of high rank in the Great Palace – perhaps herself a *zōstē patrikia*[9] –

---

6 R. Hall, *Book of Viking Age York* (London, 1994), pp. 85–7, 102. See also above, p. 129.

7 *DAI*, ch. 2.5–6, pp. 48–51.

8 *PVL*, I, 129, p. 46.

9 *DC*, p. 597; A. Poppe, 'Once again concerning the baptism of Olga, Archontissa of Rus'', in A. Cutler and S. Franklin, eds, *Homo Byzantinus. Papers in Honor of Alexander Kazhdan*, DOP 46 (1992), 273.

Sviatoslav was unmoved by such cultural blandishments. He did not accompany his mother and cousin to Constantinople, although aged fifteen or more by the mid-950s, the earliest likely date of the visit. Sviatoslav's lifestyle is presented in the *Primary Chronicle* as follows: 'Moving light as a leopard, making many wars, he did not take wagons on his travels, nor kettles, neither did he have his meat boiled. But he would cut off a strip of horseflesh, game or beef, roast it on the coals and eat. There was no tent for him, he just laid him out a sweat-cloth, with a saddle at his head.'[10]

This picture of a rough-riding warrior, though legendary in style, fits well with the image of Sviatoslav in an almost contemporary Byzantine chronicle. At the time of his surrender to the emperor on the Danube in 971, Sviatoslav wore a plain white garment – 'differing from those of the others only in its cleanliness' – and a bejewelled gold ring in one ear, while his scalp was shaven save for a long strand of hair, 'displaying the nobility of his kin'.[11] A similar hairstyle was sported by contemporary Hungarian warriors, by leading Bulgarians and probably also by Turkic steppe nomads. In the thirteenth century a shaven scalp with a few hairs hanging over one ear was 'a sign of nobility' among the Zichians living in and around Tmutorokan (a later name for S-m-k-r-ts),[12] and later still the Cossacks styled their hair this way. Sviatoslav seems deliberately to have taken on the appearance of a nomad chieftain and although this eye-witness description pictures him at the end of his campaigning days, it is compatible with his conduct earlier in his brief yet hectic reign.

Some time in the mid-960s, after finally taking over from his mother, Sviatoslav launched an attack on the Khazars and broke their power. The inhabitants of the principal town, Itil, fled before the Rus, who pushed further south to the Caspian port of Samander. An Arab visitor to the Caspian a few years later heard that after the onslaught there remained 'not even the leaf on the stalk'; the vineyards had all been devastated and the terror-stricken inhabitants fled.[13] The Rus captured the main fortress of the Khazars on the Lower Don, Sarkel, and they most probably sacked S-m-k-r-ts on the Straits of Kerch. Excavators of the latter observed 'a mighty conflagration layer' in strata datable to around the mid-tenth century.[14] According to the *Primary Chronicle*,

---

10 *PVL*, I, p. 46.

11 Leo Deac., pp. 156–7.

12 A. Theiner, ed., *Vetera monumenta historica Hungariam sacram illustrantia* (Rome, 1859), I, p. 152.

13 ibn Hawkal, *Kitab Surat al-Ard* [*Book of the Configuration of the Earth*], *Opus Geographicum: 'Liber imaginis terrae'*, ed. J. H. Kramers (Leiden, 1939), II, p. 393; tr. J. H. Kramers and G. Wiet, *Configuration de la terre* (Beirut, Paris, 1964), II, p. 384.

14 A. V. Gadlo, 'Vostochnyi pokhod Sviatoslava (k voprosu o nachale Tmutarakanskogo kniazheniia)', in *Problemy v istorii feodal'noi Rossii* (Leningrad, 1971), pp. 61–2. See also above, pp. 107–8.

Sviatoslav also 'defeated the Alans and the Kasogians'.[15] The latter lived east of the Straits while the Alans' abode was in the foothills of the northern Caucasus. This was an extraordinary feat of arms, achieved against a power which was still a major player in the steppes in the mid-tenth century. Constantine VII had regarded the Khazars as potential aggressors against Byzantium's possessions on the Crimea, although themselves vulnerable to attack by the Uzes (Oghuz), the Black Bulgars and, above all, the Alans.[16]

Modern historians have debated Sviatoslav's aims in lashing out against Khazaria, but there is no need to look beyond the *Primary Chronicle* and the *DAI* and the background of mounting commercial activity. According to the chronicle, Sviatoslav visited the Viatichi, who lived well to the north-east of the Middle Dnieper, along the Oka. They told him that they paid tribute to the Khazars at the rate of one 'shilling' – presumably really a dirham – per wooden ploughshare. The following year, 'Sviatoslav went against the Khazars' and in the year after that he 'defeated the Viatichi and imposed tribute on them'.[17] In other words, Sviatoslav attacked the Khazars in order to wrest from them the overlordship of an important and relatively prosperous grouping of Slavs.

The Viatichi consisted in part of fugitives from the Slav forts and settlements on the left bank of the Dnieper or their descendants. They had withdrawn before the Pechenegs' razzias to the relative security of the forests beyond the Oka, but they apparently maintained ties with the Khazars of a sort not greatly different from their predecessors' in the ninth century (see above, p. 77). This did not in itself preclude trade between the Viatichi and areas under Rus overlordship, and the route between Kiev and Volga Bulgaria mentioned in tenth-century oriental sources passed through their lands (see above, p. 109). At the same time, the Khazars were manifestly vulnerable to raids from neighbouring steppe peoples. This made them fair game for a prince intent on continuing Olga's policy of expanding the catchment area of tribute-payers. Sviatoslav may well have been driven by a further ambition which the chronicle does not spell out, but which the 944 treaty intimates: the Rus desire to mitigate the hazards of the long haul south with a foothold on the Black Sea. By removing Khazar influence from the steppes to the south-east, Sviatoslav could take advantage of routes along the Donets and Don valleys which had been in use when contacts were first struck up between Staraia Ladoga and Khazaria (see above, pp. 25–6). Sviatoslav's subjugation of the Kasogians and Alans also opened up possible routes across the Kuban

15 *PVL*, I, p. 47.
16 *DAI*, chs 10.3–6; 12.3–4; pp. 62–5.
17 *PVL*, I, s.a. 964 (6472), 966 (6474), pp. 46–7; cf. A. N. Sakharov, *Diplomatiia Sviatoslava* (Moscow, 1991), p. 93.

steppes to the Caspian, while the destruction of S-m-k-r-ts brought unrestricted access to the Black Sea. This fortress had been the object of attention from the Rus leadership in the 930s, perhaps partly for similar reasons (see above, p. 116).

Sviatoslav's strike against the Khazars removed from the scene a debilitated but still intrusive neighbour. According to ibn Hawkal, he also attacked the Volga Bulgars and the Burtas[18] and if, as is likely, this report is accurate, it suggests that Sviatoslav was trying to clear, if not control, the existing outlets leading to the Samanids' silver, as well as opening up new ones via the Caspian. He can hardly have conducted these fast-moving operations solely in the customary fashion, by boats and footsoldiering. Sviatoslav and his men probably did much of their campaigning on horseback, nomad-style, as the chronicle pictures them. This was not a total innovation, in that the Rus had been using the nomads' riding-gear, presumably picking up something of their horsemanship, for two generations. Sviatoslav also formed an alliance with the Oghuz, and it was probably a coordinated attack on the Khazars from two sides which overwhelmed them.

Soon after Sviatoslav's campaigns in the Don and Kuban steppes he was invited by the Byzantine government to attack remote relatives of the Volga Bulgars, the Bulgarians on the Danube. Sviatoslav was not expected to leap at the opportunity, judging by the size of the sweetener presented to him in advance – 1,500 lb of gold. There was nothing inherently new or remarkable in the emperor's bribing of the Rus (see above, p. 116). The Rus sack of S-m-k-r-ts seems to have been received with equanimity or approval in Byzantium. What the Byzantines did not foresee was that Sviatoslav would take a liking to the Danube region, and their habitual methods of containing the Rus proved ineffectual.

Sviatoslav's awakening to the advantages of a Balkan base is reported in quite similar terms by the *Primary Chronicle* and Byzantine chroniclers. According to John Skylitzes, the Rus 'marvelled at the fertility of the region', while the *Primary Chronicle* puts the following words into Sviatoslav's mouth: 'It is not my pleasure to be in Kiev, but I will live in Pereiaslavets on the Danube. That shall be the centre of my land; for there all good things flow: gold from the Greeks, precious cloths, wines and fruit of many kinds; silver and horses from the Czechs and Hungarians; and from the Rus furs, wax, honey and slaves'.[19] Clearly, one of the area's attractions for

---

18 ibn Hawkal, ed. Kramers, II, pp. 393, 397–8; tr. Kramers and Wiet, II, pp. 384, 388.
19 PVL, I, p. 48; Leo Deac., p. 105; Skyl., p. 288. The Byzantine chronicles depict Kalokyras, the emperor's emissary, as egging on Sviatoslav in order to gain backing for his own bid for the throne. This aspect of Sviatoslav's drive into the Balkans is probably historical, but while Kalokyras may have encouraged Sviatoslav to exceed the terms of his Byzantine brief, he was probably not decisive in inducing him permanently to relocate. For Pereiaslavets, see below, p. 147.

Sviatoslav was its choice of convenient trade-routes. As has been emphasized above (pp. 119–20), the Middle Dnieper had never been a particularly convenient assembly-point. The Rus came to it late, probably after they had begun trading on the Middle Danube as well as the Volga. Now, the defeat of the Hungarians by Otto I in 955 and the subsequent work of Byzantine and German missionaries opened up opportunities for continuous trading with Central Europe via the Danube. Lulled, perhaps, by the Rus' evident appetite for their goods, the Byzantines failed to realize the alacrity with which the Rus could change the directions of their trade. Sviatoslav's feat in forging an alliance with the Oghuz should perhaps have been a warning that the Rus now had an outstandingly versatile chief.

Sviatoslav invaded Bulgaria in, probably, late summer 968 and his forces encountered little resistance as they devastated its towns. Sviatoslav outstayed the term of what the Byzantines considered appropriate and, probably at Byzantine instigation, the Pechenegs raided up to Kiev, blockading the town. The inhabitants, whose numbers had been rising over the past half-century, faced starvation, and the ageing Olga is said to have contemplated surrender. According to the *Primary Chronicle*, the day was saved by a 'boy' who 'knew Pecheneg and they took him for one of their own', as he ran through the nomads' lines, carrying a bridle and pretending to look for his horse.[20] Once at the Dnieper's bank, he stripped off his clothes and plunged in, swimming across the river under Pecheneg arrow-fire. He persuaded Pretich, the leader of the armed men on the opposite bank, of the gravity of the Kievans' plight. Pretich duped the Pechenegs into believing that his was merely the advance guard of Sviatoslav's host, coming to the relief of Kiev. An agreement was reached; subsequently Sviatoslav did arrive 'and drove the Pechenegs out into the steppes and there was peace'.[21]

This tale registers some change in the condition of the Rus on the Dnieper. The boy's knowledge of Pecheneg implies fairly commonplace intercourse with them, while Pretich's ritual exchange with the Pecheneg chief of sword and shield for sabre and arrows suggests some ability to treat with the nomads. Sviatoslav soon proved capable of building upon this achievement, forging an alliance with significant groupings of them. Presumably by this time, if not before, he was sporting his shaven scalp and single lock of hair. Moreover, this story of the mustering of an armed force from the left bank of the Dnieper could be linked to the archaeological evidence from burial-grounds in and around Chernigov. The inhabitants of the region were capable of fielding a kind of militia which was lighter-armed than members of the elite, and unaccustomed to following closely upon events at Kiev. It was now nonetheless able

20 *PVL*, I, p. 47.
21 Ibid., p. 48.

and willing to go to the Kievans' aid, albeit not in pitched battle (see above, p. 114).

Sviatoslav returned to the Lower Danube, intent on occupation, probably in the autumn of 969. Rus women accompanied the men to the south, as the Byzantines would later discover while stripping the dead of their possessions. Byzantine writers impute to Sviatoslav the ambition of seizing Constantinople and, according to Leo the Deacon, he denied the Byzantines' right to the European provinces of their empire.[22] But his actions fit in well enough with the *Primary Chronicle*'s version of his aims: to establish himself at Pereiaslavets, in the Danube delta. Pereiaslavets has been identified with modern Prislava (Nufărul), on a branch of the Danube.[23] It would not have been in Sviatoslav's interest to make an attempt on the imperial capital itself. He cannot have been unaware of the difficulties of storming the sea-walls from small boats (see above, p. 114).

Sviatoslav showed judgement in confining his ambitions to lands outside the imperial frontiers. He probably hoped to do business with the Greeks from a new position of strength. Both the *Primary Chronicle* and a Byzantine chronicle register his interest in the forts and towns along the Danube. Sviatoslav assigned garrisons to the more important of them, such as Dorostolon (Dristra, modern Silistra). The inhabitants of others acknowledged his overlordship.[24] There is little evidence of commerce from the Lower Danube to Central Europe before this time. Such exchanges as there were probably crossed the river and were between the Bulgarians and the steppe peoples. But, as we have seen, the Middle Dnieper did not carry many trading boats before the Rus spotted an opportunity and installed themselves (see above, pp. 92–3).

Quite recently, the Rus had sought control of a trading centre of strategic significance in the Caucasus. Their seizure of the fortified city of Barda'a c. 944 throws sidelights on Sviatoslav's enterprise. The episode seems to represent the reaction of a group of Rus led by H-L-G-W to the failure of Igor's attack on Byzantium (see above, p. 117). But these Rus, like Sviatoslav's warriors, took their women with them and they may well have been on the look-out for a lucrative new

22 Leo Deac., p. 105.
23 N. Oikonomides, 'Presthlavitza, the Little Preslav', *Südost-Forschungen* 42 (1983), 7–9. The identification was denied by S. Baraschi, 'Unele probleme despre Proslavita', *Peuce, Studii şi communicări de istorie veche, arheologie şi numismatică*, Tulcea, 10.1 (1991), 399–409; ibid., 10.2 (1991), fig. 1, 373 (map). However, the site was of particular importance – and is thus a strong candidate for Sviatoslav's base – judging by the abundant finds there of late tenth-century Byzantine copper coins, suggestive of a sizable garrison after Tzimiskes' conquest: G. Mănucu-Adameşteanu, 'Circulaţia monetară la Nufăru în secolele X–XIV', *Peuce* 10.1 (1991), 497–501. But see V. B. Perkhavko, 'Gde zhe nakhodilsia dunaiskii grad Pereiaslavets?', *Byzantinoslavica* 55 (1994), 278–90.
24 *PVL*, I, pp. 47, 50; Skyl., pp. 301, 310.

base. They offered both intimidation and order to the inhabitants of Barda'a. Just after arriving, they issued a proclamation to the citizens: 'There is no dispute between us on the matter of religion, we only desire sovereignty; it is our duty to treat you well, and yours to be loyal to us'.[25] Subsequently, they resorted to harsher measures, being greedy for valuables; but once a ransomed man had persuaded them he had no more belongings, he was released with 'a piece of stamped clay to serve as a safe-conduct'.[26] These Rus proved capable of supervising and, for many months, defending a large, prosperous town.

A similar mix of intimidation and *laissez-faire* was shown in the Balkans. One of Sviatoslav's first actions on his return served to strike terror into the Bulgarians. Some 20,000 captives are said to have been impaled in Philippopolis so as to terrify into submission those still holding out. However, Sviatoslav saw the advantage in attaching important Bulgarians to his cause. He allowed their ruler, Boris, to remain in Preslav and to retain the trappings of imperial status, such as crowns and purple robes. Such indulgence helped gain acceptance from many Bulgarians and their warriors were to fight obstinately by the side of the Rus. They were all the more useful in that the Rus numbers were probably modest, for all the Byzantine sources' extravagant claims. But allying with large numbers of nomads was Sviatoslav's outstanding feat of diplomacy. Pechenegs and also Hungarians from Central Europe joined him to form a huge host.[27]

Sviatoslav's recruitment of numerous Hungarians highlights his interest in the Danube route to Central Europe. Commercial interests were thus attuned to politic calculation: Sviatoslav at 'Little Preslav' (the meaning of Pereiaslavets) would keep his distance from Boris' court at Preslav; the Bulgarians' antipathy towards the Byzantines and loyalty towards their own royal family would thus be harnessed to him. Meanwhile Sviatoslav could hope for revenues from trade along the Danube and past its mouth, which his governors in the strongpoints on the river could tap and stimulate. These revenues in turn would finance gifts for the steppe peoples, bringing security to the routes between the Danube and the lands of the Rus. The military presence which he seems to have established on the Upper Dniester provided one means of retaining contact with, and hegemony over, the northern lands.

Sviatoslav's mounted hordes ranged south into Byzantine territory, but no attempt was made to install garrisons south of the Haemus. Sviatoslav was probably beguiled into believing that the Byzantines acquiesced in his presence in Bulgaria. At any rate, he did not post

25 Miskawayh, *Tajarib al-umam* [*The Experiences of the Nations*], in *The Eclipse of the Abbasid Caliphate*, ed. H. F. Amedroz (Oxford, 1921), II, p. 63; tr. D. S. Margoliouth (Oxford, 1921), V, p. 68.
26 Miskawayh, ed. Amedroz, p. 64; tr. Margoliouth, p. 70.
27 Leo Deac., p. 108; Skyl., p. 288.

guards to the Haemus passes. Emperor John Tzimiskes exploited this oversight to lead a cavalry force through the mountains and at once attack Preslav, the Bulgarian capital. Not even the fierce resistance led by the Rus commander of the garrison, one Sphangel or Sphenkel, could prevent the Byzantines from storming the walls. The Bulgarian royal family, complete with their regalia, were led off into captivity.

Sviatoslav himself was in Dristra and it seems that many other Rus were stationed on or near the Danube. The number of warriors at Sviatoslav's disposal was still substantial, though he now summoned and executed 300 leading Bulgarians whose loyalties he doubted. He felt confident enough to fight a pitched battle and there are said to have been 'twelve turns of the tide',[28] but eventually the Rus fled back into the town. The Rus had reportedly been fighting on foot until this point, holding their ground with the help of long shields joined together to form a shield-wall. They now sallied forth from Dristra on horseback and suffered heavy losses, whereas Byzantine casualties amounted to just three horses.[29] This suggests that Sviatoslav's army was of a different make-up from the one which had devastated Khazaria and, perhaps, from that of his first Bulgarian campaign. If he opted initially to deploy the Rus as infantry in 971, it was probably because he was counting on his nomad confederates to provide cavalry, swamping the enemy through weight of numbers. Now, however, the Pechenegs and Hungarians drifted away, encouraged, probably, by imperial bribes. Meanwhile the Byzantine fleet sailed up the Danube to bar escape by water, and famine set in.

What did not happen next is more remarkable than what eventually did. Dristra, although crowded with people, did not succumb to starvation, disease or the emperor's storm-troopers. More than two months of inconclusive fighting followed and as late as 21 July 971 the Rus proved momentarily capable of driving the Byzantine forces back. As a Byzantine chronicler admits, 'the outcome of the war was in no way decided'.[30] The emperor, in challenging Sviatoslav to settle the issue by single combat, showed his desperation. Sviatoslav is reported to have spurned Tzimiskes' offer and the fighting went on. However, a few days later he sent a message, offering to release prisoners-of-war and withdraw to the north, provided that he and his people received grain and safe-conduct; significantly, the right of the Rus to bring their goods for sale in Constantinople itself was also to be reaffirmed. All Sviatoslav's requests were granted and, after terms had been agreed, there was a meeting between the two leaders. Tzimiskes rode his horse to the bank. Sviatoslav arrived in a small boat, rowing 'as one of the

---

28 Skyl., p. 300.
29 Leo Deac., pp. 133, 143; Skyl., pp. 300–1.
30 Skyl., p. 307.

others' of his crew; he conversed with the emperor while sitting on the main-thwart.[31]

Sviatoslav's appearance was noted down by a Byzantine observer: grey-eyed and snub-nosed, he had a straggling moustache, wispy beard, and was of middle height. More significantly, his failure to stand or show other marks of deference before the emperor befitted a meeting between two fully empowered rulers, if not equals. Sviatoslav had offered terms, but he had not surrendered. The *Primary Chronicle* incorporates the text of a sworn undertaking written down by a Byzantine official in Dristra and, in its original form, sealed with Sviatoslav's seals. Sviatoslav pledged to maintain 'peace and perfect love' and to fight against anyone committing aggression against the empire. He probably did not consider it demeaning to swear to the treaty in the company of 'those who are with me and under me', by their gods. The undertaking is in key with the terms which he had, according to a Byzantine chronicle, proposed: that he should be enrolled among 'the friends and allies of the Romans'.[32] There is no mention of war-guilt, reparations or even surrender.

Sviatoslav was, it seems, still in possession of captives and loot. Mindful, perhaps, of the fate of his father, he tried to ship back these proceeds of his expedition, ignoring Sveneld, his senior commander, who urged him to return on horseback. Sviatoslav's withdrawal was slow, and autumn found him still at the mouth of the Dnieper. During the winter supplies ran low, so that 'a horse's head [was going for] half a grivna'.[33] The loot also served as a magnet for the Pechenegs, who attacked the Rus as they tried to negotiate the Rapids after the spring thaw. Sviatoslav was, like most of his men, killed. His skull was plated over, 'and they drank from it',[34] a victory rite attested among other steppe peoples. A shaven scalp had not sufficed to maintain the Pecheneg alliance, and Sviatoslav had, while negotiating at Dristra, actually asked the Byzantines to request the nomads to let him pass through the steppes unmolested.

Sviatoslav's campaigns on the Danube had much in common with earlier Rus expeditions, especially that to Barda'a. But his venture represented more than a change of direction. Sviatoslav was trying to make a fresh start in a region where the strategic odds might tilt heavily in his favour, if only he could secure enough nomads' cooperation. The towns and strongholds along the Danube offered a more numerous, and moneyed, population than the Dnieper could. Those living on the south bank, at least, were Christians and Sviatoslav expected to rule over them, while himself still swearing by Perun and Volos,

---

31 Leo Deac., p. 156.
32 Skyl., p. 309.
33 *PVL*, I, p. 52. Grivna could mean a weight or unit or value. See below, pp. 284–5.
34 Ibid., p. 53.

lord of cattle.[35] Sviatoslav was trying to better himself with Greek gold and Hungarian horses and also through presiding over several different peoples, nomads and town-dwellers, whose religions included Christianity. Among Sviatoslav's captives was a 'Greek' nun, who was brought to be coupled with members of the ruling family in Kiev (see below, p. 191).

2. SETTLING DOWN: VLADIMIR IN KIEV

Sviatoslav's venture to the Danube was unsuccessful but there is no evidence of interruption to the economic life of the Rus settlements. In fact, the aftermath shows a fair degree of continuity north of the steppes. In March 973, Rus envoys were among the ambassadors waiting upon Otto I in Quedlinburg. The regime they served was that set up by Sviatoslav before his second journey to the Danube. Sveneld remained an influential figure on the Middle Dnieper. One son of Sviatoslav, Iaropolk, had been assigned to Kiev and another, Oleg, to the Derevlians. According to the *Primary Chronicle*, the inhabitants of 'Novgorod' had demanded a prince for themselves.[36] Iaropolk and Oleg would not go, and Sviatoslav fell back on a less eligible son, born to his mother's Slav 'housekeeper' perhaps ten years or so earlier. The boy, Vladimir, was sent north together with his uncle, Dobrynia. Vladimir was still considered a youth, but his two half-brothers can scarcely have been adults, seeing that Sviatoslav himself was no more than 35 or so at the time of his death (see above, pp. 133, 143). This regime of youths received no challenge from other members of the kin or leading figures on the Middle Dnieper. Such stability suggests some sort of consensus-based hierarchy, perhaps enhanced by the heavy toll exacted by Sviatoslav's expedition. Staying behind in the north may have been the lot of the inexperienced, or the base-born.

There was, however, a question which was unresolved, partly because it had not been raised before on the Dnieper: what should be the relationship between the three princes who had been assigned towns or peoples by their father? There was no recent or relevant precedent to guide the princes as to how the prince of Kiev should exercise seniority over his siblings. The demarcation of rights to tribute, hunting or trading may not have had much territorial basis in the essentially collective structure which had hitherto served Rus interests along the north–south waterway. Within a few years of Sviatoslav's death, tension flared up between the southern brothers, Iaropolk and Oleg. It was, according to the chronicle, the consequence of a clash

---

35 Ibid., p. 53.
36 Ibid., p. 49.

between hunting parties, one led by Oleg, the other by a son of Iaropolk's *éminence grise*, Sveneld. Oleg had him put to death. If, as the chronicle implies, he considered Liut Sveneldovich guilty of trespass, this suggests uncertainty over boundaries, but the essence may have been sibling rivalries and jealousies: the land of the Derevlians offered a far less lucrative base than Kiev, which Iaropolk and Sveneld's family occupied (on inheritance disputes, see below, chapters 5 and 7).

Iaropolk then attacked and defeated his brother. The crush of fugitives was such that men and horses were pushed off the bridge leading into Ovruch. Many fell on top of one another into Ovruch's ditch, Oleg among them. His body was retrieved after a search through the corpses 'from morning to noon',[37] and was buried by Iaropolk with solemnity and tears. Vladimir, the surviving brother in power, fled 'beyond the sea' and governors were assigned to his town. Around this time, however, a reverse-flow of power-seekers was under way. There arrived 'from overseas' a certain Rogvolod (Ragnvaldr in Old Norse). He installed himself on the Western Dvina at Polotsk, reportedly enjoying princely status. Likewise, Tur or Tury set himself up in a promontory fort by the Pripet, staying there long enough to leave his name on the place, Turov. It seems to have been a recent foundation, if not his own. Other strongholds were founded further west in the second half of the tenth century, for example, Volkovysk, on a riverway linking the Pripet with the Neman.[38]

These events show the promise and the problems besetting the political structure of the Dnieper Rus. Iaropolk seems to have been fully in command of the Middle Dnieper, but he was apparently unable to prevent newcomers from setting themselves up on the fringes. Rogvolod is depicted as contemplating a marriage-tie between his daughter and Iaropolk, placing him on a roughly equal footing with his son-in-law. But the emergence of Tury and Rogvolod is also a sign of the drawing-power of the Dnieper and its feeders. This was now the axis onto which it was worth fastening, rather than the Volga or any other route. Polotsk stood at the crossroads of the north–south routes with the Western Dvina, but only during the tenth century was its fortified hilltop supplemented by a fairly extensive settlement.[39] The north–south axis attracted another would-be potentate from the Scandinavian world, the fugitive bastard Vladimir Sviatoslavich. Vladimir managed to muster a force of warriors somewhere in Scandinavia, maybe Birka, maybe further west at a Norse court. But he lacked ready means of rewarding them and presumably led them on with promises of rewards along the East Way.

---

37 Ibid., p. 53.
38 P. F. Lysenko, *Goroda Turovskoi zemli* (Minsk, 1974), pp. 44–5; I. G. Zverugo, *Verkhnee Poneman'e v IX–XIIIvv.* (Minsk, 1989), p. 70.
39 Mühle, *Städtischen Handelszentren*, p. 211.

Vladimir apparently regained control of Gorodishche-Novgorod with ease, helped by having lived there as prince for several years. With the aid and advice of, most probably, his uncle Dobrynia, Vladimir managed to raise armed men from the inhabitants, including Slavs and Chud (Finno-Ugrians). He proposed to Rogvolod of Polotsk a marriage-tie, whereby he should wed his daughter, Rogneda (Old Norse Ragnheithr). Rebuffed, he went on to attack and devastate Polotsk, putting to death Rogvolod and his two sons. He persisted even then in marrying Rogneda, who had earlier declared, 'I do not wish to take off a slave's son's shoes!'[40] Rogvolod had not been established in Polotsk for long and it had not previously been a princely seat. Vladimir was not motivated solely by vengeance or lust in taking Rogneda to wife: there were quicker ways of settling scores. More probably, he believed that his status would be enhanced, and control over Polotsk strengthened, by conspicuous bonding with the kin of a Scandinavian 'prince'. Whether or not Vladimir really received a stinging put-down, his decision to wed Rogneda suggests a man still intent on bolstering his political legitimacy.

Despite, or because of, the ambivalence of his position at Polotsk, Vladimir quite rapidly made for Kiev, 580 kilometres away. The chronicle emphasizes that he had 'many warriors'[41] but even if he had induced Slavs and Finno-Ugrians to accompany him far from their home settlements, the chances of ousting Iaropolk were unpromising. A sizable force needed food supplies and the Novgorodians could not be expected to linger so far from their homesteads and workshops. Vladimir did not presume to advance closer to Kiev than Dorogozhichi, several kilometres north of the town. Iaropolk may well have expected to see off his half-brother by means of delay, and he still had forces of his own, capable of attacking Vladimir. In fact, Vladimir only gained control of Kiev by means of trickery and treachery. He managed to suborn the commander of the defending troops, a certain Blud. Blud advised Iaropolk against a counter-offensive and duped him into flight by falsely claiming the citizens were plotting to kill him. Iaropolk fled to Rodnia, at the confluence of the Ros with the Dnieper, near Pecheneg territory. His visit was unpremeditated and food supplies soon ran out. Iaropolk turned down the advice of one of his counsellors or kinsmen, Variazhko, that he should flee to the Pechenegs and raise an army. Instead, he put his faith in negotiations with his half-brother in Kiev, in the stone hall their father had used. 'But as he walked through the door, two Varangians stabbed him in the chest with their swords. Blud closed the doors and prevented [Iaropolk's] own men from following him in. And thus was Iaropolk killed.'[42] Variazhko, still

40 *PSRL*, I, cols 299–300.
41 *PVL*, I, p. 55.
42 Ibid., p. 55.

loyal to Iaropolk, escaped to the Pechenegs and 'often' took part in their subsequent raids.

There is no reason to doubt the substance of the *Primary Chronicle*'s account of Vladimir's road to sole rule c. 978. The story of deceit continues. Vladimir's Scandinavian warriors demanded their cut, in the form of a levy on the citizens at the rate of two grivnas per person. Vladimir's position in Kiev was probably still highly uncertain, since the Kievans had been regarded as loyal to Iaropolk while Vladimir was at Dorogozhichi, and they can hardly have been unaware that Iaropolk was murdered upon arriving to discuss peace. To inflict a swingeing tax would have courted further disorder, or insurrection, while the Pechenegs were on the war-path. Vladimir pleaded with his warriors for a delay, until marten-skins could be collected for them. He broke his word and failed to distribute the furs. But apparently they merely protested, and asked to be shown the route to the Greeks. Vladimir sent messengers ahead warning, 'Varangians are coming! . . . Do not think of keeping them in your city or they will do ill to you as they have done here'.[43] Taken literally, these words imply violence or looting in Kiev. More generally, the story shows Vladimir's difficulties in remunerating and disciplining his war-band, difficulties encountered by later princely employers of Varangians (see below, pp. 203–4). The force which had brought Vladimir to power was inconstant and, in so far as it consisted of the citizens of expanding conglomerates such as Gorodishche-Novgorod, only momentarily available.

Some of the problems which Vladimir faced at Kiev sprang directly from the events related above; others were deeper-seated, while one or two new ones arose during his rule there. He acted fast to dismiss most of his Varangians, but other adventurers might home in from the Baltic world. Accordingly, Vladimir assigned his uncle, Dobrynia, to Gorodishche-Novgorod, where he could defend the polity's northern approaches. But he faced raids mounted from the steppes by the Pechenegs, Variazhko and, possibly, other former associates of his brothers, while Tury may still have been at large to the west. Vladimir constructed an imposing earthen rampart on the Starokievskaia hill, enclosing 10 hectares; its predecessor had only enclosed two.[44] This expansion is a mark of the settlement's prosperity, but also of the insecurity of both prince and townsmen, and the new rampart may well represent an attempt to link up his fate and theirs.

Vladimir was now largely reliant on the warriors and militia whom he found on the Middle Dnieper. It had been the switch in loyalty by Blud which had, in effect, opened Kiev's gates to him. Vladimir

---

43 Ibid., p. 56.
44 E. Mühle, 'Die topographisch-städtebauliche Entwicklung Kievs vom Ende des 10. bis zum Ende des 12. Jh. im Licht der archäologischen Forschungen', *JGO* 36 (1988), 352, 354–5.

reportedly won him over with promises of virtual obedience: 'I want to have you in the place of my father, and you shall receive great honour from me'.[45] Vladimir cut a figure at once youthful and isolated. His links with the Kievan region were weak, and not entirely creditable. Although his mother's family had local roots, in Liubech, she was known to be of subservient status. Vladimir brought with him Rogneda – who had derided his origins – and did not try for a prestigious local match. His position was doubly dubious: he was the product of a backstairs affair, and the ouster and, in effect, executioner of his trusting half-brother. Vladimir also faced the abiding difficulties of protecting the route to Byzantium.

What Vladimir lacked in worldly connections on the Middle Dnieper he made up for by the company of gods. Their statues were set up in a ranking order outside his hall, on the summit of the Starokievskaia hill. First among them was Perun, god of lightning and power, who was worshipped by the Balts and Slavs and had been adopted by the Rus. Perun was invoked as warrant for the 944 treaty and for Sviatoslav's treaty in 971 (see above, pp. 150–1). The new idol had a wooden body, but his head was silver, and his moustaches golden. The *Primary Chronicle* names five other gods whose statues were set up with Perun's: Khors, Dazhbog, Stribog, Semargl and Mokosh. Dazhbog was venerated by the South Slavs as well as the East Slavs as god of the sun, growth and harvest while Stribog, judging by his name, also had followers among the Slavs. But the other gods' cults originated elsewhere. Thus Semargl's cult seems to have been brought to the Middle Dnieper by Iranian-speaking peoples and adopted by later immigrants, including the Slavs.[46] This assortment of deities seems to represent an attempt by Vladimir to associate himself with cults known and respected on the Dnieper. It probably reflects the heterogeneity of Kiev in the second half of the tenth century (see below, p. 169).

Vladimir's cohabitation with the gods was most probably designed to make up for his lack of personal standing. The chronicle relates this as Vladimir's first measure after seizing power. Dobrynia is depicted as setting up an idol upon reaching Novgorod.[47] There, too, the assumption of power and promotion of cults was interlinked. The idol is not named in the chronicle, but it may well have been Perun. He had already been worshipped for a century or more just outside the town, at a sanctuary still commemorated by the place-name, Peryn.

---

45 *PVL*, I, p. 54.
46 B. A. Rybakov, *Iazychestvo drevnei Rusi* (Moscow, 1987), pp. 436–48; V. N. Toporov, 'Ob iranskom elemente v russkoi dukhovnoi kul'ture', *Slavianskii i balkanskii fol'klor. 1989* (Moscow, 1989), 34–42. On the stone foundations of a structure which may be identifiable as the site of Vladimir's 'pantheon', see Mühle, 'Topographisch-städtebauliche Entwicklung Kievs', 353.
47 *PVL*, I, p. 56.

What the cults promoted by Vladimir and his uncle had in common was that they were mandatory and public. The inhabitants of Kiev and Gorodishche were expected to carry out sacrifices to the idols before the prince or his representative. The chronicle treats this as an innovation, as well as reprehensible.

A different change, not of Vladimir's making, was under way during the earlier years of his reign. The influx of dirhams from the Samanid realm diminished. The date when the stream had begun to fail is not yet clear, nor is the consistency of the process. Dirhams continued to reach the Rus through the 970s despite Sviatoslav's devastation of Khazaria and campaigning against the Volga Bulgars. The stream seems to have fallen off during the 980s, dwindling to a trickle in the 990s, never fully to be replenished by the dirhams of other Moslem dynasties. The increasing fluctuation in the silver content of the Samanid dirham through the second half of the tenth century was probably detected by the Rus and although the overall debasement was slight, it may eventually have discouraged suppliers from putting furs on the market. The Ghaznavids' and Qarakhanids' contest for the Samanid domains anyway hindered the organization of long-distance trading in Central Asia. These changes may not have had an immediate impact on Vladimir's regime along the Dnieper. Hundreds of thousands of dirhams and dirham fragments remained in circulation and they could still trigger further exchanges. Moreover, the silver trade was, in the second half of the tenth century, carried out primarily north of the Middle Dnieper and in the north-east it seems to have been relatively lightly supervised or taxed by princes. The transformation of settlements such as Timerëvo into rural communities without significant trading ties was not of pressing concern to Vladimir.[48] But the waning of the inflow from the east affected trading centres such as Gorodishche and Gnëzdovo, where dirhams continued to be exchanged or stored, and there is evidence that Vladimir involved himself in north-eastern affairs in the mid-980s.

According to the *Primary Chronicle*'s entry for 985, Vladimir and Dobrynia led an expedition against the Volga Bulgars. This was a joint operation, with the Rus travelling by boat and 'Torks' on horseback along the banks. The latter are identifiable with the Oghuz mentioned in accounts of Sviatoslav's campaign against the Khazars (see above, pp. 144–5). The chronicle claims that Vladimir 'defeated' the Bulgars, but it also makes clear that he failed to win decisively and the two

48 A. N. Kirpichnikov et al., 'Russko-skandinavskie sviazi epokhi obrazovaniia kievskogo gosudarstva na sovremennom etape arkheologicheskogo izucheniia', *KSIA* 160 (1980), 30; I. V. Dubov, *Velikii volzhskii put'* (Leningrad, 1989), p. 205. The special significance of Timerëvo's long-distance trading connections even at their tenth-century peak was queried by A. E. Leont'ev, 'Timerëvo. Problema istoricheskoi interpretatsii arkheologicheskogo pamiatnika', *SA* 1989, no. 3, 81, 83–5.

sides arrived at a sworn agreement. Dobrynia is said to have pointed out to Vladimir that the Bulgars wore boots: 'Let us go and look for wearers of bast-shoes!'[49] In other words, the Bulgars presented too hard a target and to seek dominance over them was futile.

Vladimir's attack on the Bulgars came after several years of campaigning. He had, according to the chronicle, attacked the Viatichi on two successive occasions; the Radimichi; and the Iatviagians, who lived between the Pripet and the Neman. The former two peoples had rendered tribute earlier in the century. Vladimir can thus be seen as reimposing hegemony after a slackening since Sviatoslav's time. He also struck far to the west, seizing 'Peremyshl, Cherven and other towns' from the 'Liakhs', probably the Ledzanians, a people named as tributaries of the Rus in the *DAI*.[50] These towns lay astride routes linking the Dnieper and Pripet with Cracow, Prague and Central Europe on the one hand, and the Baltic on the other.[51] The routes had been one of the ways Moslem silver had reached the West Slavs and the Scandinavian world; it was probably in a reverse flow along the same routes that silver denarii began to trickle into the Rus lands, albeit in only very modest quantities, during the last quarter of the tenth century. Vladimir's western campaign could, together with his attack on the Volga Bulgars, be viewed as expansion on an ambitious, if less than Sviatoslavic, scale. However, it may well also register frustration or unease at the waning of an existing trade-route. Vladimir could hardly have been indifferent to the ability of tributaries such as the Viatichi to pay up in silver, while the agglomeration at Gorodishche-Novgorod ceased to receive supplies of new oriental silver. It may not be accidental that the sole expedition of Vladimir which Dobrynia, the governor of Gorodishche-Novgorod, is recorded as undertaking with him was against the Volga Bulgars. Whatever Vladimir's objectives may have been in attacking the Bulgars – and they need not have been fixed or precise – the campaign failed to avert

---

49 *PVL*, I, p. 59.
50 Ibid., p. 58; *DAI*, ch. 37. 44, pp. 168–9. The Ledzanians seem c. 980 to have been under the loose hegemony of the Duke of Bohemia: G. Labuda, 'Der Zug des russischen Grossfürsten Vladimir gegen die Ljachen im Jahre 981. Ein Beitrag zur Ausbildung der polnisch-russischen Grenzen im 10. Jh.', in U. Haustein et al., eds, *Ostmitteleuropa. Berichte und Forschungen* (Stuttgart, 1981), pp. 15–19; G. Prinzing, 'Byzantinische Aspekte der mittelalterlichen Geschichte Polens', *Byzantion* 64 (1994), 462–3.
51 V. P. Darkevich, 'K istorii torgovykh sviazei drevnei Rusi', *KSIA* 138 (1973), 98, fig. 2, p. 100; T. Lewicki, 'Le commerce des samanides avec l'Europe orientale et centrale à la lumière des trésors de monnaies coufiques', in D. K. Kouymjian, ed., *Studies in Honor of G. C. Miles* (Beirut, 1974), pp. 226–7; C. Warnke, 'Der Handel mit Wachs zwischen Ost- und Westeuropa im frühen und hohen Mittelalter. Voraussetzungen und Gewinnöglichkeiten', *UHV, Abhandlungen der Akademie der Wissenschaften in Göttingen, philolog.-hist. Klasse*, 3. Folge, no. 156 (Göttingen, 1987), pp. 560–3.

the decline in the influx of silver. One of the last silver dirhams known to have been struck by the Bulgars themselves dates from 986/87.[52]

If the drying-up of the Moslem silver influx had some effect, albeit unquantifiable, on the regime of Vladimir, the steps which he took to try and legitimize it posed problems, too. The *Primary Chronicle* records resistance leading to martyrdom. Vladimir staged a victory feast for his idols after subjugating the Iatviagians. Lots were drawn as to which boy and girl should be sacrificed, and the lot fell on the son of a Varangian 'who had come (back) from the Greeks and held the Christian faith'.[53] This man owned a residence in Kiev, to which he had retired, presumably after making his fortune in Byzantine service. He was, according to one source, called Tury, and his son's Christian name was Ivan.[54] Tury is credited by the chronicle with denouncing the gods made of 'wood which is here today and rotten tomorrow. They do not eat or drink or talk but are made by (human) hands'. He contrasted them with the God whom 'the Greeks serve and worship, who made heaven and earth and the stars . . .'.[55] This is a standard denunciation of idolatry, influenced by the Old Testament, and instances of human sacrifice are not recorded among the Slavs. However, ritualistic slaying is recorded of the Swedes as well as the early Rus (see above, p. 45), and it is quite possible that a Varangian did object to an act of worship ordained by Vladimir, and that he and his son were put to death.

Such episodes were embarrassing for Vladimir. Much as he may have wished to bind the Kievans' loyalties to his favoured cults and himself, he is unlikely to have sought either the oppression of local Christians or the ridicule of travellers from overseas. The Christian Rus of the mid-tenth century had presumably tried to raise their children as Christians. There is, moreover, evidence of Christian ritual, in the form of pendant crosses and wax candles, in chamber-graves at Gnëzdovo and Timerëvo datable to the 960s and 970s.[56] The lighting of candles on the roof of or inside the chambers was also practised among the Danes, and the rite was probably brought east by Danish adventurers

---

52 V. V. Kropotkin, 'Bulgarian tenth-century coins in Eastern Europe and around the Baltic. Topography and distribution routes', in K. Jonsson and B. Malmer, eds, *Sigtuna Papers. Proceedings of the Sigtuna Symposium on Viking-Age coinage 1–4 June 1989* (Commentationes de nummis saeculorum IX–XI in Suecia repertis. Nova series 6; Stockholm, London, 1990), p. 199.

53 *PVL*, I, p. 58.

54 A. A. Shakhmatov, 'Kak nazyvalsia pervy i russkii sviatoi muchenik?', *Izvestiia Imperatorskoi Akademii Nauk*. VI *seriia*, I (1907), 261–4.

55 *PVL*, I, p. 58.

56 D. A. Avdusin and T. A. Puškina, 'Three chamber-graves at Gniozdovo', *Fornvännen* 83 (1988), 22–4, 28–31; N. G. Nedoshivina and M. V. Fekhner, 'Pogrebal'nyi obriad timerevskogo mogil'nika', *SA* 1985, no. 2, 111–12. Cf. E. A. Mel'nikova, 'Russko-skandinavskie vzaimosviazi v protsesse khristianizatsii (IX–XIIIvv.)', *DGTSSSR* 1987 (1989), pp. 264–5.

and traders. The inhabitants of the western towns which Vladimir had seized were largely Christian, too, and presumably expected to continue worshipping their one God. The population of Peremyshl (modern Przemyśl, on Poland's border with Ukraine) were, for the most part, burying their dead according to Christian funerary rites during the tenth century; a white-stone rotunda with circular apse may date from this time.[57] Thus Vladimir had to reckon with the subject population of newly conquered towns which might resist the imposition of a compulsory pagan cult.

There was also, for Vladimir, a question of prestige. He nailed his colours to the statues of Perun and company at a time when other rulers were proclaiming their conversion to Christianity. Miezko of Poland had adopted Christianity in the 960s, and in the mid-970s the leading Hungarian chieftain Geza accepted Christianity from German missionaries and had his son baptized with the name Stephen. Harald Bluetooth, king of the Danes, had been baptized around 960 and from the mid-970s he was issuing large quantities of silver coins bearing a cross and a figure of Byzantine inspiration.[58] Among the lavishly ornamented runestones which he set up at Jelling was one near his father's burial-mound, bearing the inscription, 'King Harald commanded these memorials made to Gorm his father and Thyre his mother. That Harald who won for himself all Denmark and Norway, and made the Danes Christian'.[59] The cults which Vladimir was trying to sponsor could not equip him with imposing victory monuments, let alone a pedigree. Nor could they offer a network of sanctuaries. Most of the excavated East Slav sanctuaries lie well to the west of the Dnieper, along the Pripet or its tributaries, or towards the Carpathians and the Dniester in the south-west.[60] Vladimir remained in contact with the Baltic world, his domicile for a spell in the 970s (see above, p. 152). One saga depicts the young Olaf Tryggvason's exile at his court while Vladimir was still a pagan, and although its contents are largely tendentious, it does reflect the toing and froing of notables between Scandinavian courts and suggests that northern rulers were keenly aware of one another's religious leanings. The saga records a significant detail, Vladimir's expectation that those in his entourage would join in his sacrifices; according to the saga, the boy Olaf

---

57 A. P. Motsia, *Pogrebal'nye pamiatniki iuzhnorusskikh zemel' IX–XIII vv.* (Kiev, 1990), pp. 97, 99–101. Caution in dating the church was advocated by P. A. Rappoport, *Russkaia arkhitektura X–XIII vv.* (*ASSSR SAI*, vyp. E1–47; Leningrad, 1982), p. 112.

58 E. Roesdahl, *The Vikings*, tr. S. M. Margeson and K. Williams (London, 1991), pp. 113, 162.

59 Tr. in E. Roesdahl, *Viking Age Denmark* (London, 1982), p. 172.

60 I. P. Rusanova, 'Kul'tovye mesta i iazycheskie sviatilishcha slavian VI–XIII vv.', *RA* 1992, no. 4, fig. 1, pp. 51, 52, 58, 60–3.

politely but firmly demurred.[61] To persist with a cult unacceptable to Scandinavian notables who were Christian was to risk ridicule and social isolation from the likes of Harald Gormson (though not from Olaf himself: he was, in fact, still pagan at the time of his stay in the east).

One cannot say which of these considerations weighed heaviest with Vladimir, but there is evidence that quite soon after instituting public idol-worship in Kiev he was taking soundings about religions long-established elsewhere. The *Primary Chronicle* recounts, schematically, the efforts on the part of Byzantine, Western Christian, Moslem and Jewish Khazar spokesmen to win over Vladimir to their faith, and Vladimir is said to have sent envoys to observe the Volga Bulgars, the Germans and the Byzantines at prayer. The envoys returned and praised the rites of the Greeks to the skies: 'There is not such a sight or such beauty on earth . . . We only know that God abides there among men, and their service is greater than that of all countries'.[62] The motif of a ruler having the case for various faiths put to him occurs in Arabic and Hebrew accounts of the conversion of the Khazar khagan to Judaism and it is possible that they provided some inspiration for the chronicle's contributors.[63] But that Vladimir really did send emissaries to foreign rulers and asked for sages to expound their respective creeds is suggested by Marwazi, a late eleventh-century Persian writer. He relates that the 'king' of the Rus sent four kinsmen to the ruler of Khorezm, in Central Asia. They asked for a teacher to instruct the Rus in Islam, and a teacher was duly sent.[64] 'Vladimir' (V-ladmir) is

---

61 *Ólófs Saga Tryggvasonar en mesta* [*Saga of King Olaf Tryggvason*], ed. O. Halldórsson, (Editiones Arnamagnaeanae, Series A.1; Copenhagen, 1958), I, ch. 57, p. 106; tr. J. Sephton, *The Saga of King Olaf Tryggwason* (London, 1895), p. 67. On the various sagas concerning Olaf, and the formulaic character of some of their episodes set in the eastern lands, see T. N. Dzhakson, 'Islandskie korolevskie sagi kak istochnik po istorii drevnei Rusi i ee sosede X-XIII vv.', *DGTSSSR* 1988–89 (1991), pp. 22–3, 30, 32–3, 75–9; E. A. Rydzevskaia, 'Legenda o kniaze Vladimire v sage ob Olafe Triuggvasone', *TODRL* 2 (1935), 10–11, 14, 20.

62 *PVL*, I, p. 75.

63 See D. M. Dunlop, *The History of the Jewish Khazars* (Princeton, 1954), pp. 84–6, 90–1, 154–5, 170; J. Shepard, 'Some remarks on the sources for the conversion of Rus'', in S. W. Swierkosz-Lenart, ed., *Le origini e lo sviluppo della cristianità slavo-bizantina* (Nuovi Studi Storici 17; Rome, 1992), p. 80 and n. 53. Cf. C. Zuckerman, 'On the date of the Khazars' conversion to Judaism and the chronology of the kings of the Rus Oleg and Igor', *Revue des études byzantines* 53 (1995), 242–7.

64 Marwazi, tr. in V. Minorsky, *Sharaf al-Zaman Tahir Marvazi on China, the Turks and India* (London, 1942), p. 36; Shepard, 'Some remarks', pp. 76–7. That learned expositions of doctrine and the Scriptures could form part of Byzantine missionary practice was pointed out by I. Ševčenko, 'Religious missions seen from Byzantium', in O. Pritsak and I. Ševčenko, eds, *Proceedings of the International Congress commemorating the Millenium of Christianity in Rus'-Ukraine*, *HUS* 12–13 (1988–89), 23.

treated by Marwazi as a title rather than a name, and his assertion that the Rus were converted to Islam is false. But it is overwhelmingly probable that the story echoes Vladimir's soundings of the 980s, and if envoys were sent to a Moslem power, they were most probably also sent to the Germans and the Byzantines. What these creeds, together with Judaism, had in common was unequivocal monotheism. Each focused on a single, all-powerful God, and the worship of each was regulated by organizations of priests or judges. And all of them were formally defined, Religions of the Book.

One may doubt whether Vladimir really needed to send abroad for information. There were most probably Moslems as well as Christians and Jews living in Kiev. A stone mould bearing an Arabic inscription variously interpreted as the personal name 'Yazid' or the ethnic name 'Turk'/'Tork' has been excavated in the Podol and it presumably belonged to a Moslem craftsman working there.[65] Vladimir may have had ulterior motives for sending out 'kinsmen' or 'good men of understanding' to foreign rulers. A monotheistic cult served by an established hierarchy possessing standard writing held out obvious attractions to the would-be ruler of a vast, amorphous land, but Vladimir may not have been in a position to pick a monotheistic religion at will and impose it unilaterally. For Vladimir, as for his father – who had cited his retainers' ridicule as grounds for rejecting Christianity (see above, p. 142) – the ability to coerce was qualified by the outlook of his retainers; and even with full-time warriors behind him, he needed the compliance of at least some of the Middle Dnieper's notables. In representing Vladimir as hesitant between the rival faiths – 'I will wait a little more'[66] – the chronicle may be refracting a political dilemma.

Vladimir's final choice was in favour of the Greeks' religion. As the chronicle's account makes clear, this was not a foregone conclusion. Had he defeated the Volga Bulgars, he would have found himself in control of a network of mosques and schools (see above, p. 62); these could have provided his townsfolk with instructors. It was the Germans, not the Greeks, who had sent a mission to Olga a generation earlier, and Otto III was to prove a zealous promoter of mission work. In the 980s, however, Otto was still a boy and his regents were preoccupied with internal affairs and the aftermath of the Slav uprising east of the Elbe. The Byzantine government, too, was embroiled with internal problems. In 987 two top generals were in revolt and the forces of one of them, Bardas Phokas, controlled much of Asia Minor. Emperor Basil II, badly in need of a relief force, was in no position to repel a foreign potentate from the border regions still acknowledging his rule.

---

65 P. P. Tolochko, ed., *Novoe v arkheologii Kieva* (Kiev, 1981), pp. 307–8.
66 *PVL*, I, p. 74.

The exact course of events, including the place and date of Vladimir's baptism, is obscure. Controversy was already under way at the time of compilation of the *Primary Chronicle*: 'those who do not know the truth say that he was baptized in Kiev, but others say in Vasilev and yet others say elsewhere'.[67] The chronicle, for its part, insists on Cherson as the spot, and recounts a detailed story. Vladimir attacked this Byzantine base and eventually forced it to surrender, aided by certain inhabitants who turned traitor. Then he demanded of the emperor his sister in marriage, agreeing as a condition to become Christian. Princess Anna was sent to Cherson and Vladimir was baptized in St Basil's, which 'is (still) standing in Cherson in the middle of the town'.[68] The wedding was celebrated and Vladimir returned to Kiev with his bride. He restored Cherson to the Greeks 'as a marriage-gift'. Two of these details, the capture of Cherson and Vladimir's marriage to Anna, are verifiable from independent, non-Slavic sources; one of them reports that Vladimir sent 6,000 warriors to help Basil, and there need be no doubt that the Rus relief force played a decisive part in the suppression of Bardas Phokas' rebellion.

However, the precise sequence and interrelationship of these events remains controversial. There was, from the later nineteenth century, a fairly general consensus among scholars that Vladimir seized Cherson as a means of putting pressure on Byzantium, after it delayed implementation of the marriage agreement. More recently, however, A. Poppe argued that Vladimir attacked Cherson *in fulfilment* of his agreement with Basil II: the town supposedly sided with the rebels and Vladimir, having already been baptized in Kiev, was restoring Cherson to imperial hegemony. This 'revisionism' has gained widespread, though not universal, support.[69]

Whichever hypothesis one may prefer, the central fact is that Vladimir seized on a period of turmoil in Byzantium to drive a hard bargain with its ruler and institute a new cult on terms more or less of his choosing. Whether he captured Cherson before or after agreeing to send troops to Basil, he was exploiting a rare occasion

---

67 Ibid., p. 77.
68 Ibid., p. 77.
69 See V. G. Vasilievskii, *Trudy* (St Petersburg, 1908, repr. The Hague, 1968), I, pp. 196–200; V. R. Rozen, *Imperator Vasilii Bolgaroboitsa* (St Petersburg, 1883, repr. London, 1972), pp. 215–17; A. Poppe, 'The political background to the baptism of Rus. Byzantine-Russian relations between 986–989', *DOP* 30 (1976), 240–2, repr. in Poppe's *The Rise of Christian Russia* (London, 1982), no. 2; J. Fennell, *A History of the Russian Church to 1448* (London, New York, 1995), pp. 37–8 (broadly favourable to Poppe); D. Obolensky, 'Cherson and the conversion of Rus': an anti-revisionist view', *Byzantine and Modern Greek Studies* 13 (1989), 244–56; W. Seibt, 'Der historische Hintergrund und die Chronologie der Taufe der Rus' (989)', in A.-E. Tachiaos, ed., *The Legacy of Saints Cyril and Methodius to Kiev and Moscow* (Thessaloniki, 1992), pp. 297–300 (reservations about Poppe's thesis).

when the emperor needed Rus cooperation far more urgently than the Kievan prince needed the emperor's. Vladimir now possessed leverage whereas Princess Olga in the mid-tenth century had not. She had associated herself with the Greeks to the extent of taking the name of Helena as her baptismal name, but she had not obtained a religious mission or a marriage-tie. Her refusal to send troops or goods to the emperor, reported in the chronicle, did not have any impact (see above, p. 136). In the late 980s Basil II was bereft of troops and this made Vladimir momentarily a ruler of first-class importance, whose demands must be met. There was thus a convergence of interests between him and Basil.

Not that Vladimir was wholly dependent on the emperor's goodwill. Basil II was in no position to stop him abducting priests or church furnishings after the capture of Cherson, and there seems to have been an element of triumphalism in Vladimir's installation of the spoils in Kiev. Two bronze figures and four bronze horses were set up in a public space and were still objects of attention a century later: the chronicle rebuts 'the ignorant' who supposed them to be made of marble.[70] Vladimir also made use of Cherson's priests, perhaps because they had experience of dealing with pagans and converts. One of the Chersonites, Anastasii, was put in charge of the great church which Vladimir founded soon after his Conversion. He remained prominent to the end of Vladimir's reign. His closeness to Vladimir seems to have prompted the chronicle's report that he had earned Vladimir's gratitude through having betrayed the location of Cherson's underground water supply: it was by cutting the pipes that Vladimir had forced the town to surrender.[71]

Vladimir presided over the ritual dismantling of the cult which he had patronized, putting a positive face on his 'U-turn'. He dramatized the concept of purification through such spectacles as tying the statue of Perun to a horse's tail and having it dragged down to the Dnieper, being struck all the while by twelve men with rods. The idol was tossed in the river with instructions that it should be kept moving until it reached the Rapids. Only after being seen through them was it allowed to come to rest on a sandbank. The same river was made the means of transforming a substantial number of Kiev's inhabitants into Christians. The chronicle is unequivocal that they assembled at Vladimir's command, not through peaceful persuasion or divine inspiration. The message was passed 'round all the town: "Whoever does not turn up at the river tomorrow, be he rich, poor, lowly or slave, he shall be my enemy!"' Many obeyed and immersed themselves in the Dnieper, 'some up to their necks, others to their chests, and the

70 *PVL*, I, p. 80.
71 Ibid., p. 76.

young up to their chests near the bank, while some people held infants and adults waded out into the river and priests stood on the bank, offering up prayers'.[72]

Vladimir was able to carry out these measures from his own resources. After a decade of campaigning and imposing tribute on outlying areas, his position in Kiev was secure. His overall legitimacy was, however, still open to doubt, and in associating his rule with another cult, he needed to make the latter visibly more impressive than its predecessors or alternatives. A marriage-tie with the Greek *tsar'* was of value here. To receive a *tsaritsa* (as Anna was known) for a bride was to gain lasting recognition of one's own high standing. It opened up the prospect of gaining further legitimacy for the regime, in the form of a son and heir of imperial stock, and becoming the envy of other northern potentates. A sense of resentment is manifest in a slightly later Saxon chronicle. Thietmar of Merseburg claims, albeit falsely, that Anna had been pledged to Otto III.[73] Finally, the marriage involved a material commitment on the emperor's part towards his new brother-in-law. A princess born, like Basil himself, in the Purple Chamber of the Palace embodied imperial majesty and had to be maintained in something like the manner to which she was accustomed. Basil II's interests converged with those of Vladimir in predicating a residence where Anna could live and worship in style, with high-ranking clergy in attendance. An Arabic chronicler, Yahya of Antioch, brings out the connection, writing of the despatch to the Rus of 'metropolitans and bishops' to carry out mass baptisms at the same time as Anna's wedding to Vladimir. Yahya credits her with responsibility for the building of 'many churches', while the *Primary Chronicle* states that Vladimir himself 'fetched masters from the Greeks' in order to build a church dedicated to the Mother of God.[74]

This Church of the Mother of God was entrusted to Anastasii the Chersonite. Priests from Cherson were assigned to officiate in it, and Vladimir earmarked revenues to fund it, a sign of his commitment to its well-being. The 'Tithe church' – *Desiatinnaia* – was intended to be as directly associated with Vladimir's rule as the idols had been a decade earlier (see above, p. 155). The site of their shrine, which stood only about 50 metres away, was built over with a wooden church dedicated to Vladimir's patron saint, Basil. The Tithe church was of brick and stone and far surpassed any earlier masonry building raised north of the steppes. Its foundations measured some 27 metres long by 18 metres wide, and it had a cupola, three aisles and three

72 Ibid., p. 81.
73 Thietmar VII.72, in Holtzmann, *Die Chronik*, p. 486.
74 Yahya ibn Sa'id (of Antioch), *Histoire*, ed. and tr. J. Kratchkovsky and A. Vasiliev (*Patrologia Orientalis* 23.3; Paris, 1932), p. 423; *PVL*, I, p. 83.

apses. The lay-out and the rows of brickwork alternating with rows of stone facings together with the marble cornices and parapets gave the Tithe church the look of a Byzantine church. In the view of some art historians, its model was a church in the palace complex in Constantinople dedicated to the Mother of God, the church of the Pharos.[75]

What is unquestionable is that the Tithe church formed part of Vladimir's palace complex on the Starokievskaia hill. Two-storeyed stone halls were built to the south, west and perhaps also north-west of the Tithe church, forming a majestic ensemble. Excavations have revealed something of the rich furnishings and decorations of the church. The floor was paved with glazed ceramic tiles showing palmettes and eagles, and the altar area had a marble floor in *opus sectile*. The walls and vaults were decorated with mosaics and paintings, while marble details, such as the capitals of columns, adorned the interior. Fragments of the paintings have been found, the delicate features of a curly-haired youth among them.[76] The stone halls nearby were each over 40 metres long and their mosaic decorations and wall-paintings resembled those in the Tithe church. They were presumably the residence of Anna and a suite of ladies-in-waiting accompanying her beyond the steppes. Fifteen years or so earlier a 'splendid retinue' had gone with Princess Theophano to Saxony.[77] Anna lived in Kiev for more than twenty years. Not one action on her part is recorded in the chronicle and she does not seem to have borne Vladimir an heir (but see below, p. 191). Yet she brought class to Vladimir even in death, being laid to rest in a marble sarcophagus in what was, in effect, the palace church next to his halls. Thus in the end Vladimir far outclassed the memorial stones of Harald Bluetooth (see above, p. 159).

Vladimir graphically linked promotion of the new cult with his personal survival and also with the well-being of ordinary townsfolk. One such act was his foundation of a church at Vasilev, after narrowly escaping death at the hands of the Pechenegs there. He staged a 'great feast' lasting eight days for 'his boiars and governors, and the elders of all the towns and many people, distributing 300 grivnas to the poor'. Then, on the feast of the Dormition of the Mother of God, he travelled the 30 or so kilometres to Kiev and staged another

---

75 See F. Kämpfer, 'Eine Residenz für Anna Porphyrogenneta', *JGO* 41 (1993), 102; Rappoport, *Russkaia arkhitektura*, pp. 7–8 (map of the Starokievskaia hill: fig. 1, p. 8).

76 N. P. Sychev, 'Drevneishii fragment russko-vizantiiskoi zhivopisi', *Seminarium Kondakovianum* 2 (1928), 93–4; table XIII facing 96; I. S. Aseev, *Arkhitektura drevnego Kieva* (Kiev, 1982), pp. 34–5; V. G. Putsko, 'Vizantiia i stanovleniie iskusstva kievskoi Rusi', in P. P. Tolochko, ed, *Iuzhnaia Rus' i Vizantiia Sbornik nauchnykh trudov (k XVIII kongressu vizantinistov)* (Kiev, 1991), 81.

77 Thietmar II.15, in Holtzmann, *Die Chronik*, p. 56.

'great feast, summoning a countless multitude of people'. Through mass-entertainments such as these, carrying on 'year in, year out',[78] Vladimir played host and benefactor to a greater number of inhabitants of Kiev and its environs, with greater solemnity, than he could have managed when rounding up worshippers or victims for Dazhbog.

Vladimir's palace complex was the principal setting for these junketings, but he made an effort to reach out into the streets. He is said to have had carts built to carry 'bread, meat, fish and various kinds of fruit'. They were drawn round the town to the cry of 'Where are the sick and the lowly, those unable to walk?',[79] and each person received according to their needs. The chronicle depicts Vladimir as piously acting upon the Bible's teaching, but the carts also carried barrels of beer, which is likely to have appealed mainly to relatively robust citizens. Vladimir, acting in the name of the cult he had forced on the Kievans, was now forging convivial yet sacral ties with them. These were tenuous, but not unhelpful to one who had arrived there a virtual outsider.

Above all, the routines and ritual of the new religion focused on the uniqueness of Vladimir's role as setter of Christian standards. His relationship with his armed followers and other men of substance was affected, to his advantage. As has already been seen, the ruling elite on the Dnieper had many of the characteristics of a collective leadership. Olga was accompanied by more than twenty notables' representatives during the receptions in the Great Palace and the magnates' continuing substance is displayed by barrows such as that of an armed man and his son at Chernaia Mogila.[80] The series of campaigns to impose or reimpose tribute during the 980s gave Vladimir the chance to command in war, rewarding and promoting those who fought well. But it was his activities as mass-baptizer which constituted a one-off feat that no-one else could emulate or hope to repeat. Prominent Rus had already become Christians of their own accord, but they were now, in a sense, outflanked: Vladimir's relentless gift-givings gained him a moral lead.

It is probably not an artifice of the chronicle that makes Vladimir appear the host and lord of his 'nobles' and 'retainers' alike, as if the two terms were interchangeable. Holding court in his new palace complex, the prince gained a certain social edge over them all. A feast was held every Sunday in a large assembly-hall of the palace, presumably after a service in the Tithe church. Vladimir ordained that it should be attended by boiars, urban militia commanders and 'distinguished men'. Food was supplied in abundance and, significantly, the show was to go on 'with the prince and without the prince'.[81] Perhaps

78 *PVL*, I, pp. 85–6.
79 Ibid., p. 86.
80 Rybakov, *Iazychestvo drevnei Rusi*, pp. 307–11; J. Blankoff, 'Černigov, rivale de Kiev? A propos de son développement urbain', *RES* 63 (1991), 149–50, 152 and n. 2. See also above, pp. 121–2, 134.
81 *PVL*, I, p. 86.

Vladimir was consciously evoking the rhythms of the Great Palace, and presumably Anna Porphyrogenita attended some of the banquets. What is clear is that Vladimir used his new cult to exercise a form of social control over other members of the elite. His palace remained a focal point, even when he had to be hundreds of kilometres away, a not infrequent occurrence, judging by the saga which terms him the 'king' of Holmgarthr.[82]

The palace buildings, rites and feasts were useful means of drawing diverse inhabitants of the Middle Dnieper region into an association with Vladimir's regime. However, they were rooted to one spot, the Starokievskaia hill. There was a medium projecting Vladimir's status which could circulate through his lands: coins. Only Vladimir himself featured on them and here, too, he was in the company of a powerful god. Vladimir issued both gold and silver coins soon after adopting Christianity. Altogether, eleven examples of the former and over 200 of the latter have been found. The finds are mostly in the Upper and Middle Dnieper region, with stray examples elsewhere along the East Way from the island of Gotland to the Dnieper estuary.[83] The fineness and the weight of the gold coins corresponded to the Byzantine *nomisma*'s, but they were only struck for a short time. In most of Vladimir's 'silver' coins there was far more copper, or other base metal, than silver, and the total number of silver coins was minuscule in comparison with the eastern dirhams still in circulation. The silver content of the latest arrivals from the east, although debased, was still markedly higher than that of Vladimir's issues. But simply through the act of issuing Vladimir showed himself to be a class apart.

Vladimir's chief purpose was to portray himself as the legitimate occupant of the throne, and this his gold coins and the earliest type of his silver coins did, literally. A Byzantine-style Christ Pantokrator (the Ruler of All) was shown on the face. On the reverse was Vladimir, sitting on a throne, wearing a Byzantine-style crown with pendants and holding a cross-topped sceptre. Few Byzantine coins depicted an emperor sitting on the throne and so the moneyer had to concoct his own design, with grotesque consequences. What is significant is the desire of the moneyer and his master to demonstrate that Vladimir was on the throne. To drive the message home, most of these coins bore the legend: 'Vladimir on the throne' (*Vladimir na stole*). As in other Scandinavian polities, so among the Rus, the throne or high-seat

---

82 *Óláfs Saga Tryggvasonar* [*Saga of King Olaf Tryggvason*], ch. 46, ed. Halldórson, p. 83; tr. Sephton, p. 54. The context is before Vladimir's Conversion, but his involvement with the town probably continued: he still had to reckon with the likes of Erik Haakonson: see below, p. 169.

83 Sotnikova and Spasski, *Russian Coins*, fig. 18, p. 84; fig. 21, p. 98; p. 66.

seems to have been the principal property of kingly authority. An alternative message could be read on variants of the gold coins and the earliest of the silver coins: respectively, 'Vladimir – and this is his gold' and 'Vladimir – and this is his silver'.[84] On the subsequent types of silver coins, from the later years of the reign, the throne becomes more clearly delineated, the bust of Christ disappears and his nimbus shifts to the head of the prince. The place of Christ is taken by a trident-like device, which was Vladimir's personal symbol of authority.[85] Such marks were in use among the Khazars and it was probably from them that Vladimir's predecessors had adopted them (see above, pp. 120–1). The trident occupied the obverse of Vladimir's coins for the rest of his reign. The legends and designs of the later types of Vladimir's silver coins show many minor variations, but the outlines of the princely sign are unmistakable.

Vladimir's 'talking coins' were partly addressed to retainers and notables in the east. But he was also vying with the other magnates capable of issuing such status symbols – not so much Byzantium's emperor as fellow-rulers in the northern lands. The khagan of the Volga Bulgars ceased issuing dirhams around the time that Vladimir struck his first coins, but c. 995 the king of the Swedes, Olaf Skotkönung, began to issue silver coins imitating the designs of the Anglo-Saxon kings. A few examples of these 'Sigtuna coins' have been found in the lands east of the Baltic.[86] Coins were also being issued in the mid-990s by the Danish king and by Olaf Tryggvason, now king of Norway. As with cults, so with coin-striking, northern rulers followed one another's moves keenly. The marked decline in the quantities of dirhams arriving from the east may have prompted them to try and set their stamps on such treasure as was available.

Vladimir maintained relations – exchanging, presumably, gifts and greetings – with other established rulers. The *Primary Chronicle* states that he 'lived in peace' with rulers such as Boleslaw of Poland and Stephen of Hungary.[87] Marriage-ties were arranged. Sviatopolk, one of his sons, was married to a daughter of Boleslaw, and an attempt was made to wed Vsevolod, one of Rogneda's sons, to Princess Sigrid of Sweden. Sigrid is depicted in a saga as having both Vsevolod and Harald of Greenland put to death, saying that 'in this way she was going to break kinglets of the habit of visiting her to ask her in marriage'.[88] These long-distance links were not purely ornamental. It had been from the Scandinavian world that Vladimir had raised a

---

84 Ibid., p. 80.
85 Ibid., pp. 79, 90, 178.
86 B. Malmer, *The Sigtuna Coinage c. 995–1005* (Stockholm, London, 1989), pp. 21, 36–7, 119–20.
87 *PVL*, I, p. 86.
88 *Heimskringla* ch. 43, tr. Hollander, p. 186.

war-band to fight his way to power in the East Way, and some time in the 990s Erik Haakonson, a Norwegian Jarl, 'harried Vladimir's land with fire, stormed Aldeigjuborg [Staraia Ladoga], that was a hard fight'. The verses are borne out by traces of the violent destruction of Staraia Ladoga's defence wall and a conflagration around the turn of the tenth and eleventh centuries. Other magnates, however, treated Vladimir's milieu as a launch-pad for expeditions in quest of riches and power bases, heading in the opposite direction. Olaf Tryggvason was one such, leading a war-fleet to pillage in the Baltic and then raiding England where, in 991, he exacted 10,000 lb of silver by way of tribute.[89]

3. DIGGING IN

If Vladimir could never afford to neglect the northern approaches to his riverways, the focal point of his revenues and newly sacred places lay in the south. Here, problems of defence were compounded by demography. The built-up area of Kiev had expanded during the second half of the tenth century with people flocking in from different directions. The slave-trade played an important, if indirect, part in this. Young women were among the most highly valued slaves, and it was not uncommon for members of the armed elite to be buried with a slave-girl. Vladimir's own concubines numbered 800, lodged in villages in the vicinity of Kiev, according to the *Primary Chronicle*. They may well have been as heterogeneous as the concubines who are said to have borne Vladimir's sons. One of these was a Czech, one a Byzantine nun, another a Bulgarian. Even allowing for exaggeration by the chronicle, one may suppose that a century or so of such liaisons left their mark on the size, as well as the ethnic mix, of the Middle Dnieper's population. There were also voluntary migrants to Kiev, such as the Arabic-speaker who carved a name on the stone mould found in the Podol, or Tury the Varangian who had returned from the Greeks (see above, p. 158). A number of the graves in Kiev's burial-grounds contained Finno-Ugrians and nomads, judging by their respective goods and rituals.[90] Already, before the Conversion, the elite was beginning to gain recruits of non-Scandinavian origin, who presumably advanced on the strength of martial prowess and their employers' trust in them.

89 Eyólfs *Bandadrápa*, ed. and tr. G. Vigfusson and F. York Powell, *Corpus boreale poeticum* (Oxford, 1883), II, p. 52; Mühle, *Städtischen Handelszentren*, p. 63; *The Anglo-Saxon Chronicle*, tr. D. Whitelock (London, 1965), pp. 82 and n. 3, 83; S. Keynes, 'The historical context of the Battle of Maldon', in D. Scragg, ed., *The Battle of Maldon A.D. 991* (Oxford, 1991), 88–90; Roesdahl, *The Vikings*, tr. Margeson and Williams, pp. 250–1.

90 A. P. Motsia, 'Etnichnyi sklad naselennia pivdennorus'kykh zemel' (za materialamy pokhoval'nykh pam'iatok X–XIII st.)', *Arkheolohiia* 1992, no. 1, 43–4.

However, the expansion and cultural diversity of Kiev was not typical of the region as a whole. The number of settlements and burial-grounds situated 30 kilometres or more from Kiev and datable to the tenth century is quite small. The only other unquestionably well-populated area was along the Desna, at Chernigov and further upstream (see above, pp. 109–10). From this quarter a relief force had come to Kiev in 969, and not from the west or south-west. Archaeological evidence of settlements in the latter areas is correspondingly meagre. In the mid-tenth century the land of the Rus had been a mere 'one day's journey' from the land of the Pechenegs.[91] The raids which Variazhko and, perhaps, other ex-associates of Iaropolk mounted with the Pechenegs made the southern approaches of Kiev still less prepossessing for agriculturalists.

By the early 980s Vladimir was confident enough of Kiev's security to lead expeditions far to the north and west. The fact remained that Kiev lay on an exposed outcrop of the Rus lands. The basic handicaps prompting Sviatoslav's decision to migrate had not lifted. Vladimir determined to make good the relative lack of, in effect, a hinterland for Kiev and thus of a population-base which might pay taxes and render military service, besides producing foodstuffs. He brought about the compulsory transplant of inhabitants of the northern forests to the region south of Kiev. The chronicle puts the following words into Vladimir's mouth: 'Look! It is not good that there are few towns around Kiev'. The chronicle lists the river valleys along which 'he began to found towns . . . and he began to choose the best men from the Slovenes, the Krivichi, the Chud and the Viatichi, and with these he peopled the towns, for there was warfare from the Pechenegs'.[92]

Archaeology supports the chronicle's indication that planned works were carried out following Vladimir's Conversion. It also bears out the words ascribed to him, in that Kiev was the lynchpin. The fortifications took the form of strongholds of varying sizes and long lines of earthworks which have come to be known as 'the Snake Ramparts' (zmievy valy). Controversy long raged over their date, but the attribution of numerous earthworks to Vladimir's era is now firm. Successive lines of ramparts were raised to the south and west of Kiev, forming a series of labyrinthine loops. There was also a continuous rampart on the Dnieper's left bank, skirting the valley. At the point where the Sula flowed into the Dnieper, this rampart joined up with another rampart, which tracked the lower course of the Sula.[93] Near the confluence, at a ford across the Sula, a large fortified settlement was constructed. Within its perimeter was a harbour capable of providing

---

91 *DAI*, ch. 37.47, pp. 168–9.
92 *PVL*, I, p. 83.
93 M. P. Kuchera, *Zmievy valy srednego Podneprov'ia* (Kiev, 1987), p. 179; illustration 4, pp. 16–17.

shelter to vessels plying the Dnieper. This base, covering 27 hectares, acquired the suggestive name of Voin (*voin'* = 'military').

The area where construction work was most intense, and Vladimir's involvement most pronounced, lay directly to the south of his throne-town. (See Map 6). Immediately to Kiev's south, a Snake Rampart was thrown up, blocking access from between the river Irpen and the Dnieper. The most important line lay further south, taking advantage of the natural defences of the left bank of the Stugna. The river alone was, on its lower reaches, deemed a sufficient barrier to nomad marauders. The Snake Rampart has been traced from a point on the Stugna which lay only 'three hours' fast ride' from Kiev.[94] After skirting the Stugna, the rampart carried on westwards to join up with the river Irpen, securing Kiev in a kind of triangle, and then wound its way north-westwards as far as the Teterev. This Snake Rampart, when eventually completed in the earlier eleventh century, ran for 100 kilometres.

Two further series of ramparts stretched westwards all the way from the Dnieper's banks, where they sandwiched in Vitichev, the newly fortified marshalling-point for Rus fleets bound for Byzantium. These outer ramparts had very few forts positioned along them, and the Snake Ramparts were not in general designed to be constantly manned.[95] Rather, they served to slow down the nomad horsemen, denying them the advantages of surprise. The ramparts were not particularly high – on average between 3.5 and 4 metres – but they were fronted by ditches as wide as 12 metres; these prevented even the lithest of horses from clearing the ramparts at full trot. The winding outer sets of Snake Ramparts obstructed the nomads' line of retreat with their loot, and they risked being trapped by their pursuers.

In order to pursue effectively, the Rus had to be mounted and expert in horsemanship, some being stationed nearby. The forts strung along the Stugna could accommodate cavalry units, and relief squadrons from Kiev were not many hours' travelling distance away. Vladimir's personal commitment to the new defence lines was symbolized by the naming of one of them Vasilev, after his Christian name and patron saint, Basil. It was there one summer that he was worsted by the Pechenegs and forced to hide beneath a bridge (see above, p. 165). The defences of Vasilev and a number of other forts and population centres were strengthened with the aid of a technical spin-off from the new cult. The interiors of the Snake Ramparts and most forts were reinforced by rows of logs placed parallel to the ramparts and resting on cross-pieces, or by logs forming cages filled with earth, sand or clay scooped out of the adjoining ditches. At Vasilev, in contrast, the citadel's rampart was raised over wooden frames whose outermost section was filled with neat horizontal rows of unfired

---

94 B. A. Rybakov, 'Vladimirovy kreposti na Stugne', *KSIA* 100 (1965), 126.
95 Kuchera, *Zmievy valy*, pp. 169, 128.

bricks. Excavations have revealed a comparable brick construction in the next fort east of Vasilev, at the modern village of Zareche. The ramparts of Vladimir's new towns of Belgorod and Pereiaslavl also contain unfired bricks in their cores. These bricks are of similar shape and size to unfired bricks reportedly excavated in the ramparts near the foundations of the Tithe church in Kiev, and there is no reason to doubt that the basic technique of making bricks was introduced by the Greek 'masters' who built that church. Reinforced with these brick supports the ramparts could be raised higher without risk of subsidence. Those at Vasilev still stand approximately 8 metres high, while the ramparts of Belgorod stand at between 5 and 6 metres and rose higher still in the 990s. Topped with palisades, these earthworks were designed to be defended. The total area enclosed at Belgorod was enormous, approximately 105 hectares. In addition, a few settlements were founded on promontories overlooking the Stugna, the Irpen and other rivers which the Snake Ramparts skirted or traversed. These agrarian settlements set away from the main forts could cover 7 hectares or more.[96]

The *Primary Chronicle* is rather matter-of-fact about Vladimir's building works south of Kiev, yet their scale represents a major feat of organization. Over 500 kilometres of earthen ramparts were raised during the quarter of a century following Vladimir's decision to build, taken soon after his Conversion. Perhaps as many as 100 forts, fortified towns and unfortified settlements were built, and many thousands of people were brought to live in them and sites as far apart as Chernigov and Cherven were refortified. The defences were well established by the time Bruno of Querfurt observed them in 1008. The German missionary described 'the most firm and lengthy fence [*sepe*]' with which Vladimir had 'everywhere enclosed' his 'realm'.[97] Vladimir accompanied Bruno and his party to a 'gate', through which they passed on foot. Their journey from Kiev had taken two days, and it was only on the third day after parting from Vladimir at the gate that Bruno encountered Pechenegs. In late winter, the time of Bruno's journey, the nomads tended to gravitate to the south in quest of easier grazing, but the contrast with the mid-tenth century still stands (see above, p. 123, n. 25).

In his concern for fortification work, Vladimir had something in common with King Alfred of Wessex. Alfred managed to establish more than 30 fortified centres (*burhs*) across Wessex, providing carefully for their maintenance. Vladimir was working on a grander scale and did not have the option of refurbishing earlier towns, as Alfred did. Winchester,

96 P. A. Rappoport, *Ocherki po istorii russkogo voennogo zodchestva X–XIII vv.* (*MIA* 52; Moscow, Leningrad, 1956), pp. 82–91; Kuchera, *Zmievy valy*, pp. 71–3.
97 Bruno of Querfurt, *Epistola ad Henricum regem*, ed. J. Karwasińska, *Monumenta Poloniae Historica, series nova*, IV.3 (Warsaw, 1973), p. 99.

one of the largest of Alfred's *burhs*, was only half the size of Belgorod and Alfred had Roman walls to build upon. Vladimir also lacked implements such as the *Burghal Hidage*, a written record of the number of units of agricultural land – hides – required to maintain the particular number of defenders of each *burh*. On the other hand Vladimir's predecessors had already shown organizational talents without much reliance on the written word and he was putting longstanding powers of coercion to new uses. King Alfred had no sweeping powers to relocate free men, and his biographer and chronicle-writers lament slackness in the implementation of fortress-building.[98] Vladimir had no need of this kind of literary campaign to extract labour from his subjects. But equally, scarcely any of Vladimir's subjects possessed the writing or reading skills with which to mount or learn from such a campaign. And this was, ultimately, a limitation on Vladimir's power.

If Vladimir managed a modest thrust into the steppes on the Dnieper's right bank, his need to take advantage of existing Slav population centres on the left bank helps explain the Snake Rampart stretching down to Voin and the rampart on the Sula. This configuration served Vladimir's overriding objective, the safeguarding of Kiev. The chronicle relates a prolonged siege of Belgorod and a confrontation with the nomads at the ford where Pereiaslavl was later founded. There was 'great and unremitting strife',[99] but there is no word of the Pechenegs attacking Kiev itself, let alone of a siege. They were now being held up by the strongholds and had to be mindful of their lines of retreat. Even so, Vladimir's defence lines were not impregnable, as the fate of the small promontory fort at Zareche shows. Vladimir had reinforced its ramparts with brickwork and the gates from the fortified settlement to the citadel led through a long, narrow tunnel. This did not save it from being sacked some time in the early eleventh century and the site was abandoned. Two *srebreniki* (silver coins) of Vladimir have been excavated in or near the gate-tower. They had probably been dropped by their owners during the sack.[100] Like the attempt to utilize brickwork to reinforce earthen ramparts on the Middle Dnieper, the silver coins represent an experiment which did not take.

However, Vladimir's final cult proved more than a fad. We have seen how he was prepared to intimidate the inhabitants of Kiev into being baptized *en masse* (see above, p. 163). His threat of violence and destruction of pagan shrines won him praise from a churchman in the mid-eleventh century (see below, p. 230). In Kiev part of the burial-ground containing members of the elite disappeared beneath the foundations of the Tithe church complex, while at Gorodishche the sanctuary just outside the town was destroyed and abandoned. From

98 *Anglo-Saxon Chronicle*, tr. Whitelock, p. 54; Asser, *Life of Alfred* ch. 91, in tr. S. Keynes and M. Lapidge, *Alfred the Great* (Harmondsworth, 1983), p. 102.
99 *PVL*, I, p. 87.
100 A. A. Medyntseva, 'Serebreniki iz Novgoroda Malogo', *SA* 1969, no. 4, 259–60.

around the end of the tenth century the burial-grounds at Gnëzdovo ceased to be the scene of boat-burnings or any other kind of cremation ritual. The dead at Gnëzdovo were buried under much smaller barrows and by the middle of the eleventh century they were being laid in pits in the ground.

Spectacular as were the prince's deeds in suppressing alternative centres of organized worship and burial-grounds, they were not in themselves sufficient to induce people regularly to observe Orthodox Christian rites or to conform to the behavioural norms preached by churchmen. It was in burial practices that members of a family or community were most likely to abide by custom and their own convictions as to what would serve the deceased best. Such practices could not be policed tightly by the prince's agents.

A glance at patterns of burial ritual reveals that burials broadly in line with what can be interpreted as Christian practice are peculiar to certain areas, mainly in the south of Vladimir's lands. Such burials are of bodies in pits dug into the earth, with few, if any, grave goods. The dead usually lay on their backs, with head towards the west and hands laid beside the body or across the chest. They were placed in wooden coffins. Among the Rus the graves are often beneath small circular barrows, a pre-Christian custom which priests felt unable to suppress or treated as a relatively harmless survival. The barrows did, in fact, offer scope for the perpetuation or evocation of pre-Christian customs. Pottery and other small personal effects were often placed in them, as also ashes symbolic of cremation and food symbolizing funeral feasts. At a select number of cemeteries there were, however, no barrows at all, from Vladimir's time onwards.

Pit-burials first became predominant in areas where Christians or churches are attested in the tenth century by other forms of evidence. As we have already seen (see above, p. 159), the majority of the population of Peremyshl and the other Cherven towns were Christian by the time of Vladimir's conquest and presumably their priests remained *en poste*. The marriage of Sviatopolk to a daughter of Boleslaw brought to his seat at Turov a bishop who was a 'Latin' Christian (i.e. under Roman papal rather than Byzantine jurisdiction), Reinbern of Kolberg. So, most probably, were the priests of the western towns. The closest analogies to Peremyshl's rotunda are in Moravia, the Czech lands and Poland. In the eleventh century the archbishopric of Prague still claimed jurisdiction up to the Western Bug and the Styr.[101] The important trade-routes linking the towns with Cracow and Prague may well have brought in churchmen as well as goods. This is the background to the appearance from the later tenth century onwards of clusters of burial-grounds containing

---

101 Cosmas of Prague, *Chronica Boemorum*, ed. B. Bretholz (*MGH* SS nov. ser., II; Berlin 1923), p. 138; I. D. Isaevich, 'Kul'tura galitsko-volynskoi Rusi', *Voprosy Istorii* 1973, no. 1, 102.

pit-burials, some in the region of Peresopnitsa, between the Upper Goryn and the Upper Styr, others near the Western Bug and the San and, in substantial quantities, along the Upper Dniester valley.[102] The interest of Vladimir and of earlier Rus princes in this relatively well-populated region and its lucrative transit routes is registered by the finds of chamber-graves there, albeit in smaller numbers than in the Middle Dnieper zone. These most probably belonged to members or agents of the princely elite who died during tours of duty. Once converted to Christianity, Vladimir could call upon the services of the local clergy, and quite rapid headway could be made in introducing Christian funerary rites and observance.

The region of Kiev and the zone stretching to its east is the other main area of finds of pit-burials. Here the correlation between princely authority and the introduction of new funerary ritual is obvious and unsurprising. At Kiev and Chernigov cremation was abandoned altogether with Vladimir's Conversion, and the bodies of the dead awaited the Resurrection intact. But barrows continued to be heaped over Chernigov's graves in the traditional way, and further upstream along the Desna bodies continued to be placed at ground-level or inside the barrows, a practice already coming into vogue among the Middle Dnieper Slavs long before Vladimir's Conversion. The burial-grounds around Chernigov were well established and even Vladimir may have found it difficult to enforce a sharp break with old ways in this thickly populated – and relatively well-armed – district. The outermost town cemetery switching to pit-burials in the 990s was at Kvetun, on the Middle Desna. By c. 1000 bridgeheads for the new burial rites and, presumably, the new religion were being established to the north of Chernigov, at Sednev (Snovsk in the chronicle) and Novgorod-Seversk. Pit-burials were also soon enforced further to the east in the steppe-frontier zone, in the region of Kursk.[103] But in the region not far to the west of the Middle Dnieper the inhabitants felt free to bury their dead in distinctive ways: the Derevlians buried their dead at ground-level, under barrows.

It was in Kiev itself, and the new plantations along the steppe frontier, that adherence to Orthodox Christian norms was most thoroughgoing. In the barrowless cemeteries of new towns such as Belgorod and Voin there was little or no past to break with. The prince was near at hand, and on the surface there was no flouting of Christian decorum. Underground, however, some old ways persisted. Brazen acts of paganism such as the boat-burning with sacrifices of animals at Belgorod are rare, and they date from the last years of the tenth century.

---

102 Motsia, *Pogrebal'nye pamiatniki*, map 64, pp. 70–1; map 65, pp. 76–7; map 68, pp. 84–5.
103 Ibid., pp. 96–7.

The overwhelming majority of the dead at Belgorod were nailed down in coffins, as they were at Voin and a neighbouring fort along the Sula, in the precincts of modern Zhovnino. But many of these graves also contain potsherds and, less often, animal bones. Women were often laid out in their finery, wearing rings at their temples or ear-rings, and hooded garments tipped with Byzantine silk.[104] Silver ear-rings with seven tiny blades hanging from them have been found in cemeteries ranging from Zhovnino to a settlement north of the river Zdvizh, at modern Nezhilovichi. They were characteristic of the Radimichi, and were presumably brought by transplantees from the Upper Dnieper region. Jingling pendants of the sort favoured by the Finno-Ugrians are found in other graves.

Finds of amulets are not uncommon in the eleventh-century cemeteries and settlements south of Kiev. On the one hand, circular pendants symbolizing the sun, miniature axes and hammerlets and flints apparently connected with the cult of Perun have been found; on the other, there are more or less mass-produced pectoral or necklace crosses and stamped metal icons of saints. The bearers or donors of these objects, which are sometimes placed together in the same grave, need not have been aware of their divergent associations. But they did count for something more than ornaments. The barrowless pit cemeteries tend to contain fewest traces of potsherds, ashes or non-Christian amulets: this suggests deliberate adherence to the norms laid down by Orthodox priests. It is no accident that such cemeteries mostly fall within a 250-kilometre radius of Kiev, or lie far to the west, in the region of the Dniester basin or the Cherven towns.

The transplantees from the northern forests had been plucked out of kin-groups and communities and they were highly susceptible to the prince's will and the ministrations of his priests. Belgorod was one of the very few towns in which Vladimir installed a bishop (see below, p. 228), and a wooden church excavated in the citadel may be identifiable as the bishop's church. It is very probable that priests were assigned to other major population centres. The elaborate fortifications and chains of warning beacons could not remove the risk of Pecheneg raids. The dismembered bodies found in a number of Voin's graves attest violent death, and the male skeletons at Zhovnino sometimes bear the marks of sword-cuts.[105] Living under threat of sudden attack, mutilation or captivity, the settlers may well have looked to the new religion for solace and protection. The prince himself seems to have

---

104 G. G. Mezentseva and I. P. Prilipko, 'Otkrytie belgorodskogo mogil'nika', *SA* 1976, no. 2, 246–8; idem, 'Davn'orus'kyi mohyl'nyk Belgoroda Kyivs'koho (doslidzhennia 1974–1976 rr.)', *Arkheolohiia* 35 (1980), 106–9.

105 V. I. Dovzhenok, V. K. Goncharov and R. O. Iura, *Drevn'orus'ke misto Voin'* (Kiev, 1966), p. 65; V. D. Diadenko and A. P. Motsia, 'Zhovnyns'kyi mohyl'nyk XI–XIII st.', *Arkheolohiia* 54 (1986), 84–5.

gained reassurance from it, as after his close shave at Vasilev (see above, p. 165). Christian worship was thus close-allied to Vladimir's stance of defiance towards the Pechenegs, which seems to mark a departure from that of his predecessors (see above, pp. 123, 146). In so far as there were persons answering the *Primary Chronicle*'s salutation of 'new Christian people, chosen by God, who have received baptism and penitence for the forgiveness of their sins', they mostly lived in the southern settlements. Many were, like Vladimir himself, newcomers to the region and what he gained from the new rites in legitimacy they may have gained in security and a sense of identity as Christian folk.

Vladimir had, then, followed a path in some ways diametrically opposed to his father's. Sviatoslav had taken on the look of a nomad chieftain and rowed with his fellows to meet Tzimiskes in a manner which Scandinavian magnates would have recognized. Vladimir was more concerned to set himself apart both from other notables on the Dnieper and from the nomads. To Bruno of Querfurt in 1008 he appeared established, 'a *senior* great in wealth and realm'.[106] Bruno conveys a sense of the sharp divide between the 'limit' of Vladimir's realm and the 'path to the pagans' beyond it. Vladimir expressed to Bruno his conviction that he would soon be killed and in fact Bruno and his companions were repeatedly threatened by 'a thousand axes, a thousand swords unsheathed above our necks' amidst 'a horrible clamouring'.[107] Bruno's account also reveals the Pechenegs' acute suspicion of the Rus and their leader. Their assumption that war was the normal state of relations between them and the Rus contrasts with the situation a generation earlier. It has been said that Bruno and his companions were, in taking leave of Vladimir at the gate in the rampart, crossing the 'symbolic frontier of the Christian world'.[108] Sviatoslav's hordes had themselves rekindled Byzantine fantasies that they were one of the savage peoples of the north whose irruption Ezekiel prophesied.[109] And whereas Sviatoslav decided that Pereiaslavets should become 'the centre of my land' (see above, p. 145), Vladimir dug in at Kiev, and most of his actions after c. 988 were aimed at consolidating his position there.

It would, however, be misleading to regard the contrast between the two leaders as absolute. Equally, one must beware of taking too sanguine a view of Vladimir's achievement, real as it was. Sviatoslav and Vladimir were each, in their way, riding the tiger of economic growth and, in the northern forests, population growth. Sviatoslav's solution to the problem of exploiting this sprawling yet ultimately

---

106 Bruno of Querfurt, *Epistola*, p. 98.
107 Ibid., p. 100.
108 A. Poppe, 'Vladimir, prince chrétien', in S. W. Swierkosz-Lenart, ed., *Le origini e lo sviluppo della cristianità slavo-bizantina* (Nuovi Studi Storici 17; Rome, 1992), p. 58.
109 Leo Deac., p. 150.

economically interdependent jumble of people and communities had been to decamp. As we have seen, the regime he installed in the Balkans showed every sign of being able to cope with a prosperous region where numerous fortified settlements flanked a major navigable river near its mouth.

Vladimir's solution to the problems of governance was rather more similar to Sviatoslav's than might at first sight appear. Essentially, he created round Kiev a zone of fortified settlements skirting the Dnieper and its tributaries. His throne-town thereby gained not only a shield but also a better-populated, more prosperous hinterland. For the first time, Kiev's ruler disposed of a core of domains extensive enough to sustain a substantial fighting force yet compact and accessible enough to be supervised by the prince and a few relatives or trusted associates. To a large extent, their inhabitants were newcomers lacking in alternative loyalties or any tradition of bargaining with the prince. In a sense, Vladimir was planting on the Middle Dnieper an urbanized polity such as his father had hoped to rule from the Lower Danube. The journey to the sea remained arduous but Vladimir made protection of the southern riverway a priority. Fortified harbours capable of accommodating many boats were built at Vitichev, Voin and other major settlements in the vicinity of the Dnieper and one of the functions of the Snake Rampart flanking the Dnieper was to hinder the Pechenegs from positioning themselves on the left bank and ambushing vessels. It now became possible to send out escort vessels or cavalry units as far as the Rapids, and the Dnieper estuary became less inhospitable. A trading settlement arose on the boggy Velikopotemkin Island towards the end of the tenth century. It contained numerous warehouses and workshops, eventually expanding to cover about 4 hectares.[110] The hazards of the long haul to Tsargrad were thus reduced, and traffic increased.

Vladimir's achievement can, then, be viewed as more a development, or variant, of Sviatoslav's undertakings in the Balkans than a complete about-turn. Each was seeking a lucrative, manageable core region, having inherited a dynamic but amorphous set of rights and routes. Vladimir's initiatives, for all their ingenuity and judicious rationale, left many questions of governance unresolved. Kiev was still in the anomalous position of being at once premier town and outpost. One of the effects of Vladimir's fencing-off of his Dnieper possessions was to provoke the nomads, who may well have regarded the Dnieper valley as their summer grazing grounds. Despite Bruno of Querfurt's efforts to bring about a reconciliation, raids and counter-raids between the Rus and the Pechenegs were still in full swing in the last years of Vladimir's reign.

A permanent state of alert against the nomads yielded benefits for the political order of the Dnieper region. The Pecheneg menace gave

110 A. L. Sokul'sky, 'K lokalizatsii letopisnogo Olesh'ia', *SA* 1980, no. 1, 65–6, 71–3.

the frontier settlers a common interest in rendering services for their prince-protector. And they might well consider themselves to be members of a single Christian flock, detached from their affinities to Radimichi or other tribal customs. But the prince's involvement with them in such fundamental matters as settling disputes and protecting property was minimal, and the nature of his authority was correspondingly rudimentary. The *Primary Chronicle* obliquely acknowledges this, and also the limitations of the impact of Christian norms on everyday life, in its story of Vladimir and the bishops.[111]

Further afield, the prince's presence was fitful and his regime's impact on ordinary inhabitants of the coniferous forest zone was slight. The distribution pattern of the pit-burials of the late tenth and eleventh centuries shows up the patchiness of princely authority and Christian observances alike. Vladimir's energies and resources were probably fully stretched with the maintenance of control-points from Staraia Ladoga (which had eventually to be refortified after Jarl Erik's sack) to the Dnieper's mouth, together with the construction of an urbanized region near Kiev. The catchment areas from which slaves and primary produce could be extracted splayed out more or less indefinitely to the north and the east, and to attempt to convert the inhabitants or otherwise alter their lifestyles was not on Vladimir's agenda. Peoples such as the Radimichi, Krivichi and Viatichi retained distinctive rites and customs, even sharpening their tribal identities with the aid of distinctive ornaments which seem to have proliferated in the generations after Vladimir's Conversion. They were cowed, but not totally subjugated. Two generations after Bruno visited Kiev, for a member of the Kievan princely family to journey 'through the Viatichi' was still a noteworthy feat, at least in his own view.[112] The Viatichian land was not very much further from the Middle Dnieper than that of the Pechenegs, 'the worst and cruellest people of all the pagans on earth'.[113]

Vladimir could not supervise all his far-flung strongholds in person, but some focus of local loyalties in the most distant centres was politic. This had for some time been the case with the inhabitants of Gorodishche-Novgorod, where Vladimir could count on his capable uncle. But Vladimir seems to have made more sweeping use of his own sons than his predecessors had done, to the exclusion of such other relatives and princely families as had come through the 970s. Dobrynia was, at some stage, succeeded as power-holder in Novgorod by one of Vladimir's sons, Vysheslav, borne to him by a Czech concubine. Later, after Vysheslav's death, Vladimir assigned to the town one of his sons

---

111 *PVL*, I, pp. 86–7; D. H. Kaiser, *The Growth of the Law in Medieval Russia* (Princeton, 1980), pp. 75–6; see also below, p. 221.

112 Vladimir Monomakh, in *PVL*, I, p. 158.

113 Bruno of Querfurt, *Epistola*, p. 100.

by Rogneda, Iaroslav. Other sons – presumably chosen from the most capable as well as apparently trustworthy – stood in for Vladimir at various points where sizable populations were concentrated, magnates had appeared or foreign potentates loomed large. Princes were sent to Rostov – near the Sarskii fort (see above, p. 22) – and to Murom, where the Volga Bulgars remained as indomitable neighbours; to the nearby land of the Derevlians, which had been subdued, but not assimilated; to Turov, Tury's former base; and to one of the Cherven towns, a recent foundation which was dignified with Vladimir's original, pagan, name, perhaps indicating the date when he first took a close interest in it – the modern Vladimir-in-Volynia. So long as the undisputed patriarch of the family lived, this division of labour and attention to prosperous border areas represented an expedient and lucrative arrangement. Out of enlightened self-interest and a certain blood-loyalty, Vladimir's sons could be expected to work together with him, keeping the trade-routes open and the tribute flowing in. But not even the 'new Constantine' could live for ever.

PART II:

Kiev and Rus

CHAPTER FIVE

Martyrs and Mercenaries
(c. 1015–36)

In the late 1040s Ilarion, a priest of the church of the Holy Apostles at the princely residence of Berestovo just south of Kiev, issued a rhetorical invitation to Vladimir to rise from the grave and gaze upon his legacy, to see how worthily and gloriously he was succeeded by his son: 'whom God made heir to your rule after you . . . Arise . . . Behold your offspring! Behold him whom you loved! . . . Behold him who adorned the throne of your land, and so rejoice and be glad!'[1] This beloved son and divinely appointed heir was Iaroslav, in baptism Georgii, ruler of Kiev until 1054, renowned as Iaroslav the Wise, patron of learning, builder of a great city ('shining in splendour', enthused Ilarion), kinsman – through the marriages of his children – to royalty throughout Europe, legislator, founder of the magnificent church of St Sophia which shimmered with the gold of its mosaics, creator and emblem of the Golden Age of Kievan Rus. As the chronicler said, 'his father Vladimir ploughed and harrowed the land – that is, enlightened it by baptism. And Iaroslav sowed the hearts of the faithful with the words of the Books. And we reap the harvest . . .'[2]

Ilarion was a eulogist, not a modern historian. His job was to conjure an image of tranquillity, of virtue triumphant, of the stately fulfilment of providential design. Events, however, were grubbier than their grand summation. There was no decorous transfer of power after Vladimir's death in 1015, no smooth succession by the beloved son and heir. Instead there was a nasty and prolonged civil war, in which Vladimir's numerous children, aided by recruits from neighbouring and distant lands, set at each other's throats. Iaroslav re-established a semblance of his father's authority only after all of his eleven known brothers had either died, or been murdered, or been incarcerated. The process took twenty years, and raises important questions about the nature of dynastic legitimacy, about the basis of princely power.

---

1 Moldovan, *Slovo*, p. 98; Franklin, *Sermons and Rhetoric*, pp. 23–4.
2 *PVL*, I, p. 102.

1. BATTLES OF SUCCESSION

Sources of information on the conflicts which followed Vladimir's death are, by the standards of the period, relatively abundant. The wars of 1015–19, in particular, resonated far beyond their immediate context, and there are substantial written accounts, both native and foreign. Native interest was sharpened by the fact that two of the minor participants, the murdered brothers Boris and Gleb, subsequently turned out to have been saints. Thus the chronicles' narratives are supplemented, and sometimes contradicted, by two works of hagiography in honour of the saints: the *Lection* (or 'Legend', or 'Lesson' – *Chtenie*), written by the monk Nestor of the Caves monastery in the late 1070s or early 1080s; and an anonymous *Tale* (*Skazanie*), which has been hypothetically dated to various times between the mid-eleventh and early twelfth centuries.[3] Briefer, more distant geographically, but far closer in time, are the extracts in the Latin chronicle by Thietmar, bishop of Merseburg, who died on 1 December 1018. These were reports from eye-witnesses, Saxon soldiers in the army of Boleslaw of Poland. Parts of the surviving manuscript are in Thietmar's own hand.[4] Finally, there is the ample but remote and clouded version in *Eymund's Saga*, which is found in the late fifteenth-century manuscript collection of Icelandic sagas known as the *Flateyjarbók*.[5]

The disparate sources tell disparate stories, and the facts behind them can be pieced together in several ways. In its most likely sequence – if for the moment we leave aside the controversies – the succession of conflicts (or the conflicts of succession) can be divided into four unequal phases involving different combinations of Vladimir's sons in various political and territorial configurations.

The first phase began even before Vladimir had died. As we have seen, Vladimir's policy was to convert the lands of the Rus into a family firm, to install his sons in key towns. But there are signs that in the latter years of his reign at least some of his sons were less loyal than he might have wished. Around 1013 or 1014 Sviatopolk of Turov is alleged to have plotted against him, and Vladimir had him arrested

---

3 Texts in Abramovich/Müller, *Erzählungen*; earliest text of the *Tale* in *Uspenskii sbornik*, cols 8–26 (pp. 42–71); English translations in Hollingsworth, *Hagiography*.

4 Text in Holtzmann, *Die Chronik*; relevant extracts and most detailed commentary in A. V. Nazarenko, *Nemetskie latinoiazychnye istochniki IX–XI vekov. Teksty, perevody, kommentarii* (Moscow, 1993), pp. 131–205; also M. B. Sverdlov, *Latinoiazychnye istochniki po istorii Drevnei Rusi. Germaniia, IX–pervaia polovina XII v.* (Moscow, Leningrad, 1989). See also the generally less reliable account in the chronicle of Gallus Anonymus: below, n. 14.

5 Text in Sigurðr Nordal, ed., *Flateyjarbók* (Akranes, 1945), II, pp. 199–218; English translation in H. Pálsson and P. Edwards, *Vikings in Russia: Yngvar's Saga and Eymund's Saga* (Edinburgh, 1989), pp. 69–89.

and held – perhaps in Kiev, perhaps in nearby Vyshgorod.[6] In 1015 Iaroslav himself refused to send Vladimir the regular dues from his own town of Novgorod. Vladimir prepared to march north, but fell ill and died before setting out.[7] The circumstances of Sviatopolk's and Iaroslav's quarrels with their father are obscure, but unrelated sources (Thietmar and the chronicle) suggest that dynastic or regional tension predates the death of Vladimir.

The second phase lasted through the summer of 1015, starting on the day Vladimir died, Friday 15 July. The principal actors were Sviatopolk of Turov and three of his brothers: Boris of Rostov, Gleb of Murom and Sviatoslav of the Derevlian land. Sviatopolk's previous arrest turned out to his advantage, for it ensured that he was already in Kiev (or Vyshgorod), closest to the centre of power, and thus able to manoeuvre more quickly and effectively than his brothers. If the native narratives are to be believed, Sviatopolk bribed the locals into acquiescence, assumed authority in Kiev, and applied his energies to arranging for the murder of as many of his brothers as he could. His first victim was Boris, whom Vladimir had sent south against the Pechenegs. Returning from the steppes, deserted by his father's men (supposedly for declining their offer to take Kiev on his behalf), Boris camped by the river Alta – in the middle ages a kind of perennial Rubicon on the road to or from the lands of the nomads, now the site of Kiev's international airport, about 40 kilometres south-east of the city. Here, on Sunday 24 July, Sviatopolk's assassins found him and killed him. Gleb was next, lured by deceit from distant Murom in the north-east. He reached the confluence of the rivers Smiadin and Dnieper close to Smolensk, where he too was murdered without resistance, on Monday 5 September.[8] Sviatoslav was killed while trying to escape to Hungary; no source gives any further details of his murder.

On the economic, political, military and social seismograph this series of fraternal assassinations would barely register. Yet in Kievan political, dynastic and cultural mythology the summer murders of 1015 became immensely significant. Boris and Gleb, it seems, were saints. Like many saints, they were posthumously versatile, acquiring in and for each age the qualities and virtues sought from them by those who

---

6 Thietmar VII.72(52), in Holtzmann, *Die Chronik*, p. 486. On problems of dating see Sverdlov, *Latinoiazychnye istochniki*, pp. 80–3; Nazarenko, *Nemetskie latinoiazychnye istochniki*, pp. 171–2.

7 *PVL*, I, pp. 88–9.

8 The days of the week in the *Tale* are correct for 1015; *Uspenskii sbornik*, cols 10d.25, 14d.26; Hollingsworth, *Hagiography*, pp. 103, 110.

promoted their veneration.[9] They dominate the native narratives, and partly in consequence they tend to dominate historical investigation, although in context they were minor players and their murders no more than a prelude.

In the third phase, which stretched from late 1015 until 1019, Sviatopolk faced Iaroslav of Novgorod, a far more formidable opponent. A period of opportunistic assassination gave way to a period of episodically fierce war. The first major clash took place in the frosty autumn near Liubech, some 150 kilometres north of Kiev and about 40 kilometres from Chernigov.[10] The two brothers encamped on opposite sides of the Dnieper: Iaroslav on the right bank, with an army of Novgorodians and Varangians; Sviatopolk on the left bank, his forces augmented by Pechenegs. For three months they faced each other, until Iaroslav's men devised a strategy to split Sviatopolk's retinue from the Pechenegs and force them onto the thin ice of a lake. As the ice started breaking, 'Sviatopolk fled to the Poles, and Iaroslav sat on the throne of his father and grandfather in Kiev'.[11]

Iaroslav's first reign in Kiev lasted for two-and-a-half years (or one-and-a-half, if one prefers a later date for the battle of Liubech). In July 1018 Sviatopolk returned in strength, with a multinational army led by Boleslaw I of Poland.[12] Again the brothers battled, on this occasion by the Western Bug, near the contentious western frontier zones where the Rus and the Poles continually competed for influence. Iaroslav suffered a massive defeat and fled back to Novgorod, while Boleslaw advanced with Sviatopolk on Kiev. On 14 August they entered the city, where Boleslaw helped himself and his foreign hirelings to 'incalculable wealth'.[13] Boleslaw dismissed his auxiliaries as soon as the locals were pacified. It is not clear how long

---

9 On variations in the early cult see Gail Lenhoff, *The Martyred Princes Boris and Gleb: a Socio-Cultural Study of the Cult and the Texts* (Columbus, Ohio, 1989); on dating the origins of the cult see L. Müller, 'Zur Frage nach dem Zeitpunkt der Kanonisierung der Heiligen Boris und Gleb', in A.-E. Tachiaos, ed., *the Legacy of Saints Cyril and Methodius to Kiev and Moscow. Proceedings of the International Congress on the Millennium of the Conversion of the Rus' to Christianity* (Thessaloniki, 1992), pp. 321–39; see also below, pp. 188, 215, 249–50, 256–7.

10 For the view that the Liubech battle took place in the following year, see A. V. Nazarenko, 'O datirovke Liubechskoi bitvy', in *Letopisi i khroniki. Sbornik statei. 1984g.* (Moscow, 1984), pp. 13–19; but the *Primary Chronicle* (*PVL*, I, p. 96) may here be using a year beginning in September.

11 *PVL*, I, p. 96; but *NPL*, p. 15, reads 'to the Pechenegs'; cf. *Eymund's Saga*, in Pálsson and Edwards, *Vikings in Russia*, pp. 74–5.

12 Thietmar VIII.32, in Holtzmann, *Die Chronik*, p. 530; on the possibility of an earlier, smaller-scale intervention by Boleslaw in the previous year, see A. V. Nazarenko, 'Sobytiia 1017g. v nemetskoi khronike nachala XIv. i v russkoi letopisi', *DGTSSSR* 1980 (1981), pp. 175–84.

13 Thietmar VIII.32; cf. VII.65(48), in Holtzmann, *Die Chronik*, p. 478.

he himself stayed in Kiev,[14] but when he left he took booty, slaves and, curiously, a defecting churchman. On his way home he paused to claim the Cherven towns, which one suspects were his prime objective and which may have been ceded as part of his bargain with Sviatopolk.[15]

Without his Polish enforcers, Sviatopolk became vulnerable once more. As Iaroslav again advanced, he fled south to raise another force of Pechenegs. The final battle took place in 1019, by the Alta: 'at the place', says the chronicler, sensitive to poetic justice, 'where Boris had been murdered'. It was only proper that here Iaroslav should win a great victory. Sviatopolk made for Poland, but reportedly fell ill on the journey and died. And Iaroslav, fortunate not for the first or the last time, 'sat in Kiev with his *druzhina* and wiped away the sweat'.[16]

The end of Sviatopolk was not yet the end of fraternal conflict, nor, merely by installing himself in Kiev, had Iaroslav restored for himself the authority of his father. He was stretched. If he stayed in the south, then Novgorod in the north suffered the unwelcome attentions of his nephew Briacheslav of Polotsk;[17] but if Iaroslav stayed in Novgorod, then yet another of his brothers – Mstislav of Tmutorokan – was tempted into the vacuum on the Middle Dnieper; as, indeed, were the Pechenegs, who had previously helped Sviatopolk and Boleslaw. The fourth and last phase of the struggle for succession was also the longest, extending from 1019 to 1024 or 1026. Briacheslav of Polotsk was no more than an irritant. The really serious rival was Mstislav, who, from his base on the Straits of Kerch, had become a powerful figure in the Azov and eastern Black Sea region (see below, pp. 200–1). Mstislav seems not to have attempted a sustained assault on Kiev, but in 1024 (or thereabouts) he moved his headquarters north of the steppes to Chernigov, ominously close. True to form, the brothers mustered armies and fought at the battle of Listven. Victory went to Mstislav, the newcomer from the deep south.

The sequel, however, was unprecedented. According to formula the narrative should continue 'and Iaroslav fled, and Mstislav sat on the throne of his father in Kiev'. But it does not. Instead of giving another push to the military see-saw, the brothers decided to bring it to a halt. They agreed to co-exist, to divide the lands between them and to try to live in peace. Mstislav, based in Chernigov, would have the left (i.e.

14 The most common view is that his stay was brief, since news of his homecoming reached Merseburg before Thietmar's death on 1 December 1018; but note the textual objections of Nazarenko, 'Sobytiia 1017g.' and in *Nemetskie latinoiazychnye istochniki*, pp. 160–2. The chronicle of Gallus Anonymus, ed. C. Maleczyński (Monumenta Poloniae Historica, n.s. II, Cracow, 1952), I.7 (p. 23), unreliably indicates a stay of ten months.
15 On the churchman, Anastasii of Cherson, see pp. 163, 227. On a legend concerning one of the captives, see below, pp. 292–3; on the Cherven towns see also above, p. 157.
16 *PVL*, I, p. 98.
17 Ibid., p. 99 (s.a. 6529).

the eastern) bank of the Dnieper and the regions associated therewith, including Tmutorokan; Iaroslav would have the right (i.e. the western) bank and associated lands, including both Kiev and Novgorod. Still Iaroslav was tentative. For two years he stayed in Novgorod, until he could assemble enough men to allow him to feel secure in proximity to Mstislav. Finally, in 1026, he returned south to Kiev, reaffirmed the arrangement with Mstislav, 'and internecine strife ceased, and there was great tranquillity in the land'.[18]

Iaroslav had luck to match his caution. In 1036[19] Mstislav went out hunting, fell ill and died. He had no living son, or none of whom we know, so Iaroslav 'took over all of his domain' (vlast', volost'). Thus at last, by care and chance and the accident of survival, but certainly not by smooth succession, Iaroslav 'became autocrat [sole ruler, samovlastets] of the land of the Rus'[20] and inheritor of the legacy of his father; though he did give chance a nudge by imprisoning his one remaining brother – Sudislav – in Pskov; and a separate branch of the family still held Polotsk. Nevertheless, despite the blemishes, it was a substantial reward for two decades of graft.

The catalogue of fraternal conflicts and settlements means little in itself: a bewildering list of names, places and battles, another squalid tale of ambition and opportunism, reminiscent of Vladimir's own rise to power by dubious means nearly 40 years earlier (see above, pp. 153–4). Such is the appearance, but where is the substance? Why, after three decades of Vladimir's sole rule, was the re-establishment of dynastic order apparently so difficult, violent and haphazard? In the first instance let us look through the prism of the sources.

2. RIGHTS AND RIGHT

The native narratives encourage a moral approach, presenting the fraternal strife as a clash between good and evil. The figure of evil is Sviatopolk 'the Cursed', inspired by the devil to fratricide in his lust for power, more foul even than Cain. Boris and Gleb are figures of murdered innocence, lambs to the slaughter, offering no resistance, praying in humility and piety, Christ-like in their acceptance of suffering and death.[21] Such contrasts are proper for hagiography; but

---

18 Ibid., p. 100.

19 Or perhaps in 1034–5: the manuscripts of the Chronicle differ here in their allocation of events to years. See PSRL, I, col. 150; PSRL, II, col. 138. In favour of 1034 see M. Dimnik, 'The "Testament" of Iaroslav "The Wise": a re-examination', Canadian Slavonic Papers 29 (1987), 371.

20 PVL, I, p. 101.

21 See e.g. George P. Fedotov, The Russian Religious Mind (I). Kievan Christianity. The 10th to the 13th Centuries (Cambridge, Mass., 1946; repr. Belmont, Mass., 1975), pp. 94–110; see also above, n. 9.

other types of source reflect other values. For example, in *Eymund's Saga* Eymund's Northmen in the service of Iarisleif (i.e. Iaroslav) devise an ingenious scheme to dispose of his rival Burislaf: they bend a tree to the ground, secretly attach a rope from the tree to Burislaf's tent, and at night release the tree so that the tent is hurled into the woods. They then kill the surprised and defenceless Burislaf. Eymund reports his ruse with pride as he delivers Burislaf's severed head to Iarisleif.[22] Here heroism is measured by boldness and stratagem rather than by Christ-like humility. For all we know (which is very little), Sviatopolk might have been acting according to the expected and acceptable norms of his milieu; or he was an abomination; or a mixture of both.

How can one disentangle the values of the participants from the values of those who later told stories about them? And how far were the storytellers prepared to go in shaping the events to fit their own moral or political or literary agendas? The narratives are inconsistent. For some, the native accounts reek of conspiracy. For the most tenacious conspiracy theorists, there was collusion in a massive cover-up, in a huge lie designed not only to promote the veneration of Boris and Gleb but also to protect the true villain: Vladimir's beloved son and heir, Iaroslav himself. The key to veracity (in this theory) is to be found in *Eymund's Saga*: the character whom the saga calls Burislaf, and who is usually interpreted as a literary composite of Sviatopolk and Boleslaw[23] is identified instead as Boris. Like Boris, and unlike either Sviatopolk or Boleslaw, Burislaf in the saga was killed by hired Varangians on the orders of his brother; but in the saga the murderous brother was not Sviatopolk but Iarisleif/Iaroslav.

This conspiracy theory has been propounded in several versions, not all of which are compatible with one another.[24] It can be attractive and sometimes plausible, but it is not persuasive. Too much reliance is placed on the more derivative and distant sources. If the main native stories were concocted as a whitewash for Iaroslav's reputation, then Iaroslav is presented in an oddly unfavourable light: he vacillates, is a poor strategist, sometimes even cowardly, and guilty of several political misjudgements. Nevertheless, behind the somewhat over-enthusiastic

---

22 Pálsson and Edwards, *Vikings in Russia*, pp. 81–4.

23 Robert Cook, 'Russian history, Icelandic story, and Byzantine strategy in Eymdunar þáttr Hringssonar', *Viator* 17 (1986), 65–89; also T. N. Dzhakson, 'Islandskie korolevskie sagi kak istochnik po istorii Drevnei Rusi i ee sosedei X–XIII vv.', *DGTSSSR* 1989–90 (1991), 160.

24 See esp. N. N. Il'in, *Letopisnaia stat'ia 6523 goda i ee istochniki* (Moscow, 1957); G. M. Filist, *Istoriia 'prestupleniia' Sviatopolka Okaiannogo* (Minsk, 1990); A. S. Khoroshev, *Politicheskaia istoriia russkoi kanonizatsii (XI–XVI vv.)* (Moscow, 1986), pp. 13–36; also A. V. Golovko, *Drevniaia Rus' i Pol'sha v politicheskikh vzaimosviaziakh X–pervoi treti XIII vv.* (Kiev, 1988), pp. 23–6.

reconstructions and deconstructions there is a valid and important point. The extant native narratives do reflect hidden and not-so-hidden agendas. Their authors were not only trying to piece together a tale which may have been imperfectly known or remembered even in their own time; they were also trying to impose interpretations. Their value-judgements served a purpose, were functional; and one of their functions was to explain and justify in retrospect (and hence with much wishful thinking) both the particular dynastic succession and a wider set of dynastic (i.e. political) ethical standards; they are about rights as well as right, about legitimacy as well as morality. Behind the question of who did what to whom is the issue of how, in the early eleventh century, such a dispute was perceived: who *was* the rightful heir to Vladimir? What notions of political order were violated or confirmed in the events of 1015–36?

Vladimir was known to later chroniclers as a man of many wives and a cornucopia of concubines: he is said to have had 300 concubines in Vyshgorod, 300 in Belgorod, and 200 in Berestovo.[25] In part his reputation for sexual excess is due to pious hyperbole: the greater his vices as a pagan, the greater the miracle of his conversion to Christianity. Yet his propensities were stressed by contemporary detractors as well as by posthumous admirers, and his prowess was rumoured abroad. Thietmar calls him a 'fornicator immensus et crudelis'.[26] The total number of his children is unknown. In the native sources the names of a dozen sons are listed, born of at least five different mothers, in uncertain sequence.[27] Thietmar also mentions nine daughters,[28] though only one, Predslava, is named in the native sources.[29] It is not clear whether Vladimir truly was the first of his line to spawn such numerous offspring, or whether he was merely the first whose offspring's actions and names happen to be narrated in such detail.

When the sources try to assess the relative status of Vladimir's children, the attempt is obviously strained. The *Tale*, for example, states that Sviatopolk was not really Vladimir's son at all. His mother had been a 'Greek' (i.e. Byzantine) nun, abducted by Vladimir's brother Iaropolk and then abducted again, when already pregnant, by Vladimir after he had killed Iaropolk: 'so he was from two fathers who were also brothers, and therefore Vladimir never loved him, as not being his own issue'.[30] The *Primary Chronicle* contains a similar

---

25 *PVL*, I, p. 57; see also above, p. 169.
26 Thietmar VII.72, in Holtzmann, *Die Chronik*, p. 486.
27 *PVL*, I, pp. 56–7, 83. See below, table I.
28 Thietmar VIII.32, in Holtzmann, *Die Chronik*, p. 530.
29 *PVL*, I, p. 95; two anonymous daughters: ibid, p. 56; on daughters see Nazarenko, *Nemetskie latinoiazychnye istochniki*, pp. 196–7; also below p. 215.
30 *Uspenskii sbornik*, col. 8c.28–30; Hollingsworth, *Hagiography*, p. 98; on Vladimir's conflict with Iaropolk, see above, pp. 153–4.

story, but leaves open the possibility that the abducted 'Greek' nun was made pregnant by Vladimir and not by Iaropolk: i.e. that Sviatopolk was merely a bastard, though still Vladimir's son.[31] The story could well be fabricated, in one or both of its versions. However, even if the charge of abducting a pregnant (or non-pregnant) nun was true, it was apparently irrelevant to Sviatopolk's status among Vladimir's offspring either before or after 1015. He appears in all the lists of sons, was allocated a town along with the other sons, in no source does any participant refer disparagingly to his parentage, and Thietmar, who was informed by an eye-witness, treats him without question as one of the brothers. Forty years later Iaroslav, in what purports to be his testament to his own children, makes a point of calling them 'sons of one mother',[32] but the fact that Vladimir's children were of many mothers does not seem to have made any difference to their status either in Vladimir's lifetime or in the decade or two after his death. Although there does seem to have been a distinction between wives and concubines, nevertheless dynastic legitimacy in Vladimir's day was unaffected by notions of legitimacy within the Christian family. Even at the very end of the eleventh century, to be the son of a prince 'by a concubine' was noteworthy, but no disqualification.[33] It is curious that none of Vladimir's known children is claimed by the sources as an offspring of his only known Christian marriage.[34]

A second and more regular criterion of legitimacy in the native accounts is chronological seniority, the deference due to an elder brother. Here also, however, there are signs of strain, signs that the criterion was superimposed, sometimes rather clumsily, to fit requirements later in the century. Vladimir's sons are listed in three ways: by name, by their respective mothers, and by the towns to which they were allocated.[35] The sequences are inconsistent. For example, the list of Vladimir's sons by Rogvolod's daughter Rogneda is: Iziaslav, Mstislav, Iaroslav, Vsevolod. Yet both in the plain list of names, and in a list by allocation, Mstislav comes after Vsevolod. In the list of names Iaroslav is placed before Sviatopolk, but in a list of allocations the order is reversed. Probably the chroniclers themselves did not have precise information. This, in turn, suggests that in 1015 the relative age of the sons was not decisive in determining notions of legitimate succession.

---

31 *PVL*, I, pp. 55–6.
32 Ibid., p. 108; see also below, p. 246.
33 Ibid., p. 179, on Mstislav, son of Sviatopolk Iziaslavich. On marriage in general, see below, pp. 296–8.
34 For an attempt to 'legitimize' Boris see A. Poppe, 'Der Kampf um die Kiever Thronfolge nach dem 15. Juni 1015', in *Forschungen zur osteuropäischen Geschichte* 50 (1995) 275–96.
35 *PVL*, I, pp. 56–7 (List A in table I below), 83 (List B in table I).

A third criterion might be parental will: that rights were conferred by Vladimir's choice rather than by purity or sequence of birth. Thietmar writes that Vladimir 'left the whole of his legacy to two of his sons, while the [a?] third had been put in prison; this third son later escaped and fled to his father-in-law'.[36] The 'third' son must be Sviatopolk, whose father-in-law was Boleslaw of Poland. Thietmar's informants fought as allies of Boleslaw and Sviatopolk, and presumably Thietmar's remarks convey what they, in 1018, had been told about the *casus belli*. But who were the two sons favoured by their father (if this is what Thietmar's phraseology implies)? Iaroslav and Mstislav? In 1015 Vladimir was on the point of making war against Iaroslav, and Mstislav of Tmutorokan was at this stage remote from the central disputes. Perhaps Boris and Gleb? Or Boris and Mstislav? In July 1015 Boris was in command of Vladimir's troops, a trusted son at his father's right hand. He is also said to have been 'beloved of his father more than all'.[37] Instead of an injured innocent, could he have been a serious claimant to Kiev, his father's chosen successor?[38] Speculation is pleasant but pointless. The more important point is that even if Thietmar was right, he was also – in a sense – wrong. Whatever Vladimir's wishes may have been, they were obviously not authoritative enough to ensure a smooth succession. He could dispose of his lands when he was alive, but there is no firm evidence that his preferences carried sufficient weight once he was dead. Neither seniority nor parental injunction – two cardinal points of the dynastic ideology which emerged later in the century – seems to have constrained Vladimir's sons.

This discussion is inevitably circular. Vladimir's death was followed by civil war, and civil war by nature indicates either a lack or a breakdown of an accepted and sufficiently authoritative framework of political legitimacy. Here the evidence points to a lack rather than to a breakdown: the inconsistent attempts of later native writers to impose order and idea; the uncertain applicability of Thietmar's statement; and above all the fact that the events of 1015–24, though exceptional in scale, were part of a repeated pattern. Any surviving brother was seen as a potential threat, to be met sooner or later with greater or lesser force: thus Vladimir had dealt with his own brothers, thus Sviatopolk dealt with Boris and Gleb and Sviatoslav, thus Iaroslav dealt with Sviatopolk, thus Mstislav initially dealt with Iaroslav; and even after their agreement, Iaroslav did not dare reside too close until he could rely on force rather than merely on his brother's word to protect him; and thus, when there was no conceivable real danger, Iaroslav dealt with his last surviving male sibling, Sudislav.

---

36 Thietmar VII.73, in Holtzmann, *Die Chronik*, p. 488: 'integritatem hereditatis suae'.
37 *PVL*, I, p. 91.
38 See Poppe, 'Der Kampf um die Kiever Thronfolge', 288–9.

The participants themselves were looking for alternatives or supplements to coercion, for symbols of legitimacy and prestige beyond the sword. As we have seen, this was probably one of the impulses behind Vladimir's official introduction of Christianity, and among Vladimir's devices for legitimizing display was the issue of coinage. Both Iaroslav and Sviatopolk followed their father's lead. But whereas Vladimir's gold coins had been authentic, and hence had intrinsic value beyond their worth as propaganda, Iaroslav and Sviatopolk upheld only the tradition of their father's 'silver' coins with little or no actual silver content, all for show.[39] Even Boleslaw joined in, issuing coins with Cyrillic inscriptions, perhaps to encourage recognition of his legitimacy in the Cherven towns. However, the fashion was transient, another false start. The economy of the lands of the Rus functioned without a local coinage, and these few ceremonial issues were not subsequently copied, did not become a tradition, a regular attribute of legitimate rulership.[40]

We seem to be sliding towards the conclusion that the strife in the aftermath of Vladimir's death was just what it appears to be: a fraternal free-for-all. This may be true, but it is superficial. Thus far we have discussed the rights or wrongs of a domestic squabble between a handful of brothers, but the brothers were not free to do as they pleased. If there was no consensus on legitimacy (beyond the legitimacy conferred by being a member of the family, a descendant of Vladimir), then a brother's authority depended to a considerable extent on access to the means of coercion. What were the means of coercion, and how did a prince get them for himself? The sources on the battles of succession in 1015–24 happen to be unusually informative on issues of military recruitment, so this is a convenient place to consider the topic both in context and more generally.

3. MIGHT

Separately the brothers were weak. If there was no effective system of peaceable succession, there was no automatic transfer of loyalty, and therefore each claimant had to assemble support almost from scratch. In conflict a prince's forces were potentially composed of three distinct

39 On Vladimir's coins see above, pp. 167–8; on the coins of Sviatopolk and Iaroslav see Sotnikova and Spasskyi *Russian Coins*, pp. 107–35.
40 On Boleslaw's coins see M. B. Swerdłow, 'Jeszcze o "ruskich" monetach Bolesława Chrobrego', *Wiadomości numizmatyczne* 13 (1969), 175–80; B. B. Szcześniak, 'The Cyrillic Deniers of Boleslaw I of Poland', *American Numismatic Society. Museum Notes* 18 (1972), 70–1. Note also the brief exception: coins minted at Tmutorokan by Iaroslav's grandson, Oleg Sviatoslavich: M. Dimnik, 'Oleg's status as ruler of Tmutarakan': the sphragistic evidence', *Mediaeval Studies* 55 (1993), pp. 137–49.

groups: his own personal followers; the people of his 'town'; and outside auxiliaries. In any major confrontation, all three were essential, yet only the first – the personal retinue – could be taken more or less for granted. Every source for this period stresses repeatedly the extent to which each prince was dependent on his capacity to augment his forces by recruitment both locally and abroad.

The general word for a prince's followers is *druzhina* ('group of friends', 'comrades'; cf. *comitatus*, or 'host'). It was a flexible term, whose meanings and composition could vary.[41] The core of the *druzhina*, the prince's permanent personal retinue (sometimes called the 'small [*malaia*] *druzhina*') could range from perhaps a couple of dozen men to perhaps a couple of hundred, depending on the wealth and status of the prince. It was sufficient for routine protection, enforcement and administration,[42] but in a land divided, the individual prince's retinue was not a force for serious campaigning. When Boris was abandoned by Vladimir's *druzhina* he was left only with his own personal followers (here his *otroki* – lit. 'youths' (cf. 'squires')), and was easy prey for the assassins. Gleb travelled from Murom with his 'small *druzhina*', because he suspected no danger.[43] At the other end of the century, in 1094, Vladimir Monomakh (Iaroslav's grandson) retreated from Chernigov to Pereiaslavl with a personal following of fewer than 100 (see below, p. 267). In 1097 Prince David Igorevich roamed the western lands with approximately 100 men.[44] In 1093 the new prince of Kiev, notionally the most powerful in the land, boasted of being able to field 700 *otroki*, which probably included men from his former town of Turov.[45] Such numbers are typical of the age: comparable, for example, to those which one might find in Anglo-Norman England.[46]

Throughout the pre-Mongol period most inter-princely conflicts (of which there were very many) involved fairly small groups of warriors, bands of armed men rather than anything on the scale or with the logistical complexity suggested by the word 'army'. In a vast country the prince with his personal retinue needed to be highly mobile. In

---

41 S. D. Lediaeva, *Ocherki po istoricheskoi leksikologii russkogo iazyka* (Kishinev, 1980), pp. 14–18; applicable not only to the retinue of princes: cf. Ratibor's *druzhina*, *PVL*, I, p. 148 (s.a. 1095, 6603).

42 On the evolution of the *druzhina* see Uwe Halbach, *Der russische Fürstenhof vor dem 16. Jahrhundert: eine vergleichende Untersuchung zur politischen Lexikologie und Verfassungsgeschichte der alten Rus'* (Quellen und Studien zur Geschichte des östlichen Europa 23; Stuttgart, 1985), pp. 94–113; A. A. Gorskii, *Drevnerusskaia druzhina* (Moscow, 1989).

43 *PVL*, I, p. 92.

44 Ibid., p. 179.

45 Ibid., p. 143.

46 See e.g. J. O. Prestwich, 'The Military Household of the Norman Kings', in Matthew Strickland ed., *Anglo-Norman Warfare* (Woodbridge, 1992), pp. 100–5.

his account of his own career, written in the early twelfth century, Vladimir Monomakh claims to have made '83 great journeys, not to mention the lesser ones'.[47] On most of these 'journeys' he was a kind of roving enforcer: collecting tribute, assisting or confronting troubled or troublesome cousins. The personal retinue was too precious to risk regularly in real battles. Dynastic squabbles often involved armed confrontation but serious fighting was relatively rare: rivals sized each other up and the weaker backed down. Far more disputes were settled by a show of arms than by their use. A military ethos was maintained, while fatal violence was contained. For the period up to the mid-eleventh century the chronicles also preserve tales of single combat: perhaps in part heroic legend, but probably a reflection of an actual practice as well. Single combat could be an effective device for concluding a battle without a battle, for armed resolution with minimal casualties.[48]

After his victory at Listven in 1024 Mstislav is reported as saying: 'Who would not rejoice in this? Here lies a Severian [Mstislav's auxiliaries], and here a Varangian [Iaroslav's auxiliaries], but the *druzhina* is intact'.[49] Care for one's *druzhina* was among the highest virtues praised in the chronicles. Vladimir 'loved his *druzhina*, and took counsel with them concerning the governance of his land, and about campaigns'. He also feasted them and gave them silver spoons.[50] Such praise is not surprising, given that members of the *druzhina* were among the chroniclers' informants.[51]

To commit the small *druzhina* to anything more than a skirmish was not only undesirable; it was also usually ineffective. In the field they could be outnumbered. Against fortified settlements they were ill-equipped. The Rus had no siege engines. Once the inhabitants had 'shut themselves into the town', behind their earthen ramparts topped with a wooden palisade, it was extremely rare for an ordinary *druzhina* to make any impression.

---

47 *PVL*, I, p. 162.
48 On the avoidance of battle as a common feature elsewhere see e.g. J. Bradbury, 'Battles in England and Normandy, 1066–1154', in Strickland, ed., *Anglo-Norman Warfare*, pp. 183–4; ibn Rusta, *Kitab al-A'lak al-nafisa [Book of Precious Jewels]* ed. T. Lewicki, *Źródła arabskie do dziejów słowiańszczyzny*, II. 2 (Wroclaw, Warsaw, Cracow, Gdansk, 1977), pp. 40–1; tr. G. Wiet, *Les atours précieux* (Cairo, 1955), p. 164, mentions duels among the Rus c. 900; for wider references to single combat and judicial duels in East Slav medieval writings see P. Brang, 'Der Zweikampf im russischen Leben und in der russischen Literatur', *Zeitschrift für slavische Philologie* 39 (1961), pp. 315–24.
49 *PVL*, I, p. 100.
50 Ibid., p. 86.
51 On the possible provenance of some of these stories see Ad. Stender-Petersen, *Die Varägersage als Quelle der altrussischen Chronik* (Aarhus, 1934); D. S. Likhachev in *PVL*, II, pp. 14–36; B. A. Rybakov, *Drevniaia Rus'. Skazaniia, byliny, letopisi* (Moscow, 1963), pp. 336–45.

For wider recruitment, the prince's first resources were local, the people of his own 'town' or 'towns'. The townspeople figure in the sources as a distinct group whose loyalty – and whose willingness to fight – could not be taken for granted by a new would-be-prince. When Vladimir died, Sviatopolk's first action was to come to an arrangement with the men of Kiev: 'and he gave them possessions; they received him, but their hearts were not with him, because their brethren were with Boris'.[52] In other words, Sviatopolk bribed them into acquiescence, but not into positive support or loyalty. By contrast, when Mstislav marched on Kiev in 1024, 'the Kievans did not receive him', so he had to withdraw.[53] There is a consistent implication that the prince ruled by assent. Loyalty, however, required something more. The Kievans' 'hearts' were not with Sviatopolk: this is no emotional confession, but a formula of the personal loyalty of the *druzhina*. For example, in the chronicle's narrative for 980, Blud pledges himself to Vladimir with the words: 'I will join you in heart and in loyalty [*priiazn'stvo*]'. Sviatopolk himself asks the men of Vyshgorod, 'Will you receive me with your heart?'[54] In an interregnum the primary loyalty of the townspeople was to each other. They negotiated with their potential princes before deciding on whom they would 'receive' or to whom they would commit their 'hearts'; whom they would not resist, whom they would assist in coercion. Here, in local urban recruitment, was another source of legitimacy, perhaps the most persuasive in the absence of a broad consensus on dynastic or moral rights.[55]

In July 1015 (according to the chronicle's dating) Iaroslav was not on the best of terms with the men of his own town, the Novgorodians. He took the side of the Varangians in a dispute in which several Novgorodians were killed. However, when Iaroslav needed Novgorodian support to raise an army against Sviatopolk, he changed his approach. He appealed to the fractious Novgorodians as 'my dear *druzhina*', and they in reply promised that they would fight for him despite the fact that their 'brethren' had been killed. This anecdote has elements similar to those in the stories of Sviatopolk and the men of Kiev and Vyshgorod: local recruitment for special purposes; an expanded sense of the term *druzhina* to include townspeople;[56] the close collective identity of the relevant group of townspeople, expressed in terms of kinship; negotiated service rather than unconditional

52 *PVL*, I, p. 90.
53 Ibid., p. 99.
54 Ibid., pp. 54, 90; cf. the same formula used in an inter-princely agreement at Liubech in 1097: *PVL*, I, p. 170; see also below, p. 291.
55 See also below, p. 347.
56 *PVL*, I, p. 95; cf. *NPL*, p. 174, where the term is defined as including the 'leading men' (*narochitye muzhi*).

support; and, crucially, the fact that loyalty was not bestowed gratis: the Novgorodians, like Sviatopolk's Kievans and Vyshgorodians, expected to be paid for their services (although Sviatopolk gave out gifts in advance whereas Iaroslav paid the Novgorodians from the spoils of victory).[57] The way to a townsman's 'heart' was through his pocket. This was genuine recruitment, not just the calling-in of personal obligations.

How broad was the base for such recruitment? In the early eleventh century a prince's capacity for local recruitment was still fairly limited. Later, as towns proliferated and dynastic authority was more widely established, a prince could send for troops from several towns under his patronage.[58] But in the 1010s and 1020s there were still not many towns to be shared out. The narratives show each prince raising troops from one town only. Some have argued that this was not so restrictive as it may appear, since recruitment from a town stretched deep into its rural hinterland; that villagers were organized – by the townspeople – into fighting units, that there were, in effect, 'popular armies'.[59] Forces are on occasion described in generalized ethnic rather than urban terms: in 1018 Iaroslav marched against Boleslaw with 'Rus, Varangians and Slovenes'; in 1024 Mstislav's troops comprised his *druzhina* and the Severians.[60] Often the chroniclers use a vague formula to the effect that the prince 'gathered many warriors' (*voi*). Do such words imply rural levies? Probably not. The most likely reading is that Iaroslav's 'Rus' were either Kievans or his personal retainers, his 'Varangians' were his overseas recruits, and his 'Slovenes' were the same as his formerly disgruntled 'Novgorodians'. Similarly, Mstislav's 'Severians' were men recruited from Chernigov. The term *voi* is too indeterminate to support any particular theory as to the social basis of recruitment.

Archaeological evidence for rural weaponry is equally thin. Questions are raised as to whether working axes might have been used as battle-axes, but nothing points persuasively to an armed peasantry either in the early eleventh century or at any other time in pre-Mongol Rus.[61] Obviously one cannot assert that no peasants were ever pressed into fighting, or (more likely) into providing logistical support for fighting men, or (most probably) into helping to defend a city into which they had fled for protection during an attack.[62]

---

57 *NPL*, p. 175.
58 For example, *PVL*, I, p. 169, where Mstislav, son of Vladimir Monomakh, assembles a *druzhina* from Novgorod, Rostov and Beloozero.
59 I. Ia. Froianov, *Kievskaia Rus'. Ocherki sotsial'no-politicheskoi istorii* (Leningrad, 1980), pp. 185–215.
60 *PVL*, I, pp. 96, 100.
61 A. N. Kirpichnikov, *Drevnerusskoe oruzhie*, I–IV (Moscow, Leningrad, 1966–73).
62 For the use of peasants to defend a town see Nazarenko, *Nemetskie latinoiazychnye istochniki*, pp. 201–2, with reference to Thietmar's phrase 'ex fugitivorum robore servorum' (Thietmar VIII.32). Note also, however, the isolated but suggestive mention of the *smerdy* rewarded by Iaroslav after the battle of Liubech: *NPL*, pp. 15, 175.

But neither the written nor the archaeological sources support the assertion that there was systematic rural recruitment. The attraction of the more densely populated areas was not that the villages directly provided more soldiers but that they could supply more populous towns. However, the underlying issue here is about more than just military history: debates on rural recruitment reflect various notions of the social, political, economic and administrative structures of the lands of the Rus. We shall return to the broader issues later, from another angle.

Numbers under arms are hard to assess, because they are rarely stated and still more rarely reliable. Nevertheless the signs are consistent enough to suggest that the largest towns could provide, *in extremis*, men in the low to mid-thousands for long-distance campaigns, and presumably rather more for defensive duties if ramparts were to be manned. In 1015 Iaroslav is said to have marched south with 3,000 Novgorodians.[63] In 1068 his son Sviatoslav apparently mustered a *druzhina* of 3,000 troops from Chernigov.[64] In 1093 the prince of Kiev was advised that he would need over 8,000 men for a campaign into the steppes, and that he would therefore have to join forces with other princes since his own resources were insufficient.[65] Nestor, writing the *Lection* on Boris and Gleb in the late 1070s or early 1080s, stated that Boris took 'up to 8000 men' into the steppes to seek out Pechenegs. The more reliable sources state only that Boris had Vladimir's *druzhina*, but the figure in the *Lection* neatly confirms that, in the late eleventh century, 8,000 was thought a plausible number for an expedition into the steppes.[66] In 1043, when Iaroslav was 'sole ruler' and thus able, in principle, to muster more men than any regional prince in a divided land, he sent an army against Constantinople. The expedition was heavily defeated. The chronicle mentions 6,000 survivors, out of an original force which probably numbered over 10,000.[67] The figures tally: around 3,000 from a single large town, around 8,000 for a combined campaign into the steppes, somewhat more for the exceptional expedition of 1043. By contrast with the routine skirmishes between *druzhina* and *druzhina*, these were indeed substantial forces.

There was no regular 'national' army, only the retinue of each

---

63 *NPL*, p. 175; cf. the corrupt figures of '40' and '40,000' in manuscripts of the *Primary Chronicle*: *PSRL*, I, col. 141; *PSRL*, II, col. 128.

64 *PVL*, I, p. 115.

65 Ibid., p. 143.

66 Abramovich/Müller, *Erzählungen*, p. 10; *PVL*, I, p. 90 ('*druzhina* and warriors'); cf. *Uspenskii sbornik*, col. 10d.13; Hollingsworth, *Hagiography*, pp. 13, 102.

67 *PVL*, I, p. 103; on the size of the forces in 1043 see J. Shepard, 'Why did the Russians attack Byzantium in 1043?', *BNJ* 22 (1978/9), 157–8.

prince and the auxiliaries which he could from time to time raise locally. Writers in the pre-Mongol period persistently urged that princes should join forces to combat outsiders (see below, p. 365); in 1015–24 the brothers did the opposite, joining forces with outsiders to combat each other. Besides their *druzhina* and their townsmen, they recruited foreigners. At Liubech in 1015 (or 1016) Sviatopolk and his Pechenegs fought Iaroslav and his Varangians. At the battle on the Bug in July 1018 Sviatopolk defeated Iaroslav and opened the way to Kiev with an army of Poles which also included 300 Germans, 500 Hungarians and 1,000 Pechenegs.[68] Mstislav of Tmutorokan came from beyond the steppes with Kasogians and 'Khazars'. The recruitment of foreigners brought the brethren into a wider network of regional and international alliances; the family squabble had political and military repercussions from the Caucasus to the Rhine.

Why should troops from so many lands have become involved in the disputes between Vladimir's sons? Certainly not because of any interest in dynastic succession, and still less through outrage at the murder of Boris and Gleb. There was no single reason. Let us recall dynastic geography, the disposition of 'towns': Iaroslav was prince of Novgorod in the north; Sviatopolk had Turov, to the west of Kiev, on the road to Poland; and Mstislav was in Tmutorokan, the Rus' southern Alaska, beyond the steppes. The brethren clashed over their claims to the centre, but they were also regional warlords in quite distant and distinct geopolitical zones. Each recruited an army from his closest neighbours and surrounding peoples, each in separate circumstances, and each had his own angle of vision on the Middle Dnieper region where all paths crossed. Each also recruited by different means: Sviatopolk took Kiev in collaboration with a foreign ruler; Mstislav used tributaries; and Iaroslav hired mercenaries. Together they provide an unusually full set of contrasts, convenient enough to warrant a brief tour round the regions.

Sviatopolk's Turov was on the river Pripet, which flows east from close to the Bug, then south into the Dnieper upstream from Kiev at modern Chernobyl. Turov was a link in a long-established trade-route from Kiev to Cracow and Prague. Boleslaw I's main objective in helping Sviatopolk was probably to acquire (or perhaps to recover) the Cherven towns, which had been taken by Vladimir in c. 981. His first attempt was in 1013. In May of that year, in Merseburg, he reached a peace agreement with Germany, and was able to direct his efforts eastwards. An inconclusive campaign (with Pecheneg support) against Vladimir produced a diplomatic solution: Vladimir's son Sviatopolk married Boleslaw's daughter, who brought with her to Turov a bishop, Reinbern, known for his missionary ardour. However, Vladimir's

---

68 Thietmar VIII.32, in Holtzmann, *Die Chronik*, p. 530.

subsequent arrest of Sviatopolk and his Polish wife (and Bishop Reinbern) suggests that the solution had failed. On Vladimir's death, Sviatopolk and Boleslaw renewed their partnership. As we have seen, the detailed movements of the princes between 1015 and the start of 1018 are controversial and hard to reconstruct, but there is no doubt of the favourable conditions for Boleslaw in 1018. In January he had further negotiations with Germany, which perhaps enabled him to procure his Saxon and Hungarian contingents for a campaign in the east, where, by contrast with 1013, he could exploit the weakness of the divided brethren. In the short term the alliance was successful for both parties: Sviatopolk gained Kiev, and Boleslaw gained the Cherven towns.[69]

However, formal intervention on such a scale was most unusual. On only one other occasion did a foreign army, led by the ruler of a neighbouring land, fight its way to take Kiev in cooperation with a local claimant. This was in 1069, when another prince of Turov sought help from another Boleslaw of Poland (see below, p. 253).

Far to the south, of no interest whatever to the king of Poland or to a chronicler in Merseburg, was Mstislav. After Vladimir's death the Rus continued to consolidate and extend their interests in the Azov region, among the Black Sea traders, among the peoples of the Kuban and the northern Caucasus. The Byzantine historian John Skylitzes tells of a certain Sphengos, prince of the Rus, who cooperated with a Byzantine naval expedition against 'Khazaria' in 1016. 'Sphengos' is probably a Greek enunciation of a Scandinavian name such as Svein or Sveinki. At around the same time Mstislav himself is reported to have subjugated the Kasogians (the Adyge of the Kuban region and northern Caucasus).[70] According to the story Rededia, prince of the Kasogians, proposed that he and Mstislav should fight in unarmed single combat: '"and if you prevail, you will take my possessions and my wife and my children and my land; and if I prevail I shall take all that is yours." And Mstislav said, "So be it."' The Kasogian prince was naive in his heroics. He had not reckoned with Mstislav's two deadly advantages: unscrupulous guile, and the Christian faith.

Mstislav began to grow weak, for Rededia was mighty and strong. And Mstislav said, 'O most pure Mother of God, help me! If I prevail, I shall build a church to your name.' And, having spoken thus, he dashed Rededia to

---

69 See V. D. Koroliuk, *Zapadnye slaviane in Kievskaia Rus' v X–XI vv.* (Moscow, 1964), pp. 216–61; Golovko, *Drevniaia Rus' i Pol'sha*, pp. 15–32; Sverdlov, *Latinoiazychnye istochniki*, pp. 75–7, 80–3.

70 *PVL*, I, p. 99, in a cluster of episodes related to Mstislav in the entries for 1021–2; on the likelihood of a somewhat earlier date see A. V. Gadlo, 'Tmutorokanskie etiudy': III ('Mstislav'), *Vestnik Leningradskogo gosudarstvennogo universiteta. Seriia 2*, 1990, *vypusk* 2 (no. 6), 21–33; Shepard, 'Why did the Russians attack Byzantium in 1043?', 204–7.

the ground, and drew a knife, and cut him to death, and went to his land, and took all his possessions, and his wife and children, and he imposed tribute on the Kasogians. And when he returned to Tmutorokan he founded a church of the Holy Mother of God, and the church which he founded stands to this day.[71]

Mstislav's victory over Rededia became one of the legendary episodes in the Rus' retelling of their past, and this version of it, with its blend of epic heroism and Christian piety, dates from no earlier than the 1070s.[72] However, though the tale is literary rather than literal, it was not conjured out of nothing. Together with Skylitzes' independent references to Sphengos it confirms that the Rus were active in the north-eastern Black Sea region in the late 1010s or early 1020s. Indeed, Sphengos and Mstislav could well be the same person. Some princes of the Rus are known by as many as three names: Slav, baptismal and Scandinavian.[73] Sphengos campaigned against 'Khazaria'; Mstislav subjugated the Kasogians and took wealth and prisoners and land. When Mstislav marched north of the steppes from his base at Tmutorokan, he augmented his forces with Kasogians and Khazars. Conquest was an effective mode of recruitment.

At the opposite extremity of the land, in Novgorod, Iaroslav was part of an entirely different network of regional interests, which at first sight were as remote from his brother on the Kimmerian Bosporos as Mstislav was remote from squabbles over the Cherven towns and Polish border zones. Iaroslav was unequivocally a man of the north, whose closest and most persistent ties were with Scandinavia, and whose coercive potential was in fair measure derived from his capacity to recruit Varangians. Iaroslav was the last great patron of the Varangians among the Rus. Native chronicles, Scandinavian sagas and archaeological finds all indicate that the period of Iaroslav's reigns in Novgorod, and to a lesser extent in Kiev, saw both a flowering and a fading, though not a complete withering, of the special relationship between the Varangians and the Rus princes.

Iaroslav had been appointed to Novgorod by his father. Apart from his brief spell in Kiev during the war with Sviatopolk, Novgorod remained his base until 1026. Even subsequently, after Mstislav had conceded Kiev, Iaroslav probably spent a fair proportion of his time in the north, at least until Mstislav's death in 1034/6. In the sagas, by

---

71 *PVL*, I, p. 99.
72 On tales of Tmutorokan in the *Primary Chronicle* see D. S. Likhachev in *PVL*, II, pp. 57–8; for somewhat fanciful versions of the history and spread of the legend see Gadlo, 'Tmutorokanskie etiudy, III', 24–5; A. P. Tolochko, 'Chernigovskaia "Pesn' o Mstislave" v sostave islandskoi sagi', in *Chernigov i ego okruga v IX–XIIIvv. Sbornik nauchnykh trudov* (Kiev, 1988), 165–75.
73 J. Shepard, 'Yngvarr's expedition to the East and a Russian inscribed stone cross', *Saga-Book of the Viking Society* 21 (1984–5), 250–1.

marked contrast with Ilarion's Kievan eulogy, Iaroslav – as Iarisleif – is associated almost exclusively with Novgorod, where he was host to many an itinerant Jarl or *konungr* in search of refuge or employment. For example, Olaf II of Norway (Olaf the Fat, St Olaf) came to Iarisleif with his son Magnus when fleeing from Canute in 1028 or 1029; Olaf stayed a couple of years, but Magnus was brought up among Iarisleif's retainers. Harald Sigurdson (Harald Hardraada) arrived at the court of Iarisleif, who made him 'chieftain of the men charged with the defence of that country'; when Harald went on to seek his fortune in the service of the Byzantine emperor, he sent his wealth back to Iarisleif in Holmgarthr for safe keeping; eventually, c. 1044, he married Iarisleif's daughter Elisabeth.[74] And of course there was Eymund, who sold his services to Iarisleif in the wars of succession after the death of Vladimir in 1015.

Coin finds tend to confirm the regularity of Scandinavian travels to the Rus in this period. English coins, paid to Denmark in tribute, turn up in the lands of the Rus from the late tenth century, but there is a sharp increase in finds of coins minted during the early years of Canute (1017–23). Canute's later coins (until 1035) are still numerous, but then there is a decline; or a levelling-off, if one adds Danish coins, which are found more commonly than English in mid-century. The vast majority of finds are from the Novgorodian and adjacent lands.[75] It has been argued that in 1018–19, in the midst of his dispute with Sviatopolk and Boleslaw, Iaroslav formed a temporary alliance with Canute, sealed by the marriage of his son (by a deceased first wife) to Canute's sister, and resulting in an attack by Canute on Poland.[76] In 1018, after his heavy defeat on the Bug, Iaroslav apparently intended to flee 'across the sea' to Scandinavia, but was prevented by the Novgorodians.[77] In 1019 he married Ingigerd (Irina in Rus sources), daughter of Olaf of Sweden.

Not all Varangians were gathered around Iaroslav. Sviatopolk of Turov had Varangians among his retainers: two of them were the instruments of Boris' martyrdom (unless of course they also were Iaroslav's men!). Thietmar mentions 'swift Danes' among the defenders of Kiev.[78] In the 1030s bands of Varangians probed and raided in

74 *Heimskringla* VIII.187–92; IX.1; X.2, 16–17; tr. Hollander, pp. 474, 482–6, 538–9, 578, 590–1; see H. Ellis Davidson, *The Viking Road to Byzantium* (London, 1976), pp. 158–73; H. Birnbaum, 'Iaroslav's Varangian Connection', *Scandoslavica* 24 (1978), 5–25; on the date of Elizabeth's marriage see M. Hellmann, 'Die Heiratspolitik Jaroslavs des Weisen', *Forschungen zur osteuropäischen Geschichte* 8 (1962), 21.

75 V. M. Potin, *Drevniaia Rus' i evropeiskie gosudarstva v X–XIII vv. Istoriko-numizmaticheskii ocherk* (Leningrad, 1968), pp. 106–8, 134.

76 A. V. Nazarenko, 'O russko-datskom soiuze v pervoi chetverti XI v.', *DGTSSSR* 1990 (1991), pp. 167–90.

77 *PVL*, I, p. 97.

78 Ibid., p. 91; *Uspenskii sbornik*, col. 12d.7–10; Hollingsworth, *Hagiography*, pp. 106, 187; Thietmar VIII.32, in Holtzmann, *Die Chronik*, p. 530.

the northern Caucasus as far as the Caspian Sea, perhaps with the cooperation of Mstislav of Tmutorokan.[79] 'Varangian' is a single word which covers diverse groups: merchants, mercenaries, settlers, autonomous war-bands. They could be found throughout the lands of the Rus. But their closest links – geographically, diplomatically, militarily and economically – were with Iaroslav of Novgorod.

Six times between 1015 and 1036 the chronicles tell of Varangians bolstering Iaroslav's forces. In 1015, threatened by his father, Iaroslav 'sent across the sea and brought Varangians'. In the entry for the same year he is said to have 'gathered 1000 Varangians', perhaps the same men, to face Sviatopolk at Liubech. In 1018 he 'assembled Rus and Varangians and Slovenes' before the battle on the Bug. After the defeat he raised funds to hire additional Varangians, who fought with him on the Alta in the following year. In 1024, preparing to confront Mstislav, he 'sent across the sea for Varangians, and Iakun [i.e. Hakon] came with Varangians'. And finally, in 1036 he gathered many troops, 'Varangians and Slovenes', to lift the Pecheneg siege of Kiev.[80] Subsequently there are no further references in the *Primary Chronicle* to the recruitment of Varangians, or to their existence as a distinct contingent of a prince's combined forces.[81] Certainly there were still many Varangians among the Rus, but both the sagas and the native chronicles present the regular hiring of Varangians as a specific feature of the period of Iaroslav's rule in, or close association with, Novgorod, between 1015 and 1036.

Thus the dispute between three brothers (or four, if we prefer to include Boris) for the Middle Dnieper region sucked in fighting men from Poland, Hungary, Germany, Scandinavia, the steppes, the northern Caucasus, and perhaps even from England. As we have seen, Mstislav recruited by conquest, Sviatopolk by alliance, Iaroslav mainly by hiring mercenaries. The conquered had little choice, but allies and mercenaries fought for profit, and the advantages which they brought were not without cost to the Rus. Essential in war, in peace they soon became burdensome both to the prince and to the local population. The chronicle reports violent clashes between Boleslaw's Poles and the Kievans among whom they were billeted, and between the Novgorodians and the Varangians in the city. Thietmar implies that Boleslaw paid off his own foreign auxiliaries as soon as he reckoned

79 See Shepard, 'Yngvarr's expedition', 242–53.
80 *PVL*, I, pp. 89, 96, 97, 100, 101.
81 See, however, other sources on the Varangians in the expedition of 1043: *PSRL*, V, p. 137; cf. Skyl., p. 430; also, for the wider context, E. A. Mel'nikova and V. Ia. Petrukhin, 'Skandinavy na Rusi i v Vizantii v X–XI vekakh: k istorii nazvaniia "variag"', *Slavianovedeniie* 1994, no. 2, pp. 56–66.

himself safe without them[82] A leitmotif in *Eymund's Saga* is Iarisleif's meanness (from the point of view of the Varangians), his unwillingness to pay. The *Primary Chronicle* relates similar tensions under Vladimir, who left his Varangians without pay for a month and was eventually relieved to dispatch most of them to Constantinople, allegedly with a warning to the emperor about their disruptive influence.[83] So far as the evidence allows us to judge, Varangians were normally hired on fixed-term contracts (in *Eymund's Saga* twelve months). They were paid a specified sum in advance, plus a bonus for success.[84] Vladimir's showdown with his Varangians was over their demands for a share of the booty from the capture of Kiev. In 1018 Iaroslav had to impose a special tax in Novgorod to raise the advance for additional Varangians.

In a successful and brief offensive, hired outsiders more than earned their temporary keep, but in failure or idleness they were an unwelcome liability. For defence, and security in the longer term, the most cost-effective method of augmenting the reserve of manpower was by settlement, whether voluntary or enforced. In 980 Vladimir is said to have picked out the best of the Varangians and given them 'towns': that is, the means to support themselves, and perhaps a garrison role. The sagas perhaps echo a similar deal, in the story of how Aldeigjuborg (Staraia Ladoga) was given to Jarl Ragnvaldr by Ingigerd/Irina, who had demanded it from Iarisleif as her dowry.[85] The cheapest settlers were prisoners-of-war or semi-tributaries: for example, Poles settled by Iaroslav along the Ros; the Oghuz at Torchesk, and later the *Chernye Klobuki* (see below, p. 326).

* * * * *

In 1015 the sons of Vladimir were themselves, in a sense, outsiders looking in: weak, divided, scattered, lacking an effective framework to determine succession or legitimacy, and each lacking the muscle to secure his own claims. After more than three decades of apparent internal order under Vladimir – an appearance diligently fostered in the sources – the revealed flimsiness of princely power is startling. Each had to enlist outsiders in order to establish a position at the centre: in order that he would thereby no longer need to enlist outsiders.

82 *PVL*, I, pp. 95, 97; Thietmar VIII.32 in Holtzmann, *Die Chronik*, p. 530; see Nazarenko, *Nemetskie latinoiazychnye istochniki*, pp. 197–8.

83 Pálsson and Edwards, *Vikings in Russia*, pp. 73, 79–80; *PVL*, I, p. 56; see also above, p. 154.

84 E. A. Mel'nikova, '"Saga ob Eimunde" o sluzhbe skandinavov v druzhine Iaroslava Mudrogo', in *Vostochnaia Evropa v drevnosti i srednevekov'e. Sbornik statei* (Moscow, 1978), pp. 289–95; cf. *PVL*, I, p. 20, s.a. 6390 (882), on regular Novgorodian payments to the Varangians 'for the sake of peace' until Iaroslav's death.

85 *Heimskringla* VIII.93; tr. Hollander, pp. 342–3.

Beneath the surface noise of conflict, however, the fraternal rivalry was itself an affirmation of a more fundamental aspect of Vladimir's policy and legacy. Why, after all, should the brothers have bothered to fight? Each was well established in his own locality, separated by huge distances, none impeding another. A couple of generations earlier their grandfather, Sviatoslav, had been quite prepared to shift his headquarters away from the Middle Dnieper; three or four generations later their descendants were eager to explore and exploit regional opportunities, to enhance regional prestige (see below, Chapter Nine). Even in their own time their nephew Briacheslav of Polotsk set his sights on Novgorod rather than on Kiev. By contrast, the protagonists among the sons of Vladimir were not content to build on regional foundations. There is no evidence that any of the senior players ultimately regarded his regional base as a (or the) centre: no propaganda of local pride, no prominent symbols of local legitimacy, no grand public building programmes in Novgorod or (despite Mstislav's modest church) Tmutorokan. To this extent Vladimir had succeeded. There was no return to the experimentation of Sviatoslav. The main focus of authority and wealth in the lands of the Rus was firmly located in the Middle Dnieper region.

Yet the Middle Dnieper region turned out to be rich enough and capacious enough for compromise. In 1024, we recall, Iaroslav and Mstislav set the river as the boundary between their respective spheres of influence. This was the first recorded attempt to delineate areas of authority by agreement rather than by war to the death. The two brothers discovered that they could converge without clashing; that they could co-exist in close proximity at the centre while looking outwards in opposite directions – Iaroslav to the north and west, Mstislav to the south; that they could accept a divided inheritance as a workable alternative to single rule. It was a most important precedent. So far as one can tell, from the minimal annotations in the chronicles, the division of lands between Mstislav and Iaroslav was stable, even mutually beneficial. The two combined to retake the Cherven towns in 1031, possibly coordinating their offensive with Conrad III of Germany.[86] And each set about enhancing his own position without necessary threat to the other. Iaroslav strengthened his father's southern defence cordon, settling Polish prisoners-of-war along the Ros. Mstislav expanded the fortified area of Chernigov, and started an ambitious building programme.

There is, however, an intriguing asymmetry in their respective projects, which is especially curious in view of the kievocentric mythology purveyed so assiduously by subsequent chroniclers and

---

86 See Golovko, *Drevniaia Rus' i Pol'sha*, pp. 32–9, on the limited scale and objectives of this expedition.

eulogists. Despite the reticence of the sources, Mstislav of Chernigov seems to have been the senior partner. The narratives for 1024–6 indicate that he was the stronger militarily, and his plans for Chernigov would have turned it into the grandest city of its day. The new fortified area was vast by the standards of the Rus, with ramparts over 2½ kilometres in circumference, built up to an average height of over 4 metres. And he initiated work on the palace church of the Saviour: the first masonry church in the city, one of the first in any city of the Rus, and among of the most imposing structures (33.2 × 22.1 metres) in the entire pre-Mongol period.

For work on the church, Mstislav brought in architects and craftsmen from Constantinople, perhaps drawing on an alliance formed during his years in Tmutorokan. The church of the Saviour was of the cross-in-square type, with three aisles and five domes. The building technique was Byzantine: alternate layers of flat brick and unworked stone, in the manner known as *opus mixtum*, with recessed rows of brick. The interior was to be decorated with mosaics and frescoes (undoubtedly commissioned from Byzantine artists), with imported marble columns under the arcades, and with carved pink slate slabs (the only native luxury, quarried near Ovruch in the Derevlian land) on the parapets and floor.[87] This was more than a place of worship: it was designed to be impressive, to be a focus of prestige. Mstislav, Constantinople's former ally in Tmutorokan, had become Constantinople's protégé on the Middle Dnieper. When complete, Mstislav's palace complex in Chernigov would almost match that of his father Vladimir in Kiev.[88]

But Mstislav did not live to complete his project. He died, c. 1034–6, after a hunting trip: an appropriate end for a man remembered in legend for his heroic stature, his swarthy complexion, his martial valour. The church of the Saviour was still a building-site, with walls 'as high as a man standing on horseback could stretch with his hand'.[89] His only known son had pre-deceased him. It is tempting to wonder what might have been, how different the political and cultural map might have become, if Mstislav or his offspring had lived longer. But they did not, and Iaroslav did, and further speculation is irrelevant.

Even now, however, Iaroslav's triumph was not quite a formality.

---

87 On the church: A. I. Komech, *Drevnerusskoe zodchestvo kontsa X-nachala XII v.: vizantiiskoe nasledie i stanovlenie samostoiatel'noi traditsii* (Moscow, 1987), pp. 134–68; Volodymyr I. Mezentsev, 'The masonry churches of medieval Chernihiv', *HUS* 11 (1987), 367–72.

88 On the later palace buildings see P. A. Rappoport, *Russkaia arkhitektura X–XIII vv.* (*ASSSR SAI* vyp. E1–47; Leningrad, 1982), pp. 40–1. On seals perhaps attributable to Mstislav see Ianin, *Aktovye pechati*, I, pp. 32–3. On the growth of Chernigov see J. Blankoff, 'Černigov, rivale de Kiev? A propos de son dévoloppement urbain', *RES* 63 (1991), 145–55.

89 *PVL*, I, p. 101; on Mstislav's subsequent image see above, n. 72.

With the formidable prince of Chernigov out of the way and with Iaroslav busy installing his eldest son in Novgorod, the Pechenegs tried to take advantage of the dynastic hiatus on the Middle Dnieper: they laid siege to Kiev. In his last major expedition of internal conquest, Iaroslav 'gathered many troops: Varangians, Slovenes', marched south, lifted the siege, and won a decisive victory 'in the place where St Sophia now stands . . . for it was then a field outside the town'. The Pechenegs were routed: 'some drowned in the Setoml, others in other rivers, and the remnants have been fleeing to this day.' Thus, finally, two decades after the death of Vladimir, Iaroslav 'took over all of Mstislav's domain [*vlast'*], and became sole ruler [autocrat; *samovlastets*] of the land of the Rus'.[90] He was a tardy and perhaps reluctant southerner. But when at last he was unrivalled he purposefully and with remarkable success promoted not only the image of Kiev as the definitive city of the Rus but also the image of himself as a definitive ruler of Kiev. Ilarion's eulogy, cited at the start of this chapter, set the tone for the future, but at the expense of the recent past.

90 *PVL*, I, pp. 101–2; on controversies concerning the date of the Pecheneg attack, and its relevance for dating Iaroslav's activities in Kiev, see the convincing arguments in A. V. Poppe, 'The building of the Church of St Sophia in Kiev', *Journal of Medieval History* 7 (1981), pp. 15–66; repr. in Poppe, *The Rise of Christian Russia* (London, 1982), no. 4. For the contrary view see e.g. P. P. Tolochko, *Drevnii Kiev* (Kiev, 1983), pp. 71–8.

CHAPTER SIX

Cracked Facades (1036–54)

From 1036 until his death in 1054 Iaroslav was unchallenged and unchallengeable in his political, military, economic and territorial dominance. With the defeat of the Pechenegs he obtained, at least for a while, relative security from attack. With the death of Mstislav (and the remote imprisonment of Sudislav) he inherited sole dynastic authority. And with the acquisition of Mstislav's 'left-bank' territories, with control over Chernigov and Tmutorokan, Iaroslav had substantially augmented his own resources. His response to this new freedom was decisive: Iaroslav embarked on the most ambitious programme of construction and public patronage in the history of his clan. In scope and scale Iaroslav's initiatives in Kiev and Novgorod comfortably, and doubtless deliberately, surpassed Mstislav's unfinished project for Chernigov. His transparent aim was to lay the physical and cultural foundations on which to secure his own status and prestige as ruler in Kiev, to secure the status and prestige of Kiev above other cities of the Rus, and to secure the status and prestige of the Rus among the peoples of the known world.

Already in the early 1030s, while still only prince of the 'right-bank' towns, Iaroslav had extended his father's outer shield of defences to the south, with a line of settlements along the river Ros, a right-bank tributary of the Dnieper.[1] In his plans for the inner shield – the city's own ramparts – Iaroslav emulated Mstislav rather than Vladimir. In effect he redefined the city, by hugely expanding the fortified area and by relocating focal points within it. Vladimir's citadel on the Starokievskaia hill became merely the northern extremity of the new fortified town, whose ramparts stretched in a south-facing semi-circle for some 3.5 kilometres and enclosed an area of around 70 hectares. The earthworks were up to 30 metres wide at the base, and up to 11 metres high, and they were topped by a palisade which in places took the total height to 16 metres. It has been estimated that if 1,000 men worked 300 days per year, they would have needed four years to shift the requisite volume of earth.[2] Three gate-towers pierced the ramparts:

---

1 *PVL*, I, p. 101.

2 A. Poppe, 'The building of the Church of St Sophia in Kiev', *Journal of Medieval History* 7 (1981), repr. in Poppe, *The Rise of Christian Russia* (London, 1982), no. 4, 30–1.

the Jews' Gate in the south-west, the Poles' Gate in the south-east (both probably of wood), and the masonry edifice of the Golden Gate at the southern tip. Iaroslav's new fortifications not only protected the city within them, but also helped to shield the low-lying Podol area beyond them to the north-east.[3]

The distinctive character of Iaroslav's Kiev, however, was not just its size. Inside the new enclosure, beyond the teams of labourers heaving earth up the ramparts, others were devising more exotic structures – architectural, artistic, verbal, administrative, ideological. In the previous chapter we looked at the means of coercion. It was essential to possess such means, but desirable not to have to use them, to dress power in a cloak of legitimate authority and prestige. In the game of power Iaroslav had been lucky; in constructing an edifice of authority he was innovative and immensely influential. In his methods he was eclectic. The result, not unusual in programmes of monumental propaganda, was a mixture of solid achievement and somewhat incongruously projected wishful thinking: a deliberately impressive set of facades, in which it is not always easy (or possible, or appropriate) to separate structural features from *trompe-l'oeil*.

1. CONSTANTINOPLE-ON-DNIEPER?

Like Vladimir, Iaroslav had been a northern prince, who borrowed a southern style when imposing himself on Kiev. The models for his cultural patronage were Byzantine. In a very broad sense this is also true of virtually all the 'high' culture of pre-Mongol Rus. When Vladimir accepted Byzantine Christianity, he accepted not so much a distinct theology or set of doctrines (eastern and western Churches were not yet in formal schism), but rather a distinct cultural filter through which inner faith (whatever that may have been) passed into outward form; the flesh for the Word. This is reflected in the extent to which the native legends of Vladimir's Conversion stress the ethical and aesthetic dimensions along with the theological and the political. The cultural vocabulary of the new faith – whether in building or in worship or in painting or in writing – was that of eastern Christianity, and thus was derived directly or indirectly from

---

3 For the view that the Podol was also fortified at this stage see Volodymyr I. Mezentsev, 'The territorial and demographic development of medieval Kiev and other major cities of Rus': a comparative analysis based on recent archaeological research', *The Russian Review* 48 (1989), 145–70; cf. E. Mühle, 'Die topographisch-städtebauliche Entwicklung Kievs vom Ende des 10. bis zum Ende des 12. Jh. im Licht der archäologischen Forschungen', *JGO* 36 (1988), 350–76; also M. A. Sahaidak, *Davno'-kyivs'kyi Podil: problemy topohrafii, stratihrafii, khronolohii* (Kiev, 1991), pp. 39–56. Note that the names for the gates may be later.

Byzantium. Byzantium was the source, the measure, the prototype of Christian civilization; a Byzantine provenance was a guarantee of authenticity and authority. In this general sense the Christian culture of the Rus, like that of the other peoples who had followed the same path to faith, was formed in the Byzantine image, as a likeness – an icon – of the Byzantine prototype.[4]

The model and main source for most of Iaroslav's programme of urban construction was, quite specifically, Constantinople, the Imperial city, Tsargrad. His principal device for elevating the authority of Kiev, and of himself as its ruler, was to focus his new city around visible and tangible reminders of the Byzantine capital and, where necessary, to import experts to do the job. In part he was merely following the precedent set by his father Vladimir and (in Chernigov) by his brother Mstislav, but the conception was larger and its realization called for fresh solutions.

Vladimir had focused resources on his palace complex. His citadel had been dominated by the church of the Mother of God, perched next to the princely residence at the northern end of Starokievskaia hill (see above, pp. 164–5). The prince and his followers thus had their splendid masonry church, the rest had to make do with unprotected wood. Iaroslav reshaped the urban landscape. He gave Kiev a new heart, both geographically and spiritually. The centrepiece of Iaroslav's new Kiev was the new church of St Sophia, the Holy Wisdom, built and decorated between 1037 and c. 1047/8.[5] St Sophia was located away from the prince's residence, on the road south to the Golden Gate. It was the church of the metropolitan, the head of the Kievan Christian hierarchy, just as the Constantinopolitan St Sophia was the church of the patriarch, the head of the Byzantine hierarchy. As St Sophia was by far the largest and most magnificent church in Constantinople, so Iaroslav made St Sophia by far the largest and most magnificent church in Kiev, replacing an earlier wooden version in the old town. By shifting the balance of patronage from the palace church to the metropolitan's church (with a new residence for the metropolitan built next to it), by shifting the focus of religious splendour away from the prince's courtyard and into the expanded town, Iaroslav moved the symbolic centre of the new faith out into the urban community. His was to be a Christian city, rather than just a Christian citadel; to emphasize the point and announce it to all-comers, Iaroslav had a church (of the Annunciation) built on top of the Golden Gates.

The prince's residence remained where it had been before, but his authority moved outwards with the Church, a presence in signs and symbols rather than in domicile. Just to the south of St Sophia Iaroslav

---

4 See esp. Dimitri Obolensky, *The Byzantine Commonwealth: Eastern Europe 500–1500* (London, 1971), pp. 272–370.
5 Poppe, 'The building of the Church of St Sophia in Kiev', 26–50.

built a church to St George, and a little to the west a church of St Eirene (echoing imperial foundations in Constantinople as well as the baptismal names of Iaroslav and his wife). The visitor to St Sophia could see, large and prominent in a painted frieze above the columns round three sides of the central nave, the 'donor portrait' of Iaroslav and his family, the pious ruler as patron of the church. This frieze was just below the gallery where the prince's family is thought to have stood: image and prototype visible together.

Reminders of Constantinople were pervasive, and not only in the dedication. At core the Kievan St Sophia was a simple cross-in-square church: that is, basically a cube with a central dome supported on four columns and with a series of curves in the eastern wall to form apses. The cross-in-square (or domed cross), one of several Byzantine church styles, became the standard architectural type for masonry churches in pre-Mongol Rus. But the Kievan St Sophia was also built to impress, and the technique for enlargement was to amplify the structure outwards and upwards. By adding rows of columns, the central cube was given five aisles and apses instead of the usual three; there was an interior first-floor gallery round three sides (all but the east), with access via staircase towers at the north-west and south-west corners; and the roof bulged with thirteen domes. The cube measured 29.3 × 29.3 metres at the base, and 28.8 metres to the top of the central dome. To stretch the dimensions further, there was a double ambulatory round the southern, western and northern sides, taking the total width to 56.4 metres and the total length west to east, including the apses, to 41.7 metres.[6] This was not vast by comparison with many West European cathedrals, and all thirteen domes would have fitted underneath the vast main dome of the church's Constantinopolitan namesake. In context, however, it was a very major building. It is the largest extant Byzantine church of the eleventh century; none of its size had been seen before among the Rus, nor would any be built again for the next 500 years.[7] In Constantinople it would have been noteworthy; on the hills above the Dnieper it must have been a strange and powerful sight.

The interior was luxurious, richly covered with images. The central

6 On the entire building as a single project, rather than as separate phases, see Iu. S. Aseev, I. F. Totskaia, G. M. Shtender, 'Novoe o kompozitsionnom zamysle Sofiiskogo sobora v Kieve', in A. I. Komech and O. I. Podobedova, eds, *Drevnerusskoe iskusstvo. Khudozhestvennaia kul'tura X–pervoi poloviny XIII v.* (Moscow, 1988), pp. 13–27; A. I. Komech, *Drevnerusskoe zodchestvo kontsa X–nachala XII v.: vizantiiskoe nasledie i stanovlenie samostoiatel'noi traditsii* (Moscow, 1987), pp. 178–232; Poppe, 'The building of the Church of St Sophia in Kiev', 43–4.

7 For scale plans see P. A. Rappoport, *Russkaia arkhitektura X–XIII vv.* (*ASSSR SAI*, vyp. E1–47; Leningrad, 1982), pp. 118–32; on conventions of measurement see L. N. Bol'shakova, 'Metricheskii analiz drevnerusskikh khramov XI–XII vv.', in Komech and Podobedova, eds, *Drevnerusskoe iskusstvo*, pp. 112–19.

upper sections were decorated with mosaics: the main apse dominated by a full-length frontal figure of the Mother of God above a mosaic frieze of Christ administering the Eucharist; the massive face of Christ Pantokrator gazing down from the heaven of the central dome; prefigurative and narrative cycles from Old and New Testaments above the transepts – together a classic Byzantine microcosm, holding the worshipper in the simulated presence of sacred history. Some 177 colour shades have been identified, mainly deep blues and greens and shimmering gold. The lower walls were filled with frescoes: in fact more economical than the marble facing which one might find in an equivalent Byzantine church (in Kiev there was no local marble), but in effect no less sensuous.[8]

Iaroslav's St Sophia was a Byzantine church in almost all but location. It was built by Byzantine architects and craftsmen – probably by the same team that had started work on Mstislav's church of the Saviour in Chernigov – using Byzantine techniques. It was decorated by Byzantine artists, often using Byzantine materials: some of the smalt for the mosaics was imported, some was made locally under the guidance of Byzantine masters.[9] And in adapting the church to its locality, its decorators, presumably with Iaroslav's approval, did not try to conceal its sources of inspiration. On the contrary, its 'Greekness' was flaunted, even where it might have been modified. All the mosaic inscriptions were in Greek, not in Slavonic. More privately, the stairwells to the gallery were painted with scenes from the life of the Constantinopolitan court: the Hippodrome, musicians, the hunt – reminders of imperial presence in the place where the prince's family ascended to their gallery.[10]

This was the most direct form of cultural transference, and in the mid-eleventh century it was the fashion. Having finished St Sophia in Kiev, the Byzantine team was dispatched to build a lesser St Sophia in Novgorod. Here too, following the Kievan example, the construction not only altered the landscape but helped to shift the focus of prestigious space: the new church dominated one bank of the 'New Town' (*novgorod*), grander by far than anything in old Gorodishche.[11] At around the same time, even though not under

---

8 See V. N. Lazarev, *Old Russian Murals and Mosaics* (London, 1966), pp. 31–64, 225–43; idem, *Mozaiki Sofii Kievskoi* (Moscow, 1960); V. L. Levitskaia, 'Materialy issledovaniia palitry Sofii Kievskoi', *Vizantiiskii vremennik* 23 (1963), 105–57.

9 On the type of manufacture see Poppe, 'The building of the Church of St Sophia in Kiev', 42–3.

10 Often thought to represent native pastimes; but see I. F. Totskaia and A. M. Zaiaruznyi, 'Muzykanty na freske "Skomorokhi" v Sofii Kievskoi', in Komech and Podobedova, eds, *Drevnerusskoe iskusstvo*, pp. 143–55.

11 On the transfer from Gorodishche to the New Town see E. Mühle, 'Von Holmgardr zu Novgorod. Zur Genesis des slavischen Ortsnamens der Ilmensee - Metropole im 11. Jahrhundert', in *Ex oriente lux. Mélanges offerts en hommage au professeur Jean Blankoff, à l'occasion de ses soixante ans* (Brussels, 1991), I, pp. 245–52.

Iaroslav's patronage, a St Sophia was built in Polotsk (see below, p. 251). The only surviving prestige objects from the early years of the century – the coins issued by Vladimir, Sviatopolk and Iaroslav – had their main messages inscribed in Slavonic; but from mid-century, princes and churchmen had their seals inscribed in Greek. Greek was the script of public display, and public monuments were produced in Byzantine style under the tutelage of Byzantine masters and with conspicuous symbolic reminders of the Byzantine presence. It is possible that Greek was also used in St Sophia in the liturgy.[12]

These were the visible, tangible products of Iaroslav's patronage. At the same time, at the prince's out-of-town residence at Berestovo, the priest Ilarion, from the church of the Holy Apostles (also, incidentally, a church dedication with distinguished imperial Constantinopolitan echoes), produced an equivalent monument in words. Ilarion's *Sermon on Law and Grace* is the first and finest extant work of Kievan rhetoric. Its main aims were, in the first place, to explain and celebrate the status of the converted Rus in sacred history; and, secondly, to praise the achievements of Vladimir and, by extension, of Iaroslav.

The acceptance of the new faith implied, among many other things, the acceptance of a completely new notion of time and space. Instead of local paganisms with local cosmologies conveyed in oral tradition, the Rus were presented with universal history as charted and interpreted in centuries of Jewish, classical and Christian writing. By accepting Christianity the Rus put themselves on somebody else's map of time and space. Ilarion took on the task of finding a place for the Rus, of showing that they were there by design rather than by chance, and thus of giving dignity, purpose and divine sanction to the policies of the rulers. While Iaroslav's architects and craftsmen built images of Christian and princely authority for the ruler, Ilarion – Iaroslav's ideologue – laid the foundations for a myth of collective Christian identity for the Rus. In both cases the assertion of local dignity was inseparable from the display of wider affiliation; to be was to belong.

The first stage of Ilarion's argument was theoretical, explaining the nature and shape of sacred history, the two great chapter-headings of the book of the world: Law and Grace, the Old Testament and the New, justification and salvation, bondage and freedom, the shadow and the truth. He illustrates by means of biblical typology: that is, the art of reading the Bible both historically (as a linear sequence of events) and figuratively (whereby events in the Old Testament prefigure those of the New Testament). In particular, Ilarion analyses the story of Abraham's handmaid Hagar and his wife Sarah, and of their respective children Ishmael and Isaac: Hagar the handmaid and her son Ishmael represent bondage and the age of the Law, Sarah the wife and her son

---

12 Simon Franklin, 'Greek in Kievan Rus", *DOP* 46 (1992), 69–81.

Isaac represent freedom and the coming of Grace. The second stage in Ilarion's exposition is historical: just as the New Testament was prefigured over time, so it was fulfilled in time; the Law was for the Jews, Grace was for all the nations of the gentiles; and so the Rus, too, became Christian. Vladimir's decision was thus an integral part of the divine plan for mankind; in this sense the future Christianity of the Rus was already present in the story of Hagar and Sarah. From theory and history, Ilarion proceeds to eulogy: to the miracle whereby Vladimir – inspired by tales of the 'pious land of the Greeks' – came to believe; and finally to Iaroslav's own cultural patronage (and hence, by convenient implication, to Ilarion's own endeavour in writing the sermon!).

Thus in buildings, pictures and words, through his architects, artists and bookmen, Iaroslav contrived to bring an aura of Constantinople to Kiev.

Yet the image was not purely Constantinopolitan. In significant minutiae it was blended to local specifications. For example, in establishing the dignity of the Rus under Providence, Ilarion managed to construct a scheme whose elements were all borrowed from Byzantium, but which nevertheless avoided the byzantinocentric imperial teleology of Byzantium itself: the idea that the Byzantine empire, as the Christian continuation of the Roman empire (in the reign of whose first ruler God had become man), was divinely pre-ordained as the earthly embodiment of the universal faith. For the Byzantines history led to the triumph of Byzantium; for Ilarion the Rus took their own place among 'all the nations' visited by Grace, not as an appendage to the empire of the *Rhomaioi* (as the Byzantines called themselves).[13]

In furthering the dignity, prestige and legitimacy of Iaroslav's rule, his collaborators produced a complex amalgam, drawing on a variety of sources – some new, some old – with reminders not only of Constantinople but also of the Old Testament, of Khazar rulership, and of local ties of kinship. Vladimir was a 'likeness of Constantine the Great', a 'new Constantine of great Rome', a David, decked with kingly virtues ('adorned with charity as with a necklace and gold regalia'),[14] but Ilarion also lauds him as the 'great *kagan* of our land', and praises his 'glorious' (though pagan) father and grandfather.[15] Iaroslav's status was enhanced through a similar

---

13 On the basis of Byzantine imperial teleology see G. Podskalsky, *Byzantinische Reichseschatologie* (Munich, 1972); also C. Mango, *Byzantium. The Empire of New Rome* (London, 1980), pp. 189–217.

14 Moldovan, *Slovo*, pp. 96, 99 (fols 191a, 194a); Franklin *Sermons and Rhetoric*, pp. 23, 25. On the topos in Byzantium see Paul Magdalino, ed., *New Constantines. Papers from the Twenty Sixth Spring Symposium of Byzantine Studies. St Andrews, March 1992* (Aldershot, 1994).

15 Moldovan, *Slovo*, p. 91 (fol. 184b); cf. pp. 78, 92 (fols 168a, 185a, 186a); Franklin, *Sermons and Rhetoric*, p. 17; cf. pp. 3, 18.

multiplicity of associations: with Constantinople through the palace frescoes in St Sophia and through the entire architectural project; with Christ through the donor portrait; with Vladimir both by kinship and by spiritual equivalence. For Ilarion he was Solomon to Vladimir's David; a graffito in St Sophia commemorates him as *tsar'*, the Slavonic word derived from *caesar*, used both of Old Testament kings and of Byzantine emperors; another graffito refers to a *kagan*.[16] According to the extant narratives, Iaroslav actively promoted the cult of his murdered brothers Boris and Gleb, whose death in family strife became martyrdom and a lesson in Christian humility, innocence and fraternal deference. It could do him no harm to stress the divine favour shown both to his father and to two of his brothers, testimony to the status of his kin: individual princely succession may have been troubled, but a family which could boast three recent candidates for sainthood must be due special honour. Kinship was not yet a significant component of Byzantine notions of legitimate rule. Suitably modified, however, the imported faith could reinforce, rather than replace, native political convention.

According to Ilarion, Iaroslav's kin, his glorious forefathers, 'ruled not some feeble, obscure, unknown land, but in this land of Rus, which is known and renowned to the ends of the earth'.[17] And indeed rulers abroad apparently shared Iaroslav's assessment of his prestige and of his place among them. His sister Maria/Dobronega married Casimir of Poland; three of his daughters – Elizabeth, Anastasia and Anna – were married to, respectively, Harald Hardraada, Andrew I of Hungary and Henry I of France. Among his sons, Iziaslav married Casimir's sister Gertrude, Sviatoslav probably married a grandniece of the German emperor Henry III, and Vsevolod married into the family of the Byzantine emperor Constantine IX Monomakhos.[18]

The overall impression, or facade, created by Iaroslav's programme of patronage and political networking is one of completeness, of accomplishment, of grand themes grandly stated, of grand goals grandly achieved. The Rus, it seemed, had arrived; perhaps not as a new breed of conquerors and innovators, but at least as a distinct though authentically Christian people with an authentically Christian ruler dwelling in his Second Constantinople, protected by the Mother of God and St Sophia, on the hills above the right bank of the Dnieper, as St Andrew himself had prophesied (see above, p. 3). If this was

---

16 S. A. Vysotskii, *Drevnerusskie nadpisi Sofii Kievskoi XI–XIV vv.*, *vypusk* 1 (Kiev, 1966), nos 8, 13; pp. 39–41, 49–52 (but dating no. 13 to mid-century).

17 Moldovan, *Slovo*, p. 92 (fol. 185a); Franklin, *Sermons and Rhetoric*, p. 18. On the origins of the cult of Boris and Gleb see above, p. 186, n. 9.

18 Manfred Hellmann, 'Die Heiratspolitik Jaroslavs des Weisen', *Forschungen zur osteuropäischen Geschichte* 8 (1962), 7–25.

what it looked like to the locals and to visiting traders and dignitaries, Iaroslav would probably have been well pleased.

In 1043, however, at the very time when the Kievan St Sophia was taking shape, Iaroslav launched a major military campaign against Constantinople. A flotilla carrying well over 10,000 troops, under the command of Iaroslav's eldest son Vladimir, prince of Novgorod, set off down the Dnieper and across the Black Sea to attack Constantinople. The result was utter defeat for the Rus. The causes have been a topic of much discussion. If we knew nothing of Iaroslav's Kievan propaganda, the campaign might provoke little surprise: here was a northern prince of the Rus, with strong Varangian connections, renewing the custom of his forefathers. But how can the attack on Constantinople be explained in the context of Iaroslav's Constantinopolitan project for Kiev? Was his entire cultural programme in fact directed *against* Constantinople, as an assertion of Kievan equality, as a reaction to Byzantine imperial pretensions?[19]

Such questions, which are frequently posed, stem from an over-simplified view of the relations between ideas and policies. Byzantium never posed any direct threat to Kiev. All the military traffic was in the opposite direction. The civil war of 1015–19 sucked in troops from most of the Rus' known world, but the Byzantines were notable absentees. Even as an idea, Byzantine universalism was effectively limited to the lands of the old Roman empire (hence the existence of an independent Bulgaria was an affront) and did not stretch north of the steppes to the lands of the peoples whom the Byzantines tended to term 'Scythians' or 'Hyperborean Scythians'.[20] On the other hand, as these terms imply, the Byzantines were perfectly capable of being supercilious. Byzantine writers rarely accorded to the Rus as much dignity as the Rus accorded to themselves, and Iaroslav manifestly cared about prestige and respect. According to Byzantine sources the pretext for the 1043 campaign was trivial: a distinguished 'Scyth' had been killed as a result of a market-place altercation in Constantinople. We do not know what deeper resentments prompted Iaroslav to launch such a major response to such an apparently minor incident, but the response is compatible with Iaroslav's desire to be taken seriously, a reaction to Byzantine *in*attentiveness more than to Byzantine *over*-attentiveness.[21] There is no necessary contradiction between the demonstratively Constantinopolitan style of Iaroslav's public patronage and his campaign against Constantinople in 1043.

19 For example, P. P. Tolochko, *Drevniaia Rus'. Ocherki sotsial'no-politicheskoi istorii* (Kiev, 1987), pp. 82–3.

20 On Byzantine names for the Rus see M. V. Bibikov, 'Vizantiiskie istochniki po istorii Rusi, narodov Severnogo Prichernomor'ia i Severnogo Kavkaza (XII–XIII vv.)', *DGTSSSR* 1980 (1981), pp. 34–78.

21 J. Shepard, 'Why did the Russians attack Byzantium in 1043?', *BNJ* 22 (1978/9), 147–212.

The 1043 campaign was the last of its kind, the last in the series of occasional Rus raids which had begun nearly two centuries earlier. Whatever the causes of the rift, relations seem to have been mended for the later years of Iaroslav's reign. The Byzantines finished St Sophia in Kiev, and went on to supervise the building and decoration of its smaller equivalent in Novgorod – city of Vladimir Iaroslavich, who had led the attack. By 1053 Iaroslav's son Vsevolod was married to his Byzantine bride. There is no recorded Byzantine objection to the appointment of Ilarion himself as metropolitan of Kiev in 1051, one of possibly only two natives of Rus, rather than Byzantines, to occupy that post in the entire period from the Conversion to the early thirteenth century.

Iaroslav put a great deal of money and effort into his public image. To what extent was the image matched by substance? The Byzantines were snobs, and historians have to be sceptics. In the previous chapter we looked at the military machinations behind the facade of stately and peaceable dynastic succession. Here we shall consider the civil and the spiritual; or rather, with a slight twist of Ilarion's meaning, Law and Grace.

2. 'LAW': THE PRINCE'S WRIT

Iaroslav is credited with having issued the earliest version of the first written code of civil law among the Rus: the *Russkaia Pravda*. Unfortunately, though unsurprisingly, Iaroslav's code cannot be read as a separate document in its original form. *Russkaia Pravda* became the generic name for accumulated princely rulings. As new decisions were added, so the code was periodically re-edited and reshaped. All existing texts of *Russkaia Pravda* are later compilations. The most common extant version, known as the 'Expanded Pravda' (EP, containing over 120 articles), was put together in the late twelfth or early thirteenth century on the basis of previous edicts. An earlier version, the 'Short Pravda' (SP, with 43 articles), was probably compiled in the late eleventh or early twelfth century. SP is rare because its functioning provisions were absorbed into EP and it therefore ceased to be a working document. Just under half the provisions of SP (articles 1–18, perhaps 42 and 43) are commonly attributed to Iaroslav, while the remainder (articles 19–41, and perhaps the compilation of SP itself) are ascribed to his sons. Iaroslav's code of civil laws – sometimes known as the 'Earliest Pravda' – is thus a hypothetical extrapolation from SP.[22]

---

22 On the history of compilations see Daniel H. Kaiser, *The Growth of the Law in Medieval Russia* (Princeton, 1980), pp. 29–46, and the account in *ZDR*, pp. 28–44. Texts cited hereafter according to *ZDR*, pp. 47–129; cf. English translations in Kaiser, *The Laws*, pp. 15–34.

If Iaroslav did issue a written code (and we shall assume for the moment that he did), then it was a modest but momentous innovation. The Rus had of course known about uses of writing for many decades, but had apparently not seen a need to adopt it for themselves to any significant extent. By the time of Iaroslav's reign, Slavonic writing had existed for nearly two centuries since the Scriptures were first translated by Sts Cyril and Methodios for their mission to Moravia in the 860s. St Cyril is credited with inventing an alphabet for the Slavs. The Rus used the alphabet now known as the 'Cyrillic', although – confusingly – the earliest Slavonic alphabet was probably not the Cyrillic (based on Greek) but the Glagolitic (more eastern in style).[23] Until the mid-eleventh century, traces of East Slavonic writing are extremely rare. The earliest locally discovered fragment in the Cyrillic alphabet dates from the mid-tenth century: a barely decipherable word (guesses include 'mustard', 'oil', or perhaps a name) incised on a pot unearthed at Gnëzdovo.[24] Add the inscriptions on a couple of small wooden blocks, thought to have been used to secure sacks of goods and tenuously dated to the 970s, and we have the full corpus of extant pre-Conversion specimens of Cyrillic writing from the lands of the Rus.[25]

One might expect the flow of writing to swell in the aftermath of the official Conversion to Christianity. In the story of the Conversion, Vladimir abandoned his synthetic pagan pantheon and investigated Religions of the Book (see above, pp. 160–1). For a ruler intent on establishing a fixed focus of authority in a large and multi-ethnic land, writing provided a huge technological advantage: the word became an object, ceased to die at the moment of utterance, ceased to depend on the presence of its bearer, could be standardized, preserved, contemplated and replicated across time and space. The Conversion can be seen, *inter alia*, as the start of a revolution in information technology. But it was a slow start. In the native uses of writing there was no abrupt discernible change in 988 or thereabouts, no rapid

---

23 For the proposition that the Glagolitic alphabet existed before St Cyril see G. M. Prokhorov, 'Glagolitsa sredi missionerskikh azbuk', *TODRL* 45 (1992), 178–99.

24 See H. Lunt, 'The Language of Rus' in the Eleventh Century. Some Observations about Facts and Theories', *HUS* 12/13 (1988/89), 279–80.

25 For details see S. Franklin, 'The writing in the ground: recent Soviet publications on early Russian literacy', *SEER* 65 (1987), 414–16; also possibly the seals attributed to Sviatoslav, and to Iziaslav Vladimirovich: Ianin, *Aktovye pechati*, I, pp. 38–41. The tenth-century treaties with Byzantium (see above, pp. 103–6, 117–19) first appear in the early twelfth-century version of the *Primary Chronicle*, and hence cannot be counted in a list of extant authentic original specimens of writing. It is in any case far from certain that they were (a) translated at the time they were produced, or (b) if they were translated, that they were rendered into Slavonic (rather than into the Scandinavian 'Rhos language' illustrated in the *DAI*).

expansion of the technology of the Word. For half a dozen decades after the Conversion the surviving fragments become only slightly more numerous than for the decades before it: the brief experiment with inscribed coinage (see above, pp. 168, 193); an alphabet scratched on a piece of birch bark from Novgorod; the maker's inscription on the blade of a sword; three saints' names on the lid of a reliquary from Chernigov.[26] Naturally more was produced than has survived. Styluses have been found at several sites even from the tenth century.[27] However, the significant change did not occur under Vladimir, but only in the mid-eleventh century, after which the range and volume of evidence increases dramatically. Before the age of Iaroslav traces of any native uses of writing, though not entirely negligible, are barely visible; after the age of Iaroslav all forms of native writing – ephemeral or otherwise – steadily proliferate (see also below, pp. 237–43). One symptom of the change is the earliest code of written law. What does it contain, and why was it issued?

Article 1 of SP deals with homicide. It allows revenge-killing by a close relative (brother, father, son or nephew), or a payment of 40 grivnas if nobody is available (or able, or willing?) to exact revenge. Articles 2–10 specify sums to be paid in respect of assault or physical injury: 12 grivnas, for example, is the payment for a blow with a sword-handle or goblet, 40 grivnas for serious injury to an arm, 3 grivnas for a finger, 12 for a beard. Articles 11–18 deal with procedures and payments for violation of property: how to recover a slave who has fled to a Varangian, or who has been taken and illicitly sold; payment for stealing a horse; a master's obligation to pay for injury caused by his slave.

With the possible exception of Articles 1 and 43 (on payment in lieu of revenge-killing, and on fees for the *virnik*, the collector of such bloodwite), the payments listed in 'Iaroslav's code' are likely to have been in the form of compensation, rather than in the form of fines to the prince.[28] The prince issues the code, but apparently has little part in procedures or sanctions; the code implies that conflicts were mainly to be resolved within the community, or between communities, based on horizontal ('dyadic') social relations. Very broadly, the history of legislative growth in medieval Rus shows the gradual encroachment

26 A. A. Medyntseva, *Podpisnye shedevry drevnerusskogo remesla* (Moscow, 1991), pp. 9–10, 50–2; *NGB*, no. 529; J. Shepard, 'Ingvarr's expedition to the East and a Russian inscribed stone cross', *Saga-Book of the Viking Society* 21 (1984–5), 222–92.

27 A. A. Medyntseva, 'Nachalo pis'mennosti na Rusi po arkheologicheskim dannym', in *Istoriia, kul'tura, etnografiia i fol'klor slavianskikh narodov. IX mezhdunarodnyi s"ezd slavistov. Kiev, sentiabr' 1983 g. Doklady sovetskoi delegatsii* (Moscow, 1983), pp. 86–97.

28 Daniel H. Kaiser, 'Reconsidering crime and punishment in Kievan Rus'', *Russian History* 7 (1980), 283–93; for a different view see M. B. Sverdlov, *Ot Zakona Russkogo k Russkoi Pravde* (Moscow, 1988), pp. 48–50.

of the prince and his agents into the community, the strengthening of vertical (or 'triadic') social relations: the growth of investigative, judicial and administrative procedures, the use of monetary sanctions (fines) and eventually physical punishment in place of compensation.[29] In 'Iaroslav's code', by contrast, the prince is so reticent as to be almost absent. His formal participation is limited to issuing the code itself. In other words, this code of written law is not a definition of the mechanisms or extent of princely power.

'Iaroslav's code' was derived from custom. Like all subsequent versions of *Russkaia Pravda*, it was written in the vernacular, owing nothing to the Church Slavonic of imported learning. Church Slavonic was a written language which had been devised specifically for the purpose of translating the Scriptures from Greek. The local vernacular was East Slavonic, the language of those Slavs among whom the Rus had become linguistically assimilated (or at least functionally bilingual) over the course of the tenth century. Church Slavonic was the language of 'high' culture, of Christian discourse; East Slavonic was the language of civil administration. The gap between Church Slavonic and East Slavonic was, however, more cultural than formal. There was a common core of grammar and vocabulary. Some sounds were distinct, but to no greater extent than is often the case between dialects. But Church Slavonic brought a mass of concepts which were alien to the pagans north of the steppes, and it often expressed them in elaborately structured sentences brimming with participles and subordinate clauses. A totally untutored East Slav would certainly have found Church Slavonic strange, in places opaque, and in order to *use* it he would have needed special training. But there was scope for degrees of familiarity. Church Slavonic was probably perceived as a functional variant of the native tongue, at some level accessible, though with an aura of solemnity.[30]

One should not imagine, however, that the vernacular was rough and unformed, just because it had not been shaped by writing. The terse and (to historians) enigmatic formulae of *Russkaia Pravda* suggest that the Rus already had a structured language of civil regulation long before it was written down. The history of written law is not identical with the history of civil authority or of functioning social norms. The search for precise origins, however, leads to obscurity. Provisions analogous to those in *Russkaia Pravda* have been found in Germanic and Anglo-Saxon codes, and in parts of the tenth-century treaties with Byzantium.[31] The obvious inference is that the norms of behaviour

29 Kaiser, *The Growth of the Law*, pp. 3–17.
30 H. Lunt, 'On the language of Old Rus: some questions and suggestions', *Russian Linguistics* 2 (1975), 269–81. On Church Slavonic/East Slavonic 'diglossy' (functional differentiation) see B. A. Uspenskii, *Iazykovaia situatsiia Kievskoi Rusi i ee znachenie dlia istorii russkogo literaturnogo iazyka* (Moscow, 1983), pp. 32–54.
31 For example, Sverdlov, *Ot Zakona Russkogo k Russkoi Pravde*, pp. 52–66.

implied by *Russkaia Pravda* reflect Varangian custom, the North European traditions of the early princes and their entourages. But it is hard to measure the extent to which, by the mid-eleventh century, Varangian and Slav customs among the ruling elites had converged. The language of the formulae, after all, was East Slavonic.

Whatever the precise mix of fertilizers, *Russkaia Pravda* was home-grown. The customs and procedures implied in 'Iaroslav's code' were local, not borrowed from Byzantium. By contrast with Iaroslav's other public initiatives, there is not the merest hint of Byzantine-style window-dressing. An anecdote in the *Primary Chronicle* relates how 'the bishops' briefly persuaded Vladimir that it was the pious duty of the ruler to punish malefactors rather than to fine them. Vladimir obliged, but the consequent loss of income meant that there was not enough money for weapons and horses, so the prince reverted to the ways of his father and grandfather.[32] The story is probably a later fabrication, supporting the increased use of fines in the late eleventh or early twelfth century. But it nicely catches an awareness that local practices were distinct, resistant to imported injunction even from the most authoritative sources. Borrowing was necessarily selective. To change the face of a city was simpler than to change the habits of society. The aura of Constantinople emanated from the ruler, but not from the rules.

Written codes are not intrinsically more effective than unwritten customs. If the code reflects custom, and if the prince was a conspicuous absentee from its provisions, why did Iaroslav bother to issue it at all? 'Among all peoples', declares a chronicler near the start of the twelfth century, 'some have written law, others have custom; the lawless think that ancestral custom is law'. The neat formula is in fact cited directly from a translated Byzantine source ('As Georgii says in his chronicle . . .') and in context applies to the contrast between a single Christian law and the multiplicity of pagan customs.[33] But it would be consistent and in character if Iaroslav had been motivated partly by the prestige of lawgiving itself as an attribute of a Christian ruler: the legitimacy of the legislator. In this case the significance of 'Iaroslav's code' would be more symbolic than practical.

Symbolism may be part of an explanation, but it is not sufficient. The articles of 'Iaroslav's code', like all other versions of *Russkaia Pravda*, are glaringly practical, almost mundane. Iaroslav and his successors used the new technology (writing) not merely to give a princely gloss to customary behaviour, but also – increasingly – to intervene, standardize

---

32 *PVL*, I, pp. 86–7; see Kaiser, 'Reconsidering crime and punishment'.
33 *PVL*, I, pp. 15–16. On the *Primary Chronicle*'s quotations from the ninth-century chronicle of George the Monk (Georgios Monakhos, alias George Hamartolos – 'the Sinner') and its tenth-century *Continuation* see O. V. Tvorogov, 'Povest' vremennykh let i Khronograf po velikomu izlozheniiu', *TODRL* 28 (1974), 99–113.

and modify. The articles generally (but hypothetically) attributed to Iaroslav give little scope for anything more than guesswork. We may speculate, for example, that the standard tariffs for compensation may have been imposed. It is conspicuous, moreover, that several articles deal with disputes which cross community boundaries, disputes which were inter-communal rather than intra-communal: if the victim was a Varangian or other foreign resident; if a Varangian or foreigner hid a slave;[34] the complex procedure for dealing with theft and sometimes resale (e.g. of a horse or slave) by a member of another community,[35] by contrast with the simple resolution of the equivalent dispute within a single community (the *mir*).[36] Still, however, this is not sufficient. Princely intervention in inter-communal urban disputes could be covered by custom.

A clearer picture emerges if we move forward in time and consider SP as a whole: the articles ascribed to Iaroslav, together with the section attributed to his sons. The latter part of SP is far more directly concerned with princely interests and involvement. In the first place, nearly half of its provisions in effect constitute a charter for the protection of the prince's own men and property, listing the penalties if they are killed or violated: from 80 grivnas for the murder of a prince's senior steward (*ognishchanin*) down to 5 grivnas for a slave and 1 nogata (0.05 grivnas of 'fur') for a lamb.[37] Secondly, and partly in consequence, far more of the articles specify fines; in effect, additional compensation for the prince. Thirdly, at least in one place it is made plain that new articles were reactive and normative, rather than descriptive; that the code grew in response to problems as they occurred: thus the penalty for killing the prince's senior stablemaster was set at 80 grivnas, 'as Iziaslav established when the residents of Dorogobuzh killed his stablemaster'.[38] Fourth, SP shows how the community was responsible *for* its members, but *to* the prince, and that the prince was particularly concerned to press his authority in cases of homicide. If the murderer of a prince's man was not found or delivered, then the bloodwite was to be paid by the community where the corpse lay. It was permissible to kill a murderer at the scene of the crime, or to kill a thief while he was being apprehended; but once a thief was caught and bound, he must be taken to the prince's residence.[39]

A later text, in EP, appears to state that Iaroslav's sons actually abolished

---

34 SP, Articles 10, 11: ZDR, pp. 47, 54–5; Kaiser, *The Laws*, p. 16.
35 SP, Article 14, perhaps also 15–16: ZDR, pp. 47–8, 56–7; Kaiser, *The Laws*, p. 16.
36 SP, Article 13, perhaps also 12: ZDR, pp. 47, 56; Kaiser, *The Laws*, p. 16.
37 SP, Articles 19–28, 32, 33: ZDR, pp. 48, 58–62; Kaiser, *The Laws*, pp. 17–18.
38 SP, Article 23: ZDR, p. 48; Kaiser, *The Laws*, p. 17.
39 SP, Articles 20, 21, 38: ZDR, pp. 48–9; Kaiser, *The Laws*, pp. 17–18.

revenge-killing and replaced it entirely with monetary sanction.[40] This is not borne out by SP, but it does add to the impression that written law was being used to modify or standardize custom, if not to abolish it. Article 1 of SP, on the degrees of consanguinity within which revenge-killing was allowed, was perhaps an attempt to limit custom. An anecdotal reflection of princely concern is found in the *Saga of Olaf Tryggvason*. One day the boy Olaf, who was living in Holmgarthr (Novgorod), chanced to recognize his foster father's murderer, so in vengeance he struck him to death with an axe. The law in Holmgarthr required that the boy, in turn, should forfeit his own life, so 'according to their custom and laws all the populace rushed to find what had become of the boy'. But the queen took Olaf into her care, and the prince/king commuted his penalty to a fine, which was paid by the queen.[41] Here we find revenge-killing prescribed by custom and commuted to a fine by the prince. The tale, though fictional, nicely echoes Article 1 of *Russkaia Pravda*.

Finally, SP helps to shed light on a practical reason for recording princely intervention in writing. The latter part of SP is said to have been produced in conference, as a form of agreement between three of Iaroslav's sons and their senior servitors.[42] Article 23, as we have seen, states a decision by one of those sons, Iziaslav, which was to be incorporated into the code of common practice for all three. The code therefore stipulated, *inter alia*, equal protection for the princes' men, regardless of which prince they happened to serve. Possibly it was intended partly to avert cross-recruitment. If rules were to be standard across separate communities and principalities, and in the absence of the particular prince who laid down the precedent, then writing did indeed have qualities lacking in orally recorded custom. This puts into a somewhat different perspective the prince's apparent absence in 'Iaroslav's code'.

Why, then, was 'Iaroslav's code' issued? We find *an* answer in the *First Novgorod Chronicle*, in its narrative of the events which followed the murder of Boris and Gleb. In 1016, after driving Sviatopolk out of Kiev, Iaroslav paid off his Novgorodian troops and sent them home, 'having given them a *pravda* and having written an *ustav* [statute], saying to them thus: "Live by this document which I have written for you."' There then follows the full text of SP.[43] The story in the Novgorod chronicle is strictly inaccurate: Iaroslav could not have issued the whole of SP, including the agreement between sons as yet unborn. Furthermore, the Novgorodian source tends to shift events of Iaroslav's main period of rule in Kiev (post-1036) back by a couple of

---

40 EP, Article 2: *ZDR*, pp. 64, 82–3; Kaiser, *The Laws*, p. 20.
41 *Heimskringla* VII.8; tr. Hollander, p. 148.
42 Text between Articles 17 and 18: *ZDR*, pp. 48, 58; Kaiser, *The Laws*, p. 17.
43 *NPL*, pp. 175–6.

decades, and also to project back into the past the later contractual relations between Novgorod and its prince (see below, pp. 343–5). But the underlying assumption is at least plausible: that Iaroslav issued the written code for Novgorod while ruling in Kiev; that writing was his surrogate presence, a substitute for his word in his absence, for the periphery rather than the centre, perhaps as a memory-aid for his agent rather than as a prestigious ornament to his personal rule.

The *social* context of early written law is plainer: the legislation in SP, taken as a whole, was aimed at free urban males. No revenge-killing, compensation or fine was laid down for the murder of a woman, except for the murder of a slave wet-nurse (listed among valuable chattels, just before a horse).[44] The specified monetary sums would have been beyond the means of all but the free urban men. A miscreant slave was to be beaten, unless he could take refuge with his master, who was then obliged to pay on his behalf.[45] In effect, as implied in the Novgorod tale, princely written legislation functioned in the same social sphere as princely military recruitment: where else would it be necessary to specify a standard penalty for striking with a goblet or a drinking-horn or a sword-hilt?[46] The prince legislated for the 'townsmen', in the rather narrow sense discussed in the previous chapter; and, in the case of Iaroslav's sons, to protect his own retainers *from* the townsmen.

Iaroslav's written code of secular law, if it existed, was a modest but significant beginning: a small number of articles which confirmed and moderated custom within a small social group; a limited experiment in the new technology; a reminder of the prince's interest, even at a distance, in the prince's men's behaviour towards each other. It was not a charter for radical social and administrative change. In scope and concept, in jurisprudential sophistication, and in the type of society which it presupposed, it was not remotely comparable to the reform projects in legal training and administration which were being introduced by Iaroslav's contemporary and kinsman-by-marriage, the Byzantine emperor Constantine IX Monomakhos (1042–55).[47] The building of a few Byzantine churches and the commissioning of a few Byzantine-style pictures and the patronage of some Byzantine-style rhetoric did not instantly transform Iaroslav into a Byzantine ruler supported by an elaborate hierarchy of fawning bureaucrats, quibbling theorists and document-producing quill-pushers. A Byzantine visitor

---

44 SP, Article 27: *ZDR*, p. 48; Kaiser, *The Laws*, p. 17.
45 SP, Article 17: *ZDR*, p. 48; Kaiser, *The Laws*, pp. 16–17.
46 SP, Articles 3, 4: *ZDR*, p. 47; Kaiser, *The Laws*, p. 15.
47 See e.g. N. Oikonomides, 'L'évolution de l'organisation administrative de l'empire byzantin au XI siècle', *TM* 6 (1976), 125–52.

might well have found the discrepancy between style and substance more than a shade incongruous.[48]

3. 'GRACE': SPREADING THE FAITH

Christianity among the Rus spread from the top down. Though there had been individual Christians and perhaps small communities before the official Conversion under Vladimir, the institutional establishment of the new religion was a result of princely policy, and the spread of Christianity was closely linked to the spread of princely authority. The Church can be viewed as one of the prince's means of legitimization, his non-coercive instrument of authority. The leaders of the Church worked with, and in some respects for, the prince. This is not to say that all churchmen were in all respects docile towards all princes: in return for moral support, the prince had moral and material obligations. The Church needed to be nurtured. The growth of its effectiveness depended, paradoxically, on the growth of its autonomy: on its ability to build and sustain its own institutions, and on its ability to gain acceptance for its own precepts among the population. The Conversion of the Rus was an event, a single decision; but the Christianization of the Rus was a long and complex process.

How widely and how deeply had the new faith become established over the first half-century of its official existence? This begs the question of how one measures the spread of the faith. One can imagine many ways in which a forced dunking in the Dnieper may or may not have affected beliefs. The problem is that faith itself – inner faith – is invisible and cannot be measured at all. We can only look at outer faith: at institutions, at customs and ritual observance, at deeds and words and objects. None of these are perfect mirrors of the mind, but they are adequate reflections of Christian topography if not of substance. Through the external signs we can trace a rough map – both social and territorial – of the spread of Christianity from the Conversion to the time of Iaroslav. We shall proceed like the faith: from the top downwards, from the centre outwards.

Who was the head of the Church, and what was his status in the Christian hierarchy? Unfortunately, the *Primary Chronicle* contains no information whatever on the Church's central organization for fully 50 years after the Conversion. In Iaroslav's time and thereafter the Church was headed by a metropolitan based in St Sophia in Kiev and under the authority of the patriarch of Constantinople.

48 Compare the studies in Angeliki E. Laiou and Dieter Simon, eds, *Law and Society in Byzantium. Ninth–Twelfth Centuries* (Washington, D.C., 1994); on the mid-eleventh century see Michael Angold, 'Imperial renewal and Orthodox reaction', in Magdalino, ed., *New Constantines*, pp. 231–46; W. Wolska-Conus, 'Les écoles de Psellos et de Xiphilin sous Constantin IX Monomaque', *TM* 6 (1976), 223–43, esp. 233–43.

The metropolitanate of *Rhōsia*, as it was termed by the Byzantines, was an ecclesiastical province of the Constantinopolitan patriarchate. Three metropolitans are known from the period of Iaroslav's reign: Ioann I, who collaborated with Iaroslav in promoting the cult of Boris and Gleb;[49] Feopempt (Theopemptos), who reconsecrated Vladimir's church of the Mother of God (the Tithe church) in 1039;[50] and Ilarion, who held the office from 1051 to c. 1054. Before Iaroslav, however, the native sources are silent, contradictory, or plainly wrong.[51] In August 1018, according to Thietmar of Merseburg, the victorious Boleslaw and Sviatopolk were greeted on their arrival in Kiev by the 'archiepiscopus civitatis illius', who honoured then 'in sancte monasterio Sofhiae' (a wooden structure, repaired after a fire the previous year).[52] The native stories of the Conversion, some 30 years earlier, mention only the church of the Mother of God, where Vladimir installed Anastasii of Cherson.

The gap between the Conversion and Metropolitan Ioann I (or Thietmar's *archiepiscopus*) is filled with ingenious guesses. It has been suggested that in the early decades the Church in Rus was subject to the Bulgarian patriarch at Ochrid (which was suppressed in 1018 after the conquests of Basil II 'the Bulgar-Slayer'); or to Tmutorokan; or to Cherson; or to Rome; or that there was a metropolitan resident in Pereiaslavl rather than in Kiev, or that the Church was autonomous.[53] However, the most persuasive single piece of evidence is a late eleventh-century Byzantine list of metropolitanates in chronological order of foundation. The sequence implies that the metropolitanate of *Rhōsia* was established under Byzantine patriarchal jurisdiction before 997: that is, at or soon after the time of the official Conversion under Vladimir.[54] Later Greek texts indicate that the first incumbent might

---

49 Abramovich/Müller, *Erzählungen*, pp. 17–19, 53–5; Hollingsworth, *Hagiography*, pp. 20–3, 119–21; *NPL*, p. 473; see Ludolf Müller, 'Zur Frage nach dem Zeitpunkt der Kanonisierung der Heiligen Boris und Gleb', in A.-E. Tachiaos, ed., *The Legacy of Saints Cyril and Methodius to Kiev and Moscow. Proceedings of the International Congress on the Millennium of the Conversion of the Rus' to Christianity* (Thessaloniki, 1992), pp. 321–39.

50 *PVL*, I, p. 103; see also Ianin, *Aktovye pechati*, I, p. 44.

51 For texts with the names Mikhail and Leontii see e.g. Ia. N. Shchapov, *Drevnerusskie kniazheskie ustavy XI–XV vv.* (Moscow, 1976), pp. 15–22; *NPL*, p. 473.

52 Thietmar VIII.32, in Holtzmann, *Die Chronik*, p. 530.

53 For a summary see A. Poppe, 'The original status of the Old-Russian Church', *Acta Poloniae historica* 39 (1979), 4–45, repr. in idem, *The Rise of Christian Russia*, no. 3; the list in J. Darrouzès, *Notitiae episcopatuum Ecclesiae Constantinopolitanae* (Paris, 1981), p. 343.

54 Poppe, 'The original status', 26–35 (proposing 987–90); Ia. N. Shchapov, *Gosudarstvo i tserkov' Drevnei Rusi X–XIII vv.* (Moscow, 1989) (advocating c. 996–7); cf. Sophia Senyk, *A History of the Church in Ukraine, I, To the End of the Thirteenth Century* (Orientalia Christiana Analecta 243; Rome, 1993), pp. 82–94; for a defence of a Mikhail as first metropolitan see O. M. Rapov, *Russkaia tserkov' v IX–pervoi treti XII v. Priniatie khristianstva* (Moscow, 1988), pp. 281–5.

have been a certain Theophylaktos of Sebasteia, though no such figure is recalled in any native source.[55] The Byzantine hypothesis is without doubt the strongest of those on offer. However, in the quest for missing metropolitans we risk missing the more significant point: whether or not there was a metropolitan under Vladimir, it is clear that he was not the most prominent churchman in Kiev at that time. Vladimir's flagship project was his generously endowed palace church of the Mother of God (see above, pp. 164–5). Anastasii of Cherson in the church of the Mother of God had a far more conspicuously favoured position than the metropolitan (if one existed) in the wooden St Sophia. After Vladimir's death there was a shift in the balance of prestige: in 1018 we find the 'archiepiscopus' from St Sophia acting as the chief ecclesiastical representative of Kiev, and in the same year Anastasii of Cherson deserted the church of the Mother of God and defected to Poland with Boleslaw. Thence we arrive at the metropolitan Ioann and eventually at Iaroslav's reshaped city. In other words, the early reticence of the native sources is possibly neither accident nor cover-up, but a fair (though faint) reflection of ecclesiastical politics and policies.

Beneath the metropolitan were the bishops. The spread of organized urban Christianity can to some extent be measured by the spread of bishoprics. In 1051 Iaroslav appointed Ilarion as metropolitan, 'having assembled the bishops' – a plurality. In his sermon, written a few years earlier, Ilarion also praised the 'bishops, shepherds of Christ's spiritual flock', who appeared in Vladimir's newly converted realm.[56] However, if the early metropolitanate is obscure, the early bishoprics are invisible. The bishop of Belgorod, Vladimir's new town, occupies first place both in the *Primary Chronicle*'s entries for 1088 and 1089, and in a twelfth-century Byzantine list of the bishoprics of *Rhosia*.[57] Luka Zhidiata, bishop of Novgorod, is reasonably attested from the mid-1030s, and a persistent local tradition traces the line of Novgorodian bishops back to Ioakim of Cherson, apparently brought in by Vladimir.[58] Bishops of Chernigov, Pereiaslavl and Iurev are all mentioned in sources for the second half of the eleventh century; the stone cathedral of St Sophia in Polotsk was built in the 1050s or 1060s, and is assumed to have been the residence of a bishop, although no incumbent is known before 1105. The case for an early bishopric of Turov rests mainly on a fourteenth-century list which is of dubious value.

Any precise chronology of the earliest foundations is very speculative.

55 The preferred candidate of Poppe, 'The original status', 26–35.
56 *PVL*, I, p. 104; Moldovan, *Slovo*, p. 93 (fol. 187a); Franklin, *Sermons and Rhetoric*, p. 19.
57 *PVL*, I, p. 137; Darrouzès, *Notitiae*, p. 367.
58 On lists of Novgorod bishops see A. S. Khoroshev, 'Letopisnye spiski novgorodskikh vladyk', *Novgorodskii istoricheskii sbornik* 2 (12) (1984), 127–42.

Recent estimates of the number of bishoprics established in Vladimir's reign range from one (Belgorod) to five (adding Novgorod, Chernigov, Polotsk and Pereiaslavl or Turov); estimates of the number in existence by the time of Iaroslav's death in 1054 range from four (Belgorod, Novgorod, Chernigov, Iurev) to seven (adding Polotsk, Pereiaslavl and Turov).[59] Historians can surmise what might have been the likely circumstances, or haggle over the trustworthiness of late sources, but it is difficult to find persuasive reasons for preferring one hypothesis to another. Whatever the details, Iaroslav's assemblage of bishops in 1051 consisted of no more than six or seven people, who together represented a very restricted area. Apart from Novgorod (and Polotsk, if it is to be included) all the established mid-century bishoprics were clustered in the Middle Dnieper region; and Belgorod and Iurev were, in effect, adjuncts of Kiev.

To what extent does the spread of an ecclesiastical organization reflect the spread of actual Christian observance in the community? One guide to religious identity among the populace is the way in which people buried their dead. By a pleasing coincidence, a tour through the graveyards of the late tenth to late eleventh centuries broadly confirms the ecclesiastical topography: where there were bishops there was a Christian flock; where there were no bishops the land was largely pagan. Thus Christian inhumation proliferated in the Middle Dnieper region and in sporadic sites eastwards along the Sula and Seim towards Kursk, while in the Derevlian land to the north-west of Kiev the inhabitants retained their traditional forms of burial (see above, pp. 174–5).

Outside the Middle Dnieper region and the northern outposts (Polotsk, Novgorod), paganisms still prevailed, and the Church had to struggle longer and harder to establish itself. Legends of Rostov in the north-east, for example, tell of missionary hierarchs persecuted in mid-century by hostile locals.[60] Bishops of Rostov are recorded for the 1070s and 1080s, but then the see appears to have fallen vacant again for a further half-century.

The wildness of the untamed north-east (from the point of view of a southern Christian) is colourfully evoked in a tale told to a compiler

---

59 At the sceptical end: J.-P. Arrignon, 'La création des diocèses russes des origines au milieu du XII siècle', *Mille ans de christianisme russe, 988–1988. Actes du colloque international de l'Université Paris-Nanterre 20–23 janvier 1988* (Paris, 1988), pp. 27–49; compare A. Poppe, 'Werdegang der Diözesanstruktur der Kiever Metropolitankirche in den ersten drei Jahrhunderten der Christianisierung der Ostslaven', in K. C. Felmy et al., eds, *Tausend Jahre Christentums in Rußland. Zum Millennium der Taufe der Kiever Rus'* (Göttingen, 1988), pp. 251–90; Senyk, *A History of the Church in Ukraine*, I, pp. 130–9. See also Rapov, *Russkaia tserkov'*, pp. 277–329, arguing unconvincingly for a bishop of Rostov as early as 992.

60 See Gail Lenhoff, 'Canonization and princely power in northeast Rus': the cult of Leontij Rostovskij', *Die Welt der Slaven* N.F. 16 (1992), 359–80.

of the *Primary Chronicle* by his most famous informant, the Kievan *tysiatskii* Ian Vyshatich (see below, p. 286, on the term). According to the chronicle's entry for 1071, there was a famine in the Rostov Land, and a pair of *volkhvy* (sorcerers, pagan priests) from Iaroslavl travelled along the Volga and the Sheksna persuading people that the blame lay with rich women who were hoarding supplies. So the people 'brought to them their sisters, their mothers and their wives; and in a dream [a trance?] the sorcerers cut them behind the shoulder and took out grain or fish. And they killed many women, and took away their property'.[61] Ian Vyshatich was in Beloozero at the time, collecting tribute for a southern prince. The sorcerers were thus direct rivals for control over the local surplus produce, not to mention local hearts and minds, and they had effective support. The people of Beloozero refused to hand them over, despite Ian's insistence that they were under the authority of his prince. A bungled attempt to capture the *volkhvy* ended in the murder of Ian's own priest. Eventually the townspeople complied only when Ian threatened that he would stay a full year unless they surrendered the sorcerers to him. After a curious theological debate, which ended with a conventional contest of prophecies (in which the pagan is unable to foretell his own death), Ian had the sorcerers killed; but only when he had travelled a fair way downstream, a safe distance from the grudging Beloozerans.

The spread of the faith was restricted socially as well as geographically. Just as its expansion outwards from the political centre was slow, so its spread downwards from the political elite could be uncertain. Anecdotal evidence from as late as the 1070s and 1080s, almost a century after the official Conversion, suggests that even in the main cities the masses could be fickle both in their observance and in their adherence. In Novgorod in the 1070s a *volkhv* so impressed the townspeople with his prophecies that they 'divided into two: Prince Gleb and his *druzhina* went and stood with the bishop, but all the people went to follow the *volkhv*. And there was great strife between them'. To defeat his pagan rival for authority, the prince used the same device as Ian, a rather one-sided contest of prophecies: 'Gleb said, "Do you know what will be today?" And he said, "I shall perform great miracles." But Gleb took out his axe and struck him and he fell dead, and the people dispersed'.[62]

A similar social contrast emerges from a more reliable contemporary witness, Metropolitan Ioann II (c. 1077–89). One of Ioann's duties was to give practical guidance to his clergy on problems which they encountered in their pastoral work. To this end he wrote a series of *Canonical Responses*, with his views and rulings on miscellaneous

---

61 *PVL*, I, p. 117.
62 Ibid., p. 120. On the political context see below, pp. 256, 260.

issues on which his advice was sought. This is the earliest such work to survive, and it gives a rare glimpse of the everyday concerns of the clergy, of Christianity as it was lived, without a rhetorical or historiographical or hagiographical wrapping. Most of Ioann's responses are on matters of ritual or sexual purity: for example, is it acceptable to use for clothing the skins of animals which it is not permitted to eat? Should a woman who has been abducted in a pagan raid be treated as an adulteress? But John can also be socially revealing: 'You say that only boiars and princes get married with proper ceremony and blessing, while the common people do not; that the common people take wives as if by abduction, with much leaping and dancing and hooting'.[63]

Ilarion stressed that the Conversion of the people was instantaneous and universal: 'not one single person resisted [Vladimir's] command', and 'at one single time all our land began to glorify Christ', and 'the thunder of the Gospels resounded throughout all the cities'.[64] This claim is not borne out by the regional and social geography of the new faith. Even a century after Vladimir's decision, Christian organization was patchy; and even in the main centres of princely authority Christian observance was a thin social veneer. The Kievan Church was still a missionary Church in a pagan land: urban in focus, mainly foreign in its senior administrative personnel, the religion of the ruling social strata. Gradually it spread to more towns and seeped down the social scale, but the age of peasant piety throughout the lands of the Rus was far in the future.

Yet Christianity did become established and the Church did grow. Ilarion exaggerated, but within its widening limits the Church was busy. It had buildings to erect and maintain, a hierarchy to support, a flock to tend, waverers to reassure, doubters to convince, a faith to interpret.

All this had to be paid for. As a non-coercive consumer the Church was unable to sustain itself – still less to expand – without provisions made for it by those whom it served and by those who sought to promote it. Its main source of material sustenance was the princely tithe, a tenth part of princely income. The institution of the tithe is ascribed to Vladimir. In 996, according to the *Primary Chronicle*, Vladimir declared that he would 'give to this church of the Holy Mother of God a tenth part from my possessions and from my towns'.[65] For this reason Vladimir's palace church of the Mother of God is called the Tithe church. A more detailed account of Vladimir's

---

63 Questions 14, 26, 30: *RIB*, VI, cols 7, 14–15, 18.
64 Moldovan, *Slovo*, p. 93 (fol. 187a); Franklin, *Sermons and Rhetoric*, p. 19.
65 *PVL*, I, p. 85; for related texts see Shchapov, *Gosudarstvo i tserkov'*, p. 76.

donation is found in a document known as 'Vladimir's Church Statute' (*Ustav* – see below, pp. 234–6). Unfortunately, 'Vladimir's Statute' was revised many times in later centuries, for it was used to lend legitimacy and the appearance of antiquity to the dispositions of rulers in different circumstances. Its many surviving versions reflect practices from the twelfth to the fifteenth centuries. Vladimir probably did donate *a* tithe, but 'his' Statute is not a reliable guide to what his tithe comprised. We cannot even be sure that Vladimir issued a *written* document at all. The *Primary Chronicle* tells of him depositing a written 'oath' (*kliatva*) in the church, but there is no other evidence for the use of written documents in princely administration at this stage.

Nevertheless the practice of giving tithes, if not the exact form, is well attested through the eleventh century. In the *Lection* on Boris and Gleb, Nestor relates that Iaroslav sponsored the building of the church to his brothers in Vyshgorod, and then instructed his local governor to 'give to the two saints a tenth part of the tribute [*dan*']'.[66] With the income thus assured, the metropolitan could set the church to work: 'he appointed priests and deacons and ordered them to sing vespers and matins in the church of the saints and to celebrate the holy liturgy every day . . .'. In a eulogy to one of Iaroslav's grandsons, Iaropolk Iziaslavich (d. 1087), the *Primary Chronicle* lists among the deceased prince's virtues the fact that he regularly paid 'a tenth part of all his wealth to the Holy Mother of God'. A tithe from fines is mentioned in SP.[67]

The custom of supporting the Church with a tithe was not borrowed by the Rus from Byzantium. Tithes were one form of tax payment in Byzantium, but were not a staple source of income for the Church. Nor is it likely that Vladimir was directly inspired by Old Testament injunctions to donate a tithe (e.g. Gen. 28:22; Lev. 27:30–32). Noting equivalent practices among the Poles and the Czechs, some have suggested that Vladimir followed an ancient Slav custom of allocating a tithe towards the maintenance of the official cult.[68] However, tithes have been widespread both within and outside Judaeo-Christian tradition, whether in taxation or in tribute or in support of religious institutions and personnel, and it is probably futile to guess at the origins of the practice among the Rus.

More important than the origins of the tithe is its substance. 'Vladimir's Statute' sets forth an ideal norm in retrospect: a tenth part annually from the prince's possessions, and from income from

---

66 Abramovich/Müller, *Erzählungen*, p. 19; Hollingsworth, *Hagiography*, p. 23 (translating as 'treasury').

67 *PSRL*, II, col. 198; cf. *PSRL*, I, col. 217. SP Article 41: *ZDR*, p. 49; Kaiser, *The Laws*, p. 18.

68 Shchapov, *Gosudarstvo i tserkov'*, pp. 85–7; B. N. Floria, *Otnosheniia gosudarstva i tserkvi u vostochnykh i zapadnykh slavian* (Moscow, 1992), pp. 5–20.

the courts (a proportion of fines) and from the markets.[69] Practice in fact was more varied. The narrative references from the eleventh century are somewhat vague and imply that the tithe was simply a tenth part of the prince's regular annual income, which was derived largely from tribute (i.e. direct community taxation). Article 41 of SP gives the church 20 per cent of the prince's share of fines; but the foundation charter of the bishopric of Smolensk (1136) specifically excludes court income ('bloodwite and fines') from its detailed calculation of the main tithe from each region.[70] Court income was unpredictable, and comparatively small, as is clear from an additional set of provisions in the Smolensk charter.[71] Also in the late 1130s the prince of Novgorod issued a charter which in effect replaced the bishop's tithe of 'bloodwite and fines' (as established 'by our great-grandfathers and grandfathers') with a guaranteed fixed sum: if the tithe from the Onega land did not reach 100 'new' grivnas (=25 old grivnas of silver), then the balance would be made up from the prince's treasury.[72]

As both princely and ecclesiastical revenue gradually became more diverse – including fines from the Church's own courts, and direct donations of property – so the simple tithe gradually gave way to more complex arrangements. For example, a mid-twelfth-century prince in the north-east is reported as giving a tithe from his herds and from the market, as well as tribute from trading settlements, and 'the best villages'; by the 1220s the local bishop could boast of extensive land-holdings. But change was slow. The tithe from princely tribute remained the most sizable and stable element of Church income well into the twelfth century. Crudely speaking, this means that the Church remained conspicuously dependent on the secular powers.[73]

In return, the Church sought to affect parts of life which direct princely authority could not reach. Whereas SP touched on a few aspects of the public behaviour of free urban males, the Church sought to extend its guidance deeper into the community, into daily life, into the home, to the poor as well as the rich, to women as well

---

69 Article 3: ZDR, pp. 141, 148; Kaiser, The Laws, p. 42.

70 SP as above, n. 67; Article 4 of the Smolensk charter in ZDR, p. 213; with translation in Kaiser, The Laws, p. 51. It is not clear whether a share of court income was to be paid in addition to the main tithe, or not at all: see V. L. Ianin, 'Zametki o komplekse dokumentov Smolenskoi eparkhii XII veka', Otechestvennaia istoriia 1994, no. 6, 104–20; Ianin also argues that the document on tithes should be dated a few years later than the founding of the bishopric.

71 ZDR, p. 214; Kaiser, The Laws, p. 53.

72 Articles 1–3 of the charter of Prince Sviatoslav Olgovich (ZDR, pp. 224–5; Kaiser, The Laws, p. 57; see also V. L. Ianin, Novgorodskie akty XII–XIV vv.: khronologicheskii kommentarii (Moscow, 1991), pp. 138–42. On money, see below, pp. 284–5.

73 PSRL, I, col. 348, s.a. 6665 (1158/9); cf. the landed wealth boasted by a bishop of Vladimir in the 1220s: Abramovich/Tschižewskij, Paterikon, p. 103; Heppell, Paterik, p. 119.

as men: what clothes to wear, what food to eat; when, with whom and in what manner to have sexual intercourse; how to conduct the rituals of birth, marriage and death. Here was the chronicler's 'one law', which 'we Christians, of whatever land' hold in common. This kind of law, by contrast with *Russkaia Pravda*, was derived from Byzantium. The Church brought with it a graduated structure of encouragement by which to promote adherence to the rules: from exhortation and instruction, through penances imposed by the priest, to penalties imposed by the bishop's court. The scope of ecclesiastical jurisdiction was defined in the form of privileges granted by princely statute. And the authoritative source of reference, which was used to validate both the Church's own rules and this collusion between prince and Church, was Byzantine canon law.[74]

In Byzantium the most widely copied compendium of canon law was the *Nomocanon of Fourteen Titles*. The bulk of this nomocanon consists of a compendium of the major texts: the Apostolic Constitutions, the decisions of the ecumenical and local councils, the rules of Basil the Great and other Fathers of the Church, as well as imperial legislation on ecclesiastical affairs. Besides the texts themselves, the nomocanon provides a detailed thematic index, a kind of concordance, arranged under fourteen headings (the 'titles' which give the work its name). For example, under the third Title ('Concerning prayers, psalmody, reading, communion') we may find: 'Chapter 17, on not giving communion to the bodies of the deceased – canon 18 of the Council of Carthage, canon 83 of the Synod under Justinian'. Or in the thirteenth Title ('Concerning laymen'): 'Chapter 20, on those who gamble or drink – the 33rd Apostolic Canon, canons 6 and 28 of the Synod under Justinian'.[75] With this handy form of reference the user could turn to the full text of the relevant canon and thus have easy access to concise and authoritative opinion on a huge miscellany of topics. A version of the *Nomocanon of Fourteen Titles* was translated into Slavonic, probably in Bulgaria in the tenth century.[76] This translated nomocanon formed the core of the Slavonic *Kormchaia kniga* ('Helmsman's Book', 'Chart', 'Book of Guidance', 'Rudder'), which, through many recensions and modifications, became the principal repository of legal texts in the lands of the Rus throughout the middle ages.[77]

---

74 See Floria, *Otnosheniia gosudarstva i tserkvi*, p. 20, comparing with practices among the Czechs and the Poles. Also on church income see Shchapov, *Gosudarstvo i tserkov'*, pp. 76–90.

75 V. N. Beneshevich, ed., *Drevneslavianskaia Kormchaia XIV titulov bez tolkovanii* (St Petersburg, 1906–7), cols 16, 53.

76 Strictly, the *Syntagma*: see Ia. N. Shchapov, *Vizantiiskoe i iuzhnoslavianskoe pravovoe nasledie na Rusi v XI–XIII vv.* (Moscow, 1978), pp. 52, 88–100. An earlier translation, attributed to Methodios, was probably of the *Synagoge of 50 Titles*.

77 Occasionally including *Russkaia Pravda*, as well as Byzantine digests and commentaries such as the *Pandektai* of the eleventh-century monk Nikon of the Black Mountain.

Notionally the Conversion to Christianity implied an acceptance of canon law. Even among the faithful, however, canon law did not and could not become an enforceable code. In the first place, Byzantine canon law was not a simply enforceable type of document. It was a paradoxical mixture of fixity and flexibility. There was no absolutely fixed corpus or arrangement of texts, no set rules of procedure, no consistent division between law (in a narrow sense) and ethics, no clear separation of ecclesiastical from secular. In the second place, the *Kormchaia* among the Rus can barely be traced to within a hundred years of Vladimir's Conversion. The oldest surviving copy was made in the early twelfth century by the Novgorodian scribe Efrem, known for his endearing marginalia ('Efrem, you sinner, don't be lazy', 'Efrem, don't let your mind wander').[78] Thirdly, imported injunction could not in any case displace native custom overnight. The process of mutual adaptation (of custom to law and of law to custom) was continual, and perhaps never complete.

Vladimir and Iaroslav are credited with issuing the first Church Statutes. The Statutes were not systematic measures for the introduction of canon law; they were princely grants, backed with reference to canon law, defining the extent to which the Church had a claim over the lives and property of the people. They therefore reveal more about authority than about piety. In their extant form the Statutes are also facades, albeit constructed by posterity rather than by Vladimir and Iaroslav themselves, for they were frequently revised while retaining the attribution to their supposed original authors. Nevertheless, by comparing the Statutes with other (avowedly later) documents, one can trace the main stages through which the Church's material and juridical status was established.[79]

'Vladimir's Statute', by far the briefer, concerns the basic allocation of resources: the tithe; a list of 'church people' (categories of person over whom the Church was to be given exclusive jurisdiction); and a list of church offences (categories of behaviour which the Church was to be given the exclusive right to judge). 'Church people' included monks, priests and their wives and other clergy, widows, pilgrims, the lame and the blind. The areas covered by ecclesiastical jurisdiction

---

78 *Svodnyi katalog slaviano-russkikh rukopisnykh knig, khraniashchikhsia v SSSR. XI–XIII vv.* (Moscow, 1984), no. 75, pp. 116–17; cf. Shchapov, *Vizantiiskoe i iuzhnoslavianskoe pravovoe nasledie*, pp. 255–6. There are earlier references to the nomocanon, but they do not necessarily relate to the full translation.

79 'Vladimir's Statute' in various versions: Shchapov, *Drevnerusskie kniazheskie ustavy*, pp. 12–84; here cited from the annotated text in *ZDR*, pp. 137–62; cf. Kaiser, *The Laws*, pp. 42–4. 'Iaroslav's Statute': versions in Shchapov, *Drevnerusskie kniazheskie ustavy*, pp. 85–139; here cited from annotated texts in *ZDR*, pp. 163–208; Kaiser, *The Laws*, pp. 45–50, uses a text of the 'long redaction' only, and from a different MS to that in *ZDR*, with some divergences of wording and numeration.

included divorce and sexual relations, adultery, abduction, incest, rape, sorcery, heresy, domestic violence, and disputes over inheritance.

At first there was little potential for confusion between the civil and ecclesiastical spheres of competence. With the possible exception of public-order offences (abduction, rape), the prince in the late tenth or mid-eleventh centuries had no direct authority in the areas allocated to the Church. This was not a division of powers, more an attempt to extend central influence by alternative means. The powers of the Church were in any case limited by the pace of Christianization. A full century after the start of Iaroslav's sole rule, in the Smolensk charter of 1136, joint competence (shared by prince and bishop) was still restricted only to cases of abduction.[80] However, as the Church's constituency expanded and as princely administration became more intrusive, so the princely and ecclesiastical spheres of judgement increasingly overlapped.

The mechanisms are nowhere described. Routine pastoral admonition for laymen is to some extent reflected in the penitentials. Very occasionally the treatment of the Church's own miscreants was spectacular enough to be mentioned in narrative sources. In 1058 Dudika, a 'slave' (*kholop*) of Bishop Luka of Novgorod, had his nose and hands cut off for slandering his master. A quarter of a century later Metropolitan Ioann II specified that recalcitrant sorcerers 'must be severely punished . . . but should not be killed, nor should their extremities be cut off, for this is contrary to the teaching of the Church'. In the late 1160s a bishop accused of malpractice was surrendered by his prince to the metropolitan (Konstantin II), who ordered his tongue to be cut off and his right hand to be severed and his eyes to be gouged out 'as a malefactor and heretic'. At the turn of the thirteenth century a charismatic monk in Smolensk, accused by clergy and the bishop, was tried and cleared in the presence of the local prince. Not surprisingly at this high level, where several of the participants were Byzantines, there are echoes of Byzantine practice: the involvement of the civil authorities in trying serious ecclesiastical cases (especially where there was a charge of 'heresy'); both the use of mutilation and arguments against the use of mutilation.[81]

---

80 Article 11: *ZDR*, p. 215; Kaiser, *The Laws*, p. 54. On such issues in Byzantine law see Patricia Karlin-Hayter, 'Further notes on Byzantine marriage: raptus – *harpagē* or *mnēsteiai?*' *DOP* 46 (1992), 133–54; more widely A. Laiou, 'Sex, consent and coercion in Byzantium', in A. Laiou, ed., *Consent and Coercion to Sex and Marriage in Ancient and Medieval Societies* (Washington, D.C., 1993), pp. 109–221.

81 *RIB*, VI, col. 4 (Question 7); *PSRL*, I, col. 356; *PSRL*, II, cols 552–3; *NPL*, pp. 182–3; Rozanov/Tschiżewskj, *Avraamij*, pp. 10–11. On Byzantine discussion see e.g. R. Macrides, 'Nomos and canon on paper and in court', in R. Morris, ed., *Church and People in Byzantium* (Birmingham, 1990), pp. 61–85 (esp. 83); I. P. Mezentsev, 'Smertnaia kazn' v tolkovanii Feodora Val'samona', *Vizantiiskii vremennik* 53 (1992), 53–61.

We hear nothing of such issues in the Statutes because the issuers of the Statutes were concerned with something different. A consequence of overlapping authority was a potential increase in what might now be called the 'opportunity cost' to the civic purse. Princes therefore devised more flexible ways of sharing income. The changes are reflected in 'Iaroslav's Statute'. Although Iaroslav may have been responsible for a distant and irrecoverable prototype of the Statute which bears his name, the surviving versions embody norms from no earlier (and mainly later) than the twelfth century.

There were three main innovations in 'Iaroslav's Statute'. First, the document does not merely list offences (as do 'Vladimir's Statute' and the Smolensk charter); like *Russkaia Pravda* it also specifies the penalties – whether restitution, a fine, or incarceration (but not mutilation). Article 3, for example, lays down the fines for rape: 'If someone rapes a boiar's daughter or a boiar's wife, [then he is to pay] 5 grivnas of gold for the dishonour, and 5 grivnas of gold to the bishop; and if she be [a daughter or wife] of lesser boiars [then he is to pay] 1 grivna of gold, and 1 grivna of gold to the bishop ... [if she be the daughter or wife] of common people, [he is to pay] 15 grivnas [of fur] to her and 15 grivnas [of fur] to the bishop'.[82] Through introducing fixed penalties to the ecclesiastical courts, the prince was generous and restrictive at the same time. Secondly, the Statute makes it clear that in many cases the specified fines were not the only punishments for the offence: that, in addition, the Church might impose its own (unspecified) penances according to canon law,[83] and that further (also unspecified) punishment might be imposed by the prince.[84] Joint jurisdiction over ecclesiastical offences had therefore expanded. It now covered divorce, adultery and bigamy as well as abduction. Thirdly, and conversely, 'Iaroslav's Statute' gave the Church the main fines, rather than a tithe, for a range of civil cases of a type also covered by *Russkaia Pravda*: arson, the cutting of a beard, and certain cases of theft.[85]

'Iaroslav's Statute' was therefore neither a systematic code for the imposition of canon law, nor a statement of all penalties which might be imposed for any particular offence; it was, we would argue, basically a grant of income, whether from conventionally ecclesiastical sources or from princely revenues. By comparison with 'Vladimir's

---

82 In the 'Short Redaction': ZDR, p. 168; the 'Long Redaction' reads 'metropolitan' for 'bishop' throughout: e.g. Kaiser, *The Laws*, p. 45 (= ZDR, p. 189).

83 'Short Redaction', Articles 12, 14, 15, 18, 19: ZDR, p. 169; cf. Kaiser, *The Laws*, pp. 46–7 (= 'Long Redaction', Articles 14, 16, 17, 21, 23).

84 'Short Redaction', Articles 2, 3, 4, 7, 8, 13, 16, 26ff.: ZDR, pp. 169–70; cf. Kaiser, *The Laws*, with 'Long Redaction', Articles 2, 3, 4, 7, 9, 15, 18, 32ff. Cf. the letter of Patriarch Germanos to Metropolitan Kirill I (c. 1224–33) objecting to secular interference: RIB, VI, cols 82–4.

85 'Short Redaction', Articles 13, 27, 28; 'Long Redaction', Articles 15, 32, 33.

Statute' or with the Smolensk charter, it represents a fusion of princely and ecclesiastical spheres of authority, a division of spoils rather than an allocation of clearly separate powers, a development of the same process through which, as we have seen, the tithe itself came to be redefined.

In pursuing 'Iaroslav's Statute' we have strayed a long way from Iaroslav himself, from the mid-eleventh century, and from the Grace of the spread of the Faith. Sometimes we can only reach Iaroslav's Rus by investigating a *double* facade: that which he erected personally through his patronage, and that which was constructed around him by generations of his progeny. We were forced into the detour by ascriptions in the written record. This is no accident. By contemporaries, successors and historians, the age of Iaroslav is presented as the age of the first flowering of written culture, when the social and spiritual uses of writing multiplied and diversified, when the seeds planted by Vladimir burst into bloom. How fertile was the garden of the Word?

4. 'THE SWEETNESS OF BOOKS'

Near the summit of Starokievskaia hill, a few yards west of the remains of the church of the Mother of God (the Tithe church), there is a small granite monument commemorating Vladimir as the founding father of education in the lands of the Rus. The roughly cut modern inscription is extracted from the *Primary Chronicle*, which states that Vladimir took the children of leading families and 'gave them over to book-learning; and the mothers of these children wept for them . . . as if for the dead, for they had not yet become firm in faith. And when these had been given over to book-learning, in the land of the Rus the prophecy came to pass: "In those days the deaf shall hear the words of the book, and the tongue of the stammerers shall be plain."'[86] This monument to Vladimir by the church of the Mother of God has its twin just to the west of St Sophia, commemorating Iaroslav as the founder of the first library among the Rus. Again the modern dedication is prompted by the chronicle, which tells of how Iaroslav 'loved books, and caused many books to be written out, and he placed them in the church of St Sophia'.[87] The modern memorials reflect the image created by the early eulogists, who had fully assimilated the common medieval notion of ruler-as-patron, ruler-as-enlightener enabling his people to reap the harvest, drink from the spring, sip the nectar. In the words of the chronicler: 'Great is the benefit of book-learning . . . From the words of books we attain wisdom and continence; the words of books are rivers that water the whole

86 *PVL*, I, p. 81; cf. Isaiah 29:18; 32:4.
87 *PVL*, I, p. 103.

earth, they are the wellsprings of wisdom; the depth of books is unfathomable'. 'We do not write for the ignorant', declared Ilarion, 'but for them that have feasted to fulfilment on the sweetness of books.'[88]

Ilarion was preaching to the converted, so – with allowances for the rhetorical flourish – his claim must be true. But true in what sense? In the pre-Mongol period 'books' and 'book-learning' (*knizhnoe uchenie*) meant, above all, *the* Book, Scripture, the Bible (Gk. *biblia*>Slav. *knigi*). By definition Christianity was the Religion of the Book. To treasure and disseminate book-learning meant to treasure and disseminate the true faith. Paganisms were oral and, in the vocabulary of the converted, ignorant. Ilarion himself stated that he had in mind 'the predictions of the prophets concerning Christ, and the teachings of the apostles concerning the age to come'. The *Primary Chronicle* likewise specifies Iaroslav's love of books as embracing 'the discourses of the prophets and the teachings of the Gospels and of the Acts and Epistles, and the lives of the holy fathers'. Ilarion and the chronicler were therefore referring not to a local culture of creative writing, but to translations.

Throughout the middle ages the book culture of the Rus was almost entirely a culture of translations. The overwhelming majority of all that was read, copied, cited, mimicked and revered for over half a millennium consisted of Church Slavonic translations from Greek. The Rus saw nothing demeaning in this. Rather it was a source of pride: to have the truth of the Books made accessible in the Slavonic tongue, to share in the miracle of Pentecost, when the Holy Spirit descended and entered the apostles so that the nations of the gentiles exclaimed 'we do hear them speaking in our tongues the mighty works of God'.[89] Through Cyril and Methodios the Slavs, too, were enabled to 'hear God's greatness in our own tongue'. According to the version of the legend in the *Primary Chronicle*, the Moravian princes had complained that 'we understand neither Latin nor Greek, and some teach us one way and others another way'. Opponents of vernacular Christianity allegedly objected that 'it is not fit that any tongue should have its own letters except the Hebrews, the Greeks and the Latins' (for these were the languages of the inscription on the Cross). But the Holy Spirit triumphed over linguistic exclusivity: 'if any should slander Slavonic letters, let him be cut off from the Church until he mend his ways'.[90]

---

88 Ibid., pp. 102–3; Moldovan, *Slovo*, p. 79 (fol. 169b); Franklin, *Sermons and Rhetoric*, p. 4.

89 Acts 2:1–11. On this theme see Dimitri Obolensky, *Byzantium and the Slavs* (New York, 1994), pp. 219–42.

90 *PVL*, I, p. 22. On the so-called 'trilingual heresy' see F. J. Thomson, 'SS. Cyril and Methodius and a mythical Western heresy: trilinguism. A contribution to the study of patristic and renaissance theories of sacred languages', *Analecta Bollandiana* 110 (1992), 67–122.

The Church's immediate and constant need was for the books which would enable it to perform its core function of celebrating the liturgy: Scriptural readings, collections of hymns and prayers and homilies and brief lives of saints, arranged to fit the rhythms and sequences of services through the year. But the pastoral, monastic, social, spiritual and ideological mission was of course broader. There were teachings to be explained, anxieties to be allayed, lives to be changed. Though the setting was new, the tasks were familiar, and the Church brought the well-tested tools of its profession. The repertoire of available Slavonic translations was, or became, far more extensive than Ilarion's list.

For general edification vast numbers of Greek sermons made their way into Slavonic, bringing the teachings of the most revered Fathers of the Church, mainly in thematic compilations and miscellanies. For those who may have found the Scriptures confusing or obscure, collections of questions and answers were on hand to provide reassurance and further enlightenment. Where the Scriptures skimped on detail, the missing pieces and the fuller stories could be gleaned from apocryphal narratives such as the *Apocalypse of Abraham* or the *Protoevangelium of James*. Or, better still, one could see the whole history of the world unfolding according to Divine Providence and revealed in a Byzantine chronicle; or in a blend of chronicle, Scripture, apocrypha and homily. For further instruction and even entertainment, some of the great moments of the past could be amplified with, for example, exotic tales of Alexander the Great, or with Josephus' account of the Romans' conquest of the Jews. For moral example and ascetic encouragement there were compendia of anecdotes on the lives of the early saints, and extensive narratives of many others, not to mention the detailed rules for living as set forth in canon law. The wondrous allegories which the Lord shows through plants and animals were decoded in the *Fiziolog*; or one could tour the world via the *Christian Topography* of Kosmas Indikopleustes. Or, for handy reference and ease of memory, there were assemblages of brief snippets of sagacity, with wise words for every occasion. And so on.[91]

Was this a lot or a little? The answer, like the length of a piece of string, depends on one's standard for comparison. For the neophyte Rus – conscious of their recent 'ignorance', and conscious of the preciousness and precariousness of their islands of faith surrounded by pagans – it was evidently sufficient (see below, pp. 315–17). It was also broadly comparable to the range of reading-matter which, as surviving inventories show, one might have found in a contemporary

---

91 For lists and surveys see F. J. Thomson, 'The nature of the reception of Byzantine Christian culture in Kievan Russia in the tenth to thirteen centuries and its implications for Russian culture', *Slavica gandensia* 5 (1978), 107–39; G. Podskalsky, *Christentum und theologische Literatur in der Kiever Rus' (988–1237)* (Munich, 1982), pp. 56–72.

Byzantine library, whether in a monastery or in the home of a wealthy layman.[92] Nevertheless, if one looks at the full spread of writing in Byzantium or in contemporary Western Europe, then there were very significant gaps in the 'library' available to the Rus in translation. In particular, there was no trace here of one of the most characteristic and treasured pursuits of the Constantinopolitan literary elite, of the types of reading and styles of writing through which this elite affirmed its cultural and imperial descent from Old Rome: the rhetorical exercises and learned disquisitions in pseudo-classical 'atticizing' Greek, the classical imagery and allusions, the quotations from the ancient tragedians, the secular poetry in a range of metrical forms, the structures of argument formed through a schooling in the pre-Christian arts of persuasion. To put it crudely, the Rus did not read *The Iliad*, either in Greek or in Slavonic.[93]

Why not? If a knowledge of the classics is a criterion of intellectual merit, then this is a troublesome question (see below, p. 316), but from the perspective of the Rus there was no compelling practical or cultural reason why they *should* have extended their mimicry of Byzantium into these areas.

In the first place, the Rus differed fundamentally from the Byzantines in their sense of historical identity, and hence in their cultural self-image. Unlike the Constantinopolitan elite, the Rus did not trace their origins back to imperial Rome. Their lands had never been part of the Roman empire. For them the world of pre-Christian Rome and of Hellenistic culture was alien and remote, with no emblematic significance for themselves, and therefore with no special status in their scale of values. Their concern was with the faith, not with symbols and fetishes of imperial continuity. They had quite enough of a job contextualizing and re-assimilating their own pagan past, and coping in the present with their own pagan counter-culture. Churchmen and merchants travelled between Kiev and Byzantium. The Rus did have opportunities to be aware of how Byzantine intellectuals displayed their erudition. If they had regarded it as important, there would have been no insuperable obstacle to prevent them from studying Attic Greek and introducing classical education in Kiev. One must assume that they were uninterested, rather than incapable.[94]

---

92 Thomson, 'The nature of the reception', with reference to monastic libraries; on the similarity of a private library see Mango, *Byzantium*, pp. 239–40, citing the Testament – dated 1059 – of Iaroslav's contemporary, Eustathios Boilas.

93 On the range of Byzantine writing in this mode see H. Hunger, *Die hochsprachliche profane Literatur der Byzantiner*, I–II (Munich, 1978).

94 S. Franklin, 'The empire of the *Rhomaioi* as viewed from Kievan Russia: aspects of Byzantino-Russian cultural relations', *Byzantion* 53 (1983), 507–37; on faint echoes of Byzantine debate among the Rus see also Franklin, *Sermons and Rhetoric*, pp. lviii–lxiv.

Secondly, the practicalities of translating written culture into a new language are different from the practicalities of translating visual culture into a new setting. Buildings and pictures can be copied, artists and artisans can be invited or paid, objects can be purchased or donated, all without the prior training of local personnel. Iaroslav imported his visible Christianity directly from Byzantium. To import book-learning directly would have been more complex, but in fact there was no need, since a convenient alternative route was available. Written Christianity reached the Rus at two removes: first because it had to pass through the linguistic filter from Greek into Slavonic; and second, because all the essentials had already been pre-packaged elsewhere, in Bulgaria. A tradition of written Slavonic Christianity had already been established. There would have been little point in re-inventing it, with or without a classical education. Church Slavonic provided both a bridge and a barrier: a bridge to the faith, and therefore a barrier (or at least a disincentive) to direct participation in the cultures of the other learned languages of Europe. A reliance on second-hand Slavonic for written Christianity is perfectly compatible with the prestige of Greek in the visual Christianity of the mid-eleventh century.

Quite apart from the issue of pseudo-classical learning, there has long been a debate as to whether or to what extent the Rus themselves did nevertheless translate fresh works, or translate works afresh, in addition to those which they inherited. An enigmatic and corrupt sentence in the *Primary Chronicle*'s eulogy to Iaroslav declares that he 'gathered many scribes, and transferred from the Greeks into Slavonic writing'. This has usually been read as a plain statement that Iaroslav sponsored a programme of translation, caused Greek books to be rendered into Slavonic. With the chronicle for authority, linguists have devised criteria by which to identify dozens of works as the products of Iaroslav's 'school of translators' (or in some versions, 'academy'). Yet the phrase in the *Primary Chronicle* may mean merely that Iaroslav ordered the transposition of Church Slavonic texts from Glagolitic into Cyrillic, or that he brought scribes from the Byzantine lands (which in his day included Bulgaria) 'for the purpose of Slavonic writing': i.e. that he recruited copyists, not translators.[95]

The question is unresolved and probably unresolvable. On the one hand, no known Church Slavonic translation can conclusively be proved to have been produced in Kiev by a native of Rus.[96] On the other hand, since the linguistic criteria for localizing a text are often

---

95 *PVL*, I, p. 102; see H. Lunt, 'On interpreting the Russian Primary Chronicle; the year 1037', *SEEJ* 32 (1988), 251–64; D. Ostrowski, 'What makes a translation bad? Gripes of an end user', *HUS* 15 (1991), 441–2.

96 See F. J. Thomson, '"Made in Russia". A survey of translations allegedly made in Kievan Russia', in G. Birkfellner, ed., *Millennium Russiae Christianae. Tausend Jahre Christliches Rußland* (Cologne, Weimar, Vienna, 1993), pp. 295–354.

inconclusive, it can be just as difficult to prove that certain works were *not* translated in Iaroslav's Kiev. On the one hand, native writers generally show no signs of having read any Byzantine literature in the original Greek, which suggests that a Kievan education did not equip its alumni to be translators.[97] On the other hand, although this is a broadly valid comment on the culture of the Rus which emerged over time, it is questionable with regard to Ilarion;[98] that is, with regard to the mid-eleventh century. Yet the mid-eleventh century was also the period of the most conspicuous and prestigious displays of Greek in Kiev, as well as being the period to which the disputed phrase in the *Primary Chronicle* actually refers.

A medieval Kievan posthumously eavesdropping on this kind of discussion might well be puzzled by the values which it implies and by the heat which it can generate. Church Slavonic was not a *national* language of culture. There was an acknowledged common debt to Cyril and Methodios, but otherwise the question of who made what translation where and when was a trivial technicality. The words of books flowed like rivers over the whole earth – a kind of medieval Internet on the information super-highway? – and the Slavonic tongue was one.[99]

Although book culture was overwhelmingly a culture of translations, by the mid-eleventh century the Rus had also begun to apply its language for local purposes. Whereas the continuous history of official faith can be traced to the reign of Vladimir, the continuous history of native Christian literature can be traced to the reign of Iaroslav. We shall consider the development of native literature in later chapters, but for the mid-eleventh century the outstanding figure is of course Ilarion, majestic like St Sophia above the wooden dwellings, with a confidence and elegance of conception and execution that was never quite repeated. As for Ilarion's contemporaries, they are so dimly visible as to be barely even shadows. One brief homily, a string of pious commonplaces, is attributed to Luka Zhidiata, bishop of Novgorod (c. 1035–59).[100] Otherwise there is much speculation and

97 F. J. Thomson, 'The implications of the absence of quotations of untranslated Greek works in original early Russian literature, together with a critique of a distorted picture of early Bulgarian culture', *Slavica gandensia* 15 (1988), 63–91.

98 L. Müller, 'Eine weitere griechische Parallele zu Ilarions "Slovo o zakone i blagodati"', *TODRL* 48 (1993), 100–4.

99 See *PVL*, I, p. 23; Moldovan, *Slovo*, p. 88 (fol. 180b); Franklin, *Sermons and Rhetoric*, p. 14.

100 S. Bugoslavskii, ed., 'Pouchenie ep. Luki Zhidiaty po rukopisiam XV–XVII vv.', *Izvestiia ORIAS* 18, ii (1913), 196–237; translated by F. J. Thomson, 'On translating Slavonic texts into a modern language', *Slavica gandensia* 19 (1992), 216–17. On Ioann I and the Boris and Gleb literature see Gail Lenhoff, *The Martyred Princes Boris and Gleb: a Socio-Cultural Study of the Cult and the Texts* (Columbus, Ohio, 1989), pp. 56–65: on theories of mid-eleventh-century components of the chronicles see e.g. D. S. Likhachev, in *PVL*, II, pp. 36–77.

hypothesis: were some of the constituent narratives of the *Primary Chronicle* written in mid-century? Or the *Tale* of Boris and Gleb? Did Metropolitan Ioann I adapt a set of Byzantine liturgical hymns for a service in honour of Boris and Gleb? If so, in what sense could such works be categorized as native or original?[101]

The type of question is by now familiar. But even without definitive answers the basic contrast between the age of Vladimir and the age of Iaroslav, as drawn both by Ilarion and in the chronicle, is in essence valid: Vladimir, who had lacked book-learning, made the decision that the Rus should receive it; Iaroslav, its second-generation beneficiary, promoted its active usage and dissemination. Vladimir would 'listen to the Gospel being read', whereas Iaroslav would himself 'read books, day and night'; Vladimir forced children to read, whereas Iaroslav hired bookmen to write.[102] The precise extent of Iaroslav's patronage is obscure, but its direction is clear. Before Iaroslav there is very little evidence of any native use of writing in general and of Slavonic Christian writing in particular. From the mid-eleventh century the signs and products of native book-learning become steadily more numerous and diverse.

❖   ❖   ❖   ❖   ❖

By standing under the main dome of St Sophia in Kiev, and facing away from the apse, one should be able to examine the the donor-portrait of Iaroslav and his family. To the left and right (above the south and north sides of the aisle) a procession of painted figures advances in the direction of the central group beneath the western gallery. The problem is that the central group of figures, including the donor himself, is not there. The original western gallery is one of the few parts of the interior lost in alterations. The procession processes into empty space, and Iaroslav is absent from his own donor-portrait. He must have been there once, but his form and surroundings have to be imagined.[103]

In effect we have followed an analogous path several times in the course of this chapter: tracing the lines which lead to or emanate from Iaroslav's reign, and finding that they break off in empty space. The arrangement of lines shows *roughly* what must have been at the place where they converge, but most attempts to fill the gap have to be hypothetical. What, if any, was Iaroslav's written law code? Or his

---

101 For extreme speculation concerning esp. chronicle notes as early as the mid-ninth (!) century see e.g. B. A. Rybakov, *Drevniaia Rus'. Skazaniia, byliny, letopisi* (Moscow, 1963), pp. 159–82.

102 *PVL*, I, pp. 86, 102; cf. 153.

103 Poppe, 'The building of the Church of St Sophia', 39–41; S. A. Vysotskii, *Svetskie freski Sofiiskogo sobora v Kieve* (Kiev, 1989), pp. 63–112.

Church Statute? Did he or did he not sponsor translations? How much native Christian literature was produced in Kiev at the time?

The gap at the centre is not wholly misleading. Behind the rhetoric, Iaroslav's Rus could not match the image conjured by contemporary and subsequent propaganda. Iaroslav's route to power had been less than majestic, and even when established in Kiev he exercised limited rule over a limited area with fairly basic institutions of government. His much-proclaimed faith was a social gloss for the urban elite in a largely pagan land, and his literary culture – almost entirely borrowed – bears little comparison with the elite intellectual pursuits which might be found in centres of Greek and Latin learning. Despite the triumphal image-building, Kiev was not Constantinople.

But nor is the facade entirely an illusion. Claim outstripped achievement, but Iaroslav's initiatives were real and multi-faceted: in urban planning and construction, in legislation, in the promotion of the Faith, in the ideology of dynastic rule, in the acquisition and use of technologies. Though in many respects the project was imitative, it was also distinctive. Even in scrupulously faithful cultural borrowing some adaptation is inevitable, just as a literal translation cannot avoid losing nuances of its original *and* cannot avoid picking up nuances from its new language and context. Change is mutual in such processes.[104] In this chapter we have seen various kinds of interplay – and of resistance to interplay – between the old and the new, the borrowed and the local. The result was a characteristic synthesis which, with modifications over time, was to become almost definitive, setting the parameters of collective identity among the Rus, for whom the reign of Iaroslav came to represent a kind of Golden Age. The synthesis meshed features derived from the Scandinavians, the Slavs and the 'Greeks'. Its components were linguistic, aesthetic, confessional and political. The various elements had emerged and converged slowly and by no means inevitably. The package was put together deliberately, in Iaroslav's programme of patronage and public works.

Naturally the presentation was neater than the substance, the wrapping than its contents. Nothing fitted quite as comfortably as the packagers might have wished, as Iaroslav's successors were to discover.

---

104 See e.g. S. Franklin, 'The reception of Byzantine culture by the Slavs', *The Seventeenth International Byzantine Congress. Major Papers* (New Rochelle, New York, 1986), 383–97.

CHAPTER SEVEN

The Inner Circle:
the Development of Dynastic
Political Culture, 1054–c. 1113

1. TESTIMONIES AND TESTAMENTS

At the start of its narrative of the events of 1097, the *Primary Chronicle* tells of a solemn family meeting:

Sviatopolk and Vladimir, and David Igorevich, and Vasilko Rostislavich, and David Sviatoslavich and his brother Oleg, came and gathered at Liubech for the settlement of a peace, and they spoke to one another saying: 'Why do we ruin the land of the Rus, making strife among ourselves, while the Polovtsy pillage our land and rejoice that there is war amongst us? Now and henceforth let us be of one heart, and let us protect the land of the Rus. Let each keep his own patrimony [*otchina*]: let Sviatopolk have Kiev, the patrimony of Iziaslav; and let Vladimir have the patrimony of Vsevolod; and let David and Oleg and Iaroslav have the patrimony of Sviatoslav. And for those to whom towns were allocated by Vsevolod – David shall have Vladimir[-in-Volynia]; and for the two Rostislavichi – Volodar shall have Peremyshl and Vasilko shall have Terebovl.' And on this they kissed the Cross: 'And if any henceforth shall turn against another, then we all and the Holy Cross shall turn against him.' And they all said, 'May the Holy Cross and all the land of the Rus be against him.'[1]

If Ilarion or Iaroslav could have been transported over half a century to witness this little scene, they might have been perplexed. Where was the 'great *kagan*' of the land, the 'sole ruler'? What exactly was implied by the term *otchina*? Who were these proliferating princelings, parcelling out the lands among themselves? What was this peculiar consultative procedure? And who were the pillaging Polovtsy? To deepen the sense of bewilderment, Iaroslav might have learned that the father of one of these earnest Cross-kissers, and the son of another, had been killed in battles against a third. And hardly had the pious words

---

1 *PVL*, I, pp. 170–1.

faded before another of the participants had his eyes poked out with a knife on the orders (or with the assent) of two more of them. Was this the glorious legacy of Iaroslav the Wise?

In a sense, it was. Iaroslav would have found here echoes of a dynastic arrangement which he himself had sanctioned. Aware that he had become sole ruler partly by chance when ten of his eleven known male siblings were dead, and anxious to avoid the fratricidal free-for-all that had followed both the death of his grandfather and that of his father, Iaroslav apparently tried to regulate the affairs of the next generation shortly before he died in 1054. The chronicle records what purports to be his last will and testament. Compare its provisions with those of the Liubech conference of 1097:

'My sons, I am departing from this world. May there be love amongst you, for you are brothers by one father and one mother. And if you abide amongst yourselves in love, then God will be in you and will subdue your enemies to you, and you will live in peace. But if you should live in hatred, in strife and at war with one another, then you yourselves shall perish, and you will ruin the land of your fathers and of your grandfathers, which through their great labours they acquired. So remain in peace, brother hearkening to brother.

'I hereby entrust the throne of Kiev to my eldest son and your brother Iziaslav, in my place. Hearken to him as you have hearkened to me. May he be for you in place of me. And to Sviatoslav I give Chernigov, and to Vsevolod Pereiaslavl, and to Igor Vladimir[-in-Volynia], and to Viacheslav Smolensk.'

And he divided the towns among them, instructing them not to transgress a brother's boundary, nor to expel [him]. And he said to Iziaslav, 'If any should offend against his brother, then you must help the one who is offended against.' And thus he enjoined his sons to abide in love.[2]

The provisions of the Liubech conference between Iaroslav's grandsons echo those of Iaroslav's Testament for his sons. Together the two texts help to set the parameters for a discussion of the political culture which emerged over the second half of the eleventh century. The Testament enunciates three clear principles. The first is that the lands of the Rus were a family firm, with legitimacy and responsibility derived from the 'fathers and grandfathers'. The second is that inheritance was divided, rather than being passed on intact to a single heir. The third is a notion of seniority among the brethren. The tailpiece adds a fourth: that each brother's allocation should be inviolable. The role of the eldest son Iziaslav was to preserve good order, to guarantee the provisions of the Testament.

Conspicuous by its absence is the concept of 'sole rule'. It appears that Iaroslav, though ostentatiously a monarch, was no monarch*ist*

---

2 Ibid., p. 108; the reference to Igor may be a later insertion or alteration: see *PSRL*, I, col. 164, and below, p. 269.

bent on perpetuating a monarchic system of rule. The facade of quasi-imperial imagery, constructed under Iaroslav's cultural patronage, was not to be underpinned by the construction of a quasi-imperial polity. Back in the practical world, even the imagery was abandoned. From the second half of the eleventh century political discourse was dominated by the terminology of kinship, and the ideologues of the elite turned their quills to the task of matching Christian justification to dynastic convention.[3] This sort of transition is not unparalleled among early medieval monarchies.

The picture would be plain enough, were it not for four awkward points. In the first place, it is not clear what dynastic convention had been. There is no earlier account of any attempt to divide inheritance *before* (rather than in the wake of) armed hostilities, but the lack of evidence – apart from a possible hint in the chronicle of Thietmar of Merseburg (see above, p. 192) – may mean no more than that we are ignorant. Thus it is difficult to say to what extent Iaroslav's arrangement for his sons was traditional or innovative.

Secondly, the Testament itself is not as clear or as comprehensive as it at first seems. Its principles potentially contradict one another: if the eldest son was 'in place of a father', then how inviolate were his younger brothers' possessions? If a brother died, was his allocation from Iaroslav to be regarded as the permanent possession of his branch of the family, as patrimony, to be inherited in turn (and further subdivided) by his sons and grandsons? Or should the senior brother decide on a new disposition? Or does the Testament list the towns themselves in a fixed order of seniority, implying that they could be redistributed – not at will, but with changes in seniority among Iaroslav's descendants? Then there are the omissions. For example, there is no mention of the family of Iaroslav's older son Vladimir, who had pre-deceased his father; no mention of Iaroslav's long-incarcerated brother Sudislav; no mention of Polotsk. Indeed, the list of towns looks odd: Kiev and Chernigov predictably fill the first two places, but there is no reference to Novgorod, or to Turov, or to Tmutorokan, while the previously obscure Pereiaslavl figures high in the list.

Third, the texts are cultural constructs rather than archival records. Many of the phrases of Iaroslav's Testament are commonplace formulae.[4]

---

3 On the lands as the collective inheritance of the entire dynasty, with comparisons with equivalent custom elsewhere, see A. V. Nazarenko, 'Rodovoi siuzerenitet Riurikovichei nad Rus'iu (X–XI vv.)', *DGTSSSR* 1985 (1986), 149–57; see also below, pp. 290, 313–19.

4 In relation to translated literature see S. Franklin, 'Some apocryphal sources of Kievan Russian historiography', *Oxford Slavonic Papers*, N.S. 15 (1982), esp. 6–15; in relation to later East Slav literary and princely testaments see Daniel E. Collins, 'Early Russian topoi of deathbed and testament', in Michael S. Flier and Daniel Rowland, eds,

Continued

The *Primary Chronicle* reports the Testament only as a speech, not stating whether it was also written down. The Testament does correspond to the arrangements made among Iaroslav's sons after his death, but as a legitimizing document it could well have been composed or edited in retrospect. It is stranded just beyond the period from which we at last begin to have reliably (which is not quite the same as 'reliable') contemporary or near-contemporary native narrative sources. From the mid-1060s the chronicle changes its character: it becomes less of a patchwork of traditions, more of a continuous record. The chroniclers were closer to their own sources and to events. But they also had their own ethical and political agendas, in support of which Iaroslav's Testament could be invoked, or rephrased, or even devised.

Fourth, whatever dynastic convention or Iaroslav's intention may have been, no temporary arrangement for Iaroslav's sons in 1054 could amount to a fixed set of rules for the family as a whole, over time, since the family was constantly having to adapt to unconventional circumstances. Over the second half of the eleventh century, and still more over the twelfth century, the dynasty expanded in number and in intricacy of relationship, across generations and across territories. Iaroslav's laconic guidelines could have given rise to contradictory claims even in a well-ordered, well-meaning, self-contained and un-disturbed family; and none of these epithets is unreservedly appropriate to the princes of the Rus.

It is a common mistake to suppose that there was a fixed political 'system' from which the unprincipled princelings occasionally (or regularly) deviated. Under Iaroslav and his forebears a political culture for an expanded, sedentary dynasty did not exist. Iaroslav's successors had to improvise, adapting custom, precedent and precept to contingencies as they arose. There were *ad hoc* arrangements, false starts, compromises and accommodations, and ingenious devices through which to dress innovation as tradition. The result was by no means chaotic. There *were* certain repetitive patterns and consistent assumptions.[5] But the ideologues and apologists who produced our written sources had a hard time keeping pace, as the southern brethren and their offspring struggled to preserve, defend and continually reconstitute the legacy of their fathers and grandfathers. Such was the path from Iaroslav's

---

Continued

Medieval Russian Culture II (= California Slavic Studies 19; Berkeley, Los Angeles, London, 1994), pp. 134–59; see also above, p. 188 n. 19; also Martin Dimnik, *The Dynasty of Chernigov* 1054–1146 (Texts and Studies 116, Pontifical Institute of Mediaeval Studies; Toronto, 1994), pp. 18–34.

5 See e.g. Nancy Shields Kollmann, 'Collateral succession in Kievan Rus'', *HUS* 14 (1990), 377–87; A. P. Tolochko, *Kniaz' v Drevnei Rusi: vlast', sobstvennost', ideologiia* (Kiev, 1992), pp. 22–66; in detail for the period covered by this chapter, but with a slightly different approach, see Dimnik, *The Dynasty of Chernigov*, pp. 34–276.

Testament to the Liubech conference of 1097, from Iaroslav's sole rule to the far more elaborate political culture of the expanded dynasty of the Rus.

2. BROTHERS AND OTHERS
(1054–76)

Iaroslav's eldest son had died in 1052. In the late 1050s the family firm, which consisted of the five surviving sons, lost its two most junior directors. In 1057 Viacheslav died, and Igor was transferred from Vladimir-in-Volynia to take Viacheslav's place in Smolensk, where he remained until his own death in 1060.[6] In 1059 the unfortunate uncle Sudislav was released from his long incarceration and allowed to spend his final years in comparative dignity, as a monk. In 1063 he, too, died. And then there were three: Iziaslav, Sviatoslav and Vsevolod, princes in Kiev, Chernigov and Pereiaslavl; the inner circle of the dynasty in their tight cluster of southern towns in the Middle Dnieper region.

By contrast with their father, Iziaslav, Sviatoslav and Vsevolod tended and still tend to be presented through a structure of ideas which stress fraternal harmony as the paramount dynastic (i.e. political) virtue. It was a notion which they themselves took steps to promote. The junior brothers' cities, Chernigov and Pereiaslavl, were given a semblance of Kiev's dignity by having their bishops designated titular metropolitans (here a purely honorific title, without implying that they could appoint suffragan bishops).[7] In the case of Pereiaslavl, a somewhat exposed outpost on the fringes of the steppe, the artifice must have been transparent.[8] To bolster Pereiaslavl's resources, Vsevolod, the youngest of the brethren, was given the tribute from Smolensk, and probably a notional swathe of potentially tribute-bearing lands in the remote north-east. In 1060 the three brothers joined forces to campaign in the steppes, 'on horseback and in boats', against the Oghuz. Jointly the brethren agreed on additions to *Russkaia Pravda*.[9] Together, in 1072, they presided over the celebration of the sanctity of their murdered uncles Boris and Gleb, and the transfer of their relics to a new church

---

6 *PVL*, I, p. 109.

7 Sophia Senyk, *A History of the Church in Ukraine, I, To the End of the Thirteenth Century* (Orientalia Christiana Analecta 243; Rome, 1993), pp. 95–7; Ia. N. Shchapov, *Gosudarstvo i tserkov' Drevnei Rusi X–XIII vv.* (Moscow, 1989), pp. 56–62.

8 See J. Lind, 'The Russo-Byzantine treaties and the early urban structure of Rus'', *SEER* 62 (1984), 362–70; for the view that Pereiaslavl was a far more ancient centre see N. N. Korinnyi, *Pereiaslavskaia zemlia. X–pervaia polovina XIII veka* (Kiev, 1992), pp. 44–7, 144–8.

9 *ZDR*, pp. 48, 58; Kaiser, *The Laws*, p. 17.

in Vyshgorod:[10] Boris and Gleb who had by now come to represent not just exemplary piety in the face of death, but exemplary compliance with the will of their older brother. Chroniclers and hagiographers found quasi-biblical phrases which echoed Iaroslav's Testament, about loving one's brother, about the inviolability of a brother's lot (see below, pp. 256–7).

Ideas often become most forcefully developed not when they are most smoothly applied but when they are most precarious. The fraternal cooperation, matching Iaroslav's reported last wishes, lasted for twenty years, more or less; at times rather less than more. Over its second decade, the only period for which we have any detailed narratives, a series of external and internal developments strained the integrity of the 'inner circle' beyond breaking point.

In the winter of 1066–7 Vseslav Briacheslavich of Polotsk attacked Novgorod.[11] In the affairs of the Rus one might reckon such an incident to be peripheral, no more grating than the ordinary background noise of distant skirmishes. Some rivalry between Polotsk and Novgorod was, after all, traditional (see above, p. 133). This was an old regional rivalry, important locally but without broader resonances. But now, when Vseslav of Polotsk imposed himself on Novgorod he triggered a series of events which culminated in the biggest political crisis in the lands of the Rus for half a century, arguably even the most serious threat to dynastic order in the entire pre-Mongol period. And although the crisis itself was fairly brief, Vseslav of Polotsk became magnified in near-contemporary and subsequent legend as a figure of demonic darkness striding across the land.

Vseslav was an outsider. He was a great-grandson of Vladimir, but, as we have seen, even in Vladimir's lifetime Polotsk was set apart from the reshuffling and reallocation of possessions among the brethren. Vseslav's father Briacheslav played no recorded part in the civil wars of 1015–19. When Iaroslav and Mstislav divided the lands between themselves, Polotsk retained its autonomy. When Briacheslav died in 1044, Polotsk was not gathered in by Iaroslav but passed to Vseslav as his patrimony. Polotsk was not mentioned in Iaroslav's Testament, and was not among the lands held or claimed by Iaroslav's sons.

Nevertheless, Polotsk was not a foreign country: it shared in the political, economic and cultural developments of the other lands of the clan. By the mid-eleventh century the prince of Polotsk had authority over other settlements not just on the Western Dvina (e.g. Vitebsk) but as far south as Minsk. In other words his authority extended through

---

10 *PVL*, I, p. 121; see Gail Lenhoff, *The Martyred Princes Boris and Gleb: a Socio-Cultural Study of the Cult and the Texts* (Columbus, Ohio, 1989), pp. 48–54; see also above, p. 231.

11 *PVL*, I, p. 111. Vseslav's campaigns began in 1065.

a substantial part of what in the distant future came to be Belorussia and eventually Belarus. Polotsk was also the seat of a bishop, and it had its cathedral of St Sophia, which was probably built in the early years of the reign of Vseslav, so that it is roughly contemporary with the cathedrals of St Sophia in Kiev and Novgorod.[12]

Vseslav of Polotsk was therefore an outsider from within. He was kin, but not a Iaroslavich; he did not fit the neat scheme of filial relations constructed by the southern brethren and their propagandists. Animosity was not automatic: in 1060 Vseslav had joined the southern brethren on their expedition into the steppes. But the rift, when it came, was violent. We hear the first rumblings in a report of an unsuccessful foray by Vseslav against Pskov in 1065.[13] Then, in the winter of 1066–7, he took Novgorod.

For more than a century the princes of Novgorod had been either the princes of Kiev or their sons. Novgorod was not mentioned in Iaroslav's Testament, because it was automatically in the gift of Iziaslav as prince of Kiev. In the colophon to the *Ostromir Gospel*, the earliest extant dated manuscript from Rus (1056–7), the scribe Grigorii speaks of Iziaslav as holding 'both domains' (*vlasti*; = East Slav *volosti*) – that is, Kiev and Novgorod.[14] The *Novgorod First Chronicle* contains a list of princes which at this point in the sequence mentions Iziaslav's son, Mstislav. Mstislav was probably born at the start of the 1050s, and was therefore appointed while still a child, like other Kievan appointees to Novgorod before him and after him (see above, pp. 130, 151, 264).[15]

In view of the traditionally intimate connection between Kiev and Novgorod, Vseslav of Polotsk can hardly have expected to attack without provoking a response from the south, and the manner of his attack suggests that he was prepared for serious confrontation. He ransacked and burned his way through the city. He even took the bells from St Sophia in Novgorod and carried them off to St Sophia in Polotsk: according to legend, the peal of those bells in Polotsk echoed down to Kiev, whither the young Prince Mstislav had fled.[16] This was more than a minor episode in a regional squabble. It can be seen as an attempt to neutralize Novgorod, to subordinate it to Polotsk, to take control of the gateway to the Baltic, to cut off the Iaroslavichi from their northern base, to split the lands of the Rus into distinct northern

---

12 P. A. Rappoport, *Russkaia arkhitektura X–XIII vv.* (*ASSSR SAI*, vyp. E1–47; Leningrad, 1982), pp. 94–5 (no. 161).

13 *Pskovskie letopisi*, ed. A. N. Nasonov (Moscow, 1955), II, p. 18; *NPL*, p. 17; cf. *PVL*, I, p. 110, s.a. 6573.

14 *Ostromirovo Evangelie. Faksimil'noe izdanie* (Moscow, 1988), fol. 294v.

15 *PVL*, I, p. 122; see O. M. Rapov, *Kniazheskie vladeniia na Rusi v X–pervoi polovine XIII v.* (Moscow, 1977), pp. 85–6.

16 See *PVL*, II, p. 396; *NPL*, p. 161; *PLDR* XII v., p. 382.

and southern zones of influence, and hence to impose a major political and territorial realignment.

The Iaroslavichi responded in unison and with brutal urgency. Marching north through the late-winter frosts, they first reached Minsk: 'and the people of Minsk shut themselves into the town. And the brethren took Minsk, and slaughtered the men, and the women and children they took captive. And they went to the [river] Nemiga, and Vseslav went to oppose them. And the two sides came together on the Nemiga, on the third day of March [1067]. And there was heavy snow. And the two sides went against one another. And there was great slaughter, and many fell, and Iziaslav, Sviatoslav and Vsevolod prevailed, and Vseslav fled.' The battle became embroidered in legend: 'the bloody banks of the Nemiga are not sown with blessings; they are sown with the bones of the sons of the Rus'.[17] A formal truce was concluded, at a ceremony of 'kissing the Cross', on 10 June.[18] In a show of friendship, Iziaslav invited Vseslav to his encampment near Smolensk – and promptly had him and his two sons arrested, removed to Kiev and incarcerated. So much for the authority of a kissed Cross.

The burning of Novgorod and the slaughter on the Nemiga were mere preludes. The real crisis was precipitated by a quite separate event at the opposite extremity of the land: an incursion of the Polovtsian nomads of the southern steppes. The Polovtsy (in Byzantine sources Cumans, in other sources Qipchaks) are first mentioned, rather innocuously, in the *Primary Chronicle*'s entry for 1054–5, when a group of them made peace with the most southerly of the brethren, Vsevolod of Pereiaslavl. After Vsevolod and his older brothers routed the Oghuz in 1060, the Polovtsy were there to fill the vacuum: in February 1062 'for the first time the Polovtsy came to plunder the land of the Rus'. Vsevolod, who was most vulnerable to attack from the steppes, even suffered a defeat in a skirmish.[19] These were small but unpleasant beginnings. The Polovtsy were to dominate dealings between Rus and the steppes for the next 160 years.

In 1068 the Polovtsy advanced into the lands of the Rus from the south-east and defeated the combined troops of the Iaroslavichi on the river Alta, the strategic crossing-point on the road to and from the steppes (see above, p. 185). Suddenly the cities of the inner circle were dangerously exposed. Sviatoslav retreated further north to Chernigov. Vsevolod, who was cut off from Pereiaslavl by the advance of the Polovtsy, retired with Iziaslav to Kiev.[20] But in Kiev the retreat provoked alarm and indignation. On 15 September there was a *veche*,

17 *PVL*, I, p. 122; *PLDR* XII v., p. 382.
18 Or July: compare *PSRL*, I, col. 167; *PSRL*, II, col. 156.
19 *PVL*, I, p. 109.
20 Ibid., pp. 112–14.

a gathering of townspeople, on the market square (on the *veche* see below, p. 289). Iziaslav was urged to go out and fight the marauders, but he refused to budge from his palace, refused even to negotiate. One frustrated group of Kievans decided that if their prince would not listen to them they would get themselves another prince. They stormed the place where Vseslav of Polotsk was incarcerated, released him, took him to the palace courtyard, acclaimed him as their prince, and plundered the palace of 'an incalculable quantity of gold and silver and squirrel furs and marten skins'. Iziaslav fled to Poland.[21]

Iaroslav's order appeared to have collapsed. His sons were divided, the steppe nomads were roaming and raiding in the very heartlands of the Rus, a faction of the townspeople had revolted, the senior Iaroslavich had been forced by his own people to quit his city, and the outsider, Vseslav of Polotsk, had risen from defeat and imprisonment to become ruler of Kiev. Truly the world had turned upside down.

Nor had the humiliation yet reached its nadir. This came in the spring of the following year (1069), and it was like an echo of the archetypal dynastic catastrophe, the civil war of 1015–19 (an echo made more resonant by some cross-contamination in the sources). Like Sviatopolk 'the Cursed', Iziaslav had his own patrimony as prince of Turov. Like Sviatopolk he took refuge in Poland. Like Sviatopolk he was linked to the king of Poland by marriage: Sviatopolk had been married to a daughter of Boleslaw I. Iziaslav was married to Gertrude, the aunt of Boleslaw II.[22] And just as in 1018 Sviatopolk had reclaimed Kiev by invading with the aid of Boleslaw I, so in 1069 Iziaslav marched to reclaim Kiev with the aid of Boleslaw II.

Vseslav had had greatness thrust upon him. He had not sought rule in Kiev, and now he lacked either the will or the local support to defend it. He fled secretly, at night, back to his native Polotsk, leaving the Kievans leaderless in the face of a vengeful prince and his Polish allies who were encamped at Belgorod, just 25 kilometres to the west of the city. According to the *Primary Chronicle*, the younger brothers Sviatoslav and Vsevolod sent to Iziaslav asking him to show restraint. Iziaslav partially acquiesced, keeping his main forces outside the city and sending instead his son, Mstislav of Novgorod: 'and Mstislav slaughtered those who had freed Vseslav, seventy of them in number; and others he blinded, and others he put to death without cause'.[23] Thus Mstislav, whose expulsion from Novgorod by Vseslav had precipitated the crisis, exacted his father's punishment on Kiev after Vseslav had bolted. Iziaslav was received back with due honour

---

21 Ibid., pp. 114–15.

22 See V. Meysztowicz, ed., 'Manuscriptum Gertrudae Filiae Mesconis II Regis Poloniae', *Antemurale* 2 (1955), 103–57.

23 *PVL*, I, p. 116.

by his people and on 2 May once more 'sat upon his throne'. The dynastic disruption had been traumatic but brief. Legitimate order, according to the terms of Iaroslav's Testament, was restored.

This was the appearance, and it was surely what Iziaslav would have wished to believe, or would have wished others to believe, but the series of disasters had exposed and exacerbated tensions which could not readily be eased by the show of restored good order. The deeper impact of the Vseslav affair can be seen both in fact and in perceptions of fact, both in the politics of the next few years and in the ways in which contemporaries and successors interpreted and reinterpreted the crisis.

Let us look first at the interpretations. Vseslav of Polotsk was an anomaly: he was the only non-Iaroslavich to be prince of Kiev in the entire period between the death of Iaroslav in 1054 and the Mongol invasions in the thirteenth century. Even in or soon after his own lifetime (he died in 1101) he was seen as a phenomenon in need of explanation, an object-lesson in something, a warning. The Vseslav affair, like the murder of Boris and Gleb, quickly came to be presented as a prototypical manifestation of political deviancy. The curious feature of this affair, however, is that it was interpreted in diametrically opposed ways. Vseslav has two quite different reputations. For the chronicler who wrote the *Primary Chronicle*'s account of the years 1067–9, Vseslav was a figure of injured piety. He trusted in the protection of the Cross, which was kissed as a sign of truce by the Iaroslavichi, yet he was perfidiously arrested when he entered Iziaslav's camp. In his imprisonment he cried out in piety, 'O honoured Cross, I have faith in you'. Through Vseslav's release 'God showed the power of the Cross, as a lesson for the land of the Rus; that having kissed the honoured Cross it should not be transgressed; that if any should transgress against it, he shall receive punishment here and eternal punishment in the age to come'.[24]

This was an important programmatic statement. Cross-kissing was the main procedure by which the family and/or its churchmen attempted to lend Christian authority to dynastic dealings. It may well have been an innovation, introduced by the Iaroslavichi. The procedure is mentioned in the context of the tenth-century agreements between the Rus and the Byzantines, but in native politics there is no reference to its use until the sons of Iaroslav in the second half of the eleventh century: in their truce with their uncle Sudislav on his release from prison in 1059; and at the peace with Vseslav on 10 June 1067. There were continuing refinements and modifications: the Liubech agreement of 1097 combines the kissing of the Cross with the traditional pledging of 'hearts'; from the mid-twelfth century there are references to the use

24 Ibid., p. 115.

of written documents in relation to Cross-kissing. Vseslav of Polotsk is the first recorded victim of a violation of Cross-kissing; Iziaslav Iaroslavich is the first recorded violator. Hence their prototypical significance, and hence the lesson in political morality.[25]

At the same time a completely different view of Vseslav was being articulated: as a part-pagan, part-demonic figure of active evil, as the cause (rather than the instrument) of the dynasty's distress. First, there were dark mutterings about Vseslav's birth: that he was born from sorcery, with a mark on his head: that 'after his birth the sorceress said to his mother, "Bind this mark on him, that he may bear it to the end of his life". And he bears it upon himself to this day, and for this reason he is pitiless in bloodshed'.[26] This magical and grotesque image of Vseslav was developed until, by the late twelfth century, he had become a perverted force of nature, who 'stalked the night as a wolf, ran at midnight like a wild beast, galloped as a wolf the path to the great Khors'. Vseslav the wolf (*volk*) and Vseslav the sorcerer (*volkhv*) fuse in the figure of Volk (or Volkhv) Vseslavich in folk epic and in tales of Vseslav the Werewolf.[27]

Vseslav cannot be held entirely responsible for his own subsequent image, but the perception of Vseslav as exemplar, whether of injured innocence or of sinister sorcery, is not accidental. In the first place, the very existence of an autonomous and evidently quite prosperous Polotsk was a continuing implicit challenge to the kievocentric ideology propagated by the southern brethren. Among the routine campaigns of the princes, campaigns against Polotsk and its associated towns, especially Minsk, stand out for their violence and brutality.[28] The challenge was diminished and diffused when the towns of the Polotsk region were split among Vseslav's sons after his exceptionally long reign (1044–1101), but it was not extinguished until Vseslav's son Gleb was defeated and imprisoned by Vladimir Monomakh in 1119.[29] Secondly, of more immediate concern to the chroniclers, the Vseslav affair cast a long shadow over southern politics. It shifted the balance of power among the Iaroslavichi.

The man who gained most was Sviatoslav of Chernigov. While his older brother Iziaslav had refused to confront the Polovtsy and was driven from Kiev, Sviatoslav, in the late autumn of 1068, engaged the

---

25 Ibid., pp. 29, 38, 109.
26 *PVL*, I, p. 104.
27 *PLDR* XII v., pp. 382, 384; see R. O. Jakobson and M. Szeftel, 'The Vseslav Epos', in *Roman Jakobson: Selected Writings* (The Hague, 1966), IV, pp. 301–68; A. A. Kosorukov, 'Liubimye idei – legendy – fakty. (Obraz Vseslava Polotskogo v letopisiakh, v "Slove o polku Igoreve" i obraz Vol'kha Vseslavicha v bylinakh)', *Germenevtika drevnerusskoi literatury XI–XIV vv. V* (Moscow, 1992), pp. 124–228.
28 See Vladimir Monomakh's own reminiscences of plundering Minsk: *PVL*, I, p. 160.
29 *PSRL*, II, col. 285; see Rapov, *Kniazheskie vladeniia*, pp. 54ff.

Polovtsy in battle, defeated them and captured their leader. When Iziaslav returned with a Polish army, Sviatoslav, along with Vsevolod, was credited with restraining him. Such signs of Iziaslav's loss of face may be dismissed as attributable merely to the bias of a chonicler; but Sviatoslav's political gains were tangible and substantial. During Iziaslav's absence abroad, Sviatoslav installed his own son Gleb as prince of Novgorod, transferring him from a rather troubled tenure in Tmutorokan (which was still a southern satellite of Chernigov). More significantly, Gleb remained prince of Novgorod even after Iziaslav's reinstatement in Kiev; indeed, in October 1069 Gleb successfully defended Novgorod, as Iziaslav's son Mstislav had failed to do, against yet another raid by Vseslav of Polotsk.[30]

The confirmation of Gleb's appointment to Novgorod is the first recorded occasion on which the acknowledged prince of Novgorod came from Chernigov, or from anywhere other than Kiev. It was an unprecedented concession on the part of Iziaslav. In this post-Vseslav deal the sweetener for Iziaslav was that his own son Mstislav received the prize of Polotsk. Mstislav died soon afterwards, and Polotsk passed to another of Iziaslav's sons, Sviatopolk; but in 1071 Sviatopolk was expelled by the old enemy Vseslav, who thus returned into his inheritance after a gap of some four years, while Iziaslav was left without any compensation for the loss of Novgorod to his younger brother. As in the late 1020s and early 1030s, so now in the late 1060s and early 1070s the balance seemed to be tipping from the prince of Kiev towards the prince of Chernigov.

The men of influence followed the men of power. Besides his lack of political deftness, Iziaslav had a knack of alienating people whom it might have been sensible to soothe. Nikon, one of the elders of the Kievan monastery of the Caves, quarrelled with Iziaslav and went off to found a new monastery in Tmutorokan, where he also acted as an intermediary for Sviatoslav in negotiations with some junior princes. Antonii, the most venerable of the Caves monks, likewise deserted to Sviatoslav, after Iziaslav had accused him of sympathy for Vseslav of Polotsk. Antonii, too, founded another monastery, under Sviatoslav's patronage, in Chernigov.[31]

On 2 (or 20) May 1072 the brethren made a solemn show of unity, legitimacy and perhaps reconciliation, at the ceremony for the translation of the relics of Boris and Gleb. The cult of Boris and Gleb,

---

30 *NPL*, p. 17; on Gleb in Tmutorokan and Novgorod see Dimnik, *The Dynasty of Chernigov*, pp. 57, 64–5, 72–3, 93.

31 *PVL*, I, p. 128; II, pp. 84–95; cf. D. Likhachev, *The Great Heritage: the Classical Literature of Old Rus* (Moscow, 1981), pp. 95–104; *Uspenskii sbornik*, fols 35b.20–4, 41c.17–41d.19, 60c.4–18; Hollingsworth, *Hagiography*, pp. 60–1; Abramovich/Tschiżewskij, *Paterikon*, pp. 110–11; Heppell, *Paterik*, pp. 36–41; see Dimnik, *The Dynasty of Chernigov*, pp. 111–13, 123–4.

symbolizing self-sacrificial obedience to an elder brother, provided a splendid agenda for Iziaslav, but ceremonial piety could not cement his fragile authority. A mere ten months later, on 22 March 1073, Iziaslav was again driven out of Kiev: not by any interloper from the north, but by his own younger brothers, Sviatoslav of Chernigov and Vsevolod of Pereiaslavl. 'The devil stirred strife amongst the brethren.' Sviatoslav and Vsevolod 'sat on the throne' at the princely residence at Berestovo.[32] So far as we can tell, the coup was bloodless. Iaroslav's Testament had been violated from within, and nobody was prepared to fight to defend it.

The opposition to Sviatoslav was merely verbal. For Kievan political moralists each crisis was an excuse for a lesson. The Vseslav affair prompted a disquisition on the sanctity of Cross-kissing; now the theme was the iniquity of transgressing one's father's instructions and one's brother's boundaries. Biblical and quasi-Biblical precedents were busily discovered, and Sviatoslav was duly castigated both by name and by implication. Nestor's *Lection* on Boris and Gleb, written in the late 1070s or early 1080s, laments the disobedience of younger princes towards their elders. A contributor to the *Primary Chronicle* peppered key narratives with suitably censorious phrases. Feodosii, hegumen (superior) of the Caves monastery, rebuked Sviatoslav in public and demonstratively boycotted his feasts.[33] It is possible that Sviatoslav even agreed with his critics, at least in principle. He tolerated Feodosii's reproaches, and bought the monastery's acquiescence, if not approval, with a grant of land and money towards the construction of a splendid church.[34] When he died he was buried in the church of the Saviour in Chernigov, not in Kiev like his father and grandfather.

What issue of policy or practice outweighed principle, prompted Sviatoslav to act, and ensured such moderate opposition? Three reasons have been suggested, or suggest themselves. The first is religious: Sviatoslav was obliged to eject his brother, because the latter was close to apostasy. Suspicions are aroused by Iziaslav's subsequent movements. He fled again to Poland, to his wife's nephew Boleslaw II, who had been so helpful during his difficulties with Vseslav of Polotsk a few years earlier. On this occasion, however, Boleslaw was less generous. He took Iziaslav's bribe money but gave no aid in return.[35] In January 1075 Iziaslav turned up at the court of Henry IV in Mainz. Henry was cautious, and sent an emissary to Kiev to

32 *PVL*, I, p. 121; see Hollingsworth, *Hagiography*, pp. 199–200.
33 Abramovich/Müller, *Erzählungen*, pp. 8, 10, 25, 33; Hollingsworth, *Hagiography*, pp. 12–13, 30, 102; cf. *PVL*, I, p. 90; *Uspenskii sbornik*, fols 57d.25–60c.4; Hollingsworth, *Hagiography*, pp. 83–6.
34 Abramovich/Tschižewskij, *Paterikon*, p. 8; Heppell, *Paterik*, p. 9; *Uspenskii sbornik*, fol. 60d.8–19; Hollingsworth, *Hagiography*, p. 86. See also below, pp. 279, 308.
35 *PVL*, I, p. 122.

find out more.[36] In the spring of the same year Iziaslav sent his son Iaropolk to Rome to enlist the support of Pope Gregory VII both in affirming the legitimacy of his own grievance and in order to mediate with Boleslaw for the recovery of Iziaslav's confiscated money.[37] Was Iziaslav perhaps suspiciously latinophile, so soon after the Pope and the Constantinopolitan Patriarch had excommunicated each other in the schism of 1054? Why did he and his Polish wife baptize one of their sons as Peter? Such suspicions are attractive but probably misplaced. Western alliances were common and carried no stigma, and there are sufficient indications of Iziaslav's Orthodoxy.[38]

Sviatoslav's second hypothetical excuse might be Iziaslav's incompetence. Iziaslav does seem to have had a talent for political misjudgement and for inducing disaffection even among his allies, be they the townspeople of Kiev or the monks of the Caves or the Polish king. Praise of Iziaslav tends to sound decorous rather than warm.

A third potential stimulus for breaking brotherly ranks was straightforward greed. Kiev brought very substantial wealth. In an array of unrelated sources, both native and foreign, the theme of Kievan wealth recurs with unusual frequency during this period. We recall that in 1068 the revolting Kievans had plundered Iziaslav's palace of 'an incalculable quantity of gold and silver . . .'. By 1073 Iziaslav had re-accumulated enough to take with him to Poland 'much wealth', whose significance is confirmed in the letter of Pope Gregory VII to Boleslaw in 1075. In Germany Iziaslav's wife Gertrude commissioned luxurious miniatures for a Psalter.[39] When Burchart, the envoy of Henry IV, visited Sviatoslav, he was shown 'an incalculable quantity of gold and silver and fine garments'. And lest we think this is the native chronicler's hyperbole, the German annalist Lambert of Hersfeld confirms that Sviatoslav sent Henry IV a bribe to dissuade him from helping Iziaslav, and that the bribe consisted of 'more gold and silver and fine garments than anybody could remember ever having been brought into the German kingdom at one time' (the gift was wasted, since Henry was far too preoccupied to bother about Iziaslav).[40] Another German contemporary, Adam of Bremen, sees Kiev's splendour as worthy of Constantinople.[41] Vsevolod's son

36 M. B. Sverdlov, *Latinoiazychnye istochniki po istorii Drevnei Rusi. Germaniia, IX–pervaia polovina XII v.* (Moscow, Leningrad, 1989), pp. 158–72.

37 Gregory's letter in E. Caspar, ed., *Das Register Gregors VII.* (Berlin, 1920), I, pp. 233–5.

38 J.-P. Arrignon, 'A propos de la lettre du pape Grégoire VII au prince de Kiev Izjaslav', *RM* 3 (1977), 5–18.

39 The 'Trier Psalter', or 'Psalter of Bishop Egbert': see Meysztowicz, 'Manuscriptum Gertrudae'.

40 *PVL*, p. 131; Sverdlov, *Latinoiazychnye istochniki*, pp. 162–3.

41 Adam of Bremen, *Gesta Hammaburgensis ecclesiae pontificum*, in W. Trillmich and R. Buchner, eds, *Quellen des 9. und 11. Jahrhunderts zur Geschichte der Hamburgischen Kirche und des Reiches* (Ausgewählte Quellen zur Deutschen Geschichte des Mittelalters 11); (Darmstadt, 1961), p. 254.

Vladimir, known as 'Monomakh' after the family name of his Byzantine mother, boasted in his autobiography of the gold he brought south in tribute from Smolensk in 1077–8.[42]

This exceptionally consistent cluster of references in wholly independent sources cannot of course reveal Sviatoslav's motives in 1073, but it does remind us that the moral and political doom-gloom of the chronicles and hagiographers is not an economic indicator. The political crises took place against a background of rapidly growing urban prosperity (see below, Chapter Eight). One could plausibly suspect a link between the two.

In 1073 Sviatoslav Iaroslavich came close to reconstituting an authority as extensive as that of his father. Chernigov and Kiev were once again under one prince. The younger brother, Vsevolod, was pliant. And through his own sons Sviatoslav spanned the lands from Novgorod right down to Tmutorokan. Whether he was a grasping profiteer or a reluctant steward, he did not enjoy the fruits or bear the burdens for long. On 27 December 1076 Sviatoslav died. Vsevolod enthroned himself in Kiev for a few months, but then withdrew under threat. On 15 July 1077 his elder brother Iziaslav returned yet again to rule in Kiev. Dynastic order, as conceived in Iaroslav's Testament, was restored.

3. UNCLES AND NEPHEWS
(1076–93)

The third reign of Iziaslav Iaroslavich was his briefest, and for him it was terminally disastrous. The death of the usurper and the restoration of the senior Iaroslavich to the senior throne did not signal the restoration of dynastic order. On the contrary, it precipitated yet another dispute unforeseen, or un-provided for, in the Testament of Iaroslav.

Sviatoslav was the first of the senior Iaroslavichi to die. In the 22 years since the death of Iaroslav, this was the first generational breach in the inner circle. What were the rules of succession? Who should receive Chernigov? Different sections of the family produced fundamentally opposed answers. On one side, in the deal struck between the remaining two Iaroslavichi, Chernigov passed to Vsevolod; on the other side Oleg Sviatoslavich, son of the deceased, claimed Chernigov for himself. Both sides could have produced a plausible case: Vsevolod should have Chernigov by right of seniority, as inheritance passed from brother to brother down the scale; uncles ranked above nephews; and in any case the agreement of Iziaslav acting 'in place of a father' should be binding. Yet for Oleg Chernigov was the 'throne of his father' and

42 *PVL*, I, p. 159.

his own patrimony; in family history uncles did not always have precedence over nephews (witness the fate of Sudislav), and the prince of Kiev was not everybody's father-substitute (witness the princes of Polotsk). In brief, divergent claims were tenable, both on grounds of custom and precedent and within the terms of Iaroslav's Testament. The tension between patrimonial and collateral claims was to become a constant theme in the politics of the expanding dynasty, growing ever more intricate across the generations. The solutions were various. Even among the Sviatoslavichi, although Oleg pressed his case more persistently, the sources are vague as to whether he was older or younger than his more pliant brother David. It is not up to us to pronounce on who was more right, and certainly not to posit the pre-existence of a fixed system on the basis of who happened to emerge the winner.

After a few months of uneasy amity, Iziaslav and Vsevolod moved to marginalize their nephews. In April 1078 Oleg Sviatoslavich fled south 'from Vsevolod' to Tmutorokan. In the summer Oleg's brother Gleb, who had previously been sustained in Novgorod with Vsevolod's support, was driven from the city and killed. Iziaslav's son Sviatopolk was posted to Novgorod in Gleb's place, so that the traditional link between Novgorod and Kiev was restored. In July Vsevolod had Gleb duly buried in the church of the Saviour in Chernigov, but the convenient result, for the uncles, was that the Sviatoslavichi were now either distant or dead.[43]

Now and repeatedly over the next two decades Oleg Sviatoslavich showed that he was not a man who could lightly be marginalized. Rather than brood in isolation beyond the steppes, he recruited support from the Polovtsy, and in the summer of 1078, together with a shadowy accomplice, Boris Viacheslavich, he returned northwards to take Chernigov by force. On 25 August Oleg and the Polovtsy defeated Vsevolod on the river Sozh, just to the east of Pereiaslavl.[44] The way to Chernigov was clear, and Vsevolod fled to Kiev to seek aid from his older brother. Iziaslav complied: not, claims the chronicle, because he desired to gain revenge for the wrongs done him by Sviatoslav, but because he felt impelled to do his fraternal duty under the terms of his father's instructions, to preserve order and guarantee the inviolability of his brother's boundaries.[45] It was to be Iziaslav's last and most ironically self-destructive action. In 1067 he had been ejected from Kiev by disgruntled citizens; in 1073 he had been ejected from Kiev

---

43 Ibid., p. 132; on the date see Berezhkov, *Khronologiia*, p. 228; also Dimnik, *The Dynasty of Chernigov*, pp. 142–7.

44 On Boris Viacheslavich, and this incident in general, see Dimnik, *The Dynasty of Chernigov*, pp. 134–52; on the location see *PVL*, II, p. 412.

45 *PVL*, I, pp. 133–4.

by his younger brothers; finally, on 3 October 1078, doing battle on behalf of one of those brothers against the son of the other, at Nezhatin Meadow near Chernigov, Iziaslav Iaroslavich was killed. He was the first acknowledged prince of Kiev to die a violent death since his great-grandfather Sviatoslav a hundred years before. Indeed, despite the chronicle-fed impression of continual crisis, Iziaslav was the first and only reigning prince of Kiev to be killed in battle against his kin.

The outcome was unexpectedly felicitous for Vsevolod. Despite Iziaslav's death, Oleg Sviatoslavich was defeated; and as a result of Iziaslav's death, Vsevolod found himself the last of the Iaroslavichi. Rather like his father, he eventually gained Kiev by default and survival. Over the years he had waited, probed, modified his stance, seeped into the available crannies of power, backed winners and strategically retreated as appropriate. Twice he had established a tentative foothold in Kiev: at his joint enthronement with Sviatoslav in 1073, and for a few months before Iziaslav's return in 1077. After the battle of Nezhatin Meadow Vsevolod at last 'sat on the throne of his father and of his brother in Kiev, and received the entire domain [*vlast*'] of the Rus'.[46]

In theory Vsevolod might appear to have reinstated 'sole rule'. In practice the distribution of power had become more complicated. Though Vsevolod was the sole surviving direct first-generation heir to Iaroslav, he did not and could not directly inherit all that Iaroslav had possessed. In the time of the 'sole rule' of Vsevolod's father and grandfather, the dynasty was no more than the nuclear family: the prince of Kiev ruled through his sons and appointed agents. Iaroslav had eleven known brothers, but only one of his nephews – Briacheslav of Polotsk – managed to remain on the political map. Iaroslav's descendants were either more fertile, or less successful at excluding the extended family. The result was that in each generation the dynasty became more numerous and politically more intricate. The effects, in their very simplest but already somewhat confusing form, were visible in the reign of Vsevolod.

Vsevolod and his sons (Vladimir Monomakh and the eight-year-old Rostislav) had vacant possession of the Middle Dnieper region: of the inner circle of cities – Kiev, Chernigov and Pereiaslavl – and probably also of Smolensk.[47] Spread around the outer circle were his nephews. Vsevolod was therefore uncomfortably land-locked. His nephews controlled too many of the strategic entrances and exits to trade-routes: Novgorod to the north, Vladimir-in-Volynia to the west, Tmutorokan to the south. In resolving the dilemma Vsevolod remained, as before, a patient opportunist: flexible in the extent to

---

46 Ibid., p. 135.
47 On Rostislav's birth: *PVL*, I, p. 116; on the status of Smolensk: L. V. Alekseev, *Smolenskaia zemlia v IX–XIII vv.* (Moscow, 1980), pp. 194–5.

which, according to circumstances, he was prepared to force change, or to bide his time, or simply to ratify the *status quo*.

Vsevolod's most urgent concern was with the southern Sviatoslavichi, his nephews Roman and Oleg, princes of Tmutorokan and – in their view but not his – Chernigov. Tmutorokan was a flourishing centre of trade and manufacture, and a place where the Rus had traditionally been in close contact with the Byzantines (see above, p. 200). Tmutorokan was a channel for Byzantine exports to the Rus, and there were probably Byzantine craftsmen in the town itself, as well as a nearby Byzantine administrative presence in the Azov region. In Tmutorokan Oleg Sviatoslavich even issued his own coins. Clearly the town was a highly desirable possession.[48]

Vsevolod preferred manipulation to confrontation. He always fought his best fights by proxy. In the summer of 1079, when Roman Sviatoslavich advanced towards Pereiaslavl with a force of Polovtsy, Vsevolod bribed some of the Polovtsy to murder him as they returned across the steppes. Roman was the second of Sviatoslav's sons, after Gleb in the previous year, whose violent death was convenient to Vsevolod. Vsevolod then hired Khazars to kidnap Oleg and ship him off to Constantinople. Thus with judicious use of petty cash two troublesome nephews were removed and Vsevolod gained a profitable *pied-à-mer* in Tmutorokan, where he now installed his own agent. Unfortunately, Vsevolod's neat manoeuvres were frustrated by his messy clan. In 1081 his agent, Ratibor, was thrown out of Tmutorokan by a different pair of predatory princelings: David Igorevich and Volodar Rostislavich, a nephew and great-nephew respectively (see below, pp. 263, 269). And within a couple more years Oleg Sviatoslavich himself reappeared and threw out these new interlopers. The net gain for Vsevolod was nil.[49]

The Byzantine episode in the colourful life of Oleg Sviatoslavich is intriguing but obscure. Apparently he spent two years on the island of Rhodes. Some have suggested that he married an aristocratic Byzantine bride. We do not know whether the Byzantines received him as a favour to himself, or detained him as a favour to Vsevolod, who had family ties with Byzantium through his first wife (see above, p. 215). Nor do we know why he was able to return to Tmutorokan with sufficient resources to oust his cousins. Perhaps Oleg's reversal in fortune was linked to Byzantine internal politics: he was exiled to Constantinople in the brief and turbulent reign of Nikephoros III Botaneiates (1078–81) and released in the reign of his successor Alexios I Komnenos. One may speculate at will, but the result for the Rus is

---

48 On Oleg in Tmutorokan see Dimnik, *The Dynasty of Chernigov*, pp. 162–75.
49 *PVL*, I, p. 135; see A. V. Gadlo, 'K istorii Tmutorokanskogo kniazhestva vo vtoroi polovine XI v.', *Slaviano-russkie drevnosti, I, Istoriko-arkheologicheskoe izuchenie Drevnei Rusi* (Leningrad, 1988), 208–10.

plain: despite Vsevolod's best efforts, the Sviatoslavichi kept their hold on Tmutorokan.[50]

In the north and west a more passive diplomacy paid better dividends in the long term. On succeeding to Kiev, Vsevolod confirmed the allocations of his senior nephews, the sons of Iziaslav: Sviatopolk Iziaslavich kept Novgorod, and Iaropolk Iziaslavich received Vladimir-in-Volynia and probably Turov. By waiting, Vsevolod eventually received Novgorod almost by accident, as a by-product of turbulence in the western lands. The main local participants, besides Iaropolk Iziaslavich, were David Igorevich and Riurik Rostislavich – Vsevolod's nephew and great-nephew from parts of the family which dynastic custom had left on the sidelines. If a prince died before his father or his elder brother, his offspring were usually excluded from the main division of inheritance. This was the convention by which Iziaslav and Vsevolod attempted to exclude Oleg Sviatoslavich. David's father Igor (Vsevolod's younger brother) had died in 1060; Riurik's grandfather Vladimir (Vsevolod's older brother and sometime prince of Novgorod) had died in 1052, too early to be included in Iaroslav's Testament.

In 1085 relations between Vsevolod and Iaropolk had soured, for reasons on which the chroniclers maintain their habitual reticence. Vsevolod sent his son Vladimir Monomakh westwards against Iaropolk, who fled to Poland. Iaropolk's possessions were confiscated, his throne was allocated to David Igorevich, and his wife, his servants and his mother (Iziaslav's widow Gertrude) were taken to Kiev. In the following year,[51] for equally unexplained reasons, Iaropolk came to an agreement with Monomakh, returned to replace David Igorevich in Vladimir-in-Volynia, and was promptly murdered.[52] The chronicler makes a great show of Vsevolod's grief and of the devilish perfidy of the murderer, but once again (for the third time) the mysterious murder of a nephew, apparently by an outside agent, turned out to Vsevolod's advantage. The removal of Iaropolk Iziaslavich gave room for a reshuffling of thrones. Vladimir-in-Volynia was probably given back to David Igorevich; in 1088 Sviatopolk Iziaslavich was moved from Novgorod to his father's old town of Turov, and Novgorod was at last clear for allocation by the prince of Kiev. Vsevolod restored the custom of installing a child as nominal prince of Novgorod: he

---

50 On Oleg in Rhodes see K.-D. Seemann, introd., *Abt Daniil. Wallfahrtsberichte. Nachdruck der Ausgabe von Venevetinov 1883/5* (Slavische Propyläen 36; Munich, 1970), pp. 8–9; on speculation as to marriage see A. P. Kazhdan, 'Rus'-Byzantine princely marriages in the eleventh and twelfth centuries', *HUS* 12/13 (1988/89), 417–18; on Vsevolod's likely remarriage see *PVL*, II, p. 426.

51 Or possibly 1087; *PSRL*, II, cols 197–8; *PSRL*, I, col. 206, with different distribution around a 'blank' year.

52 *PVL*, I, p. 135, implying the complicity of Riurik Rostislavich; cf. p. 185, implying the complicity of Riurik's brother Vasilko.

appointed his twelve-year-old grandson, Mstislav, son of Vladimir Monomakh.[53]

Thus by 1088 several of Vsevolod's most significant nephews were dead, and the rest were reduced to Turov and Tmutorokan. The prince of Kiev had reconstituted a somewhat diminished version of the incomplete 'sole rule' of his father. Like Iaroslav, Vsevolod outlived his father by nearly 40 years; and like Iaroslav he shared power in the inner circle for over half of that period before running out of brothers. Longevity was and would continue to be a great bonus for a prince of the Rus. He who dies last rules longest. Convention and/or ideology favoured the older; demography could tip the balance in favour of the younger.

A eulogist claimed in the chronicle that Vsevolod had been Iaroslav's favourite son.[54] However, on the death of Iaroslav in 1054 Vsevolod might well have felt that he had drawn the short straw. Pereiaslavl was the least enviable of the designated senior possessions, an uncomfortably exposed outpost near the steppe frontier, vulnerable to attack and easily isolated. As prince of Kiev, however, Vsevolod provided the funds to dignify and magnify his original patrimony, to turn Pereiaslavl into what it was supposed to be. In collaboration with the local bishop, a former monk of the Kievan Caves monastery named Efrem, he sponsored an extensive and intensive programme of public building through which Pereiaslavl acquired a physical and visible grandeur commensurate with its political status as the third city of the inner circle. Efrem oversaw the completion of a large and luxuriously decorated church of St Michael, a church of Theodore the Martyr above the gates, a church of St Andrew, and for the first time among the Rus (according to the chronicler) a stone bath-house. Nowhere outside the southern triangle was there such lavish patronage of monumental building in this period.[55] The nephews were demonstrably the poor relations.

Vsevolod, the last of the sons of Iaroslav, died on 13 April 1093 and was buried the following day in St Sophia. As usual the end of a generation signalled a new set of problems. The terms of Iaroslav's Testament had expired. Custom provided guidance, experience had shaped a form of political culture, and moral precepts were available wherever there was a monk to be consulted. But there was no precedent for distribution among the expanded cousinhood, and the

---

53 Mstislav was born c. 1076: see *PVL*, I, p. 159; also *PSRL*, II, col. 190; cf. Rapov, *Kniazheskie vladeniia*, pp. 139–40. Emblematic child-princes were not limited to Novgorod: e.g. *PSRL*, II, col. 535.

54 *PVL*, I, p. 142.

55 Ibid., p. 137. On Efrem see *Uspenskii sbornik*, fol. 35b.31–c.7; Hollingsworth, *Hagiography*, p. 50. On a slightly later Kievan bath-house see Rappoport, *Arkhitektura*, pp. 13–14; also Korinnyi, *Pereiaslavskaia zemlia*, pp. 209–25.

political geography of the lands of the Rus was beginning to acquire new features. Even continuity would require change.

4. THE COLLEGIATE COUSINHOOD?: THE LIUBECH ACCORD AND ITS IMPLICATIONS (1093–1113)

Succession to Kiev was not the problem. On Vsevolod's death his son Vladimir Monomakh 'began to reflect, saying, "If I sit on the throne of my father, then I shall be at war with Sviatopolk [Iziaslavich], for it was previously the throne of his father". And having thus reflected, he sent to Sviatopolk in Turov . . . and on 24 April Sviatopolk arrived in Kiev, and the Kievans went out to greet him and received him with joy, and he sat on the throne of his father and uncle.'[56] It is not absolutely clear from this text whether Vladimir withdrew in principled respect for dynastic precedence, or whether he was more cogently persuaded by a calculation of the costs of a fight. But the action here is more important than the motives. Kiev crossed the generation-gap peacefully and uncontroversially. As had been and would remain the custom. In the dense narratives of internecine strife it is easy to forget that, with very brief interruptions, the succession to Kiev was in fact quite stable, and *almost* consistent in principle, for over 100 years, through eight rulers and three generations, from the agreement between Mstislav and Iaroslav in 1026 right down to the mid-twelfth century. The complications came lower down the scale: to some extent in Chernigov and Pereiaslavl, but especially in the ever-widening and more populous outer circle of family and territory, as the peripheral princes began to branch out from the Middle Dnieper and the old north–south axis into the eminently exploitable lands of the west and the north-east.

We began this chapter at the gathering of the cousins at Liubech in 1097. The Liubech conference determined that Sviatopolk Iziaslavich, the three surviving Sviatoslavichi (David, Oleg and Iaroslav) and Vladimir Vsevolodovich Monomakh should each have their *otchina*, the land of their fathers: in practice, the cities which their respective fathers had been allocated in the Testament of Iaroslav the Wise. Thus Sviatopolk was to keep Kiev, the Sviatoslavichi had Chernigov, and Monomakh had Pereiaslavl. For the inner circle, therefore, Liubech looks like a mirror of Iaroslav's Testament across the generations. For the outer circle the authoritative precedent was different: not *otchina* (or by implication Iaroslav), but the allocations of the late prince Vsevolod.[57] Liubech thus confirms, or imposes, a distinction

56 *PVL*, I, p. 143.
57 Ibid., pp. 170–1.

in status and authority between the inner and outer circles of princes and lands.

Like Iaroslav's Testament, the recorded words of the Liubech agreement are as enigmatic as they are helpful. There is no mention of provision for the future, no explanation of its own terms, no explicit reference to seniority. It is open to interpretation in diverse ways: as a traditional document, or as an innovation; as confirming a system of collateral succession according to a strict hierarchy of seniority, passed down the line of brothers before reverting to the son of the oldest brother, or as subdividing the lands into quasi-autonomous patrimonies; as binding the clan together, or as splitting the cousinhood into separate brotherhoods.[58] Such issues should be less vexing than historians have made them. Like the Testament, Liubech was an arrangement for its time rather than a tract on arrangements in general; a treaty, not a treatise. It was both principled and necessarily improvised, the next stage in adapting custom and precept to changing life. It has loose ends, but it should be assessed not in terms of its theoretical nuances but in relation to the specific problems which it was called to resolve. Why was the Liubech conference held? And to what extent, or in which of its several aims, was it effective?

Let us consider first the inner circle, and return to the reported musings of Vladimir Monomakh in Kiev after the death of his father in April 1093. If the chronicle's account is designed to show a decision of principle rather than expediency, then it is a none-too-subtle piece of retrospective humbug. Vladimir said, '"If I sit on the throne of my father, then I shall be at war with Sviatopolk, for it was previously the throne of his father." And having thus reflected he sent to Sviatopolk in Turov, and he himself went to Chernigov, and [his brother] Rostislav went to Pereiaslavl.' Vladimir was apparently not concerned with the fact that Chernigov had been 'previously the throne' of the father of the Sviatoslavichi. Were there different standards of legitimacy for Kiev and Chernigov, or merely different assessments of the risks? Oleg Sviatoslavich was in Tmutorokan, and his brother David was bought off with the substantial concession of Novgorod.

Vladimir Monomakh's move to Chernigov in 1093, presumably with Sviatopolk's acquiescence, was a rare miscalculation. David Sviatoslavich was passive, but Oleg of Tmutorokan was not so easily mollified. His opportunity came barely a month after Vsevolod's death. On 26 May Monomakh's young brother Rostislav drowned in the river Stugna while retreating from the Polovtsy.[59] Oleg recruited Polovtsian

---

58 E.g. I. Ia. Froianov and A. Iu. Dvornichenko, *Goroda-gosudarstva Drevnei Rusi* (Leningrad, 1988), pp. 90–2; B. A. Rybakov, *Kievskaia Rus' i russkie kniazhestva XII–XIII vv.* (Moscow, 1982), p. 449; George Vernadsky, *Kievan Russia* (New Haven, 1948; repr. 1972), pp. 89–90; Dimnik, *The Dynasty of Chernigov*, 207–23.

59 *PVL*, I, p. 144.

allies, and in 1094 advanced on Chernigov. For eight days the opposing *druzhiny* battled at the ramparts, while the Polovtsy plundered the outlying regions. Finally, as Vladimir later wrote, 'I gave to my cousin the throne of his father, and I myself went to the throne of my father at Pereiaslavl'. On the humiliating journey to the city of his father's throne on 24 July 'we went between the ranks of the Polovtsy, about one hundred of the *druzhina*, and with children and women, and the Polovtsy licked their lips at us like wolves as they stood at the crossing and on the hills'.[60]

The retreat was tactical. In the following year David Sviatoslavich was transferred to Smolensk, Novgorod reverted to Vladimir's son Mstislav (who had been temporarily posted to Rostov), and Oleg was driven out of Chernigov in a combined offensive by Vladimir and Sviatopolk. Their excuse was that Oleg had refused to join them against the Polovtsy; if he was to be a prince of the inner circle he must accept the responsibilities along with the rights. In spite of defeat, Oleg refused either to negotiate or to withdraw his claim. He turned his attention to what he regarded as Chernigov's (and therefore his family's) secondary possessions in the north-east, and there from the summer of 1096 and into 1097 he waged continual war with the sons of Monomakh, one of whom was killed in the fighting at Suzdal.[61] The Liubech conference of 1097 was therefore a response to an escalating and bloody conflict of interests and claims within the clan, not a routine ratification of a standard principle of inheritance.

Although Oleg was repeatedly beaten in the war, he did well in the peace. Monomakh conceded Chernigov as the *otchina* of the Sviatoslavichi. But Oleg was not quite allowed to triumph. The trade-off was that he accepted the moderating presence, in Chernigov, of his more amenable brother David.[62] With regard to the cities and families of the inner circle, the Liubech compromise was an outstanding success. A major crisis was defused, and for the remainder of Sviatopolk's reign in Kiev (1093–1113) there is no evidence of any serious attempt to break the accord.

This was the simple part. Beyond the inner circle, however, the periphery was changing. In the last quarter of the eleventh century there is a noticeable shift in the focus of disputes, a marked intensification of activity away from the north–south axis between Novgorod and Tmutorokan, outwards into the lands of the west and the north-east.

Over the first half of the eleventh century the family had maintained little more than a token presence in the north-east. The towns of Rostov, Suzdal or Murom were very junior postings, difficult to reach

---

60 Ibid., pp. 148, 160–1.
61 Ibid., pp. 149–50, 165, 168.
62 On David's reputation as a peace-maker see the *Slovo o kniaziakh* [= 'Homily on Princes'] in *PLDR XII v.*, pp. 338–42, also below, p. 365.

and sometimes dangerous to hold amid a sparse yet alien population. Their most natural geographic and economic alignment was with Novgorod and the Baltic, not with Kiev. They were split from the south by the unassimilated and unhospitable land of the Viatichi (see below, pp. 366–7), and the safer route was circuitous, higher up the Dnieper via Smolensk. Between 1015 and the late 1080s the *Primary Chronicle* refers to the area only twice, on both occasions stressing trouble with the natives. In 1024 'sorcerers [*volkhvy*] rebelled in Suzdal . . . There was great turmoil and famine throughout that land, and all the people went down the Volga to the Bulgars, and brought food, and thus they revived'. Iaroslav went to quell the 'rebellion'.[63] In the mid-1070s Ian Vyshatich was gathering tribute along the rivers in the Rostov region when he, too, encountered sorcerers who were stirring up the people (see above, p. 229). In the 1070s and 1080s an attempt was even made to found and maintain a bishopric for Rostov and Suzdal, but repeated missions failed and at least one incumbent, Leontii, was reputed to have been murdered by the locals. The post lapsed for over half a century.[64]

These were the wild forest frontiers, where tribute-gathering was by armed gang, where the Bulgars could sometimes offer a more attractive deal than the Rus, where the customs and beliefs of the locals were strange and threatening, and where a churchman might fear for his life. Yet there were profits to be had, and the fur-bearing expanses of the north-east became more and more attractive as the more and more numerous princes of the dynasty were crowded out of the Middle Dnieper. From 1095 to early 1097 Rostov, Suzdal and Murom were scenes of intense fighting between Oleg Sviatoslavich and the sons of Vladimir Monomakh. The dispute was over demarcation. In 1095 Monomakh's son Iziaslav, whose own posting was at Kursk, a strategic town near the southern edge of the land of the Viatichi, took Murom. Oleg Sviatoslavich had maintained an agent (*posadnik*) in Murom, and after his expulsion from Chernigov he retaliated in the north-east, against Rostov and Suzdal. He thereby also provoked Monomakh's older son Mstislav, who had recently (1093–5) been in Rostov between spells as prince of Novgorod.

This was the conflict which led most directly to the Liubech conference of 1097. Liubech brought a cessation of hostilities, and apparently an acceptance by all parties that Oleg had prerogatives in Murom, and that Monomakh's family held Rostov and Suzdal.[65]

63 *PVL*, I, pp. 101–2.
64 See Gail Lenhoff, 'Canonization and princely power in northeast Rus': the cult of Leontij Rostovskij', *Die Welt der Slaven*, N.F. 16 (1992), 359–80.
65 On the conflict see *PVL*, I, p. 150; also Monomakh's letter to Oleg in *PVL*, I, pp. 163–6. It is unlikely that there were clearly zoned spheres of tribute-allocation in the north-east by this period.

The accord appears to have been stable. Liubech therefore helped to provide a consensual political framework for the further development of the north-east.

Unlike the north-east, the fertile western lands between the Carpathians, the Upper Pripet and the Western Bug, well placed for trade and with fairly dense clusters of population, had long since attracted both the Rus and their western neighbours into rivalry, as the Cherven towns had been taken, lost and retaken under Vladimir Sviatoslavich and Iaroslav (see above, pp. 157, 187, 205). In the politics of the princes this was not virgin territory. There had been time for claims and counter-claims to take root and mature. And unlike the north-east, but like Tmutorokan in the 1060s and 1070s, the claimants were not only the senior princes and their sons, but also the offspring of the relatively dispossessed peripheral relatives, sons and grandsons of the sons of Iaroslav the Wise who had died either before their fathers or before their elder brothers, and had thereby fallen or been pushed off the ladder of seniority. In 1054 Vladimir-in-Volynia was apparently held by Sviatoslav (later of Chernigov). One version of Iaroslav's Testament, quite possibly with hindsight, allocates it to Sviatoslav's brother Igor. From 1078 to 1086 it was the seat of a son of Iziaslav. From 1086 it was held by Igor's son David, whose rule was confirmed at the Liubech summit. The smaller thrones of Peremyshl and Terebovl were occupied by descendants of Iaroslav's oldest son Vladimir, who died in 1052. Vladimir Iaroslavich had campaigned with his father to retake the Cherven towns in 1031. Peremyshl and Terebovl were the seats of his grandsons, Iaroslav's great-grandsons, Volodar and Vasilko Rostislavichi.

In the west, instead of compromise and concession, the aftermath of the Liubech summit brought three years of escalating civil war. Besides the local combatants the war at various stages sucked in Poles, Hungarians and Polovtsy, and at one stage threatened even to smash the accord between the senior cousins and so destroy the very foundations of the Liubech conference. The chronicles preserve an exceptionally vivid account of scenes from this conflict, told by an eye-witness.[66]

In 1097, not long after the Liubech summit, Vasilko Rostislavich of Terebovl was arrested and blinded by agents of his older cousins Sviatopolk Iziaslavich of Kiev and David Igorevich of Vladimir-in-Volynia. To hold him still enough to put the knife to his eyes, four of his assailants placed planks across his chest and sat on them 'until his ribs cracked'.[67] The excuse was that, according to David, Vasilko had been plotting against Sviatopolk. David also hinted at Vasilko's complicity in the murder, ten years earlier, of Sviatopolk's brother (see above, p. 263). Vasilko himself later claimed to the narrator that he

---

66 PVL, I, pp. 171–80.
67 Ibid., p. 173.

had no interest in such plots, that all he wanted to do was attack and kill Poles and attack and enslave Bulgarians on the Danube, preferably with the help of forces recruited from the peoples of the steppes.[68] The claim hints plausibly at a clash of policies in the region. For over 40 years the right-bank princes – Sviatopolk and his father Iziaslav – had maintained fair relations with the Poles, whereas in 1092 Vasilko had mounted a raid into Poland with the Polovtsy.[69]

The blinding of Vasilko was shocking in itself, a Byzantine punishment unprecedented among the princes of the Rus (but see above, p. 235). It was also an immediate challenge to the Liubech accord. Monomakh and the Sviatoslavichi had resolved their differences at Liubech; yet now Liubech was being undermined by the man who should be its main guarantor, Sviatopolk, prince of Kiev. In an echo of the action of their fathers in 1073, the newly allied princes of Pereiaslavl and Chernigov marched against Kiev. There was alarm and despair among the townspeople, and moral appeals for unity by the metropolitan, and emotional appeals for peace by Vsevolod's widow. Monomakh and the Sviatoslavichi backed down. In effect they accepted a policy of non-interference, of the regional containment of regional disputes to the left and right of the Dnieper, of separable spheres of interest. Sviatopolk's problems on the western rim of the dynastic and territorial outer circle need not call for intervention. The inner circle held firm, just.

However, the senior cousins did persuade Sviatopolk to ditch his friend David Igorevich, and this led to the escalation and diversification of conflict. Besides Sviatopolk, David and the two Rostislavichi, the list of *dramatis personae* includes: two of Sviatopolk's sons, Mstislav and Iaroslav; two sons of Sviatopolk's murdered brother Iaropolk (Iaroslav and Viacheslav); Sviatosha, son of David Sviatoslavich of Chernigov; Duke Wladislaw of Poland, who took bribes both from Sviatopolk and from David Igorevich; King Kalman of Hungary, who reputedly but implausibly sent an army of 100,000 men to help Sviatopolk; Boniak, a Polovtsian leader whose 300 troops and superior tactics (an ambush following a mock retreat) led to a massacre of the massed Hungarians.

Readers may well be confused, though this is a relatively simple version of what was to become normal politics in the expanded dynasty. Better to tie the threads than to unravel them: the policy of non-intervention had failed, so the senior cousins called another conference. On 30 August 1100 Sviatopolk, Vladimir Monomakh and a brace of Sviatoslavichi (David and Oleg) summoned David Igorevich to appear before them at the southern frontier post of

---

68 Ibid., p. 176.
69 Ibid., p. 141. For a comparable clash of policies involving another maverick junior prince in the western lands, also involving the Polovtsy and links to the Danube, see below, p. 230.

Uvetichi (normally identified at Vitichev). The protocol clearly shows the distinctions of status within the clan. The princes of the inner circle conferred on horseback together with their *druzhiny*, while 'David sat apart, and they did not allow him access to themselves, but they conferred about him separately'.[70] They had authority, David did not: '"We do not wish to give you the throne of Vladimir[-in-Volynia]"', they told him via messengers. But still they settled on compromise rather than punishment. The main prize, Vladimir-in-Volynia, went to Sviatopolk's son Iaroslav. David received a scattering of smaller towns in the west, plus cash compensation of 400 grivnas, the cost to be shared by Monomakh and the Sviatoslavichi.

After the conference at Uvetichi all the towns mentioned in Iaroslav's Testament were back in the hands of the senior cousins. The princes of the left-bank cities, Chernigov and Pereiaslavl, agreed on their respective zones of interest in the north-east, while Sviatopolk secured his right-bank predominance from Kiev through Turov to Vladimir-in-Volynia. Uvetichi affirmed and sharpened the distinction between these princes and their cousins of the outer circle, for here they acted as arbiters and reallocators on their own authority rather than as guarantors of precedent. This was an extension of Liubech, modified by experience, and in its main provisions it was successful. David Igorevich complied and sat on his throne at Dorogobuzh without recorded complaint until his death in 1112. Sviatopolk patched up any damage with Poland, and in 1102 his daughter Sbyslava married Boleslaw III.[71] As an unrelated bonus, in 1101 Vseslav of Polotsk died, and for a few years at least some of his sons joined the southern alliance, the broader community of the clan of Vladimir Sviatoslavich.

The aims of Liubech were not yet fulfilled. Dynastic harmony was perhaps desirable in itself, but it was also a means to an end. The larger and most compelling need, according to the preamble to the Liubech agreement, was to unite in response to the danger from the steppes, which threatened all alike: '"Why do we ruin the land of the Rus, making strife among ourselves, while the Polovtsy pillage our land and rejoice that there is war amongst us?"'

By the late 1080s the various groups of Polovtsy had between them come to dominate the steppes from the Don to the Danube, having destroyed, displaced or subjugated the remnants of the Khazars, Pechenegs and Oghuz. In 1091 a large force of Polovtsy, under their evocatively named leader Maniak, even penetrated Thrace, where at the behest of the emperor Alexios I they smashed the last great host of the Pechenegs who had migrated into the territory of the empire. In Byzantium they gained a reputation for awesome ruthlessness.[72]

---

70 *PVL*, I, p. 181.
71 Ibid., p. 183.
72 Anna Komnene, *Alexiad* VII: iv–v: ed. B. Leib (Paris, 1943), II, pp. 135–44.

In 1092 Polovtsy plundered outposts of the Rus along the Middle Dnieper. In the same year Polovtsy joined Vasilko Rostislavich in his foray into Poland. In 1093 they once more raided up the Dnieper, and for the first time they were confronted by the combined troops of the senior southern princes: Sviatopolk, Vladimir Monomakh and his younger brother Rostislav. The princes were routed, and in the retreat across the river Stugna Rostislav was drowned. In July of the same year Sviatopolk faced the Polovtsy again, and again he was defeated. The Polovtsy sacked Torchesk, a garrison settlement of the Oghuz ('Torks') in the service of the Rus. And in the following year Polovtsy ravaged still further to the north, in the heartlands of the dynasty, taking the side of one prince of the Rus against another, having been induced by their old ally Oleg Sviatoslavich to oust Vladimir Monomakh from Chernigov.[73]

The Polovtsy were parasitic raiders rather than colonists, but their plunderings were unpleasant enough. Armed resistance had proved inadequate, so the senior princes dabbled with diplomacy instead. Sviatopolk married the daughter of Tugorkan, a Polovtsian khan, and in February 1096 Monomakh also entered negotiation. Or he pretended to do so: in fact he had two of their leaders, Itlar and Kytan, killed while they were ostensibly under his protection. This could hardly signal a peace offensive. But if the Polovtsy were to be forcibly denied access to the booty of the Middle Dnieper, then it was imperative for the princes of Kiev and Pereiaslavl to have the support of the prince of Chernigov. Oleg Sviatoslavich, however, continued to cultivate friendly relations with the Polovtsy, just as he had when prince of Tmutorokan. He even gave refuge to the son of the murdered Itlar. For him, as for earlier princes of Chernigov and Tmutorokan, the peoples of the steppes were a useful pool of recruits, and they could also be guarantors of a southern trade-route which bypassed Kiev. The Kievan sources tend to depict the Polovtsy as inherently hostile, but this was more a matter of local perspective than an overall consensus.[74]

Oleg declined to desert his Polovtsian allies and join his cousins. In the view of Sviatopolk and Monomakh, Oleg was endangering them all by refusing to accept the obligations which went with the privilege of being prince of Chernigov. They therefore united against him and drove him from his city. But this in itself was no solution, for while they were fighting against Oleg they left their own possessions exposed, and the Polovtsy poured into the breach. In late May 1096 Tugorkan, Sviatopolk's 'father-in-law and enemy', raided the regions around Pereiaslavl, while Boniak ('godless, mangy, a predator') reached

---

73 *PVL*, I, pp. 141, 143–5, 148; see also above, pp. 266–7.
74 See above, pp. 200–1; below, pp. 326-7.

the outskirts of Kiev itself. Boniak left in flames the princely residence at Berestovo, and he overran and plundered three jewels in Kiev's spiritual crown, the monasteries of Klov, Vydubichi and the Caves, within easy walking distance of the city's ramparts.[75]

In an odd way, however, the tactics of Sviatopolk and Vladimir turned out to be effective. Oleg gained nothing. His efforts in the north-east were poor compensation for the loss of Chernigov. It may be no coincidence that Tmutorokan disappears from the chronicles at about this time, perhaps acquired by the Byzantines in dealings of which we know nothing. At any rate, Oleg forfeited more through the enmity of his cousins than he gained from the friendship of the Polovtsy, who were in any case useless to him in the northern forests. Apparently he realized that he needed Sviatopolk and Monomakh as they needed him, for the tried alternatives had proved near-catastrophic for all parties. By 1097 the princes of the inner circle accepted that there was little choice but to compromise. They were forced back on each other. Hence the urgency of the Liubech summit, its insistence on a common interest, its doctrine of the acceptance of communal decisions.

At first the new alliance was defensive, and it apparently worked well as a deterrent. Boniak found alternative diversion slaughtering Hungarians for David Igorevich. In 1101 the cousins of the inner circle conferred again, by the river Zolotcha near Kiev.[76] They offered the Polovtsy peace, and the offer was formally accepted at a meeting on the southern frontiers at Sakov near Pereiaslavl. A policy formed in desperation had brought stabilization.

Stability allowed a change of strategy towards the Polovtsy, a shift from defence to aggression. The inner circle was intact, the territorial dispute in the north-east had been resolved, the disorder in the west had been contained. In the spring of 1103 Sviatopolk and Vladimir met again to confer; on this occasion by Lake Dolobskoe. The *Primary Chronicle* tells of an earnest debate on the balance of advantage:

And Sviatopolk sat with his *druzhina*, and Vladimir with his, in one tent. And they began to take counsel, and Sviatopolk's *druzhina* said, 'It is not suitable to go now, in spring, for we will ruin the peasants and their ploughing.' And Vladimir said, 'I am surprised, *druzhina*, that you are so concerned to spare the horse with which one ploughs. Why do you not consider this: that if the peasant starts to plough, a Polovtsian may come and shoot him with an arrow and take his horse and ride into the village and take his wife and his children and all that he has? Are you concerned for the horse but not for the peasant himself?' And Sviatopolk's *druzhina* could not answer. And Sviatopolk said, 'Now I am ready.'[77]

75 *PVL*, I, p. 151.
76 Ibid., p. 182.
77 Ibid., p. 183.

The assessment was that the potential cost of inaction was higher than the cost of mobilization for a pre-emptive strike.

Sviatopolk and Vladimir summoned the Sviatoslavichi. Oleg pleaded illness. This time, at least, he did not actively obstruct the plan, and it was sufficient that his brother David participated. The clan gathered at Pereiaslavl: the senior cousins, 'and David Vseslavich, and Igor's grandson Mstislav, and Viacheslav Iaropolkovich, and Iaropolk Vladimirovich; and they set off on horseback and in boats . . .'. The aim was deep penetration, a campaign far into the steppes to weaken the Polovtsy in their own homelands. In the event, both sides in the debate on the economics of war had been too pessimistic. A clutch of Polovtsian princes were killed, and there was plunder in plenty: 'cattle and sheep and horses and camels and tents with their contents and slaves . . .'.[78]

The expedition of 1103 was the first of a series of effective counter-offensives into the steppes, which reached as far as the Polovtsian encampments on the Donets and the Don: in 1109 (led by a certain Dmitr Ivorovich), 1110 (Sviatopolk, Vladimir and David, the senior cousins), 1111 (the same, plus their sons), 1116 (the sons of Monomakh and David Sviatoslavich).[79] The Polovtsy were far from vanquished, and this was far from the end of the story of their relations with the Rus, but by comparison with the near-disasters of the mid-1090s life in the south felt secure. Two of Monomakh's sons, and a son of Oleg Sviatoslavich, were married to Polovtsian princesses.[80] Here also, in helping to secure the steppe frontiers, as in regulating the internal affairs of the dynasty, the Liubech summit of 1097 was a success, at least in the short and medium term.

Besides its decisions, the Liubech summit is important for its procedures. Cooperation was in itself not new, but Liubech reaffirmed the principle of joint regulation in more complex times. Inter-princely conferences are a feature of the period of Sviatopolk's reign in Kiev, in a sequence starting with Liubech: 1097, 1100, 1101, 1103, 1111. Sviatopolk's name appears first in any list, but relations in the inner circle are presented as more collegiate than hierarchical. It is surely significant, for example, that none of the conferences took place within the Kievan citadel, or in any princely building or court. The cousins gathered in Liubech, at Uvetichi, on the Zolotcha, by Lake Dolobskoe.[81] They met on common ground to resolve

---

78 Ibid., p. 185.
79 Ibid., pp. 187, 190–2, 201.
80 Ibid., pp. 187, 197, 202: in 1108 (s.a. 6615, January), 1113, 1117.
81 Liubech was associated with Chernigov; the Zolotcha and Lake Dolobskoe were just outside Kiev: see map 10.

common problems, rather than to be assembled round the throne of a 'sole ruler' or of a senior cousin whom they were to regard 'in place of a father'. There was no ostentatious ceremonial. At Úvetichi in 1100 Vladimir Monomakh started by asking David Igorevich to account for his dissatisfaction: '"You have come here, and now you are sitting on one rug with your brethren [i.e. his cousins]; what is your complaint?"' At Lake Dolobskoe the princes and their *druzhiny* gathered and deliberated in a tent. These meetings were not casual campaign discussions. They had authority, they were reported and recorded, they were effective mechanisms for dynastic self-regulation, for the management of the family firm. One is struck by the lack of a geographical focus, of a permanent prestigious head office. One may also recall the occasion in 980 when Iaropolk Sviatoslavich did enter the hall of his brother Vladimir: he was murdered. Beside the symbolism of meeting on common ground there was prudence in being surrounded by one's *druzhina*.

Not that Sviatopolk or his cousins neglected the prestige of the 'mother of the cities of the Rus'. In the later years of his reign he sponsored the construction of one of the most sumptuous of all Kievan churches: the church of St Michael 'with the golden domes', with its shimmering mosaics and gilded cupolas.[82] And we should not forget that the *Primary Chronicle* itself was conceived and compiled by Kievan monks substantially in and just after the reign of Sviatopolk. The status, honour and wealth of the centre were not in doubt (see below, pp. 279–82). Indeed, the titular metropolitanates of Chernigov and Pereiaslavl probably reverted to ordinary bishoprics during this period. Spiritual and material culture radiated outwards from Kiev, but the political culture which matured in the time of Sviatopolk placed more stress on the cohesion and mutual responsibility of the inner circle of the dynasty than on the pre-eminent authority of the ruler of Kiev.

The idea of an emerging political culture is more appropriate to the times than that of a fixed political system. There were constant features: the exclusive legitimacy of the dynasty; divided or shared inheritance; the importance of seniority. But as the family grew and as the political and human geography became more intricate, so custom could provide guidelines but not solutions. There were too many variables: the primacy of Kiev versus the inviolability of a brother's share; reallocation versus *otchina*, and the effect of reallocation on subsequent claims to *otchina* across generations, especially in the outer circle; the place of the sons of sons who pre-deceased fathers or older brothers. In many cases precedents were either non-existent or multiple, to be set rather than followed, and to be justified with retrospective logic. The inner circle could accommodate rule by one person, or two, or three, without ideological implications.

---

82 V. N. Lazarev, *Mikhailovskie mozaiki* (Moscow, 1966).

Pragmatic opportunism made the actual arrangements more flexible than chroniclers liked to reveal. Seniority was politically manipulable; it was not a mechanical extrapolation from a family tree. No moralizing chronicler dwells on the seniority of Iaroslav's brother Sudislav after Iaroslav's death; or on the apparent fluctuations in the order of preference between Oleg Sviatoslavich and his brother David; or on why Vladimir Monomakh appears above Oleg Sviatoslavich in lists of the cousins from the 1090s and 1100s despite the fact that Vladimir acknowledged Oleg's claim to Chernigov, and despite the fact that Vladimir's succession to Kiev after Sviatopolk's death is pointedly not attributed to seniority.[83]

It is easy to underestimate the reign of Sviatopolk Iziaslavich. He is often obscured in the long shadow cast by the more glamorous heroes of epic, ecclesiastical, imperial and nationalist legend: Vladimir Sviatoslavich for the conversion to Christianity, Iaroslav for his glorious city and for refounding the dynasty; Vladimir Monomakh for his military energies and for his self-promoting patronage and writings. Sviatopolk personally did not have a good press even in the earliest sources, whose attitude towards him tends to have been adopted uncritically by subsequent commentators. However, one should look beyond the prejudices of writers loyal to Vladimir Monomakh whose patronage and whose progeny shunted the family and the name of Sviatopolk to the sidelines of dynastic history.[84]

The impact and influence of Sviatopolk's twenty-year reign was profound. The late eleventh and early twelfth centuries saw the emergence among the Rus of a political culture which quickly came to be treated as the definitive model. When the Rus looked back for a set of guiding principles and practices conducive to good order, security and prosperity, they rarely recycled the formulae of 'sole rule'. Instead in their political discourse they tended to stress collective action, communal care for the lands, a unity in the extended kin, mutual obligations sanctified by kissing the Cross: ideas which were formulated vaguely in the Testament of Iaroslav, sharpened in the cult of Boris and Gleb, developed through the *Primary Chronicle*, demonstrated at the Liubech summit in 1097, and maintained through the series of conferences and joint enterprises in the ensuing years. More revealing than a list of heroes is a list of villains: Sviatopolk Vladimirovich 'the Cursed', Vseslav 'the Wolf' (or 'the Sorcerer') of Polotsk, Oleg

---

83 Seemann, ed., *Abt Daniil*, pp. 140; cf. the rather fixed notion of precedence in V. L. Ianin, 'Mezhdukniazheskie otnosheniia v epokhu Monomakha i "Khozhdenie igumena Daniila"', *TODRL* 16 (1960), 112–31; see also Dimnik, *The Dynasty of Chernigov*, pp. 213–17.

84 On criticism of Sviatopolk see below, p. 286; often accepted uncritically: e.g. Vernadsky, *Kievan Russia*, pp. 92–4; P. P. Tolochko, *Drevniaia Rus'. Ocherki sotsial'no-politicheskoi istorii* (Kiev, 1987), pp. 99–100.

Sviatoslavich 'Son of Woe' – villains not because they opposed great men, or even (with the possible exception of Sviatopolk Vladimirovich) because they did great evil; villains because they were perceived to have violated the basis of political order, the political identity of the lands of the Rus, the unity of the brethren.

Here was the root of a persistent fallacy. The Liubech summit was impressively effective. It provided a framework for peace among the inner circle of princes in the Middle Dnieper region, and for the settlement of disputes among princes of the expanding outer circle to the west and north-east; it enabled the southern rulers to reverse their defeats at the hands of the Polovtsy and to secure the steppe frontiers; it consolidated the synthesis of dynastic custom, tactical improvization and Christian sanction. Yet Liubech, like Iaroslav's Testament, was a response to the moment, not a dynastic 'constitution'. It was a way of coping, an exercise in containment, but even in the moderately enlarged dynasty it was hard to sustain as a form of comprehensive oversight. Though there may have been a continuing interest in community, there was not necessarily a continuing community of interests.

A political narrative of the late eleventh century can seem tortuously complicated, but it is a model of simplicity by comparison with what might follow, if one were to pursue all the strands in equivalent detail. Happily there is no need to repeat the exercise. Changes are more interesting than repetitions, and other themes are more pressing. Certain norms of political culture had been established, and aspects of the narratives in this chapter can therefore be taken as generic. Over the twelfth century the dynasty became vastly more diverse and diffuse, and in larger and smaller scale the various branches of the family replicated and adapted among themselves the basic patterns of interaction which emerged among the sons and grandsons of Iaroslav.

On a different reading, all that we have surveyed is superficial: just family tiffs among a handful of warlords with pretensions, parochial tales of a tiny elite. The dynasty did not find its solutions in a social vacuum, with no constraints outside its own codes and churchmen's warnings. How extensive, or restricted, was princely 'rule'? What social space did the prince fill? What other groups of people were there, and what did they do or think or make or buy? To what extent did they and the prince impinge on one another? If the political culture of the rulers is to have substance it must be considered in a larger social, economic and cultural context.

CHAPTER EIGHT

The Prince and the City
(c. 1070–c. 1120)

Sviatopolk died on 16 April 1113. On the following day, according to the *Primary Chronicle*, the Kievans conferred amongst themselves and sent to Vladimir Monomakh saying: '"Come, prince, to the throne of your father and grandfather."' In his grief, Vladimir hesitated, whereupon a riot broke out in the city: 'the Kievans plundered the compound of Putiata the *tysiatskii*, and attacked the Jews and plundered them. And again the Kievans sent to Vladimir, saying: "Come, prince, to Kiev. If you do not come, know that much evil will be stirred: not only the plundering of Putiata's compound [*dior*], and of the *sotskie* or of the Jews, but they will attack your sister-in-law and the boiars and the monasteries; and you, prince, will be responsible that they plunder the monasteries."' Vladimir succumbed to these urgings, and was duly received 'with great honour' by the metropolitan and 'all the Kievans'. And thus he 'sat on the throne of his father and of his grandfathers, and all the people were glad, and the turbulence subsided'.[1]

Most of the elements in this tale look traditional enough. We have seen urban violence before; and we have also seen how the assent of the townspeople, whether given freely or under duress, could be a component of princely legitimacy: a new prince ruled both by inheritance from his 'father and grandfathers', and through being 'received' by the townspeople (see above, p. 196). As recently as 1102 the chronicle tells an analogous story about how the Novgorodians insisted on retaining Monomakh's own son Mstislav as their prince, instead of a candidate from Sviatopolk's family appointed from Kiev.[2] These stories of popular urban support were perhaps embellished by a chronicler favourable to Monomakh and his son, but their value is in no way diminished by possible bias: on the contrary, it may be especially significant that the chronicler chose to stress urban assent as an important factor in justifying a given prince's rule, rather than dynastic succession alone. In dynastic convention

---

1 *PVL*, I, pp. 196–7; cf. the *Tale* of Boris and Gleb: Abramovich/Müller, *Erzählungen*, p. 64; Hollingsworth, *Hagiography*, p. 132.
2 *PVL*, I, p. 182.

ambiguity was almost the norm: in 1113 both Monomakh and the Sviatoslavichi could have produced plausible excuses for claiming Kiev.[3] In the twelfth century stories of urban unrest, of invitations, negotiations with the townspeople, and of settling old scores with the dead prince's servitors, are commonplace components of the chronicles (e.g. see below, pp. 347–8). Urban assent was, after all, at the core of the dynastic myth itself, as recorded in the chronicle, in the tale of the summoning of Riurik to Novgorod.

Yet the tale of the civil unrest of April 1113 is unusually specific, among those encountered hitherto, in its listing of urban personalities and groups: the 'Kievans' attack or threaten Putiata the *tysiatskii*; the Jews; the *sotskie*; the boiars; the monasteries; even Monomakh's sister-in-law. It seems a more complex city than the one in which we last paused at the start of Iaroslav's reign. How had the city's human geography changed, and how did such changes affect the city's relations with its rulers?

1. THE MONEYMEN

The late eleventh and early twelfth centuries were boom years for the Kievan economy, both in itself and relative to the other cities of the Rus. Kiev had the most numerous and the most opulent public monuments, the most sophisticated and fastest growing urban crafts, strong local markets, a monopoly over significant areas of internal trade, as well as a flourishing international and transit trade. It also had the most successfully articulate educated elite, who set fashions both for provincial contemporaries and for posterity.

The most visible signs of Kievan surplus wealth were its public buildings, as princes continued to pour their largesse into masonry to the glory of God and themselves. Sviatoslav contributed to the church of the Dormition of the Mother of God at the Caves monastery (1073), Vsevolod to the church of St Michael at the Vydubichi monastery, Sviatopolk to the church of the Mother of God at the Klov monastery and, most spectacularly, to the 'golden-domed' church of the archangel Michael, whose mosaics almost matched those of St Sophia.[4] Kiev was the acknowledged focus: Iaropolk Iziaslavich, though not based in Kiev, nevertheless paid for the church of St Peter in the Kievan monastery of St Demetrios. Visible spiritual patronage extended to the princely outposts around Kiev: at Berestovo the church of the Saviour,

---

3 On the ambiguities in 1113 see Martin Dimnik, *The Dynasty of Chernigov 1054–1146* (Texts and Studies 116, Pontifical Institute of Mediaeval Studies; Toronto, 1994), pp. 267–72.

4 On smaller churches see P. A. Rappoport, *Russkaia arkhitektura X–XIII vv.* (ASSSR SAI, vyp. E1–47; Leningrad, 1982), nos 15, 22, 23, 29.

and at Vyshgorod a large new stone church to house the relics of Boris and Gleb, endowed by Oleg Sviatoslavich. Nowhere else was there such a conspicuous and continual proliferation of prestigious architecture. Indeed, it is not certain that *any* further major new masonry churches were built during the second half of the eleventh century in Novgorod, Chernigov or Polotsk.[5] The only significant exception seems to have been the bishop Efrem's programme to beautify Pereiaslavl (see above, p. 264).

Where did the money come from? Much of it doubtless came from traditional sources – tribute and booty. But new wealth was also being created, wealth which the rulers were keen to tap. And where there was new wealth, there were the new wealthy treading on the sensibilities of the old. The result was a gradual change in the economic, social and cultural geography of the city, both within itself and in relation to its prince.

Over the eleventh century, stimulated in part by princely patronage itself, there was a notable growth in Kievan craft production. Of the craft workshops discovered in Kiev, those which started production in the eleventh century are twice as numerous as those which started production in the tenth century.[6] At the luxury end of the market, imported skills and technologies took root locally. The Byzantine mosaicists and painters who worked on St Sophia, and on the church of the Dormition at the Caves, helped the Kievans to develop the capabilities for themselves. The *Paterik* of the Caves monastery tells of the painter Alimpii, who learned his art from the 'Greeks' in Kiev.[7] The eleventh century saw the beginning of a local glass industry, where previously glass had been imported from Byzantium and the Near East. By mid-century the Kievans were manufacturing their own glass beads and rings and window glass. They also started to produce glazed pottery: glazed vessels, ceramic tiles, *pisanki* (miniature 'eggs' of painted and glazed clay) and probably enamelware. From the 1120s they turned out large quantities of glass bracelets.[8] Jewellers worked with amber, bronze, silver and gold, acquiring the techniques of niello and filigree. For the discerning secular client they made bracelets, ear-rings, necklaces and pendants, while for the spiritually minded,

---

5 See Volodymyr I. Mezentsev, 'The masonry churches of medieval Chernihiv', *HUS* 11 (1987), 372; on possible small structures see V. P. Kovalenko and P. A. Rappoport, 'Etapy razvitiia drevnerusskoi arkhitektury Chernigovo-Severskoi zemli', *RM* 7.i (1992), 39–59; also A. I. Komech, *Drevnerusskoe zodchestvo kontsa X–nachala XII v.: vizantiiskoe nasledie i stanovlenie samostoiatel'noi traditsii* (Moscow, 1987), pp. 233–97.

6 P. P. Tolochko, *Drevnii Kiev* (Kiev, 1983), p. 139; T. S. Noonan, 'The flourishing of Kiev's international and domestic trade, ca. 1100–ca. 1240', in I. S. Koropeckyj, ed., *Ukrainian Economic History. Interpretive Essays* (Cambridge, Mass., 1991), pp. 108–9.

7 Abramovich/Tschiżewskij, *Paterikon*, pp. 192–9; Heppell, *Paterik*, pp. 172–9.

8 Iu. L. Shchapova, *Steklo Kievskoi Rusi* (Moscow, 1972).

and for the expanding ecclesiastical market, there were bronze pectoral crosses, icon-lamps and chalices.

Most such craftsmen probably still worked to order in the residential compounds (*dvory*) of the urban elite, both secular and spiritual. But there are signs that their markets were not only expanding but also diversifying. Thus Kievan potters refined and extended their repertoire of clay vessels: bowls, scoops, pitchers, mugs and small amphorae alongside the traditional pots; and they also simplified their methods so as to turn out lower-quality products (thinner, more brittle) in larger quantities. There was a similar change in the techniques of metalware production in the twelfth century. This is usually taken to indicate the development of more 'open' markets.[9]

The growth in Kievan craft production cannot be accounted for by growth in local demand alone. Kiev was dominant in internal trade. In a survey of glassware found at over 30 sites as far apart as Beloozero, Suzdal and Drutsk, a substantial majority of all finds turn out to be of Kievan manufacture.[10] Indigenous glass-making was in any case a Kievan monopoly until the early or mid-twelfth century, when glass workshops began to appear in other cities. But even when glass beads and bracelets were already being made elsewhere, Kiev still monopolized the production of glass vessels and of window glass, and Kievan 'everyday' grey glazed pottery was ubiquitous.[11] Brass pectoral crosses, too, seem to have been made exclusively in Kiev. Inlaid enamel, also a technique borrowed from Byzantium, was at first a Kievan speciality, though it is possible that some of the later specimens were made elsewhere. Almost all major excavations in Rus unearth large quantities of pink slate spindle-whorls: the slate was from Ovruch, but at least a proportion of it was taken to Kiev before being turned into spindle-whorls.[12]

Besides its own produce, Kiev distributed goods from abroad. Just as in the tenth century, Kiev was the main depot and transit-point for trade between the Rus and Byzantium and the Black Sea. Fragments of Byzantine amphorae – remnants of trade in wine and olive oil – have been found in substantial quantities not only around the Middle Dnieper but at dozens of sites in western and northern Rus. Such traffic was of course traditional, but in volume it expanded rapidly in the eleventh century.

The grand monuments were mostly concentrated in the upper town and in the cluster of monasteries on the southern outskirts, but the

9 P. P. Tolochko, *Drevnerusskii feodal'nyi gorod* (Kiev, 1989), pp. 108–15; B. A. Kolchin, 'Remeslo', in idem, ed., *Drevniaia Rus'. Gorod, zamok, selo* (Moscow, 1985), pp. 243–97.

10 Noonan, 'The flourishing of Kiev's trade', pp. 123–5.

11 T. I. Makarova, *Polivnaia posuda. Iz istorii keramicheskogo importa i proizvodstva Drevnei Rus* (ASSSR SAI, vyp. E1–38; Moscow, 1967).

12 Noonan, 'The flourishing of Kiev's trade', pp. 132–4.

lower town, the Podol, was an important generator of the new wealth. It is hard to gauge precisely the rate of settlement and expansion in the Podol, but at least by the early decades of the twelfth century it had the appropriate signs of solidity. Defensive fortifications are mentioned in a chronicle entry for 1161, though some scholars argue that they had been constructed as early as the third quarter of the eleventh century.[13] The first recorded masonry church in the Podol is that of the 'Pirogoshcha' Mother of God (1131–5), which overlooked the main market and housed a miraculous icon from Constantinople, but this church seems to have been built over the foundations of an earlier masonry church.[14] Brick and stone were statements of affluence and permanence, but Kiev remained largely a city of wood, impressive in quantity even if not in durability: the chronicles record a massive fire which raged 'in the Podol and on the Hill' for two days, on 23–24 June 1124, and which is said to have destroyed around 600 churches.[15] Wood was quickly replaceable, and the city could absorb such disasters. The number 600 is unverifiable, but one can accept it at least in the general meaning of 'a lot'. Modern estimates for the total population of Kiev range from around 20,000 to around 100,000. A figure towards the lower end of this scale is most plausible, and would still leave Kiev among the larger European cities of the time.[16]

For direct insights into this world of mounting urban prosperity we have to travel to Novgorod, where year after year the sodden mud yields ever more specimens of the most celebrated finds in modern Russian archaeology. Visually these objects are unglamorous: little scraps of curled-up birch-bark. Their remarkable feature, wholly unsuspected until the first discoveries in 1951, is that they bear scratched written messages. It turns out that increasing numbers of the urban rich were literate, and that they applied their literacy in the ordinary conduct of their business. This mundane vernacular literacy is far removed from the Church Slavonic of the traditional written sources on parchment, and far more varied than the formulaic vernacular of legal codes, though its chronology matches and confirms the chronology of virtually all other specimens of writing from pre-Mongol Rus: there is next to nothing from before the mid-eleventh century, a growing trickle after c. 1050, swelling to a fair stream through the twelfth century. After the barrenness of the age of Vladimir and the ambiguities and conjectures of the age of Iaroslav, urban writing – real writing, writing which survives – seems to

---

13 *PSRL*, II, col. 515; see above, 209, n. 3.

14 See K. N. Gupalo, *Podol v drevnem Kieve* (Kiev, 1982), pp. 111–25.

15 *PSRL*, I, col. 293; cf. Thietmar's figure of 400: Holtzmann, ed., *Die Chronik*, p. 528.

16 Volodymyr I. Mezentsev, 'The territorial and demographic development of Kiev and other major cities of Rus': a comparative analysis based on recent archaeological research', *The Russian Review* 48 (1989), 145–70; Tolochko, *Drevnii Kiev*, pp. 182–92.

proliferate almost wherever one looks, on the most varied types of object and in a wide range of techniques: scratched graffiti on the walls of churches; incised names on pink slate spindle-whorls; stamped legends on the seals of princes, churchmen and functionaries; texts on mosaics and frescoes; craftsmen's inscriptions on luxury objects; even the earliest extant dated parchment manuscript from Rus fits the pattern – a gospel lectionary (readings arranged for the liturgy) written in 1056–7 for Ostromir, governor (*posadnik*) of Novgorod. This was not yet a literate society in the modern sense, but among the urban elites varied uses of writing were becoming commonplace, almost habitual.[17]

The birch-bark documents happen to be found mainly in Novgorod, because Novgorodian conditions are particularly favourable for medieval archaeology (post-medieval urban decline, hence not much over-building; water-saturated ground which preserves organic matter). But the general implications of the birch-bark documents can be extended to other cities and *a fortiori* to Kiev. A few inscribed birch-bark fragments have also been found in Smolensk, Staraia Russa and other northern settlements. Moreover, several of the Novgorodian letters show that the horizons of the senders and recipients were far broader than the location of the finds. In the early twelfth century, for example, a certain Giurgii writes to his parents, 'sell the house and come here to Smolensk, or to Kiev; bread is cheap':[18] a nice reminder that, besides manufactured and imported goods, the south supplied the north with grain; hence the comparatively high price of bread in Novgorod. At the turn of the twelfth century Semok writes to Kulotka: 'as to what you said to Nesda about the *veveritsy* [a unit of money]: when you came to Rus [here = the south, the Middle Dnieper region] with Lazovk, he (Lazovk) took them from me in Pereiaslavl'. An anonymous sender reminds Miliata of their agreement reached in Kiev, where 'God was our witness', that Miliata should hand over nine pieces of luxury cloth.[19] The specimens of birch-bark literacy are found mainly in Novgorod, but the world of the birch-bark *literati* was broader, extending throughout the cities of the lands of the Rus.

In the birch-bark documents from the pre-Mongol period the most common single topic is money. The senders ask for payment, haggle about payment, dispatch payments and compare payments. A particularly frequent type of document is a plain list of dues, or of debtors. For example:

In Russa Boian [owes] one grivna, and Zhitobud the capital sum of one grivna and thirteen kunas. On the Luga Negorad [owes] one grivna and three kunas

---

17 See S. Franklin, 'Literacy and documentation in early medieval Russia', *Speculum* 60 (1985), 1–38.
18 *NGB*, no. 424; see also in *NGB* VIII, pp. 206–7.
19 *NGB*, nos 105, 675 (Proper names as in *NGB* VIII, pp. 205–306).

with interest; Dobrovit and his people – one grivna and thirteen kunas. On the Prozhnevitsa half a grivna from Nezhko, from Sirom a grivna less two nogata. On the Shelon ten kunas from Dobromysl, two grivnas in small sums from Zhivotko. On the [Lake] Seliger five grivnas less one kuna from Khmun and Drozd; six grivnas and nine kunas from Azgut and those of Pogost. In Dubrovno two grivnas and nineteen kunas from Khripan.

This is one of the very earliest of all the birch-bark documents, from the mid- to late eleventh century. It can stand for many others on the subject of monetary debt.[20]

Talk of money should not be confused with talk of coinage. The sums so punctiliously calculated by the Novgorodian creditors or in the expanding *Russkaia Pravda* – the grivnas and the kunas and the veveritsas and the nogatas and the rezanas – should not be visualized as loose change jangling in the merchant's purse. They were units of value, related to a silver-standard, but realizable in many forms. It is a paradox that at the turn of the twelfth century, as the economy flourished and financial activity apparently thrived, the supply and use of actual coins virtually ceased. This was the start of what is sometimes known as the 'coinless' period in the economy of Rus. The Rus had in any case never produced a regular functional coinage of their own, for they had no native supply of silver. And now the flow of imported coins dried up. Dirhams had long been rarities; West European *denarii*, which had circulated mainly in the north, stopped appearing in Rus from the early twelfth century, while Byzantine coins turn up sporadically until around 1130.[21] But the absence of coinage does not indicate the end of prosperity or a decrease in metallic wealth. Silver was melted down and recast into ingots (silver grivnas). Such ingots survive in very large quantities. They could be used in high-value transactions, and might thus in a sense be regarded as a kind of high-denomination coinage, but routine payment and exchange was conducted without metal.

The variety of exchange-objects is indicated even in the vocabulary. *Grivna* did mean a metallic weight, but *veksha*, *veveritsa* and *kuna* were originally types of fur (squirrel and marten-skins). Though furs certainly were used as currency, the words also came to denote values relative to each other, rather than specific objects. Thus 1 grivna =

---

20 Ibid., no. 526; see commentary in *NGB* VIII, p. 212 and IX, p. 176; cf. *NGB*, nos 84, 119, 120, 231, 235, 238, 246, 336, 421, 525, 613, 630, 631, 673, as well as those from Staraia Russa nos 5, 12–23, and from Pskov, no. 3: all from the mid-twelfth century or earlier.

21 T. S. Noonan, 'The monetary history of Kiev in the pre-Mongol period', *HUS* 11 (1987), 384–443; but note a report of a few late-twelfth-century Byzantine coins apparently found in 1986: V. N. Zotsenko, 'Vizantiiskaia moneta v srednem Podneprov'e', in P. P. Tolochuko, ed., *Iuzhnaia Rus' i Vizantiia. Sbornik nauchnykh trudov (k XVIII kongressu vizantinistov)* (Kiev, 1991), pp. 57–78.

20 nogatas = 25 (or from the early twelfth century 50) kunas = 50 rezanas = 150 veveritsas. To confuse matters, there was some variation – geographical and temporal – in the weight of silver ingots. The majority of Kievan ingots weigh around 155–165g, probably related to the Byzantine half-litron of c. 164g. Yet the 'grivna of silver' in legal texts is more likely to refer to the 'northern' (or 'heavy') grivna: the heavier ingots weigh around 196–205g, and are probably related to the half-pound (c. 205g). In the twelfth century the 'new grivna' (or 'grivna of kunas', or 'new kunas') was equivalent to one quarter of a 'grivna of silver': i.e. equivalent to around 51g of silver. Besides metal and furs, many different kinds of object could function as currency. It was useful if such objects could be durable, transportable and replicable. Glass beads may have served the purpose, and conceivably the slate spindle-whorls.[22]

The Novgorodian creditors had long memories: 'From Zhirovit to Stoian. It is over eight years since you swore to me on the Cross, yet you do not send me the *veveritsy*. . .'.[23] Doubtless the spread of literacy helped to keep the memory sharp. Delay was no escape, an inability to pay was no excuse, and the Cross – here recorded for the first time in native financial as well as political dealings – was not the only guarantor. If the debtor lacked the means, then a guarantor was obliged, by force if necessary, to square the account. Zhirovit continues: 'If you do not send me 4½ grivnas, I shall confiscate your debt from a distinguished Novgorodian'. Not surprisingly, such methods could lead to further disputes: 'From Sudisha to Nazhir: Zhadko sent two officials, and they plundered me for my brother's debt. But I am not Zhadko's guarantor for my brother. Stop him from setting the officers on me.'[24]

Which brings us back to Vladimir Monomakh and the urban unrest of 1113. The dissatisfaction of the Kievans was not entirely new or spontaneous. Economic success was socially and politically ambivalent. It brought obvious benefits, but it could also lead to tension, both within the city and in the relations between sections of the townspeople and their rulers. On the one hand, financial strains within the city increased the scope for princely intervention; but on the other hand, princely intervention had a price. For some while prior to 1113 there are signs of periodic friction on economic grounds. In 1069, after the 'Vseslav affair', the chronicle hints that Iziaslav tried to impose closer supervision on market activities.[25] In the early 1090s Vsevolod's 'young'

22 V. L. Ianin, *Denezhno-vesovye sistemy russkogo srednevekov'ia. Domongol'skii period* (Moscow, 1956), pp. 42–56, 187–8; Noonan, 'The monetary history of Kiev', 429–39.
23 *NGB*, no. 246, from the eleventh century.
24 Ibid., no. 235; on the date see *NGB* IX, p. 144.
25 'He drove the market up onto the [Starokievskaia] Hill': *PVL*, I, p. 116; see M. N. Tikhomirov, *The Towns of Ancient Rus* (Moscow, 1959), pp. 199–200.

servitors 'began to plunder . . . the old' by imposing taxes and fines, allegedly (according to the favourable chronicler) without Vsevolod's knowledge, such that the land was being ruined not only by wars but also by financial impositions. Towards the turn of the century Sviatopolk 'destroyed the houses of the powerful and took away many people's goods'.[26] One man's arbitrary confiscation is another man's prudent taxation, just as one man's wealth-creation is another man's exploitation. In siphoning off some of the new wealth for himself, the prince developed new means (taxation and fines, market regulation) and trod on old toes. An anecdote in the *Paterik* of the Caves monastery perhaps reveals Sviatopolk's financial sympathies. In 1097, during the disputes which followed the blinding of Vasilko, the normal supply of salt from Galich and Peremyshl was apparently disrupted. Sviatopolk supported the merchants who tried to profit from the ensuing shortage. His scheme was foiled only by a miracle-working monk of the Caves, a certain Prokhor, who continued to create salt out of ash and thus forced the merchants to slash their exorbitant prices by 80 per cent.[27]

The prince had never been able to take the townspeople absolutely for granted, and one assumes that there had always been a link between the loyalty of their 'hearts' and the fullness of their pockets. But this cluster of references suggests a gradual shift of emphasis, whose implications become clearer in the events of 1113 and their aftermath.

The first objects of the Kievans' anger in 1113 are listed as: Putiata the *tysiatskii*, and the Jews. The *tysiatskii* (lit. 'thousander', 'chiliarch') was the prince's man with responsibility over the city.[28] The *sotskie* (lit. 'hundreders', 'centurions') were lower-ranking functionaries. It is worth noting that in 1068 the Kievans' first target had similarly been the prince's senior man (the *voevoda* Kosniatin). The coupling of the *tysiatskii* and the *sotskie* with the Jews suggests that there was perceived to be an alliance between the prince's own staff and certain types of money-making.[29] The expanded version of *Russkaia Pravda* (EP) records that 'after Sviatopolk, Vladimir Vsevolodovich [Monomakh] summoned his *druzhina* at Berestovo: Ratibor the *tysiatskii* of Kiev [who had presumably replaced Sviatopolk's man Putiata], Prokopia the *tysiatskii* of Belgorod, Stanislav the *tysiatskii* of Pereiaslavl, Nazhir, Miroslav, and Oleg [Sviatoslavich]'s man Ivanok Chudinovich'. The

---

26 PVL, I, p. 142; Abramovich/Tschiżewskij, *Paterikon*, p. 149; Heppell, *Paterik*, p. 169.
27 Abramovich/Tschiżewskij, *Paterikon*, p. 152; Heppell, *Paterik*, p. 172; see also below, p. 327.
28 See Tolochko, *Drevnerusskii feodal'nyi gorod*, pp. 206–31; also U. Halbach, *Der russische Fürstenhof vor dem 16. Jahrhundert: eine vergleichende Untersuchung zur politischen Lexikologie und Verfassungsgeschichte der alten Rus'* (Quellen und Studien zur Geschichte des östlichen Europa 23; Stuttgart, 1985), pp. 162–4.
29 On studies of Jews in Kiev see the survey by L. Chekin, 'The role of Jews in early Russian civilization in the light of a new discovery and new controversies', *Russian History* 17 (1990), 379–94.

result of this conference was a ruling which placed a limit on the collection of interest on debts: if money was lent 'at a third', then the creditor could collect the interest twice while still retaining a claim on the capital sum; but if the interest was collected three times, then the debt was cancelled. Interest 'at a third' is variously glossed as meaning 50 per cent or 33 per cent. Whether or not the Church actively disapproved of usury, references in several birch-bark letters make it clear that lending at interest was common and accepted practice, and that interest 'at a third' was a standard annual rate.[30]

This is the only article in EP which is explicitly ascribed to Monomakh, but it is part of a larger pattern. Where the eleventh-century short *Pravda* (SP) had dealt mainly with physical injury and with the protection of the prince's own men, twelfth-century provisions, in EP, suggest a growing concern for the orderly management of disputes over money and property. A cluster of articles deals with interest rates and loan procedures.[31] For example, Article 52, which some attribute to Sviatopolk, specifies that for an agreement on a loan of up to three grivnas an oath is sufficient guarantee, but that a larger loan is not binding unless witnessed. Article 55 gives the order of preferential claims on the assets of a bankrupt debtor: first claim lies with merchants from another town or land, and the residue (including the proceeds from selling the man into slavery) is to be divided among local creditors, minus whatever may be owing to the prince. Another series of articles relates to inheritance, and there is quite a large section on slavery. The perils of financial dependency are shown in a set of rulings on the treatment of *zakupy*, hired or indebted labourers. Unlike a slave, a *zakup* was an acceptable witness in litigation ('in small cases, if essential'). Unlike the slave, the *zakup* was entitled to the same compensation as a free man if his lord beat him 'without thinking, when drunk, without cause' (though not if he was beaten 'for good reason'). One imagines this might have been a tricky distinction in practice; better, by and large, to be a lender than to be a borrower.[32]

What, then, was the social background to the tensions of 1113? The *Primary Chronicle* labels the aggrieved citizens merely as 'the Kievans'. The *Tale* of Boris and Gleb has a slightly different nuance: the plea to Monomakh was supported by 'all the people', but they were led by 'the powerful'. Modern historians vary the emphasis

---

30 EP, Article 53: *ZDR*, pp. 67–8; Kaiser, *The Laws*, p. 26; *NGB*, nos 75, 170, 332; Smolensk, no. 12: see *NGB* IX, pp. 154–5; also EP, Article 51; cf. Sreznevskii, *Materialy*, III, col. 992, for later examples.
31 EP, Articles 47–8, 50–3, 55: *ZDR*, pp. 67–8; Kaiser, *The Laws*, pp. 25–6.
32 On inheritance: Articles 90–5, 98–106; on slavery: Articles 110–21; on *zakupy*, Articles 56–62, 64.

according to taste: some see Monomakh supporting the traditional magnates against Sviatopolk's new speculators; others see him as the people's choice, protecting the exploited from the new exploiters; others see here the symptoms of emerging social classes.[33] In a broader perspective, however, both Sviatopolk and Monomakh, and indeed Vsevolod before them, merely present different aspects of a single process: the adaptation of prince and city to economic growth. The effect was to diversify and extend somewhat further the prince's involvement in the economic life of the town, whether by participation, or by taxation, or by regulation and arbitration. The process continued through the twelfth century and is reflected, albeit imperfectly, in the provisions of EP. EP as a whole is more intrusive than SP. It covers a wider range of disputes across a wider social spectrum. Different measures ruffled different feathers. These were the strains of success.

As in his relations with his kin, so in his relations with the city the prince had to adapt in practical ways merely to keep pace; to improvise merely to maintain the precarious equilibrium. But as in the dynasty, so with the city, improvisation was packaged as custom. Dramatic episode was contained within structural constants.

In the first place, the secular social hierarchy of the city was able to adjust to change without radically altering its complexion. The basic economic and social unit remained the *dvor*, the family compound or homestead, which could enclose craft workshops as well as enough land to grow some basic foods. Despite the expansion of public markets and the signs of growing affluence in the Podol, the primary producers and movers of the new wealth did not develop strong forms of collective identity or organization. Certain types of traders and craftsmen were probably clustered by street or district, but otherwise there is little evidence of craft guilds.[34] Craftsmen (and craftswomen) are mentioned in EP, but only in a list of princely servitors: the murderer of a (prince's) craftsman or craftswoman had to pay 12 grivnas – rather more than for a slave-girl (6 grivnas), far less than for the prince's junior retainer or *otrok* (40 grivnas).[35] Visiting merchants and exogenous communities always constituted a 'special case' and may have been segregated (hence the ease with which Jews could be identified as a target by the angry Kievans in 1113).[36] Home-based

---

33 See e.g. B. D. Grekov, *Kievskaia Rus'* 4th edn (Moscow, Leningrad, 1944), pp. 296–8; G. Vernadsky, *Kievan Russia* (New Haven, 1948; repr. 1972), pp. 93–4; I. Ia. Froianov and A. Iu. Dvornichenko, *Goroda-gosudarstva Drevnei Rusi* (Leningrad, 1988), pp. 50–60; cf. V. M. Rychka, 'Pro kharakter sotsial'nykh konfliktiv v Kyivs'kii Rusi', *Ukrains'kyi istorychnyi zhurnal* 1993, nos 2–3, 28–36.

34 See Tolochko, *Drevnerusskii feodal'nyi gorod*, pp. 117–18.

35 EP, Article 15: *ZDR*, p. 65; Kaiser, *The Laws*, p. 21.

36 See e.g. *Uspenskii sbornik*, fol. 57a.3–23 (Hollingsworth, *Hagiography*, p. 81) on the Jews berated by Feodosii as a sign of his zeal; *PSRL*, II, col. 288 on Jews' property destroyed in a fire of 1124.

merchants could and did operate in groups, and some groups acquired collective labels and even had their own churches, but there is little clear evidence that effective cooperation was converted into formal corporation.[37]

The standard vocabulary of urban stratification altered little: boiars (sometimes 'greater' or 'lesser'); (free)men (*muzhi*); townsmen (*liudi gradskie*); sometimes also the 'simple' folk (*prostaia chad'*); hired and contracted workers (*zakupy, riadovichi*); slaves (*kholopi*).[38] The collective voice of the city was its *veche*, the gathering of (free) citizens. This was where many of the strains of urban life found open expression. For example, it was from the *veche*, in the market-place, that the Kievans set out to free Vseslav of Polotsk in 1068. There has been a great deal of controversy as to who controlled the *veche*, how widely representative it was or was not, whether it was a forum for the masses or an instrument for the elite, or both.[39] To generalize about the workings of the *veche* is difficult and may well be misleading. There are very few early references: apart from the narratives about Kiev in 1068–9 and 1113, and about Vladimir-in-Volynia in 1097, the *Primary Chronicle* mentions the *veche* only in quasi-legendary tales of Belgorod in 997 and Novgorod in 1015. From the slightly more frequent twelfth-century references it seems that the composition, procedures and functions could vary. One should probably not ascribe a fixed and formal 'constitutional' role to the *veche* during this early period: *veche* was a generic word for the means of mobilizing urban opinion, a periodic event rather than an institution of government.[40]

Secondly, the city remained largely self-regulating, according to custom. EP grew slowly, over a century, and even when complete it can hardly be called voluminous. The birch-bark letters make it abundantly clear that townspeople were vigorous and scrupulous in pursuing their grievances against one another according to customary practices and without necessary recourse either to the prince or to any judicial personnel. There were mutually understood procedures concerning, for example, the use of witnesses, or of oaths, or the position of

---

37 On the *grechniki* and *zalozniki* in Kiev, and the *shchetintsy* in Novgorod, see below, p. 325.

38 The exact definitions are of course disputed: see e.g. Vernadsky, *Kievan Russia*, 2nd edn, pp. 131–57; I. Ia. Froianov, *Kievskaia Rus'. Ocherki sotsial'no-politicheskoi istorii* (Leningrad, 1980), pp. 118–49, and on rural groups idem, *Kievskaia Rus'. Ocherki sotsial'no-ekonomicheskoi istorii* (Leningrad, 1974), pp. 100–58; also S. V. Zavadskaia, 'K voprosu o "stareishinakh" v drevnerusskikh istochnikakh XI–XIII vv.', *DGTSSSR* 1987 (1989), 36–42, on *stareishiny gradskie* ('civic elders') as a bookish phrase rather than a technical term.

39 See e.g. Grekov, *Kievskaia Rus'*, pp. 222–36; Froianov, *Kievskaia Rus'. Ocherki sotsial'no-politicheskoi istorii*, pp. 150–84; Tolochko, *Drevnerusskii feodal'nyi gorod*, pp. 170–1.

40 *PVL*, I, pp. 87, 95, 177, 180. Twelfth-century usage was flexible enough to apply even to a secret conspiracy: see *PSRL*, II, col. 537 (s.a. 6677).

guarantors,[41] or the mechanism for retrieving stolen property. In cases of recalcitrance, individuals and communities could have their own officers (*otroki*) to assure enforcement.[42] Though many could now write, or at least have access to the uses of writing, nevertheless writing was slow to intrude into urban self-regulation: witness was oral, proceedings and decisions were unrecorded.

Thirdly – obvious, but worth stressing – the prince remained a prince: a *kniaz'*. The borrowed concepts of *kagan* or *tsar'* turned out to be redundant, inappropriate to the political culture of the extended family. Nor was there any significant development of titles or ceremonial. Some princes in some narratives are sometimes labelled 'great'; a particular prince may have been regarded as senior, or – to borrow a phrase – first in honour, but (*pace* quite a lot of modern popular histories) there was no formal title of 'Grand Prince' for the ruler of Kiev, no string of honorific epithets. A prince was addressed simply as 'prince', or at best 'prince and lord'. The dominant terminology remained that of kinship rather than of kingship.[43] Nor was there yet any substantial proliferation of functions and offices among princely servitors, no elaborate court hierarchies, no bureaucratic chanceries, none of the paraphernalia of a centralized monarchy. The prince still 'sat' with his *druzhina*, taking counsel, making war, feasting.

Change, therefore, was to a large extent absorbed into traditional structures. Trouble was at the margins. Nevertheless the margins were widening. It was not just a matter of some princes wanting a larger rake-off. Take the case of Zhiznomir. In the late eleventh century, Zhiznomir wrote a birch-bark letter to a certain Mikula in Novgorod: 'You bought a slave-girl in Pskov. Now the princess has detained me for that. The *druzhina* has vouched for me. Send a letter to that man [to find out] whether he has the slave-girl. I shall now buy a horse for the prince's man to ride, and then to the confrontation [*svod*]. If you have not yet received the money [for reselling the slave-girl?], do not accept any.'[44] The situation is well known from *Russkaia Pravda*: a stolen slave is resold several times, and the chain of sale is retraced through a series of confrontations. The problem here is that the chain

---

41 See H. Dewey and A. Kleimola, 'Russian collective consciousness: the Kievan roots', *SEER* 62 (1984), 180–91.
42 *NGB*, nos 241, 235, 509; Staraia Russa, nos 6, 7, 8.
43 A. Poppe, 'Words that serve the authority. On the title of "Grand Prince" in Kievan Rus", *Acta Poloniae Historica* 60 (1989), 159–84; see M. Colucci and A. Danti, eds, *Daniil Zatočnik. Slovo e Molenie* (Studia historica et philologica 4, sectio slavica 2; Florence, 1977): 'Slovo', II.1; VI.1; VII.1; VIII.1; A. Dölker, ed., *Der Fastenbrief des Metropoliten Nikifor an den Fürsten Vladimir Monomakh* (Skripten des slavischen Seminars der Universität Tübingen 25; Tübingen, 1985), fols 257a.17; 276b.15; 278b.18; 279a.6, 9, 19, etc. The label *kogan* for Oleg in the *Tale of Igor's Campaign* (*PLDR XII v.*, p. 386) is a deliberate archaism, or perhaps a reflection of his links with the nomads.
44 *NGB*, no. 109.

stretches beyond community boundaries: Mikula was in Novgorod, the slave-girl was bought by him in Pskov, linguistic features of the letter suggest that Zhiznomir himself was a southerner; he was also close to – perhaps a member of – the *druzhina*; and the princess had an interest (might the slave-girl have been hers?). Custom laid down the procedure, but custom could not cope with the circumstances; so the 'prince's man' was required, at a price, to sort things out. That, *inter alia*, was what princes were for.

The urban secular elite had a double identity: both as part of the city, and as part of the personal network surrounding the prince. The city's boiars could also be members of the *druzhina*. Personal ties with the elites were the essence of the prince's relationship to the city, but the double identity could be volatile. In Novgorod the *posadnik*, originally the prince's agent, became a local elective office. There were changes in the outward forms through which this personal relationship was affirmed. In the days of Iaroslav the townspeople – or a sufficient fraction of them – received the prince with their hearts (see above, p. 196). Later the formalities became Christianized: in 1117 Monomakh made the Novgorodian boiars 'kiss the Cross' to him, just as squabbling members of the princely family kissed the Cross to each other. Eventually, at least in Novgorod and possibly elsewhere, Cross-kissing was backed up by written contract, just as in the late twelfth century dynastic Cross-kissing came to be confirmed in writing.[45] Form did not become fossilized into inert ritual, and the periodic revision of form was another sign of insecurity and of underlying change. The extension of princely economic and legislative activity should not be mistaken for an extension of princely power. On the contrary, the strengthening of the self-sustaining urban elites made it all the more necessary for the prince not to have to rely on power and secular patronage alone.

Boiars, townsmen and princely servitors were the prime but not the lone players on the urban stage, nor were they the only groups with access to the new money. Besides the *tysiatskii* and the *sotskie*, the chronicle's account of the disturbances of 1113 mentions the prince's (unnamed) sister-in-law, and 'monasteries'. Let us continue through the list.

---

45 *NPL*, pp. 21, 205 (s.a. 6626); hence A. P. Tolochko, *Kniaz' v Drevnei Rusi: vlast', sobstvennost', ideologiia* (Kiev, 1992), pp. 78–9 erroneously argues that Cross-kissing was exclusive to princes while townspeople pledged loyalty by kissing icons. On Cross-kissing and documents see Franklin, 'Literacy and documentation', 23–4.

2. DAUGHTERS, SISTERS, WIVES AND WIDOWS

Both in Western Europe and in Byzantium urban growth in the eleventh and twelfth centuries provided a context for an expansion of women's involvement in economic and cultural life.[46] To what extent was there an equivalent trend north of the steppes?

'Love your wife', wrote Vladimir Monomakh in his *Instruction* to his sons, 'but do not give them power over you'.[47] Among the powers not given to women was power over major written sources. Women could certainly be literate and participate in written culture, but direct traces survive only in inscriptions, not in the more ample and prestigious world of parchment manuscripts. The virtue of a woman's silence was a commonplace among medieval moralists, and regret at the relative silence of medieval women is a commonplace among modern historians. But the extant writings of the Rus are far more thoroughly dominated by men than are writings from contemporary Byzantium or Western Europe. No surviving narrative, theological or literary text is known to have been written by a woman. There is no Kievan Anna Komnene, Hildegarde of Bingen, Hroswitha or Héloïse.

Writings *about* women are almost as restricted as writings *by* women. Women did not fight, nor did they 'sit on the throne of their fathers and grandfathers', so there was little room for them in the chronicles. As far as we can tell, there was no literature of courtly love, hence no romantic pedestal for women.[48] Where they do figure, women are usually anonymous, identified not by name but by their affiliation with a man: X's wife, Y's daughter. The account of the disturbances of 1113 is typical in naming Putiata the *tysiatskii* while leaving Monomakh's sister-in-law nameless, and this habit of female anonymity extends across the spectrum from learned disquisition to casual inscription. Finally, most writing about women was by men who deliberately excluded women from their own lives: that is, by monks. References to women tend to be didactic, or normative, or polemical, rather than descriptive or documentary: women as they were imagined, or women as they ought or ought not to be, rather than women as they were. It is difficult to sift fact from attitude.

Attitude, however, is also a fact, and the didactic stories are not to be discarded merely because they are biased.

Moisei Ugrin (Moses the Hungarian) served Iaroslav, but was taken captive by Boleslaw of Poland in 1018. After five years a rich young Polish widow saw him and bought him and offered him wealth and

---

46 See e.g. Erika Uitz, *Women in the Medieval Town* (London, 1990); A. Laiou, 'The role of women in Byzantine society', *JÖB* 31/1 (1981), 233–60.

47 *PVL*, I, p. 158; cf. e.g. Ephesians 5:22, 25; Colossians 3:18–19.

48 Even by comparison with Scandinavia: see Judith Jesch, *Women in the Viking Age* (Woodbridge, 1991), pp. 182–202.

honour as her husband. Steadfastly he refused, despite torture and despite the prudent urgings of those who reminded him of St Paul's words: 'it is better to marry than to burn' (I Cor. 7:9). But Moisei recalled Eve, and Potiphar's wife, and yearned to become a monk, since 'whom is it better to serve, Christ or a wife?'. His wish was granted, for he was tonsured in secret by a monk from the 'Holy Mountain' And yet the woman 'shamelessly dragged him off into sin. On one occasion she forced him to lie down with her on her bed, kissing and embracing him . . . but the blessed one said to her, "Your efforts are in vain . . . For fear of God I shun you as an unclean woman." Hearing this, the woman ordered him to be beaten with a hundred strokes every day. Finally she ordered his private parts to be cut off, saying "I shall not spare his beauty, so that no one else may enjoy it."' Moisei had his reward: the woman died, he returned to Kiev and lived out his days in the Caves monastery.[49]

This looks like a fairly straightforward specimen of piously prurient misogyny, a simple choice between marriage and the cloister, where marriage is presented primarily in terms of sexual temptation instigated by a woman. Such tales have a long pedigree.[50] The monks of the Caves were proud of their abstinence. One young recruit, Varlaam, was the son of a Kievan boiar. His father managed to retrieve him from the monastery, and tried to tempt him back to the life of the world. He dressed Varlaam in fine clothes, fed him fine food, and then set him alone with the greatest temptation, Varlaam's own wife. She begged him to come to her bed, but Varlaam, seeing her 'foolishness . . ., prayed in the secrecy of his heart to the merciful God who could save him from this trial'. With the Lord's help he resisted, and returned to the Caves.[51]

Eve, the first to be tempted, became the first temptress. But the sexual motif is not the main point of these stories. From the age of thirteen, when his father died, young Feodosii lived with his mother, but felt called to serve the Lord. He tried to set off on a pilgrimage to the Holy Land, but his mother stopped him. He left home and went to Kiev to enter a monastery. After four years his mother tracked him to the Caves, where she threatened to kill herself unless she was allowed access to him. Desperately she urged him: 'Come home, child . . . do not leave me . . . I cannot bear to live without seeing you.' Of course Feodosii refused, but there was a decorous ending: his mother entered a nearby convent.[52] Feodosii's mother is portrayed as humanly sympathetic, but the human, family sympathy was a spiritual

---

49 Abramovich/Tschiżewskij, *Paterikon*, pp. 142–9; Heppell, *Paterik*, pp. 162–9.
50 See Gail Lenhoff, 'Hellenistic erotica and the Kiev Cave Patericon "Tale of Moses the Hungarian"', *Russian History* 10 (1983), 141–53.
51 *Uspenskii sbornik*, fol. 34c.23–32; Hollingsworth, *Hagiography*, p. 48.
52 *Uspenskii sbornik*, fols 28a.27–33b.14; Hollingsworth, *Hagiography*, pp. 37–45.

impediment. The common theme in these stories is the ascetic rejection of the family, rather than the ascetic rejection of sexuality.[53]

The perils of family life (that is, of life with a woman), like its attractions, were not portrayed as exclusively sexual, nor were the potential victims exclusively monastic. Daniil 'the Exile', the possibly pseudonymous originator of a satirical petition to a prince, produced a different set of commonplaces. Should he seek to improve his position by marrying a rich woman?

A man is not a man who is dominated by his wife . . . I would rather bring an ox into my home than take an evil wife. For an ox speaks no evil and thinks no evil, but an evil wife becomes wild when beaten and becomes haughty when subdued . . . Hear, wives, the words of the apostle Paul, who says, 'Christ is the head of the Church, and a man is the head of his wife' [cf. Eph. 5:23] . . . It is better to travel in a leaky boat than to tell secrets to an evil wife: a leaky boat wets one's clothes, but an evil wife ruins her husband's whole life.[54]

This, in more florid form, echoes Monomakh's maxim for his sons: 'do not give them power over you'.

The female suitor, the wife, the mother, all hindering the man from becoming a monk; the domineering wife preventing the man from being a man: the outlook for women seems fairly bleak. To complete the gloomy picture, a woman powerful in body or mind was not really a proper woman at all. Feodosii's mother was 'strong in body, and powerful, like a man; for if anybody heard her talking, but could not see her, he would reckon that she was a man'. In a parable retold by Kirill of Turov in the mid-twelfth century a particularly perceptive princess is complimented for having a 'manly mind'.[55]

The rare positive voices of women tend to be the voices of women in grief, of women expressing not their power but their devotion, when the male object of that devotion is beyond reach; the voices of women bereaved. Vladimir Monomakh's son Iziaslav was killed in battle against Oleg Sviatoslavich in 1096: Vladimir writes to Oleg that he himself will take consolation in God, while his (unnamed) daughter-in-law will mourn 'like a dove'.[56] In the *Tale of Igor's*

---

53 For some Byzantine variants of the theme see A. Kazhdan, 'Hagiographical Notes, 8', in idem, *Authors and Texts in Byzantium* (Aldershot, 1993), no. 4, pp. 188–92.

54 Colucci and Danti, eds, *Daniil Zatočnik*, pp. 156–61; on Byzantine equivalents see S. Franklin, 'Echoes of Byzantine elite culture in twelfth-century Rus'?', in A. Markopoulos, ed., *Byzantium and Europe* (Athens, 1987), pp. 177–87; for the topos in Western Europe see e.g. Uitz, *Women*, p. 156.

55 *Uspenskii sbornik*, fol. 28b.19–22; Hollingsworth, *Hagiography*, p. 37; I. P. Eremin, ed., *Literaturnoe nasledie Kirilla Turovskogo* (Monuments of Early Russian Literature 2; Berkeley, Ca. 1989), p. 41; Franklin, *Sermons and Rhetoric*, p. 70; cf. Kerstin Aspegren, *The Male Woman. A Feminine Ideal in the Early Church* (Uppsala, 1990).

56 *PVL*, I, p. 165; cf. e.g. Isaiah 38:14; Nahum 2:7.

Campaign the hero's (unnamed) wife weeps for her husband, pleads with the elements (not to God) for his safe return. Thrice she pleads, to the winds ('O wind, wind! why, lord wind, do you blow so strongly?'), to the personified river ('O Dnieper Slovutich [=Son of Glory]!'), and to the sun ('O bright and thrice-bright Sun . . . Why have you spread forth your hot rays over the warriors . . .?').[57] Here, in women's ritual lament, Christian and pagan traditions could merge without threat. A sermon by Kirill of Turov picks up a patristic theme, Mary's lament before the Cross, with a similar appeal to the elements: 'All creation shares my suffering, O my son . . . O that I could have died with you . . . Now I have been deprived of my hope, my joy and delight, my son and my God . . . Hear, O ye heavens and sea and earth! Pay heed to the weeping of my tears!'[58]

Depictions of women, like depictions of men, varied according to their social context. Writers were not concerned with gender as such, but with status and role. Men were portrayed on a single scale of social status (prince, member of the *druzhina*, monk, etc.), while women were tied to a dual scale: social status (princess, female slave, etc.) plus family status (daughter, wife, mother, widow). In other words, the scope for a woman – her scope for autonomous action, for 'power' – changed according to her relations to men. Monks shunned the family, and hence women (or *vice versa*), but the Church also reached out in the opposite direction, into the world of women. A part of the Christian mission was the colonization of the family, its definitions and its norms.

The boundaries of this colonization were never precise, and women, perhaps more acutely than men, could be caught in the zone of uncertainty between two cultures, Christian and pagan. 'Diabolical sorcery', opines the chronicler, 'is performed above all by women', using 'charms and potions'.[59] The supercilious generalization may mask a mundane conundrum: what should one do, asks a priest in the mid-twelfth century, when a mother takes her sick child to be healed by the sorceress's potions rather than by a priest's prayers? The bishop prescribes a mere three to six weeks' penance, while a version of 'Iaroslav's Statute' lays down that a woman who uses potions should be chastised by her husband but should not be excluded from communion or subject to any further penalty.[60] It was not always easy for zealots to accept or explain the efficacy of herbal remedies, of women's role as healers in the home. Sickness might be God's punishment, health was certainly His gift: hence the prominence of

57 *PLDR XIIv.*, p. 384; cf. the lament of the widow of Roman Rostislavich of Smolensk: *PSRL*, II, col. 617 (s.a. 6688).
58 Eremin, *Literaturnoe nasledie*, pp. 65–6; Franklin, *Sermons and Rhetoric*, pp. 116–18.
59 *PVL*, I, p. 120.
60 *RIB* VI, col. 60; *ZDR*, p. 191 (Article 38); cf. Kaiser, *The Laws*, p. 48 (Article 40).

healing miracles in the cults of saints, the contests between monks and pagan or secular or heterodox or foreign healers in an edificatory work like the Caves *Paterik*,[61] or the chronicle's mini-diatribe on women and their diabolical potions.

Christianity and paganism adapted to each other. Indeed, there was not always necessarily a vast gulf between the two.[62] Traditional domestic medicine was an obvious problem, but monastic didacticism does not mean that women's status and scope – in the structure of the family – was profoundly changed by the new religion. No society can live up to the values of its own moralists. On a wide range of topics the normative sources (codes and penitentials) reflect the shifting balance between the desirable and the practicable, between zealous abstraction and pastoral accommodation. Sometimes the prelates felt they had to take a stand on vain principle: Metropolitan Ioann II in the 1080s insisted that it was 'unworthy and improper' for an Orthodox prince to give his daughter to a Latin Christian in marriage, but the record of dynastic marriages shows that piety took second place to policy. Sometimes one senses a reluctant compromise: 'the custom of the land may permit marriage to a second cousin, but those who do it must accept the punishment of the Church'.[63] Yet just as often the bishops seem to have had a fair feel for what was worth pushing and what was not. On the subject of sex at weekends, for example: 'I read to the bishop from certain *Instructions*, which said that if a man lies with his wife on a Sunday or a Saturday or a Friday, and if a child is conceived, then that child will be a thief or a fornicator or a robber or a coward, and his parents should do penance for two years; and the bishop said to me: "those books of yours should be burned"'.[64]

Morality was not the only issue here. Penances weighed more or less heavily according to faith, but the rules and customs on marriage were also the rules and customs which determined the scope and nature of women's 'power', the extent of their dependency and their access to property. It is just about possible to trace the main lines of a woman's path through the stages of family status, at least for that social group which was within reach of the surviving sources: that is, the relatively affluent, relatively Christianized urban families.

An unmarried daughter was at the disposal of her kin. 'Iaroslav's Statute' makes a gesture towards protecting daughters from the extremes of parental pressure: if a girl did herself an injury either because her parents forced her into an unwanted marriage, or because her

---

61 See e.g. Abramovich/Tschiżewskij, *Paterikon*, pp. 114–17, 128–34, 174–5; Heppell, *Paterik*, pp. 132–5, 147–52, 194–5.

62 Eve Levin, *Sex and Society in the World of the Orthodox Slavs, 900–1700* (Ithaca, London, 1989), p. 302.

63 Ioann II, Questions 13, 23: *RIB* VI, cols 7, 12–13.

64 Kirik, Question 74: *RIB* VI, col. 44.

parents forcibly restrained her from the marriage of her choice, then the parents were responsible for her injuries and were answerable to the bishop.[65] These articles deplore abuses, but nevertheless assume that arranged marriage was the norm. The expanded *Russkaia Pravda* allows that if parents died, then an unmarried daughter (of 'boiars and members of the *druzhina*') might have a share of their property to sustain her *only* if she had no brothers. If she had brothers she received nothing and they were to marry her off as best they could.[66]

On marriage a woman or girl[67] received a dowry from her kin, and might also be allocated a portion by her husband. In principle this was her property, her insurance, her pension, for her to keep or use as she chose. In practice she could be vulnerable to her husband if the marriage ran into difficulties. In a birch-bark letter from the late eleventh century the unfortunate Gostiata complains that her husband has abandoned her to take a new wife, and that he has taken all that she had been given by her father and her kin.[68] According to 'Iaroslav's Statute' a man who committed moral crimes (adultery, incest) was to be fined, a woman was to be cast out (divorced; sent to a convent).[69] Law, and probably custom, set penalties to protect a woman from physical and verbal abuse by a man who was *not* her husband; a version of 'Iaroslav's Statute' punishes a woman who hits her husband, but says nothing of a husband who beats his wife.[70]

The normative documents, though hardly equitable, were concerned to uphold monogamy, to discourage divorce in general, and to protect women in particular from arbitrary divorce.[71] The birch-bark letters indicate that concern was justifiable. For example, 'Iaroslav's Statute' states that a man could not cast out his wife merely because she was chronically ill, while on birch-bark a certain Domazhir wrote to his brother-in-law Iakov, alarmed at Iakov's dissatisfaction with his sick wife (i.e. with Domazhir's sister).[72] 'Iaroslav's Statute' stipulates fines for calling another man's wife a whore (which, if true, would be grounds for divorce); on birch-bark Anna wrote to her brother Klimiata about a dispute over a loan: a certain Kosniatin had called her a cow and her daughter a whore, as a result of which her husband Fedor had thrown her and her daughter out of the house

---

65 Short redaction of 'Iaroslav's Statute', Articles 24, 33: *ZDR*, pp. 169, 170.
66 EP, Articles 91, 95: *ZDR*, pp. 70, 71; Kaiser, *The Laws*, pp. 30, 31.
67 See *PSRL*, II, col. 658, s.a. 6695, on marriage ceremonies and gifts for the eight-year-old Verkhuslava Vsevolodovna on her marriage to Rostislav Riurikovich.
68 *NGB*, no. 9; on Gostiata's gender see *NGB*, IX, pp. 126–7.
69 Short redaction, Articles 8–23; *ZDR*, p. 169; cf. N. L. Pushkareva, *Zhenshchiny Drevnei Rusi* (Moscow, 1989), pp. 80–5.
70 Short redaction, Articles 2, 3, 25; long redaction, Articles 40, 42: *ZDR*, pp. 168, 191; cf. Kaiser, *The Laws*, pp. 48, 49.
71 Short redaction, Articles 4, 9, 17: *ZDR*, pp. 168–9.
72 Short redaction, Article 10: *ZDR*, p. 169; *NGB*, no. 705; see *NGB*, IX, pp. 97–8 for identification of this Iakov.

and had threatened to kill them.[73] It is surely significant that, although both these cases are apparently covered by the rules of the Church, nevertheless there is no suggestion of an appeal to any court or bishop. The aggrieved women turn for protection to their brothers. Anna even gives her brother precise instructions as to the words which he is to use when confronting Kosniatin, presumably according to approved formulae. The wives were dependent first on their husbands, second – in case of difficulty – on their blood-relatives (their natal family), and their disputes were dealt with man to man. Here too, therefore, law seems to have been grafted gradually onto custom rather than replacing it.

The strongest and the weakest of women were widows. They held their husbands' property in trust until their children's majority; and then they retained their dowry and – if they were lucky – an allocated portion of their husband's estate, which was theirs to keep, use or dispose of as they pleased, regardless of their children's wishes.[74] A widow of a wealthy husband, and from a wealthy family, could be truly independent at last. But a widow without such benefits was vulnerable, more reliant on remarriage or charity. In the middle ages widows comprised a far larger proportion of the population than they do today, in places perhaps as much as 20 per cent, depending on comparative rates of mortality and on the frequency of remarriage.[75] The Church taught charity towards widows. The protection of widows' inheritance helped to lessen the burden of charitable duty.

The status of women is just about perceptible, but the activities of women are largely conjectural. The far richer literary and artistic sources from Western Europe reveal multiple roles for women in the household and in the urban economy: in domestic crafts and administration, in retail trade. The sources for Rus reveal virtually nothing about women's work. Inscriptions on spindle-whorls show that many of their owners were women, which suggests – unsurprisingly – that women were involved in cloth-production. EP mentions craftswomen among categories of dependents,[76] but it is not clear whether or to what extent women made things for the market, to what extent they were involved in the urban economy as *producers*.

The scope for women as *consumers* of goods and services is rather more clear. To varying degrees women could have autonomous access to money and property, and there is ample evidence to show that

---

73 Short redaction, Article 25: *ZDR*, p. 169; *NGB*, no. 531; see *NGB*, IX, pp. 213–14; cf. Eve Levin, 'Women and property in medieval Novgorod: dependence and independence', *Russian History* 10 (1983), 167–8.
74 EP, Articles 93, 102–3, 106: *ZDR*, pp. 70, 71; Kaiser, *The Laws*, pp. 30–2.
75 Laiou, 'The role of women', pp. 247–8.
76 EP, Article 5: *ZDR*, p. 65; Kaiser, *The Laws*', p. 21.

they used it. Birch-bark lists of creditors and debtors include the names of women. In one letter Ivan's wife (or widow) threatens a defaulter with additional interest unless he pays his debt.[77] Some letters list *only* women.[78] The letter from Anna to Klimiata shows that a married woman (Anna's daughter) could enter into a binding financial contract, and that another married woman (Anna herself) could act as guarantor, even though Anna in this case denies that she had agreed to do so.[79] It may be significant that Anna's husband Fedor was away at the time, which suggests that here, as elsewhere in medieval Europe, women could have the authority to manage the family finances while their husbands were absent.[80]

Wealthy women, as consumers and patrons, were a far from negligible force in the urban economy. They helped to sustain the demand for luxury goods: for jewelry, fine furs and cloth.[81] And not all of them were decked out merely at their husbands' whim. In the early twelfth century Nezhka complains on birch-bark to her brother Zavid: it is intolerable that he has taken so long to send her the decorative pendants for which she had supplied the gold.[82] A remarkable document in Kiev records a more permanent investment: Vsevolod's wife (or widow) purchased 'Boian's land' for 700 grivnas of sable fur. The buyer's (late) husband was probably either Vsevolod Iaroslavich (whose second wife died in 1111) or Vsevolod Olgovich (d. 1146). The document is the first extant contemporary record of the private purchase of land, and it was evidently reckoned of some importance: it survives not as writing on parchment but as an inscription on a wall of the church of St Sophia.[83]

Princesses could be lavish patrons. Often the patronage of wives was associated with that of their husbands, but wives as well as widows could also give independently. Sviatopolk's mother Gertrude, wife of Iziaslav Iaroslavich, commissioned the miniatures for the Trier Psalter. On Sviatopolk's own death in 1113 his widow 'gave great riches to monasteries and to priests and to the poor, such that all were

---

77 *NGB*, Staraia Russa, no. 11; cf. *NGB*, VIII, p. 216.

78 *NGB*, Staraia Russa, nos 21, 22, from the early twelfth century; cf. *NGB*, nos 84, 228, 449, 657, 682.

79 Reading the letter as suggested in *NGB*, VIII, p. 214; cf. Levin, 'Women and property', 167.

80 For mainly later evidence see Levin, 'Women and property', 160–2; cf. the eleventh-century 'woman in charge of Vsevolod's household', who sent three wagon-loads of wine to the Caves monastery: *Uspenskii sbornik*, fol. 51c.13–16; Hollingsworth, *Hagiography*, p. 74.

81 Pushkareva, *Zhenshchiny Drevnei Rusi*, pp. 155–76.

82 *NGB*, no. 644.

83 S. A. Vysotskii, *Drevnerusskie nadpisi Sofii Kievskoi XI–XIV vv.*, vyp. 1 (Kiev, 1966), no. 25, pp. 60–71; Franklin, 'Literacy and documentation', 24–5; A. L. Nikitin, 'O kupchei na "zemliu Boianiu"', *Germenevtika drevnerusskoi literatury XI–XIV vv. Sbornik V* (Moscow, 1992), pp. 350–69.

astonished, for nobody can perform such charity'.[84] Sviatopolk's niece (the daughter of his brother Iaropolk) and her husband Gleb (son of Vseslav of Polotsk) jointly donated 600 grivnas of silver and 50 grivnas of gold to the Caves; and after her husband's death she willed – on her own account – five villages to the Caves, plus a further 100 grivnas of silver and 50 of gold. In 1161 Princess Evfrosiniia of Polotsk commissioned a luxurious cross for the church in the monastery which she had endowed. An inscription on the cross gives details of her generosity: '100 grivnas for the gold and the silver and the stones and the pearls, 40 grivnas [for the enamel]'. In a more manipulative mode, and somewhat later, the widowed Verkhuslava, daughter of Vsevolod Iurevich of Suzdal, apparently offered to pay up to 1,000 silver pieces to procure a bishopric for her favoured candidate.[85]

Evidence for women's wider participation in public life is fragmentary, but not quite negligible. In 1089 Vsevolod's daughter Ianka – a nun – was sent to Constantinople to accompany the new metropolitan (Ioann III) back to Kiev. In 1097 the Kievans, rather like the Romans in *Coriolanus*, asked Vsevolod's widow to act alongside Metropolitan Nikola as envoy and intermediary to Vladimir Monomakh, urging him to end his dispute with Sviatopolk.[86] Some public role is suggested by the survival of a few seals tentatively ascribed to princesses.[87] As to the mundane exercise of power and influence: we recall the birch-bark letter of the unfortunate Zhiznomir, arrested by a princess pending inquiries about a stolen slave-girl, or indeed the saga anecdote on the queen of Novgorod (see above, p. 223). Ianka and Evfrosiniia were both nuns. Aristocratic nuns should be grouped with aristocratic widows (who sometimes also became nuns): women with access to wealth and with an acceptable reason for lacking a husband.[88]

It would be odd to conclude a consideration of the women of Rus without mentioning the most prominent of them all, the obvious apparent exception: Olga, regent of Kiev in the mid-tenth century, who smashed the Derevlians, travelled to Constantinople, out-negotiated the

---

84 *PVL*, I, p. 196.
85 *PSRL*, II, cols 492–3; see also below, p. 306; B. A. Rybakov, *Russkie datirovannye nadpisi XI–XIV vekov* (*ASSSR SAI*, vyp. E1–44; Moscow, 1964), no. 27, pp. 32–3; Abramovich/Tschiźewskij, *Paterikon*, p. 102; Heppell, *Paterik*, p. 117. Note that Verkhuslava apparently returned to her natal family in the north-east after the death of her husband.
86 *PVL*, I, pp. 137, 174. See *PSRL*, II, col. 197 on Ianka as a nun. Like Sviatopolk, she died in 1113.
87 Ianin, *Aktovye pechati*, I, nos 23, 39, 78, 116, 121a, 226; Pushkareva, *Zhenshchiny Drevnei Rusi*, pp. 36–7.
88 See e.g. the princess who admitted Feodosii's mother to the convent; or the princess Evpraksia Vsesolodovna (tonsured 1106) or Predslavna (died as a nun 1116), *PVL*, I, pp. 186, 201.

emperor, and converted to Christianity (see above, pp. 133–8). Olga has ample space in the *Primary Chronicle*, and she also became the subject of a quasi-hagiographical eulogy. Yet Olga emphatically confirms the rule. In the first place, her status is within the norms: she is shown as holding power not in her own right, but as her husband's widow during her son's minority, and her actions against the Derevlians were her revenge for her husband's murder. Secondly most narratives about her have a curiously 'feminine' texture, unlike equivalent narratives about men. Mal, the prince of the Derevlians, sends envoys to Olga proposing marriage. Olga agrees and orders that the envoys be carried up to Kiev in their boat. When the envoys reach Olga's compound, the boat is cast into a pit and the envoys are buried alive in it. This is Olga's first revenge. She then requests more envoys, to escort her on her journey to her bridegroom. When they arrive, she suggests that they take a bath. The doors are then locked, the bath-house is set on fire, and the envoys are burned alive. Finally Olga goes to the land of the Derevlians, requesting only that, before marrying, she might hold a funeral feast for her husband. At the feast the Derevlians drink themselves into a stupor, whereupon Olga's men set upon them and cut them to pieces – all 5,000 of them.[89]

These are formulaic tales. Under the guise of betrothal, Olga sets a series of riddles, with cryptic clues symbolizing not a marriage but a funeral (boat-burial, washing the body, cremation, the funeral feast). The penalty for not decoding the riddle is death, and the Derevlians drink at their own funeral feast. There are many other saga-like tales of stratagem and deceit in the chronicle, but none like these, because none about a woman.[90] Men's stratagems involve cunning and bravery; Olga's stratagems are mostly filtered into the womanly rituals of betrothal and mourning.

The theme continues. Olga travels to Constantinople, where the emperor, struck by her beauty and intelligence, suggests that she rule with him. She points out – as if the emperor did not know – that she is a pagan and would first need to be baptized, and she asks him to baptize her personally. When he has complied, he proposes marriage, whereupon Olga springs the trap: by the law of the Christians a man cannot marry his goddaughter. "'Olga,'" says the emperor, "'you have outwitted me.'"[91] Olga's conversion was a fact, as was her reception

---

89 *PVL*, I, pp. 41–2; she also has a fourth revenge, somewhat differently structured.

90 On saga-like material in the *Primary Chronicle* see A. Stender-Petersen, *Die Varägersage als Quelle der altrussischen Chronik* (Aarhus, 1934); on Olga and Scandinavian tradition see Jesch, *Women in the Viking Age*, pp. 111–15; though there was perhaps less fixity of role in the sagas: see Carol J. Clover, 'Regardless of sex: men, women and power in early Northern Europe', *Speculum* 68 (1993), 363–87; cf. the saga-like tale of Rogneda and Vladimir in *PSRL*, I, cols 299–301.

91 *PVL*, I, p. 44.

by the emperor in Constantinople. It is not impossible that her negotiations with the emperor (or indeed her dealings with the Derevlians) did involve some kind of projected marriage alliance. The rest is good anecdote but shaky history; or rather, history translated into the anecdotal form appropriate for a woman, another riddle of false betrothal. Here the story is given respectable precedent: Olga was like the Queen of Sheba at the court of Solomon. Compare the story of Vladimir's Conversion, which involved ethical investigation, theological disquisition, intelligence reports, a military campaign, a miracle, and even an *actual* betrothal, but no 'feminine' riddles. Vladimir's betrothal to his Byzantine bride was a fact, Olga's multiple pseudo-betrothals, or quasi-betrothals, came to be dressed up as literary affirmations of her gender role. By the twelfth century Olga was a remote and safe ancestral memory, exotically magnified, but hardly a model for women of the chroniclers' own time. Never again was the dynasty left with only a child male claimant to Kiev.

The stories of Olga do not change the overall picture of women's roles. Some women, at least, were more active and influential in the economic and public life of the city than the sources readily reveal, and to this extent their 'silence' is misleading. Nor do aristocratic women seem to have been secluded to the extent that became customary in many parts of Europe, including Muscovy, in the later middle ages. It is not utterly strange to find a princess among the figures of controversy in the urban unrest of 1113. But one should also beware of exaggeration. The scope for husbandless women was strictly circumscribed both by custom and by law, and in marriage women were far more vulnerable to their husbands than were husbands to their wives. To this extent the relative silence of the sources is, so to speak, fair comment. The notion of women's subordination and generally lesser status is not, as has recently been claimed, a myth.[92] Monomakh's warning was widely heeded.

Nevertheless the landscape changes. In the summer of 1993 one of the largest of the birch-bark documents was retrieved from the Novgorodian mud. It dates from the late eleventh or early twelfth century, and its sender was a woman. It reads: '[I have written] to you three times. What is it that you hold against me, that you did not come to see me this Sunday? I regarded you as I would my own brother. Did I really offend you by that which I sent to you? I see you are displeased. If you had been pleased you would have torn yourself away from company and come to me ... Write to me ... If in my inconsiderateness I have offended you and you should spurn me, then God is my judge.'[93] The letter is unique in its

92 Pushkareva, *Zhenshchiny Drevnei Rusi*, p. 211.
93 *NGB*, no. 752: E. A. Rybina, 'Otkrytiia arkheologov 1993 goda', *Vestnik Moskovskogo Universiteta. Seriia 8, Istoriia* 1994, no. 2, p. 44.

direct expression of personal feeling. It highlights the extent to which our vision is narrowed to what the sources allow us to see, and its discovery gives hope that in time the silence may, gradually, begin to be filled with authentic voices.

3. MONKS

In their message to Monomakh in 1113 the disgruntled Kievans made a special point of the threat to attack the monasteries: if Monomakh did not come to rule in Kiev, and thereby prevent the plundering of the monasteries, then he himself would bear the responsibility for such an outrage. The growth of monasteries and monasticism was among the most prominent signs of urban transformation over the second half of the eleventh century. They were a sign of prosperity, since monasteries were founded and adorned mainly through grants and donations from rich patrons anxious to raise their spiritual stock and to have a burial-place for themselves and their kin. In their turn monasteries came to play an important part in the economic, social, political and religious life of the city. They contributed to the demand for, and production of, certain types of luxury goods; some of them became substantial self-supporting enterprises, with their own workshops, lands and dependents; monks had the ear of princes and boiars, both as confessors and more publicly on moral and political issues; monastic buildings had an impact on the urban environment, contributing to the sense of Christian space; and the monks' own labours profoundly influenced the shape and character of the emerging Christian culture.

When did native monasticism begin? As usual, we can follow a reasonably clear trail back as far as the mid-eleventh century, beyond which the evidence dissolves into ambivalence. This is not altogether inappropriate. Native monasticism probably does not have *a* beginning. Monasticism is a continuum: from the individual ascetic who chooses the life of contemplation, to the large organized community. Ilarion writes of monasteries appearing in the reign of Vladimir, but the *Primary Chronicle* states that 'monasteries began to exist' only in the reign of Iaroslav.[94] According to the chronicle a certain Antonii, having been tonsured on the 'Holy Mountain' (usually taken to mean Mt Athos), returned to Kiev and 'went round the monasteries' before settling in a cave at Berestovo, site of what was to become the Caves monastery: a version of the Caves *Paterik* tells of Antonii visiting the Holy Mountain while Vladimir was still alive (that is, not later than 1015), but the chronicle has him embarking on his pilgrimage only

---

94 Moldovan, *Slovo*, p. 93 (fol. 187a.11–12); Franklin, *Sermons and Rhetoric*, p. 19; *PVL*, I, p. 102.

after Ilarion had been appointed metropolitan (that is, not earlier than 1051).[95] An Athonite document from 1016 includes the signature of a certain 'Gerasimos ... hegumen [superior] of the monastery of the *Rhōs*'. The chronological compatibility with the *Paterik* tale of Antonii is alluring, but '*Rhōs*' is here in the singular – 'the *Rhōs* man' – so that one cannot be sure whether it refers merely to the founder, or whether it implies anything about the origin of the monks therein; or what kind of *Rhōs* (Scandinavian or Slav) this man was.[96]

The earliest history of native asceticism is therefore obscure, but by the time of Iaroslav's death in 1054 there was a plurality (probably small) of monastic communities (also probably small) in and around Kiev. In the early 1050s Feodosii, like Antonii before him, is said to have 'gone round all the monasteries' before deciding to settle in the Caves, and four years later his mother settled in a convent of St Nicholas nearby. One might be sceptical of hagiographical commonplaces, but Iaroslav himself founded monasteries of St George and St Irene; and a notice in the chronicle's entry for 1113 refers to the death, at the age of 92, of a woman who had been a nun for 60 years: i.e. who had entered a convent in 1053.[97]

After Iaroslav monasteries and monks indeed proliferated. All the princes of the 'inner circle' founded and supported monasteries in and around Kiev, regardless of where they themselves happened to rule. Iziaslav endowed the monastery of St Demetrios (not after 1062), Sviatoslav a monastery of St Symeon; and Vsevolod founded the monastery of St Andrew in Kiev (before 1086)[98] and the monastery of St Michael at Vydubichi on the hills to the south. The monastery of the Saviour at Berestovo was a princely foundation, first mentioned in 1072. Iziaslav's sons added to his monastery of St Demetrios: Iaropolk built a church there, dedicated to St Peter, and in 1108 Sviatopolk sponsored the construction of the sumptuous 'golden-domed' church of St Michael. The monastery of the Caves was not a princely foundation,

---

95 *PVL*, I, p. 105; Abramovich/Tschiževskij, *Paterikon*, pp. 16–17; Heppell, *Paterik*, p. 19.

96 P. Lemerle, A. Guillou and N. Svoronos, eds, *Actes de Lavra* I: *des origines à 1204* (Archives de l'Athos, 5; Paris, 1970, p. 155 (no. 19, l. 37). For the conventional identification of this as the Xylourgou monastery see e.g. D. Nastase, 'Les débuts de la communauté oecuménique du Mont Athos', *Symmeikta* 6 (1985), 284–90; S. Senyk, *A History of the Church in Ukraine*, I; *To the End of the Thirteenth Century* (Orientalia Christiana Analecta 243; Rome, 1993), pp. 243–4; for a sceptical view of the evidence linking the Rus, or Antonii, to Athos, see Francis J. Thomson, 'Saint Anthony of Kiev – the facts and the fiction: the legend of the blessing of Athos upon early Russian monasticism', *Byzantinoslavica* 56 [1995, forthcoming].

97 *PVL*, I, pp. 104, 197; *Uspenskii sbornik*, fol. 31a.29–31; Hollingsworth, *Hagiography*, p. 41.

98 See Ia. N. Shchapov, *Gosudarstvo i tserkov' Drevnei Rusi X–XIII vv.* (Moscow, 1989), p. 138.

but it was given land by Iziaslav and money for its church by Sviatoslav. The locations of these monasteries are revealing. They were clustered either in the upper town, or else in and around the princely residence at Berestovo. The escape from the world was under the eyes of the mighty of the world. The monks of the Caves and of Vydubichi could feel close to the authentic roots of monasticism, as hermits on hillsides in a symbolic wilderness; but they were also close neighbours of the prince, within a few minutes' walk from his out-of-town residence.

The monks of the Caves took pride in the fact that their community had been founded not 'by tsars and boiars and wealth . . . but by tears and fasting, prayer and vigil'.[99] Tales of its earliest holy men likewise make much of the notion that monks were a new and distinct social group, that to choose the monastic life meant to reject and in a sense to challenge traditional social structures and obligations. As they turned their backs on the ways of the world, monks left behind them a trail of aggrieved relatives and patrons: Feodosii's mother; Varlaam's father and wife; even Prince Iziaslav himself, who was reportedly furious when his eunuch Efrem defected to the monastery.[100] But despite such assertions of autonomy, monasteries were not independent. Monks had a degree of moral authority with the prince, yet princes could exert a degree of administrative authority over monks, even to the extent of hiring and firing. Iziaslav took Varlaam from the Caves and made him hegumen of St Demetrios. Antonii was forced to leave the Caves, having displeased the prince during the Vseslav affair (see above, p. 256). In 1112 when the Caves needed a new hegumen, 'all the brethren assembled and named the priest Prokhor as their choice, and they told the metropolitan [Nikifor I] and Prince Sviatopolk about him. And the prince ordered the metropolitan to appoint him . . .'.[101] Monks constituted a new and influential social group, but purity of origin did not set the monastery outside the political and economic nexus.

Large monasteries during this period were concentrated in and around Kiev. From the late 1060s and early 1070s there are references to small communities in Chernigov, Pereiaslavl and Tmutorokan, as well as to a monastery of the Holy Mountain near Vladimir-in-Volynia. However, the growth of monasticism on any significant scale outside the 'inner circle', or even outside the environs of Kiev itself, does not become visible until the twelfth century. The pattern is

---

99 *PVL*, I, p. 107; cf. Abramovich/Tschiżewskij, *Paterikon*, p. 19; Heppell, *Paterikon*, p. 22.
100 Abramovich/Tschiżewskij, *Paterikon*, pp. 33–4; Hollingsworth, *Hagiography*, pp. 46–7.
101 *PVL*, I, p. 195; cf. ibid., p. 187 (the prince 'ordered' the metropolitan to authorize the commemoration of Feodosi); or the trial of the monk Avraamii of Smolensk, at the bishop's court but in the presence of the prince: see above p. 235, n. 81; Hollingsworth, *Hagiography*, pp. 147–8.

the same as that for the spread of masonry churches, or of bishoprics, or of organized Christianity in general.[102]

The growth of monastic wealth is best documented with regard to the monastery of the Caves. Nestor's *Life of Feodosii* relates that the early disciples of Antonii lived in relative poverty, surviving by the work of their own hands: partly by tilling the soil to grow their own food, partly by small-scale craft production: 'sometimes they would weave sandals and cowls and would fashion other handicrafts, which they would bring to town and sell and thereby purchase grain, which they then divided among them so that at night each might grind his own portion to make bread'. The labour and the proceeds were communal.[103] But then the donations started to flow in. Some gave food and drink: wine-jars, bread, oil.[104] Some gave money or luxury objects, like the boiar Kliment, who gave two gold grivnas, an icon-setting and a gospel book.[105] Some gave villages. In Nestor's *Life of Feodosii*, written in the 1080s, there are already several references to the monastery's villages.[106] Although the brethren's avowed aim was self-sufficiency rather than luxury or profit,[107] nevertheless the Caves had clearly become an economic entity worth taking seriously. It was creditworthy, able to borrow money from Kievan merchants; it had money to spend on the acquisition of icons 'and other necessities' in Constantinople.[108]

Through donations the Caves acquired property in widely scattered regions of the lands of the Rus. Iaropolk Iziaslavich willed 'all his wealth', specifically: 'the Nebelska domains, and the Derevlian, the Lutskian, and around Kiev'. His son-in-law Gleb Vseslavich of Minsk gave 100 grivnas of silver and 50 grivnas of gold, and financed the building of the monastery's refectory, which was completed in 1108, while after Gleb's death his widow pledged 'five villages together with the peasants'. Efrem – former eunuch of Iziaslav, monk at the Caves and in Constantinople, and titular metropolitan of Pereiaslavl – gave villages near Suzdal.[109]

The formula 'together with the peasants' is significant. The higher clergy were sustained largely through an allocated proportion of the income from princely lands. By contrast, monasteries more frequently

---

102 See above, n. 96 and pp. 227–8; see also below, pp. 352–3.

103 *Uspenskii sbornik*, fol. 36a.5, 20–2; cf. Hollingsworth, *Hagiography*, p. 51.

104 *Uspenskii sbornik*, fols 36d.28–30; 51a.32–b.23; 52c.21–22; 53a.19–c.15; also 47c.28–31; Hollingsworth, *Hagiography*, pp. 52, 74, 76–7; cf. 69.

105 *Uspenskii sbornik*, fols 47c.31–48b.29; Hollingsworth, *Hagiography*, pp. 69–70.

106 *Uspenskii sbornik*, fols 40a.15–23; 50d.10–51a.4; 54b.10–c.27; 57a.24–c.25; 62a.25–32; 64d.21–25; Hollingsworth, *Hagiography*, pp. 58, 73, 78, 81–2, 88, 92.

107 *Uspenskii sbornik*, fol. 49b.4–29; Hollingsworth, *Hagiography*, p. 71.

108 *Uspenskii sbornik*, cols 44d–45d; 41b; Hollingsworth, *Hagiography*, pp. 65–6; 59–60.

109 *PSRL*, II, cols 492–3; *PVL*, I, pp. 187, 169.

(in the surviving evidence) received land outright, including the services of those who lived and worked there and the full income derived therefrom. The earliest authentically documented donations – real administrative records, rather than summary statements in hagiography or chronicle – date from the 1130s and relate to a series of grants from Monomakh's grandsons to the monasteries of St George (the Iurev Monastery) and Panteleimon outside Novgorod. St George received Buitsy 'together with the tribute and bloodwite and fines' (i.e. the totality, not a tithe), and Liakhovichi 'with the land and the people and horses and forest and hives and hunting-grounds'; Panteleimon received neighbouring land 'together with the peasants'.[110]

The hegumens (superiors) of the major monasteries enjoyed high social status. Hegumens had confidential access to princes, as their confessors and spiritual fathers. They were guests at princely feasts alongside the boiars and the *druzhina*. In 1072 they took part, alongside the princes and the bishops, in the festivities for the translation of the relics of Boris and Gleb.[111] In 1096 Monomakh and Sviatopolk suggested that they resolve their dispute with Oleg Sviatoslavich at a grand gathering which was to consist of 'the bishops, the hegumens, the men of our fathers [i.e. the *druzhina*] and the townspeople'. In 1097 'the hegumens' tried to intercede with Sviatopolk to free Vasilko. 'The hegumens' were presumably a select group from prestigious monastic houses. On the few occasions when the hegumens are listed individually, the superior of the Caves is placed first. However, only from c. 1170 is the hegumen of the Caves regularly described as an 'archimandrite' – that is, as the superior superior of a group of monasteries.[112]

These are externals. For the substance of monasticism, rather than the social and economic status of monks, we need to adopt a more credulous attitude to the monks' tales of themselves, in particular to the acknowledged exemplar: the account of the origins and emergence of the monastery of the Caves. This story came to have the same function with regard to native monasticism as the early tales in the *Primary Chronicle* had with regard to the dynasty: as an expression of legitimacy and authenticity. It is worth summarizing.[113]

By the early 1050s the hermit Antonii had finally settled in his cave at Berestovo. The sources offer confused hints as to his earlier life, but

---

110 *GVNP*, nos 79–82, pp. 138–41; V. L. Ianin, *Novgorodskie akty XII–XV vv.: khronologicheskii kommentarii* (Moscow, 1991), pp. 135–8; cf. the strict tithes in the 1136 charter for the bishopric of Smolensk: see above, p. 232.

111 *PVL*, I, p. 121; cf. *PSRL*, II, col. 530, s.a. 6676. See also above, p. 257, n. 33.

112 See *PVL*, I, pp. 150, 172, 199; *PSRL*, II, cols 535–6 on the Caves as a place for negotiations between princes; on the status of archimandrite see Shchapov, *Gosudarstvo i tserkov'*, pp. 58–60.

113 Abramovich/Tschiẑewskij, *Paterikon*, pp. 1–20; Heppell, *Paterik*, pp. 1–23.

agree that at some stage or stages he had visited the Holy Mountain, where he was tonsured. Whatever his actual wanderings, the Holy Mountain meant – or at least came to be assumed to mean – Mt Athos (see above, n. 96). At Berestovo his reputation as a holy man grew, and others settled around him, to be near him and learn from him, and he tonsured them also. And when he had gathered twelve disciples they built a small church, and 'with the blessing of God and the Holy Mountain' Antonii appointed one of their number, Varlaam, to be their hegumen. Thus the first monastery of the Caves is represented as a small assemblage of anchorites inspired by the Holy Mountain. But the assembly of brethren grew rapidly. By c. 1062, when Feodosii was appointed in place of Varlaam (who had been transferred by Iziaslav to St Demetrios), there were twenty. By the mid-1060s there were already about 100. Success brought reorganization, in a sense refoundation. To the blessing of the Holy Mountain Feodosii added the 'Rule of the monks of Stoudios . . . And all monasteries took the Rule from that monastery, therefore the Caves is honoured above all'.[114] Thus Feodosii re-formed the over-populated *skit* (gathering of ascetics), turning it into a *koinobion* (an organized monastic community). The grander institution required a grander place of worship, and with princely financial assistance Feodosii initiated the building of the splendid new *katholikon* dedicated to the Dormition of the Mother of God. The church was the fulfilment of a miraculous vision which had appeared some years previously to a Varangian named Shimon. Shimon had even observed and noted the exact measurements of the church that was to be.

Thus, as they told and elaborated the tales of their foundation, the monks of the Caves gave themselves many types of origin, all lending a sense of authenticity: anchorites reminiscent of the Desert Fathers of the earliest monasticism; Athonite inspiration; Stoudite organization; Varangian vision; princely donation; and of course miracle. It was a potently prestigious mixture on which to build a native tradition. In many respects, however, the Caves was a typical outgrowth of eleventh-century Byzantine monasticism, closely following contemporary fashion. Mt Athos, the eastern prong of the Chalcidic Peninsula, was one of several Byzantine 'holy mountains'. Originally a retreat for individuals or groups of ascetics, from the late tenth century it became a focus for large cenobitic foundations which enjoyed imperial privileges. The Stoudite Rule was derived from the precepts of Theodore of Stoudios (d. 826); but by the eleventh century it had spread well beyond the Stoudios monastery itself, and versions of it were produced for many *koinobia* both in Constantinople and on Athos. The surviving Slavonic translation of the Stoudite Rule was

114 *PVL*, I, p. 107.

not taken from the pristine ninth-century text but from a version issued by Patriarch Alexios ('the Stoudite') for a monastery of the Mother of God which he founded in Constantinople in 1034.[115] The Constantinopolitan presence was enhanced and made visible in the monastery's main church, whose decoration was entrusted to Byzantine artists.[116] There were even contemporary Byzantine equivalents to the location of the Caves monastery, a couple of kilometres outside the city.[117]

The main imperatives of the *koinobion* were Divine worship, manual labour, and obedience to the hegumen. But the Caves, like its Byzantine equivalents, was a complex institution. The cenobitic community of brethren was hierarchical, not egalitarian. There were set stages of spiritual attainment from the novitiate up to the Great Habit (*skhima*; Gk. *megaloskhēma*), and there was a fairly elaborate division of labour among the monks.[118] Each monk had his assigned task: the porter, the cooks, the cellarer, the choirmaster, the priests, the deacons, the steward (*ikonom*; Gk. *oikonomos*). Some acquired specialist skills: icon-painting, the copying or binding of books. Every aspect of daily life and worship was, in principle, covered by the Rule, from how to knead the dough, to a warning that readers must take care not to splatter books with candle-wax or saliva.[119]

Koinobia were not perfect automata. Contemporary Byzantine monasteries, even within the Stoudite tradition, engaged in earnest and sometimes acrimonious controversy: on the precise requirements for fasting; on whether or to what extent individual asceticism should or should not be allowed; on discipline and indiscipline; on whether Monks could retain personal wealth; on the extent to which monasteries should rely on secular protection. The Caves *Paterik* reveals differences of opinion and practice within the Caves on several of these points. Because of the apparent discrepancy between the Caves stories and a notionally perfect Stoudite *koinobion*, some have suggested that the Caves was not really a Stoudite monastery at all: that its monks' behaviour was more idiorhythmic than cenobitic; that the retention of

---

115 The liturgical Rule: D. M. Petras (tr.), *The Typicon of the Patriarch Alexis the Studite: Novgorod-St. Sophia 1136* (Cleveland, 1991); extracts on monastic discipline in D. S. Ishchenko, '"Ustav studiiskii" po spisku XII v. Fragmenty', in S. I. Kotkov and V. Ia. Deriagin, eds., *Istochniki po istorii russkogo iazyka* (Moscow, 1976), pp. 109–30.

116 Abramovich/Tschiżewskij, *Paterikon*, pp. 5–8, 9–12, 172; Heppell, *Paterik*, pp. 6–8, 11–12, 172.

117 See Lyn Rodley, 'The monastery of Theotokos Evergetis: where it was and what it looked like', in M. Mullett and A. Kirby, eds, *The Theotokos Evergetis and Eleventh-Century Monasticism* (Belfast, 1994), pp. 17–29.

118 *Uspenskii sbornik*, fol. 37c.30–d.13; Hollingsworth, *Hagiography*, p. 54; cf. *PSRL*, II, col. 340; see the symbolic interpretations by Kirill of Turov: Eremin, *Literaturnoe nasledie*, pp. 47–54; Franklin, *Sermons and Rhetoric*, pp. 82–96.

119 Ishchenko, '"Ustav studiiskii"', pp. 124–5, 130.

wealth by some monks violated Stoudite ideals (and Feodosii's urgings); that perhaps Feodosii only introduced the liturgical practices from the Stoudite Rule, not the full prescription for monastic discipline.[120] However, this is to ignore the fact that there were divergences on precisely these issues in Byzantine Stoudite *koinobia* as well. For example, the strict reformist Rule for the Evergetis monastery in Constantinople, founded at almost exactly the same time as the Caves, was in part a reaction to the practice of allowing monks to retain some personal wealth.[121] Eastern monasticism was in general more variable than its West European equivalent. There were common models but no fixed Orders. Each community followed – or failed to follow – its own foundation Rule, its *typikon*.[122] Even in its apparent deviations the Caves was close to the Byzantine mainstream.

The monastery of the Caves, like several Byzantine urban *koinobia*, took on responsibilities for others besides its own members. The *vita contemplativa* was not self-contained, and *philanthropia* was a traditional duty in eastern monasticism. Alexios' Rule followed standard precedent in requiring that leftover food should be given to the hungry rather than be thrown away. More formally, Feodosii established an alms-house for the poor and the sick, and he allocated to it a tithe of the monastery's income. Once a week he sent food for those in captivity. In the absence of secular institutions for social welfare, the monastery absorbed some of the strain of urban growth.[123]

The monastery of the Caves happens to be the best documented of all the Kievan communities, but it was also in fact by far the most important. The range and variety of its influence would be hard to overemphasize. In the first place, it played a large part in the spread of monasticism itself. As we have seen, Varlaam, Feodosii's predecessor as hegumen of the Caves, was appointed to be the first hegumen of St Demetrios, and his successor in that post, Isaia, was also a monk of

---

120 Senyk, *A History of the Church in Ukraine*, I, pp. 261–2; cf. F. von Lilienfeld, 'The spirituality of the early Kievan Caves monastery', *California Slavic Studies* 16 (1993), 63–76. See e.g. Abramovich/Tschiżewskij, *Paterik*, pp. 120–2; Heppell, *Paterikon*, pp. 139–40.

121 See D. Krausmüller, 'The monastic communities of Stoudios and St Mamas in the second half of the tenth century', in Mullett and Kirby, eds, *The Theotokos Evergetis*, pp. 67–85; J. P. Thomas, 'Documentary evidence from the Byzantine monastic *typika* for the history of the Evergetine Reform Movement', ibid., pp. 246–73; J. P. Thomas, *Private Religious Foundations in the Byzantine Empire* (Washington, D.C., 1987), pp. 148–243; A. Kazhdan, 'Hermitic, cenobitic and secular ideals in Byzantine hagiography of the ninth through twelfth centuries', *Greek Orthodox Theological Review* 30 (1985), 473–87.

122 C. Galatariotou, 'Byzantine *ktetorika typika*: a comparative study', *Revue des Études Byzantins* 45 (1987), 77–138.

123 *Uspenskii sbornik*, col. 51a.14–22; Hollingsworth, *Hagiography*, p. 74; Ishchenko, '"Ustav studiiskii"', p. 118 (fol. 200v.6–18); on Byzantine practices see D. Constantelos, *Byzantine Philanthropy and Social Welfare* (New Brunswick, 1968), pp. 88–110.

the Caves.[124] In the late 1060s Antonii established a small community at Chernigov. In the 1070s Feodosii's successor, Stefan, founded the monastery and church of the Mother of God of Blachernae (another explicitly imperial model) on the Klov, also on the southern outskirts of Kiev. Stefan's successor, Nikon, together with two of the Caves brethren, formed a community in Tmutorokan. By the end of the century the Caves had an associated community – a *metochion* – in Suzdal.[125] And the Caves Rule, introduced by Feodosii, carried Caves practices further than the personal peregrinations of Caves monks, for it became the model for cenobitic houses elsewhere.

Secondly, the status of the Caves was underpinned by the widespread veneration of Feodosii, both as a model of piety and spirituality and as the father of native organized monasticism. In 1108, at the urging of hegumen Feoktist, Sviatopolk 'ordered the metropolitan to write [Feodosii's name] in the *sinodik*' (Gk. *synodikon*), that is, in the list of those to be commemorated in the liturgy; and all the bishops were ordered to do the same, and they obeyed 'with joy', and thus Feodosii became commemorated in all the cathedrals.[126] This was the 'official' establishment of Feodosii's cult, and we note again the intriguing chain of command: on the initiative of the monastery, on the orders of the prince, with the compliance of the metropolitan (Nikifor I, a Byzantine). The cult was successful. Subsequent writers with no direct link to the Caves praised Feodosii as, for example, the 'beacon of all Rus', and as the 'archimandrite of all Rus'.[127]

Thirdly, monks of the Caves came to occupy important positions in the hierarchy of the Church. Indeed, the bishops' agreement to commemorate Feodosii may have been all the more easily obtained because many of the bishops were themselves former monks of the Caves. Priests could be married, but bishops had to be celibate, and the monasteries were training grounds for native recruits to the higher clergy. In the late eleventh century the Caves enjoyed a virtual monopoly. Thus around 1089–91 at least six out of seven known bishops were Caves alumni: German of Novgorod, Luka of Belgorod, Marin of Iurev, Isaia of Rostov, Efrem of Pereiaslavl and Stefan of Vladimir-in-Volynia.[128] This level of domination was not quite sustained. Between 1105 and 1123, for example, two successive

---

124 *Uspenskii sbornik*, fol. 41c.4–17; Hollingsworth, *Hagiography*, p. 60.
125 *Uspenskii sbornik*, fol. 60c.4–18; Hollingsworth, *Hagiography*, pp. 60, 86; *PVL*, I, p. 169.
126 *PVL*, I, p. 187.
127 *Kirill von Turov. Gebete* (Munich, 1965), pp. 334, 336; the *Life of Avraamii of Smolensk*, in Rozanov/Tschiżewskij, *Avraamij*, p. 4; Hollingsworth, *Hagiography*, p. 139.
128 The incumbents of Turov and Polotsk in these years are unrecorded. On Ioann of Chernigov, bedridden for 25 years before his death in 1111, see *PSRL*, II, cols 273–4; Dimnik, *The Dynasty of Chernigov*, pp. 247–8.

bishops of Pereiaslavl, Monomakh's patrimony, were appointed from Monomakh's family monastery of St Michael at Vydubichi, the Caves' near neighbour. Nevertheless Bishop Simon of Vladimir, writing c. 1225–6, estimated that up to and including himself nearly 50 bishops had been alumni of the Caves. For the entire pre-Mongol period we know the names of approximately 100 bishops.[129] There are gaps in the record, but even if we were to double the total number, still the Caves would have a hugely disproportionate share. It is often said that, as the separate branches of the princely dynasty increasingly pursued their separate interests and aims, so the unity of the lands of the Rus was embodied only in the unity of the Church under a single metropolitan. But perhaps the more pervasive and effective links were those of the extended spiritual brotherhood, the old boy network of ex-inmates of the monastery of the Caves.

Fourthly, and partly in consequence, the Caves influenced the physical and spiritual landscape far beyond Kiev. The mid-eleventh-century vogue for St Sophia was transient. No major dedications to St Sophia are known after those early cathedrals in Kiev, Novgorod and Polotsk. From the 1070s to the 1220s all other known bishoprics subsequently had cathedrals dedicated instead to the Dormition of the Mother of God, taking their lead from the *katholikon* of the monastery of the Caves. This was the case in Rostov, in Vladimir-in-Volynia, in Turov, in Smolensk, in Galich, in Riazan and in Suzdal. Legend records that Monomakh, when planning the church in Rostov, even copied the exact measurements of its Kievan prototype and the details of its iconographic programme, and that Monomakh's youngest son Iurii did the same in Suzdal.[130] Thus the prestigious focus of Christian life and worship through many of the principal cities of the Rus came to be modelled not on Vladimir's palace church, nor on Iaroslav's metropolitan church, but on Feodosii's monastic church.

Finally, monks in general, and monks of the Caves in particular, played the dominant part in shaping the written culture of East Slav Christianity, both in the use of Church Slavonic translations from Greek and in the production of such native works as have survived. The repertoire of translations – at any rate those which were most widely copied – was dictated to a significant extent by the reading prescribed or encouraged in the monastic *typikon*. Most of the known authors of native literature were monks (or bishops – i.e. former monks). And an extraordinary proportion of extant native literature derives from the monastery of the Caves itself: Nestor's *Life of*

129 Abramovich/Tschiżewskij, *Paterikon*, pp. 102–3; Heppell, *Paterik*, pp. 118–19; lists of bishops by Poppe in Shchapov, *Gosudarstvo i tserkov'*, pp. 207–13.
130 Gerhard Podskalsky, *Christentum und theologische Literatur in der Kiever Rus' (988–1237)* (Munich, 1982), p. 281; Abramovich/Tschiżewskij, *Paterikon*, pp. 11–12; Heppell, *Paterik*, p. 13.

Feodosii of the Caves; his *Lection* on Boris and Gleb; the monastery's own sizable *Paterik* with tales of its greatest members; and of course and above all our constant companion the *Primary Chronicle*, compiled at the Caves around the end of the reign of Sviatopolk, copied in 1116 by Silvestr, hegumen of Vydubichi next door (and future bishop of Pereiaslavl), and for centuries used throughout the lands of the Rus as the basic narrative of early native history. Even today it is difficult to avoid viewing the history and culture of the Rus up to the early twelfth century through spectacles heavily tinted by the monks of the Caves.

The rise of monasticism was a feature of urban economic growth from the mid-eleventh century. The proliferation of monks and monasteries was among the most conspicuous developments in the human, architectural and spiritual geography of the city. Monasteries were major beneficiaries of the new wealth, and monks were the new cultural elite. It is perhaps not fortuitous that the reports of fractious Kievans in 1113, by contrast with the reports of fractious Kievans in 1068 and before, included monasteries in their list of high-profile targets (see below, p. 347).

4. GOING NATIVE

Nikifor I, Byzantine metropolitan of Kiev (1104–21), wrote a Lenten homily addressed to Prince Vladimir Monomakh, instructing him in Christian virtue and on the duties of a ruler. By convenient coincidence, Monomakh himself also wrote on the same theme: his *Instruction* (*Pouchenie*) to his sons, likewise expounding his views on Christian virtue and on how a prince should behave. Yet these two contemporary 'mirrors of princes' could hardly be more different from one another.

According to the Byzantine churchman, the prince is to his lands as the soul or mind is to the body.

The soul sits in the head, having within it the mind like a bright eye filling the whole body with its power. Just as you, prince, sitting here in your land act throughout all the land by means of your commanders [*voevody*] and servants while you yourself are the lord and prince, so the soul acts throughout all the body by means of its five servants, that is by means of the five senses.[131]

The conventional simile presents the ruler as essentially static, stately, active by proxy and authority rather than in person.

Contrast Monomakh's own advice:

Be not lazy in your household, but oversee everything yourself; do not look to your steward [*tiun*] or to your *otrok*, lest those who come to you should

131 Dölker, ed., *Der Fastenbrief*, pp. 38–40.

laugh at your household and at your repast. When going to war, be not lazy, nor look to your commanders [*voevody* – cf. Nikifor!] . . . Set the guards yourself . . . Whatever my *otrok* was to do, I have done myself, in war and in the hunt, night and day, in the heat and in winter, not giving myself rest. I myself have done what has been necessary, not looking to my *posadniki*, nor to my *birichi* [types of agent or representative]. I have made all the dispositions in my household, and on the hunt . . . whether in the stables or regarding the falcons and hawks . . .[132]

No stately 'sitting' here; the ruler is constantly mobile, the strict and repeated imperative is explicitly to be active in person, not by proxy.

Monomakh's *Instruction* is barely concerned at all with the abstractions of rule. He depicts five categories of princely activity: war (a long list of his own campaigns); the hunt (he lists his most impressive kills, and boasts of his wounds); running the household; dispensing charity, hospitality and patronage; and praying to God. He is a warlord, heroic in battle and in recreation, pious in faith, and concerned above all for his honour and good name. He is surrounded by danger, both to his person ('do not remove your weapons hastily and without circumspection, for by inadvertence a man dies suddenly') and to his reputation ('do not allow your *otroki* to commit atrocities . . . lest you should start to be reviled . . . Honour a guest, from wherever he may come . . . If you cannot honour him with a gift, then honour him with food and drink, for these passers-by will praise a man through all lands').[133] There is no reference to the city, or to any administration beyond the estate and the battlefield. In one brief phrase Monomakh mentions 'conferring with the *druzhina* and dispensing justice to the people'. Then he passes on to more interesting matters.[134]

One could ask: who was right, the prince or the metropolitan? Who was more accurate? The differences between Nikifor's homily and Monomakh's didactic autobiography are rhetorical as much as factual. Identical procedures can be filtered through variant images. On the one hand, the metropolitan was well aware of Monomakh's unceremonious, 'hands on' approach to military and domestic affairs: he alludes to the prince's habit of sleeping on the ground, preparing his guests' food with his own hands, and putting on fine clothes only 'of necessity' when he had to go into the city.[135] On the other hand, Nikifor's

---

132 *PVL*, I, p. 157.
133 Ibid., pp. 157–8; cf. ibn Rusta, *Kitab al-A'lak al-nafisa* [*Book of Precious Jewels*] ed., T. Lewicki, *Źródła arabskie do dziejów słowiańszczyzny*, II.2 (Wroclaw, Warsaw, Cracow, Gdansk, 1977), pp. 42–3; tr. Wiet, *Les atours précieux* (Cairo, 1955), p. 165: the Rus would not go to relieve themselves unless accompanied by three armed men, see above, p. 40.
134 On the *Instruction* see A. S. Orlov, *Vladimir Monomakh* (Moscow, Leningrad, 1946); D. Obolensky, *Six Byzantine Portraits* (Oxford, 1988), pp. 102–8.
135 Dölker, ed., *Der Fastenbrief*, pp. 44–6.

simile of the soul and the senses is notionally compatible with the scene of the deliberations at Berestovo, as described in EP: Monomakh sits at his princely residence, surrounded by his *tysiatskie*, who then carry his decisions to the remote parts of his lands. Yet the Byzantine churchman chose to filter the ruler's activities through well-cultivated courtly imagery more reminiscent of the ethos of Iaroslav's propaganda, or indeed of his own Byzantine presuppositions about rulership.[136] By contrast, Monomakh amalgamated piety with robust practicalities. His tone is more reminiscent of the somewhat gruff paternal advice written by his older contemporary, the Byzantine commander Kekaumenos.[137] Or, more pertinently: travelling with Monomakh one might almost be back in the saddle with his great-great-grandfather Sviatoslav. He articulates the work ethic that was characteristic of his clan. He apparently felt no need to authenticate his role as ruler, even as Christian ruler, with quasi-imperial allusions. A prince was a prince was a prince. His rhetoric of self-presentation matches the political culture of his dynasty.

Monomakh's choice of self-presentation is symptomatic of a shift in emphasis throughout the Christian culture of the Rus in the late eleventh and early twelfth centuries. This was the passing of what might be called the age of primary borrowing, of the age when the elite had based its images of authority and authenticity on a sense of direct *translatio* from Byzantium, on ostentatiously appearing to reconstitute the presence of Byzantium in Kiev. By the end of the century *translatio* was increasingly giving way to *traditio*, as the Scandinavian, Byzantine and Slav strands fused into a less declamatory, more confident and self-sustaining synthesis. From birch-bark to parchment, Slavonic literacy and literature spread in the city. Greek lost its aura of prestigious display. By the early twelfth century Slavonic had replaced Greek in liturgical inscriptions; Monomakh's early seals were inscribed in Greek, his later seals in Slavonic. Slavonic spirituality produced its own heroes, as Feodosii's status was publicly affirmed in 1108 by Sviatopolk, and as the status of Boris and Gleb was publicly reaffirmed at the retranslation of their relics in 1115. Native monks and native bishops ministered to an expanding urban elite which had come to take its Slavonic Christianity and letters for granted. The Rus came to rely on traditions which they had begun to make their own. There was little interest in drawing fresh water from the source. Under Iaroslav's children and grandchildren the Christian culture of the Rus, so to speak, went native.

The change was not sudden or total, and certainly there was no deliberate or principled rejection of Byzantium. On the contrary,

---

136 I. S. Chichurov, *Politicheskaia ideologiia srednevekov'ia. Vizantiia i Rus'* (Moscow, 1990), pp. 140–6.
137 G. G. Litavrin, ed., *Sovety i rasskazy Kekavmena* (Moscow, 1972).

despite the development of local skills, Byzantium continued to provide luxury objects, such as the enamel on an opulent binding for a Gospel lectionary ('God only knows the price of this book', exclaims the appended note by Naslav, who was sent to Constantinople to commission the work), or the 'Suzdal amulet', commissioned later in the twelfth century by Princess Maria Shvarnovna.[138] It is virtually impossible to discern a distinct local school of native icon-painting in the pre-Mongol period. Despite the emergence of native trainees, such as the monk Alimpii of the Caves, there were Byzantine painters among the Rus well into the late twelfth century. The most famed miracle-working icons of the twelfth century – the Mother of God of Vladimir and the 'Pirogoshcha' Mother of God – were imported from Byzantium. Teams of Byzantine builders continued to work on Rus churches. Greek remained the language of bishops' seals until the mid-twelfth century, Byzantium remained a valued supplier of expertise and craftsmanship, and Constantinople itself remained a city of wonders fit for pilgrims. But locally the fashions, once set, became habitual, blended into context, accumulated local nuances; Byzantine by provenance but no longer so explicitly Byzantinist in emphasis.[139]

For some this is a tragedy. Rather than settling into self-sufficiency and isolation, the Rus could have become more inquisitive, could have deepened their direct participation in Byzantine culture, could have studied Attic Greek, could and should have commented on classical rhetoric and philosophy, could have read Homer and Aristotle, could have joined the intellectual life of Europe instead of condemning themselves to linguistic and hence intellectual provincialism; instead of swimming with the stream, they drifted into a backwater (see also above, pp. 240–2; below, pp. 354–8). Alternatively, the Rus managed to avoid the facile pseudo-intellectualism of Byzantine snobs, to find spiritual enlightenment for themselves while resisting Byzantine attempts to impose an identity; their lack of interest in Constantinopolitan cultural fashion and in the niceties of theological debate allowed them to remain admirably ecumenical in outlook, able, for example, to regard 'Latins' amicably as fellow-Christians despite the best efforts of Byzantine churchmen to propagate polemics after the schism between Constantinople and Rome in 1054. For others, the Rus were excessively complacent in possessing the outer trappings of eastern Christianity, disproportionately concerned with ethics and with forms of observance rather than with systematic inquiry and interpretation. Alternatively,

138 L. P. Zhukovskaia, ed., *Aprakos Mstislava Velikogo* (Moscow, 1983), fol. 213b (p. 289); A. A. Medyntseva, *Podpisnye shedevry drevnerusskogo remesla* (Moscow, 1991), pp. 134–48.
139 See e.g. V. G. Putsko, 'Vizantiia i stanovleniie iskusstva kievskoi Rusi', in P. P. Tolochko, ed., *Iuzhnaia Rus' i Vizantiia. Sbornik nauchnykh trudov (k XVIII kongressu vizantinistov)* (Kiev, 1991), pp. 79–99; P. A. Rappoport, 'Stroitel'nye arteli Drevnei Rusi i ikh zakazchiki', *SA* 1985, no. 4, pp. 80–90.

the Rus did join the wider community of byzantinoslavonic Orthodoxy, and the details which set them apart are less significant than the fundamentals which were shared.[140]

Here we are not concerned with the larger consequences of 'going native', and still less with questions of comparative evaluation. There were losses and there were gains, as in any translation of culture across space, time and language. In the present context the relevant point is that the emergence of a self-sustaining, self-imitating cultural synthesis was closely linked to the process of continuing urban growth. Production and consumption had become more diverse, and cultural institutions, though owing much to princely patronage, had become more autonomous. Under Vladimir Sviatoslavich Christian culture and propaganda had radiated primarily from the palace; under Iaroslav it shifted to the metropolitanate; by the end of the eleventh century it had spread its roots in the city, among the monks and the elites of the townspeople. In other words, 'going native' was part of a social process, not a purely cultural phenomenon.

The transition is most fully realized in the growth of native writing and literature, and its richest and most complex single product is the *Primary Chronicle* itself, as compiled in the early 1110s. By contrast with Ilarion's stylish display, the material in the chronicle is strikingly heterogeneous, as if the compiler had thrown together all he could find without bothering too much as to whether the result was consistent or pretty. There was no attempt to harmonize or homogenize the various styles, no attempt to disguise compilation as composition. Terse factography jostles with florid periphrasis, heroic anecdote with arid document, eye-witness detail with commonplace formula. There is no obvious sense of measure or proportion. After the dateless narrative from the Flood to the mid-ninth century, the formal control is annalistic rather than thematic. In its kaleidoscopic capaciousness the chronicle is far more informative than Ilarion's tightly shaped argument. It preserves layers and fragments of culture and a diversity of perspectives and perceptions which a more homogeneous literary composition would destroy or disguise.

One should not, however, imagine the chronicle as an unedited scrap-book, a random assemblage of whatever snippets happened to be available. The compiler had a coherent approach to Providential history, a coherent perspective on native history, and a critical concern for accuracy. Particularly revealing in this respect is his use of the legacy of Byzantium.

In the first place, the chroniclers of the Rus took from Byzantium the basic ordering of linear time. Local tradition probably counted

---

140 See above, pp. 240–2; also e.g. D. Obolensky, *Byzantium and the Slavs* (New York, 1994), pp. 75–107; idem, *The Byzantine Commonwealth Eastern Europe 500–1500* (London, 1971), pp. 353–75; Senyk, *A History of the Church in Ukraine*, I, pp. 314–26.

the years of rulers or generations; contemporary Latin Christianity already counted years from the birth of Christ; Ilarion had highlighted the typological and thematic coherence of Divine Providence; current events in Constantinople were commonly dated according to the fifteen-year 'indiction' cycle, but on the larger scale of universal history the Byzantines counted the continuous sequence of years from the Creation. Just as man was created on the sixth day, so God became man in the middle of the sixth millennium (the sixth cosmic day). The exact calculations varied somewhat. The 'Constantinopolitan era', which was the version adopted by the Rus, set the Creation at what would now be the equivalent of 5508 BC.[141] This became the standard scale of historical chronology among the Orthodox East Slavs right down to the time of Peter the Great. And this was the scale on which, in the early twelfth century, the main compiler of the *Primary Chronicle* tried to find a place for the Rus. Yet Time in the chronicle was not entirely Byzantine. It was a synthesis. The linear scale was imported, but the regular cycles were local: the chronicle's year normally begins in March, while the Byzantine year was reckoned from the start of September.

In order to find the place of the Rus in linear time the compiler again produced a synthesis, meticulously collating the two main types of source at his disposal: on the one hand, local dynastic and military legend, and on the other hand such information on the Rus as could be gleaned from translated Byzantine narratives and documents. So far as he could establish, the two types of information converged around the middle of the fourth century of the seventh millennium, in the reign of the emperor Michael III, in what we would call the mid-ninth century, whence he begins both the continuous sequence of years and the continuous sequence of the generations of the dynasty. As we have seen, this marriage of universal chronology with dynastic legend is flawed in detail but impressively durable in outline.

Secondly, the chronicler set local description in a framework of received interpretation. For example, local legend told of how Prince Oleg had died in accordance with a pagan prophecy. A *volkhv* predicted that Oleg would die on account of his horse. Oleg therefore banished the steed from his presence. Many years later he visited its corpse and in scorn placed his foot upon its skull – from which a serpent promptly slithered out and bit Oleg to death. The tale was puzzling, since elsewhere the Christian chronicler habitually derided paganism on the grounds that *volkhvy* could not predict the future. He could have rejected the legend as 'ignorant' (his standard epithet for pagan opinion), but instead he cites a long passage from the translated Byzantine chronicle of George the Monk on the subject of Apollonius of Tyana, a specialist in apotropaic talismans. The passage explains,

---

141 On various systems and calculations see V. Grumel, *La Chronologie* (Paris, 1958).

with reference to impeccable patristic authority, why sometimes God does indeed allow it to appear that pagan prophecy works. Thus the local legend is validated through Byzantine exegesis, not displaced by it; and at the same time the borrowed sources unobtrusively acquire local resonances.[142]

Thirdly, from translated sources the compiler found Christian justification for local dynastic politics. Ilarion had sought to do something similar, but Ilarion had dealt in macro-historical abstractions, whereas the chronicler sought again to validate – and to find a moral basis for – the political culture of his day. The chronicle begins with the division of lands among the sons of Noah after the Flood: Shem received the east, Ham the south, and Japhet the north and west. The Rus were therefore part of Japhet's 'lot' and descended from the peoples therein. This is medieval commonplace. But in one version of the tale of Noah's sons the chronicler noted that they were said to have sworn their father an oath 'not to transgress into a brother's lot'.[143] Here was justification both for divided inheritance and for the inviolability of each part of the patrimony: deeply un-Byzantine concerns, but crucial to the emerging political culture of the Rus. As local custom dressed itself in Christian garb (e.g. Cross-kissing instead of oaths), so imported culture was moulded to the local contours. Christianized custom blended with customized Christianity.

The result is a work which in conception and execution is deeply indebted to Byzantium yet no less deeply native. The *Primary Chronicle* fits the larger pattern, in which the elite culture came to look and sound less and less like an obvious superimposition, more and more like an effective and distinctive synthesis of three originally quite separate strands – Byzantine, Scandinavian and Slav. Such a synthesis may well have been a distant aim of the rulers of the Rus since the time of Vladimir, and it may well have been encouraged and facilitated by princely policy and patronage; yet it eventually emerged not as a simple product of princely propaganda but in the thriving urban diversity of the late eleventh and early twelfth centuries.

Ilarion had written as if history was complete. The annalistic form of the chronicle is by nature open-ended (at any rate until the end of linear time). Patterns had been set, but there was rather less starry-eyed declamation of accomplishment. The *Primary Chronicle* told the story of Kiev and the Rus; but even as the story reached its climax it was starting to become uncomfortably diffuse. Cultural integration – both of the dynasty and of the city – was a useful counterbalance to the quickening social, economic and political diffusion which we encounter as we move further into the twelfth century.

---

142 *PVL*, I, pp. 29–31; see S. Franklin, 'The reception of Byzantine culture by the Slavs', in *The Seventeenth International Byzantine Congress. Major Papers* (New Rochelle, New York, 1986), 386–92.

143 *PVL*, I, p. 10.

PART III:

The Rise of the Regions

PART III

The Rise of the Regions

CHAPTER NINE

Integration and Diffusion
(c. 1130–c. 1170)

For two days they ransacked the whole city: the Podol and the Hill and the monasteries and St Sophia and the Tithe Church of the Mother of God. And there was no mercy from anywhere to anyone as churches burned and Christians were murdered or bound and women were taken into captivity, parted from their husbands by force, and infants wept as they watched their mothers being taken. And they looted a multitude of property, and they stripped the churches of icons and books and vestments and took away the bells . . . And among the people of Kiev there was wailing and grief and unquenchable sorrow and unceasing tears.[1]

Thus the Kievan chronicler describes the capture and sack of his city in early March 1169, not by Poles or Polovtsy, but by a coalition of a dozen native princes of the dynasty. It was unprecedented, but not the end of the world. Despite the chronicler's vivid clichés of disaster, it did not even make much of a dent in Kiev's prosperity. The immediate consequence was that Gleb Iurevich, grandson of Vladimir Monomakh and prince of Pereiaslavl, was installed as prince of Kiev. Almost business as usual, just another reshuffling among princes of the inner circle.

Except for two points. In the first place, the allies were an oddly disparate bunch from a wide scattering of major and minor princely seats. They were led not by Gleb but by his nephew, who brought troops from Suzdal, Rostov and Vladimir-on-the-Kliazma in the north-east, with support from princes of Smolensk, Ovruch, Vyshgorod, Novgorod-Seversk (in Chernigov's hinterland) and Dorogobuzh. If one's expectations are formed by the Liubech summit, then the list looks incongruous. Secondly, Gleb Iurevich was quite openly a placeman, a surrogate, an appointee. The strings were pulled by his older brother Andrei of Suzdal (known as Andrei Bogoliubskii, because of his residence at Bogoliubovo). It was Andrei who assembled the coalition, under the command of his own son Mstislav; Mstislav who, with Andrei's authority, 'installed his uncle Gleb'. Envoys from the

---

1 *PSRL*, II, col. 545; on the date see Berezhkov, *Khronologiia*, pp. 180–1, 335–6; comparison with other accounts of the incident in J. Pelenski, 'The sack of Kiev in 1169: its significance for the succession to Kievan Rus'', *HUS* 11 (1987), 303–16.

Polovtsy, in Kiev for negotiations, were clear that Gleb owed his appointment to 'God and Prince Andrei'.[2] This was all the wrong way round. In the days of Sviatopolk and Monomakh princes of the south delegated their juniors to postings in the north-east, not the reverse.

Historians have pronounced dramatic judgements: Andrei Bogoliubskii 'introduced the principle of Byzantine absolutism into Russian political life';[3] his goal was the 'neutralization of Kiev',[4] or its 'subordination to Vladimir-on-the-Kliazma',[5] such that the Kievan prince would become his 'vassal';[6] he even 'transferred the capital from Kiev to the northeast'.[7] The sack of Kiev in 1169 is often presented as a symptom of, and a stage in, the 'collapse of the Kievan state', which made way for the age of 'feudal disintegration'.[8] At the very least it is seen as a sign of the 'decline of Kiev'.[9]

Commentators at the time produced a different type of explanation. Why was Kiev sacked? 'For our sins', says the Kievan chronicler. 'For their sins', concurs the Suzdalian chronicler, adding 'and because of the metropolitan's injustice' in a dispute over the rules for fasting.[10] Perhaps true, but not very helpful. Clearly there had been a change in the complexion of the dynasty and in the balance of regional power. However, the change was far less dreary than is suggested by the dirge of the Kievan chronicler or by the sanctimoniousness of his Suzdalian counterpart; and it was less systemically traumatic than is suggested by most of the modern verdicts. The twelfth century was a period of continuing economic, dynastic and cultural expansion. Change created new strains; but beneath the surface noise of family conflict there is a story of growth and sustained success.

1. THICKENING NETWORKS OF TRADE AND SETTLEMENT: A BRIEF TOUR

'There was a route', says the *Primary Chronicle*, 'from the Varangians to the Greeks'.[11] The chronicler uses the singular (*a* route) and the past

2 *PSRL*, I, col. 357; II, col. 555.
3 G. Vernadsky, *Kievan Russia* (New Haven, 1948; repr. 1972), p. 220.
4 Ellen Hurwitz, *Prince Andrej Bogoljubskij. The Man and the Myth* (Studia historica et philologica 12, sectio slavica 4; Florence, 1980), p. 18.
5 Pelenski, 'The sack of Kiev', 315.
6 Iu. A. Limonov, *Vladimiro-Suzdal'skaia Rus'* (Leningrad, 1987), p. 73.
7 H. Birnbaum, *Aspects of the Slavic Middle Ages and Slavic Renaissance Culture* (New York, 1991), pp. 78, 90, 359.
8 B. D. Grekov, *Kievskaia Rus'* 4th edn (Moscow, Leningrad, 1944), pp. 299–306.
9 See the discussion in I. Ia. Froianov and A. Iu. Dvornichenko, *Goroda-gosudarstva Drevnei Rusi* (Leningrad, 1988), pp. 77–83, 237–8.
10 *PSRL*, II, col. 545; I, col. 354.
11 *PVL*, I, p. 11.

tense ('there was'). He conceives of his country's origins and bearings as lying along a north–south axis of long-distance trade. As we have seen, the Rus had long been interested in exploring and securing paths eastwards and westwards as well: from the earliest expeditions between the Baltic and the Upper Volga, to the efforts of Vladimir Sviatoslavich to control the Cherven towns (see above, p. 157). In the chronicler's own time the dynastic difficulties tackled by the Liubech conference had been partly caused by increasing competition over the opportunities offered by the north-east and south-west. The subsidiary or peripheral routes were already being more keenly exploited and settled. During the twelfth century they became still less subsidiary, still less peripheral, as energetic and resourceful traders, both by themselves and with the encouragement of the princely elite, developed a thickening network of links throughout and across and within the territories which the dynasty aspired to rule. As a result the economic, political, geopolitical and cultural complexion of the lands of the Rus became subtly but significantly altered. A brief tour is in order, moving clockwise, starting in the south.

In 1168 Mstislav Iziaslavich, prince of Kiev, bewailed the disruptive influence of the nomads: 'they are taking away from us the Greek Route, the Salt Route and the Route of the Vines'. The prince summoned his kin to help protect 'the routes of our fathers and grandfathers'.[12] Two of these three routes were indeed long-established. The way to the 'Greeks' still led to Constantinople via the Lower Dnieper and the Black Sea, while the 'Vine' route also followed the Dnieper for some distance before branching off southwards towards the Crimea and the Sea of Azov.[13] Wine never came close to replacing beer as a commonplace tipple, but it was drunk by those who took communion in growing numbers of churches, and the wine-traders who travelled to and from the Crimea were numerous enough to have acquired a generic label, the *zalozniki*, just as those who plied the 'Greek' route were known as the *grechniki*.[14] The *zalozniki* not only supplied the towns of the Middle Dnieper but also brought wine for re-export to other Rus settlements. Fragments of amphorae from the Crimea and the northern Black Sea coast have been found as far to the north-west as Grodno, Novogrudok and Volkovysk and as far to the north as Beloozero. The *grechniki*, too, dealt in wines, as well as in oil and other agricultural produce such as walnuts and dried fruit.

---

12 *PSRL*, II, col. 538; Berezhkov, *Khronologiia*, pp. 159–60.
13 See e.g. A. Spitsyn, 'Torgovye puti Kievskoi Rusi', in *Sbornik statei posviashchennykh S. F. Platonovu* (St Petersburg, 1911), pp. 246–8; V. P. Darkevich, 'Mezhdunarodnye sviazi', in B. A. Kolchin, ed., *Drevniaia Rus'. Gorod, zamok, selo* (Moscow, 1985), pp. 387–411.
14 *PSRL*, II, cols 528, 541.

They also brought luxury commodities such as silks and gold crosses and silver bowls and enamelled medallions.

The Dnieper remained the single most important route to the south. Serious disruption would certainly have been inconvenient, but in the mid-twelfth century trade along the Dnieper seems to have thrived. On Velikopotemkin Island in the river's estuary the period of maximum occupation – over an area of approximately 4 hectares – was in the twelfth and early thirteenth centuries, and excavations have revealed many fragments of amphorae and glazed pottery.[15] During the same period there arose a very large number of Slav settlements near the Rapids and along the Lower Dnieper. The volume of trade, and the mushrooming of Slav settlements along the route, suggest that the main feature of dealings between the southern Rus and the steppe nomads over the middle decades of the twelfth century was not disruptive conflict but relative stability.

This relative stability had been established partly by force, in the steppe campaigns of the 1100s and 1110s (see above, p. 204). It was maintained by diplomacy and common interest. Two sons of Vladimir Monomakh were married to Polovtsian brides; but the most effective security device was the gradual creation of a kind of buffer zone peopled by semi-sedentarized nomads themselves. At least from the late eleventh century, with the settlement of 'Torks' near the purpose-built fortifications at Torchesk, nomadic horsemen had been enlisted to serve as frontiersmen. Many Pechenegs and Berendei (the 'Baiandur' of oriental sources, formerly part of the Oghuz federation) also assumed the role of borderers. They were concentrated along the valley of the river Ros, feeding their herds off the fertile pastures. To a certain extent their encampments replaced the fortified settlements, some of which were voluntarily abandoned. Well-armed and numerous, with an elite decked out in silken headgear with silver chains and ear-rings made by Rus craftsmen, they played a key role in guarding the right-bank approaches to Kiev and in restraining the Polovtsy of the Lower Dnieper and beyond. They could also act as scouts and guards for travellers. It was their presence which ensured the continuity and intensification of trade along the river, and made possible the development of the large unfortified Slav settlements. From around the mid-twelfth century the semi-sedentarized borderers under some sort of service obligation to the Kievan princes were known by the collective name of 'Black Caps' (*Chernye klobuki*), a translation of the Turkic name *Karakalpak*.[16] By the end of the century a substantial proportion of the Black Caps had become Christian.

---

15 This was probably the place called Oleshe in the sources: see A. L. Sokul'skii, 'K lokalizatsii letopisnogo Olesh'ia', *SA* 1980, no. 1, 66–71, 73; see also above, p. 178.

16 S. A. Pletneva, *Kochevniki srednevekov'ia. Poiski istoricheskikh zakonomernostei* (Moscow, 1982), p. 63.

The nomads, therefore, did not constitute a single, undifferentiated people. The more distant of the Polovtsy, mostly living on the Don steppes, were known to the Kievan chroniclers as the 'Wild (*dikie*) Polovtsy'.[17] They were 'wild' in that they were no great friends – but also no imminent threat – to Kiev. However, they also were employed regularly as allies by the Rus: in particular by their closer neighbours the princes of Chernigov. By the early twelfth century Chernigov had lost its maritime outpost at Tmutorokan, and the Don Polovtsy dominated the lines of communication to the Azov and Black Seas. We recall that in the 1090s Vladimir Monomakh and Sviatopolk of Kiev had been incensed by the reluctance of their cousin, Oleg Sviatoslavich of Chernigov, to break his alliance with the Polovtsy.[18] Between 1128 and 1161 the Polovtsy intervened to support Oleg's descendants on approximately fifteen occasions.[19] Indeed, their readiness to assist the princes of Chernigov was taken for granted by Kievan chroniclers. Yet the benefits of access to the Lower Don were not such as could compensate for major disruption of the far more lucrative Dnieper route. To that extent the economy of Chernigov was still tied to the fortunes of Kiev, and the southern princes were still locked into a common enterprise which their individual jockeyings for position or pre-eminence could not be allowed to overturn. It was not in Chernigov's interests for the Wild Polovtsy to become too ambitious. Hence in 1168, exceptionally, the prince of Chernigov responded to the call of his Kievan kinsman.

Despite the various forms of accommodation and alliance, the Polovtsy still constituted a barrier, and occasionally a severe irritant, accentuated by the loss of Tmutorokan. The Rus princes therefore sought other ways both to outflank the nomads and to develop alternative markets. Apart from the Greek Route and the Route of the Vines, Mstislav Iziaslavich alludes to the importance of the Salt Route. This led westwards, towards the region of Galich and the foothills of the Carpathians. Salt, for preserving meat and fish, was essential to the large population centres whose inhabitants could not readily scavenge or hunt for game during prolonged or harsh winters. If the supply of salt from the western lands was cut off, as happened during the dynastic conflicts in the late 1090s, then the reaction of Kievan markets (and inhabitants) could be highly volatile (see above, p. 286). But control over the salt supply was by no means the only attraction of the Upper Dniester and its tributaries. The region was of value for its own sake, in being fertile yet set back from the steppes, and it was

---

17 S. A. Pletneva, 'Donskie Polovtsy', in B. A. Rybakov, ed., '*Slovo o polku Igoreve*' *i ego vremia* (Moscow, 1985), pp. 249–81.

18 *PVL*, I, pp. 148–9; see also above, p. 272.

19 S. A. Pletneva, 'Pechenegi, torki i polovtsy v iuzhnorusskikh stepiakh', *MIA* 62 (1958), 222.

quite densely populated. There had long been Slav settlements along the river valleys, especially in the watershed between the Dniester and the Prut, and these settlements had increased in size and number over the eleventh century. Above all, however, the area was a veritable cat's-cradle of trade-routes. Besides supplying necessities to the Middle Dnieper, the western settlements bestraddled the routes by which high-value goods arrived from more distant lands: from the Lower Danube and Byzantine territories up to Peremyshl and the Cherven towns and on towards the Baltic; from the markets of Cracow, Prague and the Middle Danube towards the older heartlands of the Rus.

Regensburg, the base for merchants known as *ruzarii* and the West European centre of the fur trade, had particularly close links with the Rus. In 1179 a certain Hartwich living 'in the town of Kiev' granted to the monastery of St Emmeram in Regensburg eighteen pounds of silver which was owing to him from his debtors there.[20] Further downstream along the Danube a set of regulations instituted by Duke Ottokar V of Styria (1129–64) and confirmed by his son in 1191 stipulated that wagons travelling to and from *Ruzia* had to pay 16 *denarii* and were not to be detained.[21] Individual traders from Rus, bringing their goods by wagon and 'with a single horse', were provided for in a charter issued by King Imre of Hungary for a monastery at Esztergom in 1198: they, along with 'those who bring precious furs', were to pay half a mark by way of customs.[22] In 1176 a charter of King Casimir the Just conferred the right to thirteen cartloads of salt from the customs at Sandomierz, 'when they arrive from Rus'.[23]

One-horse traders and wagon trains setting out for the markets of the Hungarians, Czechs, Poles and Germans were in no particular need of princely protection. They escaped the spotlight of native chroniclers until they began to impinge on the princes' own disputes. Thus we learn most about them from Latin sources. Such traders, along with the inhabitants of the settlements between the Dniester and the upper reaches of the Western Bug and of the Pripet's right-hand tributaries, seem to have been quite capable of ordering their own affairs. Princes arrived to find local and transit trade as a going concern, although princes became catalysts for the concentration of wealth. For example, from the late tenth century German silver had passed through these regions on its way to the Middle Dnieper, first as *denarii*, and from the early twelfth century in the form of ingots; but only from around the

20 J. Widemann, ed., *Die Traditionen des Hochstifts Regensburg und des Klosters S. Emmeram* (Quellen und Erörterungen zur bayerischen Geschichte. Neue Folge, 8; 1943, repr. Aalen, 1969), p. 459.
21 A. Meiller, ed., *Archiv für Kunde österreichischen Geschichte* X (1853), p. 92.
22 G. Féjer, ed., *Codex diplomaticus Hungariae* VII (Budapest, 1841), no. 76, p. 143.
23 L. Rzyszczewski and A. Muczkowski, eds, *Codex diplomaticus Poloniae* (Warsaw, 1847), I, p. 12.

mid-twelfth century did a significant number of the local settlements develop into sizable towns with the purchasing and fiscal power to siphon off some of the valuables in transit. The numerous crudely made lead seals excavated at Dorogichin suggest that princely agents levied customs dues on traders entering and leaving their territories. From the late twelfth century bronze water-holders, candlesticks, church bells and chalices manufactured in Germany and France were acquired by the churchmen or better-off inhabitants of towns such as Terebovl, Plesnesk and Iziaslavl.[24]

There had been junior princes at Terebovl (on the Seret, a northern tributary of the Dniester) and Peremyshl (on the Upper San) from the late eleventh century, and at Zvenigorod (just to the south-east of modern Lviv) from the 1120s, but Galich itself (on the Upper Dniester) became the permanent residence of a prince only from the 1140s. Almost immediately, however, the prince of Galich, Vladimirko Volodarevich, whose father and uncle had been among the troublesome country cousins at the Liubech conference, joined the political heavyweights; or at least the putative heavyweights. Galich's secure promontory, rising some 70 metres above river level and fortified with ramparts which enclosed an area of about 50 hectares, was and remained the only large urban centre in the Dniester region. Fairly numerous finds of Byzantine silver and copper coins along the Dniester, and of amphorae in Galich, indicate one of the sources of Vasilko's prosperity. He was well placed to profit from, and offer protection to, trade with the Lower Danube and the Byzantine lands.

The appearance of an ambitious prince in Galich had wider reper-cussions both among the Rus and among Galich's neighbours to the west and south. In 1144 Vladimirko was apparently over-vociferous (*mnogoglagolivyi*) in objecting when the prince of Kiev (Vsevolod Olgovich) appointed his own son to Vladimir-in-Volynia. The Kievan response was to organize a major military expedition. Vladimirko of Galich may have been regarded as a presumptuous provincial upstart, but the scale of the operation against him shows that his potential for trouble-making had to be taken seriously. The Kievan coalition included not only a dozen other regional princes but also auxiliaries from the Polovtsy and from Poland. Although Vladimirko was able to call in a contingent from Geza of Hungary, he could not match the forces sent against him. After being chased around from Terebovl to Zvenigorod he capitulated and agreed to pay the Kievan prince a very substantial sum of silver.[25]

Besides the indignation of his elders and betters on the Middle Dnieper, Vladimirko faced resentment in his own back yard. While

24 A. V. Kuza, *Malye goroda Drevnei Rusi* (Moscow, 1989), p. 128.
25 *PSRL*, II, col. 316 (1400 grivnas); I, 312 (1200 grivnas); the details differ slightly in the two accounts.

he was on the run from the Kievan coalition, the townsmen of Galich found themselves an alternative prince in the form of Vladimirko's nephew, Ivan Rostislavich of Zvenigorod. Vladimirko managed to force his way back into Galich. Ivan escaped south to the Danube and thence to Kiev, and for more than a decade he continued to be an intermittent irritant to the prince of Galich: plundering Galician trading-vessels and fishermen from a base on the Danube, again attempting to install himself in the city.[26]

Despite such distractions, Vladimirko continued his rapid rise. By the end of the 1140s, when Kiev had a new prince (Iziaslav Mstislavich: see below, p. 347), Vladimirko had upgraded and expanded his alliances. Among the Rus he found a friend in the prince of Kiev's powerful enemy to the north-east, Iurii of Suzdal. And to protect his Danubian interests he preferred the patronage of the Byzantine emperor Manuel I, who was also at odds with Kiev at the time, to the ineffectual aid of Manuel's enemy Geza II of Hungary (who had in any case married into the family of the prince of Kiev). In 1149 Vladimirko was at the gates of Kiev, in (temporarily) successful support of his Suzdalian ally's claim to the throne, while a Byzantine chronicler approvingly implies that he had placed himself under some form of obligation to the empire.[27] Meanwhile his city became the seat of a bishop. The prince of Galich had come a long way in a short time. His provincial crossroads was established and recognized as a significant regional centre whose zone of commercial and political interests was distinct from – though linked to – that of the Middle Dnieper.

From the deepest south-west we turn northwards, past Vladimir-in-Volynia and the Cherven towns (whose princes became increasingly covetous of Galich's successes) down rivers such as the Vistula and the Neman, on the way to the Baltic. Goods manufactured in Rus – pink slate spindle-whorls, glazed *pisanki*, and various types of rings – have been found along the coast of modern Poland at Szczecin, and at Lund and Sigtuna in Sweden. These were not especially valuable objects, and dealing in them was within the range of relatively small-time traders from the nearest of the Rus lands. The same could be said of some of the goods brought in the opposite direction, from the Baltic to the Rus (e.g. amber, and probably cloth). At Sigtuna there was a Rus community, with a stone church of St Nicholas, and on the island of Gotland there was a Rus trading hall. Both these foundations are first mentioned in the twelfth century. In 1159 Henry the Lion, Duke of Saxony, gave a fillip to commerce in the Baltic by reconstituting Lübeck as a trading centre. He is said to have sent envoys 'to the northern realms, to Denmark, Sweden, Norway and *Rucia*, offering

---

26 *PSRL*, II, col. 316; I, col. 312.
27 *hypospondos*: Kinnamos, *Historiae*, ed. A. Meineke (Bonn, 1836), p. 115; tr. C. M. Brand, *Deeds of John and Manuel Comnenus* (New York, 1976), p. 92.

them peace, and that they should have free access to his town'.[28] But the shipping and organization of the growing volume of exchanges came to be dominated by Scandinavians and by traders operating out of the north German towns. The valuable product which lured them, and which was plentiful in the northern lands of the Rus, was fur.

The town best placed to benefit from the mounting demand for furs in Western Europe was Novgorod. Unlike the more fertile and densely populated south, Novgorod's hinterland was not cluttered with satellite urban settlements. Novgorod was still surrounded by vast tracts of bog and forest, much as Gorodishche had been in the ninth and tenth centuries. The lands to its north were rich breeding-grounds for fur-bearing animals, and as the Western European market for furs expanded the Novgorodians were able to extend their catchment areas without serious local competition. They set up collection-posts along the Onega basin, then along the Northern Dvina and its tributaries, probing ever further in search of the finest furs such as sable, ermine and Arctic fox.

The *Primary Chronicle* includes a story apparently told by a Novgorodian named Giuriata Rogovich, who had sent a retainer (*otrok*) to the Pechora, 'a people who pay tribute to Novgorod', and then on to the Iugra, 'a people who inhabit the northern lands next to the Samoieds'. The journey had taken Giuriata's man north of the Arctic Circle to the tundra between the Pechora river and modern Vorkuta, about as far to the north and east as it would be possible to go before crossing into Siberia. But here the intrepid retainer heard of a still more distant people, a people trapped inside 'mountains as high as the sky and which descend to the sea shore'. These unfortunates were desperate to cut their way out of the mountain, so that 'if one gives them a knife or an axe they give furs in return; the route to these mountains is impassable with precipices and snows and forests'. The chronicler identifies them as the people imprisoned in the north by Alexander the Great, as narrated in the *Apocalypse* of Pseudo-Methodios of Patara.[29] We sense a tallish tale, which nevertheless suggests that by the beginning of the twelfth century the Novgorodians were becoming aware of the Ural mountains and the Arctic Ocean, and that they were always on the look-out for exchange. (See Map 11)

The sparse peoples of the distant north posed no great threat, and the Novgorodian fur-seekers did not have to travel in large armed groups. The exchange of axes and knives for furs is plausible. The early twelfth century – the time of Giuriata Rogovich's story – provides the first firm evidence of a number of specialized craft workshops

---

28 Helmhold of Bosau, *Chronica Slavorum*, I, ch. 86, ed. B. Schmeidler, tr. H. Stoob (Ausgewählte Quellen zur Deutschen Geschichte des Mittelalters 19; Berlin, 1963), pp. 304–5.
29 *PVL*, I, pp. 167–8.

in Novgorod, and from the 1120s and 1130s there was a steep rise in production, coupled with a change to cheaper and simpler methods for the manufacture of, for example, blades for knives, axes and shears. For the acquisition of fur from its northern hinterland Novgorod did not have to depend on produce from other Rus centres. It was self-reliant in its own nexus of crafts and trade-routes. And for the re-export of the furs thus acquired, Novgorod fed the markets of Western Europe. The city was linked via settlements and portages to the Gulf of Finland, and the presence of western traders was no novelty. There were longstanding norms for dealing with offences committed by or against westerners in Novgorod, or by or against Novgorodians overseas. The rules are recorded in a treaty made in the early 1190s with an envoy who represented the German towns, the Gotlanders and 'all the Latin tongue'.[30]

Novgorod could support its own fur trade, but not its own growing population. The city suffered from minor crop failures every four or five years. One may recall the birch-bark letter from Giurgii, who invited his parents to come from Novgorod to Smolensk or Kiev, where bread was cheap.[31] Another potential source of grain, but also a potential rival for the supplies of fur, emerged to the east of Novgorod in the region of the Upper Volga. This largely Finnic area had long attracted Slav migrants from the south and west, in a kind of counter-flow to the population transplants effected by Vladimir Sviatoslavich (see above, pp. 170, 176); but in the eleventh and twelfth centuries the Slav migration to the basins of the Volga and Oka was on a very large scale. The settlers may have been drawn partly by the fur trade (gold- and silver-foil beads and *denarii* have been found in some burial-grounds), but for the most part they lived by arable farming, stock-keeping, fishing and hunting. Princely interest in the region had been correspondingly slight by comparison with their interest in, for example, the Cherven towns. But as the potential tribute-yield increased with the growth of settlement, and as the dynasty spawned more members, and as proximity to the richest sources of fur became potentially more lucrative, so the southern princes set about establishing a more solid presence in the 'land beyond the forest'. Disputes over demarcation in the north-east had been among the causes of dynastic friction before the Liubech conference in 1097 (see above, pp. 267–9). During the first half of the twelfth century the north-east began to emerge as a prosperous trading zone in its own right, held together by a tighter political regime than the Rus or anyone else had achieved there before.

The key to commercial growth in the north-east was, on the one

---

30 *GVNP*, no. 28; dated 1191–2 in V. L. Ianin, *Novgorodskie akty XII–XV vv.: khronologicheskii kommentarii* (Moscow, 1991), pp. 81–2.
31 *NGB*, no. 424; see also above, p. 283.

hand, to have access to the main supplies of fur; and, on the other hand, to have access to the eastern markets via the Middle Volga. On the Middle Volga the Bulgars provided both a stimulus and an obstacle. Bulgar trade with the rich markets of the Caspian and beyond had continued despite the drying-up of the silver supply and despite the upheavals in Moslem Central Asia. The Arabic writer Abu Hamid, who visited Bulgar in 1135–6 and again in 1150–1, reported that the peoples living one month's journey to the north paid tribute to the Bulgars, and he described the 'silent trade' conducted by merchants among those who lived still further to the north, in the 'land of darkness'.[32] Like Giuriata Rogovich, Abu Hamid described the exchange of furs for metal blades (although in this case the blades took the form of swords or harpoons specially designed for the northerners' needs). According to Abu Hamid this trade yielded a 'huge profit'.[33]

Concerned to protect their own dealings in northern furs, the Volga Bulgars were not prepared to allow the Rus free navigation right down to the Caspian, just as they did not allow southern merchants free passage upstream. They could profit from being intermediaries in both directions, and Rus produce did reach the south in large quantities in the twelfth and early thirteenth centuries. But for the Bulgars control over the transit-points was a poor substitute for direct access to the 'lands of darkness' and to the harvest of furs and tribute. Here they were in straight competition with the Rus, since the catchment area to the north of Rostov and Suzdal verged on routes used by Bulgar merchants and tribute-gatherers along rivers such as the Unzha and the Iug. The Bulgars and the Rus colonists and traders could to a certain extent benefit from co-existence, but neither side was entirely comfortable with the strong presence of the other.[34]

There was a similar ambivalence in relation to Novgorod. The relatively fertile arable land of the Volga–Kliazma watershed was a potential source of grain for Novgorod, and also a conduit for luxury goods from the Orient. For the Rus in the north-east, Novgorod was the most accessible source of silver. But the Novgorodians, like the Bulgars, could not welcome unreservedly the development of a firm political structure on the Upper Volga: their direct access to Bulgar markets was impeded, and their virtual monopoly on northern furs was eroded. By the early twelfth century the Novgorodians had established collection-points not far to the north of Rostov along

32 O. G. Bol'shakova and A. L. Mongait (tr. and commentary), *Puteshestvie Abu Khamida al-Garnati v vostochnuiu i tsentral'nuiu Evropu (1131–1155 gg.)* (Moscow, 1971), p. 32; Janet Martin, *Treasure of the Land of Darkness. The Fur Trade and its Significance for Medieval Russia* (Cambridge, 1986), pp. 21–2.

33 Bol'shakova and Mongait, *Puteshestvie Abu Khamida*, p. 33.

34 For evidence of Rus commercial contracts with the Volga Bulgars in the twelfth and thirteenth centuries; see M. D. Poluboiarinova, *Rus' i Volzhskaia Bolgariia v X–XV vv.* (Moscow, 1993), pp. 89, 98–101, 106–8, 115–16, 119.

the river Sukhona, in areas which the ambitious traders from the Upper Volga region came to covet for themselves. The outposts and collection-points of the two powers intertwined, and competition brought friction and conflict. The view from Novgorod is encapsulated in the complaint, conveyed in a chronicle's narrative for 1148, that the prince of Rostov was 'hurting Novgorod', that he had 'taken tribute away from [the Novgorodians]' and was 'interfering with them on their routes'.[35] The complaint gained substance as the north-eastern princes gained confidence and clout. In 1159 Prince Andrei Bogoliubskii – he who authorized the attack on Kiev in 1169 – is alleged to have declared: 'Let it be known, I shall seek Novgorod by fair means or foul'.[36]

Princes in the area of Rostov and Suzdal thus had a major role as guarantors both against the Bulgars and against the Novgorodians. One of their characteristic activities in the mid-twelfth century was to build fortresses and garrisoned outposts around their central possessions and at the extremities of their stretch of route. Diplomatic and military skirmishes with Novgorod were a continual preoccupation, while victories over the Bulgars were celebrated in chronicle, eulogy, public festivity and commemorative monument (see below, p. 360). In the north-east, as previously in the south, the organization and policing of trade- and tribute-routes contributed to the consolidation and growth of a polity under princely rule. Fortresses stimulated local exchange and grew into fair-sized urban settlements with their own crafts, and by the later twelfth century the new and deliberately splendid princely city at Vladimir-on-the-Kliazma was attracting Byzantine, Jewish and West European merchants as well as Bulgars and Rus.

The tour around the old periphery is almost complete, but its final segments present a choice. The traditional route from this north-to-east trading axis would take us westwards (or southwards, if we start from Novgorod) to the Upper Dnieper and from there back down to Kiev. A straighter-flying crow would pass over the land of the notoriously inhospitable Viatichi (see above, pp. 179, 268). For the merchant both contained obstacles: the one physical, the other human. Following the path of the majority we shall choose safety first.

The expansion of commerce could not erase the major physical obstacle: the gap between the northern and southern river-systems. The traveller from Novgorod or the Upper Volga to the Upper Dnieper still had to pause at the portages, where his boats were hauled by teams of men over log rollers. The barrier was far from trivial. One of its durable indications was the fact that north and south continued to use different weight-units (see above, p. 285). However, the merchant's inconvenience was the middleman's profit, and a prime beneficiary of the thickening of trade over the twelfth century was Smolensk. As we

---

35 PSRL, II, col. 367; Martin, Treasure, p. 120.
36 PSRL, II, col. 509; Berezhkov, Khronologiia, pp. 171–2, 332–3.

have seen, Gnëzdovo (i.e. old Smolensk) had previously grown in part as a service station, control-point and boat repair centre for those who had crossed to the Dnieper by portage from the north (see above, pp. 100, 102, 127–8). From the late eleventh century the new town arose some 10 kilometres to the east, taking over the business and also the name. A substantial number of new settlements and towns – more than twenty of them – emerged along the rivers in the region between the Upper Dnieper, the Lovat and the head-waters of the Volga: many of them easing (at a price) the way of the transit traveller, and all of them passing a proportion of their income to Smolensk.

The proliferation of profitable portages can be seen in the 1136 charter for the bishopric of Smolensk, which lists the amounts due from the outlying areas. By far the largest sum, 1,030 grivnas, was payable by the district together with the town of Verzhavsk, where the upper reaches of the Dnieper are close to tributaries of the Western Dvina. The next highest sum, 400 grivnas, was due from Toropets, which also lay near a key portage, as did nearly all the other seven places owing 100 grivnas or more.[37] On the evidence of the charter, in 1136 the highest-paying portages were still those which straddled the old route 'from the Varangians to the Greeks', the route which still carried northern furs and silver in exchange for southern manufactured and luxury goods, and sometimes grain. Two of the portages, however, led to the Volga, while an item laconically labelled as the 'Suzdal tribute' also attests the prince's interest in the north-east. Taken as a whole the tribute-list in the Smolensk charter is an index of the intensified flow of goods and people between the river-systems. (See Map 9).

The rise in Smolensk's fortunes changed its political stature. In the eleventh century Smolensk occasionally had its own resident member of the dynasty, but mostly it provided supplementary income for southern Pereiaslavl. From around 1125 Smolensk became the permanent seat of an increasingly influential prince, who set about making the town worthy of himself. An earthen rampart was constructed, enclosing 90 hectares, making it one of the largest fortified areas of any Rus town.[38] The 1136 charter was linked to the establishment of a bishopric. Buildings blossomed. Such public affirmations of status can be set down to princely initiative, but the city's spectacularly fast growth – the Smolensk phenomenon – was ultimately driven by rising demand for the services of boatmen, hauliers and craftsmen at a nodal point of inter-regional trade among the Rus.

---

37 L. V. Alekseev, *Smolenskaia zemlia v IX–XIII vv.* (Moscow, 1980), pp. 44–6 and figs. 2 and 5; charter in *ZDR*, pp. 212–23; Kaiser, *The Laws*, pp. 51–5; V. L. Ianin, 'Zametki o komplekse dokumentov Smolenskoi eparkhii XII veka', *Otechestvennaia istoriia* 1994, no. 6, 110–13; see also above, p. 232.

38 N. N. Voronin and P. A. Rappoport, 'Drevnii Smolensk', *SA* 1979, no. 1, p. 85.

Smolensk, like Galich, benefited from being in a zone of intersection between several routes. But between some destinations there were alternatives. In particular, a traveller between the north-east and the Middle Dnieper, or between the north-east and the Black Sea, might notionally have preferred the more direct path through the forests of the land of the Viatichi, between the head-waters of the Oka and those of the Kliazma. The problem here was that the Viatichi had been fiercely resistant to assimilation within the dynastic network of tribute-collection and satellite settlement. The Viatichi had their own political structure and ruling elite, they could gather in promontory forts (called 'towns' in the chronicles), and their readiness to defend themselves is shown in the large number of armour-piercing arrowheads and spearheads which have been excavated at some of their settlements. For Monomakh a journey 'through the Viatichi' had been a journey worth boasting about. For the compilers of the *Primary Chronicle* the Viatichi were still the black sheep of the Slav tribes, sticking to the bad old ways with polygamy and cremation of the dead 'even now', 'not knowing God's law, but making their own law for themselves'.[39]

However, the Viatichi had never been entirely averse to trade and exchange. On the Upper Oka they had been involved in the oriental silver trade to the extent that they had been able to pay their tribute to the Khazars in the form of silver pieces (see above, p. 77). As the rulers of the Rus began to take a renewed and more persistent interest in the Upper Volga region, princes and missionaries from the Rus may still have had to be wary of the Viatichi, but bands of traders and trinket-bearers could be more welcome. Many of the Viatichian towns arose along or near a land-route from Kiev to Rostov, spaced at approximately one day's travelling distance from one another. Some of them lay at points where the route crossed small rivers, and the names of the rivers became attached to the towns: Serensk on the river Serena, Tarusa, Moskva. The latter, better known in English as Moscow, came into being as a fortified promontory settlement at the end of the eleventh century, and it seems from the start to have been involved in trading with the Dnieper region. Pink slate spindle-whorls, beads and a lead weight from a pair of scales have been found in excavations of its most ancient level, while through the next level, which preserves objects from the twelfth century, there is a continual increase in the quantity and range of manufactures imported from the south: glazed pottery, yellow glass goblets, glass bracelets, fragments of amphorae.[40]

---

39 *PVL*, I, pp. 15, 158; cf. above p. 179.

40 M. G. Rabinovich, 'O vozraste i pervonachal'noi territorii Moskvy', in *Novoe o proshlom nashei strany* (Moscow, 1967), pp. 25–6; T. N. Nikol'skaia, *Zemlia viatichei. K istorii naseleniia basseina verkhnei i srednei Oki v IX–XIII vv.* (Moscow, 1981), p. 134.

The eleventh-century towns emerged at the initiative of the Viatichi themselves. Encroachment by the Rus over the twelfth century spread from both ends, led by the princes of Chernigov to the south and by the princes of Rostov and Suzdal to the north-east. The princes' interest was still primarily in tribute: in 'slaves and goods', to use the expression which appears in a chronicle's report of negotiations over sharing out zones of tribute in 1146.[41] The land of the Viatichi had a growing population, swelled partly by migrants from areas more directly under princely rule; and the Viatichian forests were another source for that most marketable of northern commodities, fur. For their part, the Viatichi continued to develop a taste for consumer durables and exotic luxuries: silks and gold brocades from Byzantium and Central Asia, similar to those found in graves in the north-east and on the Middle Dnieper, have been excavated even in rural cemeteries in the Moscow region. Here too, therefore, the advantages of servicing the trade-routes helped to erode local resistance to tribute-seeking princely colonists. By the mid-twelfth century a prince of Chernigov could travel across large tracts of the land of the Viatichi without the old sense of danger.[42] The Chernigovan family was even installing 'governors' in towns such as Briansk and Mtsensk, while in 1147 Prince Iurii of Suzdal held a 'mighty feast' in Moskva for his Chernigovan kinsman and rival.[43] The land of the Viatichi, or at least parts of it, had ceased to be a 'no-go area'.

From the Viatichi across to Chernigov and back to Kiev, or down to the Don and the Azov and Black Seas: the circle is complete. Right round the old periphery we have seen the growth of old and the emergence of new economic centres, of new zones of active commerce, as wider areas and populations were drawn into the increasingly elaborate and lucrative networks of tribute and exchange. Traditional cities like Kiev and Novgorod prospered and the number of large towns increased, but (as, for example, in the territories of Smolensk and the Viatichi) there was also a marked rise in the number of smaller fortified settlements of between $1/2$ and $2^{1}/2$ hectares. Approximately 50 such small towns are known and excavated from the period before c. 1150, and about 80 at the turn of the next century, while others had grown into the category of larger towns.[44] The competitors on the Middle Dnieper were acquiring competitors elsewhere.

The near-monopoly of the Middle Dnieper was broken. However, this does not mean – as is often mistakenly assumed or asserted – that the Middle Dnieper itself became poorer. The rise of the regions did not lead to, or result from, a decline of Kiev. The Dnieper route

---

41 *PSRL*, II, col. 337.
42 On the journey of Sviatoslav Olgovich see Nikol'skaia, *Zemlia viatichei*, pp. 120–46.
43 *PSRL*, II, cols 339–40, 342.
44 Kuza, *Malye goroda*, pp. 63–4 and tables 1 and 2. (See Map 5)

remained valuable. If alternative routes between Byzantium and the north came more into play, such as the route from the Danube to Galich, or from the Azov region via the Don, it was not because the Polovtsy had made Kiev inaccessible (they had not), or because the Byzantines were losing the Black Sea to Italians – the emperor Manuel I made sure to exclude the Genoese from free access to trade from Tmutorokan and the region of *Rhōsia* on the Azov Sea.[45] The opening and exploitation of new opportunities did not imply the end of the old. Indeed one could argue that Kiev's very success may have prompted Black Sea traders to look more keenly at the alternative routes, since many of the traditionally imported items were now being manufactured in, and exported northwards from, Kiev itself (see above, pp. 280–1). The alarm of the Kievan prince in 1168 may well have been genuine, but it should not be taken as a sign of impending catastrophe. Economic life on the Middle Dnieper was resilient enough to withstand the ebb and flow of frontier politics, and the physical danger lay elsewhere: it was not the Polovtsy who sacked Kiev in 1169; nor did the sack of the city lead to its impoverishment.

Nevertheless the rise of the regions did alter the balance and the focus. Each new centre had its distinct local interests and orientation: for Rostov and Suzdal, for example, the priority was to secure a position between the fur-bearing north (and Novgorod) and the Middle Volga; Galich needed to balance its relations with Hungary and Byzantium, while Chernigov's vital interests were linked both to the Polovtsy and to the Viatichi. This was growth through diffusion as well as expansion. Rivalries were inevitable, perhaps necessary. But at the same time the pattern of commodities and resources favoured a fairly high degree of cooperation – between traders, between local population centres, and between those who wished to be accepted as rulers. No single town had a stranglehold on an important route, so there was no advantage in making tolls exorbitant. Even Smolensk and Novgorod could be circumvented. And as the Viatichi discovered, to insist on self-sufficiency and isolation was not in the longer term profitable. The writers of the birch-bark letters appear to take for granted the fact that travel was easy and cheap.

The burgeoning regional economies were to some extent, therefore, both interdependent – thriving on the links between them – and driven from below. The princes lacked the administrative apparatus for detailed intervention. In any case, in several areas regional economic activity began to intensify before the regular presence of a member of the ruling dynasty. Migration and rising populations stimulated local

---

45 I. Zepos and P. Zepos, eds, *Ius Graecoromanum* (Athens, 1931), I, p. 420; T. S. Noonan, 'The flourishing of Kiev's international and domestic trade, ca. 1100–ca. 1240', in I. S. Koropeckyj, ed., *Ukrainian Economic History. Interpretive Essays* (Cambridge, Mass., 1991), pp. 139–40, 143–6.

exchange, enterprising and mobile traders probed and developed new markets, settlements grew at key points on their routes. The low level of supervision and interference was probably beneficial to business confidence in the small settlements among the 'one-horse traders' who played such a crucial role in regional wealth-creation over the twelfth century. When princes did arrive to skim off the profits, drawn by the prospect of fresh tribute, they were often obliged to negotiate their claims with care, or else to suffer the undignified consequences of presumptuousness. However, princes did not have to be purely parasitic: they could also serve as catalysts. In the north-east, for example, the prince's role as founder and protector of towns was of decisive importance. Besides offering some measure of defence and arbitration, princes also tended to re-invest part of their profits in ways which further stimulated local crafts and markets: in construction, in the demand for luxury goods and cultural accessories.

Clearly the princes could not just sit back and wait for the fruits to fall into their laps. In their own way they had to be as enterprising as the itinerant traders. Insinuating themselves into the regions was one problem; dealing with their own kin was another. It was no simple matter for the ruling family to remould itself to the new economic geography, to adapt to the rise of the regions. The change affected many levels of life among the Rus. Let us first consider the political dimension.

2. A GROWING FAMILY: THE POLITICS OF DYNASTIC DIVERSITY

Along the routes and into the settlements spread the ever more numerous members of the dynasty: collecting tribute, sitting with their *druzhina*, building ramparts and churches, cajoling and trying to impress the locals, propagating their culture, and squabbling with each other. As their own numbers multiplied, it was just as well that there were new opportunities to be exploited and new spaces to be filled. Over the entire eleventh century there had been little more than a couple of dozen known princes of the ruling family, and their interrelationships were quite complex enough. From the twelfth century we know of a couple of hundred, every one of them a prince. As the generations extended and degrees of consanguinity allowed, so the separate branches of the clan could begin to intertwine as princes exchanged offspring for intermarriage. The twelfth-century chronicles are intimidatingly convoluted tales of acrimony between brothers, cousins, uncles and nephews, whose patterns of alliance and counter-alliance were in perpetual transmutation. But this was the noise on the surface, the creaks and cracks and strains of the successful dynasty as it adapted to growth. If the family had had to keep dividing and subdividing the same cake among its ever more numerous members, then the scuffles for crumbs might have been far more critical.

Through the 1110s, 1120s and 1130s, especially under Vladimir Monomakh (1113–25) and his eldest son Mstislav (1125–32), the rise of the regions seemed to reflect and enhance the status of Kiev as the hub of the dynasty's operations, whose spokes reached out into the periphery. In 1113 Monomakh, either personally or through sons and grandsons, already controlled Kiev, Novgorod, Pereiaslavl, Smolensk, Rostov and Suzdal. He soon dispossessed or subordinated the offspring of his elder cousin Sviatopolk, first by taking Turov and then (in 1118) by forcing Sviatopolk's son Iaroslav out of Vladimir-in-Volynia, where he installed one of his own sons (at the request of the townspeople, according to the chronicle).[46] In 1119 Monomakh ousted Gleb Vseslavich from Minsk and made him and his family live in Kiev.[47] In 1130 Mstislav rounded up the more recalcitrant Vseslavichi of Polotsk and exiled them to Byzantium. The Chernigov branch of the family had been fairly pliant since the days of the Liubech agreement. In the mid-1120s it was divided against itself, and Mstislav managed to procure Kursk by playing one faction against another.[48] Thus by the early 1130s the Monomakhovichi – Mstislav and his sons and younger brothers – dominated most of the main dynastic centres: from Kiev and Pereiaslavl over to Kursk in the south-east, to Rostov and Suzdal in the north-east, Novgorod in the north, Polotsk and Minsk and Smolensk across the centre, west to Turov and Vladimir-in-Volynia; and the prince of Chernigov had become Mstislav's son-in-law. The age of Monomakh and Mstislav can seem like an embodiment of the conventional kievocentric vision of the lands of the Rus.

Yet Monomakh and Mstislav helped to precipitate, indeed they actively promoted, regional developments which significantly reshaped the political and cultural landscape in ways which they probably neither desired nor foresaw. The new prosperity of the regions outside the Middle Dnieper had paradoxical consequences. It brought both integration and diffusion.

In the first place, regional prosperity brought a new solidity and dignity to previously peripheral towns. Both Monomakh and Mstislav reversed the earlier pattern of patronage, investing in buildings and cultural institutions to raise the prestige of the outlying dynastic strongholds (see below, pp. 353–5). In time the outposts came to look and feel less peripheral; new masonry churches, monasteries, princely

---

46 *PSRL*, II, cols 284–5.
47 Ibid., col. 285: see also above, p. 255.
48 On the problem of dating see Martin Dimnik, *The Dynasty of Chernigov 1054–1146* (Texts and Studies 116, Pontifical Institute of Mediaeval Studies; Toronto, 1994), pp. 316–17.

residences and even new bishoprics contributed to the emergence of more self-sustaining local identities. Secondly, regional prosperity gave fresh scope for one of the traditional means of easing the pressure caused by dynastic growth: tributary colonies were hived off as separate patrimonial possessions. Like Vladimir and Iaroslav, Monomakh controlled a network of towns through his sons; and like the sons and grandsons of Iaroslav, the sons and grandsons of Monomakh treated the more desirable of those towns not as reallocatable common holdings but as permanent bases for themselves and their own descendants. For example, Smolensk and Suzdal had been sources of income for Monomakh's family based in Pereiaslavl; by the mid-twelfth century they had become the patrimonial seats of separate branches of the Monomakhovichi, leaving Pereiaslavl to rely on its own hinterland. Thirdly, the Monomakhovichi, though dominant in the early decades of the century, did not have the stage to themselves. After temporary quiescence the ambitions of Chernigov revived under the second generation of Sviatoslavichi in the 1130s. And by the 1140s and 1150s the Galician family in the west had acquired substantial political and military clout.

The result, in the absence of any centralized mechanisms of political control, was that the dynasty and its territories became increasingly polycentric. As the families of the Middle Dnieper exploited the new opportunities in the regions, so the hegemony of the Middle Dnieper gradually gave way to a network of patrimonies stretching from the Volga to the Carpathians: Rostov and Suzdal, Riazan, Pereiaslavl, Chernigov, Smolensk, Polotsk, Turov and Pinsk, Vladimir-in-Volynia, Galich. These patrimonies – cities with princely seats ('thrones' – *stoly*) plus an associated hinterland – are given various labels by modern historians: principalities, appanages, city states, according to the historian's choice of extraneous model. In the sources they are 'lands': the Suzdal Land, the Smolensk Land, etc. There was no single collective name for the agglomeration of patrimonies. In twelfth-century sources the 'Rus Land', or simply 'Rus' (*Rus'*, *Russkaia zemlia*) usually meant just the territory around Kiev itself. Thus, for example, a journey might be said to lead 'from the Suzdal Land to Rus'.[49]

Though in absolute terms the Middle Dnieper continued to prosper, in relative terms its power declined. The network of patrimonial lands could no longer be managed by a cosy consortium of inner-circle cousins. The regions were too strong, and their interests too divergent. Yet nor, for the most part, could the regional princes afford to cut themselves off entirely from their extended kin. The military capacity

49 See A. A. Gorskii, 'Rus' v kontse X–nachala XII veka: territorial'no-politicheskaia struktura ("zemli" i "volosti")', *Otechestvennaia istoriia* 1992, no. 4, 154–61.

of the individual lands was inadequate; and their interests, though far from identical, were still to a considerable extent interdependent. Dynastic alliances and power-blocs emerged and dissolved and reshaped themselves with bewildering ease, and strategic coherence is often obscured in tactical detail. The political culture of the dynasty preserved certain conventions and guidelines, but it provided no precisely fixed system of precedence, seniority or subordination. At every change of ruler the pack was at least partially reshuffled. To confuse matters further, the larger pattern of relations *between* patrimonial princes was replicated in microcosm *within* the patrimonial lands, as each patrimonial prince had to accommodate or contain the ambitions of his own younger brothers or nephews, cousins or sons: the cousins from Putivl or Novgorod-Seversk vying for Chernigov; the nephew from Zvenigorod with his eye on Galich. The proliferation of princelings led to a process of continual dynastic and territorial cell-splitting.

Not all 'lands' were the same, not all changes occurred simultaneously, and not all princes responded identically. By the mid-twelfth century the dynasty as a whole had grown too successful, too numerous and too diffuse to be fitted into any single linear narrative. Yet it is possible to follow some of the main features of political and ideological adaptation over the middle decades of the century, through episodes from the places which – as may have been noted – are absent from our list of patrimonial lands but where most dynastic paths still tended to cross: Novgorod and Kiev.

Though princes of Kiev claimed ancestral justification to the 'throne of their fathers and grandfathers', the Kievan land – despite the efforts of some of its rulers – did not revert to any one branch of the extended family. The contenders had patrimonial bases elsewhere. From the late 1130s until the end of the century (that is, until the unification of Vladimir-in-Volynia with Galich) the main players in this game came from four branches of the dynasty in four patrimonial lands: Monomakh's son Iurii and his offspring based in the northeast; Monomakh's grandson Iziaslav Mstislavich and his offspring based in Vladimir-in-Volynia; another grandson, Rostislav Mstislavich (Iziaslav's brother) and his offspring, based in Smolensk; and the descendants of Oleg and David Sviatoslavichi based in Chernigov. Notable by their absence are the offspring of Sviatopolk Iziaslavich, senior partner at the Liubech conference in 1097, although in the later twelfth century his descendants recovered his regional patrimony as princes of Turov and Pinsk.[50]

Succession to Kiev was competitive but not random; it was constrained by a sense (or by competing senses) of legitimizing convention.

---

50 O. M. Rapov, *Kniazheskie vladeniia na Rusi v X–pervoi polovine XIII v.* (Moscow, 1977), pp. 81–93; P. F. Lysenko, 'Kiev i Turovskaia zemlia', in L. O. Pobol' et al., eds, *Kiev i zapadnye zemli Rusi v IX–XIII vv.* (Minsk, 1982), pp. 81–108.

Novgorod, by contrast, was a growing economic magnet which fell into a dynastic vacuum. Partly in consequence the dynastic succession in the patrimonial lands was relatively stable – if rarely smooth – whereas the turnover of princes in Kiev, and even more dramatically in Novgorod, became quite rapid. Between 1000 and 1150 there were about twenty changes of power in Kiev, involving some sixteen princes: the average continuous reign was thus approximately 7.5 years, while the average total 'reign expectancy' of a given prince was a little under ten years, perhaps with an interruption in exceptional circumstances. Compare this with the second half of the twelfth century (1150–1200), during which there were 30 changes of power involving a total of eleven princes: an average continuous reign of less than two years, and an average total 'reign expectancy' of under five years, usually with at least two interruptions.[51] In Novgorod a similar change occurred slightly earlier. From 1000 to 1136 there were no more than a dozen princes of Novgorod, giving an average reign of over a decade. In the 50 years from 1136 there were about 30 changes of prince, giving an average continuous reign of less than two years.[52]

At the end of May 1136 the Novgorodians, together with their neighbours from Pskov and Staraia Ladoga, decided to rid themselves of their prince, Vsevolod Mstislavich, grandson of Monomakh and nephew of the prince of Kiev. Vsevolod had been appointed to Novgorod when his father Mstislav was transferred to the south in 1117. In May 1136 he and his family were arrested and held under armed guard in the bishop's residence for two months while the Novgorodians negotiated with other members of the dynasty for an alternative. After his expulsion Vsevolod tried to return and reclaim his post. He only got as far as Pskov, where, despite Novgorodian threats, he was protected until his death in 1138.[53] Over the next few years the Novgorodians changed tack several times, renegotiating, expelling and accepting a series of candidates from various patrimonial lands.

The events of May 1136 have attracted a great deal of comment. Some have seen the detention and expulsion of Vsevolod as nothing less than the start of a social revolution in which the townspeople took control of their own city and reduced the subsequent role of the prince to little more than that of a hired defence contractor;[54] but this interpretation is now widely regarded as untenable, an attempt to project onto the 1130s some distinctive features which Novgorod

---

51 See lists in G. Podskalsky, *Christentum und theologische Literatur in der Kiever Rus' (988–1237)* (Munich, 1982), pp. 302–3.
52 See lists in M. Hellmann, ed., *Handbuch der Geschichte Russlands, I. i: von der Kiever Reichsbildung bis zum moskauer Zartum* (Stuttgart, 1981), pp. 481–3.
53 *NPL*, pp. 24–5; Vsevolod was subsequently venerated as Pskov's first saint.
54 On 1136 as signalling a major change see e.g. M. N. Tikhomirov, *The Towns of Ancient Rus* (Moscow, 1959), pp. 220–2.

acquired in the later middle ages. In the twelfth century a prince of the dynasty was as essential to the dignity, legitimacy and practical functioning of Novgorod as he was in any other major city. And Novgorod was by no means the only place where the townspeople invited, rejected or negotiated terms with princes: on the contrary, such incidents are almost commonplace in the chronicles' narratives of political life right across the lands of the Rus: for example, in Vladimir-in-Volynia in 1118, Polotsk in 1127 and 1132, Galich in 1145, the north-east in 1174, Kiev in 1146–7 (see below, pp. 347–8), and of course the Vseslav affair of 1068–9.[55] Others explain the expulsion of Vsevolod as just the start of a long struggle to reduce princely power; or as part of a factional struggle between supporters of different branches of the dynasty (Vsevolod did have personal supporters in Novgorod, and in line with the common pattern their possessions were plundered once their patron was removed);[56] or a conflict between proponents and opponents of princely rule; or, by complete contrast, as an institutional boost for future princes in Novgorod, who could subsequently claim to rule with the people's mandate.[57]

Most of this is speculative. The main change signalled by the Novgorodian events of 1136 was in inter-regional politics and power rather than in local society or institutions. In 1136 Prince Vsevolod Olgovich of Chernigov inflicted a series of defeats on the Kievan ruler Iaropolk Vladimirovich (Mstislav's younger brother). Novgorodians, sensitive to the shifting wind, asked Vsevolod to send them his brother in place of the nephew of the prince of Kiev. In 1138, when Vsevolod Olgovich's position appeared more precarious, Novgorod turned to Iurii Vladimirovich of Suzdal, requesting his son as their prince. This was the first occasion on which Novgorod aligned itself with an established prince of the north-east,[58] and it reflects what was to be the consistent policy of the princes of Suzdal: to gain access to both ends of the routes between the Baltic and the Middle Volga. But on Iaropolk's death in 1139 Vsevolod Olgovich managed to install himself in Kiev, and the Novgorodians decided not to send troops in support of Iurii's attempt to oust him. Any choice was risky.

---

55 *PSRL*, I, cols 288–9, 301–2, 371–2; II, cols 316–17, 497; see also above, pp. 252–3, 278–9, and below on Kiev in 1147; see Tikhomirov, *Towns*, pp. 196–228.

56 *NPL*, p. 24.

57 See V. L. Ianin, *Ocherki kompleksnogo istochnikovedeniia* (Moscow, 1977), pp. 60–77; I. Ia. Froianov, *Miatezhnyi Novgorod. Ocherki istorii gosudarstvennosti, sotsial'noi i politicheskoi bor'by kontsa IX–nachala XIII stoletiia* (St Petersburg, 1992), pp. 186–208; O. V. Martyshin, *Vol'nyi Novgorod: obshchestvenno-politicheskii stroi i pravo feodal'noi respubliki* (Moscow, 1992), pp. 58–94.

58 In 1095 Mstislav Vladimirovich moved to Novgorod from Rostov, but he had previously been prince of Novgorod for five years and his north-eastern posting was temporary: see above, p. 267.

Iurii, in annoyance, took the Novgorodian outpost of Novyi Torg (lit. 'Newmarket'), but still the Novgorodians judged it prudent to petition for the return of Vsevolod's brother. And so on and so on through the century and beyond.[59]

For Novgorod, therefore, the lack of a local branch of the dynasty was both an advantage and a disadvantage. On the one hand, the Novgorodians had the hinterland to themselves, untroubled by a network of princely settlements with fast-breeding and quarrelsome junior incumbents. This was a significant economic bonus for the Novgorodian boiar families as they harvested the profits of the fur trade. But on the other hand, the dynastic vacuum made Novgorod especially vulnerable, for it had no 'natural' patron, no succession of local princes with an inherited family commitment to defending their Novgorodian *otchina*. Until the 1130s the best protector available was usually the prince of Kiev, sometimes another prince from the Middle Dnieper.[60] With the rise of the regions and the decline in the relative power of the Middle Dnieper, Novgorod gained a kind of independence but also a more precarious and unstable kind of dependence. It was wooed or cajoled by the princes of most of the main 'lands': Chernigov, Smolensk, Suzdal, Vladimir-in-Volynia. The Novgorodians had to play the field with care, with a close eye on the changing balance of power. This, and not Novgorodian social attitudes, is the main reason for Novgorod's accelerated turnover of princes after 1136. Nevertheless the accelerated turnover, together with the absence of princely settlement in the huge and profitable hinterland, did have social consequences. In time the city's continuity and identity did come to be associated, rather more closely than elsewhere, with the local Novgorodian elites – the boiars and the bishop.

Kievan political ingenuity was applied to a slightly different problem: how to accommodate expediency while cloaking it as convention. As we have seen, dynastic convention had always been more flexible than some of its contemporary apologists or modern theorists would lead one to expect (above, Chapters Five and Seven). In the mid-twelfth century its flexibility was pushed to new limits. There was no such thing as *the* legitimate successor to Kiev. Rather there was a range of potentially legitimate rulers. The range was quite small, some claims were in principle more cogent than others, but principles and facts had to find ways of bending to each other. Seniority was acquired, or even conferred, not automatically inherited.

When Monomakh's son Mstislav died in 1132 he was succeeded by his younger brother Iaropolk. When Iaropolk died, early in 1139, two

---

59 Froianov, *Miatezhnyi Novgorod*, pp. 218–24; Dimnik, *The Dynasty of Chernigov*, pp. 333–48.
60 On previous non-Kievan incumbents see above, pp. 256, 263.

more of his brothers still lived. The elder of the two was Viacheslav (of Smolensk, then of Turov), and the younger was Iurii. Viacheslav seems to have been either unable or unwilling to press his claim vigorously. After occupying Kiev for just a couple of weeks (24 February–4 March 1139) he ceded the city to his second cousin, Vsevolod Olgovich of Chernigov. Over the spring and summer Vsevolod managed to negotiate and bribe his way to alliances with potential opponents in the south and west, and the digruntled Iurii – who failed to get support from Novgorod – had no choice but to retire to the north-east in frustration.

For many modern historians Vsevolod was a 'usurper', since his father Oleg had never been prince of Kiev and his grandfather Sviatoslav Iaroslavich had himself usurped the throne.[61] But there is no compelling reason for us to interpret rights and wrongs from a purely Monomakhovich perspective. Over the remainder of the twelfth century the house of Chernigov provided three more rulers of Kiev. Two of them reigned very briefly, but the third – Vsevolod's son Sviatoslav – was prince of Kiev for a total of seventeen years (1176–80, 1181–94), longer than any Kievan incumbent since before the days of Monomakh. If Vsevolod bent the Monomakhovich version of the rules, he did so with the acquiescence of the Kievans who mattered, and indeed with the acquiescence of most of the Monomakhovichi themselves. Monomakh's grandson Iziaslav Mstislavich (prince, successively, of Vladimir-in-Volynia, of Pereiaslavl, and then of Kiev) subsequently explained: 'I held Vsevolod to have the rights of an elder brother, since he was my brother [brat: the word for both 'brother' and 'cousin': actually Vsevolod was Iziaslav's second-cousin-once-removed!] and my brother-in-law [Vsevolod was married to Iziaslav's sister], senior to me as a father'.[62]

This might well have perplexed the compilers of the Primary Chronicle, back in simpler days. The Testament of Iaroslav the Wise had emphasized the fact that his successors were 'brothers by the same father and mother' (see above, p. 246). Iziaslav's convoluted self-justification shows how in the expanded dynasty close political kinship could be created out of fairly distant natural kinship, and even (a new factor in internal dynastic politics) by marriage. It is difficult to tell which, in context, was more contrived: Iaroslav's stress on the nuclear family, or his great-great-grandson's obviously contingent manipulation, variants of which were to become almost standard practice from the mid-twelfth century.

Such flexible kinship, though doubtless prudent Realpolitik, reopened old uncertainties about future succession. Vsevolod followed the

---

61 See e.g. Dimnik, The Dynasty of Chernigov, pp. 349–62; N. S. Kollmann, 'Collateral succession in Kievan Rus'', HUS 14 (1990), 383.
62 PSRL, II, col. 323.

example of his great-grandfather Iaroslav the Wise in trying to tie up the future succession before his own death, but the difference in procedure and result highlights the gulf between the times. Iaroslav had merely given instructions to his sons. Vsevolod's nominated successor was his younger brother Igor. In 1145 Vsevolod arranged for his own close kin (the Chernigov family) to 'kiss the Cross' to Igor, and in 1146, during his final illness, he had the 'townspeople' of Kiev and Vyshgorod perform the same ceremony. Vsevolod died on 1 August 1146.[63]

However, Crosses kissed at the behest of a reigning prince could easily be unkissed when he was out of the way. Igor had to renegotiate the deal in his own right. As usual, the townspeople's main complaint was against the deceased prince's senior servitors: in this instance not the *tysiatskii* as in 1113 or the *voevoda* as in 1068 but the stewards (*tiuny*) Ratsha and Tudor ('Ratsha has ruined Kiev and Tudor has ruined Vyshgorod').[64] Igor promised that the Kievans would be able to choose the new *tiuny* for themselves, and on this assurance the townspeople rekissed the Cross. The Kievans thus won a concession in some respects analogous to the Novgorodian right to elect their own *posadnik*. This was evidently a topical agenda.

But Crosses kissed in one set of negotiations could be unkissed in another. Iziaslav Mstislavich (he of the convenient multiple kinship definition) was meanwhile putting together a coalition of more effective support around Kiev: from Belgorod, Vasilev, the *Chernye klobuki* and the garrisons along the Ros.[65] Some of the Kievan notables also defected to his side. Igor's attempt to disperse Iziaslav's forces was a pathetic failure, as he and his troops became bogged down (literally, in a marsh). Igor was captured in ignominy, and Iziaslav Mstislavich, grandson of Monomakh, was received in Kiev by 'a multitude of the people and hegumens and monks and priests of the whole city of Kiev', and he prostrated himself before the Mother of God in St Sophia and 'sat on the throne of his grandfather and of his father'.[66] As was often the case after a change of prince, there was a forcible redistribution of resources: the Kievans 'plundered the *druzhiny* of Vsevolod and Igor . . . and took much wealth both in their houses and in the monasteries'.[67] Igor was imprisoned, first in the monastery of St Michael at Vydubichi outside Kiev, then in Pereiaslavl. At his own request he was tonsured as a monk, and returned to a monastery in Kiev, where in 1147 he was hacked

---

63 Ibid., cols 317–18.
64 Ibid., col. 321.
65 Ibid., col. 323.
66 Ibid., col. 327.
67 Ibid., col. 328; cf. above, pp. 278, 303, on the Kievan threat to plunder monasteries in 1113; in both instances the threatened 'monasteries' may well have been small private foundations sustained by the out-of-favour servitors of the former prince, rather than the larger, self-sufficient communities.

to death by a Kievan mob, a scapegoat at a time of tensions with Chernigov. When Igor's body was recovered from the market-place in the Podol and laid in the church of St Michael, candles spontaneously ignited. Igor Olgovich came to be venerated as a saint.[68]

Igor's death did not make Iziaslav safe. The more protracted challenge was from his closer relatives. His two uncles, Viacheslav and Iurii, were still very much alive. They were Monomakh's sons, whereas Iziaslav was merely a grandson. Iziaslav was from the older line (his father had been their older brother) but Viacheslav and Iurii were senior in generation. Strict theory of collateral succession ought to tell us that Viacheslav and Iurii were right. But in fact analogous struggles between uncles and nephews were very common among Iziaslav's contemporaries right across the regions. The results of such struggles were mixed. Uncles tended to win, but this did not stop nephews trying their luck, often with some support in the towns. In Chernigov, for example, Vsevolod Olgovich was a successful nephew in 1127.[69] In Galich in 1144–5 Ivan Rostislavich 'Berladnik' was a repeatedly unsuccessful nephew, despite having at least one group of backers in the town.[70] In Kiev Mstislav Iziaslavich managed to oust his uncle Vladimir Mstislavich in 1167.[71] In the north-east Andrei Bogoliubskii's brother Vsevolod Iurevich spent two years, from 1174 to 1176, competing with his nephews for succession. There was nothing absolutely new here: we recall that in 1054 the sons of Iaroslav the Wise had bypassed their uncle Sudislav. Just to complicate matters in the Kievan conflicts after 1147, Viacheslav was the older of the two uncles, but the younger – Iurii of Suzdal – was Iziaslav's most aggressive competitor for Kiev. Iurii cultivated alliances (cemented by marriage) with the families of Chernigov and Galich, with whose assistance he twice managed to gain a temporary hold on the city: for nearly a year from August 1149, and then again from September 1150 to March 1151.

The chronicle narratives of these events reveal more of the growing ambivalence in the relations between natural kinship and political kinship. In 1146, before Iziaslav had become firmly established, the chronicler states that Viacheslav – the oldest surviving son of Monomakh – 'hoped for seniority': thus position in the natural family was plainly assumed to be distinct from status in the political family.[72]

---

68 Detailed narrative in *PSRL*, II, cols 328–54; see D. S. Likhachev, *Russkie letopisi i ikh kul'turno-istoricheskoe znachenie* (Moscow, Leningrad, 1947), pp. 219–26.

69 See Dimnik, *The Dynasty of Chernigov*, pp. 313–21.

70 Summary of Ivan's career in Rapov, *Kniazheskie vladeniia*, pp. 75–6.

71 *PSRL*, I, cols 353–4; cf. II, cols 532–4.

72 *PSRL*, I, col. 314; see A. P. Tolochko, *Kniaz' v Drevnei Rusi: vlast', sobstvennost', ideologiia* (Kiev, 1992), p. 90; cf. e.g. *PSRL*, I, 373, when a family gathering 'gave' seniority to one of its members.

Yet it is equally clear that position in the natural family still carried moral weight, even if it was not the only or the paramount criterion. Thus in 1150 Iziaslav found a novel way to deflate Iurii's challenge. An agreement was reached whereby 'Iziaslav would have [his uncle] Viacheslav as his father and that Viacheslav would have Iziaslav as his son . . . "You are my father", said Iziaslav, "and Kiev is yours"'.[73] Not that Iziaslav had any intention of yielding Kiev or of giving up actual power. The deal was that *both* princes, Iziaslav and his 'uncle and father'[74] Viacheslav, would stay in Kiev but at different residences: Viacheslav could have the honour and the 'Great' palace, while Iziaslav in the Ugorskii palace ran all practical princely business. Iziaslav was the executive; Viacheslav was the figurehead, or the fig-leaf. It was an ingenious device to recognize and reconcile the difference between power and authority. Iurii was morally outflanked, and eventually he acknowledged the arrangement.

The deal between Viacheslav and Iziaslav was copied only twice by later princes. Once, briefly, by Viacheslav with Iziaslav's brother Rostislav (of Smolensk) after Iziaslav's death in November 1154, but Viacheslav himself died soon afterwards. And once, more effectively, in the next generation: in 1180 Sviatoslav, son of Vsevolod Olgovich (of Chernigov and Kiev), accepted 'seniority and Kiev' while Rostislav's son Riurik 'took all the Rus land' – that is, actual power over the Kievan territory. On this latter occasion the agreement bridged a far larger gap in natural kinship (Riurik was Sviatoslav's third-cousin-once-removed, junior in generation), yet it held for fourteen years until Sviatoslav's death in 1194.[75] These are not signs of a system in chronic crisis, but of a continual flexibility through which the dynasty was able to exploit and adapt to economic and territorial change.

In March 1155, after the death of his older brother Viacheslav and after more than fifteen years of intermittent frustration, Iurii of Suzdal – now the only surviving son of Vladimir Monomakh – was at last able to brush aside the local princelings ('Kiev is my patrimony, not yours')[76] and enter Kiev relatively unopposed. He died just two years later, in May 1157. Iurii Vladimirovich is best known as the man who allegedly built the first fortifications at Moskva, and who thereby found aggrandisement in later political mythology as Iurii 'Long-Arm' (Dolgorukii), the founder of Moscow. But in his own life, despite substantial projects to secure, develop and embellish his north-eastern patrimony (see below, p. 355), still the peak of aspiration was to 'sit on the throne of his grandfather and father' in Kiev.

---

73 *PSRL*, II, col. 399.
74 Ibid., col. 418.
75 Ibid., cols 471, 623–4; see Tolochko, *Kniaz' v Drevnei Rusi*, pp. 46–54, on these 'duumvirates', with a critique of claims to detect more numerous examples.
76 *PSRL*, I, col. 345.

Against this background it does not seem odd that Iurii's son Andrei should have mobilized an assortment of allies to take Kiev in 1169. Indeed, Andrei's career broadly follows the norms of the age. In 1157 he ensconced himself in Suzdal by means of a fairly conventional kind of unconventionality: Iurii had instructed – and Andrei had accepted – that a different son should succeed to Suzdal; on Iurii's death Andrei ignored his pledge (urged on by the townspeople, naturally).[77] Once in office he set about the traditional tasks of nullifying any threat from his nearest and dearest: in 1161 a mass expulsion to Byzantium of a couple of his brothers, his stepmother and his nephews;[78] defeating Volga Bulgars (1164), keeping a foothold in Novgorod, and fortifying and beautifying his towns. He had no reasonable excuse to pick a major territorial fight with his senior cousin, Rostislav Mstislavich, who was prince of Kiev for much of this time (1159–67), nor did he try to do so. He turned to the south only after Rostislav's death, and when Rostislav's younger brother had been expelled from Kiev by yet another ambitious nephew. Andrei's campaign, spearheaded by his son, had support from Rostislav's own family in Smolensk.

All this looks quite ordinary. What was not quite ordinary was Andrei's decision to put his younger brother Gleb in Kiev while he himself remained in the north-east. The arrangement was convenient and perhaps politic for both brothers. Andrei had always been mainly concerned with the development of his patrimony, whereas Gleb – prince of Pereiaslavl for the previous fifteen years – was well established in the south.[79] But Andrei nevertheless broke with the practice of his father and grandfathers. For at least 150 years no other senior prince, when given the opportunity to rule in Kiev, had chosen instead to rule elsewhere. Nor was there any question of Andrei regarding the Kievan prince 'as a father'. On the contrary, he clearly reckoned that he, in the north-east, had the status and the authority to tell the southern princes what to do. After Gleb's death (20 January 1171) Andrei 'ordered' candidates in or out of Kiev, castigated them if they failed to act 'according to his will', was acknowledged as their 'father', 'gave' Kiev to the prince of his choice.[80]

Up to a point. In 1173 a brace of young Rostislavichi, Riurik and Mstislav, decided that they had had enough. When a messenger from Andrei brought the usual peremptory instructions, they publicly humiliated the man by having his hair and beard shaved off, and sent him home with the message: 'Until now we have had you as

---

77 *PSRL*, II, cols 478, 490, 595.
78 Ibid., cols 520–1, s.a. 6670, probably 'ultra-March': see Berezhkov, *Khronologiia*, p. 175; but the chronicles' chronologies for events throughout the 1160s are exceptionally confused.
79 Biographical resumé in Rapov, *Kniazheskie vladeniia*, p. 151.
80 See esp. *PSRL*, II, cols 566–70.

a father ... but you have addressed such speeches to us, as if not to a prince but to a subordinate (*podruchniku*) or commoner (*prostu cheloveku*). Do what you will'.[81] Andrei was furious. He put together another coalition to reimpose his demands by force, but this time he failed. The Rostislavichi, previously his allies, switched their support to the prince of Vladimir-in-Volynia (Iaroslav Iziaslavich), to whom they offered Kiev. Andrei's forces retreated in disgrace. In pressing his authority Andrei had miscalculated the extent of his power. In the following year he was murdered by his own servitors in his palace at Bogoliubovo.[82]

Andrei's motives and aspirations have been much debated, but a summary of events is not in itself an adequate guide to the climate of ideas, and we shall return to the issue later. However, in the narrow context of dynastic and regional relations Andrei's actions fit a consistent pattern of change. His grandfather, Vladimir Monomakh, was a southern prince who energetically worked at developing north-eastern settlements which were still fairly remote and dangerous. Iurii was Monomakh's youngest son, allocated to one of these junior postings, equally active in promoting local growth, but always – in more than 30 years of north-eastern rule – with the idea that south was best. Andrei Bogoliubskii was a north-eastern prince whose priority was his patrimony, though he retained a residual and ultimately self-defeating interest in pressing his family's authority in the south. Andrei's brother and eventual successor Vsevolod 'Big Nest' (d. 1212) completed the cycle. He had participated in the disastrous campaign of 1173, and he learned from his brother's failure. From time to time he pulled levers and exerted influence and even issued threats, but in general he showed little inclination to become directly involved in southern affairs.[83] After 1173 the competition for 'the Rus land' was left to the princes of Smolensk, Chernigov, Vladimir-in-Volynia and eventually Galich. For the north-eastern family the more critical competition was over Novgorod.

In the mid-twelfth century the success of the regions and the proliferation of princes and patrimonies posed new challenges for the dominant political culture. The family responded by continually reshaping and redefining itself. Occasionally, however, the strain did seem to push the dynasty close to the limits of its identity. In 1173 the Rostislavichi complained that Andrei was ignoring their dignity as princes, treating them as subordinates or commoners. Some twenty years later Vsevolod's peremptory treatment of the Olgovichi brought

---

81 Ibid., col. 578; cf. *Russkaia Pravda* on the dignity of beards: see above, p. 219.
82 *PSRL*, II, cols 580–95; Limonov, *Vladimiro-Suzdal'skaia Rus'*, pp. 80–98; note that the chronology of the summary in Hurwitz, *Prince Andrej Bogoljubskij*, pp. 18–20, is suspect.
83 Limonov, *Vladimiro-Suzdal'skaia Rus'*, pp. 99–116.

the aggrieved response: 'we are not Hungarians or Poles, but grandsons of one grandfather'.[84] In both cases the chronicle implies that there was a perceived threat to the sense of the ruling family as a distinct, privileged and coherent community: in the first case socially, and in the second case geopolitically. In both cases the complainants worried that the proper distinction between 'us' and 'them' was being blurred. These are issues of perception rather than fact. But cultural perceptions are integral components of political stategy. What, then, was the cultural context for, or consequence of, the political and economic processes of the mid-twelfth century?

3. FAITH IN THE LANDS:
IMITATION, EMULATION AND LOCAL IDENTITIES

Economic and dynastic growth brought religion to the regions. As the patrimonies flourished, so the faith was nourished. Money permitting, a prince came as a political and cultural package. As the network of princes thickened, so more and more of the burgeoning cities and settlements became equipped with the paraphernalia of the official culture, which now began to seep out – both above ground and below – into the countryside. By the end of the century almost all urban graves were Christian, while rural burial-grounds even in the previously retarded land of the Viatichi had begun to include some Christian pit-graves as well as traditional barrow-graves containing crosses and other Christian symbols.[85] Some 200 years after Vladimir Sviatoslavich the process of Conversion was close to becoming plausibly, rather than just eulogistically, complete. The gaps were being filled, the skeleton had grown more flesh, the facade had a depth of structure behind it. By the late twelfth century the lands of the Rus were predominantly, at least ostensibly, and in some cases ostentatiously, Christian.

One index is the rate and distribution of ecclesiastical building programmes. In the eleventh century, for example, at any given time there was perhaps just one team of builders working on masonry churches for the ruling family. Monuments were constructed in sequence, not in parallel. The builders hired by Mstislav for the church of the Saviour in Chernigov were transferred by Iaroslav to work on St Sophia in Kiev and then on St Sophia in Novgorod. About 25 masonry churches are known from the eleventh century, in just five cities. By 1150 there were at least four teams building in parallel. About 50 new monuments are known, scattered among eighteen towns. Construction continued or resumed in the old centres (Kiev,

---

84 *PSRL*, II, col. 689, s.a. 6703.
85 Nikol'skaia, *Zemlia viatichei*, pp. 103–6; in general see V. V. Sedov, 'Rasprostranenie khristianstva v Drevnei Rusi', *KSIA* 208 (1993), 3–11.

Chernigov, Pereiaslavl, Polotsk, Novgorod), and began not only in the newly prominent patrimonial centres such as Smolensk, Galich and Vladimir-in-Volynia but also in lesser towns like Novgorod-Seversk, Novogrudok, Pskov and Dorogobuzh. The total of known masonry churches built by the end of the century is around 200, spread across some 35 settlements.[86] The presence of solid, monumental places of Christian worship had ceased to be the privileged exception, an exotic superimposition along a narrow band of elite cities. It had become the norm, a standard feature of the urban landscape. The lands of the Rus bristled with little Kievs.

Kiev provided the definitive models, the authoritative precedents which determined, for example, what a church ought to look like. Almost every twelfth-century masonry church was constructed according to the same basic plan: the domed cross, or cross-in-square, usually with a single cupola. There were many variants in technique, and many ways in which the plan could be realized, modified and ornamented, but there was virtually no fundamental deviation, no interest in devising or importing alternative designs. Known specimens of rotundas and quadrifolia can be counted on less than the fingers of one hand (three in Galich, one in Kiev), and they remained isolated and uninfluential.[87] Not that construction was a 'closed shop', an introverted activity from which outsiders were excluded. The itinerant teams of builders were local, but it was not rare for foreign 'masters' (the sources use this borrowed term) to be hired to oversee the projects: in Peremyshl and Zvenigorod probably Poles in the 1110s and 1120s; the masters who worked in Galich in the 1140s, and then moved to Suzdal in the 1150s, may well have been from Hungary; when Andrei Bogoliubskii initiated a grandiose project for Vladimir-on-the-Kliazma and for his residence at Bogoliubovo he commissioned 'masters from all lands'.[88] The Byzantine monopoly was broken, but taste was conservative, and the imported masters based their designs around traditional local specifications.

A conspicuous exception curiously confirms the rule, or the force of habit which came to be perceived as rule. In the mid-1140s or early 1150s Niphont, bishop of Novgorod, commissioned the modestly sized but lushly frescoed church at the monastery of the Transfiguration of

---

86 P. A. Rappoport, *Drevnerusskaia arkhitektura* (St Petersburg, 1993), pp. 246–62.

87 P. A. Rappoport, *Russkaia arkhitektura X–XIII vv.* (*ASSSR SAI*, vyp. E1–47; Leningrad, 1982), nos 6, 188, 196; cf. 142.

88 *PSRL*, I, col. 351; the widespread assertion that craftsmen were sent by Frederick Barbarossa stems from dubious information given by the eighteenth-century chronicler Tatishchev; but see N. N. Voronin, *Zodchestvo severo-vostochnoi Rusi XII–XV vv.* (Moscow, 1961), I, pp. 329–42. On the possible influence of Transcaucasian (Armenian) architecture see I. R. and R. I. Mohytych, 'Osoblyvosti tekhniky muruvannia i arkhitekturnykh form Halyts'ko-Volyns'koho zodchestva (x–xiv st.)', *Arkheolohiia*, 1990, no. 4, 56–68.

the Saviour by the mouth of the Mirozha river just outside Pskov. From 1147 Nifont was in ecclesiastical dispute with Kiev, a dispute in which he received encouragement from Constantinople (see below, pp. 361–3). Whether by coincidence or no, Nifont seems to have invited a Byzantine or Balkan master to oversee his construction project at the monastery. The building was planned to look like no other church among the Rus, though the style existed in the Byzantine provinces: the corner sections at the western end were much lower than the roof of the main nave and transept, so that the church resembled a cross from the outside, rather than a cube which formed a cross on the inside. The provenance was respectable, but apparently the locals found the appearance not quite proper, not quite what they were used to, and therefore not quite what a church should be; or perhaps the low corners trapped too much snow. At any rate, whether the reason was practical or aesthetic or both, the western corners were raised to the full height of the central cross, and the church was turned into the familiar cube. Such was the power of conformity.[89]

That is not to say that all building was identical. On the contrary, dissemination over such a huge area inevitably led to differentiation, diffusion to diversity. Techniques and materials varied, itinerant teams worked under different masters or patrons, and the basic scheme proved highly adaptable. Consider, for example, the number and arrangement of domes. The majority of churches had a single dome, set on a drum whose platform was at roughly the same level as the top of the walls. Some larger churches had five domes: one above the junction of the main nave and transept, and four others symmetrically around it. In Novgorod, however, the configuration of domes was often asymmetrical. St Sophia has six: the basic five plus an additional one above a single staircase tower at the western end. The palace church of the Annunciation (1103) had two domes, one centrally and one above a staircase by the north-western corner. The church of the Nativity of the Mother of God at the Antoniev monastery just south of the town (1117) and the unusually bulky and voluminous church of St George at the Iurev monastery just north of the town (1119) both add a third dome, above the south-western corner.[90] In Polotsk in the 1150s there was a different kind of modification to the lines of the roof: in the church of the Saviour at Princess Evfrosiniia's monastery the rectangular platform for the drum was raised above the level of the rest of the roof, which thus acquired a stepped or layered appearance emphasizing the vertical elevation. By the beginning of the

89 See M. I. Mil'chik and G. M. Shtender, 'Zapadnye kamery sobora Mirozhskogo monastyria vo Pskove', in A. I. Komech and O. I. Podobedova, eds, *Drevnerusskoe iskusstvo. Khudozhestvennaia kul'tura X–pervoi poloviny XIII v.* (Moscow, 1988), pp. 77–94; N. N. Demicheva, 'O datirovke pamiatnikov domongol'skogo zodchestva v Pskove', *KSIA* 198 (1989), 112–17, dates the building to 1144–8.

90 Rappoport, *Russkaia arkhitektura*, nos 114, 100, 113.

next century there were similar layered or tiered roofs on churches in Smolensk, Riazan, Ovruch and Chernigov.[91] This extra elevation gave scope for the proliferation of *kokoshniki*, banks of superimposed arches between the tops of the walls and the platform of the drum, which became a characteristic feature of Russian churches.

The most striking local developments, however, were in the choice and use of materials. The vast majority of churches everywhere were, of course, wooden. Prestigious southern churches were built of *opus mixtum* (thin brick slabs between thick layers of rough stone and lime mortar), as were the earliest masonry churches in Suzdal and Vladimir-on-the-Kliazma (commissioned by Vladimir Monomakh using southern craftsmen). In Novgorod unworked stone was somewhat more prominent, though the basic building techniques were similar. But towards the middle of the century a few churches around Galich were constructed with a completely different kind of facade: the rough core was faced with smooth limestone slabs, which were laid flush with one another so that the whole looked as if it was made of solid limestone blocks. The masters may well have been brought in from neighbouring Hungary. From Galich the style and perhaps the same masters migrated to the north-east, where it can still be seen in the elegant white stone churches built by Iurii Vladimirovich for his fortresses of Pereiaslavl-Zalesskii (Pereiaslavl 'beyond the forests') and Iurev-Polskoi, and for his residence at Kideksha near Suzdal. The walls of Iurii's churches were plain, but the use of smooth stone presented new opportunities for decoration. The churches built for Iurii's sons in Vladimir-on-the-Kliazma and Bogoliubovo, with their relief carvings and sculpted friezes and recessed portals, are in some respects (and not coincidentally) reminiscent of the Romanesque, although the basic shape and plan was true to Kievan convention. Thus, gradually and unevenly, local hybrids became established and developed as regional and native styles.

The patrons of these churches were usually princes, like Iurii Vladimirovich and his sons, but here also there was some regional variation. Novgorod from the 1100s to the 1130s fitted the general pattern, as Vladimir Monomakh and his son Mstislav and Mstislav's son Vsevolod stamped their marks on the urban and suburban landscape, adorning the citadel and girding the city with monasteries. But after the expulsion of Vsevolod in 1136 an increasing proportion of the churches were built for merchants, bishops and local grandees.[92] The change

91 Ibid., nos 137, 40, 62, 71; see diagrams in G. K. Vagner and T. F. Vladyshevskaia, *Iskusstvo Drevnei Rusi* (Moscow, 1993), pp. 74–5.
92 N. Dejevsky, 'The churches of Novgorod. The overall pattern', in H. Birnbaum and M. Flier, eds, *Medieval Russian Culture* (California Slavic Studies 12; Berkeley, Los Angeles, London, 1984) pp. 206–23.

in the pattern of patronage reflects the peculiarities of Novgorodian political life. Few princes could expect to be resident for the two or three years needed to see a construction project through from start to finish, so that local notables assumed the role of public guardians of local continuity and prestige.

The spread of churches testifies to the spread of ecclesiastical institutions: of monasteries and bishoprics. From the early years of the twelfth century solidly built, solidly endowed monasteries began to be founded around more of the regional cities. From the 1110s there are the main churches of the Iurev and Antoniev monasteries outside Novgorod, and the church of the Dormition of the Mother of God in the Eletskii monastery at Chernigov. In Polotsk work started on a series of buildings at the Belchitskii monastery towards the end of the 1130s, and at Evfrosiniia's monastery in the mid-1140s – about the same time as Niphont's church at the Mirozhskii monastery across the river from Pskov, and as the church of Boris and Gleb in the Smiadyn monastery at Smolensk.[93] Kiev, the 'mother of the cities of the Rus', continued to be beautified, as with Mstislav's monastery of St Theodore, built c. 1129–33 as a family burial-place; or the same prince's church of the 'Pirogoshcha' Mother of God on the main market-place in the Podol (c. 1131–5), with its famous icon from Constantinople.[94] But Kiev's adolescent emulators were beginning to raid their illustrious parent's wardrobe.

Besides some impressive churches, a would-be impressive prince wanted a bishop, and the growing flocks of the faithful needed pastors. Smolensk, formerly dependent on Pereiaslavl, acquired its own bishop in 1136. By c. 1150 the new bishopric of Galich was founded, the once-precarious see of Rostov had become securely established, while bishops of Novgorod were beginning occasionally to style themselves archbishops. By the time of the Mongol invasions there were further bishoprics at Vladimir-on-the-Kliazma in the north-east and at Peremyshl and Ugrovsk – later at Kholm – in the south-west.[95] The oddity, perhaps, was that all the lands remained under just one metropolitan. The unitary structure of ecclesiastical authority, centred on Kiev, might be thought incongruous in the new polycentric political and economic order; the more so since the metropolitan of Kiev was responsible for a far vaster and more populous territory than was normal in the Eastern Church. As we shall see, this incongruity could cause friction.

Regional growth in the dominant institutions brought regional

---

93 Rappoport, *Russkaia arkhitektura*, nos 63 100, 113, 129–30, 133, 166–71.
94 On the name, possibly from the Greek *pyrgotissa*, see D. S. Likhachev, *'Slovo o polku Igoreve' i kul'tura ego vremeni* (Leningrad, 1978), pp. 211–28.
95 Ia. N. Shchapov, *Gosudarstvo i tserkov' Drevnei Rusi X–XIII vv.* (Moscow, 1989), pp. 62–9.

growth in the dominant culture. Manuscripts multiplied, the uses of writing became more diverse, in Novgorod the birch-bark post became steadily busier. The earliest surviving authentic administrative documents (a cluster of monastic and episcopal charters) date from the 1130s. From the 1140s chronicles start to note the use of documents in inter-princely diplomacy.[96] Extant native writings, though still few in number, become far more varied in topic, manner and place of origin than their equivalents from the eleventh century. The hegumen Daniil, most likely from Chernigov, wrote an account of his pilgrimage to the Holy Land in 1106–8.[97] In 1136 a Novgorodian monk named Kirik compiled a tract on chronology and paschal computation.[98] Kirill, a monk and later bishop of Turov, was a prolific author of prayers, homilies and florid sermons.[99] In mid-century a pair of churchmen conducted a public epistolary polemic on biblical exegesis via the court of the prince of Smolensk.[100] Local chronicles came to be compiled not only in Kiev and Novgorod but also in Suzdal and, by the mid-thirteenth century, in Galich.[101] A clutch of hagiographical and eulogistic writings emanated from Vladimir-on-the-Kliazma.[102] Dobrynia Iadreikovich of Novgorod, later Bishop Antonii of Novgorod, wrote of his pilgrimage to Constantinople in 1200.[103] The trials and deeds of Avraamii, a monk of Smolensk, were recorded in a *Life* by his disciple Efrem.[104]

One cannot yet speak of local 'schools' of writing. Known authors, labelled by name and place, are still rare. Anonymity was the norm, and the majority of scribes and preachers were keen to conserve the tradition, to copy and cherish and learn from the received corpus of Church Slavonic translations from Greek. Nevertheless in writing, as in building, diffusion and profusion in themselves brought variety, even though the prevailing ethos and aesthetic were conservative. The Rus had no schooling in classical rhetoric, but they were quite capable

---

96 See S. Franklin, 'Literacy and documentation in early medieval Russia', *Speculum* 60 (1985), 20–4.

97 K. D. Seemann, *Abt Daniil. Wallfahrtsberichte. Nachdruck der Ausgabe von Venevetinov 1883/5* (Slavische Propyläen 36; Munich, 1970); Podskalsky, *Christentum und theologische Literatur*, pp. 196–200.

98 See R. A. Simonov, *Drevnerusskaia knizhnost' (v svete noveishikh istochnikov kalendarno-matematicheskogo kharaktera* (Moscow, 1993).

99 See Franklin, *Sermons and Rhetoric*, pp. lxxv–xciv.

100 See ibid., pp. lviii–lxiv.

101 See Likhachev, *Russkie letopisi*, pp. 173–280.

102 See Hurwitz, *Prince Andrej Bogoljubskij*, pp. 39–84; G. Iu. Filippovskii, *Stoletie derzanii (Vladimirskaia Rus' v literature XII v.)* (Moscow, 1991).

103 See K.-D. Seemann, *Die altrussische Wallfahrtsliteratur* (Munich, 1976), pp. 213–21; also Gail Lenhoff, '*Kniga Palomnik*: a study in Old Russian rhetoric', *Scando-Slavica* 23 (1977), 39–61.

104 See Hollingsworth, *Hagiography*, pp. lxix–lxxx.

of manipulating the sounds and rhythms of language. They had little interest in systematic theological or philosophical inquiry, but they were quite capable of evoking and expressing nuances of concept and feeling: whether in the literary humour of the pseudo-petition attributed to Daniil Zatochnik ('the Exile'), or in the sharp sarcasm of Metropolitan Klim's epistle to Foma, or in the dense metaphors and rhythmic lyricism of the anonymous *Tale of Igor's Campaign*, or in the lively anecdotes of the *Paterik* of the Caves monastery, or in the brisk dialogues in the chronicles, or in the insistent crescendos and cadences of Kirill of Turov's cycle of sermons. The tradition was self-contained, but not static. There was now rather less of the declamatory self-advertisement of the parvenu, a more confident (if also more parochial) polyphony.

A sign of confidence was the emergence of debate and argument *within* the dominant culture. Writers of the eleventh century had been concerned above all to announce and explain the fact of their own Christianity, to celebrate their membership of the global club, to find themselves in time and space. Polemic, whether explicit or implicit, had been aimed mainly at non-members, at native pagans, as the *Primary Chronicle* often shows. By the mid-twelfth century the Christian Rus had become secure enough to argue with each other. There were polemics on the extent to which one may or should interpret the Scriptures allegorically; on the proper form of fasting if fast-days coincided with certain feast-days; on correct and incorrect procedures for appointing bishops or metropolitans; on the uses and abuses of certain kinds of erudition.[105] Such topics of debate were not original. They, like the variants in architecture, can be explained in terms of influence and provenance. But as in architecture, the local configuration and its forms of realization came to be distinctive.

The words, buildings, artefacts and institutions of the growing regional cultures provide rich material for historians of words, buildings, artefacts and institutions; but they also help to lend substance to an account of politics. Among the Rus, cultural politics was an integral part of the political culture. Christianity around the regions spread from the top down, as it had earlier on the Middle Dnieper. Through cultural patronage the regional princes acquired the means to enhance their dignity and prestige within their own localities, and to enhance the dignity of their localities in the eyes of their neighbours and kin. For most princes this was probably enough: they too were proper Christian rulers, they too were members of the club, they too could follow the lead of the mother of the cities of the Rus. However, there was one region in which imitation stretched beyond flattery, where

---

105 See S. Franklin, 'Booklearning and bookmen in Kievan Rus': a survey of an idea', *HUS* 12/13 (1988/89), 830–48.

emulation stretched beyond deference. In the north-east, over the second half of the century, under Andrei Bogoliubskii and Vsevolod 'Big Nest', economic and political growth was accompanied by a multi-faceted yet consistently focused programme of cultural aggrandisement unparalleled anywhere since the Kiev of Iaroslav the Wise. The cultural postures of Andrei and Vsevolod, via their clerics and builders and bookmen, reveal a changing relationship with the southern metropolis. The cultural evidence allows us at last to set the bald narrative of political conflict and economic interest into a fuller framework of ideas and attitudes and aspirations.

Andrei's second Kiev was at Vladimir-on-the-Kliazma, rather than the older cities of Rostov or Suzdal. Just as the Caves *Paterik* stresses how Andrei's grandfather Vladimir Monomakh copied Kiev when building his first churches in the north-east, so Andrei's own posthumous eulogist highlights the mimetic element: Andrei's residence at Bogoliubovo was 'as far from Vladimir as is Vyshgorod from Kiev'.[106] It was from Vyshgorod that Andrei had brought the miracle-working icon, the 'Vladimir' Mother of God, who became the protectress of the city (and later of Moscow). The region acquired its local missionary saint, in the form of Leontii, the allegedly martyred bishop of Rostov who had been sent from Kiev in the 1070s, whose uncorrupted remains were unearthed in the 1160s. The central church in Vladimir was dedicated to the Dormition (c. 1158–60), following the precedent set in the Caves monastery. To borrow a phrase from Ilarion, Andrei's city shone with splendour, with gilded domes and golden vessels and golden trimmings. Like Kiev it was entered through monumental 'Golden Gates'.[107]

Yet for their sources of authority Andrei and Vsevolod also looked beyond Kiev to Constantinople. Vladimir-on-the-Kliazma was equivalent to Kiev, not just derivative from it. The 'Vladimir' Mother of God was a Constantinopolitan icon, brought to the Rus together with the 'Pirogoshcha' Mother of God in Kiev. The earliest *Life* of Leontii of Rostov, which probably originated in the twelfth century, stresses that the bishop was himself a native of Constantinople. Most conspicuously, Andrei established and lavishly promoted a new feast for the Mother of God: the feast of the Intercession of the Veil (*pokrov*), celebrated on 1 October. Here there was no Kievan precedent, nor even an exact Constantinopolitan equivalent, though the inspiration or excuse was provided by a Byzantine source: a vision of the Mother of God in the church at Blachernae, as recorded in the *Life* of the prince's namesake Andrew Salos (Andrew the Fool).[108]

---

106 *PSRL*, II, col. 580.
107 *PSRL*, I, cols 367–8; II, cols 580–2, 593.
108 See L. Rydén, 'The vision of the Virgin at Blachernae and the feast of Pokrov', *Analecta Bollandiana* 94 (1976), 63–82.

The special status of the new cult was displayed to the world through the building of Andrei's church of the Intercession on the Nerl. Built in the mid-1160s after Andrei's victory over the Volga Bulgars, the *pokrov* church was given a most unusual location. It did not have to jostle for attention in the citadel, or in the market, or in the palace. It stood alone, on a bend in the river about a kilometre outside Bogoliubovo, as if guarding the way to the prince. Andrei's *pokrov* church tends now to be seen as a little gem of harmonious simplicity, modest yet elegant, in quiet sympathy with its rustic setting. The impression is anachronistic. It was a huge project for which nature was demonstratively transformed. The area of the building was originally much larger, for it has lost its ambulatory; and the grassy bank on which it stands, apparently so felicitous, was in fact a massive artificial construction built up to withstand the floodwaters and itself faced with limestone. This was no reticent rural shrine but a monumental statement of divinely protected princely power. A carved figure of the crowned King David stares out from every wall.

What Andrei began, Vsevolod developed. It is difficult to date precisely many of the writings associated with Andrei: the tale of his victory over the Bulgars, the texts relating to the cult of the Intercession or to the cult of Leontii of Rostov, the tale of the miracles of the 'Vladimir' Mother of God. At least some of them, and certainly the chronicle's posthumous eulogy to Andrei himself, originate in the second half of the twelfth century. Andrei had been adept enough at self-promotion, but the glory of his life was further magnified in the light of his death, which became martyrdom after the manner of Boris and Gleb. He was presented as the ideal ruler, a Solomon in his wisdom, his building, his generalship, yet generous to the needy and a patron of monks and nuns.[109] Vsevolod took up the theme. Andrei's cathedral of the Dormition (1158–60) had three aisles and a single dome; after a fire in 1183 Vsevolod rebuilt it to almost double the floor area, extending it on three sides to create a building with five aisles and five domes. Andrei had translated the relics of Bishop Leontii to a sarcophagus; Vsevolod promoted his official veneration as a saint.[110] On the facades of Andrei's church of the Intercession on the Nerl there were carved figures of King David; on Vsevolod's palace church of St Demetrios in Vladimir (1194–7) the far more elaborately carved facades showed not only David but also Alexander the Great. Vsevolod also seems to have encouraged the use

109 *PSRL*, I, col. 368.
110 Gail Lenhoff, 'Canonization and princely power in northeast Rus': the cult of Leontij Rostovskij', *Die Welt der Slaven*, N.F. 16 (1992), 364–77.

of the epithet 'great' (or 'Grand' – *velikii*) as a more regular appendage to his princely title.[111]

None of this was intrinsically threatening to Kiev, just as Iaroslav's eleventh-century programme was not intrinsically threatening to Constantinople. Any ruler could – indeed should – be a Solomon or a David, even an Alexander, in his own land. A generally unsympathetic Kievan chronicler attributes to Andrei no greater ambition than to be 'autocrat [*samovlastets*] over the whole of the Suzdal land'.[112] The difference, of course, was that Kiev had never been a mere outpost of Byzantium as the Suzdal land had been an outpost for the rulers of the Middle Dnieper. The adjustment from colonial backwater to powerful patrimony was not entirely smooth, and the strains show most clearly in Andrei's handling of the one institution which did have a centralized hierarchy: the Church.

A prince of the Rus expected to play an influential role in the running of his Church, *inter alia* in the matter of appointments to senior ecclesiastical office. He paid the piper, he put up the buildings. But the shifting balance of regional power created not only new opportunities for the regional princes (in the form of bishoprics) but also new tensions between the regions and the metropolis. Which prince had how much influence over which appointments? Was the metropolitanate a symbol and embodiment of pan-dynastic unity? Or was it an anachronism, a residual reflection of an outmoded political order? Problems arose more in practice than in theory, and Andrei Bogoliubskii was not the first to have difficulties.

If anyone can be said to have started the trouble, it was the prince of Kiev. In the autumn of 1146, shortly after 'sitting on the throne of his father and grandfather', Prince Iziaslav Mstislavich removed his uncle Viacheslav from Turov. At the same time he also removed Akim, Turov's bishop, from his see, and brought him to Kiev. This was a minor tremor, a small reminder that the ruler of Kiev assumed that he should be able to reshuffle the pack of clerics as he reshuffled the pack of princelings. The major quake took place in the following year, and it caused serious rifts both within the Church of the Rus and between Kiev and Constantinople. On 27 July 1147 Iziaslav summoned a synod of bishops to elect his own choice of candidate, a native monk by the name of Klim Smoliatich, as metropolitan of Kiev; or rather, as metropolitan of *Rhōsia*. This would have been splendid, except that the appointment and the procedure were unacceptable to Iurii

---

111 See A. Poppe, 'Words that serve the authority. On the title of "Grand Prince" in Kievan Rus", *Acta Poloniae historica* 60 (1989); see also above, 290; on the buildings of Andrei and Vsevolod see William Craft Brumfield, *A History of Russian Architecture* (Cambridge, 1993), pp. 44–56; and esp. Voronin, *Zodchestvo severo-vostochnoi Rusi*, I, pp. 193–494.

112 *PSRL*, II, col. 520.

of Suzdal, to Constantinople, and to several of the regional bishops. Bishop Manuil of Smolensk and Bishop Nifont of Novgorod were vocal opponents, the bishops of Polotsk and Rostov were probably absent from the synod, and the bishop of Turov was Iziaslav's virtual captive. In other words, the synod was rigged. Appointments to the metropolitanate were by convention confirmed by the patriarch of Constantinople. Most appointees were themselves Byzantine. Klim was a local man, elected unilaterally by the bishops of the Middle Dnieper – of Chernigov, Pereiaslavl, Belgorod and Iurev – plus the bishop from Iziaslav's own patrimony of Vladimir-in-Volynia.

Iziaslav may well have reckoned it reasonable to press Kievan authority in this way. But from a regional perspective, viewed from the 'lands' which were growing unaccustomed to taking their orders from the Middle Dnieper, Iziaslav had manipulated a pan-dynastic or supra-dynastic institution as an instrument of purely local policy.[113] The immediate effect was to make the Church a pawn in the game of regional politics. Whenever Iurii Vladimirovich took Kiev, Klim Smoliatich was driven out together with his patron. Whenever Iziaslav re-installed himself in Kiev, Klim Smoliatich was re-installed as metropolitan. After Iziaslav's death a new metropolitan was sent from Constantinople and promptly declared all Klim's ecclesiastical appointments invalid. After Iurii's death, at least until c. 1162, a succession of metropolitans continued to find themselves embroiled in princely squabbles about their suitability or acceptability.[114]

It is hardly surprising that there were regional repercussions and reactions. In 1156 Nestor, bishop of Rostov, was deposed in the purge by Klim's successor, Metropolitan Konstantin (Constantine). His replacement, Leon, arrived in Rostov in 1158, but the reception was hostile. Some felt that Leon's appointment was invalid, others accused him of self-enrichment, Andrei apparently objected to his views on fasting. Twice he was forced to leave his eparchy, on the second occasion (according to the chronicle) to defend – without success – his dietary injunctions at a hearing in front of the emperor Manuel I. Andrei had had enough. Although Leon was not formally deposed, Andrei simply set up his own man, a certain Feodorets, as bishop, to reside not in the old see of Rostov but in Andrei's city of Vladimir-on-the-Kliazma. Eventually, c. 1165–8, he sent to the patriarch of Constantinople with a proposal for a reform of the ecclesiastical hierarchy which would take account of recent political changes: not only that his candidate should officially reside in Vladimir-on-the-Kliazma rather than in Rostov or Suzdal, but that the hierarchical dependence on Kiev should be ended and his

---

113 Franklin, *Sermons and Rhetoric*, pp. li–lvii.
114 Ibid., pp. xlix–li.

bishop should be designated a metropolitan. In a sense the request for a separate metropolitanate was the logical culmination of Andrei's cultural programme on behalf of his own land. As we have seen, he had abandoned his father's obsession with the pre-eminence of Kiev. He wished neither to rule in Kiev, nor to be bothered with ecclesiastical appointments to Kiev; he took no political orders from Kiev, and nor did he see why he should accept Kiev's whims when running his own Church. It was not a request for precedence over Kiev, but for separation, for equivalent dignity.

Andrei's proposal was rejected. In his reply the Patriarch Loukas Chrysoberges elevated the *status quo* into a principle: that there should be one metropolitan for 'all *Rhōsia*'.[115]

If Andrei could not change the rules, then at least he could turn them to his own advantage. Three options had been declined or blocked: to take charge *in* Kiev; to accept instructions *from* Kiev; to exert authority *without* Kiev. The fourth option, to which he now turned, was to exert authority *through* Kiev. His request for a metropolitanate happened to be rejected at roughly the same time as Andrei's branch of the family acquired a plausible claim to seniority (see above, p. 350). For the sake of decorum Andrei sacrificed his controversial man Feodorets, who was sent to Kiev and tortured. But the underlying problem was solved in practice, if not in theory, when Andrei's younger brother Gleb was installed as the Kievan prince. The ecclesiastical dispute, though by no means the sole cause, reveals some of the nuances of inter-regional tension which lay behind the campaign of 1169. The chronicle's comment – that Kiev was sacked because of its errors in the matter of fasts and feasts – is not so wildly wide of the mark as one might at first have imagined.

Technically Andrei failed, both in his attempt to gain formal emancipation for his Church and (eventually) in his attempt to exercise remote control over Kievan politics. But there were lessons for all. The Church could not remain impervious to political change, and it, too, adapted to the pressures of polycentric power. A principle of unitary authority was articulated, but some measure of regional autonomy was increasingly accepted. When Vsevolod later queried the metropolitan's choice of a bishop, then the undesirable candidate was quickly re-posted elsewhere and Vsevolod's own choice was confirmed.[116]

The regional prosperity of the mid-twelfth century not only led to a shift in the balance of power between the Middle Dnieper and the regional patrimonies; it also forced a gradual shift in attitudes.

---

115 S. Franklin, 'Diplomacy and ideology: Byzantium and the Russian Church in the mid twelfth century', in J. Shepard and S. Franklin, eds, *Byzantine Diplomacy* (Aldershot, 1992), pp. 145–50.
116 *PSRL*, II, cols 629–30.

There was no absolutely standard pattern. Adjustments to change were neither smooth nor symmetrical, and even in the polycentric dynasty some patrimonies were more central than others. Kiev's own horizons narrowed, as did those of Chernigov and especially Pereiaslavl. Smolensk, Vladimir-in-Volynia and Galich joined the southern power-brokers. Novgorod, semi-detached, played the field. Andrei Bogoliubskii and his brother Vsevolod 'Big Nest' perhaps went furthest in their demonstrative disengagement from the Middle Dnieper, though at the same time they too are testimony to the success of the southern colonists in integrating the lands under a common dynasty and a common culture, bound to some extent in a shared nexus of economic ties. Viewed as a whole and in most of its parts, despite the continual jostling and the occasional major rows, the family conglomerate thrived in its growing diversity.

CHAPTER TEN

Prospect and Retrospect: 1185 and After

Hear, you princes who oppose your elder brethren and stir up war and incite the pagans against your brethren – lest God should reprove you at the Last Judgement – how saints Boris and Gleb endured from their brother not only the taking away of their domains but also the taking away of their lives. Yet you cannot endure even one word from your brother, and for the merest slight you stir up mortal enmity and receive aid from the pagans against your brethren.[1]

All you grandsons of Iaroslav and Vseslav! Lower your banners now and sheathe your blemished swords! For you have relinquished the glory of your grandfathers! In your seditiousness you began to incite the pagans against the land of the Rus. Violence from the land of the Polovtsy came about because of [your] strife.[2]

These and other such laments over the decline of the dynastic ethos around the turn of the thirteenth century – these nostalgic dirges over the decay of former glories – still resonate through much historical writing. The nostalgia stems from a double illusion. The first illusion relates to the writers' past: there had never been a Golden Age when brother had cooperated with brother throughout the lands, or when at least some princes had not tried to recruit outside help to put pressure on their kin.[3] For every David Sviatoslavich of Chernigov, whom the author of the *Homily on Princes* takes as the model of pacific piety, there had been an Oleg Sviatoslavich, who figures in the *Tale of Igor's Campaign* as a prime mover of fraternal strife. The second illusion relates to the writers' present. A glance around the regions in the late twelfth and early thirteenth centuries shows that the pattern of growth was being maintained.

Novgorod bustled with Baltic traders: the earliest *schra*, the document regulating the behaviour of the German community in Novgorod,

---

1 *Homily on Princes*, PLDR, XII v., p. 338.
2 *The Tale of Igor's Campaigns*, PLDR, XII v., p. 382.
3 See e.g. above, pp. 152, 199–203, 253, 271–3, 327, on the 970s, 1010s, 1060s, 1090s, etc.

probably dates from the end of the twelfth century.[4] Smolensk outgrew its reliance on transit and portages and expanded its own direct links with northern commerce, as witnessed in an exceptionally full and detailed treaty with Riga and Gotland in 1229.[5] In politics the Smolensk Rostislavichi enjoyed unprecedented successes during the 1210s and 1220s: they provided the princes of Novgorod from 1209 to 1221, of Galich from 1219 until 1227, and of Kiev from 1212 right through to 1235.[6] Both in Smolensk and in Novgorod there was a surge of building activity, a mushrooming of churches, from the late twelfth century to the eve of the Mongol invasions.[7]

In the north-east Vsevolod Iurevich 'Big Nest' lived on in pomp until 1212, having outlasted all other known grandsons of Monomakh by some 35 years. After Vsevolod's death there was the predictable scrabble for succession, perhaps rather nastier than usual (Vsevolod had at least six surviving sons), but not fratricidal.[8] As in many analogous cases, the conflicts did little strategic damage to the family interests. The eventual winner, Iurii Vsevolodovich (1218–38) set about the traditional business of a north-eastern prince with even more success than his father or than his uncle Andrei Bogoliubskii: in 1220 he launched a retaliatory attack on the Volga Bulgars, as a result of which, in 1221, he was able to establish the outpost of Nizhnii Novgorod (Lower Novgorod) at a key location on the confluence of the Volga and the Oka. From the same year (1221), at the other end of the Volga-Baltic route, he managed to secure a continuous line of his own nominees as princes of Novgorod.[9]

In the south-west the standing of Galich as a regional power was consolidated under Vladimirko's son Iaroslav 'Osmomysl' (1153–87) and grandson Vladimir (1189–99). But at the end of the century Galich stepped into a higher league: in 1199 its somewhat remote local branch of the dynasty was displaced by Roman Mstislavich, prince of

4 W. Schlüter, *Die Nowgoroder Schra in sieben Fassungen vom XIII. bis XVII. Jahrhundert* (Dorpat, 1911), pp. 50–6; W. Rennkamp, *Studien zum deutsch-russischen Handel bis zum Ende des 13. Jahrhunderts. Nowgorod und Dünagebiet* (Bochum, 1977); E. A. Rybina, *Inozemnye dvory v Novgorode XII–XVII vv.* (Moscow, 1986), pp. 24–33.

5 *Smolenskie gramoty XIII–XIV vekov*, ed. T. A. Sumnikova and V. V. Lopatin (Moscow, 1963), pp. 18–62.

6 John Fennell, *The Crisis of Medieval Russia 1200–1304* (Longman History of Russia 2; London, 1983), pp. 22–40, 51–7.

7 N. Dejevsky, 'The churches of Novgorod. The overall pattern', in H. Birnbaum and M. Flier, eds, *Medieval Russian Culture* (California Slavic Studies 12; Berkeley, Los Angeles, London, 1984), pp. 206–23; N. N. Voronin and P. A. Rappoport, *Zodchestvo Smolenska XII–XIII vv.* (Leningrad, 1979).

8 Despite the remarks of Fennell, *Crisis*, p. 46.

9 Ibid., pp. 45–51; V. A. Kuchkin, *Formirovanie gosudarstvennoi territorii severo-vostochnoi Rusi v X–XIV vv.* (Moscow, 1984), pp. 90–103; Iu. A. Limonov, *Vladimiro-Suzdal'skaia Rus'* (Leningrad, 1987), pp. 99–116.

Vladimir-in-Volynia and a descendant of Monomakh. Roman's father and grandfather had both ruled in Kiev, so that he too (unlike previous princes of Galich) was a contender for the throne on the Middle Dnieper, and the combined lands of Galich and Vladimir-in-Volynia gave him a credible base from which to achieve his ambitions and face his kinsmen from Smolensk and Chernigov. From 1200 to 1203 Roman managed to take and hold Kiev. Galich had become a highly desirable possession: when Roman died in 1205, leaving only infant sons, Galich endured some three decades of intermittent intervention by Poland, Hungary, the Chernigov Olgovichi and the Smolensk Rostislavichi. Nevertheless, its association with Vladimir-in-Volynia was eventually restored by Roman's patient son Daniil (d. 1264), under whose patronage the lands of the south-west also acquired literary and cultural trappings to match their economic and political status.[10]

In the south there was indeed a period of anxiety in the 1180s and 1190s, when some of the more distant groups of Polovtsy – the 'Wild' Polovtsy from the Donets and the Lower Don – took to raiding the Ros valley and its environs. The *Tale of Igor's Campaign* tells the story of a failed retaliatory expedition in 1185, led by Igor Sviatoslavich of Novgorod-Seversk, a prince of the Chernigov family, against the group of Polovtsy led by the energetic and capable khan Konchak.[11] Yet within a few years, after Konchak's death, calm on the steppe frontiers had been restored. True, in 1203 some of the Polovtsy finally managed to ransack Kiev, but only as allies of the Rus claimant (Riurik Rostislavich of Smolensk) who brought them in to help oust Roman of Galich. The effects of the raid, though mourned dramatically in the chronicle,[12] were as temporary as the effects of previous episodes of pillaging. Kiev remained immensely wealthy. Even its political succession became for a while quite stable.

The literary laments emerge out of the occasional anxieties in the south. Yet their nostalgia has turned out to be remarkably infectious over the centuries, as historians have lingered on the themes of disunity, decline and internecine strife. The themes have gained poignancy in hindsight because of the knowledge, not shared by the Rus, that the Mongols were soon to attack. Modern laments come in several varieties: out of a general sense that well-run states ought to progress

---

10 See G. Stökl, 'Das Fürstentum Galizien-Wolynien', in M. Hellmann, ed., *Handbuch der Geschichte Russlands, I. i: von der Kiever Reichsbildung bis zum moskauer Zartum* (Stuttgart, 1981), pp. 484–533.
11 On Konchak's career see S. A. Pletneva, 'Donskie Polovtsy', in B. A. Rybakov, ed., *'Slovo o polku Igoreve' i ego vremia* (Moscow, 1985); also S. A. Pletneva, *Polovtsy* (Moscow, 1990), pp. 146–71. From the vast literature on the Igor tale see e.g. D. S. Likhachev, *'Slovo o polku Igoreve' i kul'tura ego vremeni* (Leningrad, 1978); Robert Mann, *Lances Sing. A Study of the Igor Tale* (Columbus, Ohio, 1989).
12 *PSRL*, I, cols 418–19.

towards monarchy, or at least towards an integrated administration and a coordinated foreign policy; or out of pragmatic calculations as to the military and economic cost of division in the dynasty. The lands of the Rus were 'afflicted by the decay of feudal disunity', which led to 'catastrophic' disintegration; they were 'enfeebled by lack of unity', and their military capacity was 'exhausted by internecine war'.[13]

None of this is persuasive. In the first place, there is no evidence whatever that dynastic rivalry was harmful either to economic growth or to the princes' capacity to recruit. Rather the opposite was the case: dynastic flexibility, in which rivalry was a constant and probably essential component, was a positive advantage in the exploration and exploitation of new opportunities. If it had been otherwise, then two centuries of sustained expansion – first on the Middle Dnieper, then around the regions – would be inexplicable. Secondly, to lay an eleventh-century political template on late twelfth-century affairs, though tempting and understandable even for contemporaries, leads to distortion. The author of the *Tale of Igor's Campaign* might bewail the fact that a southern expedition into the steppes received no support from the mighty princes of Vladimir-on-the-Kliazma and Galich; but back in the good old days there would have been no princes of Galich or of Vladimir-on-the-Kliazma anyway, so nothing was actually lost. And in fact in the late 1190s and early 1200s both Vsevolod of Vladimir-on-the-Kliazma and Roman of Vladimir-in-Volynia (then of Galich, then of Kiev) did launch effective raids into the steppes. Thirdly, if the criterion for success is the ability to keep outsiders in check, then the family's conventional practice of forming *ad hoc* partial alliances proved perfectly adequate for all known contingencies, perhaps with the sole exception of Galich in the 1210s and 1220s. Indeed the record on this score was rather better in the twelfth century than in the eleventh: the only occasion on which Kiev itself had actually been occupied by outsiders was, as we recall, in the eleventh century (see above, pp. 186–7).

It may be comforting to imagine that the Rus would have repelled the Mongols if only they had behaved in the manner of their grandfathers. But the Rus, for good reason, had *not* abandoned their traditional ways. The problem was that the Mongols were a non-traditional enemy. Ultimately there is little point in looking for specific local reasons for the defeat by the Mongols, since Mongol victories were not just a local phenomenon. The Mongols in the mid-thirteenth century showed themselves capable of defeating anyone from China to Croatia. Their successes cannot be ascribed merely to routine squabbling among the princes of the Rus.

13 B. A. Rybakov, *Kievskaia Rus' i russkie kniazhestva XII–XIII vv.* (Moscow, 1982), p. 259; Fennell, *Crisis*, p. 86.

So much for the decline and decay. The issue of 'disunity' is more serious, for it affects the basic terms in which the lands of the Rus can be described and conceived. Should we be talking of an entity, or of a plurality? Of 'it' or of 'them'? The obvious answer is: both, depending on the criteria one chooses to apply. On the one hand there was no unitary 'state' by any reasonable definition. Galich, Chernigov, Vladimir-on-the-Kliazma and the rest looked after most of their internal affairs and external relations without necessary reference to one another, except when forming alliances based on self-interest. There was no fixed hierarchy of power, no central structure of administration, no institutional atrophy to stunt local economic initiatives. On the other hand there were clearly affinities between the dynastic lands which set them apart – collectively – from their neighbours.

However, to announce the obvious is not yet to solve the problem. In modern historical writings a great deal of effort and thought has been spent on trying to find more precise terms, on trying to transpose the lands of the Rus into a conceptual framework which can accommodate both their affinities and their diffuseness, both entity and plurality.[14] The terminology is usually taken from other times and other places. Such definitions by analogy can be useful and suggestive in a study of comparative history, but as labels in context they tend to obscure as much as they reveal. For example, many would like the lands of the Rus to be a 'federation', but even the most distinguished proponent of the term, Vasilii Kliuchevskii, spent less time justifying it than pointing out its inaccuracy.[15] For Soviet historians in particular, the transposition of the Rus onto a standard historiographical grid was of paramount importance. The eventual consensus was that the original 'Kievan State' underwent a process of 'feudal disintegration' characterized by the emergence of vassalage and fiefs. Debate then focused on the subsidiary issues of when and how which 'stage' of feudalism was reached. A dissident Marxist position, emerging from within the same frame of reference, was that Rus society was still at the 'slave-owning' rather than the 'feudal' stage.[16] Labels for the separate elements of the plurality thus vary

---

14 Summary in P. P. Tolochko, *Drevniaia Rus'. Ocherki sotsial'no-politicheskoi istorii* (Kiev, 1987), pp. 208–14.

15 V. O. Kliuchevskii, *Kurs russkoi istorii* (Moscow, 1904), I, p. 239.

16 I. Ia. Froianov, *Kievskaia Rus'. Ocherki sotsial'no-ekonomicheskoi istorii* (Leningrad, 1974); I. Ia. Froianov and A. Iu. Dvornichenko, *Goroda-gosudarstva Drevnei Rusi* (Leningrad, 1988); for a convenient survey see T. Kuryuzawa, 'The debate on the genesis of Russian feudalism in recent Soviet historiography', in I. Takayuki, ed., *Facing Up to the Past: Soviet Historiography under Perestroika* (Sapporo, 1989), pp. 111–47; on the problems with such terminology even with regard to Western Europe of the same period see Susan Reynolds, *Fiefs and Vassals: the Medieval Evidence Reinterpreted* (Oxford, 1994).

according to theory and taste: they were appanages, or vassal states, or city-states, or principalities, or kingdoms; they were independent, or semi-independent, or autonomous, or quasi-autonomous, or bound into a set of hierarchical and feudal obligations.

Such concepts would not have meant a great deal to the Rus. It is of course as legitimate to describe the Rus in our terms as it is to evoke them through their terms, so long as one is aware of the limitations of each and of the difference between them. While not banning extraneous vocabulary, we have for the most part preferred not to push the Rus into any fixed conceptual model derived from elsewhere. However, one fundamental point seems to emerge from almost all accounts of the period, regardless of the specific terms in which it is conceived: virtually all seem to agree that in the eleventh century (give or take a decade or three) there was relative unity (or a unity of relatives), which over the course of the twelfth century broke up into a relative plurality. This standard picture has from time to time been recoated in different colours, but the basic shape tends to remain the same. Indeed, if one is constructing a linear political narrative, no other shape seems possible. However, the consensus is in important respects misleading and should be revised.

In the first place, the dynasty's propensity for unity and cooperation and centralization was certainly no greater in the eleventh century than in the twelfth or thirteenth. There just happened to be fewer members of the family, who 'sat' in far fewer towns feeding off a less dense spider's-web of routes, and whose culture of legitimacy was shared by a far narrower band of the population: a golden age of unity only in its relative simplicity. Even then the linear narrative is more strained than the kievocentric ideologues tended to allow: strained, for example, by Sviatoslav's attempted relocation to the Danube in 969–71, or by Mstislav's Chernigov in the 1020s and 1030s, or throughout the eleventh century by Polotsk. The difference which emerged over the twelfth century was not so much in substance as in scale.

Secondly, the ways in which the lands of the Rus grew together are at least as significant as the ways in which they appear to have grown apart. Over the twelfth century the political 'story' becomes complex to the point of incoherence, but coalescence does not have to take place in straight lines. Integration – rather than disintegration – took place on several levels: through the development of regional economic zones linked by intricate trading networks; through the way in which the princes exploited the expanding economy and established themselves far more widely and densely across the territories which had previously been theirs in rhetoric and desire more than in tribute-gathering, church-building, troop-levying practicalities; through the seepage of the dominant culture – in all essentials a single dominant culture – from the urban elites of a few major cities out across the lands and down the social scale.

The earliest known native writers, in trying to locate and define themselves, devised a synthetic identity based on kinship, language and faith: the kinship of the Rus, the language of the Slavs, the faith of the 'Greeks'; the legitimacy of a single dynasty (albeit with many branches), cultural expression in a single language (albeit with variants), spiritual authority and observance from a single source. By means of this characteristic synthesis the Rus elite distinguished insiders from outsiders, who they were from who they were not, 'us' from 'them'. Far from being blown away by the passing political winds, these hopeful assertions became ever more widely and securely embedded as basic assumptions. The new regional loyalties incorporated, rather than displaced, the shared acceptance of a common dynasty, language and faith. By this measure, far more of the inhabitants of the lands of the Rus were far closer to a common identity in the late twelfth century than in any previous age. To revert to extraneous vocabulary: there was no 'state', but perhaps there were the beginnings of a nation.

Select Bibliography

This bibliography is intended to serve as a guide to further reading. It is by no means a comprehensive bibliography of the subject, nor is it an alphabetical rearrangement of the footnotes. From the works cited in the notes we have omitted the most narrowly specialized items, and also most of those dealing with the history of other places (occasionally cited in the notes for the purpose of comparison). At the same time we have included a number of works which readers may find useful but which happen not to have been cited directly. In selecting items for the bibliography we have generally given preference to: (i) major primary sources; (ii) books or articles which deal with the broader issues and problems rather than with individual points; (iii) relatively recent publications (if they include adequate references to important earlier work); (iv) where possible, material in West European languages (although the bibliography is necessarily dominated by works in Russian).

Ahrweiler, H., 'Les relations entre les Byzantins et les Russes au IX siècle', *Bulletin d'Information et de Coordination de l'Association internationale des études byzantines* 5 (1971), 44–70.

Alekseev, L. V., '"Okovskii les" Povesti Vremennykh Let', in A. N. Kirpichnikov and P. A. Rappoport, eds, *Kul'tura srednevekovoi Rusi* (Leningrad, 1974), pp. 5–11.

Alekseev, L. V., *Smolenskaia zemlia v IX–XIII vv.* (Moscow, 1980).

Ambrosiani, K., *Viking Age Combs, Comb Making and Comb Makers in the Light of Finds from Birka and Ribe* (Acta Universitatis Stockholmiensis. Stockholm Studies in Archaeology 2; Stockholm, 1981).

Annales Bertiniani (*Les Annales de Saint Bertin*), ed. F. Grat, J. Vieilliard and S. Clémencet (Paris, 1964).

Annales Bertiniani, tr. J. L. Nelson, *The Annals of St-Bertin* (Manchester, 1991).

Arne, T. J., *La Suède et l'Orient* (Uppsala, 1914).

Arrignon, J. -P., 'A propos de la lettre du pape Grégoire VII au prince de Kiev Izjaslav', *RM* 3 (1977), 5–18.

Arrignon, J. -P., 'La création des diocèses russes des origines au milieu du XII siècle', in *Mille ans de christianisme russe, 988–1988. Actes du colloque international de l'Université Paris-Nanterre 20–23 janvier 1988* (Paris, 1989), pp. 27–49.

Arwidsson, G., ed., *Systematische Analysen der Gräberfunde, Birka*, II.1–3 (Stockholm, 1984–89).

Aseev, Iu. S., *Arkhitektura drevnego Kieva* (Kiev, 1982).

Aseev, Iu. S., *Mystetstvo Kyivs'koi Rusi/Art of Kievan Rus* (Kiev, 1989).

Aseev, Iu. S., Totskaia, I. F., Shtender, G. M., 'Novoe o kompozitsionnom zamysle Sofiiskogo sobora v Kieve', in A. I. Komech and O. I. Podobedova, eds, *Drevnerusskoe iskusstvo. Khudozhestvennaia kul'tura X–pervoi poloviny XIII v.* (Moscow, 1988), pp. 13–27.

Avdusin, D. A. and Puškina T. A., 'Three chamber-graves at Gniozdovo', *Fornvännen* 83 (1988), 20–33.

Avdusin, D. A., ed., *Smolensk i Gnëzdovo (k istorii drevnerusskogo goroda)* (Moscow, 1991).

Bálint, C., *Die Archäologie der Steppe: Steppenvölker zwischen Volga und Donau vom 6. bis zum 10. Jahrhundert* (Vienna, Cologne, 1989).

Baran, V. D. et al., eds, *Slaviane iugo-vostochnoi Evropy v predgosudarstvennyi period* (Kiev, 1990).

Belyakov, A., 'The coins and monetary pendants from the barrows near Pleshkovo village (late Viking age)', in K. Jonsson and B. Malmer, eds, *Sigtuna Papers. Proceedings of the Sigtuna Symposium on Viking-Age Coinage 1–4 June 1989* (Commentationes de nummis saeculorum IX–XI in Suecia repertis. Nova series 6; Stockholm, London, 1990), pp. 35–41.

Beneshevich, V. N., ed., *Drevneslavianskaia Kormchaia XIV titulov bez tolkovanii*, I (St Petersburg, 1906); II (Sofia, 1987).

Berezhkov, N. G., *Khronologiia russkogo letopisaniia* (Moscow, 1963).

Birnbaum, Henrik, 'Iaroslav's Varangian connection', *Scandoslavica* 14 (1978), 5–25.

Blankoff, J., 'Černigov, rivale de Kiev? A propos de son développement urbain', *RES* 63 (1991), 146–55.

Blifeld, D. I., *Davn'orus'ki pam'iatky Shestovytsi* (Kiev, 1977).

Bocharov, G. N., *Khudozhestvennyi metall Drevnei Rusi X–XIII vv.* (Moscow, 1984).

Bogdanova, N. M., 'Kherson v X–XV vv.. Problemy istorii vizantiiskogo goroda', in S. P. Karpov (ed.), *Prichernomor'e v srednie veka* (Moscow, 1991), pp. 8–172.

Bol'shakova, L. N., 'Metricheskii analiz drevnerusskikh khramov XI–XII vv.', in A. I. Komech and O. I. Podobedova, eds, *Drevnerusskoe iskusstvo. Khudozhestvennaia kul'tura X–pervoi poloviny XIII v.* (Moscow, 1988), pp. 112–19.

Børtnes, J., *Visions of Glory. Studies in Early Russian Hagiography* (Slavica Norvegica 5; Oslo, 1988).

Brisbane, Mark, ed., *The Archaeology of Novgorod, Russia. Recent Results from the Town and its Hinterland* (The Society for Medieval Archaeology, Monograph Series 13; Lincoln, 1992).

Brumfield, William Craft, *A History of Russian Architecture* (Cambridge, 1993).

Bruno of Querfurt, *Epistola ad Henricum regem*, ed. J. Karwasińska, *Monumenta Poloniae Historica, series nova*, IV.3 (Warsaw, 1973), pp. 97–106.

Bugoslavskii, S., ed., 'Pouchenie ep. Luki Zhidiaty po rukopisiam XV–XVII vv.', *Ivestiia ORIAS* 18, ii (1913), 196–237.

Bulkin, V. A., Dubov, I. V. and Lebedev, G. S., *Arkheologicheskie pamiatniki drevnei Rusi IX–XI vekov* (Leningrad, 1978).

Callmer, J., 'The archaeology of Kiev ca A.D. 500–1000. A survey', in R. Zeitler, ed., *Les pays du nord et Byzance (Scandinavie et Byzance), Actes du colloque nordique et international de byzantinologie tenu à Upsal 20–22 avril 1979* (Acta Universitatis Upsaliensis. Figura, nova series 19; Uppsala, 1981), pp. 29–52.

Callmer, J., 'Verbindungen zwischen Ostskandinavien, Finnland und dem Baltikum vor der Wikingerzeit und das Rus'-Problem', *JGO* 34 (1986), 357–62.

Callmer, J, 'The archaeology of Kiev to the end of the earliest urban phase', *HUS* 11 (1987), 323–64.

Callmer, J., 'The clay paw burial rite of the Åland islands and Central Russia: a symbol in action', *Current Swedish Archaeology* 2 (1994), 13–46.

Canard, M., 'La relation du voyage d'Ibn Fadlan chez les Bulgares de la Volga', *Annales de l'institut d'études orientales* 16 (Algiers, 1958), 41–146.

Chekin, L., 'The role of Jews in early Russian civilization in the light of a new discovery and new controversies', *Russian History* 17 (1990), 379–94.

Chekin, L., 'The godless Ishmaelites: the image of the steppe in eleventh–thirteenth century Rus', *Russian History* 19 (1992), 9–28.

Chernigov i ego okruga v IX–XIII vv. Sbornik nauchnykh trudov (Kiev, 1988).

Chichurov, I. S., *Politicheskaia ideologiia srednevekov'ia. Vizantiia i Rus'* (Moscow, 1990).

Chistov, K. V., ed., *Etnografiia vostochnykh slavian. Ocherki traditsionnoi kul'tury* (Moscow, 1987).

Čiževskij: *see* Tschižewskij.

Clarke, H. and Ambrosiani, B., *Towns in the Viking Age* (Leicester, 1991).

Colucci, M. and Danti, A., *Daniil Zatočnik. Slovo e Molenie* (Studia historica et philologica 4, sectio slavica 2; Florence, 1977).

Constantine VII Porphyrogenitus, *De administrando imperio*, ed. and tr. G. Moravcsik and R. J. H. Jenkins (Dumbarton Oaks Texts 1; *CFHB* 1; Washington, D.C., 1967).

Constantine VII Porphyrogenitus, *Ob upravlenii imperiei* [= *De administrando imperio*], ed. and Russian tr. G. G. Litavrin and A. P. Novosel'tsev (Moscow, 1989).

Constantine VII Porphyrogenitus, *De cerimoniis aulae byzantinae*, ed. I. I. Reiske, I (Bonn, 1829).

Cook, Robert, 'Russian history, Icelandic story, and Byzantine strategy in Eymundar þáttr Hringssonar', *Viator* 17 (1986), 65–89.

Cross, Samuel Hazard and Sherbowitz-Wetzor, Olgerd P. (tr.), *The Russian Primary Chronicle. Laurentian Text* (Mediaeval Academy of America Publication, 60; 3rd printing, Cambridge, Mass., 1973).

Crumlin-Pedersen, O., 'Schiffe und Schiffahrtswege im Ostseeraum während des 9.–12. Jahrhunderts', *OWS*, *Bericht der Römisch–Germanischen Kommission* 69 (1988), pp. 530–63.

Darkevich, V. P., *Svetskoe iskusstvo Vizantii. Proizvedeniia vizantiiskogo khudozhestvennogo remesla v Vostochnoi Evrope X–XIII veka* (Moscow, 1975).

Darkevich, V. P., *Khudozhestvennyi metall Vostoka VIII–XIIIvv.: proizvedeniia vostochnykh torevtik na territorii evropeiskoi chasti SSSR i Zaural'ia* (Moscow, 1976).

Darkevich, V. P., 'Mezhdunarodnye sviazi', in B. A. Kolchin, ed., *Drevniaia Rus'. Gorod, zamok, selo* (Moscow, 1985), pp. 387–411.

Darkevich, V. P., 'Proiskhozhdenie i razvitie gorodov drevnei Rusi (X–XIIIvv.)', *Voprosy istorii* 1994, no. 10, 43–60.

Davidan, O. I., 'Contacts between Staraja Ladoga and Scandinavia (on the evidence of archeological material from Zemljanoe gorodishche)', in K. Hannestad et al., eds, *Varangian Problems* (Copenhagen, 1970), pp. 79–91.

Davidan, O. I., 'Etnokul'turnye kontakty Staroi Ladogi VIII–IX vekov', *Arkheologicheskii sbornik* (Gosudarstvennyi Ordena Lenina Ermitazh) 27 (1986), 99–105.

Davidson, H. Ellis, *The Viking Road to Byzantium* (London, 1976).

Dejevsky, Nikolai, 'The churches of Novgorod. The overall pattern', in H. Birnbaum and M. Flier, eds, *Medieval Russian Culture* (California Slavic Studies 12; Berkeley, Los Angeles, London, 1984), 206–23.

Demicheva, N. N., 'O datirovke pamiatnikov domongol'skogo zodchestva v Pskove', *KSIA* 198 (1989), 112–17.

Dimnik, Martin, 'The "Testament" of Iaroslav "The Wise": a re-examination', *Canadian Slavonic Papers* 29 (1987), 369–86.

Dimnik, Martin, *The Dynasty of Chernigov 1054–1146* (Texts and Studies 116, Pontifical Institute of Mediaeval Studies; Toronto, 1994).

Dobrovol'skii, I. G., Dubov, I. V. and Rozhdestvenskaia, T. V., 'Novaia nakhodka graffiti na Kuficheskoi monete', *Vestnik Leningradskogo Universiteta. Seriia 2: istoriia-iazyk-literatura*, 1982, vyp. 1, pp. 29–32.

Dölker, A., ed., *Der Fastenbrief des Metropoliten Nikifor an den Fürsten Vladimir Monomakh* (Skripten des slavischen Seminars der Universität Tübingen 25; Tübingen, 1985).

Donnert, Erich, *Das Kiewer Rußland. Kultur und Geistleben vom 9. bis zum beginnenden 13. Jahrhundert* (Leipzig, Jena, Berlin, 1983).

Dovzhenok, V. I., 'Storozhevye goroda na iuge Kievskoi Rusi', in E. I. Krupnov, ed., *Slaviane i Rus'* (Moscow, 1968), pp. 37–45.

Dovzhenok, V. I., Goncharov, V. K. and Iura, R. O., *Drevn'orus'ke misto Voin'* (Kiev, 1966).

Dubov, I. V., *Velikii volzhskii put'* (Leningrad, 1989).

Dubov, I. V., *Novye istochniki po istorii drevnei Rusi* (Leningrad, 1990).

Dunlop, D. M., *The History of the Jewish Khazars* (Princeton, 1954).

Dzhakson, T. N., 'Islandskie korolevskie sagi kak istochnik po istorii Drevnei Rusi i ee sosedei X–XIII vv.', *DGTSSSR* 1989–90 (1991), 5–169.

Dzhakson, T. N. and Molchanov, A. A., 'Drevneskandinavskoe nazvanie Novgoroda v toponimii puti "iz Variag v Greki"', *Vspomogatel'nye istoricheskie distsipliny* 21 (1990), 226–38.

Ekbo, S., 'The etymology of Finnish *Ruotsi* "Sweden"', in R. Zeitler, ed., *Les pays du nord et Byzance (Scandinavie et Byzance). Actes du colloque nordique et international de byzantinologie tenu à Upsal 20–22 avril 1979* (Acta Universitatis Upsaliensis. Figura, nova series 19; Uppsala, 1981), pp. 143–5.

Encyclopaedia of Islam I– (Leiden, London, 1960–).

Eremin, I. P., ed., *Literaturnoe nasledie Kirilla Turovskogo* (Monuments of Early Russian Literature 2; Berkeley, Ca., 1989).

Espéronnier, M., 'Le cadre géographique des pays slaves d'après les sources arabes médiévales', *Die Welt der Slaven* 31 (1986), 5–19.

'Eymundar þáttr Hringssonar', in *Flateyjarbók* II, ed. S. Nordal (Akranes, 1945), 199–218.

Fedotov, George P., *The Russian Religious Mind (I). Kievan Christianity. The 10th to the 13th Centuries* (Cambridge, Mass., 1946; repr. Belmont, Mass., 1975).

Fekhner, M. V., 'K voprosu ob ekonomicheskikh sviaziakh drevnerusskoi derevni', *Ocherki po istorii russkoi derevni, Trudy Gosudarstvennogo Istoricheskogo Muzeia* 33 (1959), 149–224.

Fekhner, M. V., 'Shelkovye tkani v srednevekovoi vostochnoi Evrope', *SA* 1982, no. 2, 57–70.

Fekhner, M. V., 'Bobrovyi promysel v volgo-okskom mezhdurech'e', *SA* 1989, no. 3, 71–8.

Fekhner, M. V. and Nedoshivina, N. G., 'Etnokul'turnaia kharakrisktika timerevskogo mogil'nika po materialam pogrebal'nogo inventaria', *SA* 1987, no. 2, 70–8.

Fennell, John, *The Crisis of Medieval Russia 1200–1304* (Longman History of Russia 2; London, 1983).

Fennell, John, *A History of the Russian Church to 1448* (London, New York, 1995).

Fennell, John and Stokes, Antony, *Early Russian Literature* (London, 1974).

G. Iu. Filippovskii, *Stoletie derzanii (Vladimirskaia Rus' v literature XII v.)* (Moscow, 1991).

Filist, G. M., *Istoriia 'prestupleniia' Sviatopolka okaiannogo* (Minsk, 1990).

Floria, B. N., *Otnosheniia gosudarstva i tserkvi u vostochnykh i zapadnykh slavian* (Moscow, 1992).

Font, Marta F., 'Politische Beziehungen zwischen Ungarn und der Kiever Rus' im 12. Jahrhundert', *Ungarn-Jahrbuch* 18 (1990), 1–18.

Foote, P. G. and Wilson, D. M., *The Viking Achievement* (London, 1974).

Franklin, Simon, 'The empire of the *Rhomaioi* as viewed from Kievan Russia: aspects of Byzantino-Russian cultural relations', *Byzantion* 53 (1983), 507–37.

Franklin, Simon, 'Literacy and documentation in early medieval Russia', *Speculum* 60 (1985), 1–38.

Franklin, Simon, 'The reception of Byzantine culture by the Slavs', in *The Seventeenth International Byzantine Congress. Major Papers* (New Rochelle, New York, 1986), 383–97.

Franklin, Simon, 'The writing in the ground: recent Soviet publications on early Russian literacy', *SEER* 65 (1987), 411–21.

Franklin, Simon, 'Booklearning and bookmen in Kievan Rus': a survey of an idea', *HUS* 12/13 (1988/89), 830–48.

Franklin, Simon (introd. and tr.), *Sermons and Rhetoric of Kievan Rus'* (*HLEUL* 5; Cambridge, Mass., 1991).

Franklin, Simon, 'Greek in Kievan Rus", *DOP* 46 (1992), 69–81.

Froianov, I. Ia., *Kievskaia Rus'. Ocherki sotsial'no-ekonomicheskoi istorii* (Leningrad, 1974).

Froianov, I. Ia., *Kievskaia Rus'. Ocherki sotsial'no-politicheskoi istorii* (Leningrad, 1980).

Froianov, I. Ia, *Miatezhnyi Novgorod. Ocherki istorii gosudarstvennosti, sotsial'noi i politicheskoi bor'by kontsa IX–nachala XIII stoletiia* (St Petersburg, 1992).

Froianov, I. Ia. and Dvornichenko, A. Iu., *Goroda-gosudarstva Drevnei Rusi* (Leningrad, 1988).

Gadlo, A. V., 'K istorii Tmutorokanskogo kniazhestva vo vtoroi polovine XI v.', *Slaviano-russkie drevnosti*, I, *Istoriko-arkheologicheskoe izuchenie Drevnei Rusi* (Leningrad, 1988), 194–213.

Gadlo, A. V., 'Tmutorokanskie etiudy': III ('Mstislav'), *Vestnik Leningradskogo gosudarstvennogo universiteta. Seriia* 2, 1990, *vypusk* 2 (no. 6), 21–33; IV ('Starshie Iaroslavichi i Rostislav'), *vypusk* 4 (no. 23), 3–13; V ('Oleg Sviatoslavich'), 1991, *vypusk* 2 (no. 9), 3–13.

Goehrke, C., *Frühzeit des Ostslaventums* (Erträge der Forschung 277; Darmstadt, 1992).

Golb, N. and Pritsak, O., *Khazarian Hebrew Documents of the Tenth Century* (Ithaca, London, 1982).

Golden, P., *Khazar Studies. An Historico-Philological Inquiry into the Origins of the Khazars*, I–II (Bibliotheca Orientalia Hungarica 25; Budapest, 1980).

Golden, P., 'The peoples of the Russian forest belt', in D. Sinor, ed., *The Cambridge History of Early Inner Asia* (Cambridge, 1990), pp. 229–55.

Golden, P., 'The peoples of the South Russian Steppes', in D. Sinor, ed., *The Cambridge History of Early Inner Asia* (Cambridge, 1990), pp. 256–84.

Golovko, A. B., *Drevniaia Rus' i Pol'sha v politicheskikh vzaimosviaziakh X–pervoi treti XIII vv.* (Kiev, 1988).

Goriunova, E. I., *Etnicheskaia istoriia volgo-okskogo mezhdurech'ia* (*MIA* 94; Moscow, Leningrad, 1961).

Gorskii, A. A., *Drevnerusskaia druzhina* (Moscow, 1989).

Gorskii, A. A., 'Rus' v kontse X–nachala XII veka: territorial'no-politicheskaia struktura ("zemli" i "volosti")', *Otechestvennaia istoriia* 1992, no. 4, 154–61.

Gräslund, A. -S., *A Study of the Graves on Björkö. The Burial Customs, Birka* IV (Uppsala, 1980).

Grekov, B. D., *Kievskaia Rus'*, 4th edn (Moscow, Leningrad, 1944).

Gupalo, K. N., *Podol v drevnem Kieve* (Kiev, 1982).

Gurevich, F. D., *Drevnii Novogrudok* (Leningrad, 1981).

Halasi-Kun, T., 'Some thoughts on Hungaro-Turkic affinity', *AEMA* 6 (1986) [1988], 31–9.

Halbach, Uwe, *Der russische Fürstenhof vor dem 16. Jahrhundert: eine vergleichende Untersuchung zur politischen Lexikologie und Verfassungsgeschichte der alten Rus'* (Quellen und Studien zur Geschichte des östlichen Europa 23; Stuttgart, 1985).

Hammarberg, I., Malmer, B. and Zachrisson, T., *Byzantine Coins Found in Sweden* (Commentationes de nummis saeculorum IX–XI in Suecia repertis. Nova series 2; Stockholm, London, 1989).

Hannestad, K. et al., eds, *Varangian Problems*, (Copenhagen, Munksgaard, 1970).

Heller, K., *Russische Wirtschafts- und Sozialgeschichte. I, Die Kiever und die Moskauer Periode (9.–17. Jahrhundert)* (Darmstadt, 1987).

Heller, K., *Die Normannen in Osteuropa*, Osteuropastudien der Hochschulen des Landes Hessen Reihe 1. (Giessener Abhandlungen zur Agrar- und Wirtschaftsforschung des europäischen Ostens 195; Berlin, 1993).

Hellmann, Manfred, 'Die Heiratspolitik Jaroslavs des Weisen', *Forschungen zur osteuropäischen Geschichte* 8 (1962), 7–25.

Hellmann, Manfred, ed., *Handbuch der Geschichte Rußlands, I.i: von der Kiever Reichsbildung bis zum moskauer Zartum* (Stuttgart, 1981).

Hellmann, Manfred, 'Die Handelsverträge des 10. Jahrhunderts zwischen Kiev und Byzanz', in *UHV, Abhandlungen der Akademie der Wissenschaften in Göttingen, philolog.-hist. Klasse, 3. Folge*, no. 156 (Göttingen, 1987), pp. 643–66.

Henderson, J. and Mundell Mango, M., 'Glass at medieval Constantinople. Preliminary scientific evidence', in C. Mango and G. Dargon, eds, *Constantinople and its Hinterland* (Society for the Promotion of Byzantine Studies Publications 3; Aldershot, 1995), pp. 333–56.

Heppell, Muriel (tr. and introd.), *The 'Paterik' of the Kievan Caves Monastery* (*HLEUL* 1; Cambridge, Mass., 1989).

Hollingsworth, Paul (tr. and introd.), *The Hagiography of Kievan Rus'* (*HLEUL* 2; Cambridge, Mass., 1992).

Holtzmann, Robert, ed., *Die Chronik des Bischofs Thietmar von Merseburg und ihre korveier Überarbeitung* (*MGH* SS, n.s. IX, 2nd edn; Berlin, 1955).

Hrushevs'kyi, Mykhailo [Hrushevsky, Mikhailo], *Istoriia Ukrainy-Rusy*, I, *Do pochatku XI vika* 3rd edn (Kiev, 1913); II, *XI–XIII vik* 2nd edn (Lvov, 1905) (repr. Kiev, 1991–2).

Hrushevsky, Mikhailo, *The History of Ukraine-Rus'. Volume I: From Prehistory to the Eleventh Century*, tr. Marta Skorupsky (Toronto, 1996, forthcoming).

Hudud al'Alam [*The regions of the world*], tr. V. F. Minorsky (Gibb Memorial Series, New Series 11; London, 1970).

Hurwitz, Ellen, *Prince Andrej Bogoljubskij. The Man and the Myth* (Studia historica et philologica 12, sectio slavica 4; Florence, 1980).

Ianin, V. L., *Denezhno-vesovye sistemy russkogo srednevekov'ia. Domongol'skii period* (Moscow, 1956).

Ianin, V. L., *Aktovye pechati Drevnei Rusi X–XV vv.*, 2 vols (Moscow, 1970).

Ianin, V. L., *Novgorodskie akty XII–XV vv.: khronologicheskii kommentarii* (Moscow, 1991).

Ianin, V. L., 'Zametki o komplekse dokumentov Smolenskoi eparkhii XII veka', *Otechestvennaia istoriia* 1994, no. 6, 104–20.

Ianin, V. L., ed., *Zakonodatel'stvo Drevnei Rusi* (Rossiiskoe zakonodatel'stvo X–XX vekov I; Moscow, 1984).

ibn Fadlan, *Risala*, ed. T. Lewicki, A. Kmietowicz and F. Kmietowicz, *Żródła arabskie do dziejów słowiańszczyzny*, III (Wroclaw, Warsaw, Cracow, Gdansk, Lodz, 1985).

ibn Fadlan, *Voyage chez les Bulgares de la Volga*, tr. M. Canard (Paris, 1988).

ibn Hawkal, *Kitab Surat al-Ard* [*Book of the Configuration of the Earth*], *Opus Geographicum: 'Liber imaginis terrae'*, ed. J. H. Kramers, 2 vols (Leiden, 1939).

ibn Hawkal, *Configuration de la terre*, tr. J. H. Kramers and G. Wiet, 2 vols (Beirut, Paris, 1964).

ibn Khurradadhbih, *Kitab al-Masalik wa'l Mamalik* [*Book of Ways and Realms*], ed. T. Lewicki, *Żródła arabskie do dziejów słowiańszczyzny*, I (Wroclaw, Cracow, 1956).

ibn Khurradadhbih, *ibn Khurradadhbih, ibn al-Faqih al-Hamadhani et ibn Rustih: Description du Maghreb et de l'Europe au III=IX siècle*, tr. M. Hadj-Sadok (Algiers, 1949).

ibn Rusta, *Kitab al-A'lak al-nafisa* [*Book of Precious Jewels*], ed. T. Lewicki, *Żródła arabskie do dziejów słowiańszczyzny*, II.2 (Wroclaw, Warsaw, Cracow, Gdansk, 1977).

ibn Rusta, *Les atours précieux*, tr. G. Wiet (Cairo, 1955).

Il'in, N. N., *Letopisnaia stat'ia 6523 goda i ee istochniki* (Moscow, 1957).

Ioannisian, O. M., 'Osnovnye etapy razvitiia galitskogo zodchestva', in A. I. Komech and O. I. Podobedova, eds, *Drevnerusskoe iskusstvo. Khudozhestvennaia kul'tura X–pervoi poloviny XIII v.* (Moscow, 1988), 41–58.

Isaevich, I. D., 'Kul'tura galitsko-volynskoi Rusi', *Voprosy istorii* 1973, no. 1, 92–107.

Jansson, I., 'Communications between Scandinavia and Eastern Europe in the Viking Age. The Archaeological Evidence', *UHV, Abhandlungen der Akademie der Wissenschaften in Göttingen, philol.-hist. Klasse*, 3. Folge, no. 156 (Göttingen, 1987), pp. 773–807.

Jansson, I., 'Wikingerzeitlicher orientalischer Import in Skandinavien', *OWS, Bericht der Römisch-Germanischen Kommission* 69 (1988), 564–647.

Jenkins, R. J. H., ed., *De administrando imperio: II Commentary* (London, 1962).

Jesch, Judith, *Women in the Viking Age* (Woodbridge, 1991).

John Skylitzes, *Synopsis Historiarum*, ed. I. Thurn (*CFHB* 5; New York, Berlin, 1973).

Kaiser, Daniel H., 'Reconsidering crime and punishment in Kievan Rus', *Russian History* 7 (1980), 283–93.

Kaiser, Daniel H., *The Growth of the Law in Medieval Russia* (Princeton, 1980).

Kaiser, Daniel H. (tr.), *The Laws of Rus' – Tenth to Fifteenth Centuries* (The Laws of Russia, Series I, Medieval Russia, vol. I; Salt Lake City, 1992).

Kalinina, T. M., 'Torgovye puti Vostochnoi Evropy IX veka. (Po dannym Ibn Khordadbekha i Ibn al-Fakikha)', *Istoriia SSSR* 1986, no. 4, 68–82.

Kalinina, T. M., 'Arabskie istochniki VIII–IX vv. o slavianakh', *DGVEMI* 1991 (1994), 211–24.

Kämpfer, F., 'Eine Residenz für Anna Porphyrogenneta', *JGO* 41 (1993), 101–10.

Karger, M. K., *Drevnii Kiev*, 2 vols (Moscow, Leningrad, 1958–61).

Kashtanov, S. M., 'O protsedure zakliucheniia dogovorov mezhdu Vizantiei i Rus'iu v X v.', in A. A. Guber et al., eds, *Feodal'naia Rossiia vo vsemirno-istoricheskom protsesse* (Moscow, 1972), pp. 209–15.

Kazakov, E. P., 'Znaki i pis'mo rannei Volzhskoi Bolgarii po arkheologicheskim dannym', *SA* 1985, no. 4, 178–85.

Kazakov, E. P., *Kul'tura rannei Volzhskoi Bolgarii* (Moscow, 1992).

Kazhdan, A. P., 'Rus'-Byzantine princely marriages in the eleventh and twelfth centuries', *HUS* 12/13 (1988/89), 414–29.

Khalikov, A. K., ed., *Rannie bolgary i finno-ugry v Vostochnoi Evrope* (Kazan, 1990).

Khoroshev, A. S., *Politicheskaia istoriia russkoi kanonizatsii (XI–XVI vv.)* (Moscow, 1986).

Kilievich, S. R., *Detinets Kieva IX–pervoi poloviny XIII vekov po materialam arkheologicheskikh issledovanii* (Kiev, 1982).

Kirpichnikov, A. N., *Drevnerusskoe oruzhie*, I–IV (*ASSSR SAI, vyp.* E1–36; Moscow, Leningrad, 1966–73).

Kirpichnikov, A. N., 'Connections between Russia and Scandinavia in the 9th and 10th centuries, as illustrated by weapons finds', in K. Hannestad et al., eds, *Varangian Problems* (Copenhagen, Munksgaard, 1970), pp. 50–76.

Kirpichnikov, A. N., 'Ladoga i Ladozhskaia volost' v period rannego srednevekov'ia', in V. D. Baran, ed., *Slaviane i Rus'* (Kiev, 1979), pp. 92–101.

Kirpichnikov, A. N. et al., 'Russko-skandinavskie sviazi epokhi obrazovaniia kievskogo gosudarstva na sovremennom etape arkheologicheskogo izucheniia', *KSIA* 160 (1980), 24–38.

Kliuchevskii, V. O., *Kurs russkoi istorii*, I (Moscow, 1904).

Kluchevsky [Kliuchevskii], V. O., *A History of Russia*, tr. C. J. Hogarth, I (London, 1911).

Kniazevskaia, O. I. et al., eds, *Uspenskii sbornik XII–XIII vv.* (Moscow, 1971).

Kokovtsov, P. K., *Evreisko-khazarskaia perepiska v X veke* (Leningrad, 1932).

Kolchin, B. A., ed., *Drevniaia Rus'. Gorod, zamok, selo* (Moscow, 1985).

Kollmann, Nancy Shields, 'Collateral succession in Kievan Rus", *HUS* 14 (1990), 377–87.

Komech, A. I., *Drevnerusskoe zodchestvo kontsa X-nachala XII v.: vizantiiskoe nasledie i stanovlenie samostoiatel'noi traditsii* (Moscow, 1987).

Komech, A. I. and Podobedova, O. I., eds, *Drevnerusskoe iskusstvo. Khudozhestvennaia kul'tura X–pervoi poloviny XIII v.* (Moscow, 1988).

Korinnyi, N. N., *Pereiaslavskaia zemlia. X–pervaia polovina XIII veka* (Kiev, 1992).

Koroliuk, V. D., *Zapadnye slaviane i Kievskaia Rus' v X–XI vv.* (Moscow, 1964).

Kotliar, N. F., 'Galitsko-Volynskaia Rus' i Vizantiia v XII–XIII vv. (sviazi real'nye i vymyshlennye)', in P. P. Tolochko et al., eds, *Iuzhnaia Rus' i Vizantiia. Sbornik nauchnykh trudov (k XVIII kongressu vizantinistov)* (Kiev, 1991), 20–33.

Kovalenko, V. P. and Rappoport, P. A., 'Etapy razvitiia drevnerusskoi arkhitektury Chernigovo-Severskoi zemli', *RM* 7.1 (1992), 39–59.

Kropotkin, V. V., *Klady vizantiiskikh monet na territorii SSSR (ASSSR SAI, vyp.* E4-4; Moscow, 1962).

Kropotkin, V. V., 'Bulgarian tenth-century coins in Eastern Europe and around the Baltic. Topography and distribution routes', in K. Jonsson and B. Malmer, eds, *Sigtuna Papers. Proceedings of the Sigtuna Symposium on Viking-Age coinage 1–4 June 1989* (Commentationes de nummis saeculorum IX–XI in Suecia repertis. Nova series 6; Stockholm, London, 1990), pp. 197–200.

Kryganov, A. V., 'Viis'kova prava rann'oseredn'ovichnykh Alaniv Podonnia', *Arkheolohiia* 1993, no. 2, 52–62.

Kuchera, M. P., *Zmievy valy srednego Podneprov'ia* (Kiev, 1987).

Kuchkin, V. A., *Formirovanie gosudarstvennoi territorii severo-vostochnoi Rusi v X–XIV vv.* (Moscow, 1984).

Kudriavtsev, A. A., *Feodal'nyi Derbent. Puti i zakonomernosti razvitiia goroda v VI–seredine XIII v.* (Moscow, 1993).

Kuryuzawa, T. 'The debate on the genesis of Russian feudalism in recent Soviet historiography', in I. Takayuki, ed., *Facing Up to the Past: Soviet Historiography under Perestroika* (Sapporo, 1989), pp. 111–47.

Kuza, A. V., *Malye goroda Drevnei Rusi* (Moscow, 1989).

Laiou, Angeliki, ed., *Consent and Coercion to Sex and Marriage in Ancient and Medieval Societies* (Washington, D.C., 1993).

Laiou, Angeliki and Simon, Dieter, eds, *Law and Society in Byzantium. Ninth–Twelfth Centuries* (Washington, D.C., 1994).

Larsson, G., 'Båtarna från Valsgärdes båtgravaar. Ett försök till tolkning', *Tor* 25 (Uppsala, 1993), 145–73.

Lazarev, V. N., *Mozaiki Sofii Kievskoi* (Moscow, 1960).

Lazarev, V. N., *Mikhailovskie mozaiki* (Moscow, 1966).

Lazarev, V. N., *Old Russian Murals and Mosaics* (London, 1966).

Lebecq, S., *Marchands et navigateurs frisons du haut moyen âge*, I–II (Lille, 1983).

Lebedeva, A. A., 'Transport, perenoska i perevozka tiazhestei', in K. V. Chistov, ed., *Etnografiia vostochnykh slavian. Ocherki traditsionnoi kul'tury* (Moscow, 1987), pp. 312–41.

Lenhoff, Gail, *The Martyred Princes Boris and Gleb: a Socio-Cultural Study of the Cult and the Texts* (Columbus, Ohio, 1989).

Lenhoff, Gail, 'Canonization and princely power in northeast Rus': the cult of Leontij Rostovskij', *Die Welt der Slaven*, N. F. 16 (1992), 359–80.

Leo VI, *Tactica*, PG 107, cols 671–1094.

Leo the Deacon, *Historia*, ed. C. B. Hase (Bonn, 1829).

Leont'ev, A. E., 'Skandinavskie veshchi v kollektsii sarskogo gorodishcha', *Skandinavskii sbornik* 26 (1981), 141–50.

Leont'ev, A. E., 'Poseleniia meri i slavian na oz. Nero', *KSIA* 179 (1984), 26–32.

Leont'ev, A. E., 'Volzhsko-Baltiiskii torgovyi put'' v IX v.', *KSIA* 193 (1986), 3–9.

Leont'ev, A. E., 'Timerëvo. Problema istoricheskoi interpretatsii arkheologicheskogo pamiatnika', *SA* 1989, no. 3, 79–86.

Leont'ev, A. E., and Riabinin, E. A., 'Etapy i formy assimiliatsii letopisnoi meri (postanovka voprosa)', *SA* 1980, no. 2, 67–79.

Levin, Eve, 'Women and property in medieval Novgorod: dependence and independence', *Russian History* 10 (1983), 154–69.

Levin, Eve, *Sex and Society in the World of the Orthodox Slavs, 900–1700* (Ithaca, London, 1989).

Liapushkin, I. I., *Dneprovskoe lesostepnoe levoberezh'e v epokhu zheleza* (*MIA* 104; Moscow, Leningrad, 1961).

Liapushkin, I. I., *Slaviane vostochnoi Evropy nakanune obrazovaniia drevnerusskogo gosudarstva* (*MIA* 152; Moscow, 1968).

Likhachev, D. S., *Russkie letopisi i ikh kul'turno-istoricheskoe znachenie* (Moscow, Leningrad, 1947).

Likhachev, D. S., 'The legend of the calling-in of the Varangians, and political purposes in Russian chronicle-writing from the second half of the XIth to the beginning of the XIIth century', in K. Hannestad et al., eds, *Varangian Problems* (Copenhagen, Munksgaard, 1970), pp. 170–85.

Likhachev, D. S., '*Slovo o polku Igoreve*' i kul'tura ego vremeni (Leningrad, 1978).

Likhachev, D. S., *Poetika drevnerusskoi literatury*, 3rd edn (Moscow, 1979).

Likhachev, D. S., *The Great Heritage: the Classical Literature of Old Rus'* (Moscow, 1981).

Likhachev, D. S., ed., *Slovar' knizhnikov i knizhnosti Drevnei Rusi. Vyp. I (XI–pervaia polovina XIV v.)* (Leningrad, 1987).

Likhachev, D. S. and Adrianova-Peretts, V. P., eds, *Povest' vremennykh let*, 2 vols (Moscow, Leningrad, 1950).

Limonov, Iu. A., *Vladimiro-Suzdal'skaia Rus'* (Leningrad, 1987).

Lind, J., 'The Russo-Byzantine treaties and the early urban structure of Rus", *SEER* 62 (1984), 362–70.

Litavrin, G. G., 'A propos de Tmutorokan', *Byzantion* 35 (1965), 221–34.

Litavrin, G. G., 'O iuridicheskom statuse drevnikh rusov v Vizantii v X stoletii. (Predvaritel'nye zamechaniia)', in *Vizantiiskie ocherki* (Moscow, 1991), pp. 60–82.

Litavrin, G. G., 'Usloviia prebyvaniia drevnikh rusov v Konstantinopole v X v. i ikh iuridicheskii status', *Vizantiiskii Vremennik* 54 (1993), 81–92.

Liudprand of Cremona, *Antapodosis*, in *Opera*, ed. J. Becker (*MGH* in usum schol.; Hanover, Leipzig, 1915).

Liudprand of Cremona, *Works*, tr. F. A. Wright (London, 1930).

Lunt, Horace, 'The language of Rus' in the eleventh century. Some observations about facts and theories', *HUS* 12/13 (1988/89), 276–313.

L'vova, Z. A., 'Stekliannye busy Staroi Ladogi: I, sposoby izgotovleniia, areal i vremia rasprostraneniia', *Arkheologicheskii sbornik* (Gosudarstvennyi Ordena Lenina Ermitazh) 10 (1968), 64–94.

L'vova, Z. A., 'Stekliannye busy Staroi Ladogi: II, proiskhozhdenie bus', *Arkheologicheskii Sbornik* (Gosudarstvennyi Ordena Lenina Ermitazh) 12 (1970), 89–111.

L'vova, Z. A., 'K voprosu o prichinakh proniknoveniia stekliannykh bus X–nachala XI veka v severnye raiony vostochnoi Evropy', *Arkheologicheskii Sbornik* (Gosudarstvennyi Ordena Lenina Ermitazh) 18 (1977), 106–9.

Lysenko, P. F., *Goroda Turovskoi zemli* (Minsk, 1974).

Mägi-Lougas, M., 'The relations between countries around the Baltic indicated by the background of Viking age spearhead ornament', *Fornvännen* 88 (1993), 211–21.

Makarova, T. I., *Polivnaia posuda. Iz istorii keramicheskogo importa i proizvodstva Drevnei Rusi* (*ASSSR SAI, vyp* E1–38; Moscow, 1967).

Makhnovets, L. E., ed. and tr., *Litopys rus'kyi za Ipats'kym spiskom* (Kiev, 1989).

Malingoudi, J., *Die russisch-byzantinischen Verträge des 10. Jahrhunderts aus diplomatischer Sicht* (Thessaloniki, 1994).

Mango, Cyril, *Byzantium. The Empire of New Rome* (London, 1980).

Marti, Roland W., *Handschrift – Text – Textgruppe – Literatur. Untersuchungen zur inneren Gliederung der frühen Literatur aus dem ostslavischen Sprachbereich in den Handschriften des 11. bis 14. Jahrhunderts* (Veröffentlichungen der Abteilung für slavische

Sprachen und Literaturen des Osteuropas an der Freien Universität Berlin 18; Wiesbaden, 1989).

Martin, Janet, *Treasure of the Land of Darkness. The Fur Trade and its Significance for Medieval Russia* (Cambridge, 1986).

Martin, Janet, *Medieval Russia, 980–1584* (Cambridge, 1995).

Martyshin, O. V., *Vol'nyi Novgorod: obshchestvenno-politicheskii stroi i pravo feodal'noi respubliki* (Moscow, 1992).

Masudi, *Muruj al-Dhahab wa Ma'adin al-Jawhar* [*Golden Meadows and Mines of Precious Stones*] 7 vols, ed. C. Pellat (Beirut, 1966–79).

Masudi, *Les prairies d'or*, tr. C. Pellat, I– (Paris, 1962–).

Medyntseva, A. A., *Drevnerusskie nadpisi Novgorodskogo Sofiiskogo sobora XI–XIV vv.* (Moscow, 1978).

Medyntseva, A. A., *Podpisnye shedevry drevnerusskogo remesla* (Moscow, 1991).

Mel'nikova, E. A., '"Saga ob Eimunde" o sluzhbe skandinavov v druzhine Iaroslava Mudrogo', in *Vostochnaia Evropa v drevnosti i srednevekov'e. Sbornik statei* (Moscow, 1978), pp. 289–94.

Mel'nikova, E. A., 'Skandinavskie amulety s runicheskimi nadpisiami iz Staroi Ladogi i Gorodishcha', *DGVEMI* 1991 (1994), 231–9.

Mel'nikova, E. A. and Petrukhin, V. J., 'The origin and evolution of the name *Rus*"', *Tor* 23 (Uppsala, 1990–91), 203–34.

Mel'nikova, E. A. and Petrukhin, V. I., 'Skandinavy na Rusi i v Vizantii v X–XI vekakh: k istorii nazvaniia "variag"', *Slavianovedenie* 1994, no. 2, 56–66.

Mel'nikova, E. A., Petrukhin, V. I. and Pushkina, T. A., 'Drevnerusskie vliianiia v kul'ture Skandinavii rannego srednevekov'ia. (K postanovke problemy)', *Istoriias SSSR* 1984, no. 3, 50–65.

Meysztowicz, V., ed., 'Manuscriptum Gertrudae Filiae Mesconis II Regis Poloniae', *Antemurale* 2 (1955), 103–57.

Mezentsev, Volodymyr I., 'The masonry churches of medieval Chernihiv', *HUS* II (1987), 365–83.

Mezentsev, Volodymyr I., 'The territorial and demographic development of medieval Kiev and other major cities of Rus': a comparative analysis based on recent archaeological research', *The Russian Review* 48 (1989), 145–70.

Mezentseva, G. G. and Prilipko, I. P., 'Davn'orus'kyi mohyl'nyk Belgoroda Kyivs'koho (doslidzhennia 1974–1976 rr.)', *Arkheolohiia* 35 (1980), 98–110.

Miller, D. B., 'Monumental building as an indicator of economic trends in Northern Rus' in the late Kievan and Mongol periods, 1138–1462', *American Historical Review* 94 (1989), 360–90.

Miller, D. B., 'Monumental building and its patrons as indicators of economic and political trends in Rus', 900–1262, *JGO* 38 (1990), 321–55.

Miller, D. B., 'The many frontiers of pre-Mongol Rus', *Russian History* 19 (1992), 231–60.

Minorsky, V., *Sharaf al-Zaman Tahir Marvazi on China, the Turks and India* (London, 1942).

Minorsky, V., *A History of Sharvan and Darband in the Tenth and Eleventh Centuries* (Cambridge, 1958).

Miskawayh, *Tajarib al-umam* [*The Experiences of the Nations*], in *The Eclipse of the Abbasid Caliphate*, ed. H. F. Amedroz and tr. D. S. Margoliouth (in separate volumes), I–VII (Oxford, 1920–21).

Moldovan, A. M., ed., '*Slovo o zakone i blagodati*' *Ilariona* (Kiev, 1984).

Mongait, A. L., 'Abu Khamid al-Garnati i ego puteshestvie v russkie zemli 1150–1153gg.', *Istoriia SSSR* 1959, no. 1, 169–80.

Mongait, A. L., *Riazanskaia zemlia* (Moscow, 1961).

Morrisson, C., 'La diffusion de la monnaie de Constantinople: routes commerciales ou routes politiques?', in C. Mango and G. Dargon, eds, *Constantinople and its Hinterland* (Society for the Promotion of Byzantine Studies Publications 3; Aldershot, 1995), pp. 77–89.

Moskalenko, A. N., *Gorodishche Titchikha* (Voronezh, 1965).

Motsia, A. P., *Naselenie Srednego Podneprov'ia IX–XIII vv.* (Kiev, 1987).

Motsia, A. P., 'Feodalizatsiia Chernihivs'koi okruhy v X st. (za danymy pokhoval'nykh pam'iatok), *Arkheolohiia* 61 (1988), 11–15.

Motsia, A. P., *Pogrebal'nye pamiatniki iuzhnorusskikh zemel' IX–XIII vv.* (Kiev, 1990).

Motsia, A. P., 'Nekotorye svedeniia o rasprostranenii khristianstva na Rusi po dannym pogrebal'nogo obriada', in *Obriady i verovaniia drevnego naseleniia Ukrainy. Sbornik nauchnykh trudov* (Kiev, 1990), 114–32.

Motsia, A. P., 'Etnichnyi sklad naselennia pivdennorus'kykh zemel' (za materialamy pokhoval'nykh pam'iatok X–XIII st.)', *Arkheolohiia* 1992, no. 1, 38–45.

Mühle, E., 'Die Anfänge Kievs (bis ca. 980) in archäologischer Sicht. Ein Forschungsbericht', *JGO* 35 (1987), 80–101.

Mühle, E., 'Die topographisch-städtebauliche Entwicklung Kievs vom Ende des 10. bis zum Ende des 12. Jh. im Licht der archäologischen Forschungen', *JGO* 36 (1988), 350–76.

Mühle, E., *Die städtischen Handelszentren der nordwestlichen Rus'. Anfänge und frühe Entwicklung altrussischer Städte (bis gegen Ende des 12. Jahrhunderts)* (Quellen und Studien zur Geschichte des östlichen Europa 32; Stuttgart, 1991).

Mühle, E., 'Von Holmgardr zu Novgorod. Zur Genesis des slavischen Ortsnamens der Ilmensee-Metropole im 11. Jahrhundert', in *Ex oriente lux. Mélanges offerts en hommage au professeur Jean Blankoff, à l'occasion de ses soixante ans*, I (Brussels, 1991), pp. 245–52.

Mühle, Eduard, 'Commerce and pragmatic literacy. The evidence of birchbark documents (from the mid-eleventh to the first quarter of the thirteenth century) on the early urban development of Novgorod', in

Michael S. Flier and Daniel Rowland, eds, *Medieval Russian Culture*, II (California Slavic Studies 19; Berkeley, Los Angeles, London, 1994), pp. 75–92.

Müller, Ludolf (introd.), *Die altrussischen hagiographischen Erzählungen und liturgischen Dichtungen über die heiligen Boris und Gleb, nach der Ausgabe von Abramovič* (=ed. Abramovich, Petrograd, 1916; repr. Slavische Propyläen 4; Munich, 1967).

Müller, Ludolf, *Die Taufe Russlands. Die Frühgeschichte des russischen Christentums bis zum Jahre 988* (Quellen und Studien zur russischen Geistesgeschichte 6; Munich, 1987).

Müller, Ludolf, 'Zur Frage nach dem Zeitpunkt der Kanonisierung der Heiligen Boris und Gleb', in A.-E. Tachiaos, ed., *The Legacy of Saints Cyril and Methodius to Kiev and Moscow. Proceedings of the International Congress on the Millennium of the Conversion of the Rus' to Christianity* (Thessaloniki, 1992), 321–39.

Müller-Boysen, C., *Kaufmannsschutz und Handelsrecht im frühmittelalterlichen Nordeuropa* (Neumünster, 1990).

Nagrodzka-Majchrzyk, Teresa, *Czarni Kłobucy* (Warsaw, 1985).

Nakhapetian, V. E. and Fomin, A. V., 'Graffiti na kuficheskikh monetakh, obrashchavshikhsia v Evrope v IX–Xvv.', *DGVEMI* 1991 (1994), 139–208.

Nasonov, A. N., ed., *Novgorodskaia pervaia letopis' starshego i mladshego izvodov* (Moscow, Leningrad, 1950).

Nasonov, A. N. ed., *Pskovskie letopisi*, II (Moscow, 1955).

Nastase, D., 'Les débuts de la communauté oecuménique du Mont Athos', *Symmeikta* 6 (1985), 251–314.

Nazarenko, A. V., 'Rodovoi siuzerenitet Riurikovichei nad Rus'iu (X–XI vv.)', *DGTSSSR* 1985 (1986), 149–57.

Nazarenko, A. V., 'Rus' i Germaniia v IX–X vv.', *DGVEMI* 1991 (1994), 5–131.

Nazarenko, A. V., *Nemetskie latinoiazychnye istochniki IX–XI vekov. Teksty, perevody, kommentarii* (Moscow, 1993).

Nedoshivina, N. G. and Fekhner, M. V., 'Pogrebal'nyi obriad timerevskogo mogil'nika', *SA* 1985, no. 2, 101–15.

Nikol'skaia, T. N., *Zemlia viatichei. K istorii naseleniia basseina verkhnei i srednei Oki v IX–XIII vv.* (Moscow, 1981).

Noonan, T. S., 'Ninth-century dirham hoards from European Russia: a preliminary analysis', in M. A. S. Blackburn and D. M. Metcalf, eds, *Viking-Age Coinage in the Northern Lands. The Sixth Oxford Symposium on Coinage and Monetary History* (British Archaeological Reports International Series 122; Oxford, 1981), pp. 47–117.

Noonan, T. S., 'Russia, the Near East and the steppe in the early medieval period: an examination of the Sasanian and Byzantine finds from the Kama-Urals area', *AEMA* 2 (1982), 269–302.

Noonan, T. S., 'A dirham hoard of the early eleventh century from northern Estonia and its importance for the routes by which dirhams reached Eastern Europe ca. 1000 AD', *Journal of Baltic Studies* 14 (1983), 185–302.

Noonan, T. S., 'Why dirhams first reached Russia: the role of Arab-Khazar relations in the development of the earliest Islamic trade with Eastern Europe', *AEMA* 4 (1984), 151–282.

Noonan, T. S., 'Khazaria as an intermediary between Islam and Eastern Europe in the second half of the ninth century: the numismatic perspective', *AEMA* 5 (1985) [1987], 179–204.

Noonan, T. S., 'Khwarazmian coins of the eighth century from Eastern Europe: the post-Sasanian interlude in the relations between Central Asia and European Russia', *AEMA* 6 (1986) [1988], 243–58.

Noonan, T. S., 'Why the Vikings first came to Russia', *JGO* 34 (1986), 321–48.

Noonan, T. S., 'The monetary history of Kiev in the pre-Mongol period', *HUS* 11 (1987), 384–443.

Noonan, T. S., 'When did Rūs/Rus' merchants first visit Khazaria and Baghdad?', *AEMA* 7 (1987–91), 213–19.

Noonan, T. S., 'The impact of the silver crisis in Islam upon Novgorod's trade with the Baltic', *OWS, Bericht der Römisch-Germanischen Kommission* 69 (1988), pp. 411–47.

Noonan, T. S., 'The flourishing of Kiev's international and domestic trade, ca. 1100–ca. 1240', in I. S. Koropeckyj, ed., *Ukrainian Economic History. Interpretive Essays* (Cambridge, Mass., 1991), pp. 102–46.

Noonan, T. S., 'Rus', Pechenegs and Polovtsy', *Russian History* 19 (1992), 300–26.

Nosov, E. N., 'Numizmaticheskie dannye o severnoi chasti baltiisko-volzhskogo puti kontsa VIII–X v.', *Vspomogatel'nye istoricheskie distsipliny* 8 (1976), 95–110.

Nosov, E. N., *Novgorodskoe (Riurikovo) Gorodishche* (Leningrad, 1990).

Novgorodskie gramoty na bereste:
    I. *Iz raskopok 1951 goda*, ed. A. V. Artsikhovskii and M. N. Tikhomirov (Moscow, 1953)
    II. *Iz raskopok 1952 goda*, ed. Artsikhovskii (1954)
    III. *Iz raskopok 1953–4 gg.*, ed. Artsikhovskii and V. I. Borkovskii (1958)
    IV. *Iz raskopok 1955 goda*, ed. Artsikhovskii and Borkovskii (1958)
    V. *Iz raskopok 1956–7 gg.*, ed. Artsikhovskii and Borkovskii (1963)
    VI. *Iz raskopok 1958–61 gg.*, ed. Artsikhovskii (1963)
    VII. *Iz raskopok 1962–76 gg.*, ed. Artsikhovskii and V. L. Ianin (1978)

VIII. *Iz raskopok 1977–83 gg.*, ed. Ianin and A. A. Zalizniak (1986)

IX. *Iz raskopok 1984–89 gg.*, ed. Ianin and Zalizniak (1993).

Novikova, G. L., 'Iron neck-rings with Thor's hammers found in Eastern Europe', *Fornvännen* 87 (1992) 73–88.

Novosel'tsev, A. P. and Pashuto, V. T., 'Vneshniaia torgovlia drevnei Rusi (do serediny XIII v.)', *Istoriia SSSR* 1967, no. 3, 81–108.

Novosel'tsev, A. P., 'K voprosu ob odnom iz drevneishikh titulov russkogo kniazia', *Istoriia SSSR* 1982, no. 4, 150–9.

Novosel'tsev, A. P., *Khazarskoe gosudarstvo i ego rol' v istorii Vostochnoi Evropy i Kavkaza* (Moscow, 1990).

Novosel'tev, A. P. et al., eds, *Obrazovanie drevnerusskogo gosudarstva. Spornye problemy* (Moscow, 1992).

Obolensky, Dimitri, *The Byzantine Commonwealth: Eastern Europe 500–1500* (London, 1971).

Obolensky, Dimitri, *Six Byzantine Portraits* (Oxford, 1988).

Obolensky, Dimitri, 'Cherson and the conversion of Rus': an anti-revisionist view', *Byzantine and Modern Greek Studies* 13 (1989), 244–56.

Obolensky, Dimitri, *Byzantium and the Slavs* (New York, 1994).

Oikonomides, N., 'L'évolution de l'organisation administrative de l'empire byzantin au XI siècle', *TM* 6 (1976), 125–52.

Øláfs Saga Tryggvasonar en mesta [*Saga of King Olaf Tryggvason*], ed. O. Halldórsson, I (Editiones Arnamagnaeanae, Series A.1; Copenhagen, 1958).

The Saga of King Olaf Tryggwason, tr. J. Sephton (London, 1895).

Oldenburg–Wolin–Staraja Ladoga–Novgorod–Kiev. Handel und Handelsverbindungen im südlichen und östliches Ostseeraum während des frühen Mittelalters. Internationale Fachkonferenz der Deutschen Forschungsgemeinschaft vom 5.–9. Oktober 1987 in Kiel, Bericht der Römisch-Germanischen Kommission, 69 (1988).

Orlov, A. S., *Vladimir Monomakh* (Moscow, Leningrad, 1946).

Pálsson, Herman and Edwards, Paul (tr. and introd.), *Vikings in Russia: Yngvar's Saga and Eymund's Saga* (Edinburgh, 1989).

Pelenski, Jaroslaw, 'The sack of Kiev in 1169: its significance for the succession to Kievan Rus", *HUS* 11 (1987), 303–16.

Petrukhin, V. I., 'Pogrebeniia znati epokhi vikingov', *Skandinavskii sbornik* 21 (1976), 153–70.

Petrukhin, V. I., 'Variagi i khazary v istorii Rusi', *Etnograficheskoe obozrenie* 1993, no. 3, 68-82.

Petrukhin, V. J., 'The early history of Old Russian art: the rhyton from Chernigov and Khazarian tradition', *Tor* 27.2 (1995), 475–86.

Photios, *Homiliai*, ed. B. Laourdas (Thessaloniki, 1959).

Photios, *Homilies*, tr. C. Mango (Dumbarton Oaks Studies 3; Washington, D.C., 1958).

Pletneva, S. A., *Ot kochevii k gorodam. Saltovo-Maiatskaia kul'tura* (*MIA* 142; Moscow, 1967).

Pletnjowa, S. A. (=Pletneva, S. A.), *Die Chasaren. Mittelalterliches Reich an Don und Wolga* (Leipzig, 1978).

Pletneva, S. A., ed., *Stepi Evrazii v epokhu srednevekov'ia* (Moscow, 1981).

Pletneva, S. A., *Kochevniki srednevekov'ia. Poiski istoricheskikh zakonomernostei* (Moscow, 1982).

Pletneva, S. A., 'Donskie Polovtsy', in B. A. Rybakov, ed., *'Slovo o polku Igoreve' i ego vremia* (Moscow, 1985), pp. 249–81.

Pletneva, S. A., *Na slaviano-khazarskom pogranich'e. Dmitrievskii arkheologicheskii kompleks* (Moscow, 1989).

Pletneva, S. A., 'Khazarskie problemy v arkheologii', *SA* 1990, no. 2, 77–91.

Pletneva, S. A., *Polovtsy* (Moscow, 1990).

Pletneva, S. A., 'Istoriia odnogo khazarskogo poseleniia', *RA* 1993, no. 2, 48–69.

Pobol', L. O. et al., eds, *Kiev i zapadnye zemli Rusi v IX–XIII vv.* (Minsk, 1982).

Podskalsky, Gerhard, *Christentum und theologische Literatur in der Kiever Rus' (988–1237)* (Munich, 1982).

Poluboiarinova, M. D., *Rus' i Volzhskaia Bolgariia v X–XV vv.* (Moscow, 1993).

Poppe, Andrzej, 'The political background to the baptism of Rus. Byzantine-Russian relations between 986–989', *DOP* 30 (1976), 197–244; repr. in Poppe, *The Rise of Christian Russia*, no. 2.

Poppe, Andrzej, 'The original status of the Old-Russian Church', *Acta Poloniae historica* 39 (1979), 4–45; repr. in Poppe, *The Rise of Christian Russia*, no. 3.

Poppe, Andrzej, 'The building of the Church of St Sophia in Kiev', *Journal of Medieval History* 7 (1981), 15–66; repr. in Poppe, *The Rise of Christian Russia*, no. 4.

Poppe, Andrzej, *The Rise of Christian Russia* (London, 1982).

Poppe, Andrzej, 'Werdegang der Diözesanstruktur der Kiever Metropolitankirche in den ersten drei Jahrhunderten der Christianisierung der Ostslaven', in K. C. Felmy et al., eds, *Tausend Jahre Christentums in Russland. Zum Millennium der Taufe der Kiever Rus'* (Göttingen, 1988), 251–90.

Poppe, Andrzej, 'Words that serve the authority. On the title of "Grand Prince" in Kievan Rus'', *Acta Poloniae historica* 60 (1989), 159–84.

Poppe, Andrzej, 'Vladimir, prince chrétien', in S. W. Swierkosz-Lenart, ed., *Le origini e lo sviluppo della cristianità slavo-bizantina* (Nuovi Studi Storici 17; Rome, 1992), pp. 43–58.

Poppe, Andrzej, 'Once again concerning the baptism of Olga, Archontissa of Rus", in A. Cutler and S. Franklin, eds, *Homo Byzantinus. Papers in Honor of Alexander Kazhdan*, DOP 46 (1992), 271–7.

Potin, V. M., *Drevniaia Rus' i evropeiskie gosudarstva v X–XIII vv. Istoriko-numizmaticheskii ocherk* (Leningrad, 1968).

Prinzing, G., 'Byzantinische Aspekte der mittelalterlichen Geschichte Polens', *Byzantion* 64 (1994), 459–84.

Pritsak, O., 'An Arabic text on the trade route of the corporation of Ar-Rūs in the second half of the ninth century', *Folia Orientalia* 12 (1970), 241–59.

Pushkareva, N. L., *Zhenshchiny Drevnei Rusi* (Moscow, 1989).

Pushkareva, N. L., and Levin, E., 'Women in Medieval Novgorod from the Eleventh to the Fifteenth Century', *Soviet Studies in History* 23 (1984–5), no. 4, pp. 71–90.

Pushkina, T. A., 'Skandinavskie nakhodki iz Gorodishcha pod Novgorodom', *Skandinavskii sbornik* 31 (1988), 96–103.

Pushkina, T. A., 'Torgovyi inventar' iz kurganov smolenskogo podneprov'ia', in D. A. Avdusin, ed., *Smolensk i Gnëzdovo (k istorii drevnerusskogo goroda)* (Moscow, 1991), pp. 226–43.

Putsko, V. G., 'Vizantiia i stanovleniie iskusstva kievskoi Rusi', in P. P. Tolochko, ed., *Iuzhnaia Rus' i Vizantiia. Sbornik nauchnykh trudov (k XVIII kongressu vizantinistov)* (Kiev, 1991), pp. 79–99.

Rabinovich, M. G., 'O vozraste i pervonachal'noi territorii Moskvy', in *Novoe o proshlom nashei strany* (Moscow, 1967), 21–32.

Rapov, O. M., *Kniazheskie vladeniia na Rusi v X–pervoi polovine XIII v.* (Moscow, 1977).

Rapov, O. M., *Russkaia tserkov' v IX–pervoi treti XII v.. Priniatie khristianstva* (Moscow, 1988).

Rappoport, P. A., *Ocherki po istorii russkogo voennogo zodchestva X–XIII vv.* (*MIA* 52; Moscow, Leningrad, 1956).

Rappoport, P. A., *Russkaia arkhitektura X–XIII vv.* (*ASSSR SAI, vyp.* E1–47; Leningrad, 1982).

Rappoport, P. A., *Drevnerusskaia arkhitektura* (St Petersburg, 1993).

Rappoport, P. A., *Building the Churches of Kievan Russia* (Aldershot, 1995).

Ravdina, T. V., *Pogrebeniia X–XI vv. s monetami na territorii drevnei Rusi* (Moscow, 1988).

Rennkamp, W., *Studien zum deutsch-russischen Handel bis zum Ende des 13. Jahrhunderts. Nowgorod und Dünagebiet* (Bochum, 1977).

Revelli, Giorgetta, *Monumenti letterarii su Boris e Gleb* (Genova, 1993).

Riabinin, E. A., 'Vladimirskie kurgany', *SA* 1979, no. 1, 228–44.

Riabinin, E. A., 'Novye otkrytiia v Staroi Ladoge (itogi raskopok na Zemlianom gorodishche 1973–1975 gg.)', in V. V. Sedov, ed., *Srednevekovaia Ladoga* (Leningrad, 1985), pp. 27–75.

Riabinin, E. A. and Chernykh, N. B., 'Stratigrafiia, zastroika i khronologiia nizhnego sloia staroladozhskogo Zemlianogo gorodishcha v svete novykh issledovanii', *SA* 1988, no. 1, 72–100.

Rimbert, *Vita Anskarii*, in W. Trillmich and R. Buchner, eds, *Quellen des 9. und 11. Jahrhunderts zur Geschichte der Hamburgischen Kirche und des Reiches* (Ausgewählte Quellen zur Deutschen Geschichte des Mittelalters 11; Darmstadt, 1978).

Roesdahl, E., *Viking Age Denmark* (London, 1982).

Roesdahl, E., *The Vikings*, tr. S. M. Margeson and K. Williams (London, 1991).

Rolle, R., 'Archäologische Bemerkungen zum Warägerhandel', in *OWS, Bericht der Römisch-Germanischen Kommission* 69 (1988), pp. 472–529.

Rusanova, I. P., 'Kul'tovye mesta i iazycheskie sviatilishcha slavian VI–XIII vv.', *RA* 1992, no. 4, 50–67.

Rybakov, B. A., *Remeslo Drevnei Rusi* (Moscow, 1948).

Rybakov, B. A., *Drevniaia Rus'. Skazaniia, byliny, letopisi* (Moscow, 1963).

Rybakov, B. A., *Russkie datirovannye nadpisi XI–XIV vekov* (*ASSSR SAI, vyp.* E1–44; Moscow, 1964).

Rybakov, B. A., *Kievskaia Rus' i russkie kniazhestva XII–XIII vv.* (Moscow, 1982).

Rybakov, B. A., *Kievan Rus* (Moscow, 1984).

Rybakov, B. A., *Iazychestvo drevnei Rusi* (Moscow, 1987).

Rybina, E. A., *Inozemnye dvory v Novgorode XII–XVII vv.* (Moscow, 1986).

Rybina, E. A., 'Otkrytiia arkheologov 1993 goda', *Vestnik Moskovskogo Universiteta. Seriia 8, Istoriia* 1994, no. 2, 40–5.

Rychka, V. M., 'Shliub i podruzhne zhittia v Kyivs'kii Rusi', *Ukrains'kyi istorychnyi zhurnal* 1992, no. 1, 131–41.

Rychka, V. M., 'Pro kharakter sotsial'nykh konfliktiv v Kyivs'kii Rusi', *Ukrains'kyi istorychnyi zhurnal* 1993, nos 2–3, 28–36.

Sahaidak, M. A., *Davn'o-kyivs'kyi Podil: problemy topohrafii, stratihrafii, khronolohii* (Kiev, 1991).

Sakharov, A. N., *Diplomatiia drevnei Rusi IX–pervaia polovina X v.* (Moscow, 1980).

Sakharov, A. N., *Diplomatiia Sviatoslava* (Moscow, 1991).

Sawyer, B. and Sawyer, P., *Medieval Scandinavia: from Conversion to Reformation c. 800–1500* (The Nordic Series 17; Minnesota, 1993).

Schramm, G., '"Gentem suam Rhos vocari dicebant"', in U. Haustein, G. W. Strobel and G. Wagner, eds, *Ostmitteleuropa. Berichte und Forschungen* (Stuttgart, 1981), pp. 1–10.

Schramm, G., 'Die Herkunft des Namens Rus': Kritik des Forschungs-standes', *Forschungen zur osteuropäischen Geschichte* 30 (1982), 7–49.

Schramm, G., 'Fernhandel und frühe Reichsbildungen am Ostrand Europas. Zur historischen Einordnung der Kiever Rus", in K. Colberg et al., eds, *Mittelalter und Früher Neuzeit. Gedenkschrift für Joachim Leuschner* (Göttingen, 1983), pp. 15–39.

Schramm, G., 'Die Waräger: osteuropäische Schicksale einer nord-germanischen Gruppenbezeichnung', *Die Welt der Slaven* 28 (1983), 38–67.

Schramm, G., 'Der Beitrag der Namenphilologie zur Rekonstruktion des normannischen Stützpunktsystems in Russland', in *UHV, Abhand-lungen der Akademie der Wissenschaften in Göttingen, Philol.-hist. Klasse*, 3. Folge, no. 156 (Göttingen, 1987), pp. 745–57.

Sedov, V. V., *Vostochnye slaviane v V–XIII vv.* (Moscow, 1982).

Sedov, V. V., ed., *Srednevekovaia Ladoga* (Leningrad, 1985).

Sedov, V. V., 'Rasprostranenie khristianstva v Drevnei Rusi', *KSIA* 208 (1993), 3–11.

Seemann, K. D. (introd.), *Abt Daniil. Wallfahrtsberichte. Nachdruck der Ausgabe von Venevetinov 1883/5* (Slavische Propyläen 36; Munich, 1970).

Senyk, Sophia, *A History of the Church in Ukraine*, I, *To the End of the Thirteenth Century* (Orientalia Christiana Analecta 243; Rome, 1993).

Shaban, M., *Islamic History: a New Interpretation*, I–II (Cambridge, 1971–76).

Shchapov, Ia. N., *Drevnerusskie kniazheskie ustavy XI–XV vv.* (Moscow, 1976).

Shchapov, Ia. N., *Vizantiiskoe i iuzhnoslavianskoe pravovoe nasledie na Rusi v XI–XIII vv.* (Moscow, 1978).

Shchapov, Ia. N., *Gosudarstvo i tserkov' Drevnei Rusi X–XIII vv.* (Moscow, 1989) tr. as *State and Church in Early Russia, 10th–13th centuries* (New Rochelle, Athens, Moscow, 1993).

Shchapova, Iu. L., *Steklo Kievskoi Rusi* (Moscow, 1972).

Shchapova, Iu. L., 'Vizantiia i vostochnaia Evropa. Napravlenie i kharakter sviazei v IX–XII vv. (po nakhodkam iz stekla)', in G. G. Litavrin et al., eds, *Vizantiia. Sredizemnomor'e. Slavianskii mir. K XVIII mezhdunarodnomu kongressu vizantinistov* (Moscow, 1991), 155–77.

Shepard, J., 'Why did the Russians attack Byzantium in 1043?', *BNJ* 22 (1978/9), 147–212.

Shepard, J., 'The Russian steppe-frontier and the Black Sea zone', *Archeion Pontou* 35 (1979), 218–37.

Shepard, J., 'Yngvarr's expedition to the East and a Russian inscribed stone cross', *Saga-Book of the Viking Society* 21 (1984–5), 222–92.

Shepard, J., 'Some remarks on the sources for the conversion of Rus'', in S. W. Swierkosz-Lenart, ed., *Le origini e lo sviluppo della cristianità slavo-bizantina* (Nuovi Studi Storici 17; Rome, 1992), pp. 59–95.

Shepard, J., 'The Rhos guests of Louis the Pious: whence and wherefore?', *Early Medieval Europe* 4 (1995), 41–60.

Shramko, B. A., *Drevnosti Severskogo Dontsa* (Kharkov, 1962).

Sinor, D., ed., *The Cambridge History of Early Inner Asia* (Cambridge, 1990).

Smirnov, A. P., ed., *Iaroslavskoe Povolzh'e X–XI vv. po materialam Timerevskogo, Mikhailovskogo i Petrovskogo mogil'nikov* (Moscow, 1963).

Smith, R. E. F. and Christian, D., *Bread and Salt. A Social and Economic History of Food and Drink in Russia* (Cambridge, 1984).

Snorri Sturluson, *Heimskringla: History of the Kings of Norway*, tr. and introd. Lee M. Hollander (2nd printing, Austin, Texas, 1967).

Sokul'sky, A. L., 'K lokalizatsii letopisnogo Olesh'ia', *SA* 1980, no. 1, 64–73.

Soloviev, A. V., '"Mare Russiae"', *Die Welt der Slaven* 4 (1959), 1–12, repr. in Soloviev, A. V., *Byzance et la formation de l'État russe* (London, 1979), no. 13.

Soloviev, A. V., 'L'organisation de l'État russe au X siècle', in A. Gieysztor and T. Manteuffel, eds, *L'Europe aux IX–XI siècles. Aux origines des États nationaux* (Warsaw, 1968), pp. 249–68; repr. in Soloviev, *Byzance et la formation de l'État russe* (London, 1979), no. 1.

Soloviev, A. V., *Byzance et la formation de l'État russe* (London, 1979).

Sorlin, I., 'Les traités de Byzance avec la Russie au X siècle (I), (II)', *Cahiers du monde russe et soviétique* 2 (1961), 313–60, 447–75.

Sorlin, I., 'Les premières années byzantines du *Récit des temps passés*', *RES* 63 (1991), 8–18.

Sotnikova, M. P. and Spasski, I. G., *Russian Coins of the X–XI Centuries A. D.*, tr. H. Bartlett Wells (British Archaeological Reports International Series 136; Oxford, 1982).

Stalsberg, A., 'Scandinavian relations with northwestern Russia during the Viking Age: the archaeological evidence', *Journal of Baltic Studies* 13 (1982), 267–95.

Stalsberg, A., 'The Scandinavian Viking age finds in Rus'. Overview and analysis', in OWS, *Bericht der Römisch-Germanischen Kommission* 69 (1988), pp. 448–71.

Stein-Wilkeshuis, M., 'A Viking-age treaty between Constantinople and northern merchants, with its provisions on theft and robbery', *Scando-Slavica* 37 (1991), 35–47.

Stender-Petersen, A., *Die Varägersage als Quelle der altrussischen Chronik* (Aarhus, 1934).

Stökl, G., 'Das Fürstentum Galizien-Wolynien', in M. Hellmann, ed., *Handbuch der Geschichte Rußlands*, I. *i: von der Kiever Reichsbildung bis zum moskauer Zartum* (Stuttgart, 1981), pp. 484–533.

Strässle, P. M., '*To monoxylon* in Konstantin VII. Porphyrogennetos' Werk *De administrando imperio*', *Études Balkaniques* 1990, no. 2, 93–106.

Sudakov, V. V., 'Sel'skie poseleniia IX–XV vv. v okruge Pereiaslavlia Riazanskogo', *KSIA* 198 (1989), 57–64.

Sumnikova, T. A. and Lopatin, V. V., eds, *Smolenskie gramoty XIII–XIV vekov* (Moscow, 1963).

Sverdlov, M. B., *Ot Zakona Russkogo k Russkoi Pravde* (Moscow, 1988).

Sverdlov, M. B., *Latinoiazychnye istochniki po istorii Drevnei Rusi. Germaniia, IX–pervaia polovina XII v.* (Moscow, Leningrad, 1989).

Theophanes Continuatus, *Chronographia*, ed. I. Bekker (Bonn, 1838).

Thomsen, V., *The Relations Between Ancient Russia and Scandinavia and the Origin of the Russian State* (Oxford, 1877).

Thomson, Francis J., 'The nature of the reception of Christian Byzantine culture in Russia in the tenth to thirteenth centuries and its implications for Russian culture', *Slavica gandensia* 5 (1978), 107–39.

Thomson, Francis J., 'Quotations of patristic and Byzantine works by early Russian authors as an indication of the cultural level of Kievan Russia', *Slavica gandensia* 9 (1983), 66–102.

Thomson, Francis J., '"Made in Russia". A survey of translations allegedly made in Kievan Russia', in G. Birkfellner, ed., *Millennium Russiae Christianae. Tausend Jahre Christliches Russland, 988–1988* (Cologne, Weimar, Vienna, 1993), 295–354.

Thomson, Francis A., 'The distorted medieval Russian perception of classical antiquity: the causes and the consequences', in A. Welkenhuysen et al., ed., *Medieval Antiquity* (Mediaevalia Lovaniensia. Series I: Studia, vol. 24; Louvain, 1995 [forthcoming]).

Tikhomirov, M. N., *The Towns of Ancient Rus* (Moscow, 1959).

Tolochko, A. P., *Kniaz' v Drevnei Rusi: vlast', sobstvennost', ideologiia* (Kiev, 1992).

Tolochko, P. P., *Drevnii Kiev* (Kiev, 1983).

Tolochko, P. P., *Drevniaia Rus'. Ocherki sotsial'no-politicheskoi istorii* (Kiev, 1987).

Tolochko, P. P., *Drevnerusskii feodal'nyi gorod* (Kiev, 1989).

Tolochko, P. P., ed., *Novoe v arkheologii Kieva* (Kiev, 1981).

Tolochko, P. P., ed., *Iuzhnaia Rus' i Vizantiia. Sbornik nauchnykh trudov (k XVIII kongressu vizantinistor)* (Kiev, 1991).

Trunte, H., 'Kyj – ein altrussischer Städtegründer? Zur Entmythologisierung der slavischen Frühgeschichte', *Die Welt der Slaven* 33 (1988), 1–25.

[Tschiževskij, D.] Čiževskij, D., *History of Russian Literature, From the Eleventh Century to the End of the Baroque* (Slavistic Printings and Reprintings 12; The Hague, 1960; 3rd printing 1971).

Tschiževskij, D. (introd.), *Das Paterikon des Kiever Höhlenklosters, nach der Ausgabe von D. Abramovič* (=ed. Abramovich, Kiev, 1930; repr. Slavische Propyläen 2; Munich, 1964).

Tschiževskij, D. (introd.), *Die altrussischen hagiographischen Erzählungen und liturgischen Dichtungen über den Heiligen Avraamij von Smolensk* (= ed. S. P. Rozanov, St Petersburg, 1912; repr. Slavische Propyläen 15; Munich, 1970).

Untersuchungen zu Handel und Verkehr der vor- und frühgeschichtlichen Zeit in Mittel- und Nordeuropa, IV, *Der Handel der Karolinger- und Wikingerzeit*, eds, K. Düwel, H. Jankuhn, H. Siems and D. Timpe, *Abhandlungen der Akademic der Wissenschaften in Gottingen, philolog.- hist. Klasse, Dritte Folge* no. 156 (Göttingen, 1987).

Vagner, G. K. and Vladyshevskaia, T. F., *Iskusstvo Drevnei Rusi* (Moscow, 1993).

Valk, S. N., ed., *Gramoty Velikogo Novgoroda i Pskova* (Moscow, Leningrad, 1949).

Vasilenko, V. M., *Russkoe prikladnoe iskusstvo. Istoki i stanovlenie. I vek do nashei ery – XIII vek nashei ery* (Moscow, 1977).

Vasiliev, A., *The Russian attack on Constantinople in 860* (Cambridge, Mass., 1946).

Veder, William R. (tr. and introd.) with Turilov, Anatolij A. (introd.), *The Edificatory Prose of Kievan Rus'* (*HLEUL* 6; Cambridge, Mass., 1994).

Vernadsky, George, *Kievan Russia* (New Haven, 1948; repr. 1972).

Veselovskii, A. N., ed., *Vita Basilii Iunioris*, in *Razyskaniia v oblasti russkogo dukhovnogo stikha*, *Sbornik ORIAS* 46 (1889), no. 6, *prilozhenie*.

Vestergaard, E., 'A Note on Viking Age Inaugurations', in J. M. Bak, ed., *Coronations. Medieval and Early Modern Monarchic Ritual* (Berkeley, Los Angeles, Oxford, 1990), pp. 119–24.

Vinnikov, A. Z., 'Kontakty donskikh slavian s alano-bolgarskim mirom', *SA* 1990, no. 3, 124–37.

Vinniker, A. Z. and Afanas'ev, G. E., *Kul'tovye kompleksy maiatskogo selishcha (Materialy raskopok Sovetsko–Bolgaro–Vengerskol ekspeditsii)* (Voronezh, 1991).

Vodoff, V., *Naissance de la chrétienté russe. La conversion du prince Vladimir de Kiev (988) et ses conséquences (XIe–XIIIe siècles)* (Paris, 1988).

Voronin, N. N., *Zodchestvo severo-vostochnoi Rusi XII–XV vv.*, I (Moscow, 1961).

Voronin, N. N. and Rappoport, P. A., *Zodchestvo Smolenska XII–XIII vv.* (Leningrad, 1979).
Vysotskii, S. A., *Drevnerusskie nadpisi Sofii Kievskoi XI–XIV vv., Vyp.* I (Kiev, 1966).
Vysotskii, S. A., *Srednevekovye nadpisi Sofii Kievskoi (po materialam XI–XVII vv.)* (Kiev, 1976).
Vysotskii, S. A., *Kievskie graffiti XI–XVII vv.*, (Kiev, 1985).

Warnke, C., *Die Anfänge des Fernhandels in Polen* (Würzburg, 1964).
Warnke, C., 'Der Handel mit Wachs zwischen Ost- und Westeuropa im frühen und hohen Mittelalter. Voraussetzungen und Gewinn-möglichkeiten', *UHV, Abhandlungen der Akademie der Wissen-schaften in Göttingen, philolog.-hist. Klasse, 3. Folge,* no. 156 (Göttingen, 1987), pp. 545–69.
Wieczynski, Joseph L., ed., *The Modern Encyclopedia of Russian and Soviet History,* 57 vols (Gulf Breeze, FL, 1976–94).
Wikinger, Waräger, Normannen. Die Skandinavier und Europa 800–1200 (XXII. Kunstausstellung des Europarates: Paris, Berlin, Copenhagen; Mainz, 1992).
Wozniak, F. E., 'Byzantium, the Pechenegs and the Rus': the limitations of a great power's influence on its clients in the 10th-century Eurasian Steppe', *AEMA* 4 (1984), 299–316.

Yahya ibn Sa'id (of Antioch), *Histoire,* ed. and tr. J. Kratchkovsky and A. Vasiliev in two parts: *Patrologia Orientalis* 18.5 (Paris, 1924), pp. 701–833; *Patrologia Orientalis* 23.3 (Paris, 1932), pp. 347–520.

Zharnov, I. E., 'Zhenskie skandinavskie pogrebeniia v Gnëzdove', in D. A. Avdusin, ed., *Smolensk i Gnëzdovo (k istorii drevnerusskogo goroda)* (Moscow, 1991), pp. 200–25.
Zverugo, I. G., *Verkhnee Poneman'e v IX–XIII vv.* (Minsk, 1989).
Zvizdets'kyi, B. A., 'Pro kordony Drevlians'koi zemli', *Arkheolohiia* 1989, no. 4, 47–58.

Maps

Map 1. Europe in the eighth and ninth centuries (showing some routes and known
Rus settlements)

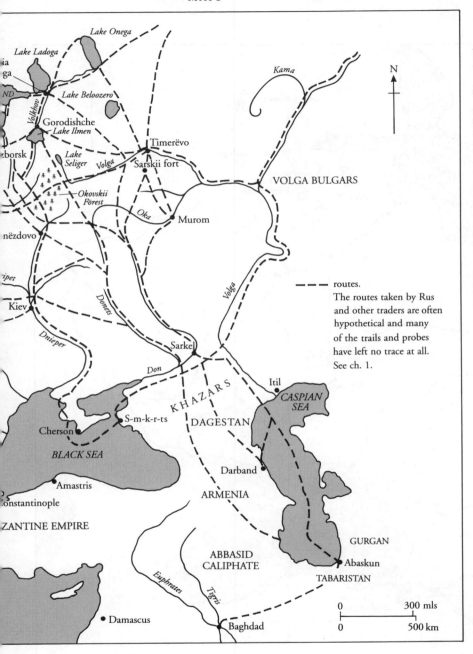

routes.
The routes taken by Rus
and other traders are often
hypothetical and many
of the trails and probes
have left no trace at all.
See ch. 1.

Map 2.   Rus settlements in the tenth century: the north-south trading axis

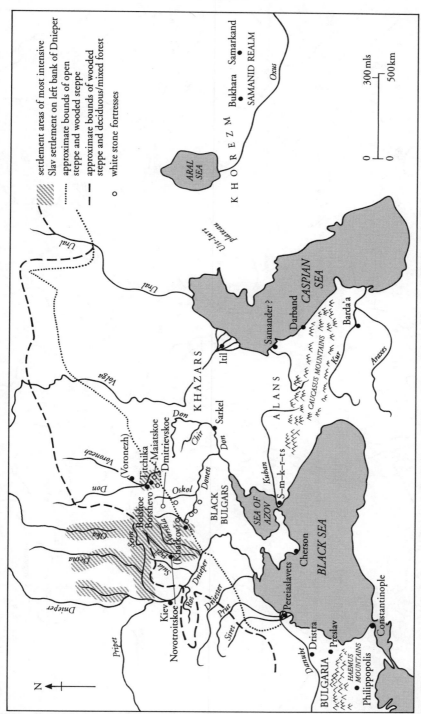

Map 3. The steppes from the Danube to Central Asia and Caucasia

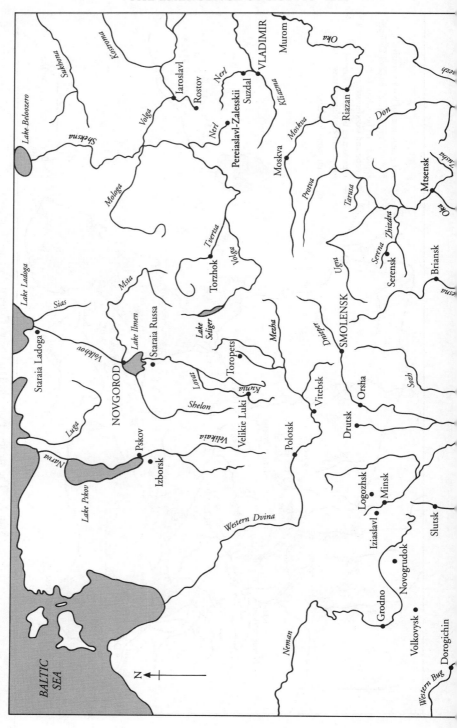

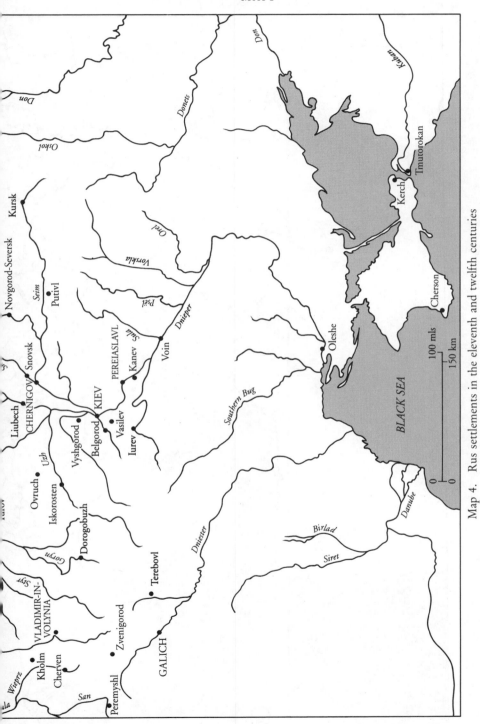

Map 4. Rus settlements in the eleventh and twelfth centuries

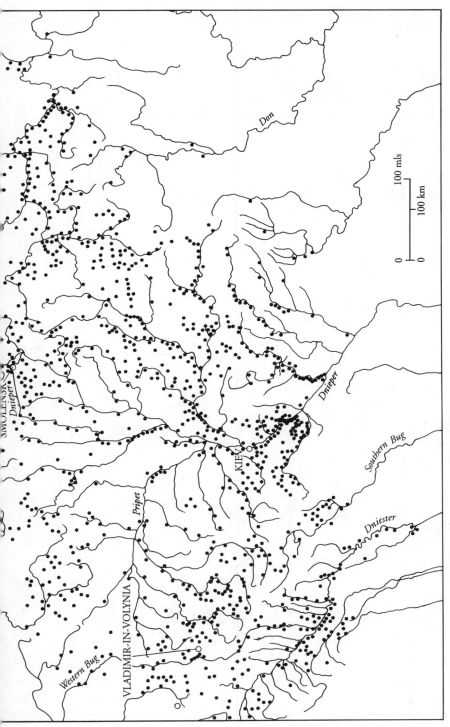

Map 5. The thickening pattern of settlement in Rus in the twelfth century

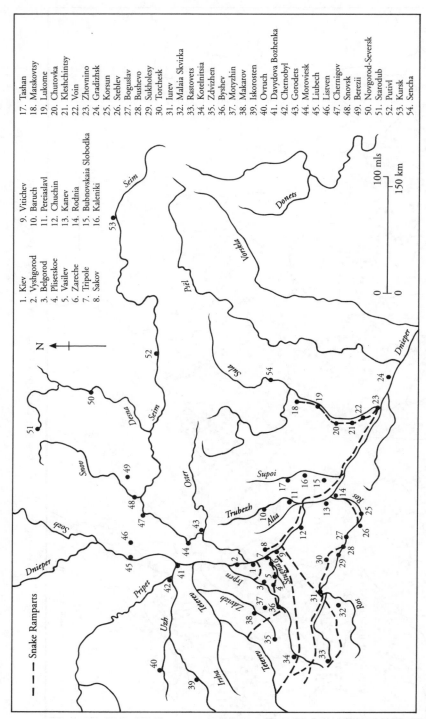

Map 6. The Middle Dnieper and the steppe frontier in the eleventh and twelfth centuries

1. Kiev
2. Vyshgorod
3. Belgorod
4. Plisetskoe
5. Vasilev
6. Zareche
7. Tripole
8. Sakov
9. Vitichev
10. Baruch
11. Pereiaslavl
12. Chuchin
13. Kanev
14. Rodnia
15. Bubnovskaia Slobodka
16. Kaleniki
17. Tashan
18. Matskovtsy
19. Lukome
20. Chutovka
21. Kleshchintsy
22. Voin
23. Zhovnino
24. Gradizhsk
25. Korsun
26. Steblev
27. Boguslav
28. Bushevo
29. Sukholesy
30. Torchesk
31. Iurev
32. Malaia Skvirka
33. Rastovets
34. Kotelnitsia
35. Zdvizhen
36. Byshev
37. Motyzhin
38. Makarov
39. Iskorosten
40. Ovruch
41. Davydova Bozhenka
42. Chernobyl
43. Gorodets
44. Moroviesk
45. Liubech
46. Lisrven
47. Chernigov
48. Snovsk
49. Berezii
50. Novgorod-Seversk
51. Starodub
52. Putivl
53. Kursk
54. Sencha

- - - Snake Ramparts

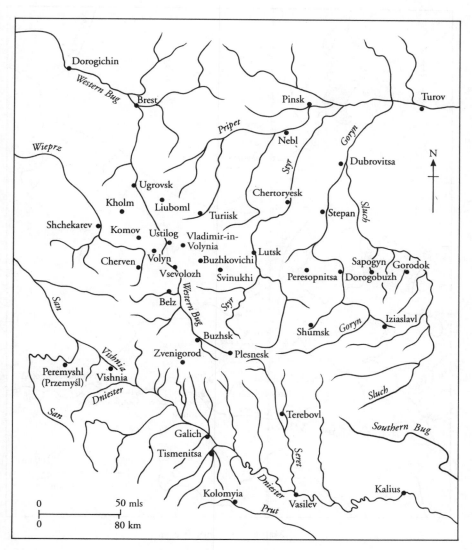

Map 7. The south-west and west

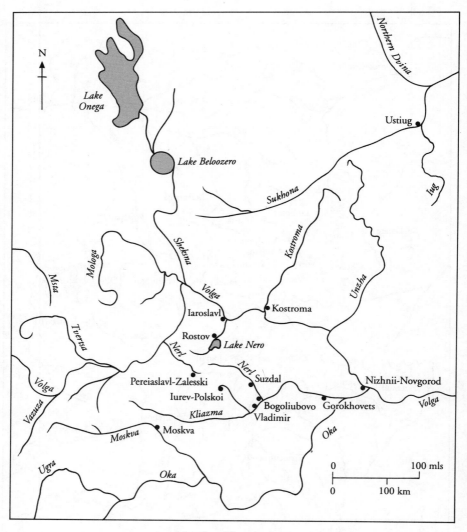

Map 8. The north-east

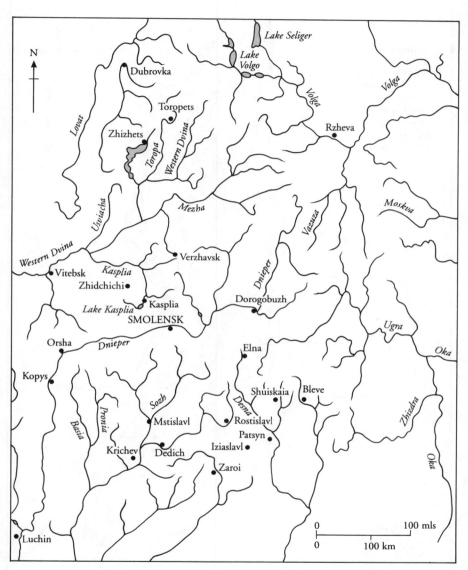

Map 9.   Smolensk and its hinterland in the twelfth century

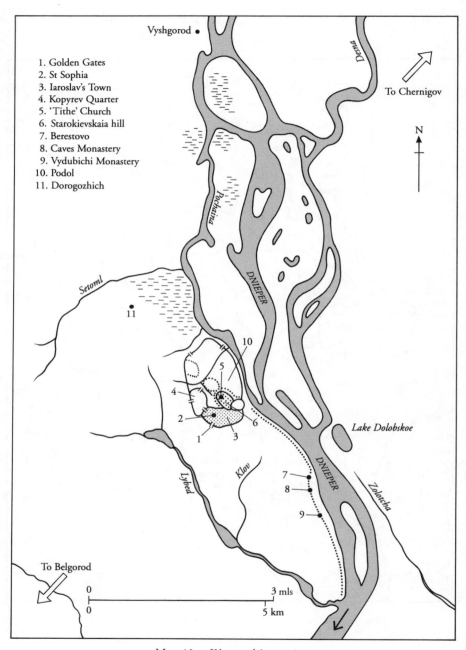

1. Golden Gates
2. St Sophia
3. Iaroslav's Town
4. Kopyrev Quarter
5. 'Tithe' Church
6. Starokievskaia hill
7. Berestovo
8. Caves Monastery
9. Vydubichi Monastery
10. Podol
11. Dorogozhich

Vyshgorod

Desna

To Chernigov

N

Pochaina

Setoml

11

DNIEPER

10

5

4

2

1

6

3

Lake Dolobskoe

7

8

9

DNIEPER

Klov

Lybed

Zolotcha

To Belgorod

0   3 mls

0   5 km

Map 10.   Kiev and its environs

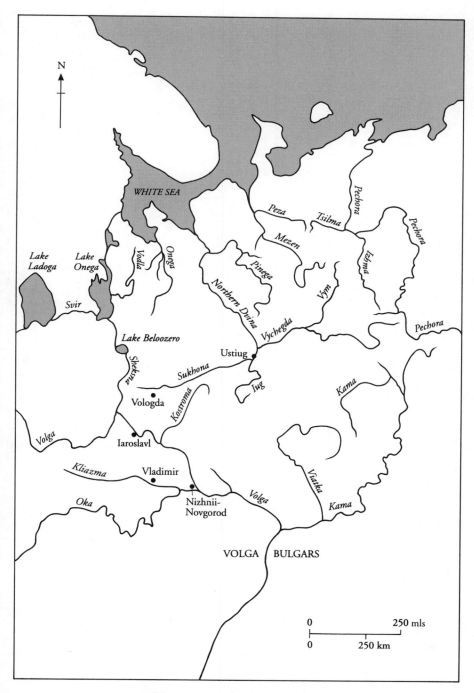

Map 11.   Lands of the far north

Genealogical Tables

No family tree of the ruling dynasty can be either comprehensive or precise in every detail. The sources are unsystematic; births are recorded very rarely indeed; deaths, though more frequently mentioned, cannot always be dated with confidence; and - perhaps surprisingly - the sources often fail to specify the sequence of seniority among siblings. The following tables should help readers to keep their bearings through the relevant parts of the narrative, but one should be aware that some of the information is more approximate than the tabular form might suggest.

Princesses and spouses are not included, except at the start of Table I. The problems of identifying female members of the family are outlined in Chapter Eight.

Capital letters are used to denote princes of Kiev. We have applied this convention liberally, with no regard for the relative brevity or contentiousness of any given prince's presence in the city.

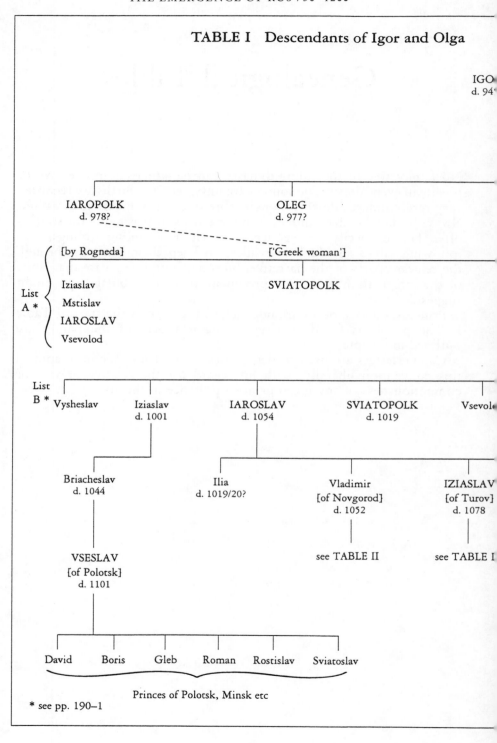

TABLE I   Descendants of Igor and Olga

IGO[
d. 94[

IAROPOLK
d. 978?

OLEG
d. 977?

[by Rogneda]

['Greek woman']

List
A *

Iziaslav

SVIATOPOLK

Mstislav

IAROSLAV

Vsevolod

List
B *

Vysheslav

Iziaslav
d. 1001

IAROSLAV
d. 1054

SVIATOPOLK
d. 1019

Vsevol[

Briacheslav
d. 1044

Ilia
d. 1019/20?

Vladimir
[of Novgorod]
d. 1052

IZIASLAV
[of Turov]
d. 1078

VSESLAV
[of Polotsk]
d. 1101

see TABLE II

see TABLE I

David   Boris   Gleb   Roman   Rostislav   Sviatoslav

Princes of Polotsk, Minsk etc

* see pp. 190–1

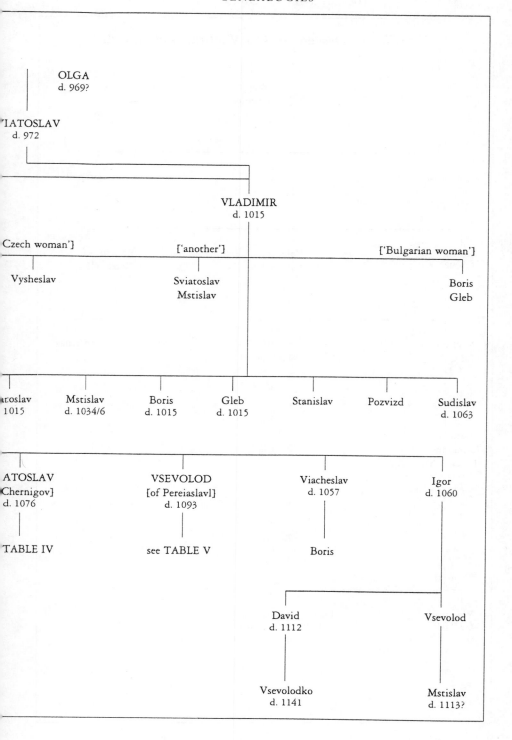

OLGA
d. 969?

'IATOSLAV
d. 972

VLADIMIR
d. 1015

Czech woman']   ['another']   ['Bulgarian woman']

Vysheslav   Sviatoslav   Boris
Mstislav   Gleb

aroslav   Mstislav   Boris   Gleb   Stanislav   Pozvizd   Sudislav
1015   d. 1034/6   d. 1015   d. 1015   d. 1063

ATOSLAV   VSEVOLOD   Viacheslav   Igor
Chernigov]   [of Pereiaslavl]   d. 1057   d. 1060
d. 1076   d. 1093

TABLE IV   see TABLE V   Boris

David   Vsevolod
d. 1112

Vsevolodko   Mstislav
d. 1141   d. 1113?

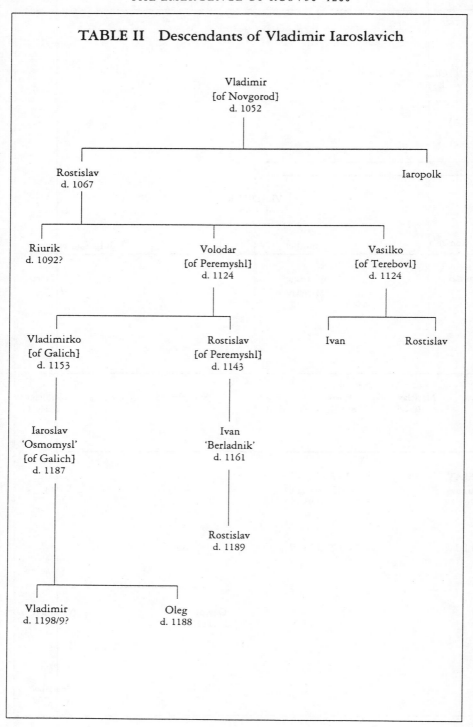

TABLE II   Descendants of Vladimir Iaroslavich

Vladimir
[of Novgorod]
d. 1052

Rostislav
d. 1067

Iaropolk

Riurik
d. 1092?

Volodar
[of Peremyshl]
d. 1124

Vasilko
[of Terebovl]
d. 1124

Vladimirko
[of Galich]
d. 1153

Rostislav
[of Peremyshl]
d. 1143

Ivan

Rostislav

Iaroslav
'Osmomysl'
[of Galich]
d. 1187

Ivan
'Berladnik'
d. 1161

Rostislav
d. 1189

Vladimir
d. 1198/9?

Oleg
d. 1188

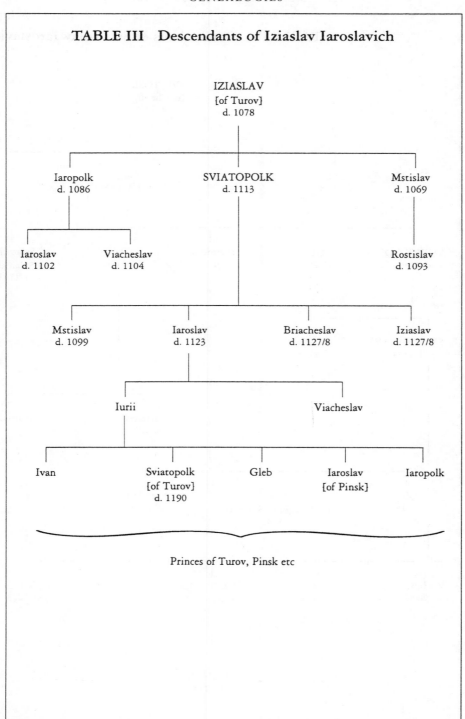

TABLE III Descendants of Iziaslav Iaroslavich

IZIASLAV
[of Turov]
d. 1078

Iaropolk
d. 1086

SVIATOPOLK
d. 1113

Mstislav
d. 1069

Iaroslav
d. 1102

Viacheslav
d. 1104

Rostislav
d. 1093

Mstislav
d. 1099

Iaroslav
d. 1123

Briacheslav
d. 1127/8

Iziaslav
d. 1127/8

Iurii

Viacheslav

Ivan

Sviatopolk
[of Turov]
d. 1190

Gleb

Iaroslav
[of Pinsk]

Iaropolk

Princes of Turov, Pinsk etc

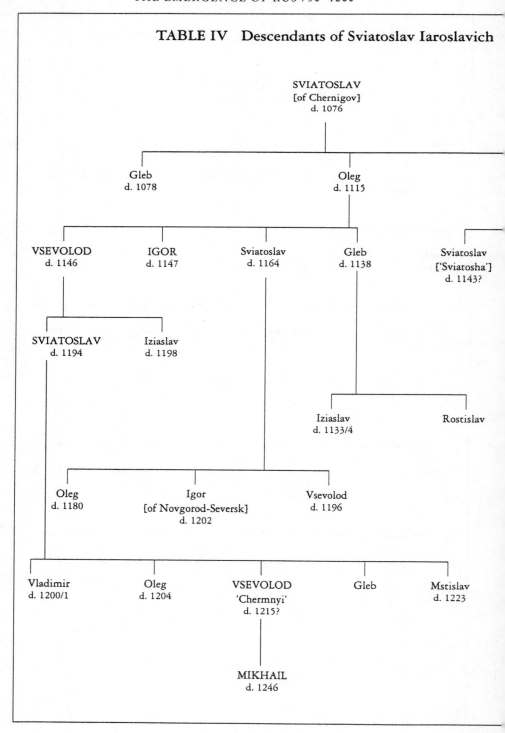

TABLE IV Descendants of Sviatoslav Iaroslavich

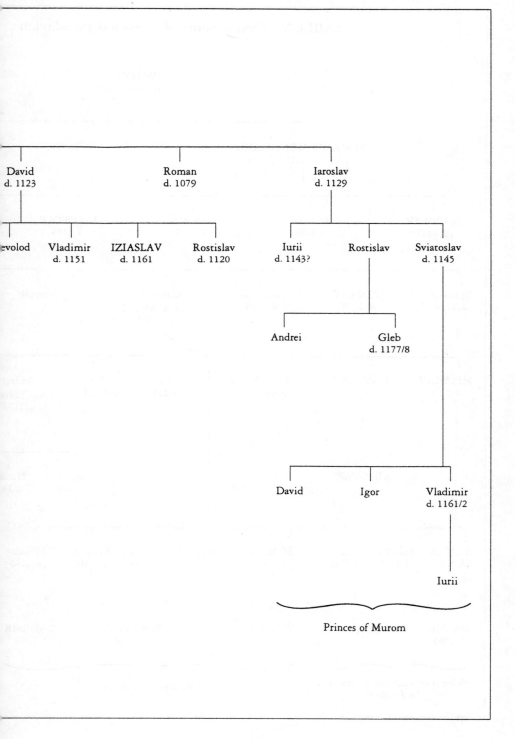

David
d. 1123

Roman
d. 1079

Iaroslav
d. 1129

evolod

Vladimir
d. 1151

IZIASLAV
d. 1161

Rostislav
d. 1120

Iurii
d. 1143?

Rostislav

Sviatoslav
d. 1145

Andrei

Gleb
d. 1177/8

David

Igor

Vladimir
d. 1161/2

Iurii

Princes of Murom

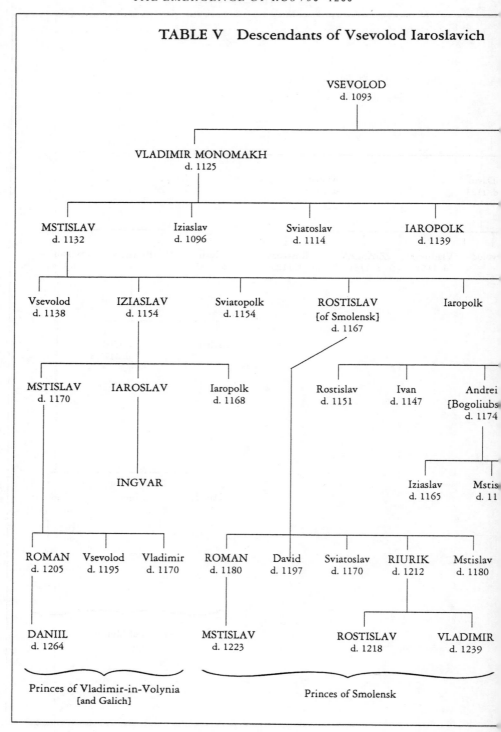

TABLE V   Descendants of Vsevolod Iaroslavich

VSEVOLOD
d. 1093

VLADIMIR MONOMAKH
d. 1125

| MSTISLAV d. 1132 | Iziaslav d. 1096 | Sviatoslav d. 1114 | IAROPOLK d. 1139 |

Vsevolod d. 1138 — IZIASLAV d. 1154 — Sviatopolk d. 1154 — ROSTISLAV [of Smolensk] d. 1167 — Iaropolk

MSTISLAV d. 1170 — IAROSLAV — Iaropolk d. 1168 — Rostislav d. 1151 — Ivan d. 1147 — Andrei [Bogoliubs d. 1174

INGVAR

Iziaslav d. 1165 — Mstis d. 11

ROMAN d. 1205 — Vsevolod d. 1195 — Vladimir d. 1170 — ROMAN d. 1180 — David d. 1197 — Sviatoslav d. 1170 — RIURIK d. 1212 — Mstislav d. 1180

DANIIL d. 1264 — MSTISLAV d. 1223 — ROSTISLAV d. 1218 — VLADIMIR d. 1239

Princes of Vladimir-in-Volynia [and Galich]

Princes of Smolensk

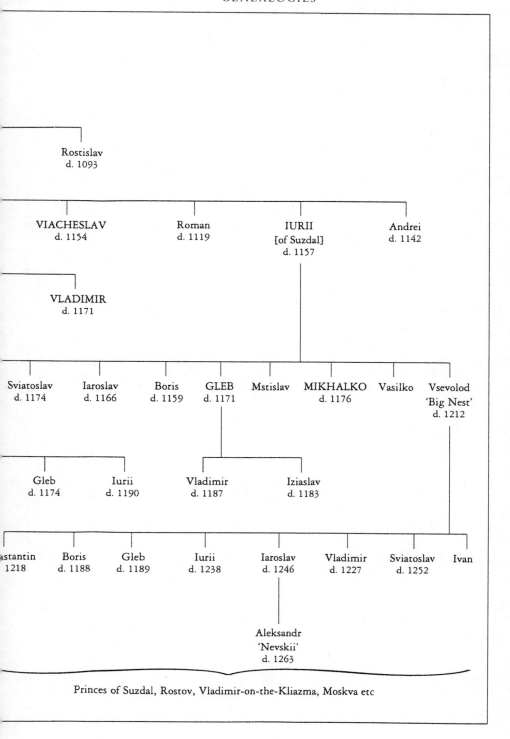

Rostislav
d. 1093

VIACHESLAV
d. 1154

Roman
d. 1119

IURII
[of Suzdal]
d. 1157

Andrei
d. 1142

VLADIMIR
d. 1171

Sviatoslav
d. 1174

Iaroslav
d. 1166

Boris
d. 1159

GLEB
d. 1171

Mstislav

MIKHALKO
d. 1176

Vasilko

Vsevolod
'Big Nest'
d. 1212

Gleb
d. 1174

Iurii
d. 1190

Vladimir
d. 1187

Iziaslav
d. 1183

stantin
1218

Boris
d. 1188

Gleb
d. 1189

Iurii
d. 1238

Iaroslav
d. 1246

Vladimir
d. 1227

Sviatoslav
d. 1252

Ivan

Aleksandr
'Nevskii'
d. 1263

Princes of Suzdal, Rostov, Vladimir-on-the-Kliazma, Moskva etc

Index

The second name of many Rus persons listed denotes a patronymic, i.e. their father's name – for example Vladimir Sviatoslavich is 'Vladimir, son of Sviatoslav' ('-ich' being equivalent to Celtic prefix 'Mc'). Members of the ruling dynasty of the Rus are listed by first name and patronymic. To assist identification, the name and patronymic of their father is given in square brackets.

A square bracket denotes a page where a person or place is referred to without being named explicitly.